TRAFFIC AND TRANSPORT PSYCHOLOGY

Related books

R. ELVIK & T. VAA (eds.)	The Handbook of Road Safety Measures
FULLER & SANTOS (eds.)	Human Factors for Highway Engineers
HENSHER & BUTTON (eds.)	Handbooks in Transport Series
HAUER	Observational Before-After Studies in Road Safety
C-H. PARK et al (eds.),	World Transport Research: Selected Proceedings of the 9th World Conference on Transport Research
ROTHENGATTER & VAYA (eds.)	Traffic and Transport Psychology: Theory and Application
J. SCHADE & B. SCHLAG (eds.)	Acceptability of Transport Pricing Strategies

Related Journals

Accident Analysis and Prevention
Editor: F.A. Haight

International Journal of Transport Management
Editor: A. Bristow

Transportation Research F: Traffic Psychology and Behaviour
Editors: J.A. Rothengatter and J.A. Groeger

Applied and Preventative Psychology:
Editor: D. Smith

For full details of all transportation titles published under the Elsevier imprint please go to:
www.ElsevierSocialSciences.com/transport

TRAFFIC AND TRANSPORT PSYCHOLOGY
Theory and Application

Proceedings of the ICTTP 2000

EDITED BY

TALIB ROTHENGATTER
University of Groningen

and

RAPHAEL D. HUGUENIN
Swiss Council for Accident Prevention bfu

2004

ELSEVIER

Amsterdam – Boston – Heidelberg – London – New York – Oxford
Paris – San Diego – San Francisco – Singapore – Sydney – Tokyo

ELSEVIER B.V.
Sara Burgerhartstraat 25
P.O.Box 211, 1000 AE
Amsterdam, The Netherlands

ELSEVIER Inc.
525 B Street, Suite 1900
San Diego, CA 92101-4495
USA

ELSEVIER Ltd
The Boulevard, Langford Lane
Kidlington, Oxford OX5 1GB
UK

ELSEVIER Ltd
84 Theobalds Road
London WC1X 8RR
UK

First edition 2004

Library of Congress Cataloging in Publication Data
A catalog record is available from the Library of Congress.

British Library Cataloguing in Publication Data
A catalogue record is available from the British Library.

ISBN: 0-08-043925-X

♾ The paper used in this publication meets the requirements of ANSI/NISO Z39.48-1992 (Permanence of Paper).
Printed in The Netherlands.

CONTENTS

MOBILITY AND ENVIRONMENT

PREFACE

This volume contains a selection of papers originally presented at the International Conference of Traffic and Transport Psychology, held in Bern, Switzerland in September 2000. For this purpose, the presentations have been reviewed and edited extensively to produce a volume that provides a balanced and representative overview of the major developments and trends in Traffic and Transport Psychology.

Traffic and Transport Psychology is more and more theory oriented. Therefore, the first part of the book contains different basic approaches and presents some integrated models. Two chapters are devoted to general theories and their implementation into Traffic and Transport Psychology.

The second part is focussed on the driver. The central issues are cognition, performance, social and differential effects and impairment. Among the cognitive factors the main aspects are treated, such as speed perception, reaction times, comprehension of perceived stimuli or interaction. The chapters on the social and differential psychology refer to the concepts of risk, self efficacy, aggression, thrill-seeking, and gender differences. Finally, the third section mainly deals with performance parameters influenced by fatigue. These chapters reflects not only the considerable development that has been made during the last years within the analysis of the most important factors for driving a road vehicle. It is also an overview of a variety of international research approaches.

Traffic and Transport Psychology is used instrumentally in various ways. Besides the promotion of environmental protection and the improvement of mobility convenience the raise of the road safety level is certainly the most important. Chapter three focuses on safety, referring to driver support systems, selection and influencing drivers by enforcement, training and rehabilitation programs. Classic ergonomic methods are discussed as well as modern telematic devices. Fortunately the authors do not only present the new tools but have already developed a critical position as far as necessary seen from the point of view of safety. As for the enforcement and training processes which are set in to enhance safety, we can note a strong trend to combine psychological and juridical methods in an interdisciplinary way. The third section of this chapter contains two methodological contributions: One refers to the accident proneness concept, the other treats test reliability problems. The rest reflects one of the most often worked field of applied traffic psychology in the German speaking countries: Assessment, selection and rehabilitation of traffic offenders.

In the last part, current developments are discussed in relation to applications of measures concerning better mobility and the protection of the environment. It shows that psychology can contribute to better life quality in traffic. Critical questions are asked, such as whether we could reduce the car use, how travel behaviour can be modified or to what extend the use of alternatives to motor vehicles, e.g. bicycles and walking, is not only a safety benefit but a win for the environment as well. These topics are seen from the psychological and the sociological point of view too.

All in all, this volume reflects the state of the art in Traffic and Transport Psychology. The tendency, to more and more take into account the role of the vehicle and the road within the traffic system by psychologists, is very well demonstrated. It is shown that it is important to adapt the system to the road user as vice versa there are limits which during the last decade have not sufficiently been considered. It is hoped that the contents of this book will contribute to a more humane traffic and transport system.

We wish to express our gratitude towards the members of the scientific committee of the ICTTP2000 who actively participated in the selection and review process:

Dr. Pierre Barjonet of INRETS, Paris
Dr. Birgit Bukasa of the Austrian Council for Traffic Safety, Vienna
Prof. John Groeger of the University of Surrey
Prof. Frank McKenna of the University of Reading
Dr. Fritz Meyer-Gramcko of the Institute for Traffic Psychology, Brunswick
Dr. Ralf Risser of FACTUM, Vienna

Thanks are especially due to Mr Chris Pringle and his staff of Elsevier who assisted us expertly and patiently in putting the book together and to those two organisations which provided us with the considerable financial support, the Swiss Council for Accident Prevention bfu, Bern and the Swiss Foundation for Traffic Safety, Bern.

March, 2004
Haren, the Netherlands / Bern, Switzerland

Talib Rothengatter
Raphael D. Huguenin

GENERAL

Traffic and Transport Psychology,
T. Rothengatter and R.D. Huguenin (Editors)

1

INTRODUCTION

Talib Rothengatter and Raphael D. Huguenin

FAIRY TALES

Accidents occur, like encounters with fairies or werewolfs, to the weary traveller, but accidents or encounters with fairies or werewolves, are random events. The behaviour of the traveller, and his mental state, are factors that influence the likelihood of occurrence. How important these factors are, is matter of debate. One extreme view is the sustainable transport philosophy maintaining that sustainable road design would virtually eliminate accidents and would ensure that those accidents that would occur will not inflict serious injury or death. No such claim is made about fairies or werewolves, but it is likely that in an orderly world they too will behave orderly. On the other hand of the spectrum remains the assertion made that 85% of the accidents occurring can be attributed to human error. Obviously, when humans are prone to imagine fairies or werewolfs, they are prone to other types of error as well.

In 1994, a special issue on traffic psychology appeared, based on presentations at the 23rd International Congress of Applied Psychology. In this issue, we contended that traffic psychology appeared a promising new area of research (Rothengatter, 1997). Research into road user behaviour and transport safety had been dominated for decades by other professions. Consequently, theoretical concepts and models dominant in mainstream psychology were not considered in the domain of road user behaviour. Application of these concepts and models would enhance our understanding of road user behaviour and would help to create the new possibilities of influencing road user behaviour.

MODELS AND THEORIES

Elsewhere, we argued that traffic psychology would benefit from developing a general domain model or theory (Huguenin, 1997). Although, a plethora of models and theories has been developed (see Ranney, 1994, for an overview), most of these are too specific to serve as a general research framework. As a result, research results often are reported without reference to any theoretical framework. We contended that a general model or theory would have to incorporate at least a component related to the disposition of the driver; a component related to social processes, cognition and motor skills, and a component related to situational characteristics (Huguenin, 1997).

Two concepts appear central in the earlier discussion on models of road user behaviour: risk and motivation (e.g. Huguenin, 1988: Rothengatter, 1988, 1990; Summala, 1988). Road user behaviour was conceptualised as adaptive to perceived risk. Road users were perceived as risk adaptors. If they perceived the risk to be high, they would adjust their behaviour to lower their risk. The debate concerned the parameters (zero risk or target risk). In Summala's zero-risk model, road users act if risk was perceived above zero; in Wilde's target risk model (1994) road users act if risk was above target risk, but also act if risk was below target risk. That road users regulated their behaviour based on perceived risk was hardly in question; road users were risk adaptors. The risk models have been criticized on various grounds (see Michon, 1989) such as the presence of a "monitor" or "comparator" in the models, the lack of definition of the risk construct (individual or aggregate) and the discrepancy between "perceived" (subjective) risk and "actual" (objective) risk. Experimental studies meanwhile have demonstrated that drivers also display adaptive behaviour when the perceived risk is low (e.g. Van der Hulst, Rothengatter & Meijman, 1998; Cnossen, Rothengatter & Meijman, 2000). Instead of adapting their behaviour to perceived risk, drivers were found to adapt their strategic and tactical behaviour to experienced task demand, the amount of effort required to maintain adequate performance. This task demand was found to fluctuate as a result of both task characteristics such as complexity or preview and state characteristics such as time-on-task or fatigue. Fuller (2000) introduced a task capability model in which drivers match performance with task demands. Although this model needs further elaboration (it incorporates a task difficulty model that again uses a comparator, this time comparing perceived task difficulty and acceptable task difficulty), it is clearly a step forward from the earlier risk models as the components of the model do allow empirical verification.

Attitudes and Driver Performance

Risk and performance models have one element in common. They all acknowledge that the quality of task performance of drivers is dependent on their aspiration level, be it in terms of perceived risk, comfort, perceived task control, workload or whatever the construct may be, and that this aspiration level is under motivational control. Summala (1988) explicitly acknowledges the importance of "external motives" in determining the outcome of the monitoring system in his model.

Attitude theory incorporates these motivational aspects as attitudes are conceptualised as psychological tendencies to evaluate aspects positively or negatively including affect and mood. Motivational processes are considered crucial to attitude formation and change (see Eagly & Chaiken, 1993). The Theory of Reasoned Action and its successor, the Theory of Planned Behavior, have been used extensively to study road user behaviour (e.g. Parker, Manstead, Stradling & Reason, 1992) albeit mostly in relation to law violations such as speeding, drink-driving and seat belt use. More recently, these theories have been applied to study aggressive road user behaviour (e.g. Parker, Lajunen & Stradling, 1998). In these theories, the motivational processes are conceptualised as a product of the estimated likelihood of the outcome of behaviour and the evaluation of that outcome. Strong, consistent positive relationships between these "motives" and intentions to display specific behaviour have been established. However, three observations must be made. The first is that these relationships have been established between attitudes and intentions, or at best, between attitudes and reported behaviour. Studies that demonstrate relationships between attitudes and actual, observed road user behaviour are rare, and these studies usually measure attitudes after the behaviour is observed, hence their predictive value can be questioned. The second observation is that the results of attitude studies have not been integrated in performance-oriented models, even though there is theoretically every possibility to do so. Finally, if attitude studies have contributed to our understanding of the motives road users have to display deviant and dangerous behaviour, they have contributed very little to measure to remedy this behaviour. This is not due to attitude theory. In other areas of applied research based on attitude theory, interventions have been developed on the basis of attitude theory, as for example in smoking and other health-related behaviour. It is a major shortcoming that needs to be addressed.

Individual Differences

Accident-prone drivers may not exist, or if they exist may not be found, (see Haight, this volume), but individual differences are a subject of substantial research. Sensation-seeking is consistently associated with risky driving (Jonah, 1997). Walton (1999) compared truck drivers' self-assessment and assessment of others on measures such as speed, safety and consideration with the averages of independently-recorded objective indicators in attempt to determine the direction of bias. He found that drivers do not demonstrate 'self-enhancement' indicative of driver overconfidence and conclude that the self-enhancement bias found operates as a negative-other rationalisation. McKenna (1993) found illusion of control but not optimism bias to affect drivers' expectancy of accident involvement. In addition to these and similar cognitive social psychology constructs, differences in accident involvement of younger versus older, female versus male, and experienced versus inexperienced drivers have attracted considerable research efforts. Groeger (2000) provides an overview of this research. It is clear that people differ in their cognitions regarding driving and differ in their driving style. How these differences determine accident-involvement is as yet largely unclear. Accident-prone driver remain elusive.

Accident-Countermeasures

The reason for carrying out applied research is not primarily to contribute to the scientific body of knowledge or to develop new models or theories; it is to contribute to solving the problem to which the research is applied. In this traffic psychology falls short. Risk theories have done little do reduce the risk of driving. Performance models may in other areas of task performance have had an impact on task design, not so in transportation. Road design still is primarily a task of road engineers, car design primarily a task of vehicle engineers. The traditional realm of traffic psychology – road safety campaigns, driver selection, training and rehabilitation – cannot claim an impressive impact on road safety.

There is one exception. The introduction of information technology in the transport system has created new opportunities for traffic psychology. In first instance, traffic psychology has concentrated on the question how the changes in task environment that resulted from the introduction of information technology would affect driving performance and safety. A very basic example is the many studies investigating the effects of using mobile telephones while driving; a more sophisticated example is the studies investigating how workload or task demand can be regulated. However, more important is the question how information technology can be used to regulate driving behaviour. An example of the latter concerns the possibility of speed regulation which now has been studied in the framework of provision of feedback, enforcement systems and systems that regulate drivers' choice (notably, intelligent adaptive cruise control and intelligent speed adaptors). Traffic psychology has contributed in the development of such systems both in terms of system effectiveness and system acceptance.

This does not imply that the impact of traffic psychology should be limited to these applications. On the contrary, it illustrates that the potential is far greater than has been achieved so far. The present volume is a statement to that effect.

References

Cnossen, F., Rothengatter, J.A., & Meijman, T.F. (2000). Strategic changes in task performance in simulated car driving as an adaptive response to task demand. *Transportation Research Part F, 3*, 123-140.

Eagly, A.H. & Chaiken, S. (1993). *The psychology of attitudes*. Philadelphia: Harcourt, Brace, Jovanovich.

Fuller, R. (2000). The task-capability interface model of the driving process. *Recherche, Transports, Securité, 66, 47-59.*

Groeger, J.A. (2000). *Understanding driving*. Hove, UK: Psychology Press.

Haight, F. (this volume). Accident Proneness: The History of an Idea.

Huguenin, R.D. (1988). The concept of risk and behaviour models in traffic psychology. *Ergonomics, 31*, 557-569.

Huguenin, R.D. (1997). Do we need traffic psychology models? In J.A. Rothengatter and E. Carbonell Vaya (Eds.), *Traffic and transport psychology: Theory and application*. Oxford: Pergamon.

Jonah, B. (1997). Sensation-seeking and risky driving. In J.A. Rothengatter and E. Carbonell Vaya (Eds.), *Traffic and transport psychology: Theory and practice*. Oxford: Pergamon.

McKenna, F.P. (1993). It won't happen to me: Unrealistic optimism or illusion of control? *British Journal of Psychology, 84*, 39-50.

Michon, J.A. (1989). Explanatory pitfalls and rule-based driver models. *Accident Analysis and Prevention, 21*, 341-353.

Parker, D., Manstead, A.S.R., Stradling, S.G. & Reason, J.T. (1992). Intentions to commit driving violations. *Journal of Applied Psychology, 77*, 94-101.

Parker, D., Lajunen, T. & Stradling, S. (1998). Attitudinal predictors of interpersonally aggressive violations on the road. *Transportation Research Part F, 1*, 11-24.

Ranney, T.A. (1994). Models of driving behaviour: A review of their evolution. *Accident Analysis and Prevention, 26*, 733-750.

Rothengatter, J.A. (1988). Risk and the absence of pleasure: A motivational approach to modelling road user behaviour. *Ergonomics, 31*, 599-607.

Rothengatter, J.A. (1990). Behaviour change on the road: the unification of platonian, draconian and pentagonian measures. *IATTS Research, 14,* 102-105.

Rothengatter, J.A. (1997). Psychological aspects of road user behaviour. *Applied Psychology: An International Review, 46,* 223-234.

Summala, H. (1988). Risk control is not risk adjustment: The zero-risk theory of driver behavour and its limitations. *Ergonomics, 31*, 491-506.

Van der Hulst, M., Rothengatter, J.A., & Meijman, T.F. (1998). Strategic adaptations to lack of preview in driving. *Transportation Research Part F, 1*, 59-75.

Walton, D. (1999). Examining the self-enhancement bias: Professional truck drivers' perceptions of speed, safety, skill and consideration. *Transportation Research Part F, 2*, 91-113.

Wilde, G.J.S. (1994). *Target risk.* Toronto (Canada): PDE Publications.

Traffic and Transport Psychology,
T. Rothengatter and R.D. Huguenin (Editors)

2

Driver Behaviour as a Hierarchical System

Esko Keskinen, Mika Hatakka, Sirkku Laapotti, Ari Katila, and Martti Peräaho

The Purpose of Theories and Models

"No comprehensive model of driving behaviour has been developed, and, given the wide variety of driving situations and associated combinations of component skills, it is unlikely that one will soon emerge" (Ranney 1994, 746). This is no wonder, because a model is always offers only one viewing angle to the subject. The basic goal of the theory is to compress the reality and generalise from it's variability.

It seems likely that one theory or model is not enough. Human behaviour is so complex that we need theories of many kind of cognitive subprocesses like perceiving, thinking, controlling attention, solving problems and acting. Motivational and emotional processes are also important and necessary when we want to construct theories of e.g. perceiving and other basic cognitive processes. A theory is always a way to direct attention to certain phenomena which are evaluated to be more important than others. In driver behaviour theories about skills or motivation has been such phenomena. But even here there cannot be one without the other.

How to Define Driving

Is driving about controlling speed and vehicle movements, where the important phenomena are lane changing and obstacle avoidance, or is it about transporting persons and goods where the important phenomena concerns decisions before and during the trip. But not all the authors regard this as a problem. However, e.g. Michon (1976, 1985) has described the hierarchical structure of problem solving in traffic and transportation (Table 1). He shows that controlling the vehicle is only one of the tasks a driver has to perform as a transporting citizen. A broader definition of driving is preferred here because many problems connected to driving actually originate from outside the very narrow definition of driving.

	Behavioural level			
	I	*II*	*III*	*IV*
Human quality as a problem solver	Road user	Transportation consumer	Social agent	Psycho-biological organism
Problem to be solved	Vehicle control	Trip making	Activity pattern (Communication)	Satisfaction of basic needs
Task environment	Road	Road network (Topographical structure)	Socio-economic structure	Nature (environment)
Task aids	Vehicles, signs, etc.	Transport mode	Transport system	"Culture", Technology

Table 1. The hierarchical structure of problem solving tasks in traffic and transportation (Michon 1985, after Michon, 1976).

Many theories of driving, however, see the driver only in a traffic situation manoeuvring the vehicle. And it is also the other way around, theories and models define driving. But perhaps the most common definition of driving comes from everyday life. Many studies concerning e.g. how driving is learned do not try to solve the problem of defining driving in a scientific way but e.g. use driving criteria for a successful performance. The result then is that car manoeuvring and managing traffic situations play the most important role. One of the applications of driver behaviour theories should also be to develop a definition of driving for example for driver training purposes and not vice versa.

A Theory of Accidents or a Theory of Normal Driving Behaviour

A fundamental concern in traffic psychology is traffic safety. Apparently it has always been so fundamental that e.g. motivational models of road user behaviour are almost synonymous with models of risk taking (Michon, 1985). Many theories describe and explain only failures in driving, i.e. accidents. Perhaps the most famous of these is the theory of accident proneness. However, we must go beyond accidents if we are to understand driving behaviour (Ranney 1994). "A theory of traffic behaviour should cover both the normal course of events in traffic and the deviations which anticipate risk situations and accidents (Mikkonen and Keskinen 1983).

A theory should describe the key elements only and make the phenomena as simple as possible without loosing it's character for understanding and pointing out the most important factors and processes. A theory should also explain empirical observations and predict behaviour on the general, group level but not on the individual level. If predicting on the individual level in a certain situation would be possible it would mean that either all individuals are equal and the situation is very simple or that the model is as complex as the real, empirical world. Neither statement is possible, at least when we speak of complex matters such as driving or even traffic behaviour in a wider sense.

Models and theories, if they have at least some of the earlier properties, should also be the base for applications. It's regrettable and sad if applications are based on everyday thinking without the aid of organising and guiding ideas of theories and models. This has often been the case because models and theories have not had so much connections to the applications of traffic psychology.

One of the ways of looking theories is to regard the theory as a tool. Then the main question will be: is a certain tool useful or should we select another one. Less important is then the question if the theory is true or not. However, often the research questions in traffic psychology concerning the theory have mainly attended to the empirical evidence supporting the theory. That is important but it is not the only way of looking at theories.

Theories and Models of Driver Behaviour

There are four big theories of driver behaviour: Wilde's (1982) risk compensation model, Fuller's (1984) risk avoidance model, Näätänen and Summala's (1974) risk threshold model, Fishbein and Ajzen's (1975) theory of planned behaviour and Ajzen and Fishbein's (1977) theory of intentional behaviour. These theories have been evaluated and criticised in review articles like Michon (1985) and Ranney (1994). Wilde's theory has been evaluated most favourable and at the same time most unfavourably. Näätänen and Summala has basically got more positive feedback, if we don't count the comments from those who have developed their own theory. But Näätänen and Summala's theory has not produced so much research which is just the opposite with Wilde's theory. Fuller's theory has perhaps got less attention than it has deserved. The theory and it's modifications by Ajzen and Fishbein has generated a lot of interest and it has been a starting point for much literature even though the theory originally does not concern driving at all. The interest in their model seems to be connected with the re-emergence of attitude studies after a more behavioristic and experimentalistic period in traffic psychology.

Hierarchical Models in Driving

There are two influential reviews concerning hierarchical models in driver behaviour, even though both deal with all kinds of theories. Michon published a very widely cited and influential paper in 1985 titled "A critical view of driver behaviour models: What do we know, what should we do?". Ranney published his evaluation almost ten years later in 1994. Both of these give a good description of models designed up to the points in time. After Ranney's article there has been two attempts to further develop a hierarchical model of driver behaviour, namely Keskinen 1996 and Summala (1996, 1997).

Michon (1985) differentiates between functional models and taxonomic models. Taxonomic models are essentially inventories or lists of facts. One example of a taxonomic model is

Rasmussen's (1987) model of human behaviour. There are no specified dynamic relations between the three levels in Rasmussen's model. An earlier but totally different example is the task analysis model by McKnight and Adams (1970a, 1970b; McKnight and Hundt, 1971) where the driving task was divided into 45 major tasks and further into 1700 elementary tasks. If the goal of a theory is to describe the most important parts of a phenomena, then McKnight's and Adams's work is not a theory, but a detailed description of the surface level of driving. More or less functional models are Janssen's (1979), Michon's (1971), Van der Molen and Bötticher's (1988), Summala's (1996), Mikkonen and Keskinen's (1980, 1983), and Keskinen's (1996) models.

A general way of dividing a driver's task is to use three levels of behaviour and control: strategical (planning), tactical (manoeuvring), and operational (control) respectively (Michon, 1971, 1979, 1985, Janssen, 1979). In Michon's (1971) and Janssen's (1979) models the strategical level defines the general planning stage of a trip, including the determination of trip goals, route, and modal choice, plus an evaluation of the costs and risks involved (Figure 1). Plans derive further from general considerations about transport and mobility, and also from concomitant factors such as aesthetics and comfort. At the tactical level drivers exercise manoeuvre control allowing them to negotiate the directly prevailing circumstances. Although largely constrained by the exigencies of the actual situation, manoeuvres such as obstacle avoidance, gap acceptance, turning, and overtaking, must meet the criteria derived from the general goals set at the strategical level. Conversely these goals may occasionally be adapted to fit the outcome of certain manoeuvres. Michon (1985) also states that a comprehensive model of driver behaviour should not only take into account the various levels , but should also provide an information flow control structure that enables control to switch from one level to the other at the appropriate points in time (p.490). Michon (1985) is also supposing that in the course of a skill learning process, performance proceeds from general and flexible but slow, to specific and rigid but fast.

Michon (1985) goes on by suggesting the mechanism behind the functions, production systems, which has clear similarity to the classical way of describing action using Miller, Galanter and Pribram's (1960) TOTE-units. However, the idea of production systems in driver behaviour has not produced any significant effects. But as we remember, he also advocated the three level hierarchy of driving and that idea has been living on fruitfully.

Van der Molen and Bötticher (1988, also Bötticher and van der Molen 1988) have created a hierarchical driver behaviour model that also incorporates three levels of traffic tasks (Figure 2). Their aim was to formulate a new model which allows calculations in terms of both behaviour alternatives and the subjective probability and utility aspects of behaviour outcomes. They continue that their purpose was to provide a structural framework which allows them to describe the perceptual, judgmental and decision processes of traffic participants at all levels of a traffic task, taking into account the subjective correlates of the probabilities of outcomes and of outcome values, explicitly distinguishing between risk judgement and other judgements. They define connections and describe processes but they also state that their model is an empty one because they have not specified how the above mentioned processes work.

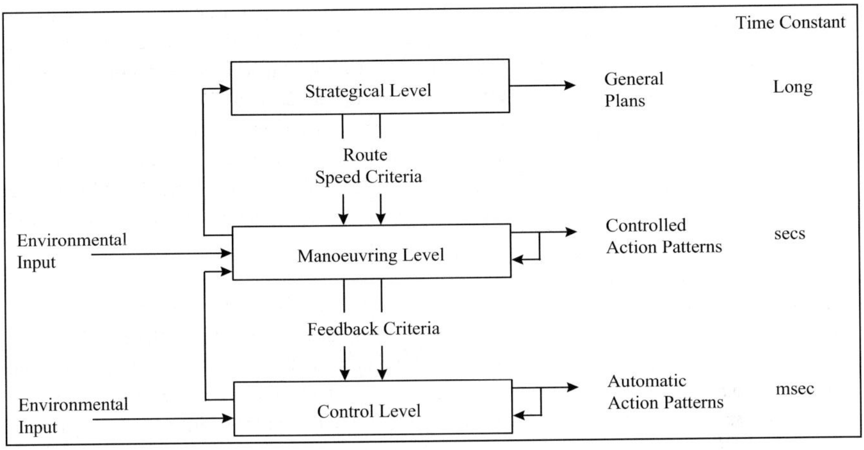

Figure 1. The hierarchical structure of the road user task. Performance is structured at three levels that are comparatively loosely coupled. Internal and external outputs are indicated (Michon 1985, after Janssen, 1979).

In their model van der Molen and Bötticher (1988) also connect a driver's behaviour to the physical environment and the perceptions made of it. In their model the Strategic Plan influences judgements at the tactical level in the form of Strategic Plan Motivation. Manoeuvring Plans from the Tactical level are carried out at the operational level as Operational Behaviour. The top two task levels have both an activity-initiating function and a supervising and correcting function. This is the normal way to describe process control in hierarchical models. Goals and feedback are used in this process as already stated by Miller, Galanter and Pribram (1960).

To avoid too much complexity the authors have used a yes or no – type of classifications. For example motivation concerns either safety or something else other, expectations are about accident or other and judgements are risk or another etc. It is easy to see, that the more elements there are in the model the more the model has to simplify things.

The authors have taken on challenging task but to describe human behaviour using such a description may simplify things too much. Also some basic assumptions in the model seem to be too simple, not unlike the assumptions by Edwards (1954) in his SEU-model (Subjective Expected Utility) as the basis for decision making. The idea to use the model as a basis for calculations is interesting but e.g. compared to the popular model by Ajzen and Fishbein, this model offers so many elements that it is difficult to control them all in an empirical study. Of course this comment does not mean that we can manage with empirical evidence better if we leave important elements out of the model. However, even if the model has been heavily criticised, e.g. by Michon (1989), it offers one starting point to the discussion of driver behaviour models which has not been all that intensive in recent years.

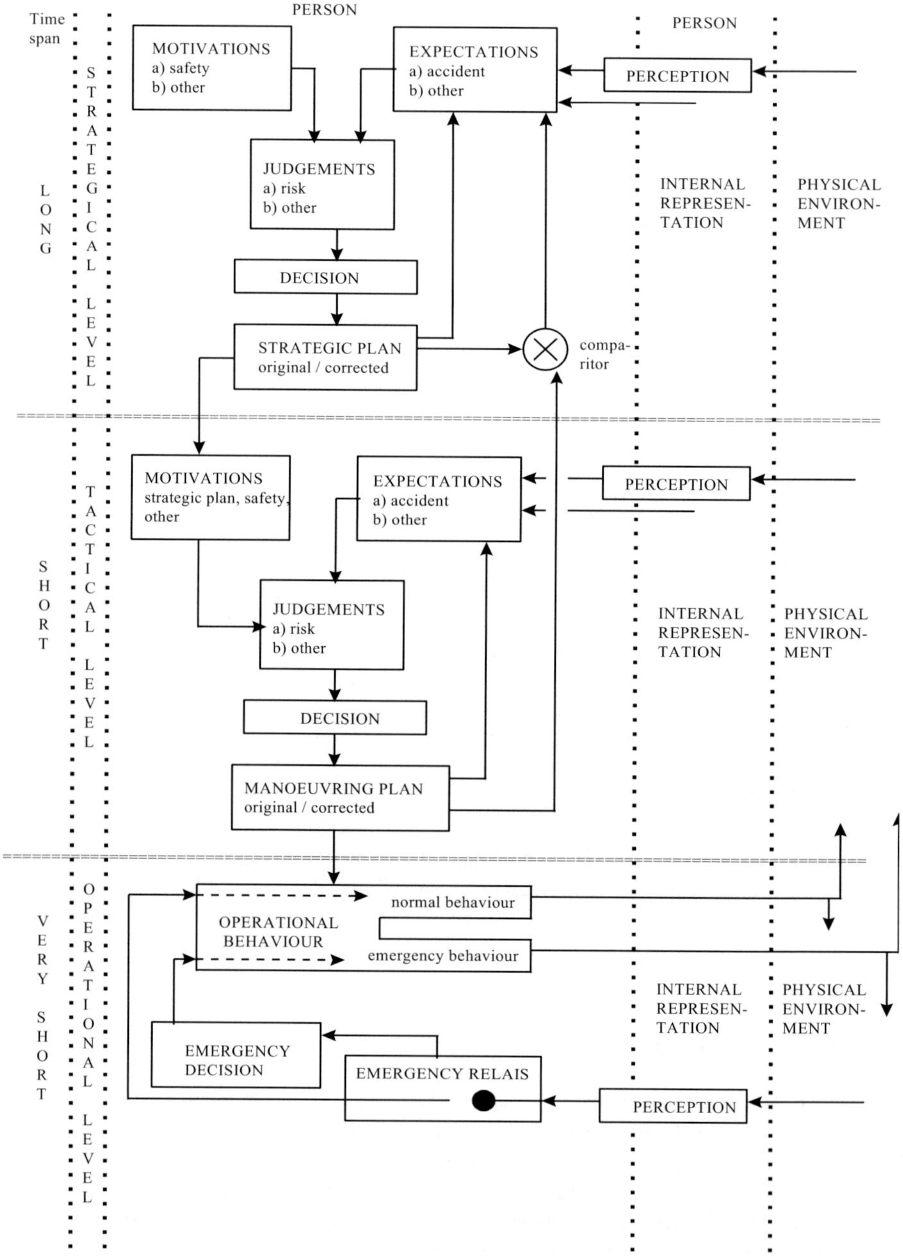

Figure 2. The hierarchical risk model for traffic participants (after Bötticher and van der Molen 1988).

Conceptualising a driver's task was also the idea behind Summala's (1996, 1997) model (Figure 3). In this model he presented a rather complicated "task cube" that combined three different concepts: a functional hierarchy of driver tasks, a functional taxonomy, and three psychological processing levels. The functional hierarchy consists of vehicle choice, trip decisions, navigation, guidance, and vehicle control. The functional taxonomy, on the other hand, includes things like passing and other manoeuvres, crossing management, obstacle avoidance etc. The three psychological processing levels were decision making, attention control, and perceptual-motor control. Separate from these concepts, but included and mentioned in the cube were also speed and time control.

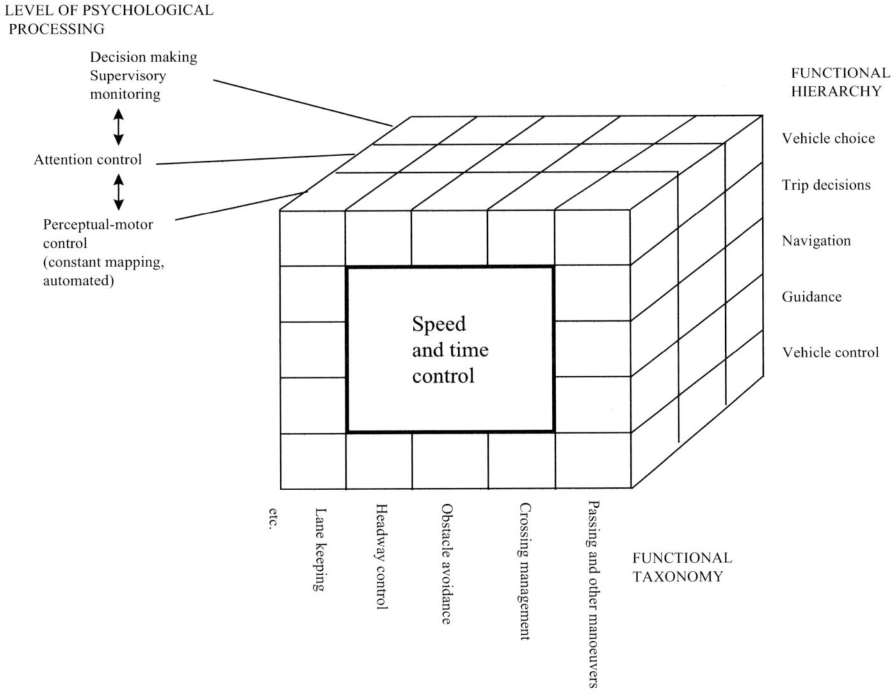

Figure 3. Drivers task cube (after Summala 1996)

The idea of using a cube dates back at least to 1967 when Altman described his classification of human error. The difference between these cubes is, however, that all the small cubes inside the big one in Altman's version bear a meaning, whereas that is not the case in Summala's version. His cube resembles more a description or a list of important variables than a solid model. Later (1997) Summala came to the same conclusion as Keskinen (1996) that the motivational factors should have a more important role in the model (Figure 4). He therefore modified it by adding motives and emotions to it and naming it the "multiple sieve model" or the "filter model of risky behaviour and road accidents". Of course we have to remember that in one of the most famous driver behaviour models, Näätänen and Summala (1974), the motivational aspects were the most important ones.

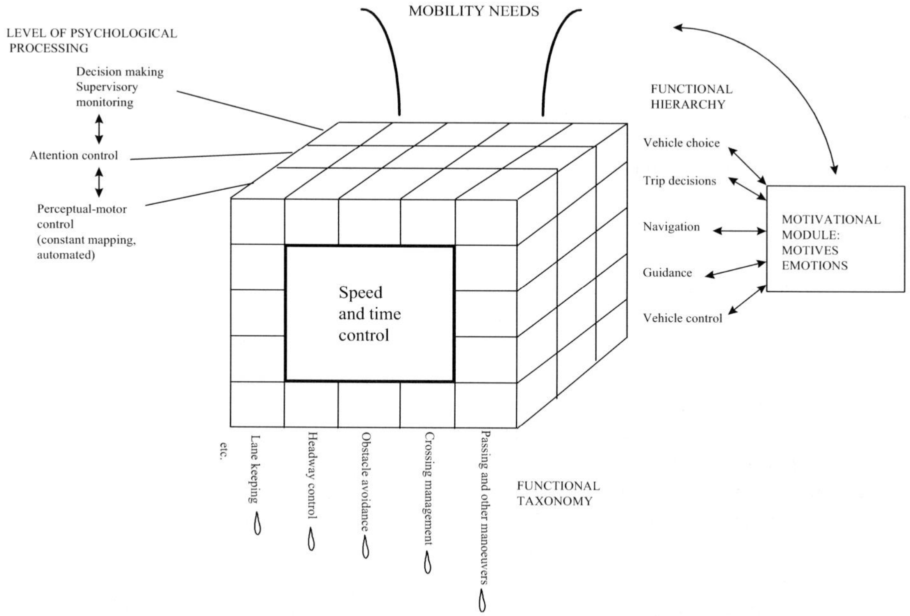

Figure 4. The multisieve model (after Summala 1997)

The fourth model to be shortly presented here is of a different kind but it has been influential in studies concerning accidents and their antecedents. Rasmussens (1980) main aim was to describe how processes, which are learned to a different degree, are controlled. He describes a taxonomy of three levels, skill-based, rule-based and knowledge-based. These levels are based on different modes of information processing and behavioural control. At the first level (the lowest), performance takes place in the form of automated schemata; at the second level, performance takes place in the form of rules or productions which are largely automated; and at the highest level, performance takes place in the form of serial, attentional and laborious processing.

Rasmussen's model, although it is a three level model, describes different phenomena than the models of Michon, Janssen and van der Molen and Bötticher. It describes three possible ways to control behaviour but it is not a description of the driving task itself, not even hypothetically. By the way, it is interesting to notice that three levels seems to be very popular. Other three level models are e.g. Fitts and Posner (1965), Leontjev (1977) and Hacker (1978). Of course it is mainly arbitrary to divide behaviour into three levels or a developmental process into the same three levels.

Reason (1985) has developed Rasmussen's (1980) model further emphasising the error side of human behaviour. His so-called Generic Error Modelling System (GEMS) has been applied to the study of accidents and violations. Studies have shown that the lowest levels of aberrant driving behaviour, self-reported slips and lapses and errors do not predict accidents rates (Parker et al. 1995a, 1995b). Violations, i.e. behaviours that involve deliberate deviations from safe driving practice, on the other hand correlate with both past and future accident rates. So again it seems that the problem of risky behaviour is re-emerging. At least do results of this kind suggest that motivational elements are highly important in predicting accidents but also in predicting driving without accidents, so called normal driving (Hatakka 1998)

Already in 1980 Mikkonen and Keskinen published their Theory of internal models in driving behaviour but unfortunately only in Finnish. The model was based on four assumptions which form the basic statements of the theory: (1) Internal models are used in the control of traffic behaviour. The models are used in the planning of actions, in the interpretation of sensory information, in guiding motor operations and in comparing feedback received from the activities; (2) Internal models develop with experience to represent typical characteristics of the traffic environment and of the flow of traffic events. Experience can be gained through personal participation in traffic e.g. as a driver, and through observing the behaviour of others, but also through verbal and pictorial description, and by imagining the course of traffic events; (3) Internal models are used interactively in two ways: some environmental key features and continuities in the flow of events arise internal models, and the anticipatory choice of model is verified by cues in the stimulus environment, and on the other hand, the choice of model is made in accordance with the motivational state; (4) In the theory of Mikkonen and Keskinen (1980; 1983) internal models are sub-ordinate to motives, as the switching of models is sensitive to changes in the goals of behaviour. In the theory internal models are regarded as purely cognitive states controlled by motivational and emotional factors. This creates an unstable element in the system; relevant models are not always in use even though they belong to the repertory of a driver; (5) Risk situations arise when the internal models in use differ from the demands of the objective situation.

Surprises and near accidents as well as accidents can be accounted for by differences between existing models (models in use) and the situational requirements. The seriousness of the consequences of risks is dependent on the magnitude and quality of the differences. The risks themselves have common roots, whether they appear as harmless surprises or as fatal accidents.

Description of the contents of a drivers' internal models is an important part of the theory. What are the aspects of a traffic environment that are represented by internal models. A system for evaluating and using information concerning the developmental level of models must also be hypothesised, otherwise the process will be controlled only by external cues or stimulus.

The other question is: How is knowledge in the models organised so that it can be used to ensure a fluent and anticipatory control of actions in driving. A hierarchical organisation seems to be necessary in which models are differentiated by their extensiveness. Theory divided the internal models into three levels. The model covering the largest range of a traffic performance was called the *route model.* It contains knowledge about roads and events between start and goal, and it is divided into several visual scenes each of which includes a *sight model.* On this level the model covers the range of road which can be tested by sensory information. Within each sight level, several *handling models* are needed. They include a map of the control equipment of the vehicle and knowledge about how it behaves when the controls are used. The route level makes possible to anticipate the type of sight models which again limit the handling models necessary for realising the performance. The model therefore assumed a control hierarchy as well as a hierarchy of representations.

It was also pointed out in the original theory that it is reasonable to assume that the internal models have a different kind of contents, e.g. social contents on the two higher hierarchical levels and contents which concern risks on all three levels. There was also an information flow diagram in the first model, but it was soon realised that there can hardly be any causal relationships in such a process diagram as almost all of the relationships are interactive by their nature. Already in the first version of the theory it was noticed that internal models has to have connections to motivational and emotional systems of the driver. The connections were, however, not specified.

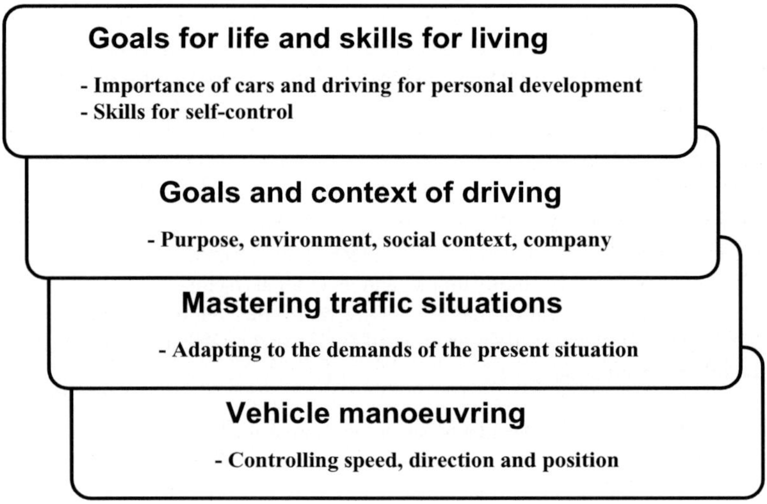

Figure 5. Hierarchical levels of driving behaviour

As a result of accident analysis, it was noted that a theory which is only concerning on knowledge and procedural bases of driving, was not successful enough. At the same time studies concerning life-style and accidents were published, as well as research results regarding the effects of self-control on accident involvement. As a consequence, a new highest level, *Goals for life and skills for living* was introduced (Keskinen 1996) into the model (Figure 5). It is possible to see already from the name of this highest level that it is especially important because it covers such a wide and not so easily described area as personality and motives. These concern especially driving but also more generally a persons relation to life and the present life situation and lifestyle. A persons goals control his or her behaviour and these goals can e.g. be more or less congruent with the norms of the society or against them. Violations against traffic regulations are important negative results of acts where the goals are not generally accepted in the society. Skills for living concerns a persons self-regulatory skills, controlling impulses and controlling effects of emotions. These are especially important to young male drivers, who often suffer from a lack of control of their driving behaviour. The three lower levels are almost identical to the original ones and the idea is that they are more like tools which a person uses when fulfilling the goals of his or her life in traffic. Of course driving is only one part of a persons life but the overall goals and skills for living also affect in his or her behaviour in traffic.

Applications and Other Use of the Extended Theory of Internal Models in Driver Behaviour

A short description of some of the applications of Mikkonen and Keskinen's (1980) and Keskinen's (1996) extended model of internal models in driver behaviour might be in order. The main focus has been on the area of driver training. This is an area which has suffered from the lack of theoretical perspectives and the applications have usually been based on the knowledge of laymen or driving instructors. At least partly because of that some training procedures have even increased the proportion of such accidents which the training was intended to prevent. Driving on slippery road is one example of that (e.g. Keskinen et al. 1992).

One application of the model has been the description of loss-of-control accidents and the differences between males and females (Laapotti & Keskinen, 1998). The results clearly show that in loss-of-control accidents (accidents which started when the driver lost the control of the car) males were suffering from inadequate self control, they were speeding and driving while intoxicated more often than females, who on the other hand had driven more often in difficult driving conditions but who were not speeding.

The theory has been applied to driver training in various ways. It has been used in defining both the goals for the training as well as the methods to be used. Driver training in Finland has partly been designed using the principles of the theory, but also other theories and empirical evidence. The content of the curriculum has been divided into three parts, i.e. handling skills, mastery of traffic situations and managing routes. And in the second phase of training, the focus is on the highest hierarchical level. Also the Swiss plan a two-phase driver training system (Bächli-Biétry, 1998) that is supported and structured theoretically using Keskinens (1996) theory.

An extension of the model was used in the EU-project Gadget (Hatakka, Keskinen, Gregersen & Glad, 1999) to describe what kind of elements a good driver should have, and this description was also used to evaluate different training methods and their advantages and disadvantages. The theory was used in the similar way in the DAN-project (Bartl, Keskinen, Hatakka & Stummvoll 2000). The projects showed e.g. that basic training still concentrates on the two lowest hierarchical levels of driving and especially on knowledge and skills. Much less emphasis is put on risks as well as on evaluation of risks in driver examination. Skills for self reflection are rarely one of the goals basic driver training, but already to some extent in driver improvement. The goals of driver improvement and especially courses for rehabilitation were clearly focusing on the two highest levels of the hierarchy.

Conclusions

Some conclusions can be drawn on the basis of the cited literature. Through its history, one of the aims in traffic psychology has been to formulate theories of driving behaviour, or for that matter, driver behaviour. It is of course the same aim as in every science. However, the aim among traffic psychologists has often been to formulate one universal theory. The first attempts focused on accident proneness, then on skills, followed by motivation. Then came the hierarchical theories, which began as skill theories but developed into theories that combined skills and motivation (Keskinen 1996, Summala 1985). It is, however, clear that the hierarchical theories cover driver behaviour only on a general level. They offer one way of structuring and conceptualising driving behaviour without giving detailed predictions on the behavioural level. Theories of basic cognitive processes like attention, perception, thinking, and problem solving are still needed. We also need basic theories of motivation, social interaction, emotions etc. In short, it means that in traffic psychology we need theories of all the basic mechanisms of human behaviour. It is not possible to construct a theory of driver behaviour without considering the connections to general psychology. The first conclusion will then be that there should be more vivid interaction between general psychology and traffic psychology.

In spite of the fact that hierarchical models were introduced into traffic psychology already some twenty years ago, these theories have not been in the focus of much research, or they have not been applied into practice. Rasmussen's (1980) and Reason's (1990) theories of skill-based, rule-based and knowledge-based behaviour, and especially the theories of errors and violations have been studied and used in the construction of questionnaires. However, these thories have not been that much tested in applied form. Nor has Summala's (1996, 1997) hierarchical theory, nor has it been the starting point for some research. Mikkonen and Keskinen's (1980) and later Keskinen's (1996) theory has been applied in driver training and in the analysis of the effects of driver training programs. It has also been used as a starting point for analysing and describing traffic accidents (e.g. Hatakka, 1998; Keskinen, 1982; Laapotti & Keskinen, 1996).

One of the reasons why hierarchical models have not been studied to any greater extent may be that these models are useful for understanding driver behaviour on a general level, whereas experimental studies as well as observational studies are mostly directed towards the study of processes on the lower hierarchical levels. This kind of studies therefore start with theories that focus on these levels. For example, studies on risk perception has been directed mainly on the traffic situation level and not on the journey level or the highest level (to use Keskinen's 1996 terminology). These levels has been outside the scope of driver training.

Motivation and skills are both necessary when trying to understand driving behaviour, but the definition of skills should also include a wide variety of higher level skills such as the ability to evaluate one's own decision making, or the ability to reflect upon one's own way of reacting to impulses. The term skill has been used to refer to low level psychomotor performance. This is of course adequate if driving is defined as activity on the handling or traffic situation levels only. A wider definition of driving would help to see the forest and not just the trees.

One topic that has been largely forgotten in driver behaviour theories is the role of emotions. Näätänen (1972) included emotions as part of what he called "extra motives" and described its effect in driver behaviour. More recently studies on driver aggression or road rage has touched upon the topic, but otherwise it has been mainly neglected. One explanation for this might be that even cognitive psychologists, not to mention the behaviorists, neglected emotions as uninteresting to the study of behaviour. However, due to the important interplay between emotions, cognitions, and motives, this topic deserves a more important role in driver behaviour models.

Finally, hierarchical models offer many possibilities to understand driver behaviour, both normal driving behaviour as well as accident behaviour. But these models should be developed to incorporate knowledge from general psychology as they cannot in themselves provide answers to all possible questions concerning driving and drivers.

References

Ajzen, I. & Fishbein, M. (1977) Attitude-behavioral relations: A theoretical analysis and review of of empirical research. *Psychological Bulletin* 84(5), 888-918.

Altman, J.W. (1967) Classification of human error. In Asker, W.B. (Ed.) *Symposium on reliability of human performance in work.* Wright-Patterson AFB, Ohio: Aeropace Medical Research Laboratories, Technical Report 67-88, 3-17, May.

Bartl, G., Keskinen, E., Hatakka, M., Stummvoll, G. (2000) Objective. In Bartl, G. (ed.) (2000) *DAN-Report. Results of EU-Project: Description and Analysis of Post Licensing Measures for Novice Drivers.* Kuratorium für Verkehrssicherheit, Vienna.

Bächli-Biétry, J. (1998) *Konkretisierung des Schweizer 2-Phasen-Modells der Fahrausbildung.* bfu-Report 37, Bern.

Bötticher, A. & van der Molen (1988) Predicting overtaking behaviour on the basis of the hierarchical risk model for traffic participants. In Rothengatter J. A. and de Bruin R. A. (Eds) *Road user behaviour. Theory and research.*

Edwards, W. (1954) The theory of decision making. *Psychological Bulletin* 51, 380-417.

Elander J., West R.. & French D.(1993) Behavioral correlates of individual differences in road-traffic crash risk: An examination of methods and findings. *Psychological-Bulletin* 113(2): 279-294.

Fishbein M. & Ajzen I. (1975) *Belief, attitude, intention and behaviour: An introduction to theory and research.* Reading, MA: Addison -Wesley.

Fitts P. & Posner M. (1967) *Human Performance.* Brooks/Cole, Belmont, California.

Fuller R. (1984) A conceptualization of driving behaviour as threath avoidance. *Ergonomics* 27(11) 1139-1155.

Hacker, W. (1978) *Allgemeine Arbeits- und Ingenieurspsychologie: Psychische Struktur und Regulation von Arbeitstätigkeiten.* Berlin: Verlag Hans Huber.

Hatakka, M. (1998) *Novice drivers' risk- and self-evaluations. Use of questionnaires in traffic psychological research. Method development, general trends in four sample materials and connections with behaviour.* Turun yliopiston julkaisuja, sarja B osa 228. Turku.

Hatakka, M., Keskinen, E., Gregersen, N.P., Glad, A. (1999) Theories and aims of educational and training measures. In Siegrist, S. (ed.) *Driver Training, Testing and Licensing – towards theory-based management of young driver's injury risk in road traffic. Results of EU-Project GADGET, Work Package 3.* bfu-Report 40, Berne.

Janssen, W.H. (1979) *Routeplanning en geleiding: Een Literatuurstudie*. Report IFZ 1979 V. 13. Soesteburg (The Netherlands): Institute for Perception TNO.

Keskinen, E. (1982) *Inhimillinen tekijä liikenteessä.* Turun yliopisto, psykologian tutkimuksia 59, Turku

Keskinen, E. (1996) Why do young drivers have more accidents? *Junge Fahrer und Fahrerinnen.* Referate der Ersten Interdiziplinären Fachkonferenz 12.-14. Dezember 1994 in Köln. (in English) Berichte der Bundesanstalt fur Strassenwesen, Mensch und Sicherheit, Heft M 52.

Keskinen, E., Hatakka, M., Katila, A. (1992) Inner models as a basis for traffic behaviour. *Journal of Traffic Medicine* 20(4), 147-152.

Laapotti, S. & Keskinen, E. (1998) Differences in fatal loss-of-control accidents between young male and female drivers. *Accident Analysis and Prevention*, Vol.30, N0. 4, pp. 435-442.

Leontjev, A., N. (1977) *Toiminta, Tietoisuus, Persoonallisuus*. Helsinki: Kansankulttuuri.

McKnight, A., J. & Adams, B. B. (1970a) *Driver education task analysis. Volume I: Task descriptions*. Alexandria VA: Human Resources Research Organization. Final Report, Contract No FH 11-7336.

McKnight, A., J. & Adams, B. B.(1970b*) Driver education task analysis. Volume II: Task analysis methods*. Alexandria VA: Human Resources Research Organization. Final Report, Contract No FH 11-7336.

McKnight, A. J. & Hundt, A. G. (1971) *Driver education task analysis. Volume III: Instructional objectives*. Alexandria VA: Human Resources Research Organization. Final Report, Contract No FH 11-7336.

Michon, J. A. (1971) *Psychonomic onderweg. Inaugural lecture*, University of Groningen. Groningen: Wolters Noordhoff.

Michon, J. A. (1976) The mutual impacts of transportation and human behavior. In Stringer, P., Wenzel, H. (Eds.) *Transportation planning for a better environment*. New York, Plenum Press.

Michon, J. A. (1985) A critical view of driver behavior models: what do we know, what should we do? In Evans, L. and Schwing, R. (Eds.) *Human behavior and traffic safety*. New York, Plenum Press.

Michon, J.A.(1989) Explanatory pitfalls and rule-based driver models. *Accident Analysis and Prevention*. Aug; Vol 21(4): 341-353.

Mikkonen, V. & Keskinen, E. (1980) Sisäisten mallien teoria liikennekäyttäytymisestä. Helsingin yliopisto, yleinen psykologia. *General psychology monographs,* no B1.

Mikkonen, V. & Keskinen, E. (1983) Cognitive theory of traffic behaviour. In Helkama, K. & Niemi, P. (Eds.) *Proceedings of the Finnish-Soviet Symposium on cognitive processes*, Turku Finland May 16-19, 1983. Helsinki.

Miller, M., Galanter, E. & Pribram, K. H. (1960) *Plans and the structure of behavior*. New York: Holt, Rinehart and Winston.

Van der Molen, H. & Bötticher, A. (1988) A hierarchical risk model for traffic participants. *Ergonomics* 31(4), 537-555.

Näätänen, R. (1972) *Maantiekuolema*. WSOY: Porvoo and Helsinki

Näätänen, R. & Summala, H. (1974) A model for the role of motivational factors in drivers' decision-making. *Accident Analysis and Prevention* (6), 243-261.

Ranney, T. A. (1994) Models of driving behavior: A review of their evolution. *Accident Analysis and Prevention* 26(6), 733-750.

Rasmussen, J. (1980) What can be learned from human error reports? In: Duncan, K., Grunenberg, M. and Wallis, D. (Eds.) *Changes in working life*. Wiley, London.

Reason, J. (1985) *Recurrent errors in nuclear plants and their implications for the design and deployment of intelligent decision aids*. Paper presented at the NATO Advanced Study Institute, San Miniato.

Reason J. (1990) *Human error*. Cambridge University Press, New York.

Reason, J., Manstead, A., Stradling, S., Baxter, J. & Campbell, K. (1990) Errors and violations on the roads: a real distinction? *Ergonomics* 33(10/11), 1315-1332.

Summala, H. (1985). Modeling driver task: a pessimistic prediction? In L. Evans and R. C. Schwing (Eds.) *Human behavior and traffic safety*. New York: Plenum.

Summala, H. (1996) Accident risk and driver behaviour. *Safety Science* 22(1-3), 103-117.

Summala, H. (1997) Hierarchical model of behavioural adaptation and traffic accidents. In Rothengatter, T. & Vaya, E., C. (Eds.) *Traffic and transport psychology*. Theory and application. Pergamon, Elsevier Science, U. K.

Wilde, G. (1982) The theory of risk homeostasis: implications for safety and health. *Risk Analysis* 2(4) 209-225.

Traffic and Transport Psychology,
T. Rothengatter and R.D. Huguenin (Editors)

3

Behavioural Adaptation to In-Vehicle Safety Measures: Past Ideas and Future Directions

Christina M. Brown and Y. Ian Noy

Introduction

The primary difference between human beings and other mammals is a predisposition towards intelligent behaviour, expressed by an ability to reason with others, plan future actions, and reflect on past conduct. Another common manifestation of intelligence is the ability to adapt to novel conditions based on one's experience, the outcome of which is typically reflected by perceived advantages, or benefits, to the individual. Despite a poor understanding of the mechanisms underlying behavioural adaptation (BA), it is often cited as an explanation for the observed discrepancies between engineering estimates of the safety benefits of collision countermeasures and actual experience. It is conceivable that BA is influenced not only by the nature and salience of the system change, but factors such as individual differences in user characteristics. In order to better understand BA and its correlates, a number of theories of BA, and driver behaviour in general, have been advanced. This collection of intuitive, and at times controversial, models has occupied a prominent position in the fields of transportation psychology and human factors engineering, and serves as the basis of this report.

A popular collection of theories, first introduced in the 1970s, posits that BA arises due to road users' attempts to maintain an acceptable level of risk. For example, the central premise of Wilde's risk homeostasis theory (RHT) is that a control mechanism operates to keep overall risk per unit time constant and, as a consequence, the number of collisions per unit of driving time remains fixed, independent of changes in the road safety system (Wilde, 1982; 1988; 1995). The determining variable in this closed-loop regulation process is the optimal, or target, risk level that is accepted and tolerated at a particular point in time (Wilde, 1988). Although RHT signified a pioneering step towards an explanation of BA, containing both face validity and intuitive appeal, it has been the subject of criticism over the years (McKenna, 1985; Evans, 1986). RHT has been accused of being overly pessimistic with respect to the potential for reducing collision and fatality statistics (McKenna, 1985). While predicting that engineering and enforcement countermeasures will be ineffective in increasing the overall level of safety, RHT does propose, however, that overall per capita costs can be reduced by countermeasures such as incentive, or educational, programmes that reduce the societal target, or accepted, level of risk (Wilde, 1995).

Another criticism of RHT revolves around the nebulous nature of the theory itself-it is unclear whether risk homeostasis occurs at the level of the individual, the community, or the nation. Similarly, RHT is vague in its assumptions regarding the time period required for risk homeostasis to take place, be it minutes, months, or years. A related concern is the choice of variables that are used in the homeostatic calculation. Does society, for instance, base its perception of risk on the per capita number of vehicle collision fatalities, the number of fatalities due to all accidents, or on the total number of deaths in the population, be they accidental or naturally-occurring? Furthermore, the theory does not explain what occurs during periods of war or during natural disasters such as droughts or floods. Presumably, if RHT was accurate in its predictions, a population would take these events into account when determining its overall assessment of risk.

RHT is based on assumptions that are not tenable. Few controlled experiments have been undertaken that empirically test the theory and, in general, results give rise to competing interpretations. Michon (1989) contends that, in the unlikely event that the same homeostat operates in all individuals, ensembles of homeostats (individual drivers) still would not necessarily produce homeostatic behaviour at the aggregate level. It also remains possible that factors other than risk underlie the behaviour changes that follow alterations to the traffic system.

Another risk-based theory, the zero-risk model of driver behaviour, proposes that drivers attempt to maintain a stable balance between subjective and objective risk (Summala & Näätänen, 1987; Summala, 1988). Thus, drivers avoid "feeling fear" (hence, experience "zero-risk") when they drive by anticipating, or expecting, some degree of risk during the performance of this task. Only when the subjective risk reaches a level that was not anticipated will drivers change their behaviour, increasing safety margins like vehicle spatial and temporal spacing (Ranney, 1994). BA is predicted to occur when there are changes to road users' perceptions regarding risk, perceptions that can change following the introduction of a novel safety measure.

Fuller (1984) presents another risk-based model of driving behaviour, which is based on learning theory and similar to both RHT and the zero-risk model. Originally named the 'threat-avoidance model', the risk avoidance model describes driving behaviour as a collection of individual stimulus-response decision processes that take place throughout the driving task-and include many determining factors that contribute to the ultimate goal of risk avoidance. Basically, when a driver is presented with a discriminative stimulus for a potential aversive event, he or she will choose a response based on its corresponding rewards and punishments. While providing a good model of the contribution of individual discriminative stimuli and their corresponding responses, risk avoidance theory has one serious limitation: it is unable to explain driving behaviour in terms of more complex, "nested" situations (Michon, 1989). For instance, it is unable to explain all of the decision points and responses that occur during a more complex driving scenario such as over-taking, which involves many considerations and decision points. As Michon so eloquently states, "the word meanwhile does not exist in the vocabulary of behaviorism(sic)" (p.346), from which risk avoidance theory takes its roots.

The notion of subjective risk, which is inherent in all risk-based theories, implies that the driver, or road user, has the capacity to consistently and accurately predict the outcome of various behavioural alternatives. In actual fact, it is extremely unlikely that individuals have the ability to accurately assess their level of risk. Furthermore, the process of estimating risk carries with it a component of conscious processing, and it is unlikely that road users perform this processing in the milliseconds that precede most driving manoeuvres. As well, while risk regulation is used to explain changes in road user behaviour, the primary construct (risk) can easily be substituted with other plausible contenders. For example, trip utility maximisation (Janssen & Tenkink, 1988) is a mathematical model that sees variables other than risk as underlying why a 'rational and well-informed decision-maker' (i.e., driver) might display behaviour counteracting the expected benefits from safety interventions. In this theory, risk homeostasis is considered to be a by-product of behaviour directed towards a reasonable purpose, i.e., to maximise the overall utility associated with a trip. Similarly, Lund and O'Neill (1986) provide a common-sense, and even more convincing, reason why drivers might compensate their behaviour according to imposed changes to the road traffic system. When driving, drivers receive feedback regarding their vehicle's handling characteristics. This information is used by the driver to determine what the car can do without losing control and crashing, with the ultimate goal being to get from the starting point to the desired destination without getting into a collision. Therefore, only those interventions that provide feedback to the driver about the driving task should affect behaviour. Unlike risk-based theories, this explanation for BA does not rely on constructs such as societal risk homeostasis, which, while interesting in nature and philosophy, remain speculative and essentially untestable. Rothengatter (1988) determined that other factors, such as pleasure in driving and the behaviour of others, also play an important role in determining the occurrence of "risky" behaviours such as speed choice.

Several theories have merged risk management with other variables in their explanations of BA. Evans (1985) proposes a human behaviour feedback formalism, the core notion of which is that when a system is changed, users do not, in general, ignore the change but, rather, respond with some type of concomitant change in behaviour. This change in behaviour is not motivated solely on risk perception, but other factors as well, and can produce one of five possible outcomes: a greater than expected change, a less than expected change, an expected change, no safety change, or a 'perverse' effect (change in opposite direction to that expected). Using a mathematical equation as illustration, the parameter f is put forth as representing the degree to which there is feedback, or interactions, in a system. The value of f is never truly known, and Evans, following an examination of 26 different engineering safety changes, can only provide likely ranges as an estimate, the actual value lying somewhere on a positive-negative continuum.

The main advantage of the theory is that it provides an explanation as to why some traffic interventions work and others do not. If a change is associated with obvious feedback to a road user, then more BA is predicted to occur. For example, marked (painted) crosswalks result in more vehicle-pedestrian collisions than unmarked crosswalks (Herms, 1972). This was believed to result from pedestrians experiencing an increased sense of security, while approaching drivers experienced no such parallel increase in caution. On the other hand, if an engineering change does not provide much feedback to the road user, it is less likely to result in BA. Driving a car that is equipped with passive restraint systems such as air bags, for instance, does not result in significant increases in risky driving practices such as reduced headway time (Sagberg, Fosser & Sætermo, 1997).

O'Neill's decision-theory model of danger compensation (O'Neill, 1977) shares components of risk homeostasis, trip utility maximisation, and human behaviour feedback models. In it, the driver is assumed to act as a rational human being; that is, one who, having relatively stable goals, attempts to maximise the total expected value of his/her actions. A mathematical formula is presented by which one can determine the degree of compensation that a driver exhibits in response to an environmental safety improvement, resulting in a value that is more than, less than, or equal, to that expected. The probability of a collision occurring per hour is proposed to equal the product of the danger occurrence rate and the probability that the danger is too close to be avoided, so long as the rate at which dangers arise is small. By assuming that all drivers act as rational and informed human beings, the theory predicts that either all drivers should increase their accident rate in response to a safety improvement, or all should decrease it. This assumption, however, like those of the risk-based theories, is not likely tenable.

Underwood, Jiang and Howarth (1993) describe a model of safety measure effects that considers effects of both engineering and motivational safety measures. Using a cost-benefit analysis model, the theory attempts to explain the compensatory process that takes place in reaction to the introduction of safety measures. Using drivers' motivations (other than safety), as well as expected accident cost, the model determines the expected benefit of a safety measure. Based on the assumption that the aim of road users in making a trip is to maximise the benefit of the action, risk compensation is posited to occur as road users respond to changes in the system. This response ultimately ensures that their personal needs are achieved. In this way, the model is similar to Janssen and Tenkink's (1988) trip utility maximisation model and O'Neill's (1977) decision-theory model of risk compensation. Underwood et al.'s model has better predictive and explanatory power, however, in that it does not rely, as O'Neill's model does, on empirically unsupported assumptions, such as that drivers can accurately predict collision probability. Unfounded theoretical assumptions are also avoided by considering what the drivers' needs and motivations are before predictions regarding the effects of safety measures on behaviour are made. By doing this, the authors generate a 'net gain curve' for each driving episode, which is a trade-off among a number of goals and costs.

In an attempt to explain driving behaviour on levels other than simple risk reduction, a set of 'hierarchical' theories emerged. Van der Molen and Bötticher's (1988) hierarchical risk model for traffic participants explicitly characterises a hierarchy of driver behaviour, in terms of three levels of control: strategic, tactical, and operational. The strategic level corresponds to actions such as route planning, mode choice, and desired cruise speed. At the tactical level, more concrete manoeuvres occur, such as overtaking. Actions chosen at the tactical level are completed at the operational level, by means of steering inputs, brake application, and emergency responses. This theory allows the calculation of individual behaviour alternatives, as well as the subjective probability and utility aspects of said alternatives, while also describing the perceptual, judgmental, and decisional processes involved in the driving task.

Summala (1997) describes a hierarchical model of BA and traffic accidents, which incorporates three levels of psychological processing and their corresponding levels of the driving task into its explanation. High level decision-making and supervisory monitoring make up the highest level of psychological processing, which refers to the more conscious decisions that are made by the driver both during, and before, a trip. BA on this level would include the avoidance of adverse conditions by certain groups of drivers, for example the elderly. The second level in the model is attention control, a level of typically unconscious processing that relates to navigation and other trip decisions. Attention control is applied either bottom-up, when sudden changes in the environment demand an attention shift, or top-down, when drivers intentionally monitor vehicle control tasks. BA on this level might take the form of a shift in attention, either from the road scene to in-vehicle tasks, or from in-car functions towards the driving task. The lowest level is that of perceptual-motor control, which is considered to occur largely without the driver's awareness. BA on this level might be evidenced by a driver altering headway distance between vehicles, or changing vehicle speed.

Although possessing some of the same weaknesses as the risk-based models, hierarchical models are generally more comprehensive, and incorporate several improvements. For example, psychological processes that may underlie BA are proposed, which, in turn, allow for predictions to be made regarding when BA will occur. Testable hypotheses can thus be generated, and empirical studies carried out.

Empirical Research to Date

In terms of human evolution, driving behaviour is a relatively recent phenomenon. Consequently, the quantity of research in the area is somewhat limited, especially when studies looking at more complex, higher-order processes are considered. The phrase 'BA', as applied to driving behaviour, was defined in 1990 with the Organisation for Economic Co-operation and Development's (OECD) report on BAs to changes in the road transport system. Since then, some researchers have chosen the term to describe changes arising from transportation safety measures; however, others continue to use it synonymously with phrases like 'risk compensation' (Underwood, Jiang & Howarth, 1993; Assum, Bjørnskau, Fosser & Sagberg, 1999). Whether the two terms are, in reality, synonymous is unlikely. The only way to answer questions such as this is by thorough scientific investigation. What follows is a review and discussion of past experimental studies designed to examine BA to in-vehicle safety measures.

Engineering safety interventions

Daytime Running Lights. Daytime running lights (DRL) are designed to make vehicles more conspicuous during daylight hours. In Canada, DRL have been regulated as mandatory equipment on all new light-duty vehicles since December 1989, while in other countries DRL apply only to certain vehicle types such as motorcycles, which are typically less conspicuous than automobiles.

While effective in reducing the number of collisions involving vehicles travelling in opposite directions or turning (Hollo, 1998; Transport Canada, 1997; Elvik, 1996; Arora, Collard, Robbins, Welbourne, & White, 1994), DRL can also create undesirable side effects. For example, vehicles not equipped with DRL are even more difficult to perceive as surrounding light levels decrease and the number of DRL-equipped vehicles increase (Atwood, 1977; 1979). Theeuwes and Riemersma (1996) suggest that this effect may also extend to more vulnerable road users such as cyclists and pedestrians; however, this notion has yet to be empirically assessed. In 1997, citing a continuing and increasing number of complaints from its members, the U.S. National Motorists Association (NMA) submitted a petition to the National Highway Traffic Safety Administration (NHTSA) requesting that the installation of hard-wired DRLs be prohibited on all new vehicles (National Motorists Association, 1997). The petition raised concerns such as: increased visual glare, reduced visibility of directional signal lights, increased visual 'clutter', reduced conspicuity of motorcycles and emergency vehicles, distorted distance perception, and drivers' decreased use of standard lights in low-light, low-visibility conditions.

Centre High-Mounted Braking Lights. Centre high-mounted braking lights (CHMBL) provide redundant information at the centre of a driver's visual field, indicating that a lead vehicle is braking. Associated with statistically shorter reaction times than typical brake light configurations (Sivak, Olson, & Farmer, 1981) and a 50% reduction in the rate of rear-end accidents in fleet studies (Malone, Kirkpatrick, Kohl & Baker, 1978; Reilly, Kurke, & Buckenmaier, 1980), the CHMBL has been mandated on all new passenger vehicles in the U.S. and Canada as of 1986. In terms of actual performance in the general driving population, however, they have not resulted in the predicted reduction of rear-end collisions. Most studies have not been able to dissociate the novelty effect of these lights, and some researchers have proposed that some of their benefit is disappearing (OECD, 1990).

In a study designed to assess the long-term effects of CHMBL, Farmer (1996) compared rear-end insurance claims for the years 1985 and 1986 with rates for 1986 to 1991. Overall odds ratios revealed that the presence of a CHMBL resulted in a 3-12% reduction in the likelihood of a rear-end claim, which does not replicate the initial predicted decrease of 50% found in the fleet studies. A number of explanations have been put forth to account for this discrepancy. Over time, the inclusion of the CHMBL in all vehicles may acclimatise drivers to not attend to it or to behaviourally adapt to it (Theeuwes, 1991; OECD, 1990). Drivers may also decrease their following distance, or headway, as they learn that less time is needed to respond. An initial trend of data from 1986 and 1987 for CHMBL-relevant collision reductions support this hypothesis: in 1986 there was a 22% reduction of CHMBL-relevant collisions, this decreased to 17% in 1987 (Kahane, 1987; 1989). As well, across six years (1986-91), the effectiveness of CHMBL was found to diminish with time; however, it was not significant enough to conclude that full acclimatisation had occurred (Farmer, 1996).

Studded Tires. Studded tires, used primarily in countries that experience ice- and snow-covered roads during winter, enable better traction and shorter braking distances than their non-studded counterparts. These advantages only exist, however, when driving on snow or ice. In fact, studded tires actually increase braking distances on dry roads and decrease lateral control of the vehicle. BA to these tires would be expected to result in speed increases in inclement road conditions, resulting from drivers' experience of increased manoeuvrability on snow and ice. Therefore, the increase in safety resulting from studded tires would be expected to be diminished if drivers concomitantly increased their speeds and decreased their following headway.

In a study designed to investigate this hypothesis, Rumar, Berggrund, Jernberg and Ytterbom (1976) found that, although drivers with studded tires drove faster in icy conditions, they drove with larger safety margins (headway) than drivers with unstudded tires. Furthermore, in dry conditions, there were no clear differences in headway or speed selection between the two groups of drivers. These results, while not demonstrating a complete reversal of the safety benefit of studded tires, can still be seen as supporting the hypothesis of BA. Since drivers with studded tires drove faster only on icy conditions (when feedback regarding the effects of their tires was present) and not when driving on dry roads, BA to the tires was concluded to have taken place. This provides an example where the safety effect of an intervention was reduced, but not completely negated.

Seat Belts. Seat belts restrain vehicle occupants, preventing them from hitting the steering wheel, dashboard, other vehicle occupants, or being ejected in the event of a collision. Consequently, they lower the probability that an individual will be seriously injured or killed in a collision by about 40% for front outboard occupants (Evans, 1991). With such a significant effect on safety, BA resulting from the use of seat belts should be readily apparent. For example, in order to negate seat belts' safety effects, seat belt-wearing drivers would need to demonstrate a much more reckless manner of driving compared to non-wearers. Most investigations looking at seat belts and driving behaviour, however, do not support this conclusion. For example, in a study looking at seat belt use and preferred headway, variables such as vehicle size, vehicle age, and the presence or absence of passengers were found to affect headway more than whether seat belts were used (MacKay, Dale & White, 1982). More support for the notion that seat belt use does not result in an increase in risky driving behaviour comes from studies looking at the pattern of collisions between protected road users (belted drivers) and unprotected users (pedestrians, cyclists, public service vehicles). One year after seat belts were made mandatory on all passenger vehicles in the United Kingdom, the number of collisions involving protected vs. unprotected road users remained the same as the preceding year (Scott & Wallis, 1985).

While seat belt use is associated with significant safety benefits, the regulation and enforcement of their use have resulted in much more modest effects on traffic fatalities (Dee, 1998). One explanation put forward to explain this phenomenon is Evans' 'selective recruitment hypothesis'. The basic premise of this hypothesis is that people who wear seat belts are inherently more risk aversive, having fewer violations and accidents than people who do not wear seat belts. Thus, when seat belt use is increased by mandatory laws, the people who comply are less likely to have accidents than those who do not comply (Evans, 1985). Janssen (1994) conducted an on-road study with groups of habitual wearers vs. non-wearers in which participants drove two 105 km routes in an instrumented vehicle. As well, a double lane-change manoeuvre and braking to a fixed obstacle were subsequently performed on a street that was closed to traffic. Habitual wearers wore their seat belts, while non-wearers wore them during one trip and not the other. Belted non-wearers tended to drive faster, on average, than belted wearers. This provides support for the selective recruitment hypothesis. Also, when non-wearers were belted, they tended to drive faster than when they were not; this is indicative of BA. Questionnaire results found that belted non-wearers felt safer on the extra tasks but not on the freeway route.

There is other evidence that seat belt use may diminish the caution demonstrated by drivers. In a controlled experimental investigation of the effects of seat belt use on 'risky' driving behaviour, Streff and Geller (1988) found that subjects driving go-carts who switched from not using a safety belt to using one increased driving speed during the second phase significantly more than subjects who used the safety belt during both driving phases. Habitual belt non-wearers did not drive faster than habitual wearers, indicating that this effect was likely due to transient effects such as putting on the seat belt, rather than on stable personality characteristics. It is difficult to know what made drivers drive faster when they wore seat belts. It is possible, for instance, that when restrained, drivers' felt more stable in the go-carts, which in turn allowed them to have better control of the vehicle. On the other hand, it is possible that drivers' aversion to sustaining an injury decreased when they wore a seat belt. There is also the possibility that seat belt-wearing drivers experienced a reduction in their aversion towards sustaining a collision; however, it is difficult to imagine that a safety measure could be capable of changing the acceptability of the outcome of an unknown, and potentially fatal, event.

Antilock Brake Systems. The technical advantage provided by antilock braking systems (ABS) ensures that, on most surface types, drivers stop sooner and in a more controlled manner than with traditional systems. ABS modulates the pressure in each wheel's brake line so that when a wheel lock-up is anticipated or occurs, the brake line pressure is released, which allows the wheel to turn. Immediately after releasing the pressure, the ABS reapplies it until the wheels begin to lock-up again. Because the wheels continue to turn during the braking manoeuvre, steering and braking continue to be effective. Without ABS, the wheels would lock-up, causing the vehicle to lose traction, resulting in the ineffectiveness of both steering and braking inputs (Grant & Smiley, 1993). In an initial study looking at its effectiveness, ABS decreased driver errors, such as leaving the marked lane and striking an object by 2.4 times over conventional brakes (Rompe, Schindler, & Wallrich, 1987). This enabled the conclusion that "the early introduction of ABS on a universal basis would effect a considerable reduction in both the severity and number of road accidents". On the basis of collision studies, Langwieder (1986, in OECD, 1990) concluded that the universal adoption of ABS in Germany could diminish the number of accidents involving property and personal loss by between 10 and 15 %. The full benefit from ABS, however, has not been realised. This is reflected in real-world collision and insurance claim data.

In a small fleet study of taxicabs in Germany, no differences were found in the crash rates of taxicabs with and without ABS (Schenbrenner & Biehl, 1992; in Williams & Wells, 1994). Interestingly, observers posing as passengers rated drivers with ABS as driving more aggressively and performing more dangerous manoeuvres than drivers without ABS. When surveyed, the taxicab drivers revealed that they thought ABS made them more likely to take risks. A more recent taxi fleet study found that drivers using vehicles equipped with ABS showed significantly shorter headway distances than those driving without ABS (Sagberg, Fosser & Sætermo, 1997). The lack of benefit of ABS is also apparent when inspecting insurance figures. Both damage liability and collision coverage insurance claims for vehicles equipped with ABS vs. those not equipped have been found to be of the same frequency and average cost (Highway Loss Data Institute, 1994).

Some authors have proposed that BA to in-vehicle safety devices will be more likely to occur if the driver is able to experience direct feedback from the device (Evans, 1991; Lund & O'Neill, 1986). Based on this premise, BA to ABS should be more likely to occur in drivers who have experienced the effect of ABS vs. those who have not. Grant & Smiley (1993) tested this hypothesis using an instrumented vehicle on a test track. Drivers who were shown the increased control available with ABS drove faster in a curve-following task, and used higher brake pedal forces than those who had not been shown the benefits of ABS. It was concluded that drivers behaviourally adapt to the effects of ABS by driving less safely. This, in turn, reduces the predicted safety benefits of such systems.

Airbags. Airbags, also known as supplementary restraint systems (SRS), are designed to protect drivers against injury during collision by providing an energy-absorbing buffer that prevents the head and upper body from striking the steering wheel, instrument panel and windshield. Rather than reducing the likelihood of a collision, airbags reduce the injury cost of a collision once it has occurred. It has been hypothesised that injury-reducing measures such as air bags are less likely to result in BA than are collision-reducing countermeasures (Lund & O'Neill, 1986). If BA were to take place in response to the presence of air bags, it might be manifest at the strategic level of driver behaviour; for example, drivers with air bags may be less likely to wear their seat belt.

Sagberg, Fosser and Sætermo (1997) looked at taxi drivers who drove vehicles equipped with air bags vs. those driving vehicles not equipped with air bags. Results showed that the presence of air bags was not related to any changes in driver behaviour, including seat belt wearing. Other behavioural measures included speed selection, headway distance, and lateral lane deviation. Another study, based on insurance data and accident reports, determined that drivers tend to drive more aggressively when a car is equipped with an airbag (Peterson, Hoffer, & Millner, 1995); however, they did not directly test driving behaviour with and without an airbag.

Intelligent transportation system (ITS) devices

Adaptive Cruise Control. Adaptive Cruise Control (ACC), an enhanced version of conventional cruise control, allows a vehicle to follow a lead vehicle at an appropriate distance by controlling the engine and/or power train and, potentially, the brake. A vehicle equipped with ACC will thus reduce speed automatically, within limits, to match the speed of a slower vehicle that it is following (Francher, Bareket, Bogard, MacAdam, & Ervin; 1997). Current ACC systems have a limited braking ability sufficient to maintain the headway distance under most driving conditions but not sufficient to avoid a collision without driver intervention. Therefore, ACC is currently marketed as a driver convenience rather than a safety feature. The goal of ACC is partial automation of vehicle control and reduction of driver workload. When used correctly, it may also have useful safety benefits. For example, ACC has the potential to reduce tailgating and, as a consequence, reduce the number and severity of rear-end accidents. Using a set of accident records from a number of jurisdictions in California, Chira-Chavala and Yoo (1994) estimated the proportion of accidents that could benefit from the use of ACC to be 7.5%. Expected behavioural changes include reductions in hard acceleration and decelerations, speed harmonisation among vehicles, and reductions in unsafe headway.

Issues of BA to ACC include whether or not drivers use the system as intended (to maintain safe headways), or whether they use it as a collision warning system, consequently accepting greater risk (e.g., speeding, following too closely). A number of dependent variables are likely to indicate that BA to ACC has taken place: 1) headway and headway variance, 2) speed and speed variability, 3) the migration of vehicles equipped with ACC to the passing lane, and 4) intrusion of other drivers into the headway gap. The effects of two types of ACC that differed in their automation capabilities were studied by Risser and Lehner (1999). Adaptive behaviours were examined at a social level of analysis, and included communication, automation responses, risk compensation, delegation of responsibility (to the ACC), and irritation/ avoidance behaviour. In general, support for changes in patterns of communication between ACC-equipped drivers and other road users was found; however, conclusions reached by the authors, while interesting, were difficult to evaluate due to the lack of elaboration regarding the methods and results.

In a more detailed simulator study, Hoedemaeker and Brookhuis (1998) tested the ability of ACC to induce BA. Regardless of driving style (speed choice and the ability to ignore distractions), results showed BA in terms of higher speed, smaller minimum time headway, and larger brake pedal forces. Although most drivers evaluated the system very positively, the potential safety effects of ACC systems are challenged by such results. Indeed, the finding that drivers rate the system so positively may make the safety-reducing BA effects even more significant, in that drivers will be more likely to a) use the system and b) be unaware of any negative behavioural correlates.

Collision warning systems. Collision warning systems have the ability to detect lane departures, hazardous road and weather conditions or obstacles in the vehicle's path, and warn drivers of potential hazards. In a recent paper examining theoretical issues associated with collision warning systems, Parasuraman, Hancock, and Olofinboba (1997) discuss the problem of setting appropriate triggering thresholds for warning signals, taking into consideration the rate of false alarms. Their analysis suggests that collision warnings may have limited effectiveness in reducing the number of collisions due to the conflicting requirements of the system to minimise false alarm rate and, at the same time, to provide sufficient time for the driver to react when there is a real event (e.g., a hazard undetected by the driver). A related concern is the degree to which BA may develop in response to collision warning systems. The most conceivable form that this behaviour could take would be drivers' ignoring the warning signal due to the system generating too many false positives. These concerns and their related, conflicting requirements may ultimately be irreconcilable; however, some manufacturers continue to ignore ergonomics principles in their eagerness to produce novel, marketable warning systems. This is worrisome, especially in view of current discussions regarding incentives that may be implemented in order to encourage the adoption of these devices. These include tax credits and the proposal to allow commercial truck drivers who use collision warning systems to drive for longer time periods without taking a break (Locker, 1999). To date, no research looking at the issue of BA in response to collision warning systems has been conducted.

Fatigue warning systems. Considerable effort is underway to develop driver monitoring systems, some of which may have dubious benefits. Fatigue warning systems employ a variety of techniques, such as measuring the frequency of driver eyelid closures, lane deviation and steering wheel activity, to detect driver drowsiness while operating a vehicle and signal a driver when critical levels of drowsiness are reached. Vincent, Noy, and Laing (1998) recently published the preliminary results of a study investigating BA to fatigue warning systems. While no evidence was found that drivers relied on these systems to keep them awake, there was similarly no evidence that the warnings produced by the system had any effect on drivers' propensity to take breaks. This is not surprising given that drivers are often well aware of their level of drowsiness. The warnings may be redundant insofar as the driver is concerned and, hence, may have no intrinsic value.

Vision Enhancement Systems. Vision Enhancement Systems (VES) use either infrared or ultraviolet sensors to enhance various aspects of the roadway and environment during low visibility conditions (Bossi, Ward, Parkes, & Howarth, 1997).

Certain drivers may behave in such a way as to negate the intended benefits of VES by, for example, driving at a higher speed, thereby increasing their mobility at the cost of safety if a collision were to occur. From the perspective of the driver, however, changes in risk associated with driving faster at night may not be perceptible. Thus, while collisions involving pedestrians and animals are expected to decrease with the use of VES, the potential increase in exposure (especially at night and in inclement weather) may result in more collisions overall.

Another form of BA that may result from VES is the tendency of drivers to focus their attention on the VES display, thereby reducing their attention to peripheral regions. In fact, Bossi et al. (1997) found that at night, but not at dusk, VES reduced target detection for peripheral targets outside the central field that was enhanced through VES. Based on these results, there will be a decreased likelihood of crashes involving hazards on or near the road (if speed increases are limited), and an increased likelihood of crashes involving hazards entering the road, when drivers use VES.

In-vehicle Navigation Systems. Navigation systems provide drivers with route-finding information in a variety of formats including map displays, visual displays of simple instructions, or systems providing auditory oral instructions (Zaidel & Noy, 1997).

BA to in-vehicle navigation systems may take different forms, depending on the level of processing involved. For example, at a strategic level, drivers using navigation aides have been found to travel more on neighbourhood streets, as compared to major arterial roads, in a effort to avoid traffic congestion (Kubota, Koyama, Iwazaki, & Monji, 1995). On an operational or perceptual-motor level, drivers spend less time looking at the road ahead when they use an in-vehicle navigation system. With a navigation system, drivers were found to glance ahead only 57% of the time, as compared to 78% of the time when using a paper map, or 85% of the time when the route was memorised beforehand (Antin, Dingus, Hulse, & Wierwille, 1990).

Future Directions

As previously outlined, available theories of BA and driving behaviour in general, while intuitively appealing and providing some useful insight, are all lacking in at least one respect. What is notably absent from the field of transportation psychology is a single, comprehensive, quantitative theory that can accurately describe, explain, and predict BA to in-vehicle, and roadway, safety measures.

While concepts such as risk adjustment and danger compensation may explain some aspects of BA, these notions are incomplete and overly simplistic. By not considering individual driver characteristics or the range of motivations that determine driving behaviour, these theories have fallen short. What is needed is a more comprehensive theory of BA with testable hypotheses and predictions. In order to develop such a theory, other concepts need to be evaluated. What follows is a description of three potential candidates: drivers' trust in automation and the psychological constructs locus of control and sensation-seeking. Finally, a model is proposed that integrates these concepts with selected features of earlier models.

Trust in automation

The human operator's role with respect to automated systems consists of: 1) device supervision, 2) performance monitoring, and 3) when required, intervention. When in-vehicle ITS devices are considered, these tasks translate to the driver's 1) awareness of the device and its purpose, 2) monitoring of the device's accuracy and performance, and 3) decision to respond to the device's output or ignore it. The concept of trust in automation, first introduced by Sheridan and colleagues (i.e., Sheridan, 1980; Sheridan, Fischhoff, Posner & Pew, 1983; Sheridan, Vamos, & Aiuda, 1983; Sheridan & Hennessy, 1984), can be used to explain individual differences in the use of, and reliance upon, a wide variety of automated equipment including ITS. A comprehensive theory of trust in automation has been developed by Muir (1994), who puts forth the notion that human operators will intervene, or override, a system when their trust in the automation falls below some point, or threshold. Alternatively, if the operator trusts the automation too much, they may become complacent and fail to override the system when it is faulty, a phenomenon known as automation complacency (Parasuraman, 2000). From Muir's perspective, trust is an intervening variable that cannot be measured directly; it is best viewed as a construct that mediates human beings' responses to various stimuli. Rather than subscribing to the simple notion that if technology works, people will use it and, if it is faulty, they will not, Muir invokes the concept of trust to describe individual differences in operator behaviour. By doing this, the theory is able to not only describe the nature of human trust in machines, but also how trust in a system changes with experience. This makes the theory more appealing to those interested in the nature and prediction of BA.

Muir combines the postulates of an earlier, general theory of trust (Barber, 1983) with a model of the dynamics of trust (Rempel, Holmes, & Zanna, 1985) to come up with an integrated model of trust in human-machine relationships. The model predicts four possible outcomes that are related to trust and the quality of automation. The first is called appropriate trust, and refers to the situation where an operator trusts and uses automation when the quality is good. The second is appropriate distrust, which refers to an operator distrusting and rejecting poor-quality automation. The third outcome is false distrust, which takes place when an operator distrusts and rejects good-quality automation. In the context of in-vehicle safety devices, these first three scenarios will not result in any dangerous conditions-although false distrust will result in a loss of the automation's potential safety benefits. It is the fourth outcome, false trust, that is of primary concern to road safety researchers. In this case, the driver trusts and uses poor-quality automation. Only one instance of the automation's inaccuracy is necessary to produce devastating effects. It is this possibility that makes BA an important construct to remember when designing and implementing novel safety-related technology.

Muir's (1994) model of trust in automation shares many features with Riley's (1989) general model of mixed-initiative human-machine systems. The latter predicts that operator trust takes longer to be rebuilt than to be destroyed, and that an operator's overall opinion of the automated device will be less sensitive to change as his/her experience with the device increases. Riley suggests that the trust that aircraft pilots have in an automated system may determine their response to either rely on, or to override, a system. Self-confidence, or a pilot's evaluation of their own capabilities to perform what the automated system can do, is also related to the use of automation. If self-confidence is higher than trust, pilots (and drivers) will shift their preference from automatic to manual control, especially in risky situations. This possibility has also been raised by authors interested in the design of effective intelligent vehicle-highway systems (Kantowitz, Hanowski, & Kantowitz, 1997; Hancock & Parasuraman, 1992).

There is empirical evidence suggesting a role for trust in the operation of automated systems. Muir and Moray (1996) used subjective ratings of trust in a simulated supervisory process. In their study, participants were assigned to control one of three simulated pumps that differed in their degree of competence: the first pump's rate was set to precisely match the requested rate (no error); the second pump's rate was set to consistently be ten per cent higher than the target rate (constant proportional error); and the third pump's rate was manipulated to be a value selected randomly from a Gaussian distribution centred on the requested pump target, with a standard deviation of two per cent of the pump target value (variable error). As expected, participants trusted the exact pump more than the pump with either a constant or variable error, and their trust in these latter two did not differ. Results showed that operators' trust in the constant proportional error pump grew with experience, but was more stable for the exact pump and the variable error pump.

A second experiment found a high positive correlation between operators' self-reported trust in the pump and the time they spent in automatic pump mode, rather than manually intervening (Muir & Moray, 1996). The authors interpret this finding to demonstrate that subjective ratings of trust provide a simple, non-intrusive insight into people's use of automation. There was also a significant negative correlation between operators' monitoring behaviour and their ratings of trust. In other words, the more an operator trusted a pump, the less intensely they monitored it. These results have two important implications for the prediction of BA: first is the possibility that drivers' simple subjective ratings of trust in an in-vehicle device may be a reliable, quantitative predictor of BA; second is the implication that, if a driver trusts a device, they will monitor it less, resulting potentially in reduced alertness and vigilance, and a consequent over-reliance on the system to maintain alertness and orientation.

As with people, trust in a machine or system develops with repeated exposure. Just as we learn to rely on those close to us to perform certain functions and fulfil various roles, we similarly learn to rely on automated systems. Driving has typically been construed as a 'closed-loop' system, with the driver acting as operator. The introduction of in-vehicle ITS devices, however, is gradually decreasing the driver's overall contribution. For example, ACC systems maintain a constant headway between the host and lead vehicles by means of engine control and, in some cases, braking. Thus, the driver's workload is decreased as these task components are removed from his/her control. The extent that an individual driver will allow a device to take over functions will depend on the amount of trust that s/he feels toward it. Trust, in turn, depends on the amount of exposure one has to a device. In the context of driving, however, one instance of false trust can result in disaster. It is important for the driver not to relinquish too much of their attentional resources.

Locus of control

The personality dimension 'locus of control' relates to an individual's assumptions regarding responsibility for positive and negative events (Baron & Byrne, 1987). A person who believes that s/he is able to act so as to maximise the possibility of positive outcomes and minimise the possibility of negative ones is described as having an internal locus of control. Conversely, someone who believes that people are helpless and at the mercy of external forces, luck, or fate, has an external locus of control.

An external locus of control is associated with a lack of caution and a failure to take precautionary steps to avoid the occurrence of unfavourable outcomes (Montag & Comrey, 1987). It seems intuitive, therefore, that locus of control should also be related to driving behaviour and involvement in traffic accidents. Indeed, individual differences in locus of control are found to affect behaviour in a variety of settings, including driving. When university students were given questionnaires that assessed their driving abilities and personality, the driving skill scale was negatively correlated with a locus of control scale measuring lack of control, or externality (Lajunen & Summala, 1995). The same driving skill scale was positively correlated with an internal locus of control. The authors interpret these findings as indicating that individuals who emphasised skilled and fluent driving and mastering the vehicle in every situation also had, or wanted to express, a sense of having control over their own lives. Thus, the need for a sense of control is generalised and is manifested in driving behaviour. Another interpretation of the same finding is that a generalised sense of control determines the calibre of an individual's driving performance.

In a study looking at accident involvement, an internal locus of control was found to be associated with lower levels of accident involvement and higher levels of cognitive ability (Arthur, Barrett, & Alexander, 1992). Similarly, a cross-cultural study including samples from the United States, India, and Hong Kong consistently found externally-oriented individuals to be characterised by such self-destructive behaviours as drinking alcohol, smoking, and driving unsafely (Kelley et al., 1986). Finally, results of a driving simulator study looking at personality attributes and driving behaviour showed that people who have an external locus of control make more road departure errors than those with an internal locus of control (Verwey & Zaidel, 2000). It is clear from the preceding evidence that the way in which one sees the world affects the way one behaves. In the case of driving, if an individual views her- or himself as being responsible for both positive and negative outcomes, s/he will be more likely to take precautionary measures such as wearing a seat belt and being vigilant to roadway cues. On the other hand, those who see themselves as playing little or no part in the unfolding of events will act in a less cautious manner, believing that fate will achieve its goals no matter what the individual does.

Following this reasoning, BA to in-vehicle safety measures may also be under the influence of drivers' locus of control. It is possible that drivers with an internal locus of control will rely more on their own skills and abilities while they are driving and, no matter how reliable a safety device, will always maintain more direct involvement with the driving task than those scoring high on the externality dimension. Conversely, those with an external locus of control may be more likely to give up control to an external device, relying on it to competently perform the task it was designed for. These individuals, therefore, would be more likely than internals to over-rely on a device to keep them oriented and alert. Consequently, they will become less involved with the driving task and be less likely to react, or react more slowly, when the device fails to perform the task it was designed to.

Sensation-seeking

Zuckerman (1994) defines sensation-seeking (SS) as the tendency to seek novel, varied, complex, and intense sensations and experiences, and the willingness to take risks for the sake of such experience. High SS has been found to correlate with a variety of risk-taking behaviours, including injury proneness, sexual activity, gambling, financial risk-taking, smoking, and risky driving (Zuckerman, Chapter 5). SS as a personality characteristic appears to increase until approximately age 16, then decreases gradually over time. It has typically found to be higher in males than in females, and there is some evidence suggesting a biological and/or genetic basis (Zuckerman, 1994; Jonah, 1997).

A number of studies have looked at the relationship between SS and risky driving behaviour (for a complete review, see Jonah, 1997). High SS drivers are more likely than low SS drivers to drink and drive, and this relationship appears to be stronger among men than women. Interestingly, it is the drivers' perceived risk of collision involvement that appears to mediate the relationship between SS and impaired driving. Risky driving behaviours, other than drinking and driving, show the same relationship with SS, again with high SS drivers tending to perceive less danger in risky driving behaviour than low SS drivers. Finally, most studies looking at the relationship between SS and the outcome of risky driving, involvement in collisions, have reported positive results, with high SS drivers being more likely than low SS drivers to experience collisions and other traffic violations.

With respect to BA, Jonah (1997) suggests that, due to their propensity for seeking out and accepting higher risk levels, high SS drivers may be more likely than low SS drivers to behaviourally adapt to in-vehicle safety devices. By sensing that a novel safety measure reduces the level of risk, high sensation seekers may demonstrate BA even more than their low SS counterparts, due to their acceptance, or, even more likely, preference, of higher levels of risk. Thus, the BA that is found in response to novel safety devices may, in this way, be manifest in only a specific portion of the population: those scoring high on SS scales. As an example, Jonah predicts that, if provided with a warning that alerts them when they are becoming tired, high SS drivers will be expected to adapt to the presence of the warning device and, consequently, drive longer and at higher speeds, take fewer breaks, and make more driving errors than low SS drivers. This hypothesis was evaluated in two separate studies (both reported in Jonah, Thiessen, & Vincent, 1997). The first study investigated the likelihood of participants adapting to ABS. Participants were asked to imagine a hypothetical situation where they were driving a vehicle equipped with ABS, which, they were informed, increase safety. They were then given a self-report questionnaire that assessed their likelihood of demonstrating BA. High SS participants were more likely than low SS drivers to report that, with ABS, they would driver faster on a highway, drive after drinking, drive faster on wet roads, and not wear their seat belt. The second study was done on-road using an instrumented vehicle. Participants were asked to drive for an extended (5 h) period of time, either while receiving a fatigue warning signal or not. It was hypothesised that, compared to low SS drivers, high SS ones would take fewer breaks, drive faster, and exhibit greater lane deviation. While overall there was very little evidence of BA, high SS drivers tended to take fewer breaks during the post-test session (where half of all subjects received fatigue warning signals) than during the pre-test session, when no warning was present. The authors interpret this finding as suggesting that high SS drivers may have felt more comfortable with the experimental situation during the post-test condition, thus deciding to complete the driving task sooner by taking fewer breaks.

A quantitative theory of behavioural adaptation

Based on the above concepts, a new model of BA is proposed (see Figure 1). In it, drivers' personality variables (such as locus of control and sensation-seeking) contribute to the occurrence of BA in two ways: first, by directly influencing a driver's mental model of the driving task and, second, by interacting with psychological processes such as trust. According to this model, a driver with an external locus of control has a different mental model of the driving task than someone with an internal locus of control, seeing him/herself as being less responsible for both positive and negative events. As well, a driver with an external locus of control (who is hypothesised to be more likely to trust a device) is predicted to alter his or her mental model of the driving task to include assumptions about the device that it will do what it was designed to do. This change in mental model, in turn, will influence driving behaviour on all levels (strategic, tactical, and operational).

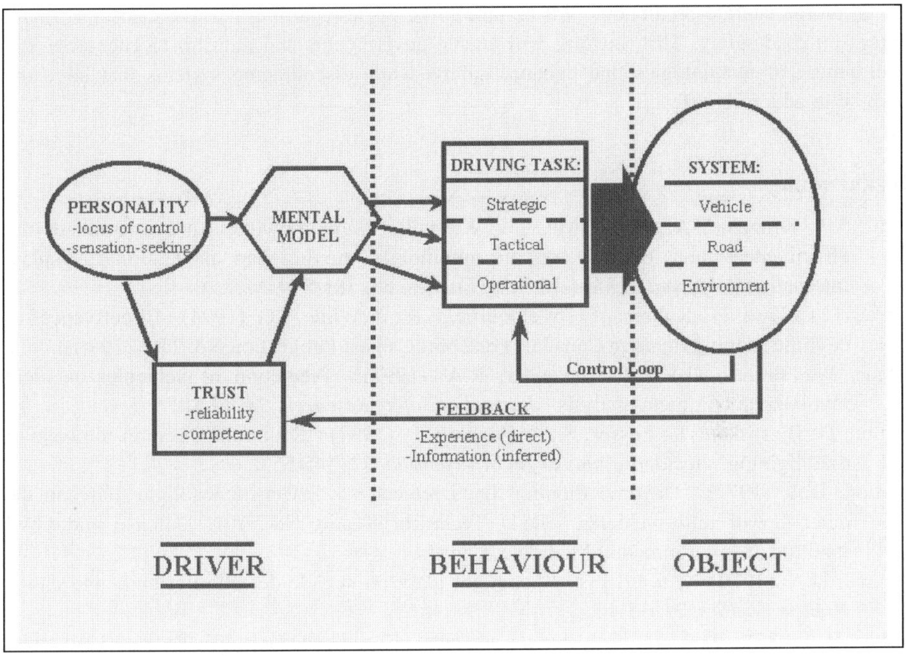

Figure 1. A quantitative model of behavioural adaptation.

The model also considers the object of the driver's behaviour, be it the vehicle, the road, and/or the environment. Feedback from each system can be either direct, through experience, or inferred, through information received from others, educational campaigns, and/or the media. Thus, if a new in-vehicle device is hailed by friends and the media as having only positive effects on safety, a driver may be more likely to trust that it will do what it was designed to do and, hence, behaviourally adapt to it. On the other hand, if a device is publicised as having negative effects, an opposite outcome would likely result, with drivers being less likely to demonstrate BA. The quality of the feedback will also determine the extent to which BA develops. For instance, timing of feedback from each system (whether it is immediate or delayed), amount of exposure, and persistence (if feedback is received indirectly through external sources) will all serve as contributing variables.

Lastly, the model is quantitative in nature, as it incorporates several testable constructs into its assumptions: 1) a driver's trust in a device, measured directly by means of simple questionnaires, 2) a driver's locus of control, measured using Montag and Comrey's (1987) driving internality/externality scales, and 3) a driver's degree of SS, measured using Zuckerman's (1994) SS scale. At the present time, in two studies looking at driving behaviour with lane departure warning devices, the model is being assessed with respect to whether, and to what extent, the above constructs contribute to BA (see Brown, 2000). It remains to be determined empirically whether this and/or other quantitative theories of BA can be validated.

If it is, more accurate predictions will be able to be made regarding the true effects of novel devices on road safety. This, in turn, will enable governments and industry to encourage the development of technologies that enhance safety, while discouraging systems that have the potential to adversely affect it.

References

Antin, J.F., Dingus, T.A., Hulse, M.C., & Wierwille, W.W. (1990). An evaluation of the effectiveness and efficacy of an automobile moving-map navigational display. International *Journal of Man-Machine Studies, 33*, 581-594.

Arora, H., Collard, D., Robbins, G., Welbourne, E.R., & White, J.G. (1994). Effectiveness of daytime running lights in Canada. Transport Canada Publication No. TP 12298(E).

Arthur, W., Barrett, G.V., & Alexander, R.A. (1992). Prediction of vehicular accident involvement: A meta-analysis. *Journal of Safety Research, 23*, 73-80.

Assum, T., Bjørnskau, T., Fosser, S., & Sagberg, F. (1999). Risk compensation-the case of road lighting. *Accident Analysis and Prevention, 31*, 545-553.

Atwood, D.A. (1977). Daytime running lights project V: Effect of headlight glare on the detection of unlit vehicles. RSU Technical Report No.77/01, Defense and Civil Institute of Environmental Medicine, Canada.

Atwood, D.A. (1979). The effects of headlight glare on vehicle detection at dusk and dawn. *Human Factors, 21*, 35-45.

Barber, B. (1983). *The Logic and Limits of Trust.* New Brunswick, NJ: Rutgers University Press.

Baron, R.A., & Byrne, D. (1987). *Social Psychology:* Understanding Human Interaction. Boston: Allyn and Bacon, Inc.

Bossi, L.L., Ward, N.J., Parkes, A.M., & Howarth, P.A. (1997). The effects of vision enhancement systems on driver peripheral visual performance. In Y.I. Noy (Ed.), *Ergonomics and Safety of Intelligent Driver Interfaces* (pp. 239-260). New Jersey: Lawrence Erlbaum Associates.

Brown, C.M. (2000). The concept of behavioural adaptation: Does it occur in response to lane departure warnings? Proceedings of the International Conference on Traffic and Transport Psychology. Berne, Sept. 4-7.

Chira-Chavala, T., & Yoo, S.M. (1994). Potential safety benefits of intelligent cruise control systems. *Accident Analysis and Prevention, 26*, 135-146.

Dee, T.S. (1998). Reconsidering the effects of seat belt laws and their enforcement status. *Accident Analysis and Prevention, 30*, 1-10.

Elvik, R. (1996). A meta-analysis of studies concerning the safety effects of daytime running lights on cars. *Accident Analysis and Prevention, 28*, 685-694.

Evans, L. (1985). Human behavior feedback and traffic safety. *Human Factors, 27*, 555-576.

Evans, L. (1986). Risk homeostasis theory and traffic accident data. *Risk Analysis, 6,* 81-94.

Evans, L. (1991). *Traffic Safety and the Driver.* New York: Van Nostrand Reinhold.

Farmer, C. M. (1996). Effectiveness estimates for center high mounted stop lamps: A six year study. *Accident Analysis and Prevention, 28*, 201-208.

Francher, P.S., Bareket, Z., Bogard, S., MacAdam, C., & Ervin, R. (1997). Tests characterizing performance of an adaptive cruise control system. Proceedings of the Society of Automotive Engineers International Congress and Exposition (SAE Technical Paper No. 970458, Special Publication SP-1230).

Fuller, R. (1984). A conceptualization of driving behaviour as threat avoidance. *Ergonomics, 27*, 1139-1155.

Grant, B.A., & Smiley, A. (1993). Driver response to antilock brakes: A demonstration of behavioural adaptation. Proceedings of the Canadian Multidisciplinary Road Safety Conference (pp.211-220). Saskatoon, June 14-16.

Hancock, P.A., & Parasuraman, R. (1992). Human factors and safety in the design of intelligent vehicle-highway systems (IVHS). *Journal of Safety Research, 23,* 181-198.

Herms, B.R. (1972). Pedestrian crosswalk study accidents in painted and unpainted crosswalks. *Highway Research Record, 406,* 1-13.

Highway Loss Data Institute (1994). Collision and property damage liability losses of passenger cars with and without antilock brakes. Arlington: Highway Loss Data Institute.

Hoedemaeker, M., & Brookhuis, K.A. (1998). BA to driving with an adaptive cruise control (ACC). *Transportation Research Part F, 1,* 95-106.

Hollo, P. (1998). Changes in the legislation on the use of daytime running lights by motor vehicles and their effect on road safety in Hungary. *Accident Analysis and Prevention, 30,* 183-199.

Janssen, W. (1994). Seat-belt wearing and driving behavior: An instrumented-vehicle study. *Accident Analysis and Prevention, 26*, 249-261.

Janssen, W.H., & Tenkink, E. (1988). Considerations on speed selection and risk homeostasis in driving. *Accident Analysis and Prevention, 20*, 137-142.

Jonah, B.A. (1997). Sensation seeking and risky driving: A review and synthesis of the literature. *Accident Analysis and Prevention, 29,* 651-665.

Jonah, B.A., Thiessen, R., & Vincent, A. (1997). Sensation seeking, risky driving and BA. Proceedings of the Canadian Multidisciplinary Road Safety Conference X. Toronto, June 8-11.

Kahane, C.J. (1987). The effectiveness of center high mounted stop lamps: A preliminary evaluation. U.S. National Highway Traffic Safety Administration, Report No. US-DOT HS-807-076.

Kahane, C.J. (1989). An evaluation of center high mounted stop lamps based on 1987 data. U.S. National Highway Traffic Safety Administration, Report No. US-DOT HS-807-442.

Kantowitz, B.H., Hanowski, R.J., & Kantowitz, S.C. (1997). Driver reliability requirements for traffic advisory information. In Y.I. Noy (Ed.), *Ergonomics and Safety of Intelligent Driver Interfaces* (pp.1-22). New Jersey: Lawrence Erlbaum Associates.

Kelley, K., Cheung, F., Rodriguez-Carrillo, P., Singh, R., Wan, C.K., & Becker, M.C. (1986). Chronic self-destructiveness and locus of control in cross-cultural perspective. *Journal of Social Psychology, 126,* 573-577.

Kubota, H., Koyama, S., Iwazaki, N., & Monji, T. (1995). Can we protect our neighborhood from "intelligent rat-runners"? Proceedings of the 2nd World Congress on Intelligent Transport Systems. (Vol.4, pp.1894-1898).

Lajunen, T., & Summala, H. (1995). Driving experience, personality, and skill and safety-motive dimensions in drivers' self-assessments. *Personality and Individual Differences, 19, 307*-318.

Locker, R. (1999). NTSB seeking better safety technology. The Journal of Commerce, September 3rd.

Lund, A.K., & O'Neill, B. (1986). Perceived risks and driving behavior. *Accident Analysis and Prevention, 18*, 367-370.

Malone, T.B., Kirkpatrick, M., Kohl, K.S., & Baker, C. (1978). Field test evaluation of rear lighting systems. U.S. National Highway Traffic Safety Administration, Report No. US-DOT HS-803-467.

McKay, G.M., Dale, K.J., & White, A. (1982). Seat belts under a voluntary regime: Some aspects of use related to occupant and vehicle characteristics and driving behaviour. Proceedings of the VIIth IRCOBI Conference on biomechanics of Impacts. Lyon.

McKenna, F.P. (1985). Do safety measures really work? An examination of risk homoeostasis theory. *Ergonomics, 28*, 489-498.

Michon, J.A. (1989). Explanatory pitfalls and rule-based driver models. *Accident Analysis and Prevention, 21*, 341-353.

Montag, I., & Comrey, A.L. (1987). Internality and externality as correlates of involvement in fatal driving accidents. *Journal of Applied Psychology, 72*, 339-343.

Muir, B.M. (1994). Trust in automation: Part I. Theoretical issues in the study of trust and human intervention in automated systems. *Ergonomics, 37,* 1905-1922.

Muir, B.M., & Moray, N. (1996). Trust in automation. Part II. Experimental studies of trust and human intervention in a process control simulation. *Ergonomics, 39,* 429-460.

National Motorists Association (1997). Petition to modify federal motor vehicle safety standard no.108: Lamps, reflective devices, and associated equipment. Available: http://www.motorist.org/issues/drl/DRL_petition.html.

OECD (Organisation for Economic Cooperation and Development)(1990). Behavioural adaptations to changes in the road transport system. Paris: OECD Road Research Group.

O'Neill, B. (1977). A decision-theory model of danger compensation. *Accident Analysis and Prevention, 9,* 157-165.

Parasuraman, R. (2000). Designing automation for human use: empirical studies and quantitative models. *Ergonomics, 43*, 931-951.

Parasuraman, R., Hancock, P.A., & Olofinboba, O. (1997). Alarm effectiveness in driver-centred collision-warning systems. *Ergonomics, 40*, 390-399.

Peterson, S., Hoffer, G., & Millner, E. (1995). Are drivers of air-bag-equipped cars more aggressive? A test of the offsetting behavior hypothesis. *Journal of Law and Economics, 38,* 251-264.

Ranney, T.A. (1994). Models of driving behavior: A review of their evolution. *Accident Analysis and Prevention, 26,* 733-750.

Reilly, R.E., Kurke, D.S., & Buckenmaier, C.C. (1980). Validation of the reduction of rear-end collisions by a high-mounted stoplamp-Final Report. U.S. Dept. of Transport Report No. DOTHS701756.

Rempel, J.K., Holmes, J.G., & Zanna, M.P. (1985). Trust in close relationships. *Journal of Personality and Social Psychology, 49*, 95-112.

Riley, V. (1989). A general model of mixed-initiative human-machine systems. Proceedings of the 33rd Annual Meeting of the Human Factors Society. (pp.124-128). Denver.

Risser, R., & Lehner, U. (1999). Evaluation of an ACC (autonomous cruise control) system with the help of behaviour observation. FACTUM: unpublished research report.

Rompe, K., Schindler, A., & Wallrich, M. (1987). Advantages of an anti wheel lock system (ABS) for the average driver in difficult driving situations. Proceedings of the XIth International Technical Conference on Experimental Safety Vehicles. (pp.442-448). Washington, DC.

Rothengatter, T. (1988). Risk and the absence of pleasure: a motivational approach to modelling road user behaviour. *Ergonomics, 31*, 599-607.

Rumar, K., Berggrund, U., Jernberg, P., & Ytterbom, U. (1976). Driver reaction to a technical safety measure-studded tires. *Human Factors, 18,* 443-454.

Sagberg, F., Fosser, S., & Sætermo, I.F. (1997). An investigation of behavioural adpatation to airbags and antilock brakes among taxi drivers. *Accident Analysis and Prevention, 29,* 293-302.

Scott, P.P., & Wallis, P.A. (1985). Road casualties in Great Britain during the first year with seat belt legislation. TRRL Research Report No.9.

Sheridan, T.B. (1980). Computer control and human alienation. Technology Review, October, 61-73.

Sheridan, T.B., Fischhoff, B., Posner, M., & Pew, R.W. (1983). Supervisory control systems. In: Research Needs for Human Factors. Washington: National Academy Press.

Sheridan, T.B., Vamos, T., & Aida, S. (1983). Adapting automation to man, culture and society. *Automatica, 19,* 605-612.

Sheridan, T.B., & Hennessy, R.T. (1984). Research and Modeling of Supervisory Control Behavior. Washington: National Academy Press.

Sivak, M., Olson, P.L., & Farmer, K.M. (1981). High-mounted brake lights and the behavior of following drivers. University of Michigan Highway Safety Research Institute Report No. UM-HSRI-81-31.

Streff, F.M., & Geller, E.S. (1988). An experimental test of risk compensation: Between-subject versus within-subject analyses. *Accident Analysis and Prevention, 20,* 277-287.

Summala, H. (1988). Risk control is not risk adjustment: The zero-risk theory of driver behaviour and its implications. *Ergonomics, 31,* 491-506.

Summala, H. (1997). Hierarchical model of BA and traffic accidents. In T. Rothengatter and E.C. Vaya (Eds.), *Traffic and Transport Psychology: Theory and Application* (pp.41-52). Oxford: Permagon Press.

Summala, H., & Näätänen, R. (1987). The zero-risk theory and overtaking decisions. In J.A. Rothengatter and R.A. de Bruin (Eds.), *Proceedings of the Second International Conference on Road Safety.* Assen: Van Gorcum.

Theeuwes, J. (1991). Center high-mounted stop light: An evaluation. TNO Institute for Perception, Report No. IZF 1991 C-3.

Theeuwes, J., & Riemersma, J. (1996). Comment on Williams and Farmer's evaluation of daytime running lights. *Accident Analysis and Prevention, 28,* 799-800.

Transport Canada (1997). Daytime running lights. Transport Canada publication No. TP13189.

Underwood, G., Jiang, C., & Howarth, C.I. (1993). Modelling of safety measure effects and risk compensation. *Accident Analysis and Prevention, 25,* 277-288.

Van der Molen, H.H., & Bötticher, A.M.T. (1988). A hierarchical risk model for traffic participants. *Ergonomics, 31,* 537-555.

Verwey, W.B., & Zaidel, D.M. (2000). Predicting drowsiness accidents from personal attributes, eye blinks and ongoing driving behaviour. *Personality and Individual Differences, 28,* 123-142.

Vincent, A., Noy, I., & Laing, A. (1998). Behavioural adaptation to fatigue warning systems. Proceedings of the 16th International Technical Conference on the Enhanced Safety of Vehicles. (Vol.1, pp.521-536). Windsor.

Wilde, G.J.S. (1982). The theory of risk homeostasis: Implications for safety and health. *Risk Analysis, 2,* 209-225.

Wilde, G.J.S. (1988). Risk homeostasis theory and traffic accidents: Propositions, deductions and discussion of dissension in recent reactions. *Ergonomics, 31,* 441-468.

Wilde, G.J.S. (1995). *Target Risk.* Kingston: PDE Publications.

Williams, A.F., & Well, J.K. (1994). Driver experience with antilock brake systems. *Accident Analysis and Prevention, 26,* 807-811.

Zaidel, D.M., & Noy, Y.I. (1997). Automatic versus interactive vehicle navigation aids. In Y.I. Noy (Ed.), Ergonomics and Safety of Intelligent Driver Interfaces (pp. 287-307. New Jersey: Lawrence Erlbaum Associates.

Zuckerman, M. (1994). Behavioural Expressions and Biosocial Bases of Sensation Seeking. Cambridge: University of Cambridge Press.

Traffic and Transport Psychology,
T. Rothengatter and R.D. Huguenin (Editors)

4

Theories of Science in Traffic Psychology

Ralf Risser and Wolf-Rüdiger Nickel

Introduction

This chapter presents and elaborates on two statements:

- problems that lead our applied scientific work in traffic are not analysed
- problem solutions are continuously developed anew, based on new empirical work; theoretical concepts are made too little use of - we do not rely on the theories we have, and work eternally to prove theories; there is no tradition to develop ideas for solutions on basis of what we have learned, more heuristically

These ideas were presented in the frame of the workshop and discussed. Below, first the statements given at the workshop are presented. Then, the results of the discussion are presented in a summarised form.

Problem Definition

"What is to be seen as a problem is, among others, a matter of philosophy", according to Winch (1990). We [WRN1] should put our empirical work in a philosophical frame. In traffic psychology, it looks as if we have not thought very much about problems connected to traffic, so far: We seem to have accepted the implicit view of many authorities in the industrial countries that traffic is mainly car traffic, which has to be safe and to flow smoothly. Thereby, in the terms of Goffman's model of role-play, safety is a matter of stage, whereas flow- and capacity-problems steer back-stage (among others see Barat 1985, Vasconcelos 1998).

This is illustrated by of the following overview. It shows usual modal split values [WRN2] in European countries/cities, the modal split of Vienna just to give one practical example, and the presentations in the Valencia proceedings (Rothengatter & Carbonell-Vaya, 1997) by the contents dealt with (Table 1):

Table 1. Modal split in European countries and in Vienna, and contents of presentations of the Valencia proceedings

Mode	*Modal split generally (%)*	*Modal split in Vienna (%)*	*Papers of the Valencia proceedings (%)*
Car	30-50	~ 33	94
Public transport	10-35	~ 33	
Walking and cycling	20-35	~ 33	
"Non-car" modes taken together	50-70	~ 66	6*

*) Waller's (1997) Keynote speech about "Transportation and society" and 2 presentations about "Mobility and car usage"

Now one could say that our focus is mainly on the car because cars cause most of the problems in traffic. But these problems are very often caused in the course of interaction with other road users: Only between 20 and 30% of all accidents are single accidents, all others are accidents between 2 or more road users. Moreover, pedestrians - in most European cities at least 1/4 to 1/3 of the fatalities - are victims of motor vehicles, after all. In the Valencia proceedings, there is not one single paper dealing with the communication of car drivers with other drivers, or with other types of road users regarding

- Interpretation of other road users' behaviour by drivers
- Presentations about other road users' situation and conditions generally
- Notion of other road users' needs and problems

So even if one is not philosophically minded and does not agree with Peter Winch, one has to admit that compared to the real world, the selection of contributions presented in Valencia is strangely odd. And the Valencia proceedings are not basically different from those of other traffic-psychology congresses.

The conclusion is: Traffic psychologists should deal more extensively with problem definition, which is not necessarily a psychological matter, but psychology could play a role, there: We could help to discover, whether basic needs and interests are frustrated or even violated in traffic, in which respect and for which groups (e.g., see Risser 2000).

Next, we have to interfere with problem solution. Probably everybody working in the field tries to do so. However, psychologists work on the problems at varying distances from practice. In many cases it almost looks as if they were afraid to apply psychology to practical problems.

Dealing with Problems: Two Different Types of Assumptions

There are at least two approaches when attempts are made to tackle traffic problems with psychological measures: Type 1) reflects the assumption that not every single implementation needs to be preceded by a case related empirical beforehand-testing of measures if one wants to apply or implement it in a special case, and Type 2) reflects the assumption that every single implementation needs to be preceded by a case related beforehand-testing of measures if one wants to apply or implement it in a special case.

Psychological theories are not mathematical, nor similar to those in physics. They are context-dependent, time-dependent, fashion-dependent, etc.. Thus, every time we apply psychological principles, there is the risk that rules we have learned in the past have changed in some characteristics. This seems to imply that we have to test the validity of measures every time before we apply them. But this would mean that we cannot compete at all with the technical disciplines in the applied areas, because we are much too slow andrigid. As a consequence psychology would lose importance in society, at least in the more technical areas of society: work place, traffic, economy. In practice, this seems to be a real problem only in the area of traffic: Natural scientists do work heuristically, they have their special universities training them to do so. Psychologists and social scientists do not.

We (psychologists) do research in order to find appropriate measures for problem solutions and in order to prove beforehand that they will be valid[1]. But we never will succeed in doing so in such a way that the sceptical, positivistic technocrat is satisfied. Our results for him, to a large degree, remain a matter of interpretation and belief (see Flyvbjerg 1999). Technicians and lawyers do research as well. But they usually also decide what is feasible in practice, and in the course of time they have gathered experience to do so because they have been implementing outcomes of their work regularly. They usually also "take care" of psychological aspects, but mostly without de facto considering psychologists and their knowledge and know-how, nevertheless always having some clichés on their lips: about the human factor, about user needs, about road user behaviour, etc..

What we need is to develop a clear alternative to the natural-scientific approach for applied psychology, because this natural-scientific approach implies that we have to prove again and again that our concepts for problem solution are valid. In the meantime, other disciplines decide what is going to happen in practice:

We need more freedom in the application of psychological rules which can only be achieved by the development of better heuristic procedures[2]: Reasoning, discussions, testing of ideas by presenting them to colleagues, pilot testing of concepts - and applications of methods and measures based on such procedures. The most important point, however, is that all applications are evaluated thoroughly.

The message is: Try to implement as many psychologically based concepts, or measures, as possible and try to evaluate as many of them as possible, and systematically. When talking about evaluation, we are back to problem definition and identification: 1) Psychologists can contribute to the identification of problems, especially when problems have to do with the

[1] What is a proof in psychology? One question that should be discussed extensively is whether it is possible to prove psychological concepts, i.e. analytical methods and problem solutions, beforehand, viz., off the practical circumstances under which they are supposed to function later on. Is the extra step between general psychological knowledge and rules, and their application, namely the experimental "proof" of their functionality, necessary, or even reasonable, in all cases? Or would not consequent application of psychological principles, and a systematic evaluation of effectiveness and efficiency of the application be more appropriate, while research (to find proofs, among other things) goes on parallel?

[2] The idea of dealing more with heuristic approaches in the frame of the education of traffic psychologists was also expressed by F. McKenna in the Symposion about Traffic psychology in Europe held at the IAAP Congress in San Francisco 1998.

frustration or violation of needs and interests, using special psychological instruments (interviews, questionnaires, etc.), based on qualitative and quantitative psychological models; and 2) they can discuss effects of measures on the basis of a more elaborated and appropriate problem definition than only so-called "objective" safety. Figure 1 presents an overview reflecting this and focussing especially on the role of evaluation.

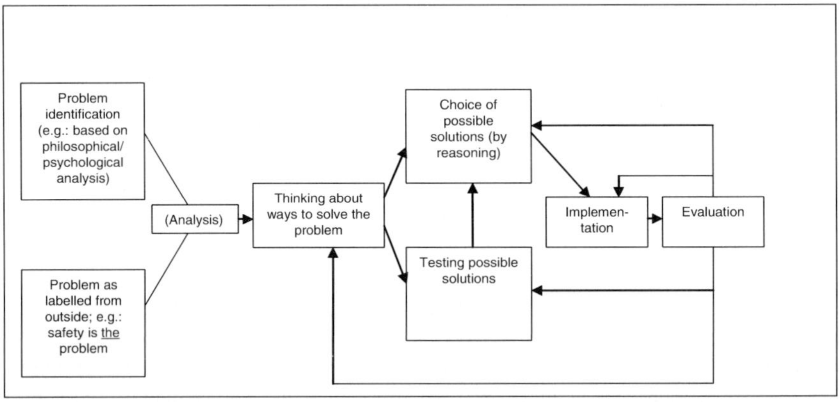

Figure 1. From problem identification to problem solution

The Practitioner's View

Every psychologist working in the field is sometimes confronted with everyday situations like:

"I have a problem, can you help me?" After exploring the problem - which is more an every-day problem type, not the AIDS or BSE type, of course -, the answer could be: "No, maybe you come back three years from now when I might have finished my research on your problem and when I can present sufficiently reliable and valid data concerning the instruments I will be using and the effectiveness of my possible interventions." One could, on the other hand, tell the client to turn to a medical doctor who very often simply cannot wait until the problem has been solved totally by international research activities. But one could also open one's toolbox and carefully select the methods most suitable for solving the client's problem, and get to work.

These alternatives apply to many situations psychologists may be confronted with: It does not really matter whether you are asked as an advisor to policy-makers, to engineers in industry or as a counsellor for an individual. The authors of this presentation consider it necessary to open the toolbox.

Of course, such an approach needs a framework within which it becomes acceptable. First of all, one has received professional training for the job that one is doing. This is usually accomplished by academic training and is finished with a diploma or a comparable certificate after having been examined. In the course of academic training one has learned about theories, some of them well established, some of them in a very questionable status. One has learned to be sceptical towards the beliefs that one has developed subconsciously, and finally one has learned to ask questions to control the processes that one is involved in. Readings in qualitative research, usually lead to the last two points (e.g. Patton 1997).

Primary training is an adequate but by no means a sufficient prerequisite for psychological work in the field. Further education and training during a lifetime of professional work is mandatory; this encompasses supervision and coaching as well as asking questions to the "most scientific" scientists - those at the university.

One's toolbox will need an update every now and then; there may be substantial changes and new scientific results affecting the applicability of the tools. Of course one is aware of the "sharpness" of the tools and of possible, yet unknown interactions of these tools with specific situations and certain types of clients and problems. One gets hopefully used to a cautious procedure in selecting tools, and to documenting procedures and processes in order to be able to relate them to the tools and to the underlying theories. This is of course nothing else than an evaluation process.

The typical procedure in science is: observing, registering, analysing, developing a theory, testing the theory, and accepting, rejecting or adjusting the theory. This procedure has often not been followed systematically. One of the reasons is that two radically different approaches may be observed. One is represented by the methodologist who - expressed in a simplified manner - is interested in the validity of a measure, an outcome and a theory. The other one is represented by those who are more interested in delivering tools for practice, designed to assist in reducing safety risk potential. While the former may be called "purist", the latter may be called pragmatic. Both positions are equally necessary as long as they communicate. Both generate valuable knowledge to science and its application, and they contribute directly and indirectly to improve traffic safety. The researcher with methodological focus gives advice and develops guidelines on how to improve observation, development of treatment techniques, registration of data, outcome measurement and theory development. The field worker is primarily interested in outcome in practice: his question is, whether the applied treatment generates results in the expected direction in reality, e.g., whether it represents a contribution to traffic safety.

These goals may be subdivided again. The effects attributed to a certain procedure depend on the defined goals. To give one example from the driver improvement area: One goal may simply be the significant reduction of the overall number of recidivists in a defined population or sub-population. A somewhat contrasting goal may be to establish or re-establish individual drivers' competence to meet more general safety needs. In the first case the attribution of effects will be facilitated by a less rigorous challenge than in the latter. In terms of safety gains, both goals, however, may lead (and have led) to equally significant contributions.

To observe, to register, to analyse, to develop a theory, to test the theory, and accept, to reject or to adjust the theory: this is what one does when one shapes one's assumptions about underlying causes of problems to be solved. This procedure is absolutely mandatory in order to select the adequate tools. One has to follow up the processes one has triggered in order to gain new experience.

The question is whether all of us working in the field will move around in this type of framework and keep it in mind. The belief and the experience of the authors is that most of us do. This is a question of ethics and morale and it is a problem of control in terms of active management of the job. In fact, if what is scientifically correct or not could be totally defined by empirical facts, ethics and morale would only be of interest with respect to those who break rules on purpose. You would not need these concepts, then, in order to make sure that you treat the right problems, and that you treat them the right way.

Wottawa (1981) states that "exaggerating methodological purism inhibits applied research" and one should add: it inhibits psychological work. The limitations in applied research are: (1) the problem(s) can hardly ever be solved at the moment they occur; (2) there is not and never will be sufficient money to establish the reliability and validity of all single procedures in, e.g., counselling, therapy, training, education; (3) one of the most remarkable notions in traffic psychology is that "they drive as they live", stating nothing else than that we have to understand the practice of the subjects we are dealing with. Understanding practice is more than just empirical research, and it is absolutely indispensable if one wants to be of help (Bourdieu 1976).

Some questions, comments and statements which were presented during the discussion in the workshop were the following:

One of the major problems in applied traffic psychology is a lack of meta-theory that allows to keep our unstable and context-dependent theories under better control. This makes the psychologist helpless, perpetuating the same type of research for decades. There is no, and there will never be any, valid unified theory of human behaviour. Therefore there will never be a convincing unified theory of driver behaviour.

Instead of basic theoretical models we should most probably have "rules & sentences of experience" which may be improved every now and then

Psychology is working with "fuzzy" concepts by nature - we are dealing with probabilities and not with certainty. However, many types of probable consequences can be formulated as trivial facts

What we need is a comprehensive overview of procedures and tools, which may become possible through application of modern technology and high-speed databases.

How do we define "tools"? Tools and procedures belong together. Tools do not work without a defined procedure and a defined procedure will not work without tools.

In attempting to evaluate individual drivers' behaviour, situational variance must not be overlooked. We can learn a lot from environmental psychology, there, which is very much theory- and concept based and does not suffer so much from the fact that many of its theorems are not empirically proven yet (see Bell et al. 1996)

Psychologists are often afraid to behave like "prostitutes": to do whatever they are asked to do. Often, simple solutions are preferred. But we are afraid of simple solutions, even if such a solution could exist in many cases. Our self-image is that we have to tell the public that simple solutions are not possible, and we should protect this image.

On the other hand, one has to explain why things often tend to be complicated. E.g., tell those who want quick solutions "if you want better road safety, change the law so that to-day's cars that are much too fast are not allowed on the road". Then you will see that there are other disciplines, as well, that tell us: Things are not that simple

Psychologists in general and traffic psychologists in particular must engage in training and education of other professions in psychology (e.g. lawyers), because colleagues from these disciplines implicitly take care of psychological questions

Anglo-Saxon literature does not mention papers published in other languages representatively; the language barrier is still effective - and a paradoxical characteristic in empirical research

Evaluation is the key to professional work in the field; evaluation may necessarily vary in design and procedure, depending on the problem to solve.

The Results of the Discussion

The results of the discussion following the presentations displayed in chapter 1 and 2 are summarised below.

Problem identification

Referring to one part of the introduction the question is repeated: What do we experience as being a problem, and therewith a task for traffic psychologists? Is the problem "forwarded" to us by statistics, do politicians tell us what has to be considered as a problem? Do affected persons or groups address us? Do we ourselves decide what has to - or could - be considered as a problem?

One should consider the following, in addition to what has been said: If someone, for instance an authority, approaches us with respect to an identified problem, is it not usual, then, that there also are other, additional problems connected to the originally identified one? Often, additional problems are such that without solving them, the original problem cannot be solved.

E.g., original problem = accidents at an intersection --> additional problem = car drivers do not want to acknowledge that their speeds are too high. A problem analysis, at least a rough one, should always be done.

Which solutions do we have?

Many solutions that we psychologists suggest aim at changing certain types of behaviour of certain people. We will need theories there in order to have ideas on how to change behaviour: Firstly, which factors in the physical environment and in the social environment steer the original behaviour and how the behaviour is anchored in the individual; e.g., attitudes, social perception, perspectives on reality, interpretation of facts, satisfaction or frustration of needs and wishes, etc. Secondly, what should be done in order to change behaviour, i.e., which factors should be modified, and by which means? Many different means will be useful,among others, social-psychological micro-theories, e.g. those dealing with communication, were mentioned in the discussion.

Which theory should we choose?

Theoretical questions are always there, in connection with psychological work in practice. Applied work in the area of psychology, especially on problem-solution, or on the improvement side, is based on the assumption that there are basic similarities in the attitudes and in the behaviour of individuals. Otherwise psychological analysis referring to more individuals at the same time, and prediction of behaviour, would be impossible. This is in a way contrary to the assumption that all individuals are different from each other.

The sheer number of theories is a handicap: Which theory is the best one to approach a certain problem? Which one should be applied in order to understand the relationship between a certain problem and possible solutions? Could there be several solutions and will all of them work equally well? Is it possible to answer these questions beforehand? When it was said that trying to answer such questions beforehand would keep us psychologists from working practically at all, it was commented that in a way this is also true for the application of natural science knowledge: Solutions are often chosen from several possible ones, and guesses of what is best are often important elements in this process. "Technicians often choose a heuristic approach"

Evaluation is the one and only empirical test of solutions

In practical work we should remember the medical cartoon-doctor who tells his patient "Try this" and the patient being happy and leaving with the intention to "try this". If it works, the doctor will not see him/her again, because the patient is healthy. If it does not work, the patient will either be dead, or will go to another doctor, who can help. I.e., when we do practical work we should act in order to keep our "patients", and to keep them alive: Tell them that we do not know the one and only solution in many cases, but that we have good guesses. Explain what the risks could be if our kind of solution is applied. But most of all, try to really implement the solutions proposed and to evaluate them. Next, make clear to the "patient" that the "therapy" will be even better after the evaluation.

Traffic psychologists should know their tools: These tools consist of working methods and procedures that have to be adapted to the actual problem situation. Whether this adaptation has to be carried out in the frame of scientific - empirical - research or can be done by reasoning, referring to models and theories, is the question. It seems to be reasonable to adapt knowledge and know-how by reasoning, to apply tools which are adapted on this base, and then to evaluate. The outcome of such a process is new experience with respect to the effectiveness and efficiency of the tool under special circumstances.

"Assuming forbidden"?

The opinion is expressed that we do not know so much about human behaviour, and therefore we should not act as if we really did. This of course leads to the question of how many of us agree that psychology is the science of human behaviour, how to understand it, and how to control it. Anyway, the comment could be interpreted as the position of an academic psychologist: It must be the primary assumption of the psychological scientist that our knowledge about behaviour is insufficient. Otherwise there would be no necessity for further research. However, one cannot tell the practical working psychologist that he/she does not know enough in order to work practically. This would prevent psychological work in practice.

In this respect there is a problem as far as co-operation with, e.g., policy makers is concerned: They want quick, clear and simple answers to their questions. The special type of problem in connection with this is that there hardly ever are such answers, certainly not in the area of psychology. But as soon as one starts hesitating, talking about probabilities and uncertainties, etc., they withdraw. This is a clear conflict of interests: On one hand one wants to help and to be involved (and also to earn a living), but on the other hand this is often only possible with "quick and dirty" solutions. In the discussion, no moralistic attitude is taken, but it is underlined, that the way of working has to be made explicit: Quick guesses based on past experience or on general theory, where explicit know-how with respect to the actual situation is missing, have to be specified as such.

Academic versus applied science, or academic and applied science?

Working under the condition that one respects scientific rules is not the same as working as an academic scientist. Dealing with problems in practice is not the same as working with "interesting scientific problems" at the university. The practical worker will be lost if (s)he will have to develop new solutions and to prove the effectiveness and efficiency of these solutions in every new situation and context, beforehand. The academic scientist, on the other hand will be more happy the more he can analyse and test things in order to differentiate as thoroughly as possible between as many different (types of) individuals, preconditions, contexts, as possible. But of course, the practical working psychologist will have some thoughts in mind why (s)he chooses certain approaches or certain solutions. Call it a model, a theory, or even experience - if one thinks that things in the future will function in the same way as they have done according to one's experience, the effect is the same as the one of a model or of a theory: one expects that under certain circumstances certain things will happen.

If prevailing academic standards according to some academic psychologists are applied, there will be no psychological work that deals with practice in the way engineering sciences do. There should be more support for the applied psychologist by academic scientists. In other words, academic science should deal more with the question of how psychological knowledge and know-how can be applied in practice in a smooth but nevertheless scientifically well-based manner. More importance will have to be attributed to the heuristic part of applying psychology: When one wants to achieve an improvement in practice, there will only be few psychological measures the validity of which has been proved beforehand. Not to allow the use of measures the validity of which under special circumstances is not absolutely certain (new subjects, new context, new preconditions, new time periods) means, not to allow evaluation and prevent progress.

The heuristic approach

Traffic psychologists must dare act and recommend problem solutions on the basis of what they know, without always launching a research project before recommendation. This does not mean that recommendations are given "aus dem Bauch" ("directly from the stomach", as it is said in German, without reasoning), because there is knowledge and know-how: The psychologist involved must work on a sound theoretical background and should have some experience himself. Moreover, a lot of problems have already been dealt with in literature. This is especially the case in traffic psychology, where obviously many researchers believe that all research ought to be conducted by themselves, or only accept "knowledge" that has been gained in the only way they declare acceptable to them. The difficulty, is that many of these researchers only would know literature on past research in the English language. Could this really be an empiricist's position: knowing that there might be knowledge which could enlighten him or her - something visible, readable, translatable - but to act as if nothing was there, because it is in a language he does not know?

Empiricism and theory

As to the question of "Empiricism versus theory": One has to have some model in mind when interpreting certain results of psychological research. Evaluation of work implemented in practice, for instance, will lead to results which have to be interpreted: certain training programs for young drivers are mentioned which, may work under some conditions and may not work under others; on the other hand, and more importantly, there may be adverse effects of training which are not captured under certain conditions of evaluation, e.g., when training effects are measured at a very early stage after the training, or even during the training; and certain effects may not be captured, when subjects know that they are tested. In order to adjust one's instruments and to do comprehensive evaluation work, one has to have a good theory to work with. There is no contradiction between empiricism and theory. The question, with respect to practical work, remains: How much empirical work is needed, before recommending the use of psychological analytical methods, and before suggesting measures in order to mitigate or to solve problems in society?

Theory is important as a basis for evaluation. The example of the rural roads in former Eastern Germany is given: In the old alleys, there, many people die in collisions with trees: The most simple solution would be to eliminate all trees there, viz. never again to plant trees along roads. If one finds this an absurd idea, it is necessary to think of other possible solutions of this problem, which have to be implemented and tested. Again, evaluation is the final empirical test of a theoretical assumption.

References

Barat J. 1985, Integrated Metropolitan Transport - reconciling efficiency, equity, and environmental improvement, Third World Planning Review 7(3).

Bell P.A., Greene T.C., Fisher J.D. & Baum A. 1996, *Environmental Psychology*. 4th Edition, Harcourt Brace College Publishers, New York, Montreal, London, Sydney, Tokyo

Bourdieu P. 1976, *Entwurf einer Theorie der Praxis*, Wissenschaftliche Sonderausgabe Suhrkamp

Flyvbjerg B. 1992, Rationalitet og magt (Rationality and power), Akademisk forlag, Copenhagen; translated as:

Flyvbjerg B. 1999, *Rationality and Power*, Chicago University Press

Fuller R. 1997, The psychology of theories and a theory of psychology, in: Rothengatter T. & Carbonell-Vaya E. (Eds.), *Traffic and Transport Psychology: Theory and Application:* Oxford: Pergamon

Goffman E. 1973, *Interaktionsrituale*, Suhrkamp, Frankfurt am Main

Patton M.Q. 1997, *Qualitative Inquiries*, Sage publication

Risser R. 2000, Ältere Verkehrsteilnehmer in der Zukunft, in: Amann A. (Ed.), *Kurswechsel für das Alter*, Böhlau Verlag, Wien

Rothengatter T. & Carbobell-Vaya E. (EDS.), *Traffic and Transport Psychology: Theory and Application:* Oxford: Pergamon

Vasconcelos E.A. 1998, *Transporte Urbano, Espaco e equidade. Analise das politicas publicas*, NetPress, Sao Paulo

Singh S. 1999, *Fermat's last Theorem*, Fourth Estate, London

Waller P.F. 1997, Transportation and society In: Rothengatter, T. & Carbonell Vaya, E. (Eds.): *Traffic & Transport Psychology / Theory and Application* (pp. 435-444). Amsterdam, New York, Oxford, Tokyo: Pergamon.

Winch P. 1990, *The idea of a social science and its relation to philosophy*, Routledge, London

Wottawa, H. und Thierau H. 1990, *Lehrbuch Evaluation*. Bern; Stuttgart; Toronto: Huber, 1990

Road User

Cognition and Performance

Traffic and Transport Psychology,
T. Rothengatter and R.D. Huguenin (Editors)

5

Cognitive Effects of Environmental Knowledge on Urban Route Planning Strategies

Sébastien Chalmé, Willemien Visser and Michel Denis

Introduction

Planning is a common cognitive activity. Before driving, for example, one is often confronted with the task of errand planning. Such a task is sometimes simple, but it may also constitute a problem, for example when a large number of errands with spatial and temporal constraints have to be planned. If an errand-planning task constitutes a problem for people, its difficulty is obviously affected by their knowledge of the city.

In the study presented in this paper, we analysed how urban route planning is affected by the planners' knowledge of the urban environment. We were guided by two main objectives: to highlight the cognitive processes involved in such planning, and to provide ergonomic specifications for onboard planning aid systems, on the basis of our results. Until now, there has indeed been little research connecting cognitive processes involved in route planning and such support systems.

Problem solving in design activities

Like other cognitive tasks, planning may or may not make up a problem for a planner. If it does, we analyse such a task as a design problem-solving task, i.e. in the present case, design of route plans. In order to construct an experimental task constituting indeed a problem for the participants in our study, a problem description was constructed so that the number of errand tasks to be accomplished just exceeded the actual time available, most tasks being submitted to temporal and/or spatial constraints.

One of the earliest insights to emerge from cognitive psychology was that problem solving -i.e. planning and other design tasks- could be considered a top-down, goal-driven and hierarchically structured process (Newell & Simon, 1972). Hierarchical planning models in A.I. were also founded upon these principles (Sacerdoti, 1974). However, most of these models were not based on significant user data or cognitive analyses of actual activities by human planners. Visser (1994, 1996) investigated the differences between design problems solved in artificially restricted conditions and those solved in real-life, professional tasks. She showed that real-life design activities are opportunistically organised (Hayes-Roth & Hayes-Roth, 1979) and identified several factors accounting for such an organisation.

Urban route planning and onboard systems

To our knowledge, there are no onboard planning aid systems. However, there are more and more commercial onboard guidance systems. It seems interesting to analyse the logic used by these systems to select the "best" route from an origin to a destination. An errand-planning problem might be compared to an errand-scheduling problem, followed by the problem to select the "best" route between consecutive errands. According to this approach, guidance systems would be efficient to solve the second problem. But what is the "best" route for these systems? For a majority of systems it is the one that reduces total travel time. This criterion is also the one that drivers who have been interviewed on their trips, present as the most important one used during their driving. Their second criterion is distance (Ueberschaer, 1971). However, the importance of these two criteria changes when one analyses what drivers actually do, rather than what they think they do. Benshoof (1970) and Van Winsum (1993) pointed to the fact that travel time indeed influences actual route selection, but is not the only factor.

Ergonomic design rules specify that, in order to ensure a high level of user acceptance, a system's logic should be compatible with the decision logic adopted by the system users, i.e. the drivers. system. The study reported in this paper is intended to both improve current onboard guidance systems, and formulate ergonomic specifications for the design of onboard planning aid systems. In order to do so, the present study focuses on the actual planning strategies adopted by people who have to plan a number of errands throughout a city.

Method of the experimental study

The experiment consisted in asking 24 participants (age: 33 (9 years) to plan a route through a French modern city, Saint Quentin-en-Yvelines, near Paris, in order to execute 13 tasks (for example, sign a paper at the bank between 2 p.m. and 4 p.m., buy flowers for an invitation in the evening, buy ice cream at Picard, visit an apartment before 1 p.m. at Elancourt, take the program at the theatre of Saint Quentin, go to the Technocenter at 3 p.m. for a 30 min. interview) (see Figure 1).

The tasks had spatial and temporal constraints and their locations were distributed all over the city. The map given to the participants was a road map, more detailed and bigger than that of Figure 1 (66 x 51 cm). Two types of participants were compared: participants with knowledge of the city (14 people) and participants without such knowledge (10 people). We used a simultaneous-verbalisation method: participants were asked to think aloud all during their planning task. The data used to analyse the participants' strategies were their recorded verbalisations and the written or graphic data that they produced during their planning.

Analysis of Results

We coded and analysed the verbalisations in order to identify the strategies used during problem solving. Some preliminary explanations are necessary. Analytically, problem solving may be decomposed into three theoretically distinct stages, construction of a problem representation, solution development and solution evaluation (Richard, 1990). In actual problem-solving activities, however, people interrupt and/or skip stages, come back to theoretically previous stages, etc.

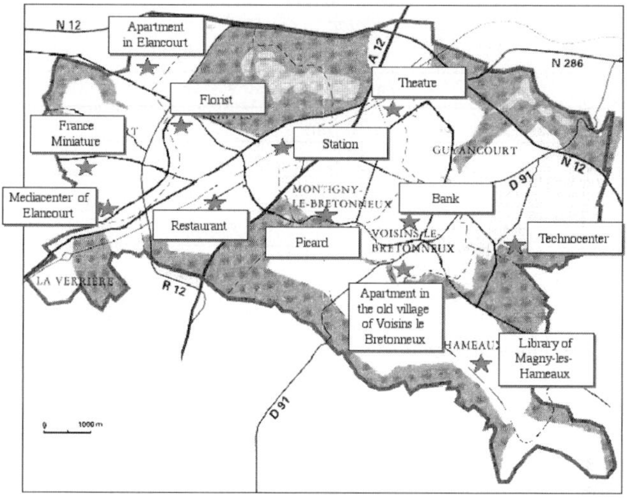

Figure 1. Distribution of the errand tasks on the map given to the participants

(i) In order to start problem solving, one needs a mental problem representation. Problem solving thus normally starts by the construction of such a representation. We coded an activity as "problem-representation construction" if the participants were analysing their task, and/or reading and analysing the data.

(ii) Solution development is the stage where a participant generates part or all of a sub-solution. The final global solution may be modelled as an array of 13 columns and six lines (see Table 1). Columns correspond to the 13 errand tasks, lines to the six characteristics defining an errand sub-solution (absolute or relative order of the errand in the plan, arrival time, departure time, time necessary to execute the errand, travel time required to reach the errand location, and composition of the itinerary to reach the errand location). The participants were free to define their solution as exhaustively as they wanted. Some boxes of the array thus could stay empty.

The values in Table 1 are some of the temporal constraints of the problem description. The participants could adjust these temporal constraints, in order to be in advance or to be late. However, they were not allowed to change four characteristics (underlined in Table 1). Some of the characteristics are non-applicable (coded -). All the others are undefined at the start (coded *).

(iii) We coded an activity as "solution evaluation" when participants used criteria to judge a solution with respect to knowledge they possessed or to the problem specification (description and map).

Table 1. Model of the solution of the errand-planning problem.

Task Characteristics	*Task 1: departure at the station*	...	*Task 6: interview at the Techno-center*	...	*Task 11: program at the theatre*	...	*Task 13: arrival at the station*
Order	1	*	*	*	*	*	13
Arrival time	-	*	3 p.m.	*	*	*	5 p.m.
Departure time	10 a.m.	*	3.30 p.m.	*	*	*	-
Performing time	-	*	0.30 p.m.	*	*	*	-
Travel time	-	*	*	*	*	*	*
Itinerary	-	*	*	*	*	*	*

Results

Here we focus on some strategies. For a presentation of all strategies, see Chalmé, Visser and Denis (2004).

Strategies used for problem-representation construction

For all participants, the global strategy used to construct a problem representation consisted in analysing part or all of the data made available to them. However, all did not proceed in the same way. They indeed applied different strategies. We categorised those strategies with respect to their result (one task, all the tasks, or a number of tasks but not all) and to their "source" (i.e. the data used to apply a strategy). This source is generally the result of the application of the previous strategy, a representation-construction or other strategy. In this section, we only present some examples illustrating our classification.

Type 1. Strategies selecting one task. These depend on the source used.
The source is the full list of tasks (problem description). A strategy to analyse this list of tasks in order to select as quickly as possible one task for which a solution is then going to be developed, is, for example, to go through the list until one identifies a task (i) without any temporal constraint and whose execution would be rapid, (ii) or with a temporal constraint and that could be executed immediately.

The source is a list of all tasks with temporal constraints. For these strategies to be applied, a preliminary analysis is required. A participant has to go through the full list of tasks in order to select the tasks with temporal constraints. A strategy to select as quickly as possible, from the resulting list, one task for which a solution is then going to be developed, is, for example, to go through the list until one identifies a task (i) with a temporal constraint and whose execution would take a long time, or (ii) for which one of the corresponding solution characteristics evokes immediately its default value on the basis of general knowledge (for example: "lunch" evokes "at noon" for "arrival time").

The source is the map with the spatial task locations. A strategy to analyse this map in order to select as quickly as possible one task for which a solution is then going to be developed, is, for example, to examine the map until one identifies a task location (i) that is the nearest neighbour of the current task location, or (ii) to which the itinerary is easy.

The result of the application of one of these strategies is a task for which the participant is going to develop a solution. In that case, analysis and development are generally so intertwined that it is hard to know if the analysis strategy gives rise to the development which ensues, or if analysis is due to a development strategy applied before analysis. Probably both patterns occur.

Type 2. Strategies selecting a number of tasks, but not all. In order to simplify the presentation of these strategies, we arranged the examples with respect to the temporal and/or spatial aspect that prevails.

- Temporal aspects prevail: select the tasks (i) with temporal constraints, or (ii) that have to be executed before lunch.
- Spatio-temporal aspects prevail: For example: select the tasks - in a particular geographic area on the map that are all temporally constrained and combine them into a spatio-temporal cluster.
- Spatial aspects prevail: select the tasks that are (i) the nearest neighbours of the current task location, or (ii) in a particular geographic area on the map and combine them into a spatial cluster.

N.B. For a number of tasks to be considered a "cluster", they must be ≥ 3.

Type 3. Strategies selecting all tasks. In this case, participants aim to modify their mental problem representation built immediately after first presentation of the data by the experimenter:

- Organise the tasks into two categories, for example: (i) tasks with and tasks without temporal constraints, or (ii) tasks in the East and tasks in the West (on the map).
- Construct a graphic representation of the data in which the relation between the spatial and temporal constraints is highlighted.

The differences between people with and without knowledge are the following. Almost all participants without knowledge (9/10) start problem solving by a quick analysis of the errand tasks (strategies of type 1 or type 2). This analysis is generally top-down, that is, they generally start by a selection of tasks with temporal constraints (type 2), or by analysis of all tasks (type 3) followed by the selection of a task with temporal constraints that could be executed immediately (in case of plan execution) (type 1). Their general approach was a top-down strategy using one same type of criterion, i.e. temporal.

Participants with knowledge generally tend to build a well-structured problem representation. They start problem solving by a long analysis of the tasks. This analysis is generally top-down, that is, they first apply strategies selecting all tasks (type 3), then follow one or more strategies selecting a number of tasks (type 2) and finally they select one task (type 1). For example, participants select all tasks with respect to their position on the map in the spatial clusters East / West, then select the tasks of the West cluster that are temporally constrained and finally select the task to which there is a quick itinerary. They apply a top-down strategy using both temporal and spatial criteria.

These differences in the construction of a problem representation may be due to participants' different global aims. To verify this hypothesis, we must first analyse the two other types of problem-solving activity.

Strategies used for solution development

In this paper, we focus on the comparison between breadth-first and depth-first strategies. N.B. For reasons of simplicity in wording, the expression "develop a task solution" is used to refer to "develop a solution corresponding to a task".

We consider that a participant applies a depth-first solution-development strategy when he/she develops a sub-solution defining several of its characteristics, before developing other sub-solutions in a comparable way. Such a development strategy may be implemented, for example, by participants defining, for a particular task solution, its order, the moment at which the task will be executed, its departure and arrival time, and sometimes also its travel time and the itinerary used to reach the task location. Only after having developed, even if but partially, such a task solution, the participant does so for another sub-solution.

We consider that a participant applies a breadth-first strategy when he/she selects a group of tasks (a list, a spatial or a temporal cluster), that is, the result of a representation-construction strategy, and fixes for each of these tasks the same solution characteristic before fixing another characteristic.

Table 2 presents the number of times that participants with and participants without knowledge apply depth-first strategies and/or breadth-first strategies to develop a solution.

Table 2. Number of times that participants in each group applied depth-first strategies and breadth-first strategies to develop a solution.

Type of strategies	*Participants with knowledge (T = 14)*	*Participants without knowledge (T = 10)*
Breadth-first strategies	16	6
Depth-first strategies	12	14

We applied the Fischer exact probability test with the H0 that the two groups of participants apply equally often depth-first and breadth-first strategies. The probability of the observed distribution of frequencies under H0 is $p = .04$. This leads us to reject H0.

Participants with knowledge apply relatively more often breadth-first strategies than do participants without knowledge. This result may be related to the problem representations they constructed. Two thirds of participants with knowledge (10/14) analysed all the data. Their analysis was temporal and spatial, whereas the participants without knowledge tended to construct a problem representation nearly exclusively based on temporal problem attributes. Therefore, the problem representations of participants with knowledge, i.e., the representations that guided their solution development, were more complete than those of the participants without knowledge. Ten participants with knowledge analysed all the data. Almost all of them applied, immediately after their data analysis, breadth-first strategies in order to develop the solution(s) corresponding to one or more tasks taking place in the morning. In order to apply a breadth-first strategy, a participant has to know which are the sub-solutions of the global solution under development (see Visser, 1996), i.e. the different tasks. The difficulty met by participants with knowledge was that they sometimes forgot a task in their global solution. To add it, they had to process once again all sub-solutions previously developed. At each new planning round, the old and new sub-solutions lost precision with respect to their characteristics.

Participants without knowledge applied relatively more often depth-first strategies than participants with knowledge. They applied local strategies related to their current solution state, the data analysed and the strategies previously applied. These local strategies generally corresponded to strategies that quickly led to a simple solution. So the strategy applied at a particular moment could be at the opposite of the previously applied local strategy, and even of the current, more abstract strategy.

In order to apply a depth-first strategy, it is possible for participants to take their decision with respect to the next task to be developed only after having developed the current task. In that case, a task can be added without any particular difficulty.

However, a problem occurred if the tasks added had implicit temporal constraints (for example, "buy ice cream" or "buy flowers for an invitation in the evening"). Contrary to participants with knowledge, those without knowledge generally did not to take into account such tasks. For example, only two participants out of 10 noticed that ice cream bought in the morning would no longer be eatable in the evening. Participants without knowledge generally applied a strategy with low cognitive cost (generally the nearest-neighbour strategy, an "optimisation" strategy as a participant called it). Most participants without knowledge therefore could position the ice-cream task at any time of the day, even in the morning. Despite a negative evaluation of this sub-solution, they maintained it, because they did not want to change their solution development.

Strategies used for solution evaluation

Participants applied both general and local solution-evaluation strategies.

General solution-evaluation strategies. Participants without knowledge tended to apply depth-first strategies both to develop and to evaluate solutions. Solution development and solution evaluation were intertwined. Participants without knowledge consecutively developed different sub-solutions and evaluated each one as it was being developed. They evaluated the spatio-temporal feasibility of each sub-solution separately. Only at particular moments, they made a temporal evaluation of their global solution. They did so, for example, just after development of a temporally constrained sub-solution, such as just after the lunch task or after the visit at the Technocenter.

Participants with knowledge tended to apply breadth-first strategies both to develop and to evaluate solutions. They developed sub-solutions with respect to a particular characteristic and evaluated them with respect to this characteristic. Participants with knowledge evaluated their sub-solutions both individually and as components of their global solution. After development of all sub-solutions, they evaluated the spatio-temporal feasibility of the global solution by simulation of plan execution.

Local solution-evaluation strategies. These strategies depended on the criteria used by the participants. Participants without knowledge only used few evaluation criteria. The criteria most often used by these participants were proximity and feasibility.

Participants with knowledge used several criteria. They used general criteria and idiosyncratic criteria. The criteria most often used were task importance (with respect to other tasks), type of the road and -their subjective estimate of- the probability to come upon a traffic jam on a road at certain hours of the day. This led them, for example, to evaluate positively a road solution because of its few traffic lights. Temporal idiosyncratic constraints concerned, for example, opening hours, lunch hour (often: at 12 a.m.), time required for task execution (for example: one hour for lunch), or waiting time. The time between two task solutions could be evaluated as too short or too long; time allocated for task execution could be considered too long.

Discussion and Conclusion

This paper presented strategies used in order to solve a route-planning problem. In order to analyse our results, we used the classical decomposition of problem-solving activities into three theoretically distinct stages, that is, construction of a problem representation, solution development and solution evaluation. We examined the effects of knowledge on strategies implemented in each of these stages.

Construction of a problem representation

Participants without knowledge clearly aimed to proceed as soon as possible to solution development: this led them to a shallow and quick analysis of the tasks with temporal constraints. Participants with knowledge aimed to construct a comprehensive problem representation: this led them to analyse carefully the available data: analysis of temporal constraints was followed by a scrupulous analysis of spatial constraints.

Participants with knowledge frequently applied data-clustering strategies according to a spatial criterion. Such spatial clustering may have been induced by a survey perspective using an extrinsic frame of reference, which particularly characterises people with good environmental knowledge (Pailhous, 1970).

Solution-development activity

Participants without knowledge generally applied depth-first strategies in order to develop their solution. They applied local strategies that generally led them to quick development of a simple solution. The local strategy applied at a particular moment could be at the opposite of the previously applied local strategy, and even of the current, more abstract strategy. This type of shift may be qualified as "opportunistic", and may be supposed to be inspired by motives of cognitive-cost reduction (see Visser, 1994).

Participants with knowledge generally applied breadth-first strategies. Their analysis was both temporal and spatial, so the problem representations which guided their solution development were more complete and global than those of the participants without knowledge.

These differences between participants with and participants without knowledge are comparable to those observed between novices and experts in other problem-solving tasks, such as computer programming (Adelson, 1981; Détienne, 2001; Ehrlich & Soloway, 1982) and physics problem solving (Simon & Simon, 1978).

Solution evaluation

Participants without and participants with knowledge tended to apply respectively depth-first strategies and breadth-first strategies, both to development and to evaluation of solutions. Participants without knowledge only used few evaluation criteria: proximity and feasibility. Participants with knowledge used much more criteria, both general and idiosyncratic ones.

The general aim of participants without knowledge may be supposed to be the reduction of the cognitive cost of their planning activity, in order to develop as quickly as possible a solution. They proceeded opportunistically, applying local strategies that directly depended on the data selected. Their activity was data-driven, generally leading them to apply a depth-first problem-solving strategy. The general aim of the participants with knowledge be supposed to be the reduction of the cognitive cost of the execution of their solution, i.e. their final plan. They therefore controlled their activity in order to construct a precise and realistic solution. Their activity was goal-driven, generally leading them to apply breadth-first problem-solving strategies.

Another interesting result is the observation that neither the type of strategy used by people with knowledge of the city (depth-first), nor that used by people without such knowledge (breadth-first) is the "best" problem-solving strategy. Each group met difficulties. Participants without knowledge met difficulties by choosing a strategy with low cognitive cost. Those with knowledge met difficulties due to their ambition to take into account all the experimental data and all the data they wanted to add, in order to construct a realistic plan that could be easily executed. This difficulty generated some planning errors, obliging the participants to replan several times the same sub-plan, reducing their planning motivation and solution satisfaction.

An onboard system could help to reduce these difficulties. On the basis of our results, three ideas can be formulated. A support system could be useful to planners on the following points: (i) facilitating the construction of problem representations, which, as we saw, was obviously difficult, especially for people without knowledge, but also for people with knowledge when proceeding to replanning; (ii) providing contextual information, facilitating people to develop and evaluate a realistic plan: for example, concerning traffic charge, travel time, and travel length; (iii) providing seamless switching between both spatial and temporal representations of the data, and between both spatial and temporal representations of the plans as they evolve. Such switching allows planners to exploit the complementary character of the temporal and spatial aspects of the representations that they use for such spatio-temporal problem-solving activities as route planning.

This paper presents the first results of a study in the context of a research program that aims to both highlight the cognitive processes involved in route planning and formulate, on the basis of the results, ergonomic specifications for onboard planning systems. Other studies will undoubtedly be necessary to refine these results.

Acknowledgements

The research underlying this paper is being conducted through collaboration between EIFFEL-INRIA, LIMSI-CNRS and LARA/IMARA-INRIA in the context of the "Cognitique" research programme of the French Ministry of Research (research action "PLANS: Studying urban route planning"). The first author's research is being partially funded by LARA/IMARA, INRIA - Rocquencourt.

References

Adelson, B. (1981). Problem solving and the development of abstract categories in programming languages. *Memory & Cognition, 9*, 422-433.

Benshoof, J. A. (1970). Characteristics of drivers' route selection behaviour. *Traffic Engineering & Control, 11*, 605-609.

Chalmé, S., Visser, W., & Denis, M., (2004). Cognitive aspects of urban route planning. *Chapter 5 of this volume*

Détienne, F. (2001). *Psychology of Software Design*. Heidelberg: Springer

Ehrlich, K., & Soloway, E. (1982). *An empirical investigation of the tacit plan knowledge in programming* (Rep. No. 236). New Haven: Yale University Department of Computer Science.

Hayes-Roth, B., & Hayes-Roth, F. (1979). A cognitive model of planning. *Cognitive Science, 3*, 275-310.

Newell, A. & Simon, H. A. (1972). *Human Problem Solving.* Englewood Cliffs, NJ: Prentice-Hall.

Pailhous, J. (1970). *La Représentation de l'espace urbain. L'exemple du chauffeur de taxi.* [The representation of urban environment: Case of the taxi-drivers]. Paris: Presses Universitaires de France.

Richard, J. F. (1990). *Les activités mentales. Comprendre, raisonner, trouver des solutions.* [Mental activities: understanding, reasoning, solution finding]. Paris: Colin.

Sacerdoti, E. D. (1974). Planning in a hierarchy of abstraction spaces. *Artificial Intelligence, 5,* 115-135.

Simon, D. P., & Simon, H. A. (1978). Individual differences in solving physics problems. In R. S. Seigler (Ed.), *Children's Thinking: What Develops?* Hillsdale, NJ: Lawrence Erlbaum Associates.

Ueberschaer, M. H. (1971). Choice of routes on urban networks for the journey to work. *Highway Research Record, 369*, 228-238.

Van Winsum, W. (1993). Selection of routes in route navigation systems. In A.M. Parkes and S. Franzen (Eds.), *Driving future vehicles* (pp. 193-204). London: Taylor & Francis.

Visser, W. (1994). Organisation of design activities: opportunistic, with hierarchical episodes. *Interacting with Computers, 6* (3), 239-274 (Executive summary: 235-238).

Visser, W. (1996). Two functions of analogical reasoning in design: a cognitive-psychology approach. *Design Studies, 17,* 417-434.

Traffic and Transport Psychology,
T. Rothengatter and R.D. Huguenin (Editors)

6

Perception of Speed and Increments in Cars

Miguel A. Recarte, Angela Conchillo and Luis M. Nunes

Introduction

The diversity of aspects focused by speed perception studies gives rise to a dearth of reference points. Several works are based on simulators (Groeger, Carsten & Blana, 1997; Harms, 1991, 1996; Manser, Carmody & Hancock, 1997). But not many investigations have been carried out by using a real car: Denton (1966) required the participants to produce a speed with a given proportional relation (double or half) to a standard speed presented, found a speed overproduction effect in all cases. Triggs and Berenyi (1982) found a general speed underestimation in researching the differences between day and night driving. Recarte and Nunes (1996) found a high correspondence between estimation and production, and no influence of driving experience on speed estimation. The symmetry between underestimation and overproduction suggests that the same psychological process underlines both estimation and production tasks. Nonetheless, the acceleration sign had no effect on estimation (the estimate was the same after accelerating and decelerating) but it did on the speed production task (over-) adjustment was higher after decelerating than accelerating. Also, along these lines Recarte, Conchillo and Nunes (1996) carried out two experiments on the production of increments, and considering the acceleration sign (increasing / reducing) the adjusted increment was less when decelerating than when accelerating.

In the present study three experiments were carried out: the Experiment 1 tries to replicate the results found by Recarte and Nunes (1996) in the same closed track, and, in addition, to extend the study to a wider range of speed increment values. Experiments 2 and 3 focus the ecological validity of the results and study the speed production under normal traffic conditions. More precisely, the aim of the first experiment is: (a) to replicate the effect of speed (common to estimation and production) and acceleration (which arises in speed production, but not in estimation) and the lack of effect of driving experience and sex; (b) to study how the acceleration process previous to target speed affects speed estimation and production when different acceleration/deceleration conditions are manipulated. c) to verify the correspondence between estimation and production methods. d) to study the perception of speed increments/decrements using a production method. Experiments 2 and 3 analyse the speed production while driving in an ordinary road and in a highway, respectively, what allows to answer the following questions: (1) whether overproduction takes place in ordinary driving conditions, (2) whether there is a speed effect, in which case speed overproduction is expected to be greater at lower speeds, (3) whether the adjusted speeds are affected by the acceleration sign, (greater overproduction after deceleration than after acceleration).

EXPERIMENT 1

Method

Participants. Thirty participants classified by sex and by three levels of driving experience: no drivers, with less than two years of driving experience, and with more than five. There were 15 participants of each sex, 10 of each experience level. The average age was 27.7.

Experimental design. Four experimental variables were considered: (i) Task: speed estimation, speed production and increment production.(ii) Target Speed: 70, 90 and 110 km/h. (iii) Acceleration sign: accelerating and decelerating. (iv) Target Increment: 20, 30 or 40 km/h. The between-subjects variables were sex and driving experience. Design: (3 Tasks x 3 Target Speeds x 2 Acceleration Sign x 3 Target Increment) x 2 Sex x 3 Experience, within-subjects in the first three variables, and between-subjects in the last two.

Instruments and procedure. The test was carried out on a circular track in absence of other traffic. An instrumented vehicle (Citröen BX-GTI) provided with a recording system was used. The speed data were collected at a 50Hz frequency. The participants were seated in the front passenger's seat and could not see the speedometer. The experimenter drove the car to set it at the experimental speeds according to the procedure for each task. The participants performed 18 trials in each task. The different tasks were performed according to the following description:

The speed estimation task. the estimation task was always performed prior to the production task to avoid giving the participants information about the target speeds. In each trial the driver set the vehicle at the previous speed for a few seconds, after he reduced or increased the speed progressively without changing gear, set the vehicle at the target, and blew the horn; that was the signal for the participant to estimate verbally the vehicle's speed in km/h, while operating a control button at the same time. The speed of the car was kept constant since the horn signal until the estimation response was given. Target speeds were attained both after acceleration and deceleration.

The speed production task. the participant had to adjust a target speed by operating a complementary accelerator pedal conveniently installed in front of the passenger's seat. The car was still driven by the experimenter, although the participant was instructed to operate the complementary accelerator. As in the estimation task, the experimenter set the vehicle at a previous speed, blew the horn and also told the participant the target speed he or she had to achieve. The participant, using the accelerator pedal, tried to reach the target speed, and pressed a control button while trying to keep the speed constant. After pressing the button the participant also released the accelerator to the experimenter. In half of the trials the target speed should be achieved by accelerating and in the other half by decelerating although no indication was given to the participant regarding whether he/she had to accelerate or decelerate.

The increment production task. the participant's task consisted of increasing or reducing actual speed in a given magnitude. Although the participant had no explicit information about the starting speed (the actual speed before a trial) there was an explicit instruction about the magnitude and the sign of the acceleration required: an increment or decrement of 20, 30 or 40 km/h. The procedure included the same steps as in the speed production task, but the instruction now was increase the speed 20 km/h or reduce 30 km/h, and so on.

Results

Firstly we present separately the results of each task and finally several comparisons between tasks are presented and commented.

The speed estimation task. The dependent variable was the proportional speed (estimated speed / target speed). The results can be seen in Table 1. The participants underestimated the speed ($M = 0.83$ km/h), thus replicating the main effect of Recarte and Nunes (1996).

A repeated measures ANOVA was done (3 Target speeds x 2 Acceleration signs x 3 Target increments) x 2 Sex x 3 Experience. The significant effects were: speed, $F\ (2,48) = 28.47$; $p < .001$; Acceleration sign x Target increment, $F\ (2,48) = 5.89$, $p < .01$; Experience x Acceleration, $F\ (2,24) = 3.79$, $p < .05$; and Sex x Experience x Speed, F (4,48) =2.71, $p < .05$. The explanation of these effects is the following: (a) Speed effect shows that as the vehicle speed increases the estimated speed comes nearer to the real one, going from an underestimation of 0.75, at 70 km/h, to 0.88 at 110 km/h; (b) Acceleration x Target increment interaction indicates a different effect of the increment depending upon whether it is made by accelerating or decelerating, but this effect is small and irregular (see Table 1); (c) Experience x Acceleration interaction indicates that the differences among the experience groups are most noticeable when decelerating rather than accelerating; (d) Sex x Experience x Speed interaction showed a small and irregular effect: it means that, in the experienced women group, the general trend of the proportional estimate throughout the range of speeds (the more speed, the less proportional estimate) is broken.

Power function between estimated speed (ES) and actual speed (AS) was: ES = .170 (AS) 1.349, and the correlation between actual speed and the estimated one was $r = .70$, which indicates that 49% of the speed estimates variance was associated with the variance of the actual speeds.

Also, the 18 trials were split into two halves of 9 trials according to the acceleration sign. The correlation between the errors in both split halves was $r = .83$. When splitting the task into three blocks of 6 trials, one for each speed, correlation ranges from .82 to .90, a higher correlation existing when the speeds are most similar. Splitting the task into three blocks of 6 trials, one for each increment value, correlation goes from .91 to .95. Such data allow the conclusion to be reached that the ability to estimate vehicle speed is a firm psychological trait.

Table 1. Mean *(M)* and Standard Deviation *(SD)* of Proportional Speed Estimation (ratio) as a function of Target Speed, Acceleration Sign and Increment (Experiment 1; $n = 30$).

Target Speed			*70 km/h*		*90 km/h*		*110 km/h*		*Total*	
			M	*SD*	*M*	*SD*	*M*	*SD*	*M*	*SD*
Acceleration	Increment	+20	0.76	0.24	0.88	0.21	0.90	0.17	0.85	0.22
		+30	0.75	0.18	0.90	0.19	0.89	0.14	0.85	0.18
		+40	0.76	0.25	0.79	0.16	0.88	0.17	0.81	0.20
		Total	0.76	0.22	0.85	0.19	0.89	0.16	0.83	0.20
Deceleration	Decrement	-20	0.76	0.24	0.86	0.24	0.87	0.16	0.83	0.22
		-30	0.70	0.25	0.80	0.22	0.86	0.18	0.79	0.22
		-40	0.78	0.28	0.84	0.21	0.88	0.17	0.83	0.23
		Total	0.75	0.26	0.84	0.22	0.87	0.17	0.82	0.22
Total			0.75	0.24	0.85	0.21	0.88	0.16	0.83	0.21

The speed production task. The dependent variable was the proportional production (produced speed/ target speed), and the clearest result is that systematically the participants over-adjusted the speed (M=1.16 km/h), as can be seen in Table 2. This over-production error is symmetrical to the under-estimation error in the estimation task.

A repeated measures ANOVA was carried out. The three experimental variables had statistically significant effects: speed, F (2,48) = 70.01, $p < .001$, acceleration sign, F (1,24) = 49.12, $p < .001$, and increment, F (2,48) = 4.20, $p < .05$. The statistically significant interactions were those of Speed x Acceleration, F (2,48) = 11.72, $p < .001$, Speed x Acceleration x Target increment, F (4,96) = 2.88, $p < .05$, and Experience x Speed x Acceleration x Increment, F (8,96) = 2.57, $p < .05$. Regarding the main effects: (a) Effect of speed consisted in the reduction of the proportional production from 1.25 at 70 km/h, to 1.08 at 110 km/h; (b) Effect of acceleration indicated that production was higher when decelerating (proportional production = 1.21) than when accelerating (proportional production = 1.11); (c) Effect of increment was much less than the two previous ones and its interpretation was not clear, no stable trend was observed.

The power function between produced speed (PS) and target speed (TS) was: $PS = 4.73\ (TS)^{.686}$, which is in agreement with Recarte and Nunes' (1996) results, where the exponent was .711. This function accounts for 44.1% of the variance.

The correlation between errors in accelerating and decelerating was $r = .87$, between errors grouped by speeds ranged from $r = .86$ to $r = .95$, and between errors grouped by increments were $r = .96$ and $r = .97$. Consequently, we can say that speed production is also a stable skill of the participants.

Speed estimation versus speed production. A repeated measures ANOVA was carried out using data from both tasks. To avoid a redundant description of the effects already analysed separately for each task we will only focus on task effects. Firstly, we have the main task effect, $F\,(1,29) = 44.05$, $p < .001$. Also, various interactions were statistically significant: Task x Speed, $F\,(2,58) = 73.62$, $p < .001$, Task x Acceleration, $F\,(1,29) = 15.91$, $p < .001$, Task x Acceleration x Speed, $F\,(2,58) = 3.22$, $p < .05$, Task x Acceleration x Target increment, $F\,(4,116) = 2.55$, $p < .05$. Task effect confirms the difference between estimated (0.83) and produced (1.16) speed. The interesting interaction, Task x Speed, which can be seen in Figure 1, shows the symmetrical results between estimation and production: the higher the speed, the lower the production, and, on the contrary, the higher the speed the higher the estimation. Both, estimated and produced proportional speeds, tending up to the unit when speed increases. Task x Acceleration interaction (see Figure 1) displays the fact that the acceleration sign does not produce significant effects on estimating, but it does in producing speed, where over-adjustment is greater after decelerating than after accelerating. Task x Acceleration x Speed, Task x Acceleration x Increment, and Task x Speed x Increment, albeit statistically significant, represent irregular effects.

An additional support to the hypothesis of a common mental representation underlying estimation and production tasks, is that predicted produced speeds from those estimated were coincident to the actual produced speeds. That is, from power function of estimation task, we set:

$$ln\text{ (actual speed)} = [ln\text{ (estimated speed)} - ln\text{ (0.170)]} / 1.349 \qquad (1)$$

From this equation, we can resolve the actual speeds for the estimated speeds equals to 70 km/h, 90 and 110 km/h. They are 86.7, 104.5 and 121.3, respectively. But, in Table 2, the produced speeds for these same target speeds were 87.6, 103.0 and 119.3, respectively, all of them very close to those predicted from equation (1).

Another argument to demonstrate that the same process underlines both tasks is that, by using just one measure of estimation error for each participant, and just another one for production error, linear correlation was $r = -.72$. This high, negative correlation shows that the more a participant underestimated speed in the estimation task, the more he/she overproduced speed in production task.

Discussion of estimation versus production. Results of both tasks agree with those of Recarte and Nunes (1996): (a) in speed estimation, underestimation is produced and the error declines with increasing speeds. The lack of significant effects of the acceleration, sex and driving experience is also reproduced. In addition, in the current research an absence of significant effects of the increment magnitude has been revealed. Along with these main findings, there is also a generalized lack of significant interactions. The lack of effect due to driving experience has been verified in other studies (Recarte & Nunes, 1996; Recarte et al., 1996). Results lead us to consider estimation of speed as a stable skill, that is essentially the manifestation of a basic perceptual process; (b) the participants overproduce the target speed, the overproduction declines as speed increases and it is also less if the maneuver requires acceleration rather than when deceleration is required. This result is undoubtedly the least understood aspect, as it does not appear in the estimation task. Nor in the production of speed are there any effects from the between-participants variables (sex and experience) nor from the increments needed to reach the target speed, except some high-level interactions of difficult interpretation; (c) When both tasks are considered jointly, the equivalence of the underlying speed representations is reaffirmed, as Recarte and Nunes (1996). This correspondence between estimation and production is manifested in the symmetry of the results (Figure 1), and particularly in the high negative correlation between errors in both tasks, which indicates that the symmetry is produced at the individual level: those who under-estimate more are also those who over-adjust more.

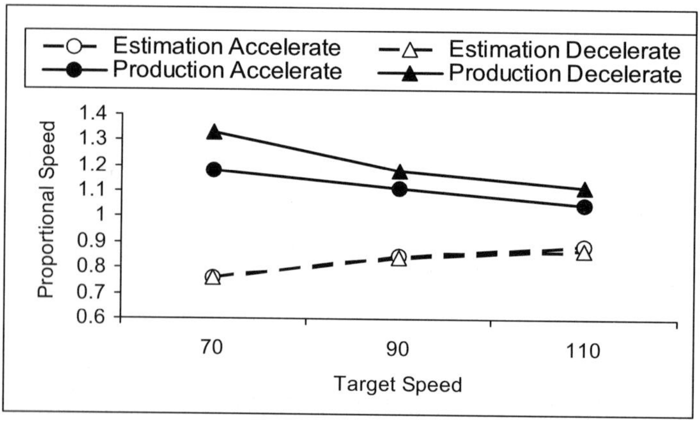

Figure 1. Proportional estimated and produced speed as a function of target speed and acceleration sign.

Speed increment production. The dependent variable was the proportional increment (increment produced/ target increment). The results can be seen in Table 2.

A repeated measures ANOVA for the three within-subject variables and the two between-subjects measures provided the following statistically significant effects: speed, $F\ (2,48) = 18.98, p < .001$); sign of acceleration, $F\ (1,24) = 17.70, p < .001$; Speed x Acceleration, $F\ (2,48) = 57.56, p < .01$; and Speed x Increment, $F\ (4, 96) = 4.57, p < .01$. The effect of speed indicates that the higher the final speed had to be reached, the lower the proportion of increment was produced; but this effect is to a certain extent a result of two opposing effects, as can be seen in the Speed x Acceleration interaction (Figure 2). This interaction indicates that magnitude of the increments carried out depended on speed and acceleration sign: in the case of acceleration, at a higher speed the proportion of increment/decrement made declines, while in deceleration, the higher the speed the greater is the proportion of increment/decrement made. The effect of acceleration sign indicates that the proportion of the increment produced is less if the manoeuvre requires deceleration than if acceleration is needed, though the Speed x Acceleration interaction qualifies this effect in the sense that it shows a slight inversion around 110 km/h.

Table 2. Mean error *(M)* and Standard Deviation *(SD)* in Proportional Speed Increment (ratio) as a function of Speed, Acceleration Sign and Target Increment (Experiment 1; $n = 30$).

Speed resulting from target increments		70 km/h		90 km/h		110 km/h		Total	
		M	*SD*	*M*	*SD*	*M*	*SD*	*M*	*SD*
Acceleration Increment	20	1.15	0.48	0.99	0.46	0.68	0.37	0.94	0.47
	30	1.22	0.35	0.87	0.35	0.77	0.30	0.95	0.38
	40	1.22	0.39	0.95	0.32	0.76	0.23	0.98	0.37
	Total	1.20	0.41	0.94	0.38	0.74	0.30	0.96	0.41
Deceleration Decrement	-20	0.63	0.37	0.74	0.48	0.69	0.42	0.68	0.43
	-30	0.58	0.34	0.62	0.24	0.82	0.34	0.67	0.32
	-40	0.57	0.20	0.72	0.27	0.91	0.26	0.74	0.28
	Total	0.59	0.31	0.69	0.35	0.81	0.36	0.70	0.35
Total		0.90	0.47	0.81	0.38	0.77	0.33	0.83	0.40

If two measures are allotted to each participant, one for all accelerating trials and another for decelerating ones, the correlation between both sets of measures is almost zero ($r = .08$; $p > .05$). This null correlation has led us to analyse reliability separately for increments and decrements. By calculating three measures for each participant (one for each of the final speeds), the correlations for accelerating trials range between .71 and .84 ($p < .001$), and for decelerating trials they range between .68 and .83 ($p < .001$). So, we can say that adjusting increments or decrements are reliable tasks, but both tasks do not represent the same skill.

As a suggestion, we hypothesise an explanation of the asymmetry between acceleration and deceleration: the acceleration manoeuvre implies a positive action of pressing the accelerator pedal, whereas deceleration (without braking) implies an act of omission, totally or partly releasing the accelerator. In any case, it appears that manoeuvres requiring deceleration lead to different results from those requiring acceleration, both in the case of producing speeds and in producing increments. This might have important practical consequences if this is also verified in ordinary driving.

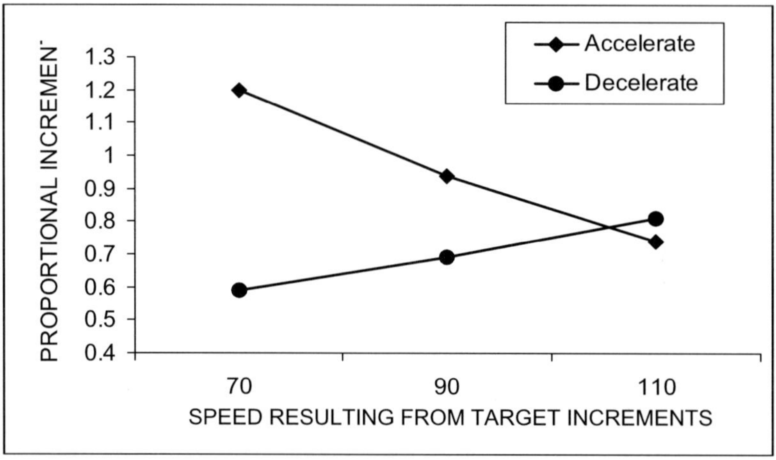

Experiment 2

Figure 2. Proportional produced increment as a function of the speed resulting from target increments.

This experiment is an exploratory study based in an extrapolation of the production task of Experiment 1 to the natural world. The participants do not only control the speed but also support the entire driving task among normal traffic conditions on a standard road of two single lanes.

Method

Participants. Ten participants (5 men and 5 women) have taken part, their ages ranging from 22 to 45 ($M = 27.3$, $SD = 5.1$). Their driving experience showed a great variability, although all of them had driven for more than two years. None of them were familiar with the route or with the particular model of car used in the experiment.

Design, instruments and procedure. The experiment was carried out on a secondary road, over a stretch of 8 km length with 12 bends and medium traffic flow and with the same experimental car than Experiment 1. Prior to the experimental trials the participants drove for about 30 minutes to become familiar with the car. The only restriction compared to ordinary driving was the concealment of the speedometer.

Once the test started the experimenter instructed the participant to adjust the speed to a target speed, with no time pressure. When the participant considered he had attained the target speed, he activated the right indicator lever. This was recorded and used to obtain the actual speed from the data recording system. The adjusted speeds were 60, 70, 80, 90 and 100 km/h. The order in which the speeds were presented was balanced so that (a) the speeds of 60, 70 and 80 were attained both after acceleration and deceleration; (b) the difference between two consecutive target speeds should be at least 20 km/h. The reason is that preliminary studies indicated that an error of over 10 km/h was relatively frequent, so the results could be skewed: for example, if a participant is requested to set the vehicle at 100 km/h and he set it at 87, if he is subsequently asked to adjust it at 90 km/h he is practically forced to reduce speed despite already being below the requested speed. A consequence of the design is that speeds of 90 and 100 km/h were never attained with a deceleration maneuver in order to respect the legal speed limit of 100 km/h.

The ordinary traffic conditions affected the regularity of the acceleration or deceleration processes: for example, a manoeuvre to increase speed should be postponed if there was another slow vehicle in front or a bend was close by, likewise a speed reduction should also be delayed to avoid a traffic conflict with vehicles coming from behind. As a result of this casuistry, the number of trials for each speed and for each acceleration sign was different, and therefore repeated measures testing could not be carried out to analyse data. In all there were 98 valid observations. To test overproduction and error reduction with increase in speed all speeds could be used; but for checking the effect of the acceleration sign only the speeds of 60, 70 and 80 km/h were used.

Results and discussion

The results, expressed as overproduction errors (positive) or underproduction errors (negative) can be seen in Table 3. All in all there is a mean overproduction of 4 km/h, somewhat attenuated compared to the experiments carried out on the closed track.

If all the speeds are considered in the statistical analysis, there is an error reduction at high speeds $F\ (4,93) = 10.31;\ p < .001$), Also, only the linear component of this trend is statistically significant $F\ (1,93) = 37.6;\ p < .001;\ r = -.53$. But if only the 60, 70 and 80 km/h speeds and the acceleration sign variable are considered the ANOVA indicates statistically significant differences for the acceleration sign, $F\ (1,57) = 27.6,\ p < .01$) but not for speed, nor for Acceleration x Speed.

The attenuation of speed overproduction can be explained because two of the speeds (90 and 100 km/h) were only reached by accelerating, which, as was previously shown, leads to lesser error.

Results, albeit with the limitations corresponding to an exploratory study and in natural traffic environment, show that the three main effects observed in speed production in a closed track are also produced when the participant drives the vehicle on a normal road and with normal traffic. They are: (a) speed overproduction, (b) reduction of overproduction at high speeds, (c) reproduction of the acceleration effect: in decelerating overproduction is noticeably higher than when accelerating (in fact, in acceleration the mean overproduction is zero). Perhaps the latter is the most noticeable finding and it is particularly important from the applied point of view: higher overproduction errors can be expected when the fulfilment of deceleration manoeuvres is needed, and particularly when lower speed limits should be respected in sites like approaching junctions, crossroads, residential areas, etc.

Table 3. Mean (*M*) and Standard Deviation (*SD*) of Speed Production Errors (Km/h) as a function of Target Speed and Acceleration Sign (Experiment 2).

Target speed	*60 km/h (n = 22)*		*70 Km/h (n = 21)*		*80 Km/h (n = 20)*		*90 Km/h (n = 18)*		*100 Km/h (n = 17)*		*TOTAL (n = 98)*	
	M	*SD*	*M*	*SD*	*M*	*SD*	*M*	*SD*	*M*	*SD*	*M*	*SD*
Accelerate (n=61)	2.0	6.5	1.4	6.8	1.8	5.7	0.8	7.9	-3.6	6.9	0.0	7.1
Decelerate (n=37)	11.1	4.7	10.9	5.4	6.9	3.9	--	--	--	--	10.2	5.0
Total	7.8	6.9	8.7	7.0	3.6	5.6	0.8	7.9	-3.6	3.9	3.9	8.6

EXPERIMENT 3

This experiment, analogous to the Experiment 2, was carried out on a dual carriageway highway with another sample and different speed values.

Method

Participants. A total of 13 drivers, 7 women and 6 men, participated in the experiment. The mean age was 27.85 years old, ranging form 23 to 40. All of them were experienced drivers with more than 5 years of experience and a mean total mileage near 150,000 km. As in the second experiment; they were not familiar with the route or with a car of the same model of the experimental vehicle.

Design instruments and procedure. The tests were run on a highway near Madrid. The participants also drove the instrumented car with the speedometer occluded and the production procedure was analogous to the one described in Experiment 2. Each participant performed 12 trials, and the target speeds were 80, 90 and 100 km/h. Each trial was performed so that half of the trials implied an acceleration manoeuvre and half a deceleration manoeuvre. The difference between previous and target speed was not systematically varied but assigned on a random basis within a range of approximately plus or minus 15 to 30 km/h respect to target speed. The experimenter, before each trial, gave general instructions to the participant like "slow down" or "speed up" until the previous speeds were in the mentioned range. Then told the participant to set the car at the target speed and press a response button when considered that the target speed was attained.

Results

The adjustment errors were calculated. In the analysis of variance only the linear component of the speed effect is statistically significant, F (1,12) = 8.04, p = .015: the over-adjustment tendency and the adjustment error is progressively reduced with increasing target speeds. The acceleration effect shows the expected trend (higher over-adjustment after decelerating than after accelerating), although in this occasion the difference was not statistically significant. (See Table 4).

Table 4. Mean (*M*) and Standard Deviation (*SD*) of Speed Production Errors (km/h) as a function of Target Speed and Acceleration Sign. (Experiment 3; *n*=14).

Target speed	*80 km/h*		*90 km/h*		*100 km/h*		*Total*	
	M	*SD*	*M*	*SD*	*M*	*SD*	*M*	*SD*
Accelerate	5.7	5.6	2.4	9.0	-1.9	8.9	2.1	6.1
Decelerate	4.6	9.6	4.0	9.9	0.2	10.2	2.9	8.6
Total	5.2	7.0	3.2	8.5	-0.9	8.6	2.5	6.9

General Discussion

The results of speed estimation and speed production tasks reproduced those of Recarte and Nunes (1996), and extended them to other conditions: (a) symmetry between speed underestimation and speed overproduction, (b) greater underestimation and overproduction for lower speeds rather than for higher ones, (c) absence of effects or slight ones from between-participants' variables (sex and driving experience).

All the symmetries in the effects suggest that same representational process underlies speed estimation or adjustment. Likewise, the lack of driving experience effects suggests the existence of a primary perceptual process, scarcely affected by learning factors, despite of the complexity of the driving context. Nevertheless, the same asymmetry is reproduced: the acceleration sign did not affect the estimation but affected the speed production task. It may be that different perceptual parameters operate when action is implied compared with passive perception. Milner and Goodale (1995) show abundant evidence that perception for action is basically different, and backed by different cerebral structures, from perception for identification or recognition. If, moreover, the reliability results, especially the lack of correlation between increments and decrements production, is borne in mind, a conclusion with practical implications can be drawn: the perception of absolute speed and speed increments is different after accelerating rather than after decelerating, but only if the speed control action is involved.

Regarding the role of increments in speed perception, the lack of effect of increment magnitude, either in estimation or in production, suggests that speed perception takes little benefit form a continuum comparative processes of speed variations along time, represented by each trial and the experiment as a whole, but rather is determined by an absolute appreciation of speed: given a complex pattern of perceptual motion at a particular time, the participant assigns a speed value (km/h), with some error and according to some regularities. Furthermore, as far as the perception of increments in themselves is concerned, when the participants are expressly to perform a particular speed increment or decrement, the task appears to be qualitatively different to one of simple target speed production: speed increments are under-produced while speed is generally overproduced, what agrees with other studies (Denton, 1966: Recarte et al., 1996).

Moreover, the reproduction of the speed effect in ordinary driving (the lower the speed the greater the overproduction) and acceleration sign (greater overproduction of speed after deceleration than after acceleration) provides ecological validity to the results obtained on the closed track. In fact, it is at low speeds and after deceleration when the most frequent, restrictive and potentially dangerous driving situations occur in real traffic, and since they coincide with more and demanding and complex environments, it is more likely to give priority to the inspection of the visual scene outside the car, to omit the speedometer inspection (Recarte & Nunes, 2000), and to rely upon intuitive speed reduction. Even assuming the drivers willingness to comply with the rules, (something in little doubt in the participants of the experiment 2 and 3), the present data show that such speed reductions give rise to gross errors in ordinary driving.

Acknowledgements

This research was supported by the Dirección General de Tráfico.

References

Denton, G. G. (1966). A subjective scale of speed when driving a motor vehicle. *Ergonomics, 9,* 203-210.

Groeger, J. A., Carsten, O. M., & Blana, E. (1997). Speed and distance estimation under simulated conditions. In A.G. Gale, I.D. Brown, C.M. Haslegrave and S.P. Taylor (Eds.), *Vision in Vehicles VII,* (pp.291-299). Amsterdam: Elsevier.

Harms, L. (1991). Experimental studies of variations in cognitive load and driving speed in traffic and driving simulation. In A.G. Gale, I. D. Brown, C. M. Aslegrave, I. Moorhead and S. Taylor (Eds.), *Vision in Vehicles III* (pp. 71-78). Amsterdam: Elsevier (North-Holland).

Harms, L. (1996). Driving performance on a real road and in a driving simulator: Result of a validation study. In A.G.Gale, I.D. Brown, C.M. Haslegrave and S.P. Taylor (Eds.), *Vision in Vehicles V,* (pp.19-26). Amsterdam: Elsevier.

Manser, M. P., Carmody, J., & Hancock, P. A. (1997). The role of environmental stimuli on driver's ability to maintain a constant velocidty through restricted environments. In A.G.Gale, I.D. Brown, C.M. Haslegrave and S.P. Taylor (Eds.), *Vision in Vehicles VI.* Amsterdam: Elsevier.

Milner, A. D., & Goodale, M. A. (1995). *The Visual Brain in Action.* Oxford: Oxford University Press.

Recarte, M. A., & Nunes, L. M. (2000). Effects of verbal and spatial-imagery tasks on eye fixations while driving. *Journal of Experimental Psychology: Applied, 6,* 31-43.

Recarte, M. A., & Nunes, L. M. (1996). Perception of speed in an automobile: estimation and production. *Journal of Experimental Psychology: Applied, 2,* 291-304.

Recarte, M. A., Conchillo, A., & Nunes, L. M. (1996). Percepción y ajuste de incrementos de velocidad en automóvil [Perception and adjustment of speed- increments in automobile] *Psicológica, 17,* 441-454.

Triggs, Th. J., & Berenyi, J. S. (1982). Estimation of automobile speed under day and night conditions. *Human Factors, 24,* 111-114.

Traffic and Transport Psychology,
T. Rothengatter and R.D. Huguenin (Editors)

7

Comparison of Reaction Times at Low and High Speeds

Tomoyuki Fuse, Katsuya Matsunaga, Kazunori Shidoji and Yuji Matsuki

Introduction

According to a previous investigation through a questionnaire, many people thought that the principal cause for car accidents was over speed driving (Fujita, 1999). Traffic accidents (collisions) occur when a car's stopping distance becomes longer than the headway distance between the vehicle and the obstacles. It's known that the stopping distance is sometimes suddenly prolonged. One of the causes of this is the extension of the driver's reaction time (RT) (Matsunaga, 1994). This results in the greater distances traveled from the time of the first appearance of an obstacle or the sudden change in the surroundings to the time when the driver initiates the braking action (Matsunaga, Kito, Kitamura, Shidoji & Yanagida, 1990). But there are few people who are conscious of this fact.

It is supposed that the driver's RT is one of the most important human factors in accident prevention. For example, the result of our previous experiment was that the mobile phone restrained the driver's view and prolonged the driver's RT (Fuse, Matsungaga, Shidoji, Matsuki & Umezaki, in press). We suggested that this prolongation could be a cause of the collisions.

It was found that accident-prone drivers have a large standard deviation value in their RTs (Matsunaga, 1988). The mean value or RT did not relate to accident-proneness. The relationship between the standard deviation of RT and the vehicle speed is not yet clear. Therefore we aimed to measure the RT in several driving speed conditions and at stimulus locations. Next, we analyzed the mean and standard deviation of the RT. In Experiment 1, the stimulus location was in the central area of the driver's view. In Experiment 2, it was in the upper area of the driver's view.

Experiment 1: The Driver's RT for Stimulation of the Central Area of the Retina

Purpose

The purpose of Experiment 1 was to clarify the relationship among the mean of RT, the standard deviation of RT for the stimulus in the central area of the driver's view, and the vehicle speed.

Method

The authors developed a computer based experimental system that measured the speed and a driver's RT where by RT means the period from the time when the light-emitted diode (LED) on the windshield was turned on until the time when drivers pushed the button on a steering wheel. Figure 1 shows the equipment for the Experiment 1. The experimenter required the subject (the driver of an experimental car) to push the button as soon as he noticed that the LED was turned on.

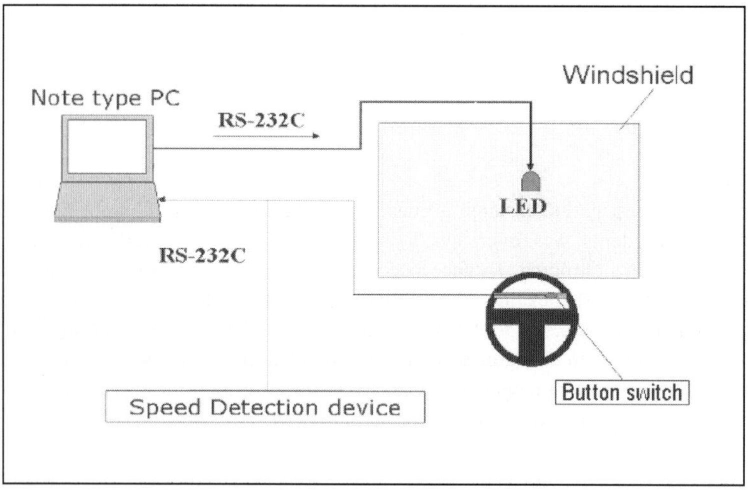

Figure 1. The equipment for Experiment 1.

Experiment 1 was conducted on a straight road. The car velocities were set as the stop condition (0km/h) and driving conditions (20 km/h, 40 km/h and 60 km/h). The subject drove the experimental car without seeing a speed meter. The experimenter in the front passenger's seat verbally assisted the driver in keeping the speed. The LED was set up in two positions, one on the windshield in front of the driver and the other on the windshield at 10 degrees on the left of the first LED position. The experiment for the central LED position was conducted first and the experiment for the LED at 10 degrees on the left was done at another time. The LED was turned on at the same random interval sequence for each speed condition. The RTs were measured 20 times under each stimulus position and speed. An experimental design was 8 (subjects) x 4 (speed conditions) x 2 (LED positions). The drivers (subjects) were eight males who were between 22 and 25 years of age.

Result and Discussion

Figure 2 shows the mean and standard deviation of RT of each subject and each experimental condition. At the centre LED position, the mean RT at 0 km/h was 339 ms (*SD* 64 ms); at 20 km/h 400 ms (*SD* 138 ms); at 40 km/h 429 ms (*SD* 122 ms); at 60 km/h 396 ms (*SD* 130 ms).

At the 10 degrees on the left LED position, the mean RT at 0 km/h was 315 ms (*SD* 48 ms); at 20 km/h 354 ms (*SD* 43 ms); at 40 km/h 367 ms (*SD* 46 ms); at 60 km/h 360 ms (*SD* 52 ms).

A two-way analysis of variance (ANOVA) led to the main effect of the speed condition ($F(3,18)=7.814$, $p<.01$), but did not reveal the main effect of the LED's position ($F(1,6) = 1.807$, *ns*). A multiple comparison with Ryan's procedure showed that the mean RTs at driving conditions of 20 km/h, 40 km/h and 60 km/h were larger than the mean RT at 0 km/h condition.

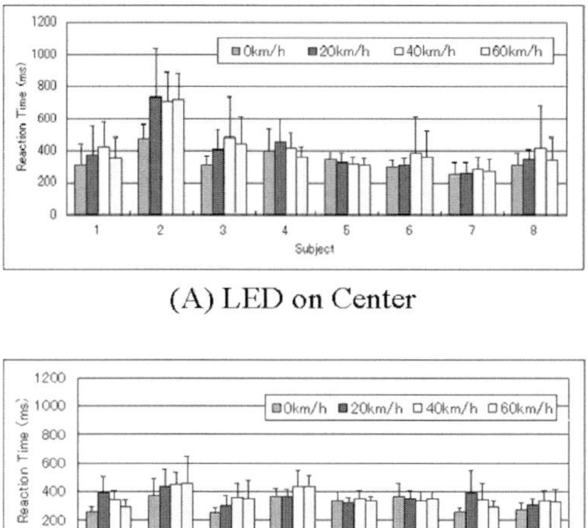

(A) LED on Center

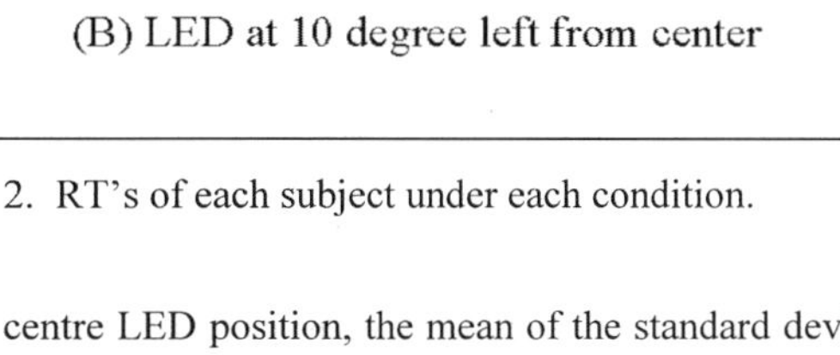

(B) LED at 10 degree left from center

Figure 2. RT's of each subject under each condition.

At the centre LED position, the mean of the standard deviation of a driver's RT at 0 km/h was 81 ms (*SD* 34 ms); at 20 km/h 126 ms (*SD* 82 ms); at 40 km/h 162 ms (*SD* 77 ms); at 60 km/h

118 ms (*SD* 47 ms). At the 10 degrees on the left LED position, the mean of the standard deviation of a driver's RT at 0 km/h was 60 ms (*SD* 30 ms); at 20 km/h 81 ms (*SD* 40 ms); at 40 km/h 83 ms (*SD* 22 ms); at 60km/h 82 ms (*SD* 50 ms).

A two-way ANOVA led to the main effect for the condition of speed ($F(3,21)=3.035$, $p<.10$), and led to the main effect of LED's position ($F(1,7)=14.626$, $p<.01$).

The mean RTs in driving conditions were larger than that in the stopping conditions. This difference suggests that driving required more processing loads for the subjects. But there were no significant differences in either the mean RT or the *SD* of RT in all the driving conditions. In this experiment, the stimulus was located in front of the driver so that they could see it at a central vision.

We could not find any differences in driving conditions because the stimulus was noticed too easily. We found that the standard deviation of RT at the 10 degrees left position was smaller than that at the central position.

Experiment 2: The Driver's RT for Upper Central Area Stimulus

Purpose

In Experiment 1, there was no significant difference in RT for the central area stimulus in all the driving conditions. In Experiment 2, we tried to measure RT for a stimulus that was located farther from the central area.

Method

We used the same measurement equipment as in Experiment 1, but installed the LED at a 15 degrees elevation from the center of the driver's visual field. Conditions of vehicle speed were at 40 km/h and 60 km/h. The reasons the authors omitted the 0 km/h, 20 km/h conditions were that the 20 km/h condition was not considered an ordinary speed on most roads, and there was no significant difference on RTs and *SD*s between the 20 km/h condition and the 40 km/h, 60 km/h and stopping conditions.

The subjects were nine men between 23 and 25 years of age. The experimental design was 9(subjects) x 2(speed conditions).

Result and Discussion

Figure 3 shows the mean and standard deviation of RT of each subject.

The mean RT of all subjects at 40 km/h was 582 ms (*SD* 162 ms), and at 60 km/h 553 ms (*SD* 230 ms). A *t*-test did not show a significant difference between those ($t(8) = .741$, *ns*). The mean *SD* of RT at 40 km/h was 254 ms (*SD* 113ms), and at 60 km/h 188 ms (*SD* 107 ms). The *SD* of the RT under the 40 km/h driving condition was larger than that of the 60 km/h driving condition ($t(8) = 2.497$, $p<.05$).

There was no difference in mean RT between two velocities. But, at the speed of 40 km/h, the *SD* of the RT was larger than that at 60 km/h. Most subjects reported that they became anxious about other vehicles at 40 km/h driving because other traffic ran at around 60 km/h. We supposed that the speed difference with the surrounding traffic gave the drivers stress and they looked frequently in the rearview mirrors while at 40 km/h.

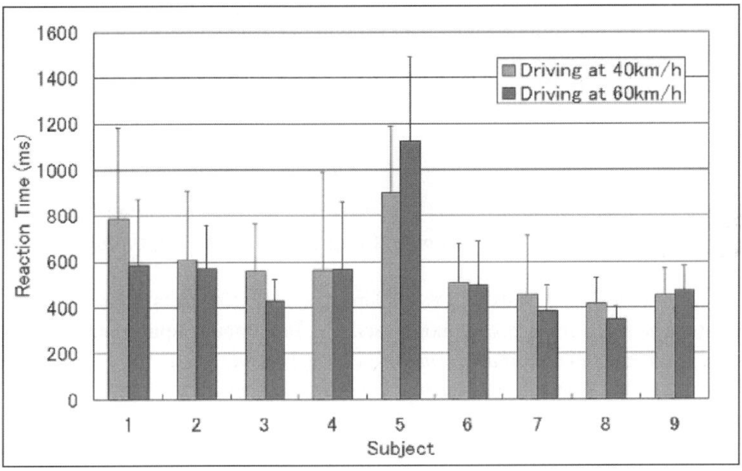

Figure 3. The RT and *SD* of each subject under each condition.

General Discussion

The result of Experiment 1 showed that the mean RTs under all driving conditions were larger than in the stopping condition. This difference suggests that subjects must process more information while actually driving.

In Experiment 1, there were no significant differences in the mean RT and the SD of RT under all driving conditions. In Experiment 1, it was supposed that the subject could drive a vehicle without any shift of a fixation point to find the stimulus since the stimulus position was in the central area of the subject view. Therefore the subject could easily check the stimulus while driving.

However, in Experiment 2, the stimulus was presented at a farther position from the central area of the subject's view. It was assumed that they could not see the direction of travel and the stimulus, simultaneously. They would frequently move their eyes from the direction of travel to the stimulus and vice versa. The task was a little more difficult than in Experiment 1. Therefore, the *SD* of RTs showed a difference between the two velocity conditions in Experiment 2. The *SD* of RT at 40 km/h was larger than that at 60 km/h in Experiment 2. It was assumed that this result was due to the traffic circumstances of the experiments. The authors did the experiments on a wide and straight road without busy traffic. Other vehicles traveled at around 60 km/h. At 40 km/h, the subjects sometimes looked in the rearview mirrors to see other vehicles. It was supposed that this produced the large *SD*. The authors believe that this would not apply on crowded or narrow roads. Drivers must be aware of many other things and will be processing too much information at a high driving speed.

Conclusions

There was no significant difference in mean RT under different driving conditions. But the *SD* of RT at 40 km/h was larger than that at 60 km/h for a near central view area stimulus. We inferred that this result was due to traffic circumstances.

References

Fujita, K., Matsunaga, K., Shidoji, K., & Matsuki, Y. (1999). The research of knowledge about safe driving. *Proceedings of the 59th Japanese Congress of Traffic Psychology*, (pp.1-4).

Fuse, T., Matsunaga, K., Shidoji, K., Matsuki, Y., & Umeazaki, K. (in press). The cause of traffic accidents when drivers use car phones and the functional requirements of car phones for safe driving. *International Journal of Vehicle Design*, *3* (1).

Matsunaga, K. (1988). *Scientific Research in Kyushu University*, 1, Kyushu University.

Matsunaga, K., Kito, T., Kitamura, F., Shidoji, K., & Yanagida, T. (1990). Reaction Time Variability and Type of Personality of Accident-Prone Drivers. In J. Misumi, B. Wilpert and H. Motoaki (Eds.), *Proceedings of the 22nd International Congress of Applied Psychology vol.1, Organization and WorkPsychology*. (p.323). East Sussex : Lawrence Erlbaum.

Matsunaga, K. (1994). Reaction Time Variability and Hastening whilst Driving as Factors for Accident-Prone Drivers. *Handout of the 23th International Congress of Applied Psychology*.

Traffic and Transport Psychology,
T. Rothengatter and R.D. Huguenin (Editors)

8

Comprehension and Evaluation of Road Users' Signalling - An International Comparison between Finland, Germany and Japan

Kazumi Renge, Gert Weller, Bernhard Schlag, Martti Peräaho and Esko Keskinen

Introduction

The present study focuses on road users' signalling (using devices and gestures on the road) as a type of non-verbal communication. Adequate social interaction and comfortable human relationships between road users should be established. It is therefore definitely necessary to understand road users not only as operators of automobiles, but also as social partners in road traffic.

"Roadway interpersonal communication" (Renge, 2000) is certainly a central area of such social interaction. This communication consists of formal and informal communication by using a variety of channels such as blinkers, headlights, passing lights, horns, hand gestures, eye contact, head movements, and vehicle movements. The process of roadway communication reflects comprehensive social interaction between drivers and other road users. In order to comprehend such signals, drivers have to analyse the patterns of the signals suitably relating to the behaviour of the cars and to the traffic situations in which the behaviour is executed. This means that comprehension of road users' signals is an important process related to driving skill.

Renge (2000) conducted a laboratory experiment of roadway interpersonal communication. Sixty-three participants (32 novice, and 31 experienced drivers) evaluated meanings of road users' signals in twenty-four traffic situations; signals included blinkers, headlights, hazard lamps, and hand gestures. The traffic scenes were shown with a slide projector in the laboratory. Confidence in answers was also evaluated by using a 5-point scale. The signals were classified into three categories; Formal Device-Based Signal (Formal Signal), Informal Device-Based Signal (Informal Signal), and Informal Gesture-Based Signal (Everyday Signal). The total comprehension scores demonstrated that experienced drivers could understand the signals better than novice drivers. There was a large difference in the comprehension scores for Informal Signal between experienced and novice drivers. Novice drivers could understand Formal Signal and Everyday Signal better than Informal Signal. Similar results were also obtained in the confidence scores. Experienced drivers were more confident in their answers than novice drivers. An effect of gender was found in the scores of confidence.

The present study concentrated more on international differences than on drivers' individual differences. An international comparison study involving three countries, Finland, Germany and Japan, was conducted in laboratories, which were chosen as representatives of northern and central Europe and East Asia. As each country is highly motorised, they were regarded as suitable for the purpose of the research.

The main purposes of the study are first to compare drivers' comprehension of the signals in each country, and secondly, to investigate how differently they evaluate the signals on scales of necessity and friendliness. If the drivers in different countries would comprehend a variety of signals on roads differently or feel them differently, e.g. more or less aggressive or necessary, road users' social interaction could be negatively influenced, which might sometimes cause drivers' aggressive behaviour on roads. The international comparison in the present study brings us useful information to establish more effective and comfortable social interaction between road users.

METHOD

Subjects

In total, 261 subjects participated in the experiment (149 in Finland, 46 in Germany, and 66 in Japan), mainly university students and staff. Using a matching method, 30 subjects from each country were selected for analysis, as the subjects in each country were different from each other regarding individual characters like driving experience. The two criteria for matching were driving experience (total driving distance after licensing) and age. Of course, it was difficult to make perfect matching of both aspects at the same time, as, for example, Japanese drivers usually drive much less per a year than drivers in Finland or Germany. The characteristics of the subjects after matching are described in Table 1.

Table 1. Description of age, sex, and mileage groups.

Country	*Sex*	*n*	*Age*	*Mileage (km)*
Japan	Male	17	27.1	51352
	Female	13	30.1	29523
	Total	30	28.4	41893
Germany	Male	11	28.5	71363
	Female	19	29.3	26694
	Total	30	29.0	43073
Finland	Male	11	23.5	45409
	Female	19	25.0	40089
	Total	30	24.4	42040

Stimuli

Twenty-two videotaped traffic scenes with road users' signalling were presented to the subjects on a video-monitor. The scenes were recorded in Finland. We used two criteria for classifying the signals, namely "formal or informal" and "device-based or gesture-based". Formal signals based on road traffic rules are taught in driving school and usually involve a tight code system. Informal signals gradually develop through drivers' interpersonal interaction on roads. Combining the two criteria, the signals in the scenes were classified into four categories such as "formal device-based signals"(an example: a driver of a red car intends to change lane and applies the right turn signal), "formal gesture-based signals"(a bicyclist signals a turn with her left hand), "informal device-based signals"(a driver waiting at an intersection sounds the horn shortly to a car in front still waiting after the traffic light turned green), and "informal gesture-based signals"(a driver shakes his fist fiercely in anger, when he is denied the right of way by another driver in an intersection). The types and meaning of the signals as stimuli are presented in Table 2.

Procedure

Each scene lasted about ten seconds. The subjects selected the correct meaning of each signal from a list of 19 alternatives. They also evaluated how sure or unsure they were of their answer, how friendly or aggressive they perceived the signal, and how necessary or unnecessary they found it in the situation. The evaluation was given on a 1 to 5 point Likert-scale. Based on the ratings on the "friendly- aggressive scale" from -2 (aggressive) to +2 (friendly) to each signal, the informal signals were further divided into two categories, which were Friendly Signals and Aggressive Signals. The former included the signals that got a mean evaluation of 0.5 or more on the scale (7 signals), and the latter the signals which got a mean evaluation of -0.5 or less on the scale (5 signals). These scores were compared by using GLM of SPSS v.10.0 between countries and by sex. The Tukey's q-tests were performed on all main-effects.

Results and Discussion

Formal Device-based Signals (FDS) and Formal Gesture-based Signals (FGS)

Comprehension scores to FDS and FGS were compared by country. Main-effects of country on Comprehension Scores in both FDS and FGS were found ($F\ (2,82) = 18.42$, $p < .001$ in FDS; $F\ (2,82) = 23.15$, $p < .001$ in FGS). Similar main-effects were also found regarding Confidence Scores in both signals ($F\ (2,82) = 8.75$, $p < .001$ in FDS; $F\ (2,82) = 45.46$, $p < .001$ in FGS). As showed in Figure 1, Japanese drivers identified the correct meanings of both FDS and FGS less often than Finnish and German drivers. They were also less confident of their answers (Figure 2) than those drivers. No main-effects of sex were found regarding both Comprehension and Confidence Scores to FDS and FGS. A signal involving hazard warning lamps and a bicyclist' turn signal could not be understood by many Japanese drivers.

Necessity and Friendliness-Aggression Scores for FDS and FGS were also analysed by country and by sex. In the analysis, only subjects' correct answers of the meanings to the signals were dealt with, because drivers' misunderstanding as to the meaning of the signals could bring different evaluation to them. As showed in Figure 3, a main-effect of countries was found regarding Necessity Scores for FGS (F (2,83) = 13.29, p < .001). Japanese drivers evaluated FGS as less necessary than drivers in the other two countries. No main-effects of sex were found regarding Necessity Scores for FDS and FGS.

Table 2. Types of signals, meaning and order of presentation.

Formal device-based signals	
04	A car is pulling out from the roadside. A red car is just about to pass and swerves in order to avoid a collision, the driver honking the horn at the same time ("Warning").
05	A red car is driving along a multi-lane road, the right blinker is flashing ("Changing lane").
17	A car is about to pull out from the side of a street, the left blinker is flashing ("Starting")
19	A red car is looking for parking space in a parking lot, when another car reverses out in front of it. The driver of the red car honks the horn. ("Warning").
20	A red car standing stationary on the roadside with the hazard warning lights flashing ("Warning").
Formal gesture-based signals	
01	A cyclist approaches an X-crossing and stretches out her left arm ("Turning left").
08	A cyclist is cycling along a bicycle road. She stretches out her right arm as she is approaching a crossing ("Turning right").
16	A cyclist approaches a priority road. She stretches out her right arm ("Turning right").
22	A cyclist is cycling along a bicycle road. She stretches out her left arm ("Turning left").
Informal device-based signals	
02	A red car is following closely behind another car on a country road. The driver of the red car honks the horn ("Give way").
03	A red car is following closely behind another car on the overtaking lane of a motorway. The driver of the red car flashes the headlights ("Give way").
07	A car is driving along a country road. The brake lights flash three times ("Too close").
10	A car is driving on a motorway holding to the extreme right and letting a red car pass. The driver of the red car flashes the left blinker immediately after passing ("Thank you").
11	The driver of a red car flashes the headlights when another car is approaching on a country road. The latter car does not have the headlights turned on ("Turn the lights on").
13	A red car is driving along a country road. The driver flashes the right blinker ("You may overtake").
15	A red car is waiting behind another car for the traffic lights to turn green. When they do, the driver of the car in front does not start off. The driver of the red car honks the horn ("Hurry up").
Informal gesture-based signals	
06	A pedestrian is about to cross a street when a car approaches. He waves to the car with his left hand ("You may go first").
09	A car is turning left in a crossing when a cyclist approaches from the opposite direction. The cyclist waves to the car ("You may go first").
12	A motorcyclist with the right of way has to brake abruptly when a car drives out in front of him from the left. He protests with his middle finger in the air ("Obey the traffic regulations").
14	A car holds to the extreme right on a motorway. A red car passes, the driver holding up his right hand ("Thank you").
18	A driver of a red car has to brake abruptly when another car drives out in front of him. He protests by shaking his fist. ("Obey the traffic regulations").
21	A driver of a red car is looking for parking space when another car reverses out in front of him. The driver of the red car waves his hand ("You may go first").

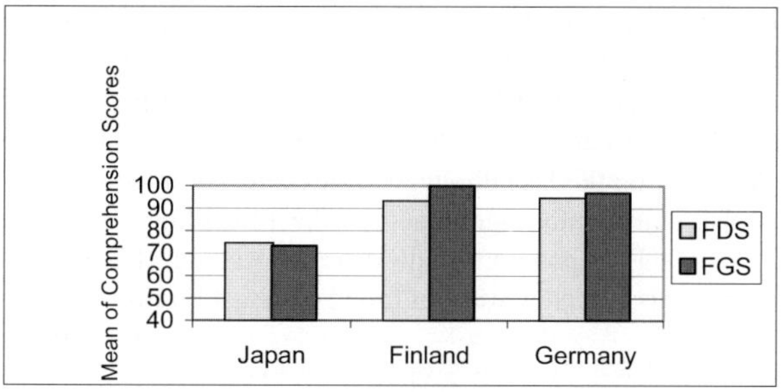

Figure 1. Comprehension scores for Formal Device-based Signals (FDS) and Formal Gesture-based signals (FGS) between countries.

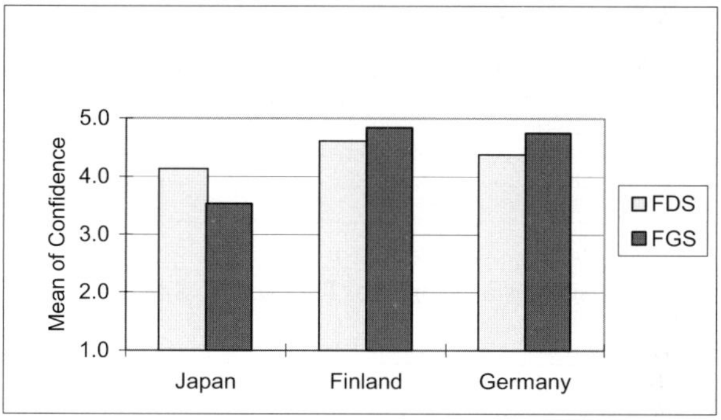

Figure 2. Confidence scores for FDS and FGS between countries.

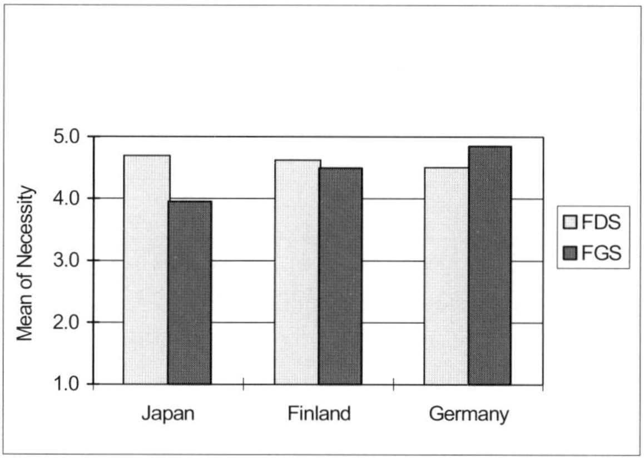

Figure 3. Necessity scores for FDS and FGS by country.

A strong main-effect of countries on Friendliness-Aggression Scores for both FDS and FGS was demonstrated (F (2,83) = 15.49, p < .001 in FDS; F (2,83) = 29.49, p < .001 in FGS). Finnish drivers evaluated FDS friendlier than Japanese drivers, who evaluated both FDS and FGS friendlier than German drivers (Figure 4). The German subjects evaluated both types of signals quite neutrally on the friendly-aggressive scale. An interaction of both factors (countries and sex) was also statistically significant on the Friendliness-Aggression Scores to FDS (F (2,83) = 3.13, p < .05). Japanese female drivers evaluated FDS as more friendly than male drivers (Figure 5). This tendency was not found amongst Finnish or German drivers.

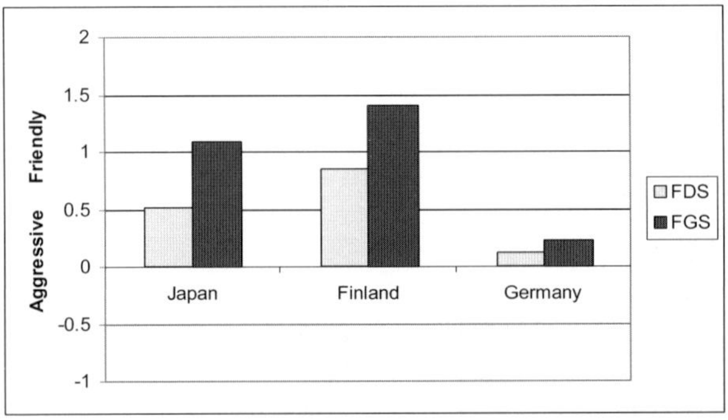

Figure 4. Friendliness-aggression scores for FDS and FGS by country.

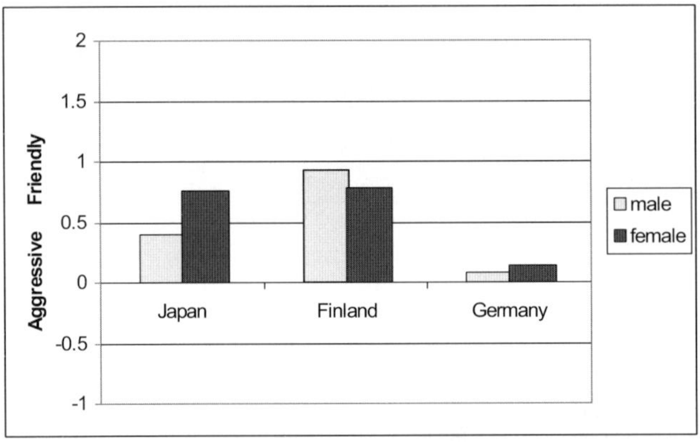

Figure 5. Friendliness-aggression scores for FDS by sex.

Informal signals

It is difficult to say what interpretation should be regarded as being "correct" as informal signals are used differently in different countries, or not used at all in a certain country. As regards comprehension of informal signals, three categories could be identified: (a) universal signals, (b) area-based signals (Figure 5), and (c) country-based signals (Figure 6). The motorcyclist in Figure 6 had to brake abruptly when a car drove out in front of him from the left. He protested with his middle finger in the air. Drivers in Europe can easily understand the signal, because they are familiar with it in their everyday life. The signal is not popular in Japan. A relatively higher proportion of Japanese drivers could not understand it at all (e.g. many of them comprehended it as "Thank you"). The signal in Figure 7 is an example of country-based signals. The signal used in Finland means "Thank you". However, almost no Japanese or German drivers could comprehend it n such a way. It means that the signal has only spread out in a certain country. As mentioned above, the drivers comprehend the signals differently, and their evaluation of the signals was also different. Therefore, we only analysed the evaluation of the signals, which were comprehended in the same meaning by the drivers.

Figure 6. An example of area-based signal ("Obey the rules" by a rider who had been denied his right-of-way).

Figure 7. An example of country-based signal ("Thank you" for letting me overtake using blinker).

Significant differences in confidence and evaluation were also found regarding informal signals. As for Confidence Scores for Friendly Signals, a main-effect of country was found (F (2,82) = 34.83, $p < .001$). Finnish drivers were more confident than drivers in the other two countries, and Japanese drivers were less confident than German drivers (Figure 8). As for Aggressive Signals, a similar result was found (F (2,83) = 10.34, $p < .001$). Japanese drivers were less confident than drivers in the other two countries.

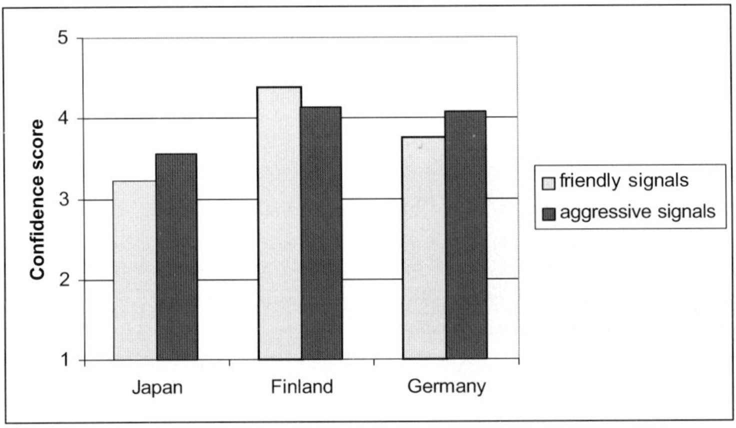

Figure 8. Confidence scores to informal signals (friendly and aggressive signals).

No main effects of country were found regarding Necessity Scores for informal Friendly and Aggressive Signals (Figure 9). A main-effect of sex was found regarding Necessity Scores for Aggressive Signals (F (1,84) = 5.19, $p < .05$). Male drivers evaluated Aggressive Signals as more necessary than female drivers (Figure 10).

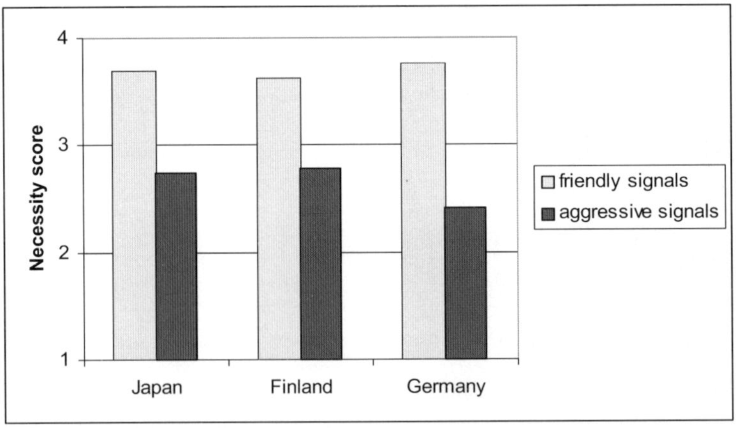

Figure 9. Necessity scores for informal signals (friendly and aggressive signals).

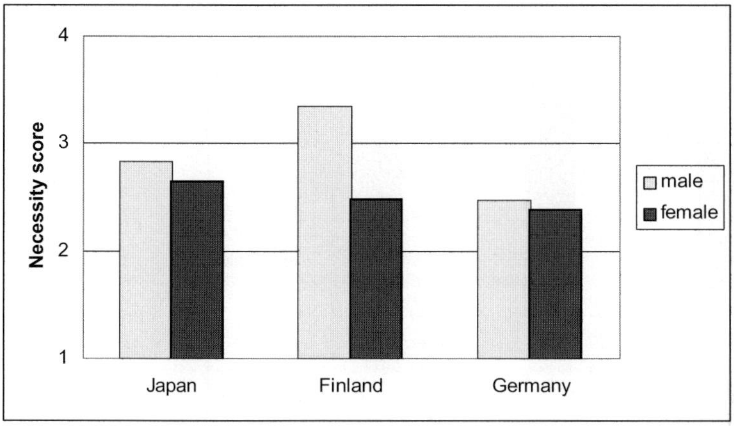

Figure 10. Necessity scores for informal aggressive signals by sex.

As for Friendliness-Aggression Scores for Friendly Signals, main effects of countries and sex were found (F (2,84) = 10.83, $p< .001$ and F (1,84) = 4.55, $p < .05$, respectively). Finnish drivers evaluated the Friendly Signals as friendlier than German and Japanese drivers (Figure 11) and female drivers evaluated the signals friendlier than male drivers (Figure 12).

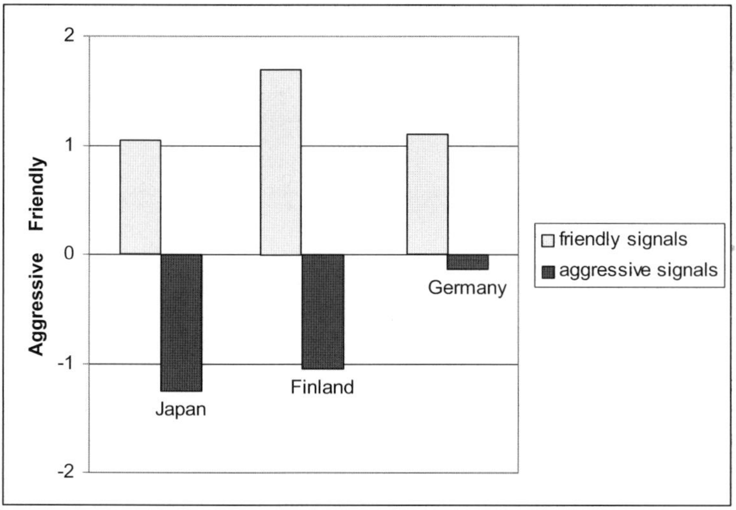

Figure 11. Friendliness-aggression scores for informal signals (friendly and aggressive signals).

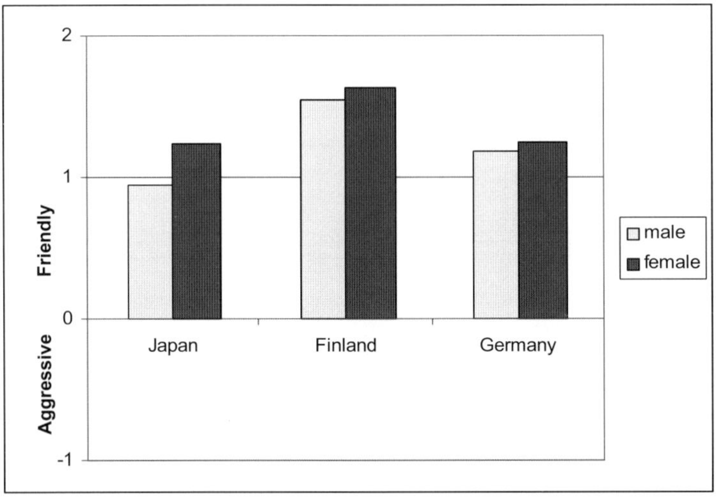

Figure 12. Friendly-aggression scores for informal friendly signals by sex

A variety of international differences in drivers' comprehension and evaluation of road users' signals were found. When drivers' cultural backgrounds were different, they easily misunderstood and evaluated the signals differently. The same signals were evaluated differently on the scales of Necessity or Friendliness-Aggression. It is supposed that these differences in comprehension and evaluation might cause aggressive behaviour or "road rage" between road users.

Reference

Renge, K. (2000). Effect of driving experience on drivers' decoding process of roadway interpersonal communication. *Ergonomics, 43,* 27-39.

Traffic and Transport Psychology,
T. Rothengatter and R.D. Huguenin (Editors)

9

Interaction and Communication in Dynamic Control Tasks: Ship Handling and Car Driving

Christine Chauvin and Farida Saad

Introduction

The purpose is twofold: to present the results of two research studies aimed at analysing operators' activity when managing their interactions with others and, on this basis, to discuss the potential impact of new support systems. These studies have been carried out in two different fields: ship handling and car driving. However, it seems interesting to parallel one study with the other, since they share several theoretical and methodological aspects: (a) In both cases, interaction management between actors was regarded as a crucial dimension of the tasks studied and of the efficiency and safety of their performance, (b) the actors' activity was studied in the complexity of real-life situations, (c) the methods used are quite similar. They are based on two complementary investigative techniques: the observation of behaviour as well as the description of their situational context and the recording of operators' verbal reports (either simultaneous or subsequent to the performance of the task), (d) furthermore, the two studies come up with comparable results that raise the same kinds of question relative to the design and evaluation of new support systems.

First, the tasks studied will be compared. Then the methods and the main findings of each study will be presented. In conclusion, we will discuss the potential impact of technological changes in the light of the results obtained.

Ship Handling and Car Driving: Similarities and Differences

Interaction management in ship handling and car driving takes place in quite similar circumstances: head-on situations, crossing situations and overtaking. Nevertheless, these tasks may differ and can be compared in three respects (Bainbridge, Lenior & Van Der Shaaf, 1993): person-related aspects, tool or device aspects and task demands.

Person-related aspects

(a) In both cases, the experience and the status of the actors involved in interaction situations may differ. At sea, they are either professional (watch officers on board merchant vessels, fishermen) or not (sailors). In the same way, private drivers coexist with professional ones on the road. However, it is important to emphasise that mariners are mainly professional, whereas road users are mainly private motorists, (b) In both cases, the actors (watch officers or drivers) are autonomous, having their own goals, knowledge and strategies. In contrast to the organisation of air traffic, for example, there is no supervisor for controlling interactions between the various actors.

Tool or device aspects

Several means do exist for supporting and organising interactions between actors. These means can be classified into four main categories, summarised in the following table (Table 1).

Table 1. Existing tools and devices to help and structure interactions between actors

	Ship handling	*Car driving*
Infrastructure	Traffic separation scheme (shipping lanes are shown on nautical charts but are not physically visible).	Road infrastructure, including traffic lanes, road signs and road marking, ...
Formal rules (governing priority and safety)	The COLREG (Collision avoidance rules)	The Highway Code
Means of communication	Navigation lights, sound signals and the VHF (Very High Frequency) radiotelephone system	Indicators, headlights, horn, ...
Onboard device	The Automatic Radar Plotting Aid (ARPA) radar, which provides useful information about the target (speed, heading, distance, bearing, DCPA and TCPA) except its identity	Similar kind of devices is being developed

(DCPA : the Closest Point of Approach [The distance off at which a target will pass]; TCPA : the Time at which the target will reach its Closest Point of Approach).

Task demands

In dynamic tasks, several factors may determine the task demands. Hoc (1991, 1996) mentioned the degree of control, access to crucial information, time constraints and the level of automation. Roth and Woods (1988) added uncertainty and risk.

(a) The degree of control refers to the extent to which operators' actions have a direct impact upon the crucial variables of the process. In ship handling and car driving, the degree of control of the vehicle is comparable and has a relatively direct effect. However, watch officers on board large vessels (such as oil tankers) have to deal with a specific problem because of the time taken for the ship to respond (Hoc, 1991). (b) Useful information (regarding interaction management) is directly accessible on board ships, since it is provided by the ARPA radar. In contrast with watch officers, car drivers have to assess crucial information, such as the speed of another vehicle. (c) The most important difference between ship handling and car driving certainly relates to time constraints, since watch officers have to deal with slower movements than drivers. (d) The level of automation is higher on board ships than on the road. The automatic pilot allows watch officers to have intermittent control of the vessel, while in the case of car driving control is continuous. (e) Finally, it has to be emphasised that, in both fields, uncertainty (mainly about other users' intentions) and risk (of critical interference with others) are common features of the situations that the actors have to deal with.

This brief comparison raises two main questions: How do the actors (watch officers and car drivers) deal with these task demands and with risk and uncertainty ? Do the differences between the two tasks (in terms of the status of the actors, of available devices, of time constraints) have an effect on their interaction management ?

We will now turn to the findings as regards interaction management in the two fields. Three main topics will be developed: the use of formal communication and formal rules, the knowledge and environmental cues referred to by the actors for understanding and anticipating others' behaviour and intentions, and the strategies they use for managing (actual or potential) interactions with others.

Ship Handling

The study presented in this paper consists of an analysis of watch officers' activity during collision avoidance. The activity lasts about twenty minutes. It begins when a risk is detected (when the projected courses and speeds of two vessels place them at or near the same location simultaneously). It entails deciding what action to take after making a diagnosis of the situation, and it ends when the danger is passed. The analysis was based on ecological data so as to highlight the difficulties encountered by watch officers.

Method

Data were collected on board two ferries in the course of 19 voyages that involved seven watch officers altogether. The ferries followed the same route, crossing the English Channel between Ouistreham and Portsmouth. Activity was observed when the ferries crossed shipping eastbound towards the Straits of Dover and shipping westbound for the Casquets. During the crossing, which takes around an hour and a half, the vessels often have to manoeuvre. Each time an interaction situation was detected (i.e. a situation where at least two vessels are on a collision course), several data were recorded, including both independent variables and dependent ones. The latter give an account of the activity of the watch officer and make up a 'scenario'. Twenty scenarios were analysed. Ten scenarios describe a crossing situation (the ferry being either the stand-on vessel or the give-way one), five describe a head-on situation and five an interaction between the ferry boat and fishing vessels.

Independent variables may have an effect on the activity. They may be: (a) features of the context (visibility, wind force and direction, strength and direction of the currents, traffic, time ahead of or behind Expected Time of Arrival), (b) a description of the type of conflict (head-on, crossing, overtaking), or (c) indications of priority, showing, for example, whether own ship is the give-way vessel or the stand-on one ?

Dependent variables are behavioural data and verbal data. Watch officer behaviour is characterised by use of ARPA functions. It is also characterised by manoeuvring features (angle of course alteration, distance from the other ship when the alteration is initiated, DCPA, distance to the original route). Thinking-aloud protocols were recorded because it was assumed that such data can be of help in determining reasoning and mental representations (Chauvin, 2000).

Findings

Fist of all, there was found to be little formal communication between the actors. Watch officers are reluctant to make contact by VHF radio, due to the difficulty of distinguishing an approaching vessel from other vessels in the vicinity and the added problem of communicating with a vessel of a different nationality. In fact, only two communications were recorded, between two ferries of the same company.

The second finding concerns formal rules. Collision Regulations include recommendations about the direction of manoeuvres (to starboard rather than to port in case of a crossing situation and in the case of a head-on situation). They also provide recommendations concerning the time and amplitude of the course or speed alteration. Studies on collision avoidance show that the possible interpretation of the Regulations generates uncertainty concerning the actions of other vessels. This uncertainty relates to: (a) evaluation of the risk made by watch officers (Hara & Hammer, 1993), (b) The distance at which the 'give-way' vessel will alter her course (Habberley & Taylor, 1989), (c) The direction to which it alters course: port or starboard (Hinsch, 1996). We found, in our research work, that the most difficult case is encountered when the 'give-way vessel' does not alter her course. In that event, the 'stand-on' vessel may take action to avoid a collision by her manœuvre alone, as soon as it becomes apparent to her that the vessel required to keep out of the way is not taking appropriate action in accordance with these rules (Rule 17). During the 19 voyages, the ferry had to alter her course four times to avoid a target that was the 'give-way' vessel. To decide if and when they have to alter course, watch officers must interpret this rule. In fact, they altered their course at a distance of around 2 nautical miles[1]. In two cases the manoeuvre entailed two actions : the watch officers altered their ferry's courses early to starboard (at 6.7 nm and 5.5 nm) to reduce the miss distance and to oblige the other one to move. They finished the manoeuvre at a distance of 2 nm. Some mariners achieve a sufficient miss distance by altering course to port. They alter course to port particularly often in the case of head-on situations (three of the five manœuvres observed), after having communicated with the other vessel (in two of those three cases). One pattern of action was misunderstood. The ferry, as a give-way vessel was altering her course to port, then to starboard, and finally to port again. As a result, the privileged vessel performed an emergency manœuvre.

---

[1] 1 nautical mile is equal to 1852 meters.

The third result concerns knowledge and strategies. To understand another user's behaviour and anticipate his future actions, the actor has to rely on his knowledge of similar situations and on the other's present behaviour. In fact, drawing on his knowledge both of such situations and of the type of actors involved, the actor develops a specific representation during the interaction. Watch officers' knowledge includes knowledge of the type of interactions, of the ships involved and of the normal stages of a manoeuvre. Knowledge of the interaction situation includes specific attributes (data concerning the safety distance to keep between the ship and the target are not the same in the case of a crossing situation as in the case of a head-on situation). Knowledge of the ship relates to the distance at which different types of ship tend to manœuvre, whether they be passenger ships, container ships, small cargoes or oil tankers. The first are known to be easy to handle and, as a consequence, are known to manœuvre quite late. Oil tankers, on the contrary, tend to manœuvre as early as possible. Such knowledge extends to presumptions about fishing vessels and sailing vessels, which are assumed not to abide by to the rules and hence to be dangerous. To activate the right classes of knowledge, the actor has to determine the type of ship involved. If he can't see it, he makes inferences on the basis of its speed and course. Knowledge of the stages of a manœuvre establish transitions between different navigational states. Koyama & Yan (1987) presented them in an algorithmic form (Figure 1). Usually, the process goes from normal (the situation at the beginning of the encounter) to avoiding (the target is changing its course to ensure a sufficient miss distance), avoided (proceeding steadily on the new course), and returning (changing direction to come back on to its original course when the risk is passed). However, any other way indicated by arrows is possible.

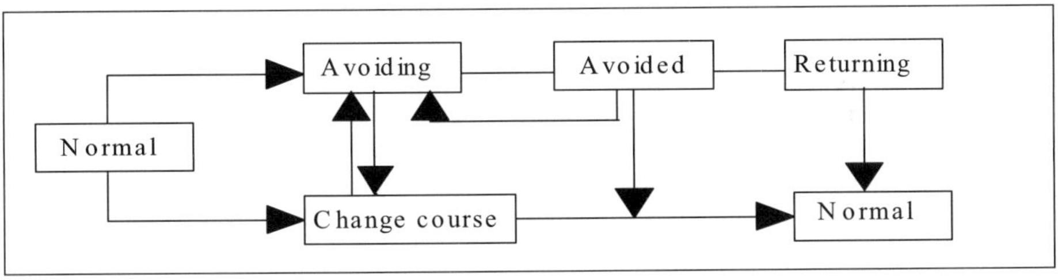

Figure 1. Possible transition of navigational states (Koyama & Chan, Ibid).

The specific representation consists of inferring from available knowledge the other's intentions and future action, on the basis of his behaviour at the time. This reasoning may lead to different conclusions. If an observed target is taking avoiding action, it is expected to change direction to come back on to its original course as soon as possible. It also leads to conclusions about whether the other's behaviour is 'normal' or not. If the other's behaviour does not correspond to acquired knowledge about navigational states (for example, when a target is avoiding after previously changing direction to come back on to its original course), its behaviour is interpreted as erratic and hence as dangerous. If a ship has passed the distance at which a vessel of its kind would normally manoeuvre (in that kind of situation), the other will infer that it is not going to alter course.

The actions and reactions of the watch officer consist of (a) adapting his behaviour to the other's immediate or expected behaviour, even if it is contrary to the rules, for example, by altering course even if own ship is the stand-on one, or by altering course to port if the other one is doing so, (b) communicating his intention to the other or influencing his behaviour by taking drastic action, for example, by increasing the amplitude of an avoiding manoeuvre to make the other user aware of it, or by adopting a collision course to force the other to alter course.

CAR DRIVING

The study presented here concerns an analysis of drivers' activity in car-following situations observed on an urban motorway. A car-following situation is generally considered to begin once a driver can no longer drive at the speed he would like to because of the presence of other users in his lane (Leutzbach, 1974). Depending on the number of vehicles on the road and the traffic lanes available, this constraint may be more or less great and more or less long-lasting.

Car-following situations call for the driver to adapt to the constraints and variations of the traffic, and in particular to detect critical variations, i.e. those which require a regulating action to restore adequate safety margins or prevent a collision. In this kind of driving situation, where motorists' actions are closely interdependent, the driver's adaptation depends on the safety margins he adopts and the way he controls his interaction with other users.

Method

The method used combined two investigative techniques: on-board observation of driver behaviour during a journey on a motorway, and subsequent interviews. The route chosen for the study was a stretch of an urban motorway, covering a distance of about 20 kms. The drivers used a vehicle equipped for video-recording the journey and for collecting data, such as driver's speed or use of brake. Immediately after completing the journey, each driver was interviewed (yielding verbal reports on the video recording of the journey and semi-structured interviews). Two groups of drivers participated in the study (three experienced drivers and three novice drivers).

An analytical grid was developed in order to provide a continuous detailed description of the various road situations encountered throughout the motorway journey (lasting on average 15 minutes) and of drivers' behaviour in relation to those situations. Drivers' subsequent verbal reports were systematically logged with regard to each specific context in which they were made. Several detailed analyses were carried out (see, for example, Saad 1996), including of the lane change manoeuvres performed by the drivers themselves (N = 121) and by others in their immediate vicinity (N = 105) and of drivers' involvement in "critical car-following episodes"[2] (N = 73).

[2] i.e. car-following episodes where the time headways with the preceding vehicle were = 1,5 second.

Findings

Managing interactions with other users calls for the driver to understand their current behaviour and anticipate their intentions, which depend on the information the others communicate either explicitly, through the use of formal signals (such as their indicator), or implicitly, through their behaviour (speed, positioning on the road, etc.). They also depend on the driver's body of knowledge, which structure his expectations and enable him to formulate hypotheses about the adjustments that other users may force him to make in his driving (Saad, Mundutéguy & Darses, 1999).

The lack of communication and deviations from the formal rules may generate uncertainty concerning the actions of others as well as the driver's own behaviour. Observation showed deviations from formal rules related to communication. When other users changed lane in the vicinity of the driver (pulling into or out of the lane he was travelling in), they did not systematically use their indicators (39% of the 105 manoeuvres performed by others were effected without preliminary communication of their intentions). The use of the indicator seems to depend on the risk of interference with the driver observed and/or with a third party (the risk being a function of several parameters, such as the relative speed and distance between the actors involved). It also depends on the extent to which the lane change manœuvre was planned: some lane changes appeared to be quite opportunistic, i.e. the other driver took the opportunity of a variation in the traffic flow for quickly carrying out his manoeuvre, and as a consequence did not give any prior signal of his intentions. Other deviations from safety recommendations and formal rules were observed during the journey, which were either due to the drivers themselves or to others. The most frequent deviation observed was in safety margins during car-following episodes, linked to the performance of lane change manoeuvres performed by the drivers themselves (mostly overtaking manoeuvres) or by others (cutting into the driver's lane). Other deviations concern the rules applied to overtaking. Drivers performed some overtaking manoeuvres using the right-hand, or inner, lane (7,5% of the total number of cases in which drivers passed other vehicles, with the experienced drivers being the ones mostly involved), while they were sometimes overtaken in the same deviant way by others (6% of cases where other vehicles passed the driver, with the novices being the ones mostly involved). Some of these deviations may be viewed as an adaptation of the formal rules to the specificity of the road situation or as a compromise between the requirements of two different formal rules (Leplat, 1998). More generally, it should be emphasised that formal rules are often interpreted or replaced by more informal rules, acquired through practice and experience of traffic situations. Drivers may be guided by these informal rules, which form part of their driving knowledge, in order to understand other drivers' actions and infer their intentions.

Analyses of drivers' behaviour and of their situational context combined with an analysis of the verbal protocols, enabled us to identify some of these informal rules as well as the range of variables that drivers take into account in managing their interactions with other users and, in particular, their safety margins in car-following situations. They include: (a) the characteristics of the infrastructure; the overall speed, density and stability of the traffic flow, (b) the vicinity, the extent and duration of safety margin variations, and (c) the nature of the immediate interactions with (and between) other drivers. More generally, the results suggest that, when managing their interactions with other road users, drivers (and especially experienced ones) draw on a number of 'reference situations' and base their decisions on a representation of the 'typical behaviour' of other road users in those situations. If they detect any deviation from that norm, they intensify their monitoring of the situation and/or take some form of anticipatory regulating action (changing lane, reducing speed). Finally, it should be stressed that the cues used by drivers to identify the interaction situation they are faced with are for the most part informal (and experienced drivers refer to them more frequently than novices). The knowledge they draw on is related to the events that could occur given the characteristics of the infrastructure and to the configuration of the traffic, as well as to the type of vehicles involved. This knowledge enables experienced drivers to manage critical interactions caused by others' behaviour more easily than novice drivers. Some 'anticipated' lane changes are indicative of this, for example when a driver anticipates that another vehicle is going to move into his lane before the other driver has made his intention known by indicating, or when he changes lane on nearing a traffic entry zone before any other road user is actually visible.

Temporal aspects and anticipation mechanisms appears to play an important role in the control of interaction situations. The regulating action that drivers take (or do not take) depends not only on their immediate interaction with the preceding vehicle but also on the overall traffic situation and its dynamics, as well as on their intentions and priorities in that context. It also depends on other users' behaviour or intentions (as observed or inferred), and is sometimes aimed at influencing that behaviour. For example : (a) When the traffic flow is highly unstable (within or between traffic lanes), or when the behaviour of one or several other drivers creates uncertainty about their intentions, drivers tend to increase their safety margin or change lane, if they have the opportunity to do so, (b) When they anticipate that a preceding vehicle is about to pull over into another lane, or that a vehicle that has just joined their lane will quickly gather speed, they are willing to accept a temporary reduction in their margin. In both cases, these temporising strategies are associated with firm expectations about other drivers' behaviour or intentions, whether backed up by formal communication or not, (c) When drivers want to prevent other drivers from cutting in, or to indicate to the driver in front that he ought to change lanes, they tend to reduce their margins. Therefore, in many cases the action taken by drivers may have a communicative value.

Conclusion

Synthesis

Although there are some differences in the tasks studied, the results obtained suggest that it is important in both cases to analyse the way actors manage their interactions with others in order to understand their behaviour and to improve the efficiency and safety of their performance.

The main difference between the two tasks lies undoubtedly in the dynamics of the situations to be managed and hence in the temporal constraints weighing on the actors' activity (at least in the conditions taken into account in the situations observed). We would stress, for example, the high degree of instability observed in driving on an urban motorway, which is seen in particular in the frequency with which the drivers or other users change lanes (on average, one lane change manoeuvre was observed every 21 seconds). It also has to do with the number of actors involved in interaction situations. The situations observed in car driving were more likely to involve several actors than those observed in ship handling. In order to control these interactions, car drivers thus need to monitor a broader field than mariners.

The main common points found in these studies relate to the manner in which the actors manage their interactions with others. They confirmed, firstly, that there exist deliberate means of communication based on manifest behaviour, which is designed to make the actor's intentions clear to other users. Examples of such means of communication, which are informal for the most part, are amplifying a manœuvre and increasing or reducing safety margins. The message may be more or less explicit to other users. They also highlighted the part played by prior knowledge in interpreting other users' present behaviour and anticipating their intentions. This knowledge, which includes a number of informal rules and stereotypes, may in some cases complement the information available to the actors, or even make up for the lack of formal communication. Several complementary studies are under way to broaden and deepen these findings. As regards ship handling, they include the analysis of new sets of data collected from another sample of mariners. In the case of car driving, they involve analyses of new data collected by means of the same observation method, as well as a more controlled investigation of the way drivers recognise the intentions of other users (Dusire & Mundutéguy, 2000).

Looking to the future

In the light of these findings, it seems important to discuss the potential impact of new support systems being developed in the fields of ship handling and car driving, essentially in terms of their impact on managing interactions with other users and on communication between the different actors involved.

The introduction in the near future of transponders on board ships larger than 300 gross tonage (gt) will overcome the problem of unreliable data. This system, also known as Automatic Identification System, will broadcast the ship's identity, position and other data at regular intervals. The AIS is aimed at making verbal communication easier. At present, vessels communicate through actions (in a rather crude, simplified manner). Verbal contacts are likely to introduce a certain complexity into the communication process, which may be time consuming and may delay actions and reactions.

Among the new motoring aids being developed are Speed Limiters, Adaptive Cruise Control or Collision Avoidance Systems. These systems are expected to have a specific impact on driver behaviour in terms of the speed practised and/or the safety margins adopted in car-following situations. These systems, if used according to the designers' objectives, will change drivers' behaviour and may thus alter the way they usually interact with other users. Several studies have shown that, in some traffic situations, drivers are reluctant to use these systems when doing so would require a significant deviation from informal rules of managing interactions and from their usual strategies of performing certain tasks (Saad & Villame, 1996). They are also worried about the way others might interpret their behaviour, when using these systems (Malaterre & Saad, 1984).

When designing new support systems or assessing their impact on behaviour, it is thus important to take into account the interactive dimension of the tasks performed as well as the communicative value of the behaviour displayed.

References

Bainbridge, L., Lenior, T.M., & Van der Shaaf, T. W. (1993). Cognitive processes in complex tasks : introduction and discussion. *Ergonomics, 36*, 1273-1279.

Chauvin, C. (2000). Analyse de l'activité d'anticollision à bord des navires de commerce : des marques linguistiques aux représentations mentales [Analysis of collision avoidance on board merchant vessels: from linguistic cues to mental representations]. *Le Travail Humain, 63*, 31-57.

Dusire, S., & Mundutéguy, C. (2000). Intent Recognition and Situation Awareness in Transportation Activities. *Proceedings of the IEA 2000 / HFES 2000, 14th Triennal Congress of the International Ergonomics Association and 44th Annual Meeting of the Human Factors and Ergonomics Society.* (Vol. 1, pp. 173-176). San Diego, USA.

Habberley, J.S., & Taylor, D.H. (1989). Simulated collision avoidance manoeuvres: a parametric study. *The Journal of Navigation, 42*, 248-254.

Hara, K., & Hammer, A. (1993). A safe way of collision avoidance manoeuver based on manoeuvring standard using fuzzy reasoning model. *Proceedings of MARSIM'93 - International Conference on Marine Simulation and Ship Manoeuvrability.* (Vol. 1, pp. 163-170). St. John's, Newfoundland: Fisheries and Marine Institute of Memorial University.

Hinsch, W. (1996). Traffic rules to coordinate collision avoidance manoeuvres at sea. *Proceedings of the International Conference on Preventing Collision at Sea - Collision'96.* (Vol. 1, pp. 166-172). Epsom Surrey : Chiavari Publishing.

Hoc, J.-M. (1991). Some dimensions of a cognitive typology of process control situations. *Paper presented at the 2nd Workshop about Cognitive processes in complex tasks*, Eindhoven.

Hoc, J.M. (1996). *Supervision et contrôle de processus - La cognition en situation dynamique* [Process supervision and process control - Cognition in dynamic situation]. Grenoble: Presses Universitaires de Grenoble.

Koyama, T., & Yan, J. (1987). An expert system approach to collision avoidance. *Paper presented at the 8th Ship Control Systems Symposium.* La Haye.

Leplat, J. (1998). About implementation of safety rules. *Safety Science, 29*, 189-204.

Leutzbach, W. (1974). Collisions par l'arrière [Rear-end collisions]. *Paper presented at the 12ème semaine internationale d'étude technique de la circulation et de sa sécurité. Thème VI : collisions en chaîne*, Belgrade.

Malaterre, G., & Saad, F. (1984). *Contribution à l'analyse du contrôle de la vitesse par le conducteur: évaluation de deux limiteurs* [Contribution to an analysis of drivers' speed control : assessment of two speed limiters] . (Cahiers d'études ONSER, N° 62), Arcueil : Organisme National de Sécurité Routière.

Roth, E. M., & Woods, D. (1988). Aiding Human performance, I : cognitive analysis. *Le Travail Humain, 51*, 39-64.

Saad, F. (1996). Driver strategies in car-following situations. In A.G. Gale (Ed.), *Vision in Vehicles* (pp. 61-70). Amsterdam: Elsevier.

Saad, F., Mundutéguy, C., & Darses, F. (1999). Managing interactions beetween car drivers : an essential dimension of reliable driving. In J.M. Hoc, P. Millot, E. Hollnagel and P.C. Cacciabue (Eds.), *Proceedings of CSAPC'99* (pp. 99-104). Valenciennes: Presses Universitaires de Valenciennes.

Saad, F. & Villame, T. (1996). Assessing new driving support systems : contribution of an analysis of drivers'activity in real situations. *Proceedings of Third Annual World Congress on Intelligent Transport System* (CD Rom).

Traffic and Transport Psychology,
T. Rothengatter and R.D. Huguenin (Editors)

10

Training of Tram Drivers in Workload Management – Workload Assessment in Real Life and in a Driving/Traffic Simulator

Matthias Normann, Günter Debus, Petra Dörre and Detlev Leutner

Introduction

Tram driving is a job which is highly demanding and strenuous in the long term. This finds expression for example in the number of working hours lost through sickness. Therefore, transport companies are eager to pay special attention to the possible reduction of workload by special courses in the drivers′ training and further vocational training. These training courses focus mainly on workload resulting from the actual driving job.

Within the framework of a research assignment, we have analysed how and with what success a training for the reduction of workload can be designed and carried out using a driving and traffic simulator. One concern of the project was the analysis of workload in real driving situations and the construction of authentic workload simulations.

The aim of our research was the assessment of (high) workload with tram drivers in three steps. First of all, we had to identify high workload in real driving situations. On the basis of these results differently strenuous driving situations were constructed and evaluated for the simulation with a driving and traffic simulator. The most interesting aspect about it was the question if the drivers′ everyday high workload situations can be implemented in the simulator in such a way that an authentic workload surrounding is created for the training. Additionally, a training for the reduction of workload was evaluated with the help of our indicators in a third step. The trainees had to complete workload-inducing simulator tasks before and after the training. Their performance and evaluation was then compared with those of a control group (Dörre et. al., 2000; Leutner & Debus, 1995).

In the following the job and structure of workload of tram drivers will be briefly described, the methods used in our research including their indicators will be explained and finally an overview of the results will be provided.

Job Characteristics of Tram Drivers

The main assignment of tram drivers consists in the safe, punctual and economical transport of passengers. Actually, the order of adjectives is important here: the transport must be safe first of all, also punctually and economical when possible. At the same time the companies expect their drivers to act customer-oriented. That means that they always have to take into account the customers' interests while planning and co-ordinating their job. The demands resulting from this job profile are varied. In general the drivers are requested to have an anticipating way of driving and a good knowledge of tram technology.

The respective high workload situations can be divided into workload resulting from either the driving job itself or the driver's social situation. High workload resulting from the actual driving job can be based for example on high density of traffic, technical failures or time pressure. Social conflicts on the other hand arise from the interaction with passengers, superiors or for example in consequence of shift-work.

Classification of Situations with High Workload

In many stress models (for example Lazarus et al., 1984) high workload situations are characterised by the high complexity, the low predictability and the low controllability of the underlying driving situations. This finds expression in several empirical studies. Generally, the increasing complexity of a driving situation leads to higher mental and cognitive strain which corresponds to an increased need of planning and co-ordination as well as higher demands on the driver´s memory and attention. The required abilities can be learnt in the course of the training. Both low predictability and low controllability lead to the well-known symptoms of distress and effort overload. The training programmes are aimed at individual possibilities of coping with stress, preventing stress and evaluating situations realistically.

Measurement of Mental Workload

Conceptually, we planned our study on the basis of resource management models. The more demanding situations are due to high complexity, low predictability and low controllability the more resources are needed for the driving task as the primary task. Consequently, less resources are left for secondary activities. Hence, we selected a secondary task to measure the remaining resources according to the assumptions of resource management models. The methodology generally follows the principles of the so called dual task paradigm as recommended by many scientists (O'Donnell & Eggemeier,1986, Wierwille & Eggemeier, 1993, Tattersal, 2000). In an earlier study (Bartmann, 1995) the speech activity of car drivers had been turned out to be a secondary activity whose temporal structure was highly sensitive to work load variations in car driving. For tram drivers speech activities are only required in some situations, for instance when passengers or superiors contact them. Most of the time the driver is doing his job silently. So there is enough time for speech activity as a secondary task. Furthermore, this activity can be studied in real life as well as in a simulation setting. Therefore, the temporal structure of speech activity was selected as the main indicator for identification of workload in real life, for constructing workload situations and for demonstrating workload reduction in the simulator. Complementary methods were included resulting in three types of methods: dual task performance, driving performance and performance evaluation.

The performance differences between the speech task carried out with (dual) and without (single) driving is attributed to the intensity of workload in the driving situation. Driving performance measures were taken by the recording of driving data in the simulator respectively observations. Eventually, drivers, trainees and instructors were asked to complete questionnaires on workload situations. Their subjective statements were then compared with the objective performance and behavioural data. For each of the three steps, identification, construction and reduction of workload, there exist results obtained by all three methods of measurement, performance, behaviour and subjective assessment (Table 1).

Table 1. Overview of the methods used in the three steps of research.

	Real life	*Driving/traffic simulator*	
	Identification of workload situations	*Construction of workload situations*	*Reduction of workload situations*
Speech task Speaking, pausing, beat length and interruptions	Single speech task vs. dual task Difficulty of track sections (4 levels)	Single speech task vs. dual task Predictability (2 levels) Workload intensity (2 levels)	Single speech task vs. dual task With vs. without training Before vs. after training
Objective driving data Speed, driving time, use of mirror, frequency of selected actions, reaction to target persons	4 transport companies with different tracks, trains and demands	Predictability (2 levels) Workload intensity (2 levels)	With vs. without training Before vs. after training
Questionnaire about workload situations (drivers, trainees and instructors)	4 transport companies with different tracks, trains and demands	Predictability (2 levels) Workload intensity (2 levels)	With vs. without training Before vs. after training

In the first step the variation of workload was based on the selection of four track sections with different grades of difficulty. Observations and subjective assessment were carried out in four traffic companies with different tracks, trains and demands on the drivers. In order to construct workload in simulated situation, the variation of workload was determined in two ways. First of all the variation was based on two different simulation exercises with high and low workload. Moreover two groups of drivers were obtained who differed with regard to the predictability of the workload situations. In the training research two groups of drivers, a training group and a control group, were observed twice in high workload simulation tasks, namely before and after the training.

The Driving and Traffic Simulator

The driving and traffic simulator was built by Krauss-Maffei, Munich, and is used by the Stuttgarter Straßenbahnbetriebe (a transport company) to train their drivers. It contains a moving system, a visual system and an acoustic system. Thus, it gets possible to reproduce the driver´s behaviour and his impressions in a realistic and authentic way. The original driver´s cabin is in working order, that means, that all (operational) instruments and displays can be used. On the screen the drivers see original tracks in Stuttgart with all relevant details (e.g. switches, signals, tunnels). According to the drivers the recognition value is quite high.

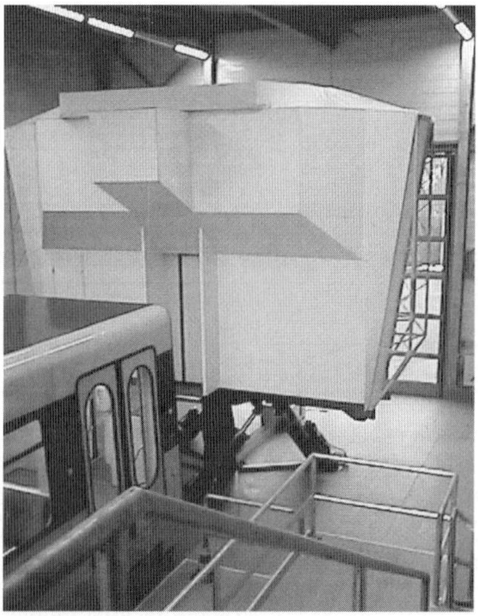

Figure 1. The driving and traffic simulator in Stuttgart (Germany), including moving, visual and acoustic systems and a driver´s cabin with all real-life functions.

The training room is equipped with one instructor´s seat and about six trainee´s seats. At the instructor´s seat the instructor programs the simulation exercises and controls them during driving. At the same time he takes on the function of the headquarters and represents the contact for the trainees. The trainees in the training room can observe the driving of their colleague in the driver cabin and follow his actions in detail. After each simulation exercise the instructor discusses the driving performance with the driver and the other trainees.

The situations on the screen contain high workload. This is especially true when the driver is diverted by other events, for example a radio message or a conversation with a passenger. The following example shows the principle of constructing a simulation exercise: First, we have to select the track section on which the planned workload situations can take place. Then we implement for example the following situations: (1) driving through a tunnel with railway construction works, (2) a technical failure occurs while a person is crossing the railway, (3) an unauthorized crossing of a lorry, (4) an incomprehensive question of a passenger, (5) People crossing the railway unexpectedly and (6) a heavy technical failure occurs in the train This exercise lasts about 20 minutes. For all of these situation local factors and other factors relevant for the action have to be determined and defined.

Dual task paradigm – the speech task

The participants had to speak the syllables „rah, reh, rih, roh, ruh" repeatedly. Not the content of the speech was recorded, but only the speech energy expressed in the sequence of speech and pausing times. This speech energy was recorded by the so called "Logoport" (Krüger & Vollrath, 1996), an instrument, which allows to measure speech times with high density. The speech signal is picked up by a condensor microphone attached to the subject's throat with a sticking ring. The condensor microphone transforms the mechanical vibrations to voltage. After rectifyication and amplification the signal is digitized to 8 bit values of "ons" and "offs" with a measurement rate of 125 Hz.

The participants had to follow a given metronome beat, to control individual differences. They had to speak 3 minutes in a raw on parts of the track where no conversation with passengers or the headquater was needed. The speech task includes several indicators which are sensitive for workload variation: the duration of speaking and pausing, the length of the spoken beats, the start of speaking according to the metronome beat and the number of interruptions (Bartmann, 1995; Normann, 1996). The mean duration of speaking and pausing either increase or decrease under workload conditions. The mean beat lenght does not change under workload conditions, but the variability increases. The start of speaking in accordance with the metronome differs decisively interindividually and its variability increases under workload conditions. After a few minutes of exercise, people can usually speak the sequence of syllables without producing any interruptions. However, under workload conditions the number of interruptions increases greatly. The drivers are often so busy with the driving task that they are not able to coordinate it with the speech task.

Results

Results of the speech task

The following diagrams illustrate some main results. In real driving situations the mean duration of pausing changes compared to speaking in single task mode. Additionally, the mean duration of pausing is longer while driving on a difficult track section in a street than on an easy track section in a tunnel.

In Figure 2 you can see that the duration of speaking can be a predictor for a successful training. For both groups (training group and control group) the mean duration of speaking increases in dual tasks in contrast to single tasks, both before and after the training. However, the extent of the increase was lower when the drivers had undergone training.

There are similar results for the number of interruptions. In real driving situations the number of interruptions depends on the difficulty of the track section. The drivers produce more interruptions in the street than in a tunnel. In single task mode the drivers did not interrupt their speech.

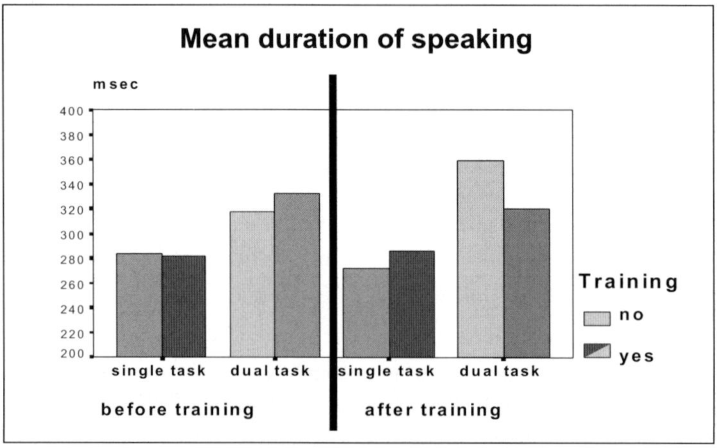

Figure 2. Mean duration of speaking a syllable in the training research. The speech task was carried out either alone (single) or during driving (dual).

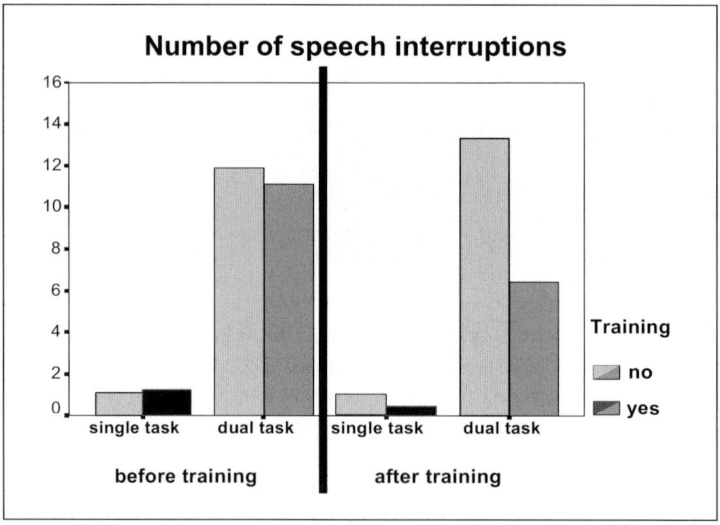

Figure 3. Number of speech interruptions in the training research. The speech task was carried out either alone (single) or during driving (dual).

In the training research, the number of interruptions proved to be a good predictor for a successful training (Figure 3). Before the training the number of interruptions was the same in the training group and in the control group. However, after the training the training group produced significantly fewer interruptions than the control group.

Results of the driving data

Under low workload conditions, the driving time in the simulator corresponds to the given time-table in reality. The drivers do not drive faster or slower than in real life. Surely, the drivers usually can not keep to schedule in simulator exercises with high worklod situations because of the installed failures and obstructions. However, the drivers with higher predictability of the situations are less behind schedule than drivers with lower predictability.

In the training research the drivers had to decide whether certain persons were standing on the left or on the right side of their view. This was another secondary task. This task is similar to the demands on an anticipating way of driving in reality. Figure 4 implies that the training group is able to react more successfully to these persons after the training than before the training and than the control group.

Figure 4. Detection rate of target persons (in percent of all relevant target persons) in the training research.

Results of the questionnaire

In the questionnaire the drivers were asked to assess their own controllability in the high workload situations. Comparing the situations including more motor demands (e.g reactions to cars or pedestrians) and those including more mental and cognitive demands (e.g. communications and technical failures), we got different answers. Drivers with high predictability claim that they have a better controllability in mentally demanding situations than drivers with low predictability. For situations with motorly demanding situations there is no difference. The same is true for the training research. After the training the training group assesses its controllability on the high workload situations higher than before the training and higher than the control group.

The instructors assess the performance of the drivers with high predictability in accordance with the previous results, that is they believe it to be better than the performance of the drivers with low predictability. In the training research we got similar results. The intructors also stated that after the training the performance of the training group was better than before the training and better than that of the control group.

Summary

To sum up, high workload situations with tram drivers can be constructed sufficiently similar to real driving situations. Equivalent simulation tasks can be programmed. The indicators used proved to be sensitive for the designed variation of workload. The training for the reduction of the drivers' workload was successful. With the help of our indicators, a success of the training could be shown. Compared to a control condition, the training led to a significant workload reduction. The data show high sensibility and diagnostic power of the workload measures in the simulated driving situations and a correspondence with real driving situations. Moreover, a high degree of correspondence between performance, behavioural and subjective data could be observed. Actually, after the training the tram drivers themselves were convinced that the training enabled them to master future high workload in everyday driving situations more experienced, more professionally and more reliably than before.

References

Bartmann, A. (1995). *Zur Erfassung von kognitiver Beanspruchung beim Führen von Kraftfahrzeugen* [Towards the measurement of cognitive workload in car driving]. Aachen: Shaker.

Dörre, P., Normann, M., Debus, G., & Leutner, D. (2000). Entwicklung eines Streßreduktionstrainings für Straßenbahnfahrer [Development of a stress reduction training for tram drivers]. Manuscript submitted for publication.

Krüger, H.-P., & Vollrath, M (1996). Temporal analysis of speech patterns in the real world using the Logoport. In J. Fahrenberg & M. Myrtek (Eds.), *Ambulatory assessment* (pp. 101-113). Göttingen: Hogrefe & Huber.

Leutner, D., & Debus, G. (1995). Psychologische Aspekte der Belastung von Schienenfahrzeugführern im öffentlichen Personennahverkehr und Entwicklung eines simulatorgestützten Belastungs-Reduktions-Trainings [Psychological aspects of drivers′ workload in local transport services and development of a simulator-based workload reduction training]. *VDI-Berichte, 1219*, 49-59.

Lazarus, R. S., & Folkman, S. (1984). *Stress, appraisal and coping*. New York: Springen.

Normann, M. (1996). *Fahrzeugführung bei temporaler Zusatztätigkeit* [Driving under temporal secondary tasks]. Unpublished dissertation. University of Aachen, Aachen.

O'Donnell, R.D., & Eggemeier, F.T. (1986). Work load assessment methodology. In K.R. Boff, L. Kaufman and J. Thomas (Eds.), *Handbook of perception and human performance: Vol. II: Cognitive processes and performance* (Chapter 42). New York: Wiley.

Tattersal, A.J. (2000). Work load and task allocation. In N. Chmiel (Ed.), *Introduction to work and organizational psychology.* Oxford: Blackwell.

Wierwille, W.W. & Eggemeier, F.T. (1993). Recommendations for mental workload measurement in a test and evaluation environment. *Human Factors, 35*, 263-281.

Road User

Social and Differential Psychology

Traffic and Transport Psychology,
T. Rothengatter and R.D. Huguenin (Editors)

11

Road Safety: What Has Social Psychology to Offer?

Dianne Parker

Introduction

The topic of this chapter is the contribution of social psychology to road safety research. I am an applied social psychologist and although a lot of my work is in the area of road safety, not all of it is. So it might be the case that my position in this field of research is not as central as the position of some. In trying to get my work published and the results disseminated I have twin, and equally important aims. The first is to make a contribution to the social psychology literature, and the second is to make a contribution to road safety through publishing in outlets read by the road safety community. Securing funding for and carrying out research that can meet those twin aims, academic and applied, equally well is far from straightforward. However I am convinced that real progress can be made only when we manage to keep those twin aims in mind at all times.

Given the difficulty of doing that, I will begin with two acknowledgements. The first is that I am conscious that in focussing on social psychology I will be omitting much discussion of the contribution of other psychological sub-disciplines, let alone other disciplines entirely, to our understanding of the traffic environment, the driver and road safety. I must apologise in advance for that. I can speak only about my own area and nothing here is meant to detract from the enormous importance of the work of cognitive psychologists, ergonomists, transport planners, engineers etc. The work I am going to describe is all relevant to behaviour rather than relevant to performance. That is relevant to understanding what people *do* do, rather than what they *can* do.

My second acknowledgement is that from the multitude of studies concerned with the concepts of social psychology, I have tried to select examples published in mainstream social psychology literature. I will also, for the sake of brevity, be sticking mainly to the work of European social psychologists, and so should apologise in advance to colleagues from other areas.

Attitudes

The place I want to start is with attitudes, one of the two main planks of social cognition, arguably the most influential perspective in current social psychology. Over the last decade or so many researchers have come to agree on the importance of attitudes in the behaviour of road users. The concept of attitude is central to social psychology. It generally refers to the thoughts and feelings that impel us to behave in one way and not in another. In Manchester one of the first distinctions we made in looking at 'bad' driver behaviour was between erroneous bad behaviour (errors and lapses) and intentional bad behaviour (violations). This distinction was first systematically applied to driving in the Manchester Driver Behaviour Questionnaire (DBQ, see Parker et al. 1995)). It has been shown that the commission of driving violations, which are at least to some extent intentional, are predictive of both future and past accident involvement. So if at least part of the road safety problem is a motivational one, caused by drivers choosing to do risky things behind the wheel, we need to persuade them not to. Social psychological theories hold that the best way to effect long-lasting change in behaviour is to change the beliefs, values and attitudes that underpin the decision to behave in that way. In short we need to change their attitudes and their behaviour will follow. Icek Ajzen's Theory of Planned Behaviour (TPB, 1988) provides a simple model of the relationships among values, beliefs, attitudes, intentions and behaviour, and is without doubt the most widely used model of its kind. Moreover, it has been usefully applied to road user behaviour several times. To summarise the theory, it holds that volitional behaviour is based on intentions and that intentions are based on three cognitive components. These are evaluations of the likely outcomes of the behaviour, (what will happen if I do it?) perceptions of the social norm surrounding the behaviour (what will people think if I do it?), and perceptions of control over the behaviour (can I actually do it without too much trouble?).

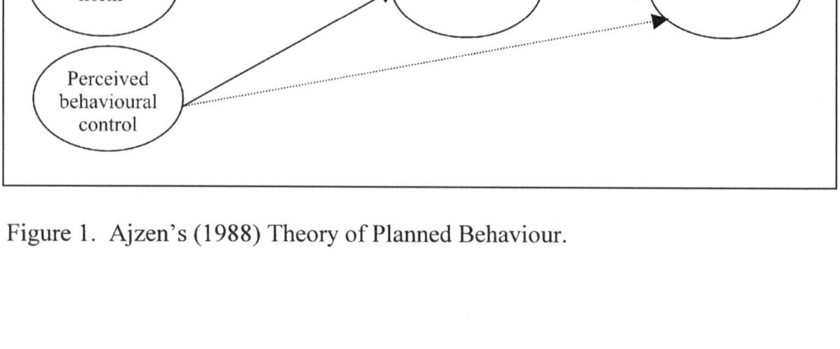

Figure 1. Ajzen's (1988) Theory of Planned Behaviour.

In Manchester, we have applied the model, and extensions of it, in several studies of the attitudes and behaviour of drivers in general and of company car drivers in particular, looking at attitudes to a range of driving violations including speeding, close following and cutting in. At the University of Swansea, Daphne Evans has used it to look at the road crossing decisions of young pedestrians. In Sweden, Lars Aberg has used the model as a theoretical framework to guide the design of survey questionnaires assessing the factors the underlie the decision to drive after drinking, and this week has given a presentation emphasising the need for a theoretical framework to guide statistical analysis of, and inference from, survey data. In the Netherlands, Talib Rothengatter has used the model several times. For example, he has adapted the model to look at speed choice, concluding that compared to non-speeders, speeders believe that they will get more pleasure from speeding, believe themselves to be at less risk while speeding, evaluate increased expense less negatively and evaluate shortened driving time more positively. He has also carried out a study based on the TPB model to show that risk avoidance was more important than detection avoidance in predicting the commission of a range of driving violations.

In most cases the TPB, sometimes supplemented with additional predictor variables, has proved a useful way of identifying the beliefs and attitudes typical of the individual who behaves in a risky fashion. Having uncovered those beliefs, we are able to target them specifically in educational or other persuasion campaigns. In this way we demonstrated that short, experimental anti-speeding videos featuring the specific beliefs suggested for targeting by a TPB analysis of attitudes to speeding lead to measurable improvement in attitudes. Similarly, Daphne Evans developed a theatre in education drama based on her TPB study of road crossing intentions and behaviour. When it was used as a road safety intervention in schools, it was favourably evaluated by pupils and teachers alike.

In short, the TPB provides a useful theoretical framework for considering the attitudes of road users to any issue. Because it is a well established theory there is a lot of published material on how to apply the model, develop a survey questionnaire, and analyse the data. Not all of that material is in the area of road user behaviour. However if all road safety researchers wanting to measure attitudes were to use the model, we have a basis for comparing results and assessing their relative significance. I suggest that anyone interested in looking at attitudes as part of their research should consider using the TPB as a starting point.

Several other attitude-behaviour models are available from the health psychology literature, although none has been as widely and successfully applied as the TPB, as noted by Sonja Forward (1994) at Upsala, in a comparative review. One example is, Protection Motivation Theory which was developed in the 1970s by Rogers and has been widely used by those investigating the reasons why people sometimes fail to protect themselves against health threats (Rogers, 1975) . The basic idea is that we are motivated to protect ourselves against such a threat only if four conditions are satisfied: (i) the threat must be perceived as severe; (ii) we must perceive ourselves as vulnerable to the threat; (iii) we must believe that something can be done to avoid the threat; (iv) we must believe that we can do it.

Another possibility is the Health Belief Model, developed initially in the 1950s and developed further by many, including Janz and Becker (1984). According to their model, the decision to undertake a health protecting behaviour will be made on the basis of the following factors: (i) general motivation for health; (ii) perceived severity of the threat; (iii) perceived susceptibility to the threat; (iv) perceived barriers to threat-reducing action; (v) perceived efficacy of the threat- reducing action.

This model shares many of the core constructs of PMT, but also incorporates a consideration of general motivation towards health protection and of perceived barriers, which are the costs of engaging in the health protective behaviour. Although I have been unable to find any examples of the use of PMT in the road safety literature, the HBM was used with some success by Derek Rutter and colleagues in Kent, to look at the safety behaviour of motorcyclists, and at older children's use of cycle helmets. It is surprising that these models have not been used more in road safety research, particularly research into driver behaviour. It is clear that risky driving involves the threat of accident involvement, and that the model could be used to try to identify which of the four basic conditions are not being met by those who drive in a risky manner. Don't they think there is a real threat of an accident? Or don't they think they are vulnerable personally to an accident? Or don't they understand how accident risk can be minimised? Or don't they believe themselves capable of driving in a manner that will minimise their personal risk? Knowing the answers to these questions would help in the precise targeting of publicity and education materials.

Cognitive Biases

The second main plank of social cognition is the notion of attribution. This is an area of research concerned with the ways in which we understand and interpret the behaviour of others. Attribution theory can help us to understand why we tend to react badly to the behaviour of other road users, even though we may not always behave well ourselves. Attribution theory holds that several cognitive biases exist that systematically colour our thinking. In the early 1990s (Baxter et al., 1990) demonstrated one such bias, the fundamental attribution error. Drivers were presented with written scenarios describing someone either shooting through lights turning red or close following (tailgating). In one version participants read about the violation as if they had committed it and in another version as if another driver had. In all other respects the scenarios were the same. Then participants had to rate possible explanations for the behaviour described in the scenario. As predicted by attribution theory, drivers tended to attribute their own behaviour to situational factors such as being in an especial hurry or having had a really bad day, and to ascribe the behaviour of the other driver to dispositional factors, such as being an aggressive person or a bad driver. I have also seen, looking at free hand accounts of aggressive driving incidents, that this tendency holds true there. Those who initiate an aggressive driving incident ascribe their behaviour to the situation (what else could I do? I had no choice) whereas those on the receiving end of aggressive driving tend to see it as the result of characteristics of the driver him or herself (he/she is an aggressive person, he/she was showing off to mates). Lars Åberg and Mat Haglund have recently demonstrated the fundamental attribution error among Swedish drivers in their opinions about the safety of their own and others' driving.

Other cognitive biases have also been investigated in the context of driver behaviour. For example, Manstead et al. (1996) showed the operation of false consensus in the minds of drivers. False consensus is the perception that our beliefs are shared by more others than is actually the case, a perception that can lend a spurious sense of social approval to violating drivers. For example, some may wrongly perceive that their belief that driving after drinking is acceptable is shared by most others.

The operation of such cognitive biases may contribute to the stress drivers feel behind the wheel. Gerry Matthews and his colleagues have done a lot of work on individual differences in vulnerability to stress among drivers, and have suggested that the use of confrontational coping strategies in interactions with other vehicles reflects a dysfunctional and aggressive response to stress while driving. Misattributions about the behaviour of others, and false consensus beliefs about the appropriate reaction, may well underpin the stress that leads to the use of such coping strategies. There has been a recent suggestion by David Shinar that driver aggression is the product of frustration caused by congestion and delay and that environmental modifications may help to eliminate the sources of frustration. While that would undoubtedly be helpful, I think it unlikely that meaningful reductions in traffic density will be achieved in the near future. A useful alternative would be to attempt to alter drivers' subjective perceptions of the situation they find themselves in and their role in it. This would probably involve attacking the attributional biases described above. Those who see other drivers as the enemy, as an aggressive or bad driver, may be more likely to become stressed by their behaviour, than those who see the other driver as someone who has probably had a bad day, just as they have.

Frank McKenna has demonstrated the operation of the illusion of control in the context of driving. This is the tendency for individuals to see themselves as having more control over their own behaviour and the environment than is actually the case. In an ingenious series of experiments, McKenna showed that drivers believe that they are at more risk as passengers in the car of a speeding driver than when they are driving at the same speed themselves. Drivers judged themselves to be relatively invulnerable compared to other people, a dangerous bias to take out onto the road and one that might lead them to pay less attention to safety than we would wish. Groeger and Grande (1996) have shown that drivers make unrealistically optimistic assessments of their own skill compared to that of a novice, assessments which may serve to preserve their sense of self-efficacy and invulnerability. A similar finding came from a study by Greening and Chandler (1997) who showed that drivers believe that accident risk base rates apply to the average driver, but, as they believe themselves to be above average as drivers, their personal accident risk must be lower than the base rate implies.

Stereotyping is another well-researched type of cognitive shortcut possibly is very pertinent to road user behaviour. Stereotyping of both the elderly and the young (especially young males) on the road occurs widely, and is likely to be very resistant to change. But at the very least, knowing about the likely biases in our thinking should help to reduce the level of stress that is provoked by the behaviour of other road users. First, though more research is needed to establish their validity in the context of road user behaviour.

To summarise, a whole range of cognitive biases and shortcuts exist that might have negative effects on road user behaviour. However, only some have been investigated in relation to road user behaviour. It could be argued that attempts to inform and educate the general public about them could be valuable, although Frank McKenna (1997) has shown that countering these biases is not easy.

Crime and Road Traffic Accidents

So far this chapter has covered ways to understand why some road users decide to behave in a risky manner, often breaking either the law or the rules of the road by doing so. It is also important to understand why some drivers comply with traffic regulations. Here the work of Tom Tyler, a social psychologist at the University of California, Berkeley is relevant. In his 1990 book *Why People Obey The Law* he differentiates between instrumental and normative motives for compliance with the law. Instrumental compliance involves complying because we fear sanctions or other negative consequences, while normative compliance involves complying because we privately believe that the behaviour prescribed by the rule is right, and that the rule has a moral force, or because we believe the law was formulated by an authority we consider to be legitimate. Normative compliance, which probably embodies intrinsic motivation, is the type we need to encourage among road users. Individuals who are intrinsically motivated to obey the law do not need the constant threat of sanctions to keep them in line. Dana Yagil (1998) carried out a study at the University of Haifa showing that levels of normative compliance were lowest among young male drivers, who were also the group who perceived traffic laws to be least important. It is my belief that normative compliance can only sensibly be fostered at an early age. By the time we come to take driving lessons our sense of what is right and what is wrong behaviour as a road user is already well-developed. If the educational system taught us that being a considerate road user is part of being a good citizen and a decent person, we may run into fewer attitudinal problems. In fact, Tyler's arguments about normative legitimacy echo the finding, in the context of a TPB study, that those who believe that the commission of driving violations is simply wrong, and who would regret doing it even if they got away with it, tend to commit fewer violations (Parker, Manstead & Stradling, 1995).

There are some good examples of work linking existing theory to the issue of road safety, in considering whether deviant road user behaviour is just one aspect of a more general deviant tendency. Junger and Tremblay (1999), publishing in the criminological literature, have produced evidence that crime has a non-spurious positive association with road traffic accident involvement. Robert West and Marianne Junger collaborated (1999) to show that school children aged 7-15 who were in the top 25% of the distribution for problem behaviour were three times more likely to be involved in a road traffic accident than were those in the lowest 25%. Interestingly, their conclusion is that community interventions should be targeted on those children for whom safety and personal responsibility are not important values. This might best be done by investigating and targeting the beliefs that underpin such notions. Again, Meadows and Stradling (1998) have shown that the relationship between extreme social deviance and accident involvement in a sample of young male offenders was partly mediated by the tendency to commit driving violations.

Travel Mode Choice

An increasingly important aspect of transport strategy today involves urging car drivers to consider alternative forms of transport. In this context there has been some work done recently by Steve Stradling and Michelle Meadows. They showed in a recent survey of English car drivers that while almost 20% stated that they would like to reduce their car use and increase their use of public transport in the following year, only 3% think that they actually would do so. Respondents were also asked which from a range of policy measures would be effective in getting them out of their cars. The measures chosen reflected an original differentiation by Steg and Vlek (1997) between push and pull factors. Those policies that involve pull factors, that is increase the attractiveness of alternative transport modes, were rated as likely to be more effective than push factors, which work by making continued car use less attractive. This suggests that education and publicity campaigns on this issue should emphasise the attractiveness of modern public transport.

There has also been experimental work in the area of travel mode from Bas Verplanken, at the Tromsö, in Norway and Henk Aarts at Nijmegen. Reasoning that the TPB is best suited to the explanation of considered (or reasoned) behaviour, they used Triandis' (1980) model of the attitude-behaviour link to investigate the role of habit on decisions about travel mode choice. Triandis' model suggests that strength of habit will attenuate the complexity of choice processes, and this was borne out in experimental studies. In fact their rather pessimistic conclusion was that the consequences of habit can be over-ruled, by forcing participants to pay more attention to the decision-making process, but this effect was only temporary, even in relatively simple context of a laboratory. It seems that if we want to avoid the need to change resistant habitual behaviours we need to stop those behavioural habits from forming at the outset, through educational interventions designed to foster desirable attitudes and behaviour.

The take-home message from all this work is that if policy makers want to persuade us to get out of our cars, it would be wise to turn to theoretically underpinned analyses of the reasons why we haven't yet done so. Some work on inoculating school children against the pervasive effects of car culture would also be worthwhile.

Targeting Interventions

Some changes in patterns of car use and driver behaviour are clearly necessary, given the environmental, social and economic problems they can bring. We need to find ways to maximise the effectiveness of the push and pull factors available to us. Here again, social psychological theory and knowledge about behaviour change might be of some help. Working in a therapeutic environment, Prochaska and DiClemente (1984) initially developed their five-stage model of behaviour change to explain the process of quitting an addiction such as smoking or drinking. However it has since been generalised to apply to other behaviours, and can serve as a useful framework for considering how to go about changing driver behaviour.

The five proposed stages can be summarised as follows, in relation to switching to public transport:

a. *pre-contemplation*, when the individual does not even recognise that their behaviour is problematic: This stage is characterised by the thought; Why shouldn't I use my car whenever I want?

b. *contemplation*, when the individual recognises the problematic nature of their behaviour, and that it is having an effect on themselves and others. A typical belief in this stage might be By using my car all the time I am contributing to environmental pollution

c. *preparation*, when they actively consider concrete strategies by which they might change their behaviour. Now the individual might resolve to take action; I will try using the bus to commute to work

d. *action*, the stage in which those strategies are acted upon

e. *maintenance*, during which the individual monitors the new behaviour and tries to ensure that the old ways are not re-adopted.

The mind-set of the individual changes as they progress through the stages, and so persuasive attempts through publicity campaigns must be tailored to suit the stage reached. For example, to shift an individual from pre-contemplation to contemplation, an awareness-raising campaign would be appropriate and effective. Such a campaign would be wasted on those already in the preparation stage, who would benefit much more from practical advice on alternative options, and encouragement to make the change. This technique was designed for use in a therapeutic setting with individuals, and might not be suitable for application to the general public. However it is clear that a matching the type of intervention used to the current stage of readiness to change would certainly be possible at a more local level, within communities, classrooms or companies.

Summary

This chapter has provided a flavour of the main theories and models that social psychology can offer to researchers interested in the reasons why road users behave as they do. I believe that these models can help in (i) uncovering the beliefs that lead to undesirable behaviour; (ii) elucidating the cognitive biases that road users are prey to; (iii) suggesting when and how to target persuasion attempts where they will be most effective.

Finding out about the values and beliefs that characterise those who behave in certain ways is more practically useful than finding out about their demographic characteristics or their personalities, which are not amenable to change. There are ways in which we can attempt to change beliefs, and thus to change attitudes and behaviour. However if such attempts are to have the best chance of success they should be grounded in the models and theories that have been shown to be successful in the past.

Good progress has been made in the last decade in applying the concepts and theories of social psychology to problems of traffic and road safety. However, if we are to maintain that progress in both theory and application, it is important that those concepts and theories are operationalised, and the data analysed in appropriate ways. The chapters in this volume by Steve Stradling – who presents a model of the personal and systemic influences crash involvement that included attitudes and perceptions – and by Ray Fuller – who referred to the motivations of the novice driver in choosing a preferred speed, as one part of a model looking at the balance between the capabilities of the driver and the demands of the driving task – sketch ambitious integrated models of the social and cognitive aspects of driving, involving both the driver and the context he/she operates in. The contention here is that we need to be confident that we understand as much as possible about each of those aspects before trying to fit them together into an inclusive model. Attitudes, beliefs and motivations play a crucial part in driver behaviour. If we are to include their influence as one aspect of a unified theory they must be conceptualised and measured in a theoretically and methodologically respectable way. One way of checking that we have done this well is by seeking publication in the social psychology literature. If much more traffic and road-safety related research found its way into, and made a contribution to, mainstream psychology journals, this would provide a good basis on which to compare results and gauge progress.

References

Åberg, L. (1993). Drinking and driving: Intentions, attitudes and social norms of Swedish male drivers. *Accident Analysis and Prevention, 25*, 289-96.

Ajzen, I, (1988) *Attitudes, Personality and Behaviour*. Milton Keynes, UK: Open University Press.

Arnold, L., & Quine, L. (1994). Predicting helmet use among schoolboy cyclists: An application of the Health Belief Model. In D. Rutter and L. Quine (Eds.) *Social Psychology and Health: A European Perspective*. Aldershot, UK: Ashgate.

Baxter, J.S., Macrae, C.N., Manstead, A.S.R., Stradling, S.G & Parker, D. (1990). Attributional biases and driver behaviour. *Social Behaviour, 5*, 185-92.

Evans, D., & Norman, P. (1998). Understanding pedestrians' road crossing decisions: An application of the theory of planned behaviour. *Health Education Research, 13*, 481-89.

Forward. S. (1994). *Theoretical models of attitudes and the prediction of drivers' behaviour.* (Rep. No. 434) The University of Upsala, Sweden: Upsala Psychological Reports.

Greening, L., & Chandler, C.C. (1997). Why it can't happen to me: The base rate matters but overestimating skill leads to underestimating risk. *Journal of Applied Social Psychology, 27,* 760-780.

Groeger, J. A., & Grande, G.E. (1996) Self-preserving assessments of skill? *British Journal of Psychology, 87*, 61-79.

Groeger, J. A., & Chapman, P.R. (1997). Normative influences on decisions to offend. *Applied Psychology: An International Review, 46*, 265-85.

Janz, N.K., & Becker, M.H. (1984). The health belief model: A decade later. *Health Education Quarterly, 11*, 1-47.

Junger, M., & Tremblay, R.E. (1999). Self-control, accidents and crime. *Criminal Justice and Behaviour, 26*, 484-501.

Lajunen, T., Parker, D., & Summala, H. (1999). Does traffic congestion increase driver aggression? *Transportation Research Part F, 2*, 225-236.

Manstead, A.S.R., Parker, D., Stradling, S.G., Reason, J.T., & Baxter, J.S. (1992). Perceived consensus in estimates of the prevalence of driving errors and violations. *Journal of Applied Social Psychology, 22,* 509-530

Matthews, G., Tsuda, A., Xin, G., & Ozeki, Y. (1999). Individual differences in driver stress vulnerability in a Japanese sample. *Ergonomics, 42,* 401-15.

McKenna, F. P. (1993). It won't happen to me; unrealistic optimism or illusion of control? *British Journal of Psychology, 84*, 39-50.

McKenna, F. P., & Myers, L.B. (1997). Illusory self-assessments - can they be reduced? *British Journal of Psychology, 88,* 39-51

Meadows, M., Stradling, S.G., & Lawson, S, (1998). The role of social deviance and violations in predicting road traffic accidents in a sample of young offenders. *British Journal of Psychology, 89,* 417-31.

Parker, D., Reason, J.T., Manstead, A.S.R., & Stradling, S.G. (1995). Driving errors, driving violations and accident involvement. *Ergonomics, 38*, 1036-48.

Parker, D., Manstead, A.S.R., & Stradling, S.G. (1995). Extending the theory of planned behaviour: The role of personal norm. *British Journal of Social Psychology, 34*, 127-37.

Prochaska, J.O., & DiClemente, C.C. (1984). *The Transtheoretical Approach: Crossing the Traditional Bounds of Therapy.* Dow Jones-Irwin: Homewood, IL.

Rogers, R.W. (1975). A protection motivation theory of fear appeals and attitude change. *Journal of Psychology, 91*, 93-114.

Rothengatter, J.A., & van der Pols, E. (1993). *High or low risk: Who cares?* Unpublished manuscript, University of Groningen, The Netherlands

Shinar, D. (1998). Aggressive driving: The contribution of the drivers and the situation. *Transportation Research Part F, 2,* 137-160

Steg, L., & Vlek, C. (1997). *The role of problem awareness in willingness-to-change car use and in evaluating relevant policy measures.* In J.A. Rothengatter and E. Carbonell Vaya (Eds.), *Traffic and Transport Psychology*. Oxford: Pergamon Press.

Triandis, H. C. (1980). Values, attitudes and interpersonal behaviour. In H.E. Howe and M.M. Page (Eds.), *Nebraska Symposium on Motivation*. Lincoln, NE: University of Nebraska Press.

Tyler, T. (1990) *Why People Obey the Law*. New Haven, CT: Yale University Press.

Verplanken, B., Aarts, H., & Van Knippenberg, A. (1997). Habit, information acquisition and the process of making travel mode choices. *European Journal of Social Psychology, 27,* 539-61.

West, R., Train, H., Junger, M., West, A., & Pickering, A. (1999). Accidents and problem behaviour, *The Psychologist, 12*, 395-97.

Yagil, D. (1998) Gender and age-related differences in attitudes towards traffic laws and violations. *Transportation Research Part F, 2*, 123-137.

Traffic and Transport Psychology,
T. Rothengatter and R.D. Huguenin (Editors)

12

Risk Taking and Self-Efficacy among Young Male Drivers: Self-Efficacy and Changing Task Demands

Patricia Delhomme and Thierry Meyer

Introduction

In road safety, it is important to "understand how drivers adapt to the driving task in such a way that they become able to adapt it to their own skills and explain why they fail to adapt themselves to the demands imposed on them by the driving environment" (Brehmer, 1994, p. 542). Self-assessment of driving skills is a central dimension of driving activity. While the most often, this self-assessment can be an effective source of regulation of driving activity (Brown, 1989; 1991), this factor can also be a source of risk when it leads driver to overestimate his driving abilities. People evaluate their own skills either at a general level or at a specific level. The evaluation of their general skills may be reflected in their choice of preferred speed (for instance, drivers who tend to overrate their skills claim to exceed legal speed limits more frequently compared to those who do not have an overly high opinion of their ability, Delhomme, 1994; Spolander, 1982), or be related to accidents (young drivers with one to two years' experience who think they are far better than the average driver claim to be responsible for more accidents compared to those who think they are much less skilled than the average driver, Maycock, 1995).

The evaluation of specific skills may be conceptualised by self-efficacy. Self-efficacy (Bandura, 1986; 1997) is probably the most popular construct among the factors predicting performance. Moreover, self-efficacy as an "exercise of control" is now a theory of self-regulation and action. Self-efficacy has been studied in many fields, such as sport and academic performance. Little work has been carried out on self-efficacy in the field of motoring, even though similar, albeit far less precise, concepts have been developed (overconfidence, self-assessment of skills; Harvey, 1994). Yet it is important to know to what extent self-efficacy is predictive of performance according to some dimensions of driving activity, and especially how this self-efficacy varies as a function of changes in task demands and according to experience.

Definition of Self-Efficacy

Self-efficacy is concerned not with actual skills but rather with what people think they can do with their skills in a future specific task. So self-efficacy is a subjective assessment of ability to attain a level of performance. Efficacy expectation differs from performance expectation to the extent that the former relates not so much to the expected outcome of the action as to the individual's evaluation of his ability to take effective action. Those who have a strong sense of self-efficacy in a particular situation will devote their attention and effort to the demands of the situation, and when faced with obstacles and difficult situations, they will try harder and persist longer. Efficacy beliefs should be measured in terms of particular judgements of ability that may vary according to the different levels of task demands (Bandura, 1997). Measures of self-efficacy must be tailored to areas of functioning and must grade task demands within those areas.

Scope of the Study

Drivers have to constantly manage greater or smaller variations in task demands. So we studied self-efficacy in driving situations in which task demands are intensified, for instance when drivers are confronted with a deterioration in driving conditions due to external factors such as fog, ice, rain. Adaptation to major and/or sudden changes in driving situations is an important component of driving task. Drivers often tend to overestimate the control they can exert over such driving situations. This is true both for experienced drivers and for novice drivers with some months of driving experience behind them. Novice drivers do not take their inexperience sufficiently into account in gauging their skills. They are overconfident probably because they lack meta-cognitive knowledge about their own skills. Self-efficacy among novice drivers is currently accurate but can sometimes be unrealistic, especially when task demands increase.

Main Objective

Our aim was to gain a better understanding of how self-efficacy contributes to performance, depending on the task demands (i.e. reduced visibility), and on changes in task demands, among young drivers with varying driving experience. While self-efficacy should normally increase with task familiarity, does it adjust commensurately to new constraints on the task, in this case reduced visibility? One may suppose that experienced drivers make better quantitative and qualitative adjustments to their self-efficacy than less experienced drivers. Experienced drivers should have gained a more stable general sense of self-efficacy, so their assessments of situations should be more accurate. Experienced drivers generally are more able to correct the mistakes they may make while driving than less experienced drivers. In particular, driving experience should result in a greater ability to maintain a high level of performance (at a subjectively acceptable level of risk), whatever the variations in the situational context.

We concentrated on the interaction between self-efficacy and driving experience among young drivers, who are the ones most frequently involved in road accidents. According to Bandura (1986, 1997), although self-efficacy judgements are functionally related to action, a number of factors can affect the strength of that link. We expected that a high level of self-efficacy among less experienced young drivers might sometimes be confused with overestimation of control.

Drivers think they can attain a high level of performance, but they do not always have the ability to perform the task as well as they would like or expect to.

METHOD AND PROCEDURE

Overview

Drivers carried out a manoeuvre task on a track at the wheel of a Renault 9. Each driver performed two experimental trials: one took place in normal visibility and the other in reduced visibility. Visibility was reduced by means of a stiff translucent plastic helmet. This was designed to make the driving task more difficult, emulating the situation of driving in fog. A daylight index (luxmeter) was calculated for each trial. The variation in task demands involved either going from a trial in normal visibility (without the helmet) to a trial in reduced visibility (with the helmet), or from a trial in reduced visibility to a trial in normal visibility.

Participants

One hundred and twenty young male drivers took part in this experiment. We differentiated the less experienced drivers from the more experienced young drivers on the basis of a median split of the kilometres they had driven since they obtained their driving license (see Table 1: Age, kilometres driven and months licensed for each of these groups). All the drivers were doing their mandatory military service near Paris and were paid for voluntarily participating in the experiment.

Table 1. Age, months licensed and kilometres driven (mean, standard deviation, minimum, maximum) for less experienced and more experienced young drivers.

	Less experienced drivers (n = 59)				*More experienced drivers (n = 61)*			
	M	*SD*	*Min*	*Max*	*M*	*SD*	*Min*	*Max*
Age (months)	255.15	11.34	230	281	258.97	10.9	233	284
Months licensed	26.23	15.18	2	61	36.13	11.90	10	57
Kilometres driven	22727	14114	500	45400	82403	46435	50000	351000

Tasks

1. The manoeuvre task consisted of driving along a winding path about 38 meters long. The path was bordered on either side by a line of 28 cones. Drivers had to drive at less than 25 km/h, knocking over as few cones as possible. The difficulty of the task lay in the narrowness of the path, which was 2.10 m wide. Participants were required to perform a familiarisation drive prior to each trial (with or without the helmet). They also had to fill in a questionnaire before each trial to register their self-efficacy, and another one after each trial to register their

subjective performance without knowing how many cones they had knocked over and their estimated speed (km/h).

2. Drivers had to complete a post-experimental questionnaire that was essentially aimed at obtaining a general self-assessment of driving ability (10 items, $\alpha = .78$), self-esteem ($\alpha = .79$, Rosenberg, 1965) and their personal driving history.

Measure of self-efficacy

Following a standard methodology for measuring self-efficacy beliefs (Lee & Bobko, 1994), drivers were shown items with different levels of performance. Drivers were asked whether they could perform at specific levels for each trial (yes or no) and assess their degree of confidence in their ability to perform at that level (on a scale from 0 to 100) (cf. Table 2). The sum of positive replies divided by the total number of items gives the magnitude of self-efficacy. The mean confidence rating represents the strength of self-efficacy. We used a composite measure of the strength and magnitude of self-efficacy. We standardised the self-efficacy strength items by converting them to z scores and then totalled them across all self-efficacy levels to which the answer was yes.

Table 2. Questionnaire to measure self-efficacy.

The path consists of 56 cones. How many of them do you think you will knock over, driving at less than 25 Km/h?	*Yes/No*	*Degree of confidence in your answer (0 % = uncertainty, 100 % = certainty)*
Less than 30 cones	Y/N	..... %
Less than 27 cones	Y/N	..... %
Less than 24 cones	Y/N	..... %
Less than 21 cones	Y/N	..... %
Less than 18 cones	Y/N	..... %
Less than 15 cones	Y/N	..... %
Less than 12 cones	Y/N	..... %
Less than 9 cones	Y/N	..... %
Less than 6 cones	Y/N	..... %
Less than 3 cones	Y/N	..... %
NO CONES	Y/N	..... %

Design

In the field of self-efficacy, it is important to test not only the effect of self-assessment on the driver's performance but also the reactivity of self-assessment on the performance itself. That is why we used a control group and an experimental group (cf. Table 3). Out of 120 drivers:

– a measure of self-efficacy was recorded for only 80 drivers (experimental group). Forty carried out the first trial in normal visibility first and the second one in reduced visibility second, while the other 40 performed them in reduced visibility first and in normal visibility second.

– the other 40 drivers (control group) did not estimate their self-efficacy before the task. Twenty of them were asked to carry out the trials in normal visibility first and in reduced visibility second, and the other 20 to perform them in the reverse order.

Table 3. Mixed experimental design.

	Trials	
	Normal-reduced visibility	*Reduced-normal visibility*
Self-efficacy assessment before trials (experimental group)	N = 40	N = 40
No self-efficacy assessment before trials (control group)	N = 20	N = 20

The cases were not significantly different in terms of age and driving experience.

Validity checks

Measure of self-efficacy. Self-efficacy is not significantly related to age, driving experience (kilometres, months of driving experience), general self-assessment of driving ability and self-esteem as a trait (Rosenberg, 1965).

Reactivity of efficacy assessment. The fact of filling out a detailed questionnaire on self-efficacy beforehand had no effect on performance (we found no significant difference in performance between the control and experimental groups).

Effect of the visibility conditions on task performance. Whatever the order of visibility conditions (i.e. with or without the helmet first), drivers knocked over an average of six cones in normal visibility and nine cones in reduced visibility. The mean correlation between the two tasks is $r = .48$ ($p <.001$).

Level of self-efficacy. On the whole, the outcome expectancies (magnitude of self-efficacy) was lower than actual performance. This means that, on average, there were 7.4 positive replies in normal visibility (approximately 10 cones knocked over) and 5.9 positive replies in reduced visibility (around 14 cones knocked over).

Results

Self-efficacy and task performance

To test the impact of self-efficacy on performance of the manoeuvre task, we differentiated drivers according to their self-efficacy scores: low self-efficacy (as a function of a zero or negative score) vs. high self-efficacy (positive score).

Self-efficacy and task performance in the first trial. Performance (number of cones knocked over) was processed by analysis of variance according to 3 between subject factors: driving experience (less experienced vs. more experienced drivers), visibility conditions for the first trial (normal vs. reduced visibility), and self-efficacy (low vs. high), and a covariant factor (index of luminosity).

Self-efficacy and driving experience had no significant effect on performance in normal visibility (i.e. without the helmet) but had an effect in reduced visibility (with the helmet) (interaction $p < .068$) (cf. Figure 1). In reduced visibility condition, low self-efficacy lead to more mistakes than high self-efficacy among the less experienced drivers, whereas high self-efficacy lead to more mistakes than low self-efficacy among the more experienced drivers ($p < .02$).

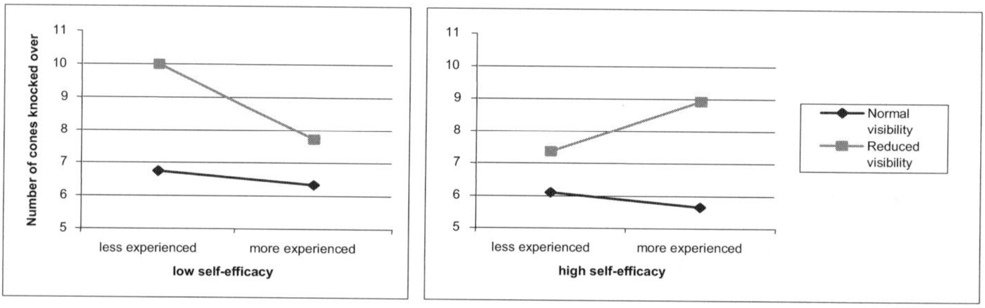

Figure 1. Number of cones knocked over according to driving experience (less experienced vs. more experienced), self-efficacy (low vs. high), and visibility conditions in the first trial (normal vs. reduced).

Self-efficacy and task performance in normal and reduced visibility. Task performance (number of cones knocked over) was assessed by analysis of variance according to 3 between subject factors: driving experience (less experienced vs. more experienced drivers), the trial order in normal visibility (first vs. second trial) (and for the second analysis of variance trial order in reduced visibility), and self-efficacy (low vs. high), and a covariant factor (index of luminosity).

Normal visibility. Whichever the order in which the normal visibility trial was performed (1st vs. 2nd trial), the less experienced drivers made more mistakes ($M = 6.7$) than the more experienced drivers ($M = 5.54$) ($F(1,71) = 3.96, p = .05$).

In normal visibility, low self-efficacy resulted in more mistakes being made in the first trial than in the second, whereas high self-efficacy lead to more mistakes being made in the second trial than in the first (cf. Figure 2) ($F(1,71) = 4.68, p < .034$).

In normal visibility, drivers with a high self-efficacy thought they were more successful in the performance of the task ($M = 6.91$) (estimation a posteriori of the number of cones knocked over without knowing their performance) compared to those with a low self-efficacy (M = 9.76) ($F(1,71) = 5.95, p = .017$).

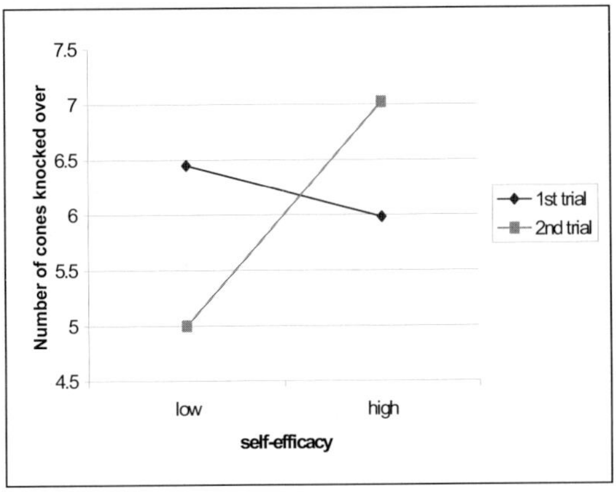

Figure 2. Number of cones knocked over according to self-efficacy (low vs. high) and the order of the Normal visibility trial (1st vs. 2nd trial).

In normal visibility, drivers thought they had driven faster in the second trial compared to those in the first ($F(1,71)$ = 3.53, p <.06). This result is attributable to drivers with a high self-efficacy who thought they had driven more quickly in the second trial compared to other groups (p<.008) (cf. Figure 3).

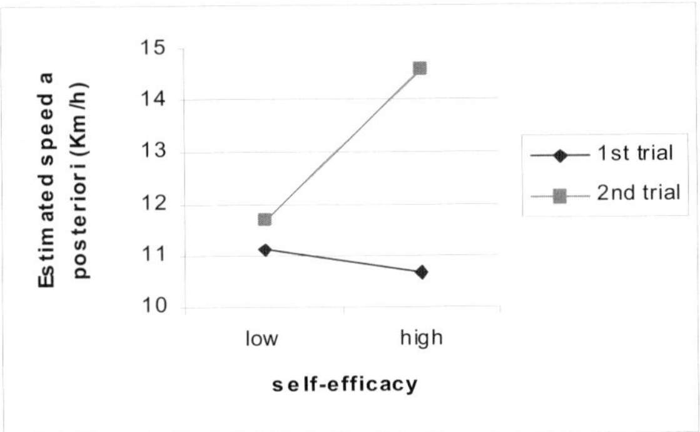

Figure 3. Speed estimated a posteriori according to self-efficacy (low vs. high) and the order of the Normal visibility trial (1st vs. 2nd trial).

Reduced visibility. In reduced visibility, the less experienced drivers did not make significantly more mistakes (M = 9.54) than the more experienced drivers (M = 8.68).

An interaction was found between driving experience, the order of the reduced visibility trial and self-efficacy $F(1,71) = 4.28$, $p = .042$) (cf. Figure 4). In reduced visibility, for the first trial the less experienced drivers with a low self-efficacy made more mistakes compared to those with a high self-efficacy, whereas for the second trial the less experienced drivers with a high self-efficacy made more mistakes compared to those with a low self-efficacy.

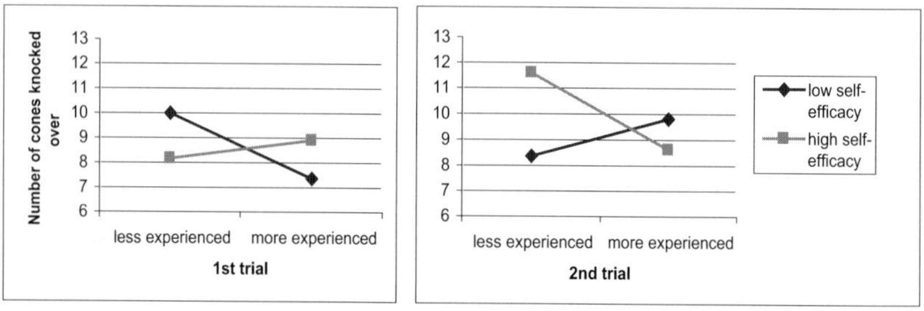

Figure 4. Number of cones knocked over according to driving experience (less experienced vs. more experienced drivers), the order of the Reduced visibility trial (1st vs. 2nd trial) and self-efficacy (low vs. high).

In reduced visibility, the less experienced drivers considered a posteriori that they had made more mistakes ($M = 13.66$) compared to the more experienced drivers ($M = 10.17$) ($F(1,71) = 3.93$, $p = .051$).

In reduced visibility, drivers thought they had driven faster in the first trial (M = 13 km/h) compared to those in the second (M = 8,5 km/h) ($F(1,71) = 22.2$, $p < .00001$).

Changes in efficacy expectation and performance

The experiment was designed to determine the changes in efficacy expectation and performance that occurred between the first and second performance of the task (cf. Figure 5). A mixed analysis of variance was carried out using a between subject factor (driving experience), a within subject factor (the trials) and a covariant factor (index of luminosity). When drivers began by the easier trial (in normal visibility), self-efficacy increased ahead of the second trial to be performed in more difficult condition (in reduced visibility) ($F(1,38) = 5.56$, $p < .024$). Although the interaction is not significant, ($F(1,38) = 1.90$), a separate analysis of variance revealed that the self-efficacy of only the less experienced drivers increased from normal visibility condition (1st trial) to reduced visibility condition (2nd trial) ($p < .024$), whereas the most experienced drivers had a constant self-efficacy rating whatever the visibility conditions of the task ($F < 1$).

When drivers began by the trial in more difficult condition and finished by the trial in easier condition, their self-efficacy increased from one to the other ($F(1,38) = 5.12$, $p < .03$), that was the case mainly for the less experienced drivers ($p = .05$) (for the more experienced ones, *ns*).

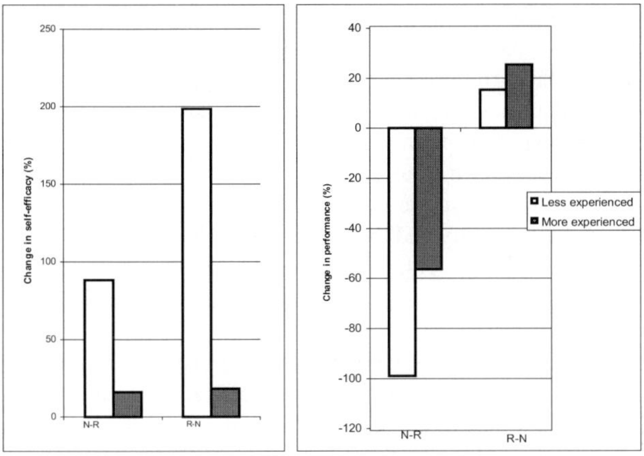

Figure 5. Change in self-efficacy and performance (%) as a function of change in driving condition (Normal visibility followed by Reduced visibility vs. Reduced visibility followed by Normal visibility).

We observed a significant positive correlation between the self-efficacy of task performance from normal visibility to reduced visibility only when drivers began in normal visibility condition (r = .76 and .77 respectively for the less experienced and more experienced drivers) and not when they began in reduced visibility condition (respectively, r = .43 and r = -.02 for the less experienced and more experienced drivers). It could be expected that self-efficacy would increase when drivers performed the first trial in reduced visibility because the second trial was in normal visibility, so drivers adapted their self-efficacy to the easier trial. It is nevertheless surprising that self-efficacy increased so much when drivers performed the first trial in normal visibility, because the second trial in reduced visibility was more difficult, as attested by their performance in the second one. Both the less experienced and the more experienced drivers made more mistakes in reduced visibility when they performed this task in the second trial.

Discussion

Our measure of self-efficacy on driving task yields good index of internal and construct validity. The absence of reactivity of the measurement of self-efficacy is corroborated for diverse activities in the field of self-efficacy: physical exercise, cognitive attainments, regulation of motivation.

How can one explain the fact that the less experienced young drivers increased their efficacy expectation so much even when visibility was reduced? The less experienced drivers probably do not distinguish sufficiently between the familiarity they gradually acquire in successive performances of the manoeuvre task and the change imposed by the new condition that render the task more difficult (first normal and then reduced visibility). Possibly the dry run they performed to familiarise themselves with the course in reduced visibility lead them to think that they could perform it better than might be expected. The more experienced drivers were able to base their expectations on a more stable conception of their abilities and a more precise knowledge of the task demand (reduced visibility). Their efficacy expectation is increased because the task is more familiar, but the task variations have less of an impact on their assessment. It can thus be seen that the more the self-efficacy of the less experienced drivers increased from the normal visibility trial to the reduced visibility one, the more mistakes they made, whereas in the case of the more experienced drivers, the more their self-efficacy increased between the normal visibility and the reduced visibility trial, the fewer mistakes they made (respectively, r = .35 and r = -.44, *ns* with a significant difference between the two correlations, p<.01).

Measures of self-efficacy are less realistic when the reduced visibility task is performed in the second trial. The less experienced drivers whose self-efficacy increased more when they performed the reduced visibility task in the second trial showed that they were unable to adjust their self-efficacy either to the task or to their performance. While such confidence in their ability could be useful in fostering a general feeling of proficiency in driving, it could at the same time represent a risk insofar as it does not engender any improvement in their driving performance.

Viewed within the framework of dynamic tasks, self-efficacy sheds light on the construction of driving skills. A more systematic study should lead to a better understanding of the extent to which efficacy expectations are based on a realistic assessment of task demands and on the preservation of a general sense of driving skills that is indispensable to the learning process and to perseverance in the face of failure, as well as of the extent to which they reflect the unrealistic assessments that are common in the field of driving (but are currently assessed away from the context of a challenging task).

A limiting condition of this research is that we looked at only one aspect of driving activity - a manoeuvre task in which the demands of the task changed in the course of the trials. But we think it is an important aspect of perceived efficacy in driving, which can be applied more generally to other driving situations. A second part of this study, not dealt with here, showed that efficacy expectations can have an effect on a subsequent task (a braking task).

Acknowledgements

The authors like to thank our experimenters N. Clauss from University Paris X & J.-J. Soubercaze from Inrets, and F. Lenoir, J-L. Mondet & C. Perrot from Inrets for their technical support.

References

Bandura, A. (1997). *Self-efficacy. The exercise of control.* New York : W.H. Freeman and Company.

Bandura, A. (1986). *Social foundations of thought and action: A social cognitive theory.* Englewood Cliffs, N.J.: Prentice-Hall.

Brehmer, B. (1994). Psychological aspect of traffic safety. *European Journal of Operational Research, 75*, 540-552.

Brown, I.D. (1989). How can we train safe driving ? Groningen : Traffic Research Centre.

Brown, I.D. (1991). Prospects for improving road safety during the 1990's. In W.T. Singleton, and J. Dirkx (Eds), *Ergonomics, Health and Safety*. Leuven : Leuven University Press.

Delhomme, P. (1994). Liens entre surestimation de ses propres capacités, expérience de la conduite et activité de conduite. *Rapport de Recherche Inrets, 187.*

Harvey, N. (1994). Relations between confidence and skilled performance. In G. Wright and P. Ayton, *Subjective probability* (pp. 321-352). Chichester : John Wiley.

Lee, C., & Bobko, P. (1994). Self-efficacy beliefs: Comparison of five measures. *Journal of Applied Psychology, 79,* 364-369.

Maycock, G. (1995). Novice driver accidents in relation to learning to drive, the driving test, and driving ability and behaviour. In G.B. Grayson (Ed.) *Behavioural Research in Road Safety* (PA3081/95, pp. 1-13). Crowthorne: Transport and Road Research Laboratory.

Rosenberg, M. (1965). *Society and the adolescent self-image*. Princeton, N.J.: Princeton University Press.

Spolander, K. (1982). *Accident risks of drivers-a model tested on man and woman* (Rapport 260). Linköping: Swedish Road and Traffic Research Institute (VTI).

Traffic and Transport Psychology,
T. Rothengatter and R.D. Huguenin (Editors)

13

Errors, Lapses and Violations in the Drivers of Heavy Vehicles

Mark J. M. Sullman, Michelle Meadows and Karl Pajo

Introduction

Early research into self-reported driving behaviour found that aberrant driving behaviour, measured using the Driver Behaviour Questionnaire (DBQ), could be classified into errors, lapses and violations (Reason, Manstead, Stradling, Baxter & Campbell, 1990). Lapses involve problems with attention and memory and include such things as switching on one thing when meaning to switch on something else (Parker, Lajunen & Stradling, 1998). Errors are a type of driving mistake involving failures of observation and misjudgement, and include such behaviours as failing to notice a Stop or Give Way sign, or failing to check your mirrors before pulling out or changing lanes (Parker et al., 1998). Violations are deliberate deviations from those practices believed to be necessary to safely operate a vehicle and include such behaviours as speeding and close following (Reason et al., 1990). More recent research has divided violations into ordinary violations and aggressive violations (e.g. Chapman, Roberts & Underwood, in press; Dimmer & Parker, 1999; Lawton, Parker, Stradling & Manstead, 1997). Aggressive violations are to do with expressing hostility towards another road user or aggressive driving.

Research using the DBQ on private motor vehicle drivers has produced relatively stable findings in terms of the factor structure and prediction of crash involvement. This stability has been found both within and across different countries and cultures. Three or four factor solutions (depending on the version of the DBQ used) have been found by researchers in Britain (Parker et al., 1995a; Reason et al., 1990), Australia (Blockey & Hartley, 1995), Sweden (Åberg & Rimmö, 1998), and in China (Stradling, Parker, Lajunen, Meadows & Xie, 1998). In the majority of studies it has been the violations factor that has been found to be significantly predictive of crash involvement (Parker et al., 1995a; Stradling et al., 1998).

For many general road users there is now considerable evidence that aberrant driving behaviour can be reliably measured and categorised using the DBQ. However, the picture is less clear in the case of professional drivers or for those driving in a work-related context. For example, in studies using drivers of company cars, researchers have failed to replicate the standard 3- or 4-factor solution, and violations have not been significantly predictive of crash involvement (Dimmer & Parker, 1999; Chapman et al., in press). Interestingly, Chapman et al. (in press) also found very different crash rates for different types of professional drivers. They found that sales staff and those driving 'perk' cars had a much higher rate of crash involvement than those driving liveried vehicles.

These findings suggest we should be cautious generalising the results of studies on conventional road users to professional drivers. This is especially the case with the drivers of trucks, as truck drivers have a different set of demographics, skill base and possibly also different attitudes. For example, it is known that professional truck drivers have a higher average age than the general driving population, engage in driving for a different purpose than the public, and spend more time on the road than the general public (Walton, 1999a; Walton, 1999b). Unlike company car drivers, who are involved in more crashes than the general public (Chapman et al., in press; Dimmer & Parker, 1999; Lynn & Lockwood, 1998), truck drivers are involved in fewer crashes per million kilometres driven than private vehicle drivers (Walton, 1999a). Trucks, however, are involved in a disproportionately large percentage of fatal crashes. While trucks account for around 6% of the total distance travelled on New Zealand's roads, they are involved in 22% of all fatal crashes. Although truck drivers are not responsible for the majority of these fatal crashes, they an important group to study if New Zealand's relatively high road toll is to be addressed.

The validity of the DBQ in the context of New Zealand road conditions and for New Zealand drivers has not been established. Furthermore, the DBQ has never been used to investigate aberrant driving behaviour amongst professional truck drivers. Accordingly, this research aimed to test the generalisability of the DBQ to a sample of New Zealand drivers of heavy vehicles. More specifically, we investigated the level of self-reported aberrant driving behaviour, the factor structure of the DBQ, and the correlation between the DBQ and crash involvement for New Zealand truck drivers.

Method

The participants in this study were full time truck drivers from forty eight different transport companies working in the logging, petroleum and dairy sectors. Questionnaires, reply-paid envelopes, and covering letters were sent to each company who distributed them to the drivers they employed. The drivers were asked to fill out the questionnaire and return it using the reply-paid envelope. To facilitate the response rate, reminders were sent to each transport company at 2-weekly intervals for a period of six weeks.

The questionnaire contained a number of demographic and background variables, including; age, gender, annual mileage, years experience driving trucks, preferred driving speed and number of crashes they were involved in over the previous three years. The four preferred driving speed items were combined to form an overall measure of preferred speed (Meadows, Stradling & Lawson, 1998).

A 28-item version of the DBQ, was included to measure self-reported aberrant driving behaviours. This version included 8 error items, 8 lapse items, 6 violation and 6 aggressive violations. Participants were asked to indicate on a six point scale (0 = never, 5 = all the time), how often they engage in each of the 28 aberrant driving behaviours (Parker, Reason, Manstead & Stradling, 1995a).

Results and Discussion

Descriptive statistics

The sample comprised more males (99.2%) than females (0.8%), with an average age of 40.4 years old. Participants had slightly more than 18 years experience driving trucks and a mean annual mileage of 95,092 kilometres (see Table 1). These figures are similar to those reported in an earlier survey of New Zealand truck drivers (Walton, 1999a).

Table 1. Descriptive Statistics for Demographic Variables.

Variable	*Mean*	*SD*	*Minimum*	*Maximum*
Age (years)	40.38	9.64	20	62
Mileage (km)	95,092	42,586	1500	251,000
Years experience*	18.43	9.68	0.2	44

* The number of years the participant had been driving trucks

Almost two thirds (62.7%) of truck drivers reported that they had not been involved in a crash over the previous 3 year period. Of the remainder, 22.5% reported being involved in 1 crash, 9.9% reported 2 crashes and 4.9% reported being involved in more than 2 crashes over the last 3 years.

Table 2 shows that in the majority of cases the truck drivers reported a lower mean level of each aberrant behaviour than the company car drivers surveyed by Dimmer and Parker (1999). The difference was more pronounced when the mean truck drivers responses were compared with research on private motor vehicle drivers conducted by Lawton et al. (1997).

Factor analysis

In order to comply with the assumptions of multivariate analysis, most of the DBQ items were transformed using either square root, logarithm or reflection. Following the removal of the outliers, Principle Component Analysis (PCA) using varimax rotations was performed to determine the factor structure. Table 3 shows a parsimonious four factor solution was produced which accounted for 35.8% of the variance. The production of a factor solution accounting for 35.8% of the variance is very much in line with that found by other researchers. For example Reason et al. (1990) produced a three factor solution which accounted for 33% of the variance, Blockey and Hartley (1995) found a three factor solution which accounted for 27.7% of the variance and Åberg and Rimmö (1998) found a three factor solution which accounted for 35.9% of the variance.

Table 2. Behaviour reported by company car drivers vs truck drivers.

		Sullman et al.	*Dimmer & Parker*	*Lawton et al. 1997:*
Type	*Behaviour*	*Mean (SD)*	*Mean*	*Mean*
Violation	Speed on a motorway	1.45 (± 1.26)	2.82	3.41
Violation	Speed in a residential area	0.80 (± 0.88)	1.71	3.31
Violation	Close following	0.69 (± 0.77)	0.84	2.09
Violation	Cross changed lights	0.54 (± 0.69)	0.60	2.09
Violation	Overtake on the inside	0.24 (± 0.59)	1.16	2.02
Violation	Drive over the alcohol limit	0.24 (± 0.54)	0.23	1.32
Aggressive	Sound your horn	1.29 (± 1.02)	0.81	2.42
Aggressive	Indicate hostility	1.07 (± 1.00)	0.93	2.89
Aggressive	Race away from the lights	0.50 (± 0.79)	0.97	2.43
Aggressive	Force your way into traffic	0.45 (± 0.68)	0.84	2.09
Aggressive	Give chase	0.28 (± 0.69)	0.19	1.31
Aggressive	Dive in lane at last minute	0.14 (± 0.44)	0.70	1.89
Lapse	Get in the wrong lane	0.99 (± 0.81)	1.50	
Lapse	No clear recollection of road	0.97 (± 0.86)	1.47	
Lapse	Switch on wrong thing	0.94 (± 0.88)	0.87	
Lapse	Hit something reversing	0.59 (± 0.64)	0.46	
Lapse	Take wrong exit	0.43 (± 0.67)	1.09	
Lapse	'Wake up' on journey	0.32 (± 0.56)	0.89	
Lapse	Forget where park	0.10 (± 0.33)	1.01	
Error	Underestimate another's speed	0.78 (± 0.67)	0.77	1.78
Error	Fail to check mirror	0.43 (± 0.67)	0.60	1.68
Error	Nearly hit car in front	0.43 (± 0.62)	0.75	1.75
Error	Brake too quickly	0.41 (± 0.60)	0.64	1.49
Error	Nearly hit a cyclist	0.40 (± 0.65)	0.31	1.38
Error	Fail to notice pedestrians	0.36 (± 0.57)	0.45	1.65
Error	Overtake right turner	0.23 (± 0.47)	0.29	1.44
Error	Miss Give Way sign	0.19 (± 0.43)	0.23	1.31

Note: 1. The item "drive off in 3rd gear" was dropped due to inconsistent interpretation. 2. Violation = ordinary violation, Aggressive = aggressive violation.

Factor 1, labelled Errors, accounted for 18.0% of the variance and consisted of six errors, one aggressive violation and one lapse. Factor 2 (Violations Factor) contained 6.9% of the variance and consisted of four violations, and one aggressive violation. The third factor, labelled Lapses, accounted for 5.6% of the variance and was comprised of four lapses and two errors. The fourth factor, labelled Aggressive Violations, consisted solely of aggressive violations and contained 5.4% of the variance.

Table 3. The factor structure and loadings of DBQ items.

Behaviour	*DBQ*	*Errors*	*Viol*	*Lapse*	*Aggres*
Nearly hit the car in front	E	.654			
Miss "Give Way" signs	E	-.617*			
Force your way into traffic	A	.572			
Fail to notice pedestrians	E	-.540*			
Overtake right turner	E	-.512*			
Fail to check your mirrors	E	.489			
Get into the wrong lane	L	.410			
Nearly hit a cyclist	E	-.410*			
Speed on a residential road	V		.770		
Speed on the open road	V		.710		
Close following	V		.621		
Race away from lights	A		.428		
Shoot (run) traffic lights	V		.404		
"Wake up" on journey	L			-.616*	
Underestimate another's speed	E			.575	
No recollection of journey	L			.567	
Brake too quickly	E			.560	
Switch on wrong thing	L			.490	
Take wrong exit	L			.490	
Indicate hostility	A				.704
Sound your horn	A				.676
Give chase	A				-.557*

* = variables transformed by reflection

It is interesting to note that Factor 4 contains only the aggressive violations which had to do with expressing hostility towards another driver. The three remaining aggressive violations, which had to do with aggressive driving, did not load on this factor. This finding is consistent with Lawton et al.'s (1997) findings and is in line with Chapman et al.'s (in press) factor three. These three findings together provide evidence that the items measuring expressions of anger or hostility are actually a separate entity from the rest of the scale.

Correlations

The relationships between crash involvement and the main variables were initially examined through the calculation of Pearson's Product Moment Correlation Coefficients (see Table 4). Table 4 shows that those who reported having had a crash in the previous 3 year period were more likely to be younger ($p < .001$), have less experience driving trucks ($p < .05$) and tended to have higher scores on the violations factor ($p < .001$).

The finding that age was significantly negatively correlated with the number of crashes reported in the previous 3 year period is in agreement with previous research (Reason et al., 1990; Parker et al., 1995a; West et al., 1993), as it means that it is the younger drivers who experience more crashes than older drivers. Years experience driving trucks was also negatively related to number of crashes reported in the last 3 years, meaning that more experienced drivers were less likely to have had a crash in the previous 3 year period than their less experienced counterparts. However, the finding that mileage was not related to having had a crash did not agree with previous research. This finding is somewhat surprising, but could be in part due to the fact that professional truck drivers have a relatively homogeneous annual mileage when compared with the general public. A second possible explanation, which Dimmer (2000) used to explain a similar finding, is the operation of some kind of ceiling effect. It is possible that there is a level of exposure to risk (annual mileage) at which no further exposure would increase that individual's chances of being crash involved.

Again in agreement with previous research (e.g. Parker et al., 1995a; Meadows et al., 1998; West et al., 1993) was the finding that only the violations factor score was significantly correlated with the number of crashes reported in the previous 3 years. Those drivers who report engaging in violations more often also report being involved in more crashes.

Table 4. Correlations with Number of Reported Crashes.

Variable	*Correlation*
Age	-0.209***
Mileage	0.068
Year experience	-0.129*
Speed preference	0.045
Errors	-0.017
Lapses	0.074
Violations	0.191***
Aggressive violations	0.005

*p< .05; **p< .01; ***p< .001; Years experience = years experience driving trucks; Preferred Speed = a combination of the four speed items.

Prediction

Finally, hierarchical logistic regression was performed to identify which of the DBQ factor scores significantly improved the prediction of crashes beyond that afforded by knowledge of demographic and background variables. The dependent variable was recoded into a dichotomous variable - not being crash involved and being crash involved within the previous 3 year period. The demographic variables were entered into the regression prior to the factor scores.

Each factor score (from the factor analysis of the DBQ data) was separately analysed by individually entering them into the regression after the demographic and background variables to find out whether it significantly added to the prediction of the crash involvement. In line with previous research (e.g. Parker et al., 1995a; Parker et al., 1995b), the violation factor was a strong predictor of whether a driver would be crash involved or not (beta = 0.4072, Wald = 8.7894, $p < .01$). The only other significant predictor of crash involvement was the drivers age (beta = -.0550, Wald = 5.0607, $p < .05$).

Table 5. Summary statistics for the prediction of crashes over previous 3 year period.

Block		*Model chi-square improvement*	*%Correctly classified*	*B*	*Wald*	*Exp (B)*
1	Mileage	3.276	62.11	.000005	3.2423	1.00
2	Age	17.599	65.26	-.0550	5.0607*	0.9465
2	Sex			-4.4501	0.1086	0.0117
2	Truck type			0.0269	0.0338	1.0272
2	Experience			0.0183	0.5396	1.0184
2	Speed			0.0200	0.1394	1.0202
2	Load			-0.0174	0.0209	0.9828
2	Employee			0.2468	2.2507	1.2799
3	Violations factor	26.719**	63.86	0.4072	8.7894**	1.5027

$^*p < .05$; ** $p < .01$ ***; $p < .001$

Conclusions

These findings indicate that New Zealand truck drivers engage in a relatively low level of aberrant driving behaviours. Despite these very low levels and the very different demographic and background variables, the factor solution produced here was very similar to the hypothetical four factor structure. The violations factor was found to be a significant predictor of crash involvement over the previous three year period. These findings indicate that the predictive strength of the violations factor remains despite the differences in culture, demographics, background variables, and vehicle types. These findings also suggest that in order to reduce the accident liability of New Zealand truck drivers, it is necessary to focus on the truck driver's attitudes and beliefs which underpin violating behaviour. Future research should investigate what these attitudes and beliefs are, and how they can be changed.

References

Åberg, L., & Rimmö, P. (1998). Dimensions of aberrant driver behaviour. *Ergonomics, 41*, 39-56.

Blockey, P.N., & Hartley, L.R. (1995). Aberrant driving behaviour: Errors and violations. *Ergonomics, 38*, 1759-1771.

Chapman, P., Roberts, K., & Underwood, G. (2000). A study of the accidents and behaviours of company car drivers. Manuscript submitted for publication.

Dimmer, A. (2000). Personal Communication.

Dimmer, A.R., & Parker, D. (1999). The accidents, attitudes and behaviour of company car drivers. In G.B. Grayson (Ed.) *Behavioural Research in Road Safety IX*. Crowthorne: Transport Research Laboratory.

Lawton, R., Parker, D., Manstead, A.S.R., & Stradling, S.G. (1997). The role of affect in predicting social behaviours: The case of road traffic violations. *Journal of Applied Social Psychology, 27*, 1258-1276.

Lynn, P., & Lockward, C. R. (1998). *The accident liability of company car drivers*. (TRL Report 317). Crowthorne; Transport Research Laboratory.

Meadows, M.L., Stradling, S.G. & Lawson, S. (1998). The role of social deviance and violations in predicting road traffic accidents in a sample of young offenders. *British Journal of Psychology, 89,* 417-431.

Parker, D., Lajunen, T., & Stradling, S. (1998). Attitudinal predictors of interpersonally aggressive violations on the road. *Transportation Research Part F, 1*, 11-24.

Parker, D., Reason, J.T., Manstead, A.R.S. & Stradling, S.G. (1995a). Driving errors, driving violations and accident involvement. *Ergonomics, 38,* 1036-1048.

Parker, D., West, R.J., Stradling, S.G. & Manstead, A.R.S. (1995b). Behavioural characteristics and involvement in different types of traffic accident. *Accident Analysis and Prevention, 27,* 571-581.

Reason, J., Manstead, A., Stradling, S., Baxter, J. & Campbell, K. (1990). Errors and violations on the roads: A real distinction? *Ergonomics, 33,* 1315-1332.

Stradling, S.G., Parker, D., Lajunen, T., Meadows, M.L., & Xie, C.Q. (1998). Normal behaviour and traffic safety: Violations, errors, lapses and crashes. Available: http://millemiglia.ce.unipr.it/ARGO/theysay/urban/.

Walton, D. (1999a). Examining the self-enhancement bias: Professional truck drivers' perceptions of speed, safety, skill and consideration. *Transportation Research Part F, 2*, 91-113.

Walton, D. (1999b). Mixed messages. *The Transportant, 28* (5), 20-23.

West, R., Elander, J.. & French, D. (1993). Mild social deviance, Type-A behaviour pattern and decision-making style as predictors of self-reported driving style and traffic accident risk. *British Journal of Psychology, 84*, 207-219.

Traffic and Transport Psychology,
T. Rothengatter and R.D. Huguenin (Editors)

14

Anger and Aggression in Driving and Non-Driving Contexts

Peter R. Chapman, Jane Evans, David E. Crundall and Geoffrey Underwood

Introduction

A series of recent surveys and press reports have suggested that anger and aggression are common features of driving in contemporary Britain. One survey reported that 90% of motorists questioned had experienced at least one "road rage" incident in the previous year (Automobile Association, 1995). It is important in such surveys to distinguish between occasions where a driver simply became angry, and those where the driver actually acted in an aggressive manner (Ward, Waterman & Joint, 1998). For example, the Lex Report on Motoring (1996) claimed that 44% of drivers questioned had suffered verbal or gesticulatory abuse in the past 12 months from other drivers and that 9% of drivers had been forced to pull off the road because of aggressive driving by others. As well as being the recipients of aggressive acts, surprisingly high numbers of drivers admit to committing aggressive driving behaviours themselves. A study by Parker, Lajunen and Stradling (1998) found that 89% of 270 drivers admitted sometimes committing aggressive violations such as chasing other drivers, indicating hostility to other drivers, or sounding the horn to indicate annoyance with other drivers.

In an attempt to explain differential accident liability rates, researchers have focused upon drivers' self-reported failures while driving. On common method for recording and classifying such failures is the Driver Behaviour Questionnaire (DBQ) devised by Reason, Manstead, Stradling, Baxter and Campbell (1990). Numerous studies have indicated that the key components from this questionnaire in terms of predicting accident likelihood tend to be deliberate violations of traffic law, rather than other errors or lapses. Parker, West, Stradling and Manstead (1995) postulate that it is reasonable to expect such a finding since young males who are consistently over-involved in accidents also report the highest frequency of violations. Blockley and Hartley (1995) found a high DBQ violations score to be correlated with the number of speeding convictions that a person reports having. Recent studies have explored the violation factor in more detail (Lawton, Parker, Manstead, & Stradling, 1997; Parker, Lajunen & Stradling, 1998). These studies suggest that the violation factor can be usefully decomposed into those that involve clear aggressive intent towards other road users (e.g. how often do you sound your horn to indicate your annoyance to another road user) and those without such intent (e.g. how often do you disregard the speed limit on a motorway).

Another way of exploring the nature of driving anger in greater detail is provided by the Deffenbacher et al. (1994) Driving Anger Scale (DAS). Analysis of responses allow researchers to determine which of the six factors of the scale: 'discourtesy', 'hostile gestures', 'slow driving', 'traffic obstructions', 'police presence' and 'illegal driving' are most associated with the experience of anger in drivers. In addition to the questionnaire measure to assess causes of anger, the study also addresses the question of the possible effect of traffic congestion on anger intensity. Heavy traffic density blocks goal directed activity and this has been demonstrated to be a cause of anger (Izard, 1991, Lazarus, 1982, Rule & Percival, 1971, Mabel, 1994).

A recent study (Underwood et al., 1999) explored the relationships between the DAS, DBQ, frequency of near-accidents while driving, and the reporting of anger on the roads. This study progressed beyond questionnaires alone in eliciting reports of anger and near-accidents using a diary study approach. This allows the reporting of such events much sooner after their occurrence and allows greater detail about such incidents to be recorded. Exploring near-accidents rather than actual accidents has the advantage that the frequency of such incidents is comparable to the frequency of anger experienced while driving, however it is particularly important to obtain such reports as soon as possible after the event because of evidence for rapid forgetting of such events (Chapman & Underwood, 2000). The original study focused on driving anger as distinct from aggression, and respondents were not asked directly about their experience of aggression from other road users, or their own aggressive acts. However, respondents were asked whether their experience of anger affected their driving in any way. Initially we had chosen not to code these data because of the open-ended nature of this questions. However, upon re-examining the transcripts of respondents' driving experiences, it was apparent that on many occasions our drivers were spontaneously reporting their own aggressive acts. To understand more about the relationship between anger and aggression on the roads, this paper starts with an extension of the Underwood et al. (1999) study to include an analysis of aggression. This is referred to below as Study 1. For purposes of comparison some of the key results from the original (1999) analysis will also be included. Two further studies which explore the relationship between anger and aggression directly are then reported.

Study 1

Method

Participants: These were 100 regular drivers. Of these 48 were male and 52 were female, and their ages ranged from 17 to 42 years (mean 23 years). Their driving experience ranged from being in their first year of driving to having been driving for 11 years (mean 3 years). Participants were paid £10 for taking part in the study.

Procedure: Data from two questionnaires are reported here. The 33 item version of the Driving Anger Scale (Deffenbacher et al., 1994) was used with minor modifications to clarify items for a British sample. A shortened version of the Driver Behaviour Questionnaire (Reason et al., 1990) was used. This version contained 18 items, consisting of six violations, six errors, and six lapses. Once participants had completed the questionnaires and provided basic demographic information they were issued with a microcassette recorder and instruction card and the procedure was explained to them. For the next two weeks they kept the recorder and card in the glove compartment of their car. Each time they completed a car journey they turned on the recorder and described details of the journey and answered a series of specific questions about incidents of near accidents, anger or aggression.

Results and discussion

Detailed results and the data from questionnaire analyses and a near-accident typology are available in Underwood et al. (1999). Here we will present a few of the key findings, followed by additional results and analyses relating to the drivers reports of aggressive acts after experiencing anger. Overall the diary technique was extremely successful in eliciting a rich and detailed description of the typical experiences of these drivers over a two-week period. In total 1778 journeys described, including 293 reports of near-accidents. A total of 383 incidents of anger were reported. This corresponds to anger being experienced on 21.5% of the journeys reported.

There was a significant correlation between anger and near-accidents, $r(98) = .500$, showing that the types of people who reported most anger, also reported more near-accidents. This relationship remained strong and significant even when exposure and reporting differences are accounted for, either by partially out the number of journeys made, $r(97) = .430$, or the total mileage driven, r(97)=0.437, or the number of incidents of courtesy reported, $r(97) = .497$. The latter method has the particular strength of controlling, not only for the amount of driving done, but also for the general tendency of drivers to report incidents reliably. However, on re-examining the raw data it was clear that claiming a causal link between anger and near-accidents would be inappropriate. In many cases it appeared that anger was being caused by being involved in a near-accident. When the 142 cases where anger immediately followed a near-accident were removed from the data, the correlation was dramatically reduced and no longer significant, $r(98) = .161$. A further analysis of these cases revealed that the type of accident played an important role in determining this relationship. For the purposes of this analysis near-accidents were divided into those where the driver admitted that near-accident was completely their own fault, and those where they claimed that the near-accident was definitely not their fault. When this is done there is a significant correlation between at-fault near-accidents and reports of anger, $r(98) = .273$, but no significant correlation for near-accidents where the driver felt that they were not at fault, $r(98) = .108$. The frequency of reporting this anger was also correlated significantly with score on the DBQ violations factor, $r(98) = .283$, and lapses factor, $r(98) = .200$, and on the overall DAS score, $r(98) = .208$, but particularly the DAS hostile gestures factor, $r(98) = .322$.

After reporting any incidents of anger, drivers were asked to report whether this affected their driving in any way, giving details. Respondents were not completely reliable in answering this question, one some occasions they gave no details at all, while on other occasions they simply responded "yes" or "no" and provided no further details. On other occasions they gave general descriptions such as "wrote it down to experience", or "I probably drove a bit more carefully afterwards". However when these data were examined in detail it became clear that there were 65 occasions where anger was spontaneously reported as leading to an aggressive act. In order of frequency these 65 acts were as broken down as follows: 20 speeding, 8 blowing horn, 6 tailgating another vehicle, 6 blocking another driver, 6 slowing down to annoy driver behind, 5 aggressively overtaking, 3 hand gestures, 3 flashing lights, 2 chasing other vehicle, and 6 other aggressive acts where insufficient detail was provided to categorise the incident, e.g. "I made sure that the other driver was aware just how angry I was".

Considering only these 65 incidents of aggression, many of the analyses performed on the anger data were repeated. The overall frequency of aggression was found to be significantly correlated with the number of near accidents where the driver admitted being at fault, $r(98) = .398$, the score on the DAS hostile gestures factor, $r(98) = .368$, and the DAS police presence factor, $r(98) = .260$, and the score on the DBQ violations factor, $r(98) = .237$. No significant relationship emerged with measures of driving experience, age or gender. Clearly this pattern is similar to that observed when occasions of anger were analysed. One possibility is that, because aggression was only reported when anger had already occurred, these relationships are inevitably the same as those observed for the anger. A more interesting question may be how likely an individual driver is to behave aggressively given that they have already experienced anger. For the purposes of this analysis the 30 drivers who never reported anger were removed from the data. For the remaining 70 drivers, the probability that they behaved aggressively, given that they had felt angry was calculated. Thus a driver who felt angry just once, and behaved aggressively on that occasion would receive a score of 1, while a driver who experienced ten occasions of anger, but only behaved aggressively on one occasion would receive a score of 0.1. The resulting probability of aggression given anger was significantly correlated with the number of near accidents where the driver admitted being at fault, $r(68) = .257$, the score on the DAS hostile gestures factor, $r(68) = .337$, and the DAS police presence factor, $r(68) = .272$, and the score on the DBQ violations factor, $r(68) = .234$. Once again there were no significant correlations with measures of driving experience, age or gender.

These analyses revealed extremely high incidences of both anger and aggression. Overall our respondents reported feeling anger on 21.5% of their journeys, and spontaneously reported that these feelings of anger caused them to commit aggressive acts on 17.0% of occasions. It should be noted that this second figure almost certainly represents an underestimate of the true frequency with which feelings of anger in driving lead to aggressive acts. We did not directly ask respondents to report aggressive acts, and it is likely that if they had been directly cued to report aggression this figure would have been even higher. It should also be noted that this study makes no record of aggressive acts which drivers may commit without any previous feeling of anger. Nonetheless we were extremely surprised at the frequency with which aggression was reported. When correlations with accident involvement and other measures of anger and violations were considered, these measures of aggressive acts seemed to behave in a similar way to reports of anger. While this strengthens the case that anger and aggression in driving are important correlates of accident involvement it also raises the questions of whether it is anger or aggression which is the more important problem. One possibility is that occasions of anger are a natural and normal part of everyday life. The key point about 'road rage' may not be that drivers get angry, but that they have the opportunity to express their anger in aggressive acts when they are driving rather than in other everyday contexts. The remaining studies explore this possibility.

Study 2

In the previous study aspects of both the DAS and the DBQ were found to related to the frequency of reporting anger while driving, and both the frequency and likelihood of this anger leading to occasions of aggression. Of course the DAS is a measure of internal feelings "how angry would you feel if", while the DBQ is a measure of self-reported behaviour "how often do you". It might have been expected that the DAS would relate more closely to reports of anger, while the DBQ would be correlated with aggression rather than anger. The nature of the previous study, with aggression only reported when linked with anger, may have prevented any such distinction emerging, however, these scales provide an interesting opportunity to distinguish between reports of anger and aggression. Our aim in Study 2 was to see whether it would be possible to extend these scales for use in non-driving contexts. This was intended to provide a way of exploring the possibility that aggression rather than anger might be particularly typical of driving situations.

Method

Participants. These were 71 drivers (33 female, 38 male), with a mean age of 21.4 years. All had held their full British driving licence for at least one year.

Materials / Procedure. All participants filled in three questionnaires, a 24 item anger questionnaire based on the DAS, a 15 item aggression questionnaire based on the DBQ, and the 29 item aggression questionnaire used by Buss & Perry (1992). The first two questionnaires were adapted to include matched items from driving and non-driving contexts.

Examples from the revised DAS were as follows:

Please rate how much anger would you feel in the following situations?
Someone in a car in front of you is slow in parking and is holding up the traffic.
Whilst on the roads someone is weaving in and out of traffic.
Someone takes an excessively long time with a bank clerk while you are waiting in the queue.
Someone runs past you and knocks you without apologising.

Examples from the revised DBQ were as follows:

Please indicate how often, if at all, you have acted in the following ways over a period of about the last year.

1. When driving along race oncoming vehicles for a one car gap on a narrow or obstructed road.
2. Have an aversion to a particular type of road user and indicate your hostility by any means you can.
3. Barge past people in a busy shop who get in your way.

4. Have a dislike for a particular type of person which you have no qualms about expressing.

In each case the first two examples refer to driving situations taken from the original questionnaire, while the final two refer to similar everyday situations. A pilot study revealed that respondents found some of the examples from everyday contexts implausible. Once these items were removed, the final questionnaires contained 13 driving anger items, 11 everyday anger items, 8 driving aggression items, and 7 non-driving aggression items. The revised DAS was answered on a five-point scale ranging from 1, none at all, to 5, very much, and the revised DBQ used a scale ranging from 1, never, to 5, nearly all the time.

Results and discussion

Table 1 shows the mean ratings and standard errors of the respondents for anger items (from the revised DAS) and aggression items (from the revised DBQ) divided into those items which were related to driving situations and those that referred to other non-driving contexts. For the revised DAS items respondents gave significantly higher ratings when the items referred to everyday contexts, $t(70) = 4.94$, $p < .01$, while for the revised DBQ items respondents gave significantly higher ratings for driving situations than other everyday contexts, $t(70) = 9.28$, $p < .01$.

Table 1. Mean anger and aggression ratings for driving and everyday situations with associated variances.

	Anger	*(var)*	*Aggression*	*(var)*
Driving	2.79	(0.26)	2.06	(0.49)
Everyday	3.20	(0.30)	1.72	(0.49)

To compare these results with a more standard instrument, respondents' overall scores for anger and aggression in driving and everyday situations were correlated with the four factors previously identified on Buss and Perry's (1992) aggression questionnaire. These correlations are given in Table 2.

Table 2. Correlations between the four factors on Buss and Perry's (1992) aggression questionnaire and overall scores on the modified DBQ and DAS for both driving and everyday events, $n = 71$, all correlations are significant ($p < .05$) except that between verbal aggression and driving anger.

	Scores on Buss & Perry (1992) Aggression Questionnaire			
	verbal	*physical*	*anger*	*hostility*
Driving Aggression	0.261	0.603	0.479	0.258
Everyday Aggression	0.285	0.465	0.394	0.330
Driving Anger	0.176	0.389	0.452	0.310
Everyday Anger	0.253	0.294	0.383	0.375

As would be expected the DBQ scores generally correlate more strongly than the DAS scores with the Buss and Perry verbal and physical aggression factors, although the pattern for anger and hostility is less clear. In general correlations with both questionnaires are particularly strong with physical aggression, and lower with verbal aggression. This seems to reflect the non-verbal nature of most of the driving situations used in both the DAS and DBQ. Particularly noteworthy is the very high correlation between driving aggression and physical aggression on the Buss and Perry questionnaire. This latter factor consists of a series of nine items which are broadly about getting into fights, for example "once in a while I can't control the urge to strike another person" and "if someone hits me, I hit back". Consistent with Buss and Perry (1992) we found significant gender differences in both verbal and physical aggression, but not in anger (there was a marginal difference, $p = .07$, on the hostility factor). It is thus perhaps surprising that we found no hint of gender differences in any of the four new scales.

Although the results from Study 2 are consistent with our expectations that driving situations are particularly likely to evoke aggressive acts, there are certain clear limitations to the study. One problem is the difficulty in ensuring that driving and everyday items are appropriately matched. There are many driving situations for which it is extremely difficult to come up with plausible matched everyday scenarios; although we attempted to remove these from the questionnaires, it is still possible that the results partly reflect the researchers' ingenuity (or lack thereof) in devising appropriate everyday anger and aggression items. A more serious problem is the nature of the DBQ and DAS in terms of the response formats required. The DBQ is essentially a behavioural frequency report, in that it requires respondents to remember how often they have committed certain acts. In contrast the DAS asks respondents to imagine how much emotion they would feel in certain hypothetical situations. Behavioural frequency reports are notoriously subject to distortion in memory (Chapman & Underwood, 2000) and by the way in which a question is phrased (e.g. Wright, Gaskell & O'Muircheartaigh, 1997). While the DAS items are less likely to be distorted by memory effects, they are probably even more sensitive to the precise wording of questions. It would thus be preferable to ensure that both anger and aggression questions are phrased similarly and asked as soon as possible after the relevant events. Study 3 is a brief pilot study which explores a methodology for doing this.

Study 3

Method

This brief study consisted of a series of 40 structured interviews which were conducted outside a busy supermarket. Drivers were interviewed between 4:45pm and 6:45pm on weekdays - times when both the supermarket and the roads approaching it were likely to be particularly busy. Half the participants were interviewed on their way into the supermarket, having just completed their drive to the supermarket, and half on their way out, having just completed their shopping. Respondents were simply asked whether anything on their drive to the supermarket / trip around the supermarket had made them feel angry, and whether they had displayed their anger in any way. If their answer to either question was yes, they were asked to describe exactly what had made them feel angry or how they had displayed their anger. Respondents also made an anger rating on a five-point scale. The structure and timing of the questions was identical for both groups of respondents, the only difference was whether the questions referred to the respondents' shopping trip, or to their drive to the supermarket.

Results and discussion

This pilot study consisted of only 40 interviews, and in the vast majority of cases respondents reported neither feeling anger nor acting aggressively. The possible analysis is thus extremely limited, however, the raw frequencies of reporting feeling anger and acting aggressively are given in Table 3.

Table 3. The number of drivers reporting having felt angry, when either driving to the supermarket, or when shopping, and the numbers who reported acting aggressively as a result of this anger. The maximum in each cell would be 20.

	Driving	*Shopping*
Felt Angry	5	4
Acted Aggressively	3	0

An example of a situation causing driving anger was "someone pulled out in front of me quickly, so I had to slam on my brakes", and in this case the driver reported showing their anger by swearing at the other driver. An example of anger in the shopping condition was "the supermarket was too busy, and other people kept bumping into me with their trolleys". There were no examples of aggressive acts in the shopping condition. The results in Table 2 suggest that we may have identified an appropriate situation in which anger is roughly equally likely to be experienced in driving and in one other everyday context. The overall high frequency of anger reports (cf. Study 1) probably reflect the immediacy of the reporting and the choice of a particularly busy time at which to conduct the study. The pattern of results also suggests that our intuitions about anger and aggression may be correct - once again it appears that driving is a context in which people are particularly likely to engage in aggressive acts, however, it should be noted that the small numbers of all report types in this pilot study preclude serious analysis.

General Discussion

The first and most noteworthy conclusions from this research are concerned with the high frequency of both anger and aggression in everyday driving. Study 1 respondents reported feeling anger on 21.5% of their journeys, a figure which is broadly comparable with the 25% of Study 3 respondents reporting anger on that particular journey. Study 1 drivers spontaneously reported that these feelings of anger caused them to commit aggressive acts on 17.0% of occasions. This is considerably lower than an estimate based on the three out of five occasions in Study 3 where driving anger was expressed. However it was noted in the discussion of Study 1 that the 17.0% figure almost certainly represents an underestimate of the true frequency with which feelings of anger in driving lead to aggressive acts. The high frequency of aggression arising from feelings of driver anger may thus suggest a direct causal explanation for the significant correlations between driving anger and accident rates reported in Underwood et al. (1999). This strengthens the case that making driving more pleasant, in terms of removing potential sources of frustration, and hence anger, may actually reduce accident rates. However, the other suggestion from this research is that it may not be anger, but aggression which is the surprising feature about contemporary driving. Studies 2 and 3 lend support to the idea that anger may be relatively common in many areas of everyday life. The unusual feature about driving may be that this is a situation in which people are particularly likely to commit aggressive acts.

Possible reasons for the high incidence of aggression in driving situations are not hard to find. Obvious factors in the driving environment which are not present in other everyday situations include the anonymity and perceived safety provided by being in a vehicle, and the physical power provided by the vehicle. Although a focus on reducing aggression rather than anger changes the types of intervention which would be considered, it should be noted that all the aggression reported Studies 1 and 3 was as a direct result of feelings of anger. Although aggression, rather than anger, may be the key feature of 'road rage', interventions focusing at either the reduction of anger on the roads, or on the possibility of expressing this anger may be equally effective in reducing accident rates.

References

Automobile Association (1995). *Road Rage*. The Automobile Association. Road Safety Unit: Basingstoke, U.K.

Blockley, P. N., & Hartley, L. R. (1995). Aberrant driving behaviour: errors and violations. *Ergonomics, 38*, 1759-1771.

Buss, A. H., & Perry, M. (1992). The aggression questionnaire. *Journal of Personality and Social Psychology, 63,* 452-459.

Chapman, P., & Underwood, G. (2000). Forgetting near-accidents: The roles of severity, culpability and experience in the poor recall of dangerous driving situations. *Applied Cognitive Psychology, 14,* 31-44.

Deffenbacher, J. L., Oetting, E. R., & Lynch, R. S. (1994). Development of a driving anger scale. *Psychological Reports, 74*, 83-91.

Gulian, E., Matthews, G., Glendon, A. I., Davies, D. R., & Debney, L. M. (1989). Dimensions of driver stress. *Ergonomics, 32,* 585-602.

Izard, C.E. (1991). *The psychology of emotions.* New York: Plenum Press.

Junger, M., Terlouw, G., & van der Heijden, P. (1994). Crime and accident involvement in young road users. In G. Grayson (Ed.) *Behavioural Research in Road Safety V.* Crowthorne: Transport Research Laboratory.

Lawton, R., Parker, D., Manstead, A. S. R., & Stradling, S. G. (1997). The role of affect in predicting social behaviours: the case of road traffic violations. *Journal of Applied Social Psychology, 27*, 1258-1276.

Lazarus, R. S. (1982). Thoughts on the relations between emotion and cognition. *American Psychologist, 37*, 1019-1024.

Lex (1996). *The Lex Report on Motoring.* London: Lex Service plc.

Mabel, S. (1994). Empirical determination of anger provoking characteristics intrinsic to anger provoking circumstances. *Journal of Social and Clinical Psychology, 13*, 174-188.

Matthews, G., & Desmond, P. (1995) Stress as a factor in the design of in-car driving enhancement systems. *Le Travail Humain, 58*, 109-129.

Maycock G., & Lockwood, J.R . (1993). The accident liability of British car drivers. *Transport Reviews, 13,* 213-245.

Parker, D., West, R., Stradling, S., & Manstead, A. S. R. (1995). Behavioural characteristics and involvement in different types of traffic accident. *Accident Analysis and Prevention, 27,* 571-581.

Parker, D., Lajunen, T., & Stradling, S. (1998). Attitudinal predictors of interpersonally aggressive violations on the road. *Transportation Research Part F, 1,* 11-24.

Reason, J., Manstead, A. S. R., Stradling, S., Baxter, J & Campbell, K. (1990). Errors and violations on the road: a real distinction? *Ergonomics, 33,* 1315-1332.

Rule, B. G., & Percival, E. (1971). The effects of frustration and attack on physical aggression. *Journal of Experimental Research in Personality, 5,* 111-118.

Suchman, E. (1970). Accidents and social deviance. *Journal of Health and Social Behaviour, 11*, 4-15.

Underwood, G., Chapman, P., Wright, S., & Crundall, D. (1997) Estimating accident liability. In J.A. Rothengatter and E. Carbonell Vaya (Eds.), *Traffic and Transport Psychology.* Oxford: Pergamon.

Underwood, G., Chapman, P., Wright, S., & Crundall, D. (1999) Anger while driving. *Transportation Research Part F, 2*, 55-68.

Ward, N. J., Waterman, M., & Joint, M. (1998). Rage and violence of driver aggression. In G. B. Grayson (Ed.), *Behavioural research in road safety VIII*, pp. 155-167. Crowthorne, UK: Transport Research Laboratory.

West, R, Elander, J., & French, D. (1993). Mild social deviance, type-A behaviour pattern and decision-making style as predictors of self-reported driving style and traffic accident risk. *British Journal of Psychology, 84*, 207-219.

Wright, D. B., Gaskell, G. D., & O'Muircheartaigh, C. A. (1997). How response alternatives affect different kinds of behavioural frequency questions. *British Journal of Social Psychology, 36*, 443-456.

Traffic and Transport Psychology,
T. Rothengatter and R.D. Huguenin (Editors)

15

Abusing the Roadway "Commons": Understanding Aggressive Driving Through an Environmental Preservation Theory

Bryan E. Porter and Thomas D. Berry

"Ruin is the destination toward which all men rush, each pursuing his own best interest in a society that believes in the freedom of the commons. Freedom in a commons brings ruin to all" Hardin (1968, p. 1244).

Driving Aggression

Enough has appeared in recent media and scientific literature to make it clear that aggression on the roadways is a growing interest to society. Driving aggressively, thought by typical safety officials to include tailgating, weaving, speeding, red light running, gesturing angrily, or in the extreme using a vehicle as a weapon (Porter & Berry, 1998) is not a recent phenomenon. In fact, Novaco (1991) found relevant research papers from the 1960s and several other works published in the following decades. What seems new, however, is the increasing emphasis that the traffic-safety community places on roadway aggression and the efforts to find personal and contextual predictors of the behaviour.

The new emphasis was evident in a recent Presidential Address of the International Association of Applied Psychology's Traffic and Transport Psychology division (Shinar, 1998). It was also evident in recent empirical investigations of attitudes, intention, stress, and traffic congestion predictors of aggressive driving (Hennessy & Wiesenthal, 1997; Parker, Lajunen & Stradling, 1998). Finally, it was evident in the convening of the Aggression symposium at the 2000 International Conference of Traffic and Transport Psychology (ICTTP). However, it should be noted that there are still disagreements concerning definitions of aggressive driving, despite the growing interest in the issue. Novaco (1991) and the American Automobile Association through its sponsorships of related research (i.e., Mizell, 1997) would suggest aggressive driving is only the most extreme case of driving behaviour with intent to harm others (i.e., "road rage"). Other authors and groups, such as Shinar (1998) and the Insurance Institute for Highway Safety in the United States (Williams, 1997), include other behaviours not often linked with intention to harm others. For instance, red light running was a focus of these authors.

The dispute over the meaning and prevalence of aggressive driving is not trivial. Legislation to outlaw aggressive driving is unlikely without a clear definition, nor are successful interventions likely to be designed to reduce it. Our peers who presented papers at the Aggression symposium during the ICTTP conference helped shed more light on the defining characteristics of aggression driving. What we offered during the symposium was a systematic theory to understand contextual causes of reckless driving behaviour, intentional or otherwise, that may lead to aggressive actions. This chapter presents our viewpoint.

The "Commons"

In 1968 Garrett Hardin published a seminal article entitled "The Tragedy of the Commons" (Hardin, 1968). As he argued, the tragedy lay in abusing our commons, or the public lands and spaces that we share as a society. Historically, the commons have been considered rivers and streams, farmland and natural resources. As community members, our survival and well-being depend upon shared coal, gasoline, foodstuffs, fresh water, and clean air. These commons, our shared resources, become abused by overpopulation.

Overpopulation is at the root of commons abuse because more and more societal members want their share of the public's wealth. There are likely finite amounts of resources, and these resources are required to support an ever-growing population. Granted, populations and resource stores differ by country, but the general principle applies: overpopulation will create shortages because there will not be enough resources to share. Hardin further argued that we should not count on technology to save us. Technology in agriculture, for example, has had great success in producing bigger yields, but some of the latest techniques with genetically altered food are controversial (e.g., see Manning, 2000 for a journalist's description of one of the many relevant issues).

Ultimately, abusing the commons becomes tragic because individual needs begin to hurt the societal or common good. Individuals learn that using more than their share increases their gains with minimal expense to themselves. As Hardin (1968) argued, herders sharing graze lands learn that adding one more sheep increases their individual profits at minimal expense (they do not have to buy land for an additional animal, for example). However cumulatively, as more farmers add more sheep to gain maximal profit at minimal expense, the common graze lands are destroyed more quickly. The tragedy of abuse is rooted in the freedom of these individuals to use public space for their own welfare.

The "Common" Roadway

Artificially constructed commons are just as susceptible to abuse (Ruckelshous, 1998). For example, roadways, particularly in the United States, are a commons (Ruckelshous, 1998). They are built and maintained with public funds and are available for the transporting public to share. We travel where we please, when we please, and for the most part how we please. There are rules of the road, of course, but these rules are bent and broken as we use and abuse the roadway commons. Frequent speeding (Boyle, Dienstfrey & Sothoron, 1998), red light running (Porter & England, 2000; Retting & Williams, 1996, Retting, Ulmer & Williams, 1998), and tailgating (Michael, Leeming & Dwyer, 2000) are particular types of abuse seen on the commons. Aggressive speeders, for example, abuse the commons by expecting an open lane in front and create risk by weaving in and out of traffic. Red light runners abuse the commons by delaying other drivers waiting to proceed on a green light and create risk by possibly hitting another vehicle in a deadly crash. Tailgaters abuse the commons by expecting other road users to let them pass, and then create risk by either weaving or being too close to others to stop if an emergency occurs.

Unfortunately, roadway overpopulation may increase the probability of these risky driving behaviours and lead to negative consequences. More frequent crashes, injuries, and fatalities are possible. Further, overpopulation on the roadways will almost assuredly decrease the space we have to transport ourselves to destinations. In fact, as roadway overpopulation increases the more likely each incident of unsafe behaviour will at best delay us and at worst hurt us.

Roadway Overpopulation

In 1997, the United States had 3.92 million miles of roadway (Federal Highway Administration [FHWA], 1996-1998). This was a 2.6% increase above 1980 roadway miles. On the other hand, in 1997 the United States had 202.87 million combined passenger cars (i.e., sedans), light trucks (i.e., sport utility vehicles, or "SUVs"; pickup trucks), heavy trucks (i.e., commercial trucks, truck-based motorhomes) and motorcycles/mopeds that were registered, up 38.6% from 1980 (National Highway Traffic Safety Administration [NHTSA], 1999). Not only were vehicle frequencies increasing on United States' roadways between 1980-1997, these vehicles, on average, were travelling more miles per year. In 1997 a vehicle was driven 12,587 miles on average, which represented a 21.1% increase above the 1980 average.

We created Figure 1 to demonstrate trends in these data over the 1980-1997 time period. Figure 1 simultaneously shows the trends for vehicles per mile of roadway and vehicle miles travelled per vehicle. Each rate consistently increased across the 28 years, indicating United States' roadways are becoming more populated by vehicles that are travelling more each year.

In addition, we analysed these rates by separating out different types of vehicles. Figure 2 compares the number of miles travelled per year by passenger cars, light trucks, heavy trucks, and motorcycles/mopeds. While passenger cars, light trucks, and motorcycles/mopeds have not shown much change over time, heavy trucks have. Specifically, the average annual mileage for heavy trucks has increased 44.2% from 1980 to 1997. The rate for light trucks has actually caught up with the rate for passenger cars, an indication of the growing popularity of these SUVs and pickup trucks in American culture. In fact, Figure 3 shows the growing popularity of light trucks. Specifically, the number of light trucks per mile has increased 118.2% from 1980 to 1997, whereas the rates for the other vehicle types have either levelled off (i.e., passenger cars) or decreased (i.e., heavy trucks and motorcycles/mopeds).

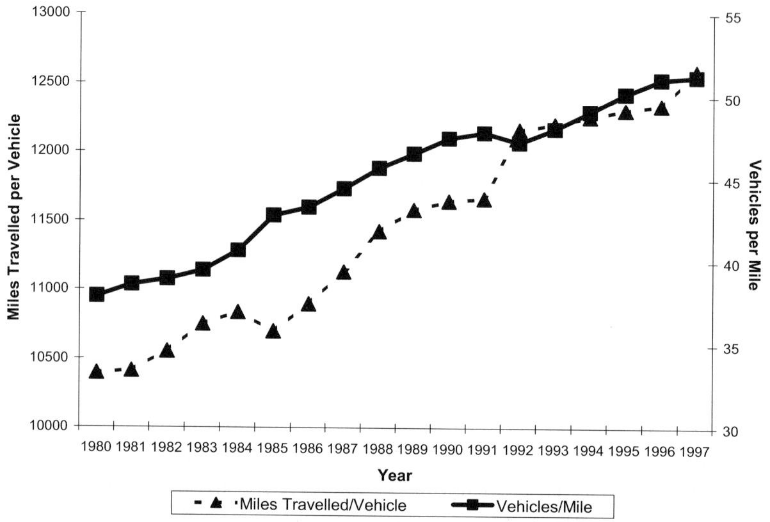

Figure 1. Roadway overpopulation as defined by miles travelled per vehicle and the total number of passenger cars, light trucks, heavy trucks, and motorcycles/mopeds per mile of roadway from 1980-1997.

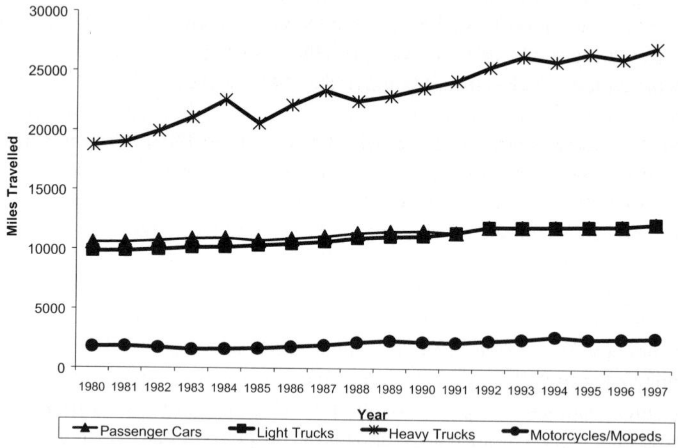

Figure 2. Miles travelled per vehicle type (passenger cars, light trucks, heavy trucks, and motorcycles/mopeds) from 1980-1997.

Figure 2. Miles travelled per vehicle type (passenger cars, light trucks, heavy trucks, and motorcycles/mopeds) from 1980-1997.

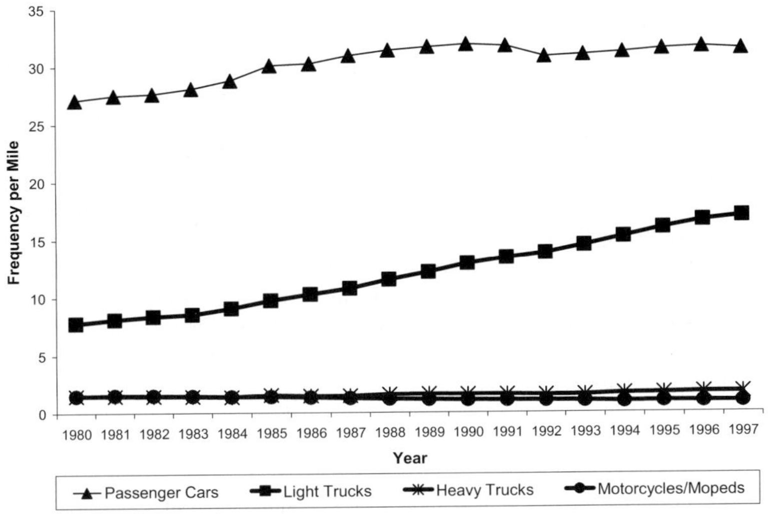

Figure 3. The number of vehicle types (passenger cars, light trucks, heavy trucks, and motorcycles/mopeds) per mile from 1980-1997.

Clearly, the additional vehicles being driven more miles per year on roadway space that is not keeping pace will eventually lead to roadway overpopulation, more congestion, and more costs to public funds. Governments have been forced to build more roads at the expense of other commons projects (even mass transportation projects, which are not well used or developed in most United States' cities). Further, as more light trucks are purchased and increasingly driven, gasoline consumption will increase because these vehicles typically are less fuel efficient. Besides the obvious environmental concern, light trucks may also be contributing to an increase in aggression. They are larger, take up more space, and make it difficult for drivers of passenger vehicles to see the road past them. These additional barriers, including those of general roadway congestion, may contribute to frustration and therefore aggression if drivers are excessively stressed (Berkowitz, 1989).

Saving the Natural Commons

How do we save the commons, whether the goal is to save natural or artificial commons? Hardin (1968) thought focusing on technology and appealing to conscience would fail. Rather, he believed "mutual coercion mutually agreed upon" (p. 1247) would be successful. Specifically, he advocated that individuals in communities should agree upon limits to what can be the commons. Hardin's views have been at times refuted or revised (Crowe, 1969; Edney, 1980), but the basic premise of saving commons by limiting or altering their laissez-faire use seems to have held. Note, however, that overpopulation itself has not been a major focus for intervention. Emphasising birth control to trim overpopulation has been difficult given the political and moral climates of the United States and many other nations. Rather, theorists and policy makers have typically discussed intelligent and managed use of our resources to save the commons.

Intelligent use and management involves balancing economic prosperity and saving resources for future generations. For the environmental commons, accomplishing this feat may be possible by increasing co-operation among users as Edney (1980) suggested. Dwyer, Porter, Leeming, and Oliver (1995), however, have more succinctly summarised Edney's (1980) ideas. Co-operation may be increased when the commons (1) have less value, (2) have not suffered much depletion, and (3) have been divided among users (increasing private interests and responsibility, and shrinking the commons). For users, co-operation may be increased when there (1) are fewer participants, (2) is more friendship among users, (3) are predisposed personalities to co-operate, (4) is a high level of "morality", (5) is prior experience managing commons, (6) is high group communication, (7) is greater amount of public disclosure regarding individuals' use of the commons, and (8) is a greater level of, or probability of, retribution for commons abuse.

Saving the Roadway Commons

Unfortunately, these suggestions for co-operation are not easily applied to roadway commons. For instance, co-operation is not easily accomplished from the commons point of view. Roads have value and have suffered depletion on many fronts, particularly in large urban cities. Further, it is impractical and impossible to divide roadways into individual user's property (although we suppose in some distant future vehicles may drive for us and may be assigned a spot in a roadway queue with specific times to complete trips; this is doubtful if not mandated by government).

Thus, co-operation to save the roadway commons and decrease the likelihood of reckless driving depends upon driver co-operation. This fact gives little hope for the community because co-operation depends on a social agreement or contract. Such agreements are mediated by a process of exchange that is rare among drivers speeding down the highway. In fact, only two of the eight means to increase user co-operation seem viable for the roadway commons: public disclosure of violators and increased likelihood of retribution for misuse. We reached this conclusion after considering the impracticality of other options. For example, if the trends of Figure 1 continue, there will be more vehicles and more driving in the United States, shattering the hope that the commons will have fewer participants. We are also unsure if enough drivers will be friendly or predisposed to co-operate, and even if there are enough such drivers there may be insufficient inter-vehicle communication to assist in reinforcing friendliness and co-operation. Further, how many of us in the United States have experience limiting our driving or having only one vehicle (i.e., experience managing the roadway commons)? Why should we do these things when our neighbours do not likewise limit themselves? Morality is even harder to dictate and control given the diversity of our drivers. Many drivers do not think speed limits are reasonable. Others see no risk when tailgating. Still others do not think breaking traffic laws is criminal behaviour.

Perceived and Real Consequences

Public disclosure of violators and increased retribution are examples of negative consequences for commons abuse. Typical negative consequences applied to the roadway commons are citations for illegal driving. Other negative consequences include increased costs for gasoline because of excessive consumption. Societies could apply positive consequences for good behaviour (i.e., reinforcement) which psychologists know to be more powerful, but most have chosen penalties for illegal or abuse behaviour as more expedient.

Perhaps more powerful than real consequences are perceived ones. What expectations do drivers have for getting caught when speeding or running red lights? Evans (1991) documented that receiving citations or being involved in crashes is rare enough to teach some drivers that there are few if any consequences for reckless driving. Porter and Berry (in press), as a specific example, found that drivers expect most red light runners to escape without consequence. Unless communities successfully increase real and perceived consequences for roadway overpopulation and reckless driving there is no reason to expect to save our transport commons and reduce reckless and aggressive driving.

Increasing Consequences

At this point we will not argue for specific techniques to keep vehicles off the road or to slow purchases of SUVs which consume excessive gasoline and road space. We call upon economists and public policy specialists to assist in these efforts, but it is likely that increased gasoline prices and improved mass transportation with powerful incentives for its use will be needed. Rather, we concentrate our discussion on altering reckless driving behaviours.

Increasing real and perceived consequences for reckless driving and roadway overpopulation is difficult using traditional means. For example, police availability is limited, and thus officers cannot be at all locations at all times to catch any and all speeders and red light runners. Communities need to be creative and at times implement unpopular policies if the roadway commons are to be respected.

One means of applying immediate consequences is to use technology-ironically so, given that Hardin did not believe technology could save us. At least in the driving environment, technology has already shown itself to be important and useful for applying consequences and changing behaviour. Photo red enforcement cameras have been successfully used to reduce red light running more quickly than any other method implemented thus far (see Retting, Williams, Farmer, & Feldman, 1999a,b). Further, Retting et al. (1999a,b) demonstrated that the majority of affected community members favour photo red cameras. Unfortunately for advocates of this technology, politicians hear enough opposition from constituents to keep many localities from using such cameras. In 2000, for example, a bill to expand the use of photo red cameras in the Commonwealth of Virginia (U.S.A.) was passed by the state legislature after several setbacks and debates, only to be vetoed by the governor ("Photo red" traffic light signal enforcement program, SB 414, 2000).

If communities cannot use powerful enforcement technology that applies immediate consequences to all violators -- which creates a powerful perception of consequences -- what are the alternatives? One is to create social norms locality by locality. Evans (1991) argued that mass media programs could create such norms. Another means of creating norms is to develop diffusion interventions with change agents. Essentially, communities could save the commons one person at a time by encouraging individuals to promote the proper behaviour to someone else. Rogers (1995) discussed the many activities of change agents, and the effectiveness of agents has been documented for several different behaviours (e.g., Burn, 1991 for recycling; Geller, 1988 for safety belt use; and Porter, 1998 for fire safety).

Another means of creating norms that has the additional benefit of linking norms to implied consequences is to manipulate rules (Malott, 1989). From the behaviour analysis literature, rules are simple "if-then" contingencies that link a behaviour with its consequence. Laws are the typical means of creating rules, and often work because many people will follow a law when they have a history of following laws or experience with law enforcers. Successful rules also assist in altering perceptions of consequences, and provide the link between a person's behaviour and society's application of a consequence for that behaviour. Of course, if individuals learn that there will be no immediate and contingent consequence to the behaviour, the rule will likely be ineffective (Baum, 1994). This is one reason why behavioural psychology has shown time and again that consequences are important for encouraging and maintaining behaviour, and antecedents such as rules are not likely to be effective alone.

Challenges to Saving the Commons

Saving the roadway commons, and the commons in general, is an enormous task. Our society is struggling with limited resources to address a multitude of problems, of which the commons is only one. Exasperating the problem are general expectations that the commons can be saved quickly, typically by building better roads. Fewer voices in the United States suggest we should reduce our driving and invest more in mass transportation. The lack of resources and the debate surrounding our personal behaviours and presumed freedoms can create such burdens that nothing really gets done and the problem continues to worsen.

We must consider two very important concepts to make a difference for roadway commons and reduce the likelihood of failure: social traps (Platt, 1973) and small wins (Weick, 1984). Social traps reflect the behavioural tendency of choosing immediate over more distant consequences. For example, we are likely to speed because the immediate reinforcement of thrill and arriving more quickly at our destination outweigh distant negative consequences such as less fuel and a shorter lifespan for the vehicle because of greater wear-and-tear. Any effort to reduce roadway overpopulation and aggressive behaviours will need to focus on the immediacy of consequences to change behaviour. Photo red camera enforcement is an example of such an effort.

"Small wins" is the philosophy needed to save the commons in spite of periodic failures and frustrations when attempting to change large-scale behaviours. Specifically, Weick (1984) argued that social problems affecting many people are too big and that failure is imminent. Large problems create such arousal in people that they cannot think as creatively or as clearly to arrive at solutions. Weick argued that success comes from breaking large problems into smaller, more manageable pieces. The smaller problems do not create as much arousal and give people more confidence and hope that solutions can be found. For saving the roadway commons and reducing aggression, small wins philosophy dictates careful selection of reckless behaviours that are of most interest to specific communities. If red light running is a particular problem, then a community should focus its limited resources to reduce it while not trying to change all reckless behaviours at once in all places. Once red light running is successfully altered or under control, then a new problem could be addressed. In such a manner progress can be documented and community members will become more encouraged with their ability to control their environments. Trying to do too much asks for failure.

Conclusions

Commons theory is helpful for understanding our behaviour in public space and with public property, particularly our consumption of such resources. We bring our desire for individual freedom into the public domain, and act as if our choices have no effects on others. However, there are no vacuums in the public domain. Individual choices have public consequences. If we choose to have three vehicles, all SUVs, and drive them as much as we can each year, we would be naïve to believe our behaviour does not influence the commons. Yet, there are individuals who hold such beliefs. There are also many others who do not realise the consequences of free consumption. Either way, society must influence the behaviours of these individuals if we are to have any expectation for commons recovery.

In fact, society -- and for now, we specifically mean the United States -- has two main choices to save the roadway commons. Our leaders can invest a great deal of money to build additional roads to relieve overpopulation. Doing so would hopefully reduce barriers that may create frustration and aggression (Berkowitz, 1989). But, when the frequency of vehicles on the road is increasing nearly 15 times faster than roadway miles are being built, it would take a substantial investment just to catch up with driver demand. Where would this money come from? What other government-supported programs would need to be sacrificed for pavement and destroyed land? Of course, even if enough money were discovered to build roads to meet current demand, by the time they were completed the demand would likely once again have surpassed supply.

The second choice is by far the less popular in American society. It involves interventions to increase immediate consequences for roadway overpopulation and aggression. Camera technology, gas taxes, disincentives for purchasing SUVs and other less efficient vehicles, and similar interventions are involved in this approach. Each of these options tries to counter an immediate reinforcer with an immediate punisher, which leads to the unpopularity (for obvious reasons). Further, even when these solutions are effective, they are more difficult to sell to the public as an alternative to building new roads because they limit individual freedoms to benefit the common good. This option is the epitome of Hardin's "mutual coercion mutually agreed upon" principle, and it is the only choice that allows for realistic small wins and a chance to break social traps. It is the choice we believe is needed to save the roadway commons.

Our recommendation aside, commons theory has shown success and applicability in the management of natural lands and fisheries (Baden & Noonan, 1998). Although it remains to be tested in the roadway commons, we find the theory an intriguing guide for developing interventions to increase driving safety and intelligent roadway use, and reduce aggressive behaviour. Perhaps in time -- and hopefully soon -- such potential can be empirically documented.

References

Baden, J. A., & Noonan, D. S. (Eds.) (1998). *Managing the commons* (2nd ed.). Bloomington, Indiana: Indiana University Press.

Baum, W. M. (1994). *Understanding behaviorism: Science, behaviour, and culture*. New York: Harper-Collins College Publishers.

Berkowitz, L. (1989). Frustration-aggression hypothesis: Examination and reformulation. *Psychological Bulletin, 106*, 59-73.

Boyle, J., Dienstfrey, S., & Sothoron, A. (1998). *National survey of speeding and other unsafe driving actions, Volume II: Driver attitudes and behaviour* (DOT HS 808 749). Washington, DC: U.S. Department of Transportation.

Burn, S. M. (1991). Social psychology and the stimulation of recycling behaviours: The block leader approach. *Journal of Applied Social Psychology, 21*, 611-629.

Crowe, B. L. (1969). The tragedy of the commons revisited. *Science, 166*, 1103-1107.

Dwyer, W. O., Porter, B. E., Leeming, F. C., & Oliver, D. P. (1995). Environmental social psychology. In S. W. Sadava and D. R. McCreary (Eds.), *Applied social psychology* (pp. 228-247). Upper Saddle River, New Jersey: Prentice Hall.

Edney, J. J. (1980). The commons problem: Alternate perspectives. *American Psychologist, 35*, 131-150.

Evans, L. (1991). *Traffic safety and the driver*. New York: Van Nostrand Reinhold.

Federal Highway Administration. [FHWA]. (1996-1998). *Highway statistics series: summary to 1995; 1996; 1997* [On-line]. Washington, DC: U.S. Department of Transportation. Available online: http://www.fhwa.dot.gov/////ohim/ohimstat.htm.

Geller, E. S. (1988). A behavioural science approach to transportation safety. *Bulletin of New York Academy of Medicine, 64*(7), 632-661.

Hardin, G. (1968). The tragedy of the commons. *Science, 162*, 1243-1248.

Hennessy, D. A., & Wiesenthal, D. L. (1997). The relationship between traffic congestion, driver stress and direct versus indirect coping behaviours. *Ergonomics, 40*, 348-361.

Malott, R. W. (1989). The achievement of evasive goals: Control by rules describing contingencies that are not direct acting. In S. C. Hayes et al. (Eds.), *Rule-governed behaviour: Cognition, contingencies, and instructional control* (pp. 269-322). New York: Plenum Press.

Manning, A. (2000, May 4). FDA plans to serve data before biotech food. *USA Today* [On-line]. Available: http://www.usatoday.com/life/health/general/lhgen030.htm.

Michael, P. G., Leeming, F. C., & Dwyer, W. O. (2000). Headway on urban streets: Observational data and an intervention to decrease tailgating. *Transportation Research Part F, 3, 55-64.*

Mizell, L. (1997). *Aggressive driving.* Washington, DC: AAA Foundation for Traffic Safety.

National Highway Traffic Safety Administration [NHTSA]. (1999). *Traffic safety fact 1998* [On-line]. Washington, DC: U.S. Department of Transportation. Available: http://www.nhtsa.dot.gov/people/ncsa/tsf-1998.pdf.

Novaco, R. W. (1991). Aggression on roadways. In R. Baenninger (Ed.), *Targets of violence and aggression* (pp. 253-326). Amsterdam: North-Holland.

Parker, D., Lajunen, T., & Stradling, S. (1998). Attitudinal predictors of interpersonally aggressive violations on the road. *Transportation Research Part F, 1*, 11-24.

"Photo red" traffic light signal enforcement program, Senate Bill 414, Virginia General Assembly, 2000 Sess. (2000).

Platt, J. (1973). Social traps. *American Psychologist, 28*, 641-651.

Porter, B. E. (1998). Predicting active and effective agents for safety: Test of the Actively Caring Approach. *Journal of Safety Research, 29*, 223-233.

Porter, B. E., & Berry, T. D. (1998). *An action report for understanding and reducing aggressive driving and boating*. Norfolk, VA: DRIVE SMART Hampton Roads.

Porter, B. E., & Berry, T. D. (in press). A nationwide self-report survey of red-light running behaviour: Measuring prevalence, predictors, and perceived consequences. *Accident Analysis & Prevention.*

Porter, B. E., & England, K. J. (2000). Predicting red light running behaviour: A traffic safety study in three urban settings. *Journal of Safety Research, 31*, 1-8.

Retting, R. A., Ulmer, R. G., & Williams, A. F. (1998). *Prevalence and characteristics of red light running crashes in the United States*. Arlington, VA: Insurance Institute for Highway Safety.

Retting, R. A., & Williams, A. F. (1996). Characteristics of red light violators: Results of a field investigation. *Journal of Safety Research, 27*, 9-15.

Retting, R. A., Williams, A. F., Farmer, C. M., & Feldman, A. (1999a). Evaluation of red light camera enforcement in Fairfax, Va., USA. *ITE Journal, 69*(8), 30-34.

Retting, R. A., Williams, A. F., Farmer, C. M., & Feldman, A. (1999b). Evaluation of red light camera enforcement in Oxnard, California. *Accident Analysis & Prevention, 31*, 169-174.

Rogers, E. M. (1995). *Diffusion of innovations* (4th ed.). New York: The Free Press.

Ruckelshaus, W. D. (1998). Managing commons and community: Pacific northwest people, salmon, rivers, and sea. In J. A. Baden and D. S. Noonan (Eds.), *Managing the commons* (2nd ed.). Bloomington, Indiana: Indiana University Press.

Shinar, D. (1998). Aggressive driving: The contribution of the drivers and the situation. *Transportation Research Part F, 1*, 137-160.

Weick, K. E. (1984). Small wins: Redefining the scale of social problems. *American Psychologist, 39*, 40-49.

Williams, A. F. (1997, July). *Causes and dangers of aggressive driving.* Arlington, VA: Insurance Institute for Highway Safety.

Traffic and Transport Psychology,
T. Rothengatter and R.D. Huguenin (Editors)

16

Characteristics and Crash-Involvement of Speeding, Violating and Thrill-Seeking Drivers

Stephen Stradling, Michelle Meadows and Susan Beatty

Introduction

We know that drivers who speed, who violate other rules of the road, and who seek thrill when driving pose greater crash risk to themselves and to other road users (Meadows, 1994; Parker, West, Stradling & Manstead, 1995). But just who are these people? Results from an extensive questionnaire survey of English car drivers for the UK Department of the Environment, Transport and the Regions (Stradling, Meadows & Beatty, 1999) allowed for a comprehensive delineation of the demographic characteristics and the vehicle use characteristics of car drivers scoring high on self-reported speed choice and on measures of violation and thrill-seeking.

Such information should assist in choosing and targeting appropriate remedial measures for those groups of drivers who engage in such risky road behaviours, as constraining any behaviour is facilitated by a better understanding of the motivations behind the behaviour and of the circumstances under which the behaviour is more likely manifested. All travel and transport decisions, from whether to use public or private transport for a trip, through to whether to speed, violate or seek thrill at a certain point in a car journey, arise from the interaction of opportunity, obligation and inclination (Stradling et al., 1999; Stradling, Meadows & Beatty, 2000; Wardman, Hine & Stradling, 2000). For example, whether a driver speeds will depend on whether there is opportunity for speeding (e.g., do the vehicle capabilities, the road layout and the traffic conditions currently allow it?), on whether driving fast at this point would fit with the lifestyle obligations being met by the trip agenda (e.g., "I am on my way to an important business appointment and I'm running late"; "I am conveying my own and other's children to a leisure activity and have a clear duty of care to these precious passengers") and on the individual driver's attitudes, beliefs and values driving their inclination to speed (e.g., "Yes! Driving fast just makes me feel good!"; "No! I don't feel in control if things are happening too quickly").

Sample

791 English car drivers responded to a postal questionnaire (response rate: 21%). Table 1 shows that the sample covered a wide range of values on all the demographic variables: driver age, gender, socio-economic status, annual household income, and place of domicile; and on all the driving variables: years of driving experience, size of engine, age of car, estimated annual driving mileage, whether the car was employer-owned, and the extent of driving 'as part of your work'.

Table 1. Range of values on demographic and driving variables for sample of 791 English car drivers.

Demographics	
Age	17 -> 83 years
Sex	M 61%; F 39%
SES	A/B, C1/C2, D/E, (economically) retired
Household Income	< £5K pa -> > £50K pa
Domicile	City, Town, Suburb, Village, Semi-rural & Rural
Driving variables	
Driving Experience	1 year -> 60+ years
Engine Size	< 1 Litre -> > 2 Litres
Age of Car	1 year -> 10+ years
Annual Mileage	< 1K -> > 20K miles pa
Company Car	Yes / No
Drive As Work	Never -> Every working day

Measures

Speeding

Inclination to speed was indexed in three ways. First by asking drivers how many speeding offences they had been penalised for in the previous three years. Second by asking respondents to write in, in miles per hour, the speed at which they normally drove on four road types - motorways, other main roads, rural roads and suburban roads. And third by asking them to nominate the speeds at which they would prefer to drive on each of these types of road. Scores on each road type were converted to z-scores with a mean of zero and a standard deviation of unity, and the z-scores then averaged across the four road types, giving each respondent 'normal speed' and 'preferred speed' scores on scales where drivers with positive scores were nominating speeds higher than the average for the sample and those with negative scores were nominating lower than the average for the sample. Some intriguing patterns of similarity and divergence between individual's normal and preferred speeds were found, which are discussed elsewhere (Stradling et al., 1999).

Violating

The tendency to violate the rules of the road was indexed by responses to the most recent form of the Manchester Driver Behaviour Questionnaire (DBQ: Lawton, Parker, Manstead & Stradling, 1997: Lawton, Parker, Stradling & Manstead, 1997; Parker, Lajunen & Stradling,

1998; Stradling & Meadows, 2000), a twenty item version consisting of 12 violation and 8 error items. Factor analysis produced two violation factors - highway code and aggressive violations - plus an error factor (Stradling et al., 1999). Table 2 gives the items loading on each of the violation factors, arranged in descending order of frequency of reported commission within each factor.

Table 2. DBQ factor structure and item means* for highway code and aggressive violations

	Mn
Highway code violations	
Disregard the speed limit on a motorway	3.1
Disregard the speed limit on a residential road	2.3
Race away from traffic lights with the intention of beating the driver next to you	1.9
Drive so close to the car in front that it would be difficult to stop in an emergency	1.9
Cross a junction knowing that the traffic lights have already turned against you	1.9
Stay in a lane that you know will be closed ahead until the last minute before forcing your way in to another lane	1.8
Overtake a slow driver on the inside	1.8
Drive when you suspect you may be over the legal blood-alcohol limit	1.3
Aggressive violations	
Become angered by a certain type of driver and indicate your hostility by whatever means you can	2.2
Sound your horn to indicate your annoyance to another driver	2.1
Pull out of a junction so far that the driver with right of way has to stop and let you out	1.9
Become angered by another driver and give chase with the intention of giving him/her a piece of your mind	1.1

*Responses to 'How often do you ...' on 1 - 6 scale from 1 'Never' to 6 'Nearly All The Time'.

Thrill-seeking

The combination of excitement tinged with fear that engages the whole person and characterises extreme forms of thrill-seeking while driving was well expressed by one of the respondents in the initial, qualitative phase or our study:

Q "What do you enjoy most about driving?"

A "The speed .... When I go really fast a sense of exhilaration and nervousness at the same time because the faster you go the more concentration is needed." (Interviewee #8, Stradling et al., 1999).

Respondents were asked to '.. think about usual or typical feelings you may experience when driving', and rated their agreement with 8 of 9 items from the thrill-seeking scale developed by Matthews, Desmond, Joyner, Carcary and Gilliland (1997). Factor analysis of the responses yielded a single factor and summing responses to the 8 items gave a thrill-seeking scale with high reliability (Standardised item alpha = .91; Stradling et al., 1999). Table 3 gives the scale items in descending order of mean score.

Table 3. Thrill-seeking scale item means*

	Mn
I would enjoy driving a sports car on a road with no speed limit	4.7
I enjoy the sensation of accelerating rapidly	4.2
I enjoy listening to loud, exciting music while driving	3.6
I get a real thrill out of driving fast	3.3
I enjoy cornering at high speed	2.8
I would like to risk my life as a racing driver	2.4
I like to raise my adrenaline levels while driving	2.2
I sometimes like to frighten myself a little while driving	1.9

*Scale range from 1 'Do not agree at all' to 11 'Agree strongly'

Potential scores on the thrill-seeking scale ranged from 8 to 88. Actual scores ranged from 8 (134 respondents: 17%) to 87 (1 respondent). This high scoring respondent was a 20 year old male driving a 5 year old 1600cc sports car which he owned himself. Domiciled in a village in the South East of England and in full-time employment he drove 14,000 miles a year, driving to and from work every working day, though rarely in the rush hour, and not driving as part of his work. He was social class A/B, and lived in a 3 adult household with a gross annual household income of over £50,000.

Characteristics of Speeding Drivers

Overall, 8% of the sample had been penalised for speeding in the previous three years. Table 4 shows the influence of each of the demographic and driving variables on this incidence.

Table 4. Demographic and driving characteristics of car drivers penalised for speeding offences 'in the past three years' (overall: 8%).

Factor	
Age Band	21-39 14%; 60+ 2%
Sex	M 9%; F 6% (but ns)
SES	D/E, Retired 3%
Household Income	<£10K 2%; >£40K 18%
Domicile	no effect
Driving Experience	no effect
Engine Size	1.8 litres+ 13%
Age of Car	1-3 years 12%
Annual Mileage	>20K miles pa 24%
Company Car	Yes, 18%
Drive As Work	Always, 16%

More male drivers than female drivers reported being penalised (9%: 6%) but the difference did not reach statistical significance (p = .056). Age of driver proved a good predictor of level of speeding offences. This was highest amongst car drivers aged between 21 and 39, and lowest for those aged 60 and over (Table 5).

Table 5. Per cent of car drivers penalised for speeding offences 'in the past three years' by age band.

Age	*17-20*	*21-29*	*30-39*	*40-49*	*50-59*	*60-69*	*70+*	*Overall*
Speeding Offences	10%	14%	13%	10%	7%	1%	2%	8%

The effect of age band remained significant ($F = 2.133$; $p = .048$) when annual mileage was controlled for by being entered as a covariate in 1-way ANOVA. The covariate - mileage - was itself highly significant ($F = 16.774$; $p < .001$).

Older drivers, those from social class D/E and the economically retired, and those from low income households (below £10,000 pa) were the least likely to have been penalised for speeding. Car drivers from high-income households (£40,000 pa and above), and high-mileage (above 20,000 miles pa) drivers of newer, larger-engined cars (1-3 years; 1.8 litres and above) who drove employer-owned cars and drove as part of their work every working day were more likely to have been penalised for speeding 'in the past 3 years'. 18% of company car drivers and 16% of those who drove as part of their work every working day had been penalised. 37% of those who drove every working day and drove more than 14,000 miles per annum had been penalised. And 60% of those who had been penalised for speeding drove cars of 1.8 litres or above.

Speeding offences and crash involvement

Why should speeding be constrained? Because, as Table 6 shows, 35% of those car drivers who had been penalised for speeding in the last 3 years reported also having been accident-involved, compared to 22% of those who had not been penalised, indicating that the kinds of drivers who have been recently caught for speeding are 59% more likely to have also been recently crash-involved. Speed kills and speeders crash. Though we do not know from this data whether they were speeding when they had their crashes (further research is needed!) this finding suggests that being detected speeding is a good indicator of a car driver's risk potential.

Table 6. Self-reported speeding offences and crash-involvement in the previous three years

	Speeding Offences last 3 years		
		None	1 or more
Accidents	None	78%	66%
last 3 years	1 or more	22%	35%

Speed choice

Separate analyses, using SPSS Answer Tree, for the two variables normal and preferred speed, resulted in similar profiles for those car drivers who do, and those car drivers who would like to, drive faster than others. This is shown in Table 7. The two variables, normal speed and preferred speed, correlate very highly ($r = 0.85$, $p < .001$), suggesting that either may be used as a proxy for the other.

Table 7. Demographic and driving characteristics of car drivers nominating high normal and preferred speeds across four road types.

Factor	*Normal Speed*	*Preferred Speed*
Age Band	17-24 > 25-58 > 58+	17-29 > 30-64 > 65+
Sex	M > F	M > F
SES	A/B > C1, C2 > D/E, Retired	A/B > C1, C2 > D/E, Retired
Income	£30K+ > £20-30K > <£20K	£30K+ > £20-30K > <£20K
Domicile	Out-of-town faster	Out-of-town faster
Experience	1-3 years faster	1-3 years faster
Engine Size	1.6 litres+ faster	1.8+ > 1.6-1.8 > below 1.6
Age of Car	1-7 years faster	1-7 years faster
Annual Mileage	>10K > 5-10K > below 5K	>10K > 8-10K > below 8K
Company Car	Yes, faster	Yes, faster
Drive As Work	Sometimes, fastest	Any, faster

Young drivers are faster, older drivers slower. Recently qualified - and thus inexperienced - drivers want to drive faster and report that they do so. Male drivers are faster than female drivers. The higher social classes, and the better-off, drive faster. Drivers who dwell out of town, who drive high mileages, in newer and larger-engined cars, drive faster. Drivers of employer-owned cars and those who drive as part of their work drive faster.

While both variables proved susceptible to age and gender differences, they were also prone to mileage effects, with high mileage drivers nominating higher normal and preferred speeds, and annual mileage varies with both age and gender. To control for these differences ANCOVA analyses were performed with age and sex as factors and annual mileage entered as covariate. Both variables showed age and sex effects, even after correcting for mileage differences. Estimates corrected for differences in annual mileage are plotted in Figures 1 and 2.

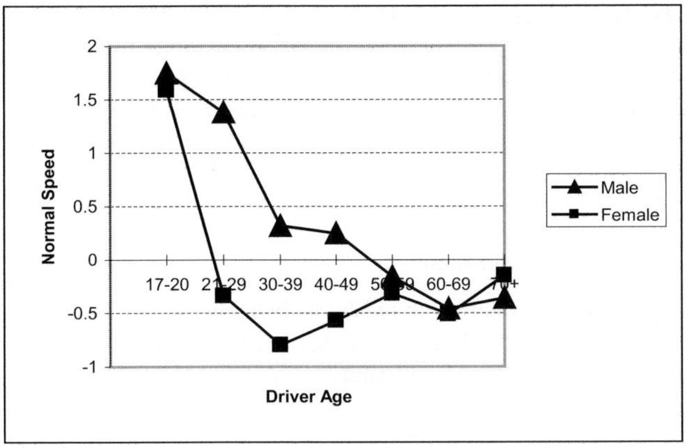

Figure 1. ZNormal speed by age band and sex, correcting for mileage.

For normal speed (Figure 1), mileage was highly significant ($F = 38.56$; $p < .001$), and there was a strong main effect for age ($F = 4.95$; $p < .001$) and a weaker effect for sex ($F = 4.71$; $p = .030$). For both sexes, 17-20 year olds report the highest normal speeds. Female drivers appear to slow down sharply in their 20s and then maintain this reduced velocity across the rest of the age range. Male drivers seemingly defer any reduction in velocity until their 30s but are still nominating higher normal speeds than age-equivalent females until male and female nominated normal speeds finally converge at around age 50.

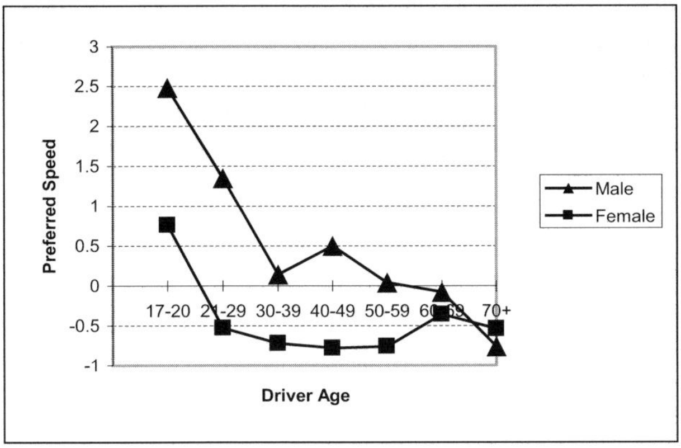

Figure 2. ZPreferred speed by age band and sex, correcting for mileage.

For preferred speed (Figure 2), mileage was again highly significant ($F = 39.98$; $p < .001$), there was a strong main effect for age ($F = 4.50$; $p < .001$) and a strong main effect for sex ($F = 12.37$; $p < .001$). Males retained their preference for higher speeds than females to age 60 and while 17-20 year old males and females were reporting the same nominated normal speeds (Figure 1), the young males nominated preferred speeds much faster (Figure 2) than the young females.

Normal and preferred speeds and crash involvement

Both z-transformed variables showed an association with crash involvement. Active crashes ('I hit [another road user] or an obstacle or lost control of the vehicle') and Passive crashes ('I was hit by [another road user]') (West, 1995) were examined separately.

Eighty-nine % of the car drivers in the sample reported no active accidents, 9% reported 1, and 1.5% reported 2 or more 'during the past 3 years'.

ANOVA analysis showed a significant main effect ($F = 4.72$; $p = .009$) and a significant linear trend ($F = 4.68$; $p = .031$) for ZNORMAL - the more active accidents you report, the faster you normally drive - and even stronger main ($F = 7.88$; $p < .001$) and linear trend ($F = 7.73$; $p = .006$) effects for ZPREFER - car drivers who have had more active crashes would like to drive faster.

Eighty-five % of the car drivers in the sample reported no passive accidents, 12% reported 1 passive crash, and 3% owned to 2 or more. ANOVA analysis for passive crashes showed an indicative trend in the mean scores but the differences were not statistically significant.

Thus the speed at which 'you normally drive' and - even more so - the speed at which 'you would prefer to drive', across a number of different road types predicted active, but not passive, crash involvement for this sample of English car drivers. Those who do, and those who would like to, drive fast are more likely to run into other road users and to suffer loss of control crashes.

Speed choice and driving as part of your work

Company owned cars make up 8% of the UK car fleet but, due to the high mileage their recipients commonly drive, contribute an estimated 20% of the UK car mileage. 1 in 9 drivers in employment in the sample (11%: 16% of male drivers in work, 4% of female drivers in work) indicated that the vehicle they normally drove was an employer-owned car.

Respondents also indicated the extent to which they drove a car as part of their work, on a 6-point frequency scale from 'Every working day' to 'Never or almost never'. Almost two-thirds of car drivers in employment (64%), three-quarters (75%) of working males and half (49%) of working females, reported that they drove a car as part of their work at least some of the time. Thus while there is a relatively small and homogeneous group of company car drivers, results from this sample suggest there is a much larger group of both males and females in employment who are driving a car - most often their own car - as part of their work (we asked separately about frequency of driving to and from work) at frequencies ranging from 'every working day' to 'less than once a month'. Figure 3 illustrates that for the males, but not for the females, those who drive as part of their work report higher normal and preferred speeds than do those in work who do not drive as part of their work.

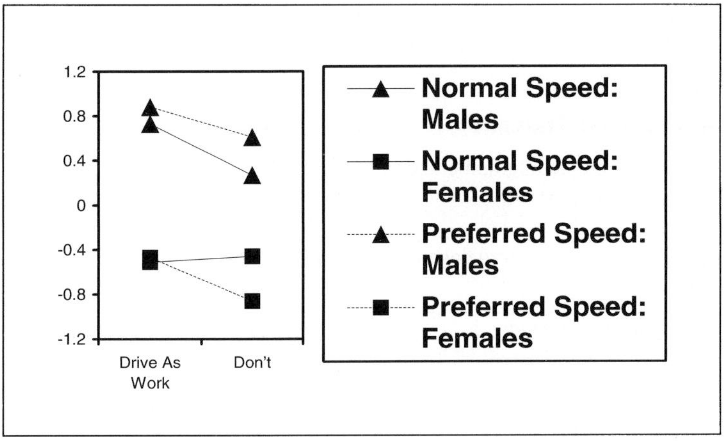

Figure 3. Normal and preferred speeds for males and females in work who do and who do not drive a car as part of their work.

Driving as part of your work and crash involvement

Table 8 shows that twice as many males (27%) as females (13%) drove every working day as part of their work, and that the differential reduces amongst those driving as part of their work less often until almost as many employed females (21%) as males (25%) report driving a car 'sometimes' as part of their work. The annual reported mileage differs substantially across the four groups, and the proportion who had been crash involved in the previous three years was highest for those who drove every working day.

Table 8. Sex, annual mileage and 3-year crash involvement by extent of driving as part of work for car drivers in employment.

	M	*F*	*Annual Mileage*	*Crash last 3 years*
Always (every working day)	27%	13%	18,600	30%
Often (> once a week)	22%	15%	14,500	22%
Sometimes	25%	21%	11,800	23%
Never or almost never	26%	51%	7,600	22%

But is this elevated crash risk for those who drive as part of their work every working day due to the type or the amount of driving that they do? This was examined using ANCOVA, with Drive As Work entered as a factor, and sex, experience (number of years a full licence had been held) and reported annual mileage entered first as covariates. Crash involvement increased with increasing mileage (p = .010), and decreased with increasing experience (p = .003) and, once the covariates had been statistically controlled for, the extent of driving as part of work made no additional significant difference.

It would thus appear that for this sample the elevated crash risk of those who drive frequently as part of their work results from the amount of driving they do as a result, and is moderated by the accumulation of driving experience (or wisdom - age and experience correlate at r = .84 for this sample; more experienced and older drivers crashed less).

Characteristics of Violating Drivers

Table 9 shows the influence of the demographic and driving variables on the factor scores for highway code and aggressive violations.

Table 9. Demographic and driving characteristics influencing car drivers' scores on highway code and aggressive violations

Factor	*Highway Code Violations*	*Aggressive Violations*
Age Band	17-24 > 25-40 > 41-59 > 60-68 > 69+	17-40 > 40-49 > 50-69 > 70+
Sex	M > F	M > F
SES	A/B > C1 > C2 > D/E, Retired	A/B, C1, C2 > D/E, Retired
Household Income	£40K+ > £20-40K > £10-20K > below £10K	£30K+ > £10-30K > below £10K
Domicile	City, Town or Suburb higher	City, Town or Suburb higher
Driving Experience	1-3 years > 4-23 > 24+	1-23 years > 24+
Engine Size	1.8L+ > 1.4-1.6L > below 1.4L	>1.4L, higher
Age of Car	1-7 years higher	no effect
Annual Mileage	20K+ > 8-20K > 3-8K > below 3K	>8K, higher
Company Car	Yes, higher	Yes, higher (p = .053)
Drive As Work	Any, higher	Any, higher

Profiles for perpetrators of the two types of violations were very similar. High violating car drivers were more likely to be young, to be male and to have less driving experience. They were of higher social class and from higher income households. They were more likely to be domiciled in-town (in city, town or suburb) than out of town. Those who report higher levels of violation tend to drive larger engined cars, to drive higher mileages, to drive company-owned cars, and to drive as part of their work.

Level of highway code violation (HCV) is strongly affected by mileage ($F = 42.83$; $p < .001$) with higher mileage drivers reporting higher levels of HCVs. Analysis of estimates corrected for mileage differences, plotted in Figure 4, shows highly significant main effects for sex ($F = 22.65$; $p < .001$) and age ($F = 13.47$; $p < .001$) with male car drivers consistently reporting a higher mean level of HCVs than age-equivalent females, and both sexes showing reduction in levels of commission as age increases.

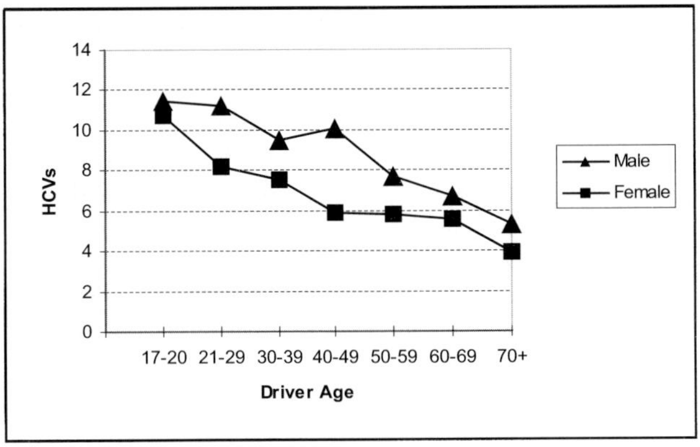

Figure 4. Highway code violations by age band and sex, correcting for mileage.

Level of Aggressive Violation (AV) is less strongly - though still significantly - affected by mileage ($F = 7.74$; $p < .010$) with higher mileage drivers tending to report higher levels of AVs. Analysis of estimates corrected for mileage differences, plotted in Figure 5, shows a highly significant main effect for age ($F = 13.21$; $p < .001$) but the sex difference does not reach statistical significance ($F = 3.76$; $p = .053$).

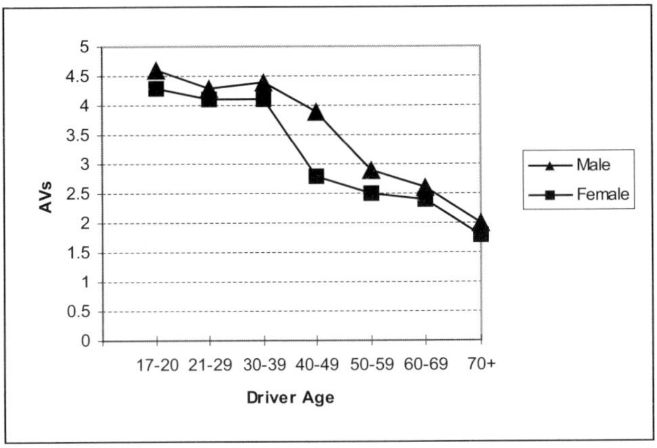

Figure 5. Aggressive violations by age band and sex, correcting for mileage.

Examination of the plot of the corrected estimates for AVs indicates that male and female car drivers show very similar trajectories across the age range. For each age-band the plotted values for males and females are similar, and the two trajectories suggest that - when comparison is made of figures corrected for mileage - both sexes show relatively high scores for aggressive violations on the road from ages 17 to 40, before declining linearly across the remainder of the age range.

Violations and crash involvement

Drivers who had been crash-involved in the previous 3 years scored significantly higher on highway code violations ($F = 19.32$; $p < .001$) and aggressive violations ($F = 11.73$; $p = .001$) compared to those who reported no crashes. This held for both active accidents (HCV: $F = 19.30$; $p < .001$: AV: $F = 4.25$; $p = .040$) and passive crashes (HCV: $F = 4.28$; $p = .039$: AV: $F = 4.17$; $p = .041$), with the effect being strongest for the influence of level of reported highway code violations on active crash involvement.

Violations and driving as part of your work

Figure 6 illustrates that male drivers who drive a car as part of their work report more highway code violations - but not more aggressive violations - than do male car drivers in work who never drive as part of their work.

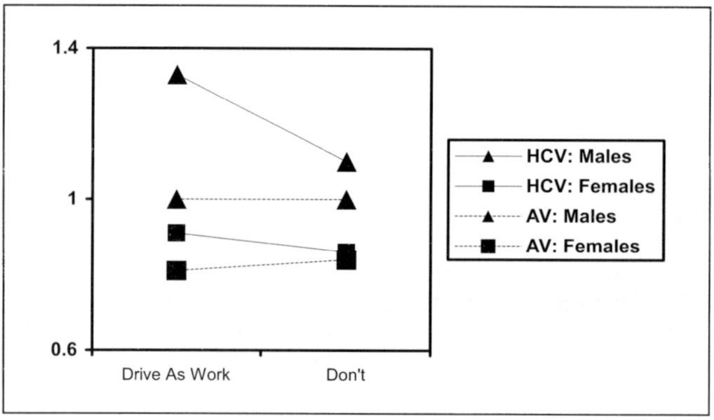

Figure 6. Highway code (HCV) and aggressive (AV) violations for male and female drivers in work who do and who do not drive a car as part of their work.

Driving as part of your work, violations and crash involvement

Of all the car drivers in the sample who were in work, 24% had been crash-involved in the previous 3 years. For those who drove a car as part of their work every working day this rose to 32%. And for those who drove a car as part of their work every working day and scored high on highway code violations this rose to 44%, compared to 15% of those who drove a car as part of their work every working day but did not report a high-violating driving style. Thus for this group highway code violation amplifies crash-risk; and refraining from highway code violations is prophylactic, even when risk-exposure, indexed by annual mileage, is high.

CHARACTERISTICS OF THRILL-SEEKING DRIVERS

Table 10 summarises the influence of the demographic and driving variables on variability in thrill-seeking scores.

Table 10. Demographic and driving characteristics influencing car drivers' scores on thrill-seeking scale scores.

Factor	
Age Band	17-23 > 23-40 > 40-59 > 59+
Sex	M > F
SES	Retired, lowest
Household Income	> £20K, higher
Domicile	no effect
Driving Experience	1-3 years > 4-23 years > 23+ years
Engine Size	2.0L > 1.4 -1.6L > below 1.1 > 1.2-1.4L
Age of Car	no effect
Annual Mileage	20K+ > 8-20K > below 8K
Company Car	Yes, higher
Drive As Work	Any, higher

Younger and inexperienced drivers, male drivers and those from households earning above £20,000 pa all scored higher on thrill-seeking, as did those driving large-engined cars, company cars, driving high annual mileages, and driving as part of their work. It is likely that persons who seek thrill in driving would seek out jobs where driving forms part of the job description.

As thrill-seeking scale scores varied with drivers' annual mileage, and drivers of different age and gender post large variations in annual mileage, differences in scale scores between younger and older drivers or between female and male drivers may simply be due to mileage effects. This was tested by using the General Factorial Model of GLM in SPSS to compute estimates of scale scores for each gender and age band, corrected for differences in annual mileage, by entering annual mileage as covariate in an ANCOVA with sex and age band as factors.

Plotting these estimates for scale scores corrected for the effects of mileage (Figure 7) shows a clear effect of age ($F = 28.402$; $p < .001$), a male advantage across the age range ($F = 64.888$; $p < .001$), and a small but statistically significant interaction ($F = 3.264$; $p = .004$) whereby female and male driver scores converge beyond age 50. The effect of the covariate, mileage, was also highly significant ($F = 22.943$; $p < .001$) with higher mileage drivers reporting more thrill-seeking from driving.

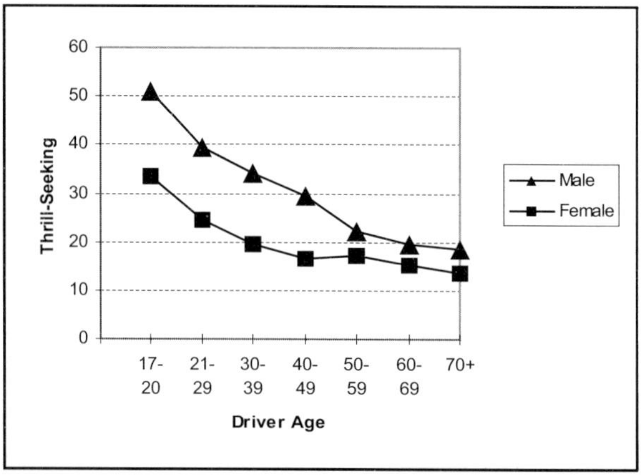

Figure 7. Thrill-seeking by age band and sex, correcting for mileage.

Thrill-seeking and crash involvement

Drivers who had been involved in active crashes in the previous 3 years scored significantly higher on the thrill-seeking scale ($F = 7.96$; $p = .005$) than did drivers who reported no crash-involvement. The effect for passive crash-involvement was in the same direction, but the difference did not reach significance. Thus thrill-seeking drivers in this sample were more likely to have run into other road users or lost control of their vehicle.

Thrill-seeking and driving as part of your work

There were no significant differences in thrill-seeking scale scores for either males or females between those in employment who did and those in employment who did not drive a car as part of their work.

Summary and Conclusions

Using data from a comprehensive study of English car drivers this report has enumerated the demographic and driving characteristics of speeding, violating and thrill-seeking drivers and documented their elevated crash risk. Across measures of recent speeding offences, speed choice, highway code and aggressive violations and of thrill-seeking while driving similar patterns emerged, identifying two population segments whose manner of driving makes them a greater risk to themselves and to other road users.

Young and inexperienced drivers - especially, though not exclusively, young and inexperienced male drivers - are well known to be over-represented in the RTA statistics. And while company car drivers have been recognised as carrying a high risk of crash-involvement, our analysis identifies a much larger at-risk group - those 75% of males in work and 49% of females in work who drive a car as part of their work at least some of the time.

Table 11 summarises these findings. Drivers at the lower end of the age range were more likely to exhibit all the measures of risky road behaviour: those who drove as part of their work (in particular the males) scored higher on many of them. And all measures of risky driving used in this study showed an association with elevated crash involvement.

Table 11. Risky road behaviours of young drivers and those who drive a car as part of their work.

	Young Drivers	*Drive (a car) as Part of Work*	*Crash Risk*
Speeding Offences	21 - 39	Yes	Elevated crash risk
Normal Speed	17 - 24	Males Yes	Elevated active crash risk
Preferred Speed	17 - 29	Males Yes	Elevated active crash risk
Highway Code Violations	17 - 24	Males Yes	Elevated crash risk
Aggressive Violations	17 - 40	No	Elevated crash risk
Thrill-Seeking	17 - 23	No	Elevated active crash risk

Different, targeted, road safety countermeasures will be needed to constrain the behaviour of these two groups. Young drivers have long been known to carry an elevated crash risk. It is now time for those who drive as part of their work to also be targeted for restraint. Health and Safety at Work legislation should be extended to cover not just how those who drive a car as part of their work bend their backs when loading the boot, but how they behave when behind the wheel.

References

Lawton, R., Parker, D., Manstead, A. S. R., & Stradling, S. G. (1997a) The role of affect in predicting social behaviours: The case of road traffic violations. *Journal of Applied Social Psychology, 27*, 1258-1276.

Lawton, R., Parker, D., Stradling, S. G., & Manstead, A. S. R. (1997b) Predicting road traffic accidents: The role of social deviance and violations. *British Journal of Psychology, 88,* 249-262.

Matthews, G., Desmond, P. A., Joyner, L., Carcary, B., & Gilliland, K. (1997) A Comprehensive Questionnaire Measure of Driver Stress and Affect. In J.A. Rothengatter and Enrique Carbonell Vaya(Eds), *Traffic and Transport Psychology.* Oxford: Pergamon.

Meadows, M. L. (1994). Psychological correlates of road crash types. Unpublished doctoral dissertation, University of Manchester, Manchester, UK.

Parker, D., West, R., Stradling, S. G., & Manstead, A. S. R. (1995) Behavioral traits and road traffic accident involvement. *Accident Analysis and Prevention, 27*, 571-581.

Parker, D., Lajunen, T., & Stradling, S. G. (1998) Attitudinal predictors of interpersonally aggressive violations on the road. *Transportation Research Part F,* 1, 1-14.

Stradling, S. G., Meadows, M. L., & Beatty, S. (1999) Factors affecting car use choices. Transport Research Institute, Napier University: Edinburgh, UK.

Stradling, S. G., Meadows, M. L., & Beatty, S. (2000) Helping drivers out of their cars: integrating transport policy and social psychology. *Transport Policy, 7,* 207-215.

Stradling, S. G., & Meadows, M. L. (2000) Highway code and aggressive violations in UK drivers. Global Web Conference on Aggressive Driving Issues. Available: http://aggressive.drivers.com.

Wardman, M., Hine, J., & Stradling, S. G. (2001). Interchange and travel choice, Vol.1, Vol. 2 and Research Summary. Central Research Unit, Scottish Executive, Edinburgh, UK.

West, R. (1995) Accident script analysis. Contractors Report CR343. Transport Research Laboratory: Crowthorne, UK.

Traffic and Transport Psychology,
T. Rothengatter and R.D. Huguenin (Editors)

17

Driver Behaviour and its Consequence: The Case of Chinese Drivers

Cheng-qiu Xie, Dianne Parker and Stephen Stradling

Introduction

Despite the ever-rising concern of traffic safety and driving related behaviour, traffic accidents remain a world-wide problem, especially in developing countries. In 1994, there were 66,362 deaths caused by traffic accidents in China, compared to 41,360 in America and 3814 (1993 figure) in Great Britain. In 1995, deaths caused by every 10,000 vehicles in Japan, Germany, France and China were 1.6, 1.9, 3.5 and 22.5 respectively (Wang & Duan, 1997). In China, fatalities caused by traffic accidents had reached a striking 83,529 last year, which is almost six times the 14,096 in 1978 (Public Security Ministry, 1993, 1999) when China started its policy of reform and openness. Traffic accident casualties are only part of the problem. Serious traffic congestion affects everybody's daily life. A recent survey showed that 61% of the residents in Beijing and 43% in Shanghai believe traffic is the number one social problem (Zaobao, 2000). Moreover, Chinese drivers were rated, along with Indian drivers, the worst in Asia, in terms of traffic safety and conformity to traffic rules (Reaves, 1998). Despite the clear urgent need little psychological research has been done about this problem in China.

In the West, ever since the relationship between human behaviour and traffic accident has been established (e.g., Sabey & Taylor, 1980; Parker, Reason, Manstead & Stradling, 1995), various research has been done to distinguish driving behaviours according to different criteria (e.g., Näätänen & Summala, 1974, 1976; Reason, Manstead, Stradling, Baxter & Campbell, 1990; Lajunen & Summala, 1995; Lajunen, Corry, Summala & Hartley, 1998). Based on the Driving Behaviour Questionnaire (DBQ) study, Reason et al. (1990) proposed a three-ford typology of a wide range of aberrant driving behaviours, namely intentional violations, unintentional mistakes and lapses. Since then the DBQ has been adopted and adapted in other UK samples and several other countries (e.g., Parker et al. 1995; Blockey & Hartley, 1995; Stradling & Parker, 1996; Lawton, Parker, Stradling & Manstead, 1997; Åberg & Rimmo, 1998). The three-way structure of undesirable driving behaviour has been basically confirmed, and the relationship between demographic variables, aberrant driving behaviour and accident involvement has also been explored. Another approach to the taxonomy of driving behaviour was based on Näätänen and Summala (1974, 1976)'s perceptual-motor and safety model. With reference to the works of Spolander (1983) and Hatakka, Keskinen, Laapotti, Katila and Kiiski (1992), Lajunen et al. (1995) developed the Driving Skill Inventory (DSI). The DSI survey results (Lajunen & Summala, 1995; Lajunen et al. 1998) confirmed the perceptual-motor and safety skill distinction and suggested theoretical models of driving style, personality factors and traffic safety.

The study reported here was a questionnaire study using the Driving Behaviour Questionnaire (DBQ, Parker et al., 1995) and Driving Skill Inventory (DSI, Lajunen & Summala, 1995). It was a pilot study for a research programme concerning Chinese drivers. The aim of the study was to provide information on the applicability of these Western survey questionnaires to Chinese drivers. It was also hoped that the replication of the DBQ and DSI in an apparently rather different environment in terms of both general cultural factors and the traffic situation would provide further insight into the nature of the aberrant driving behaviours.

Method

The questionnaire administered had three sections. The first section contained items concerning the driver's demographic information. The second section was the 24-item version of the DBQ (Parker et al., 1995), with eight items measuring violations, errors and lapses respectively. The drivers were asked about how often they commit each of these behaviours on a 0-5 (never-almost all the time) scale. The third section was the 28-item version of the Driving Skill Inventory (Lajunen & Summala, 1995), measure the driver's self-view of his/her perceptual-motor skill and safety skill compared to 'average drivers' on a 0-4 scale (much worse-much better).

Three hundred and sixty three questionnaires were completed by a range of Chinese drivers including who drove professionally and privately. Bus drivers, taxi drivers and truck drivers were also included. The demographics of the sample are summarised in Table1:

Table 1. Demographic characteristics of the sample.

Variable	*Mean*	*SD*	*Min.*	*Max.*
Age (yr.)	33.4	7.71	18	60
Mileage (km)	26,150	25,000	500	100,000
Years with a license	6.96	6.73	.2	34.6

Note: N=363, Male =281, Female =73, Missing=9

Key Findings

Mean scores

DBQ: The overall means for the violation, error and lapse scales were 1.22, .98 and 1.15 respectively, indicating that the respondents committed intentional violations more often than they made mistakes. When compared with other DBQ studies, the means of each of the three categories for the current sample were higher than those in the same category for any other samples (Reason et al. 1990; Parker et al. 1995; Blockey & Hartley, 1995; Åberg & Rimmo, 1998; also see Stradling, Parker, Lajunen, Meadows & Xie, 1998). For the violation category, the items with much higher means than any other samples were all aggressive violations. The two error items with much higher means than others' were 'failing to notice pedestrians crossing' and 'on turning left nearly hit a cyclist'.

DSI: The seven items with the highest means were all safety items, indicating that respondents rated themselves as very safety-concerned. The items at the very bottom were all skill items, especially those skills needed on special, unusual occasions.

Factor structures

DBQ: Three factors with eigenvalues over 1 were extracted, together explaining 58.1% of the total variance. Factor 1 consisted of six error items and six lapse items and explained 44.56% of the total variance. All the eight violation items and one lapse item comprised factor 2 which accounted for 9.0% of the total variance. Factor 3 consisted of two error items and two lapse items and accounted for a further 4.5% of the total variance.

DSI: Factor analysis of the 28 DSI items produced a 2-factor solution that reflected the skill-safety dimensions almost perfectly and accounted for 64.2% of the total variance. Factor1 was a skill factor and explained 54% of the total variance. Factor 2 was a safety factor and explained 10.1% of the total variance.

Factor scores and accident involvement

DBQ: Whether the respondent was accident free in the previous three years was regressed on demographic variables and DBQ factor scores. In step 1, the demographic variables were entered with forced entry, including the driver's age, sex, exposure, years of holding a driving license, and whether he/she was a company driver or not. In step 2, the three DBQ factor scores were entered stepwise. The result is shown in Table 2.

The Violation factor score was the only significant predictor and explained 2.3% of the total variance. Respondents who had been involved in at least one traffic accident in the previous three years scored significantly higher on the violation factor than those who were accident free in the same period of time. None of the demographic variables entered were significant predictors. Altogether they explained a mere 1.1% of the total variance.

Table 2. Predictors of accident involvement in the previous three years.

Step	*Variable*	R^2	*Beta*
1 Enter	Age		-.003
	Sex		.039
	Mileage		.038
	Yr. of license		.049
	Company driver	.011	-.052
2 Stepwise	DBQ violation	.034	.224***

DSI: Among all the variables entered, the safety factor score was the only significant predictor for accident involvement in the previous three years. It explained 2.0% of the total variance. None of the demographic variables were significant predictors, altogether explaining only 0.4% of the total variance.

Table 3. Predictors of accident involvement in the previous three years.

Step	*Variable*	R^2	*Beta*
1 Enter	Age		.019
	Sex		.022
	Mileage		.025
	Yr. of license		.019
	Company driver	.004	-.028
2 Stepwise	DSI safety factor	.024	-.147*

Discussion

In the present study, the means of all the three categories of aberrant driving behaviours in the DBQ were higher than those of all the previous studies mentioned. There are several possible reasons for that. First of all, according to official statistics, there are less traffic facilities (e.g., road markings, signs, lights, etc.) in China than in other countries, which makes the driving task more difficult for drivers and may lead to more aberrant driving behaviours of all types.

Another possible reason could be that the current sample lacked experience and skill in terms of driving. In the current sample the average age (33.4) and years of holding a license (6.96) are both much lower than those in the previous studies (e.g., 42 and 22 respectively in the Åberg & Rimmo study, 1998). In the present sample, 33.7% of the drivers had held a driving license for less than three years, 53.0% for less than five years.

Among the reported violation frequency scores, the present sample differed from other samples most clearly in those items concerning attitudes and behaviours toward other road users rather than in those referring to the violation of the traffic regulations. This suggests that the present sample may be more interpersonally aggressive.

In terms of the factor structure of the DSI, results showed that three safety skill items loaded on the perceptual-motor skill factor. They were 'attention to others', 'attention to pedestrians and cyclists' and 'adjusting speed to the conditions'. They were all related to the driver's distribution of attention. It may be that in this sample these items were related to perceptual-motor skill as a consequence of the traffic situation. In Beijing, the likelihood of drivers encountering pedestrians and cyclists on the roadway is much higher than in any of the other countries where the DSI has been used. This makes attention distribution a demanding task, like other perceptual skills, rather than only a kind of safety concern. Also the relative lack of road signs and markings means there is much more uncertainty in terms of traffic conditions in China, which makes 'adjusting your speed to the conditions' an ongoing task. These two reasons may explain why these three items loaded on the skill factor in this sample. Apart from this, the factor structure is almost identical to the results obtained by previous studies (e.g., Lajunen and Summala 1995; Lajunen et al. 1998).

For the current sample, the perceptual-motor skill factor contributed much more to the explained variance than the safety-skill factor (54% Vs 10.1%), while in previous studies (e.g., Lajunen et al. 1998) the two factors explained variance almost equally. The most plausible reason is the current sample's diversity of driving experience.

Parker et al. (1995) found that there was a significant correlation between DBQ violation scores and accident involvement, but no significant correlation between error scores and crash involvement was found. The present study confirmed this conclusion. In the same study Parker et al. also found that males were more likely to be involved in an accident than females, and young drivers more likely than older ones. In the present study, age did not predict accident involvement or violations. This may due to the inconsistency between age and driving experience in the current sample.

Sex was not a significant predictor of accident involvement in the previous three years, a finding inconsistent with previous studies. One possible reason for the inconsistency could be that the current female sample was non-representative of females in general. In the present sample females represented only 21% of the sample population, a proportion much lower than in previous driver behaviour studies. However, this is an accurate reflection of the driving population in China. Female drivers were quite rare in China just a few years ago, with the exception of some public bus drivers in major cities. For the present female sample (n = 73) the average number of the years of holding a license was 4.63, whereas for the male sample it was 7.63, a significant difference. No difference was found in this respect in previous studies (e.g., Blockey & Hartley, 1995). However, while this sample might reflect the proportion of female drivers in the Chinese driving population, the female drivers might be far from representative of Chinese females overall. In China, only a small proportion of people have access to a car, even fewer in the case of females. For those females who do have, their SES is well above the average. They are more powerful, richer and relatively younger, characteristics that may be reflected in their driving.

The significant predictive power of scores on the DSI safety factor stresses the link between safety concern and accident involvement. Although traffic accidents are rare events and scores on the safety factor did not explain a large proportion of the variance, the fact that neither demographic variables nor skill factor scores predicted traffic accident involvement makes the importance of the safety factor among Chinese drivers remarkable.

A correlation analysis of the DBQ and DSI factor scores showed that DBQ violation factor was negatively correlated with the DSI safety factor ($r = -.40, p < .001$) but not correlated with the skill factor, indicting that violations are associated with a lack of safety concern but not with one's perceptual and motor skill. DBQ error and lapse factor scores were negatively correlated with both the skill factor and the safety factor, indicating that errors and lapses are a matter of both lack of skill and the concern of safety.

References

Åberg, L., & Rimmo, P. (1998). Dimensions of aberrant driver behaviour. *Ergonomics, 41*, 39-56.

Blockley, P., & Hartley, L. (1995). Aberrant driving behaviour: errors and violations. *Ergonomics, 38*, 1759-1771.

Duan, L. R. & Wang, G. D. (1997). Road Traffic Accidents. Beijing: The Chinese People's Public Security University Press.

Hatakka, M., Keskinen, E., Laapotti, S., Katila, A. & Kiiski, H (1992). Driver's self-confidence-the cause or the effect of mileage. *Journal of Traffic Medicine, 21*, 313-315.

Lajunen, T., & Summala, H. (1995). Driving experience, personality, and skill and safety-motive dimensions in drivers' self-assessment. *Personality and Individual Differences, 19*, 307-318.

Lajunen, T., Corry, A., Summala, H., & Hartley, L. (1998). Cross-cultural differences in drivers' self-assessment of their perceptual-motor and safety skills: Australians and Finns. *Personality and Individual Differences, 24*, 539-550.

Lawton, R., Parker, D., Stradling, S. G., & Manstead, A. S. R. (1997). Predicting road traffic accidents: The role of social deviance and violations. *British Journal of Psychology, 88*, 249-262.

Lian He Zao Bao (2000). The most concerned social problems in some Southeast Asian cities. Available: http://www.zaobao.com.

NäätäÅnen, R., & Summala, H (1974). A model for the role of motivational factors in drivers' decision-making. *Accident Analysis and Prevention, 6*, 243-261.

Näätänen, R. & Summala, H. (1976). *Road-user behaviour and traffic accidents*. Amsterdam and New York: North-Holland /American Elsevier.

Parker, D., Reason, J. T., Manstead, A. S. R. & Stradling, S. G. (1995). Driving errors, driving violations and accident involvement, *Ergonomics, 38*, 1036-1048.

Reason, J. T., Manstead, A. S. R., Stradling, S. G., Baxter, J. S. & Campbell, K. (1990). Errors and violations on the road: a real distinction? *Ergonomics, 33*, 1315-1332.

Reaves, J. A., (1998) Asia's worst drivers. Reader's Digest, Oct., 17-23.

Sabey, B. E., & Taylor, H. (1980). *The known risks we run: The Highway* (TRRL Supplementary Rep. No. 567). Crowthorne: Transport Research Laboratory.

Spolander, K. (1983). *Drivers' assessment of their own driving ability* (Rep. No. 252). Swedish Road and Traffic Research Institute.

Stradling, S. G., & Parker, D (1996). Violations on the road: Bad attitudes make bad drivers. *Paper presented at the International Conference on Road Safety in Europe*, Birmingham.

Stradling, S. G., Parker, D., Lajunen, T., Meadows, M. L. & Xie, C. Q. (1998). Drivers' violations, errors, lapses and crash involvement: International comparisons. *Paper presented at the 9th International Conference on Road Safety in Europe*, Germany.

Traffic Administration of the Public Security Ministry, (1993*). National Road Traffic Accident Statistics*. Beijing: Mass Press.

Traffic and Transport Psychology,
T. Rothengatter and R.D. Huguenin (Editors)

18

Are Female Drivers Adopting Male Drivers' Way of Driving?

Sirkku Laapotti and Esko Keskinen

Introduction

Reasons for choosing this topic

The number of female drivers is increasing. The proportion of females in Finland having a driver's licence was 38% in 1980 and it had increased to 63% by 1996 (Register of Driving Licences in Finland). In the UK the corresponding figures were under 30% in 1975/76 and around 55 % in 1995/96 (Meadows & Stradling, 1999). The proportion of 18-19 year old male and female driver's licence holders increased in Finland until 1989-90 but after that there has been a slight decrease in the proportion of drivers' licence holders among young adults. In 1997 about 66 % of all 18-19 year old females had a driver's licence, and for 18-19 year old males the corresponding figure was 79 %.

Females drive increasingly more. Not only do more and more females have a driver's licence but females also drive increasingly more. For example, in the beginning of the 1990s the average annual kilometrage by car in Finland was about 26,000 km for males and 13,000 km for females (Ernvall & Pirtala, 1992). The corresponding figures in the UK were 19,000 kms for males and 13,000 kms for females (Meadows & Stradling, 1999). In the USA males drove about 27,000 kms and females about 15,000 kms annually. The increase in annual mileage from 1969 to 1990 was 76 % for females and 46 % for males (Nationwide Personal Transportation Study, 1991).

Female drivers have more accidents than before. In Finland, drivers' gender was differentiated in accident statistics kept by the insurance companies for the first time in 1980.The proportion of female drivers' accidents was about 13 % of all accidents in 1980, and today it is about 24 % as shown in Figure 1. The accident statistics of the insurance companies in Finland cover all accidents from which damages are paid.

Many studies have not separated drivers' gender. Not separating drivers' gender in research is a problem at least when we talk about young drivers and their problems or compare young drivers to middle-aged or older drivers.

Contradictory evidence about female drivers' risky driving. S ome studies conclude e.g. that drinking and driving among young females is increasing (Popkin 1991; Wylie 1995). Forward, Linderholm and Järmark (1998) reviewed the literature on male and female drivers' way of driving and risk-taking behaviour during the time periods 1970-84 and 1985-97. They compared the results of the studies from these two time periods and concluded that female drivers' attitudes and self reported behaviour were increasingly similar to male drivers. On the other hand, McKenna, Waylen and Burkes (1998) made a comparison of male and female drivers' accidents in the UK from 1979 to 1997. Their conclusion was that (p.11): "Despite the fact that there has been a massive shift in the population of women drivers there is little evidence that the sex difference in the pattern of accident involvement is changing over the years".

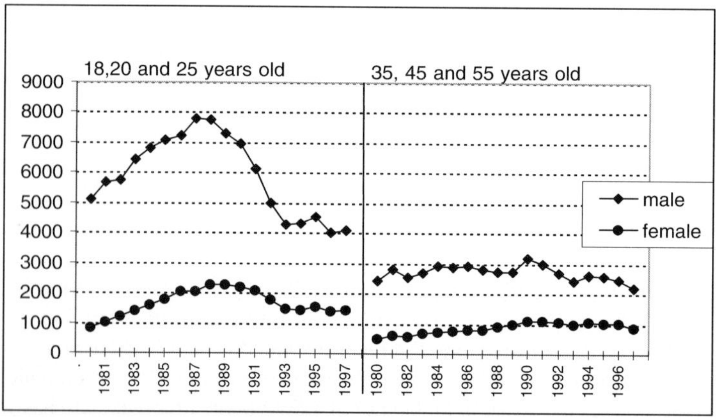

Figure 1. Number of accidents of male and female drivers in Finland in 1980-1997. (Statistics of insurance companies in Finland).

Purpose of this study

This paper examines whether the growing number of female drivers' accidents is only due to the fact that females drive more than before, or whether there are qualitative changes in the way they drive. This would imply that the accidents of female drivers are also qualitatively different. The main question was whether the proportion of female drivers' accidents involving alcohol, speeding, or night-time driving have increased during the research period compared to other types of accidents. Also the proportion of accident involved drivers with previous traffic offences was studied. The results are discussed in the framework of the hierarchical model of driving behaviour (Keskinen, 1996).

Data and method

The study is based on data on fatal accidents from the years 1984-98 in Finland. The number of accidents is shown in Table 1. The data is collected by Finnish road accident investigation teams and contains a wealth of information about all fatal road accidents in Finland during that period. Young (18-25 years) and middle-aged (35-55 years) drivers are studied separately, as the hypothesis was that if there is a change in the way female drivers drive, it should be apparent in young drivers' group first.

The study focused on four variables connected to the culpable party of an accident: (1) Proportion of accidents where the driver has exceeded the speed limit; (2) Proportion of accidents where the driver was drunk. Being drunk is defined as having a BAC-level >0.5 per mil, which is the legal BAC-level limit in Finland; (3) Proportion of accidents during night-time (between 10 p.m. and 6 a.m.); (4) Proportion of drivers with previous traffic offences. The fatal accident database includes information about how many traffic violations the driver has committed during the previous 5 years.

Table 1. Number of young and middle-aged drivers' fatal accidents in Finland in 1984-98.

	The most guilty party	*The other party*	*Single vehicle*	*Total*
18-25 year				
males	570 (36,5)	470 (30,1)	521 (33,4)	1 561 (100)
females	129 (54,7)	61 (25,8)	46 (19,5)	236 (100)
35-55 year				
males	677 (28,8)	1 323 (56,3)	351 (14,9)	2 351 (100)
females	191 (51,5)	140 (37,7)	40 (10,8)	371 (100)

RESULTS

Proportion of speeding drivers

About 58 % of all culpable young male drivers had been speeding when they had a fatal accident during 1984-98. Young female drivers had been speeding in about 24 % of their fatal accidents. There was a significant difference between the sexes (for young drivers: (χ^2=66.10, df = 1, p <.001; for middle-aged drivers: χ^2=6.61, df = 1, p <.01). There was no statistically significant year to year change as shown in Figure 2.

Accidents during evenings and night-time

Figure 3 shows that males had more often accidents during evenings and night-time than females (for young drivers:, χ^2 = 35.67, df=1, p <.001; for middle-aged drivers: χ^2 = 8.40, df=1, p <.01). There were no statistically significant year to year changes.

Proportion of drunk drivers

Figure 4 shows that male drivers were more often drunk when they had a fatal accident as culpable party (for young drivers:, $\chi^2 = 36.70$, df = 1, $p < .001$; for middle-aged drivers $\chi^2 = 28.21$, df = 1, $p < .001$). The proportion of young male drivers being drunk at the time the fatal accident took place increased from 1984 to 1998 ($\chi^2 = 16.61$, df = 4, $p < .01$). There was no statistically significant year to year change in other driver groups.

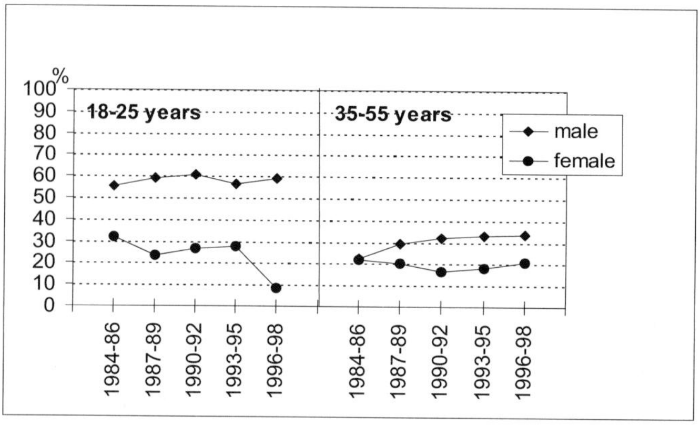

Figure 2. Proportion of speeding drivers in fatal accidents, guilty drivers

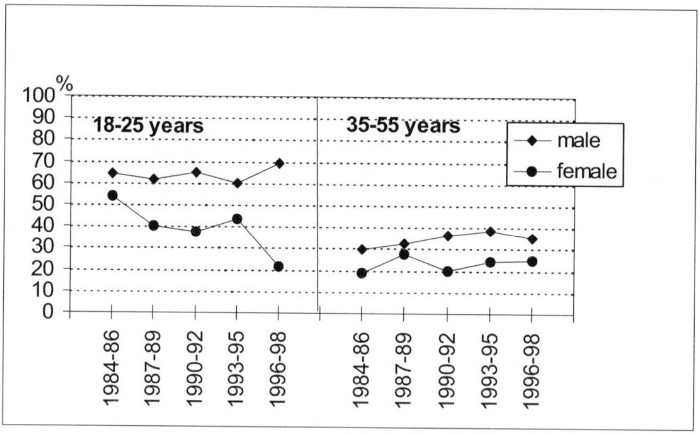

Figure 3. Proportion of fatal accidents during night-time, guilty drivers.

Male drivers were more often drunk when they had a fatal accident as culpable party (for young drivers: df=1, $\chi^2=36.70$, $p<.001$; for middle-aged drivers df=1, $\chi^2=28.21$, $p<.001$). The proportion of young male drivers being drunk at the time the fatal accident took place increased from 1984 to 1998 (df=4, $\chi^2=16.61$, $p<.01$). In other driver groups there was no statistically significant year to year change (Figure 4).

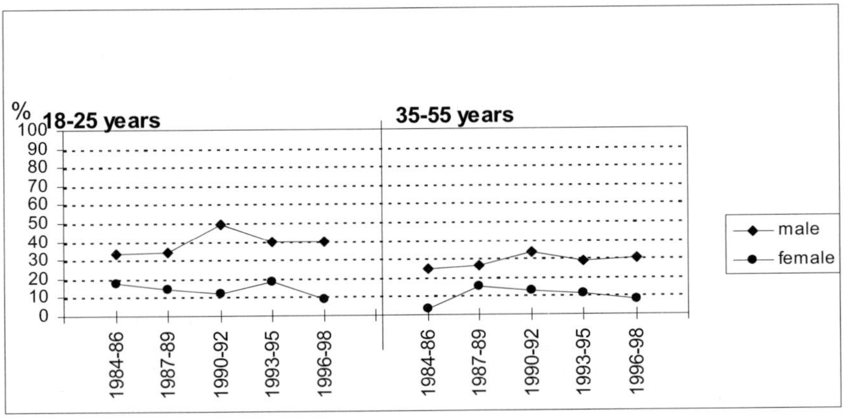

Figure 4. Proportion of drunken drivers in fatal accidents, guilty drivers.

Proportion of drivers with previous traffic offences

Figure 5 shows that male drivers had more often previous traffic offences than female drivers (for young drivers: $\chi^2 = 105.28$, df=1, $p < .001$; for middle-aged drivers: $\chi^2 = 62.92$, df=1, $p < .001$). There was no statistically significant year to year change.

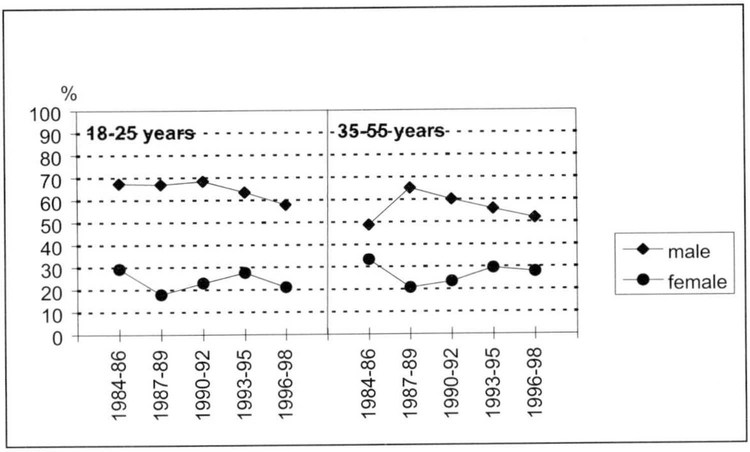

Figure 5. Proportion of guilty drivers with previous traffic violations in fatal accidents

Conclusions

Although there is an increase in the number of female drivers, in how much they drive and in the number of accidents, there were no change to be seen in the way females drive. The differences regarding what types of fatal accidents males and females were involved in remained the same during the research period. This result supports the previous result of McKenna et al. (1998). They found that in the UK the accident pattern of males and females was different and there were no remarkable changes during the research period.

The present study found that males had more accidents during night-time, and that they were more often drunk and speeding when the accident happened. Males also had more often previous traffic violations than females. Differences between males and females tend to be larger among young drivers than among middle-aged drivers.

In this study driving behaviour is considered in the light of the hierarchical model by Keskinen (1996). Apart from controlling the vehicle and the traffic situations, a driver must also be able to control him-/herself. In Keskinen's model as shown in Figure 6, the lowest level of driving behaviour is called "vehicle manoeuvring", i.e. controlling the speed, direction and position of the car. The second level is called "mastering traffic situations". The driver should adapt his/her behaviour to the demands of a traffic situation. The third level "goals and context of driving", refers to the purpose and circumstances of driving. The highest level is called "goals for life and skills for living", which refers to the importance of cars and driving for a driver's personal development and to skills for self-control. By studying this level we can answer questions like: what motives is a driver satisfying through driving, or how can a driver control him-/herself, and his/her motives and emotions when driving (see Keskinen, 1996; Hatakka, 1998; Hatakka, 2000).

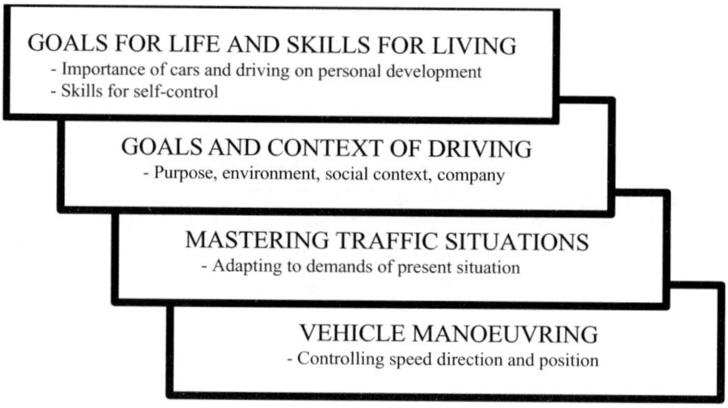

Figure 6. The hierarchical levels of driver behaviour (Keskinen, 1996; Hatakka, 2000)

Driving behaviour on the lower levels of the hierarchy (vehicle manoeuvring, mastering traffic situations) is changing according to driving experience. For example, vehicle manoeuvring becomes automated when a driver has acquired enough driving experience. The skill to master different traffic situations becomes better when a driver gains more experience. However, the driving behaviour on the higher levels of the hierarchy does not to the same extent depend on the amount of driving (Hatakka, 1998). Changes on the higher levels are connected to a driver's personal development and to the norms of a culture. Changes on the higher levels of the driving hierarchy therefore take more time than changes on the lower levels.

Young male drivers as a group exhibit more problem behaviour in traffic (speeding, drink and driving, violating traffic rules, showing off one's driving skill) than other road user groups. Risky driving may be a sign of problems in personal development but it may also be purposeful and instrumental (Jessor, 1987). Risky driving may be one way for young males to get admiration from important others. This is what "goals of driving", and even more so "goals for life" refer to in Keskinen's (1996) hierarchy. Risky driving has not been as useful for young females as for males due to different sex roles and expectancies in society.

The results of this study did not give support to the idea that female drivers are adopting male drivers' way of driving. On the contrary, there seems to be some hope that young male drivers begin to drive more like females and that the attraction of cars and driving decreases among young males. During the end of the 1990s there has been a slight decrease in Finland and a sharp decrease in Sweden in the proportion of young driver's licence holders (Register of Driving Licences in Finland; Swedish Road Administration, 1998). At the same time also the number of young drivers' traffic accidents has decreased. These are positive signs of changes in young (male) drivers' behaviour.

This study found no negative changes in female drivers' way of driving. However, this study focused only on types of fatal accidents and possible changes regarding these. It is possible that changes in how female drivers drive will first become apparent e.g. in values and attitudes. Forward et al. (1998) found that females' behaviour and attitudes are increasingly similar to males. Fatal accidents are rare events and not very sensitive to changes in traffic behaviour. More research on behaviour, values and attitudes of female drivers is therefore needed.

References

Ernvall, T.. & Pirtala, P. (1992). Kuljettajan iän, ajokokemuksen ja automallin vaikutus kuljettajan onnettomuusriskiin [The effect of driver's age and experience and car model on accident risk]. University of Oulu, publications of road and transport laboratory, 16. Oulu, Finland.

Forward, S., Linderholm, I. & Järmark, S. (1998). Women and traffic accidents, causes, consequences and considerations. *Paper presented at the 24th International Congress of Applied Psychology*, San Francisco, CA.

Hatakka, M. (1998). Novice drivers' risk- and self-evaluations. University of Turku, Department of Psychology. Painosalama Oy, Turku, Finland.

Hatakka, M. (2000). What makes a good driver? - The hierarchical approach. In G. Bartl (Ed.), *DAN-Report*. Results of EU-Project: Description and Analysis of Post Licensing Measures for Novice Drivers (pp 19-25). Austrian Road Safety Board (KfV), Vienna, Austria.

Keskinen, E. (1996). Why do young drivers have more accidents? *Proceedings of the "Junge Fahrer und Fahrerinnen"* Conference (pp 280-290 in English), Berichte der Bundesanstalt für Straenwesen, Mensch und Sicherheit, Heft M 52, Bergisch Gladbach, Germany.

McKenna, F. P., Waylen, A. E., & Burkes, M. E. (1998). *Male and female drivers: how different are they?* Basingstoke: AA Foundation for Road Safety Research.

Meadows, M., & Stradling, S. (1991) Are women better drivers than men? In J. Hartley and Branthwaite (Eds.), *The Applied Psychologist*. Milton Keynes: Open University Press.

Nationwide Personal Transportation Study 1991. Washington, DC: National Highway Traffic Safety Administration.

Popkin, C. L. (1991). Drinking and driving by young females. *Accident Analysis & Prevention 23*, 37-44.

Register of Driving Licences in Finland. Vehicle Administration Centre, Helsinki, Finland.

Statistics of Insurance Companies in Finland from 1980-97. Liikennevakuutuskeskus, Helsinki. Swedish Road Administration, 1998. Swedish National Road Safety Report. Borlänge, Sweden.

Wylie, S. J. 1995. Young female drivers in New Zealand. *Accident Analysis and Prevention, 27*, 797-805.

Traffic and Transport Psychology,
T. Rothengatter and R.D. Huguenin (Editors)

19

The Relationship between Accidents and Near-Accidents in a Sample of Company Vehicle Drivers

Katherine L. Roberts, Peter R. Chapman and Geoffrey Underwood

Introduction

Researchers investigating factors associated with accident involvement are faced with a number of methodological problems. Because observational and experimental studies are often impractical, it is common practice to use self-reports as a measure of driving behaviour (e.g. Reason, Manstead, Stradling, Baxter & Campbell, 1990) and accident liability (e.g. West & Hall, 1997). However, there are certain problems associated with this approach, in terms of its validity and practicality.

Studies have shown that a surprisingly large proportion of accidents are forgotten within a few years. Loftus (1993) reported that 14% of people do not remember an injury-provoking accident a year later. Maycock, Lester & Lockwood (1996) estimated that approximately one third of all road accidents are forgotten each year. Whether these effects are due to traumatic amnesia, forgetting of relatively minor events (Chapman & Underwood, 2000), or forward telescoping in time of events, the reliability of self reports is brought into question.

In terms of the practicality of researching accident rates using self report, the key difficulty is in the low numbers of accidents typically experienced by drivers in the UK. Maycock, Lockwood & Lester (1991) found that accident rates ranged between 0.037 per year for older females, to 0.462 per year for young males. Researchers wishing to investigate factors associated with accident liability therefore need extremely large sample sizes, particularly if they plan to use multivariate modelling techniques (e.g. Maycock, Lockwood & Lester, 1991; Forsyth, Maycock & Sexton, 1995).

Police accident reports and insurance statistics are sometimes used as a more objective measure of accident involvement. However, there are often ethical difficulties in linking these data with other personal information, and since these only provide information about relatively serious accidents, they will generally require event larger sample sizes than studies which rely on self report. As Maycock (1997) points out, the low frequency of accidents makes the statistical modelling of individual driver data very difficult. He stresses that accidents are only the tip of the driver error 'iceberg' which also includes (in descending order), near misses (conflicts), offences, errors (lapses, dangerous errors and violations) and 'normal' driving behaviours.

This paper investigates the possibility of moving down Maycock's 'iceberg' by exploring incidents which would not normally be recorded - near-accidents. A recent study conducted by the authors studied the accident liability of company vehicle drivers, using a two phase approach. Initially, 635 employees of a large British company completed a questionnaire asking about their typical driving behaviours, driving history and accident involvement. Following on from this, a subset of 98 employees completed a diary study in which they kept a microcassette recorder in their car for a period of two weeks, and recorded details of each journey they made, including any near-accidents that they experienced.

The diary study is a technique designed to provide detailed information about people's day to day driving experiences (e.g. Chapman & Underwood, 2000; Underwood, Chapman, Wright & Crundall, 1999). It allows a greater degree of immediacy, since subjects report details of their journeys straight after each drive is completed, rather than relying on estimates of typical driving patterns and memory for events. The study of near-accidents rather than real accidents has two advantages. Firstly, near-accidents are far more common, with drivers typically reporting around 1.5 near accidents in a two week period (Chapman & Underwood, 2000). In addition, because the costs of near-accidents are not as severe as those of real accidents, it is possible that subjects will be less likely to report them in a biased way. This paper will investigate the relationship between real and near-accidents. In addition to comparing real and near-accident rates, accidents will be categorised to allow a comparison of the distribution of real and near-accidents across accident types.

METHOD

The questionnaire study

A 12 page questionnaire was sent to 2000 employees within a large British company. The questionnaire contained items relating to their typical driving behaviour, driving history, demographic variables and accident involvement over the past three years. The following definition of an accident was provided:

"We are interested in the types of road accident you have been involved in as a driver over the past three years. By 'accident' we mean any incident which involved injury to another person or yourself, damage to property, damage to another vehicle, or damage to the vehicle you were driving. Please mention only those accidents in which you were involved as a driver, not as a passenger. Please include all accidents, regardless of how they were caused or how slight they were."

Subjects were first asked to report the number of accidents they had been involved in over the three year period, and then to provide a detailed description of the three most recent accidents. They then answered a series of questions relating to those accidents. Subjects were given the opportunity to take part in the second phase of the study, and provided contact details if they wished to participate.

The diary study

Microcassette recorders were sent to 136 of the respondents who volunteered to take part in the diary study. These were sent out as soon as the questionnaire was received, in order to complete the diary study while the respondents were still enthusiastic about participating.

Subjects were provided with a cue card which contained a number of questions relating to individual journeys, and were encouraged to keep this in their vehicle with the microcassette recorder. Subjects were asked to record their responses to the questions on the cue card immediately on completion of each journey, for a period of two weeks. It was stressed that subjects should not use the microcassette recorder while driving. Questions relating to each journey included a request for a detailed description of each near-accident experienced, and specific questions relating to the near accident.

Results

Of the 2000 questionnaires sent out, 635 were completed and returned (a response rate of 31.8%). A large proportion (94%) of respondents were male, reflecting the distribution of employees in the organisation. Where respondents failed to provide and answer to a specific question, they are removed from the analyses which required that information, but included in all other analyses.

Table 1. Summary Information.

	Questionnaire Study	*Diary Study*
n	635	98
Age in years (SD)	43.73 (6.83)	43.38 (6.52)
Driving Experience in years (SD)	25.91 (7.28)	25.78 (7.41)
Annual Mileage	22,592 (8,269)	24,265 (7,892)
Accidents in past 3 years	0.572 (0.837)	0.694 (0.890)
Accidents / 100,000 miles	0.909 (1.488)	0.964 (1.261)

From the initial 136 microcassette recorders sent out, 117 were returned, of which 98 contained usable data. These 98 subjects supplied information about 3,329 journeys, comprising 87,372 miles or 2,176 hours of driving. Table 1 contains summary information about the drivers in the questionnaire and diary studies.

Clearly the diary study sample is comparable to the questionnaire study sample in terms of age and experience. Those participants that took part in the diary study appear to have a slightly higher annual mileage, but since the annual mileage of the sample is very high compared to the general population in both samples, this was not considered to be a problem. Similarly, accident rates over the past three years, and per 100,000 miles were higher in the diary study sample, but considered comparable when compared to the general population, who have much lower accident rates than this company vehicle driver sample.

Following each journey, participants in the diary study were asked to report the number of miles driven. As can be seen in Table 2, this information indicates that these drivers' annual mileage estimates accord well with mileages reported on a journey by journey basis.

Table 2. Summary Information from the Diary Study.

	During Study	*Projection for 1 Year Period*
Mileage	891.55 (386.47)	23,180
Near Accidents / 2 weeks	1.816 (1.976)	47.216
Near Accidents / 100 miles	0.225 (0.238)	52.155

Near accident rates for this sample of drivers are similar to those reported by Chapman and Underwood (2000), and would provide details of approximately 47 near accidents per person over a one year period. Compared to real accident rates of around 0.6 accidents over a three year period, this methodology is clearly capable of providing a dramatically larger volume of data.

To support the hypothesis that near accident frequencies can be used as a measure of real accident involvement, a comparison was made between the number of real and near accidents experienced by the diary study subjects. A significant correlation was found (Pearson's r = 0.273, df = 96, $p < 0.01$).

Real and near accident coding scheme

As part of the questionnaire study, subjects provided detailed descriptions of the three most recent accidents they had been involved in over the past three years. Of the 397 descriptions provided, 37 were not considered to be genuine accidents (usually due to the car being parked at the time of the accident, or the accident occurring outside the three year period). Four further accidents could not be coded due to insufficient detail. This left 356 accidents which were categorised into accident types. The diary study produced 178 descriptions of near-accidents, of which 164 contained sufficient detail to allow them to be coded.

A variation of West's (1993) coding scheme was used to categorise the accident descriptions from both the questionnaire and diary studies. This divided the accidents into six accident types, based on what actually happened for the real accidents, and what would have happened had the accident not been avoided for the near-accidents. Each category can be sub-divided according to an active-passive distinction: active if the reporting driver's vehicle hit another vehicle, person or object or was committing a right of way violation. Two of the authors independently coded the real and near-accidents. Agreement between the raters was very high. Coding of the real accidents resulted in a Cohen's Kappa of 0.921 for the active-passive distinction, and 0.895 for the categorisation. Coding of the near-accidents was also very reliable, with a Kappa of 0.915 for the active-passive distinction, and 0.830 for the categorisation. The two raters then agreed together on the classification of the disputed accidents. The high level of agreement implies that the coding scheme is clear and meaningful for both real and near-accidents. The adapted coding scheme is summarised below.

Accident typology

Right of way violations: A vehicle pulls into the path of another without right of way. Active if the reporting driver's vehicle violated right of way rules, passive if it didn't. This category includes head-on incidents - active if the reporting driver was pulling out to overtake, passive if another vehicle was.

Shunts: One vehicle hits another in the same carriageway from behind. Active if the reporting driver's vehicle hits the one ahead, passive if hit from behind. In multiple car shunts the first collision involving the reporting driver's vehicle has priority.

Loss of control: Driver fails to keep the vehicle in the carriageway during normal or high speed driving. Active if the reporting driver loses control, passive if another driver does.

Manoeuvring: One vehicle hits another vehicle, person, or object while manoeuvring at low speeds (for example, when reversing). Active if reporting driver does the hitting, passive if they are stationary at the time of impact.

Lane changing: A vehicle collides with another while changing lanes (N.B. this could include changing lanes while negotiating a roundabout or junction). Active if the reporting driver's vehicle was moving lanes, passive if it remained within one lane.

Other: This would include hitting objects in the road, hitting animals, people, car doors, etc. Active if reporting driver's vehicle does the hitting, passive if it is hit.

A comparison of the number of active and passive accidents reported in the questionnaire and diary studies shows some differences between real and near-accidents. The data shown in Table 3 demonstrate the general tendency for real accidents to be active, but near-accidents to be passive.

Table 3. Distribution of Active and Passive Real and Near Accidents.

	Real Accidents	*Near Accidents*	*Total*
Active	222	52	274
Passive	134	112	246
Total	356	164	520

Pearson chi square = 42.3, df = 1, $p < .01$

The active-passive distinction provides a reasonably objective measure of responsibility. When the drivers were asked to report how much they felt they were to blame for the real or near-accident, they seem to provide a fairly accurate attribution of blame, as shown in Table 4. Table 5 compares the distribution of blame attributions in real and near accidents. In this table, and those that follow, bold type indicates that the standardised adjusted residual for that cell was significant: i.e. that the value of the cell is greater (negative residual) or lower (positive residual) than expected by chance.

Table 4. Self-Reported Culpability (Active vs. Passive Accidents).

		Not at all	*A little*	*Partly*	*Quite a lot*	*Entirely*	*Total*
Real	Active	15	38	25	24	112	214
	Passive	113	11	6	2	1	133
	Total	128	49	31	26	113	347
Near	Active	11	7	3	10	7	38
	Passive	85	6	4	0	0	95
	Total	96	13	7	10	7	133

Fewer people than would have been expected by chance said that they were 'not at all' to blame for their real accidents, while more than expected said that they were 'not at all' to blame for their near-accidents. Fewer people than expected said that they were 'entirely' to blame for their near-accidents. This pattern is similar to that found when the accidents were coded according to whether they were active or passive.

Table 5. Self-Reported Culpability (Real vs. Near-Accidents).

	Not at all	*A little*	*Partly*	*Quite a lot*	*Entirely*	*Total*
Real	128	49	31	26	113	347
(Res)	2.16	-0.34	-0.35	0.00	-1.50	
Near	96	13	7	10	7	133
(Res)	-4.03	1.06	1.18	-0.01	9.74	
Total	224	62	38	36	120	480

Pearson chi square = 57.4, df = 5, $p < .01$

Tables 6 and 7 show the distributions of real and near-accidents, respectively. The distribution of real accidents shows that there were fewer active, and more passive, shunts than expected. Conversely, there were more active, and fewer passive, manoeuvring accidents than expected. The distribution of near-accident types shows a different pattern: fewer active right of way violation accidents, and fewer active lane change accidents than expected. Near shunts were found to show the opposite pattern of results from real shunts, with more active, and fewer passive, shunts than would have been expected by chance.

Table 6. Distribution of Real Accidents.

	RofW	*Shunt*	*LofC*	*Man*	*Other*	*Lane*	*Total*
Active	15	44	25	110	22	6	222
(Res)	1.78	2.44	-0.57	-2.61	0.50	1.18	
Passive	26	62	8	8	19	11	134
(Res)	-1.74	-2.64	1.30	12.43	-0.69	-1.12	
Total	41	106	33	118	41	17	356

Pearson chi square = 88.3, df = 5, $p < .01$

Table 7. Distribution of Near Accidents.

	RofW	*Shunt*	*LofC*	*Man*	*Other*	*Lane*	*Total*
Active	10	20	7	3	7	5	52
(Res)	3.32	-2.31	-1.33	-0.84	-1.53	5.47	
Passive	53	7	2	1	0	49	112
(Res)	-0.98	2.66	1.70	0.99		-1.19	
Total	63	27	9	4	7	54	164

Pearson chi square = 69.6, df = 5, $p < .01$

A chi square was conducted on the real and near accident data, with the expected number of near accidents in each of the categories based on the reported numbers of real accidents. The adjusted standardised residuals are reported in Table 8. Negative residuals indicate that the type of accident was less likely to occur within the near-accident distribution. Passive right of way near accidents, and passive lane change near accidents were more likely to occur than expected, while there were fewer passive near-shunts and active manoeuvring near accidents than expected.

Table 8. Comparison of Real and Near Accident Types (Residuals).

	RofW	*Shunt*	*LofC*	*Man*	*Other*	*Lane*
Active	1.24	-0.05	-1.13	-5.60	-0.83	1.36
Passive	8.51	-2.49	-0.51	-0.80	-1.70	13.42

Pearson chi square = 599.9, df = 5, $p < .01$

Discussion

This main aim of the above analyses has to been to determine the degree to which near-accident reports can be used as a substitute for reports of actual accidents. The critical questions that need to be addressed are first whether the two samples of respondents were broadly equivalent in terms of overall driving habits, then whether there were significant relationships between the numbers of near-accidents and real accidents. Finally we have attempted to explore the differences that are likely to be found between real and near-accident reports in terms of the attribution of blame and the types of incidents that are reported.

Demographic variables suggest that the subset of drivers that participated in the diary study were representative of the questionnaire study sample in terms of age, experience and annual mileage. Information from the diary study supported the annual mileage estimates made in the questionnaire study. In general company vehicle drivers are likely to be unusually good at providing accurate estimates of annual mileage, because these figures may be routinely required for tax purposes or by the company. However it is worth noting that many other groups of drivers may find estimating annual mileages considerably harder. For such drivers a diary methodology is likely to provide a better estimate of exposure that a single estimate of annual mileage. Critically, in terms of matching the two samples, the accident rates appear to be similar for both groups, even when mileage is accounted for.

The questionnaire study produced information about 356 real accidents (635 participants; three year reporting period), while the diary study produced information about 164 near-accidents (98 participants; two week reporting period). There was an average of 0.572 real accidents over the three year period, and 1.816 near-accidents over the two week period. With so many more near-accidents than real accidents, there are clear advantages to being able to use near accidents as a model for real accidents, in terms of data collection and in generating a sufficiently large data set to permit multivariate modelling. On an individual level this also means that a driver's risk of near-accident can be assessed relatively rapidly. Based on these figures one might anticipate that an average respondent will experience almost 250 near-accidents before he or she is involved in an actual accident. If the frequency and type of near-accidents experienced are predictive of impending real accidents these should provide a significant opportunity to address risk factors before real accidents actually occur.

A significant correlation (r = .273) was found between the numbers of real and near-accidents experienced by drivers who participated in both the questionnaire and diary study. Although this correlation is modest in size, it is important to remember the essential variability in both accident and near-accident data. As Grayson & Maycock (1988) remind us, "low correlations are an inevitable consequence of the large random component of the accident data, and do not necessarily imply that the underlying systematic effects are small" (p.235). In principle it is accident liability (or expected accident rates) rather than true accident rates that we are interested in estimating. Even a driver with a very high expected accident rate may continue for many years before actually being involved in an accident. Conversely, many accidents, particularly passive ones, may happen to drivers whose expected accident rate is actually very low. One way to begin to address this problem is to explicitly explore different types of real and near-accident, and to attempt to account for culpability wherever possible.

Relatively few drivers reported being 'entirely' to blame for their near accidents, which accords well with the low number of active near-accidents, and high number of passive near-accidents experienced by these drivers. Similarly, fewer respondents than would have been expected by chance claimed to be 'not at all' to blame for their real accidents; and more than expected claimed to be 'not at all' to blame for their near accidents. Again, this reflects the low numbers of passive real accidents, and high numbers of passive near-accidents. The very good agreement between self-ratings of culpability and more objective assessments of active-passive lends support to the use of both these measures, though we need to remain aware of the possibility that drivers may be unconsciously biasing their accident reports or culpability ratings, or both, to maintain consistency. Nonetheless, the general tendency to report passive near-accidents rather than active ones may reflect a genuine bias at work. Drivers' illusions of control (McKenna, 1993) will generally cause them to regard incidents where they are the active party as being safer than identical incidents where they are passive. They will thus be less likely to regard active conflicts as near-accidents than passive ones. For real accidents, where the accident is more objectively defined, this bias is far less likely to operate.

The distribution of real accidents shows some interesting trends. There were fewer active shunts, than passive ones; and conversely, more active than passive manoeuvring accidents. The pattern of manoeuvring accidents is easily explained due to the large number of these accidents which involve collision with an object, rather than another road user. Such accidents will almost inevitably be active. The pattern of shunts is more difficult to interpret, however. One possibility is that participants are more likely to remember and report accidents for which they were not to blame (Chapman & Underwood, 2000). Alternatively, there may be a problem with multiple car shunts, where drivers may be inclined to report that they were hit from behind before contacting the car in front.

The distribution of near-accidents shows the opposite effect for shunts, with active shunts being more likely, and passive shunts being less likely. This is of course easily explained by what the driver is able to observe. It will generally be obvious to the responding driver when he or she has narrowly avoided driving into the back of another vehicle, but more difficult to notice when the situation is reversed.

In addition to this, there were fewer active lane changing near-accidents than expected, and fewer active right of way violations than expected. Again, this is intuitively simple to explain since the reporting driver clearly pulls out or changes lane when they believe they have enough time to conduct the manoeuvre safely, but that they may not trust other road users to make the same judgement. Such a bias could also fall under the illusion of control heading mentioned earlier.

When real and near-accidents are compared, several differences between the distributions are apparent. There are relatively high numbers of active manoeuvring accidents within the real accident distribution compared with the near-accidents distribution. This is presumably because drivers may never become aware that a near-accident occurred (e.g. a driver who nearly reverses into a concealed post will probably never know that they had a near-accident). One common feature of near-accidents is likely to be a feeling of danger. When the incident is happening at sufficiently low speeds, such a feeling is unlikely to be present, and this too may reduce the tendency to report active manoeuvring near-accidents.

The differences that have been described between real and near-accident distributions seem to be predictable based on the physical nature of near-accidents, and known biases operating in driver psychology. It should thus be possible to refine near-accident reports to weight different near-accident types appropriately. It might then be possible to make predictions, at an individual level, not just of the likelihood of accident involvement generally, but of particular accident types which present specific dangers to different drivers.

So far, we have broadly focused on the advantages of using near-accident reports as a research tool, however, near-accidents have even more significant benefits to offer in real settings. The key benefit of recording and monitoring near-accidents is that they may allow dangerous driving behaviours to be identified and modified before real accidents occur. Rather than waiting for death or injury before any remedial actions are taken, near-accident analysis offers the possibility of identifying drivers who may be in particular danger before accidents actually happen.

References

Chapman, P.. & Underwood, G. (2000). Forgetting near-accidents: The roles of severity, culpability and experience in the poor recall of dangerous driving situations. *Applied Cognitive Psychology, 14*, 31-44.

Forsyth, E., Maycock, G. & Sexton, B. (1995). *Cohort study of learner and novice drivers: Part 3, Accidents, offences and driving experience in the first three years of driving.* (TRL Project Report 111). Crowthorne, UK: Transport Research Laboratory.

Grayson, G., & Maycock, G. (1988). From proneness to liability. In J.A. Rothengatter and R. de Bruin (Eds.), *Road User Behaviour: Theory and Research.* Assen: Van Gorcum.

Loftus, E. F. (1993). The reality of repressed memories. *American Psychologist, 48*, 518-537.

Maycock, G. (1997). Accident liability - the human perspective. In J.A. Rothengatter and E. Carbonell Vaya (Eds.), *Traffic and Transport Psychology: Theory and Application.* Oxford: Pergamon.

Maycock, G., Lester, J., & Lockwood, C. R. (1996). *The accident liability of car drivers: The reliability of self report data.* (TRL Report 219). Crowthorne, UK: Transport Research Laboratory.

Maycock, G., Lockwood, C. R., & Lester, J. F. (1991). *The accident liability of car drivers.* (TRRL Research Report 315). Crowthorne, UK: Transport and Road Research Laboratory.

McKenna, F. (1993). It won't happen to me: Unrealistic optimism or illusion of control? *British Journal of Psychology, 84*, 39-50.

Reason, J. T., Manstead, A. S. R., Stradling, S. G., Baxter, J. S., & Campbell, K. (1990). Errors and violations on the road: A real distinction? *Ergonomics, 33*, 1365-1375.

Underwood, G., Chapman, P., Wright, S., & Crundall, D. (1999). Anger while driving. *Transportation Research Part F, 2*, 55-68.

West, R. (1993). *Accident script analysis.* (TRL Report 274). Crowthorne, UK: Transport Research Laboratory.

West, R., & Hall, J. (1997). The role of personality and attitudes in traffic accident risk. *Applied Psychology: An International Review, 46,* 253-264.

Road User

Impairment

Traffic and Transport Psychology,
T. Rothengatter and R.D. Huguenin (Editors)

20

Fatigue and Driving

Laurence R. Hartley

Introduction

This chapter discusses the impact of fatigue on drivers and the countermeasures which might be used to control fatigue. In a broad ranging review such as this some detail is necessarily omitted but interested readers are referred to Horne and Reyner (2001), Smiley (1998). Fatigue is a term which has come in to usage to describe a collection of symptoms or signs displayed by drivers including loss of alertness at the wheel, microsleeps (brief periods of sleep of several seconds visible in the electroencephalographic record of drivers but which they are usually unaware of), poor vehicle contrøl including lane drifting and variable speed, and finally single vehicle crashes without any avoidance manoeuvre occurring usually at night. The term fatigue is synonymous with drowsy driving and sleepy driving which are used interchangeably.

There has been renewed international interest in driver fatigue for a variety of reasons including (i) better understanding of the causes of fatigue; (ii) longer working hours in the transport industry due to (iii) longer trips; (iv) increased international economic activity; (v) globalisation; (vi) just in time delivery where a goods vehicle becomes a mobile warehouse; (vii) increasing fuel costs requiring drivers to work longer hours to pay for the fuel; (viii) increasing transport industry competition resulting from de-regulation.

The Size of the Problem; Fatigue Surveys and Crash Data

The U.S. National Sleep Foundation carried out a survey of sleep problems in 1998. The survey found that 32% of people sleep less than 6 hours a night; 66% of adults reported sleep problems such as insomnia, 8% of adults had a diagnosed sleep disorder such as sleep apnoea, 38% of people reported excessive day time sleepiness, 57% of people admitted they had driven a vehicle when they were drowsy and 23% of people admitted they had fallen asleep behind the wheel at least once. In the U.K. Maycock (1997) reported that 29% of drivers reported they had come close to falling sleep at the wheel at least once.

It is difficult to determine with complete certainty whether a crash is due to fatigue for several reasons: (i) Fatigue crashes tend to be severe because there is no avoidance manoeuvre and often kill the driver; (ii) If drivers survive they seldom admit they were sleepy, or had fallen asleep, in order to escape liability; (iii) Sleepiness or fatigue in a driver leaves little trace after the crash and the crash is likely to arouse them; (iv) Fatigue crashes usually involve a single vehicle and mainly occur during the very early hours of the morning, so there may be no witnesses to the pre-crash manoeuvre.

Nevertheless there have been many attempts to estimate the size of the fatigue crash problem. These include: (i) American Automobile Association in 1985 which investigated 221 truck crashes and attributed 40% to fatigue; (ii) The U.S. Federal Motor Carrier Safety Administration has recently estimated 15% of fatal truck crashes are caused by fatigue (FMCSA,2000); (iii) In Australia Haworth et al. (1988) estimated that 20-30% of casualty and 25-35% of fatal truck crashes were due to fatigue, and Ryan (1995) estimates 16% of truck crash fatalities are fatigue related; (iv) In the UK Horne and Reyner (1995) estimate 16-20% of all fatalities are fatigue related.

Given the uncertainties involved in these estimates some authors have used the following characteristics of a typical fatigue crash to estimate the size of the problem. Hartley (2000) analysed Australian crash data from 1990-1995, where there was no involvement of alcohol or speed, for the following characteristics: (i) * Head on crash on the wrong side of the road when not overtaking; (ii) Single vehicle run off road crash with no avoidance manoeuvre

Hartley (2000) found that 40% of rural and 15% of urban fatalities in all vehicles were fatigue related. Thirty five percent of rural and 12% or urban serious fatalities were fatigue related. Taken together 29% of all fatalities and 20% of serious injuries are fatigue related. For truck crashes alone the respective percentages are 25% and 11%. Thirty five percent of fatal and 44% serious injury crashes due to fatigue involve drivers under 25 years old, making young drivers over-involved in fatigue crashes. Seventy one percent of fatal and 64% of serious injury crashes due to fatigue involve male drivers. Interestingly these proportions of fatalities due to fatigue are closely similar to those due to excessive speed and involving alcohol. Since this analysis is almost certainly over-inclusive of all fatigue related crashes these estimates are probably the upper bound of the proportion of crashes due to fatigue.

Causes of Driver Fatigue

Three principle causes of drivers fatigue have been identified in accident investigations, self reports and controlled studies.

Sleep loss

A number of studies have identified drivers who have had little sleep as over represented in crashes. The US National Transportation Safety Board (1995) examined 107 single heavy goods vehicle crashes where the drivers survived and records of their activities over the previous 4 days were available. In 58% of those crashes the drivers admitted they crashed because fatigue; and in 18% of those crashes the driver was asleep at the wheel. In the fatigue crashes the Safety Board found that drivers had: an inverted sleep/waking cycle; driven at night with a sleep debt (chronic sleep shortage); had slept only 5.5 h in the past 24 hours compared to 8.8 h in the crashes not due to fatigue; and had fragmented between night and day.

Arnold and Hartley (1998) analysed self report data from truck drivers about hazardous incidents including crashes and their hours of sleep the previous night. Drivers having less than 6 h of sleep reported 3 times more hazardous incidents than those having more than 6 h sleep. Drivers with less than 6 h sleep reported nodding off at the wheel 21/2 times more often than those with more than 6 h sleep. Drivers with less than 6 h of sleep reported using stimulant drugs to stay awake twice as often as drivers with more than 6 h sleep.

Stutts, Wilkins and Vaughn (1999) surveyed 1400 US drivers about their sleep history and crashes. They found shift workers were at six times the risk of a crash due to fatigue. Drivers who had less than 6 hours of sleep were at three times the risk of a fatigue crash; and drivers with less than 5 hours of sleep were at five times the risk of a crash due to fatigue.

These data clearly identify restricted sleep as a major cause of crashes with 6 or fewer hours of sleep placing the driver at great risk of crash than a blood alcohol concentration of 0.05%.

Driving at different times of day

It has been known for many years that humans have a diurnal cycle of alertness and propensity to sleep. Not unsurprisingly there is a diurnal cycle of single vehicle crashes. Hamelin (1987) found truck crash rates were lowest between 08.00 and 19.00. Between the hours of 20.00 and 07.00 there was twice the risk of having a crash. If the driver had already driven for 11 hours of more, the relative risk of having a crash increased fourfold during the night-time hours. Mackie and Miller (1978) calculated the percentage of crashes at different times of day. The percentage of single vehicle crashes reached its peak at 04.00 and minimum at 19.00. The relative increase in risk is 25 fold. Keklund and Akerstedt (1995) calculated the relative risk of a crash, where alcohol was not involved, for all vehicles by time of day. The data were adjusted to take account of the number of vehicles on the road at different times of day. They found that the risk of a single vehicle crash rose to a peak of 13 times the minimum risk at 03.00-04.00. The US Federal Motor Carrier Safety Administration (2000) has published the risk of truck involved fatal accidents at different times of day. There is four times the relative risk of a fatigue related crash at 05.00 compared to 19.00.

These data point to a diurnal cycle of crash risk, which reflects the cycle of sleep propensity or drowsiness. Since some studies involved single vehicle crashes it is concluded that the crashes are due to driver sleepiness, although recent work (Balkin, Thome, Sing, Thomas, Redmond, Wesensten, Williams, Hall & Belenky, 2000) have found a poor correlation between electroencephalographic signs of sleep and crashes in a driving simulator.

Long hours of driving

Some data point to an increased risk of a crash the greater the number of hours driven. Mackie and Miller (1978) found some aspects of driving performance deteriorated after 8-9 behind the wheel. They analysed 750 truck crashes that involved fatigue or were single vehicle crashes. They found twice the risk of a crash in the second as compared to first half of a trip, and the odds of a crash started to rise after 5 hours driving. Folkard (1997) undertook a meta-analysis of several studies of hours of driving and crash risk. Folkard found that there was a rise in risk at two hours into the trip before risk dropped back to starting levels at 4 hours into the trip. Relative risk of a crash then started to rise again the more hours driven until at 11 hours the risk was higher than at any previous time. The US Federal Motor Carrier Safety Administration (2000) has published data showing the relative risk of a fatigue crash and hours driven. As in Folkard's data and Hamelin (1987) crash risk starts to seriously rise by 7 fold after 10-11 hours of driving.

These data are indicative that after several hours behind the wheel crash rates begin to rise. However, an element of caution is needed in interpreting these data as showing that hours behind the wheel causes driver fatigue and crashes. One reason for caution is, that depending on trip start time, a down turn in the circadian cycle could be influencing performance during the later hours of the trip and thus could be responsible for the risk in crash risk.

Countermeasures to Fatigue

Behavioural countermeasures

A variety of behavioural countermeasures have been reported by drivers (e.g. Hartley, Arnold, Penna, Hochstadt, Corry & Feyer, 1995). These include winding the window down, turning up the radio, walking around the vehicle, chewing gum and smoking cigarettes. Horne and Reyner (1996) have evaluated some of these measures using a driving simulator to assess performance. Only drinking 2-3 cups of caffeine beverage and taking a 15 min nap proved to have any lasting restorative benefit. All other countermeasures had only transient or no effect.

Technological countermeasures

There are a very large number of hardware devices said to alert the driver to impending fatigue or crash. These range from devices to detect head nodding, oculomotor behaviour, psychomotor performance and slow eyelid droop (PERCLOS) to computer software programs to predict sleepiness in order optimise shift rosters. The fundamental task facing the developers of these technologies is to demonstrate criterion validity and demonstrate what the safe level of the criterion is. In fact there is very little validation data available for virtually all the devices that purport to detect fatigue, with the except of a few devices. PERCLOS (percentage eyelid closure) is one device with validation data. An infra red camera is located in-vehicle and it automatically records and scores slow eyelid closures which cover 80% of the pupil. This device has high correlations of 0.8 with lapses on the psychomotor vigilance task (Dinges, Mallis, Maislin and Powell, 1998) and could be a good candidate for a fatigue detection device.

A second device for which some validation data is available is SAVE, the System for effective Assessment of the driver state and Vehicle control in Emergency situations of Brookhuis, De Waard, Peters, & Bekiaris, (1998),. It has undergone validity testing during 1998.

"The SAVE Project (Brookhuis et al., 1998) is formally known as System for effective Assessment of the driver state and Vehicle control in Emergency situations. The aim of the SAVE project is to develop a prototype that will in real time detect impaired driver states and undertake emergency handling. This will be realised by instant detection of impairment, following which the driver will be warned, drivers in the vicinity will be warned, or if need be, the vehicle will be controlled automatically to the road verge." Table 1 summarises the components and measures that are employed by the SAVE system .

Table 1. The components and measures of the SAVE system.

Components	*Physiological measures*	*Vehicle measures*	*Environmental measures*
Integrated monitoring unit (IMU)	Eyelid closure	Speed	Time of day
Human-machine interface (HMI)	Head position	Steering wheel angle	Whether it rains or not
Hierarchical manager (HM)	Grip force on steering wheel	Distance to a lead vehicle	
SAVE warning systems (SWS)		Lateral position	
Automatic control device (ACD)		Time to line crossing	

In SAVE a Principal Component Analysis to reduce the data is first conducted, then a Neural Network calculation is conducted to decide on impairment and finally Fuzzy Logic is carried out to arrange the HMI (Human Machine Interface). Currently, the system appears to be detecting around 90% of fatigue cases, suggesting good concurrent validity but there is no formal report on the evaluation of the validity of the system. The use of multiple inputs to a model to detect fatigue requires that the inputs are integrated. Multiple inputs do not increase the likelihood of false alarms but reduce them essentially by checking all inputs. At present this system is still a long way from being commercially available.

There are computer three software systems to predict fatigue. The Fatigue Audit 'Interdyne' system was is described in Dawson et al., 1998). It is a mathematical algorithm based on timing, recency and duration of work and rest periods. Its objective is to allow companies to assess and compare previous, current and possible future work schedules in terms of predicted work related fatigue (McMahon, 2000). This is achieved by inputting work start and end times for a shift system into the program (including shift start and end times for the previous 7 days, to assess recent work history and recovery). The output consists of relative fatigue scores (ranging from 'standard' to 'extreme') for each hour of the shift schedule; this allows comparisons of different shift schedules on an hour-by-hour basis (McMahon, 2000).

US army sleep management system is another mathematical model based on work/rest periods and circadian cycles (see Belenky et al. 1998). U.S. Army medical researchers at Walter Reed Army Institute of Research (WRAIR) have developed a mathematical model to predict human performance on the basis of prior sleep (Belenky, 2000). They integrated this model into a wrist-activity monitor based sleep and performance predictor system called "Sleep Watch."

The Sleep Watch system includes a wrist-worn piezo electric chip activity monitor and recorder which will store up records of the wearer's activity and sleep obtained over several days. It then incorporates the measures with circadian periodicity variables into a stored sleep and performance predictive algorithm. At any point in time, the algorithm estimates how much in need of sleep the wearer is. The Sleep Watch, via wristwatch-like display informs the wearer about his/her state of alertness based upon the presumed need for sleep, or indicates his readiness to continue to conduct his/her job until the next opportunity for rest and/or sleep. The Sleep Watch system is based predominately on the amount of sleep obtained or not obtained, over the previous 3-4 days, and the prediction of performance is based upon preconceived relationships of quantity and quality of sleep to real time readiness to perform at a particular point in time.

The U.S. Army Sleep Watch system will be one of the Fatigue Management Technologies (FMT) in a large 2-year field trial sponsored by the Federal Motor Carrier Safety Administration and American Trucking Associations Foundation (FMCSA-ATAF) beginning in the U.S. and in Canada in October, 2000. (See further description of this FMT test later in the paper). At this point, this technology is considered to be in the adolescent stage, and is not yet ready for prime time applications.

The fatigue model of Åkerstedt and his co-workers (e.g. Åkerstedt and Folkard, 1997; Folkard, Åkerstedt, Macdonald, Tucker & Spencer, 1999) is a model for predicting alertness/ performance. The model is summarised as:

The model uses sleep data as input and contains a circadian and a homeostatic component (amount of prior wakefulness and amount of prior sleep), which are summed to yield predicted alertness (on a scale of 1 to 16) as well as performance on monotonous tasks. The model includes an identification of levels at which the risk of performance/alertness impairment starts, as well as prediction of sleep latency and time of awakening of sleep episodes. It is suggested that the model may be used to evaluate work/rest schedules in terms of sleep-related safety risk. (Åkerstedt & Folkard, 1997, page 115).

While the model has been extensively evaluated and redesigned it has certainly not been widely used by transport companies or commercial drivers to assess the safety and efficiency of their shift schedules. Furthermore, as pointed out by Folkard, Åkerstedt, Macdonald, Tucker and Spencer (1999) at the moment the predictions from the model are difficult to reconcile with trends in industrial accidents or injury risks

The accuracy of the fatigue algorithm is critical. As Dinges (1997) states, "a model that mis-estimates a cumulative performance decline by only a small percentage can lead to a gross miscalculation of performance capability and alertness over the course of a working week". So while such models show potential to easily predict fatigue in operators, a large amount of validation and possible 'fine-tuning' of the models are needed before their veracity can be fully accepted. At the time of writing there are few convincing real world predictive validation data on this technology.

As with the fitness-for duty testing described above, the Fatigue Audit Interdyne technology is performed before a shift and needs no special apparatus in the vehicle, so it does not impinge on the performance of in-vehicle systems (such as route guidance) and can fit in well with other regulatory/enforcement methods. By contrast the U.S. Army sleep watch system is "continuous" and operates continuously 24 hrs per day, including within the truck cab. Drivers may consult their sleep watch at any time to determine whether they need sleep or not. Thus this model has not only the potential to predict fatigue but also detect it.

All the models do have the potential to improve the design of shiftwork rosters and even in their present state of development they could provide useful advice to inexperienced supervisors responsible for roster design. The next generation of these models will need to take account of individual differences in susceptibility to fatigue including indications of differences in circadian physiology and periodicity and the degree of fatigue caused by different job demands.

Although many fatigue detection and prediction devices are available the validity of most of them remains to be demonstrated.

Regulatory countermeasures

There are regulations in many jurisdictions to govern the working and resting hours of road transport drivers. For example in the U.S.A. regulations limit drivers to 10 hours driving and 8 hours rest in 24 hours and 60 hours duty over 7 days. In Canada longer hours of work are permitted (13) and in Australia there are a variety of schemes ranging from 12 to 14 permitted hours of work. Enforcement in these jurisdictions is by keeping a log book of hours of work to be shown on demand to a police officer. Violation of these regulations is very common and enforcement is costly and difficult and rarely occurs apart from following an accident or incident. In Europe there are a variety of permitted driving and working hours depending on the jurisdiction. Enforcement is by a tachograph which records the vehicle movement. Enforcement follows an accident or incident.

Needless to say the regulatory approach to managing driver fatigue has received a great deal of criticism not only from the transport industry. The core criticisms are that the regulations do not address the principle causes of fatigue reviewed here: the timing of work and rest, and the duration of sleep. Other criticisms are: the inflexibility of regulations which may actually compound the problem of fatigue by preventing a driver reaching home where better rest may be obtained than by sleeping in the truck; and the poor enforcement of the regulations which brings them into disrepute.

References

AAA Foundation for Traffic Safety. (1985). A Report on the Determination and Evaluation of the Role of Fatigue in Heavy Truck Accidents, Report to the AAA Foundation for Traffic Safety.

Åkerstedt, T., & Folkard, S. (1997). The three-process model of alertness and its extension to performance, sleep latency and sleep length. *Chronobiology International, 14,* 115-123.

Arnold, P.K., & Hartley. L.R. (1998). Its not just hours of work; ask the drivers. In L.R. Hartley (Ed.), *Managing Fatigue in Transportation*. Oxford: Pergamon

Balkin, T., Thome, D, Sing, H, Thomas, M, Redmond, D, Wesensten, N, Williams, J, Hall, S, and Belenky,G, (2000) Effects of sleep schedules on commercial motor vehicle driver performance. U.S. Department of Transportation, Office of Motor Carrier Safety Administration, Report No. DOT-MC-00-133.

Belenky, G., Balkin, T.J., Redmond, D.P., Sing, H.C., Thomas, M.L., Thorne, D.R. & Wesensten, N.J. (1998). Sustained performance during continuous operations: The US army's sleep management system. In L. R. Hartley (Ed.), *Managing Fatigue in Transportation*. Oxford: Elsevier Science.

Belenky, G. (2000). The Effects of Restricted Sleep on Performance and Subsequent Recovery: Implications for Managing Sleep to Sustain Performance. *Presentation made at the 4th International Conference on Fatigue and Transportation: Coping with the 24 Hour Society*. Fremantle, WA, March 2000.

Brookhuis, K., De Waard, D., Peters, B., & Bekiaris, E. (1998). SAVE - system for detection of driver impairment and emergency handling. *IATSS Research, 22*, 37-42

Dawson, D., Lamond, N., Donkin, K., & Reid, K. (1998). Quantitative similarity between the cognitive psychomotor performance decrement associated with sustained wakefulness and alcohol intoxication. In L. R. Hartley (Ed.), *Managing Fatigue in Transportation*. Oxford: Elsevier Science.

Dinges, D.F. (1997). The promise and challenges of technologies for monitoring operator vigilance. Proceedings of the International Conference on Managing Fatigue in Transportation, American Trucking Associations Foundation, Florida, USA.

Dinges, D.F., Mallis, M.M., Maislin, G., & Powell, J.W. (1998). Final Report: Evaluation of Techniques for Ocular Measurement as an Index of Fatigue and as the Basis for Alertness Management. Washington, DC: National Highway Traffic Safety Administration. Report No DOT HS 808 762.

Federal Motor Carrier Safety Administration (2000). Hours of Service of Drivers; Driver rest and sleep for safe operations. Washington D.C: Department of Transportation 49 CFR Parts 350, 390, 394, 395 and 398

Folkard, S. (1997). Black times: temporal determinants of transport safety. *Accident Analysis and Prevention, 29*, 417-430.

Folkard, S., Åkerstedt, T., Macdonald, I., Tucker, P. & Spencer, M.B. (1999). Beyond the three-process model of alertness: estimating phase, time on shift and successive night effects. *Journal of Biological Rhythms, 14*, 577-587.

Hartley, L.R. Arnold, P.K. Penna, F., Hochstadt, D., Corry, A., & Feyer, A-M. (1995). *Fatigue in the Western Australian Transport Industry, Part 1.* Perth, Australia: Murdoch University.

Hartley, L.R. (2000). Fatigue and Driving. *Invited paper International Congress of Traffic and Transport Psychology.* Berne, Switzerland.

Haworth, N.L., Triggs, T.J., & Grey, E.M. (1988). *Driver Fatigue: Concepts, measurements, and crash countermeasures.* (Report #CR-72). Canberra, Australia: Department of Transport and Communications, Federal Office of Road Safety.

Horne, J.A., & Reyner, L.A. (1995). Sleep related vehicle accidents. *British Medical Journal; 6979,* 565-567.

Horne, J.A., & Reyner, L.A. (1996). Counteracting driver sleepiness: effects of napping, caffeine and placebo. *Psychophysiology, 33*, 306-309.

Horne, J.A., & Reyner, L.A. (2001). Sleep Related Vehicle Accidents: Some Guides for Road Safety Policies. Transportation Research F (in press)

Kecklund, G., & Akerstedt, T. (1995). Time of day and Swedish road accidents. *Shiftwork International Newsletter, 12*(1), pg. 31..

Mackie, R.R., & Miller, J.C. (1978). Effects of hours of service regularity of schedules, and cargo loading on truck and bus driver fatigue. Washington D.C.: U.S. Department of Transport Report No. HS-803 799..

McMahon, M. (2000). *Critical evaluation of a predictive model of work-related fatigue*. (Draft report). Perth, Australia: WA Department of Transport.

Maycock, G. (1997). Sleepiness and driving: the experience of U.K. Car drivers. *Accident Analysis and Prevention, 29*, 453-462.

National Sleep Foundation (1998). *Drive Alert, Arrive Alive.* Washington: National Sleep Foundation.

National Transportation Safety Board. (1995) Safety study: Factors that affect fatigue in heavy truck accidents. Washington D.C.: NTSB PB95-917001 - SS-95/01.

Ryan, G. A., & Spittle, J. (1995). The frequency of fatigue in truck crashes. *National Road Safety Research and Enforcement Conference.* Perth: Promaco Conventions.

Smiley, A. (1998). Fatigue Management: Lessons from Research, In L. R. Hartley (Ed.), *Managing Fatigue in Transportation*. Oxford: Elsevier Science.

Stutts, J.C., Wilkins, J.W., & Vaughn, B.V. (1999). Why do people have drowsy driving crashes. Washington: AAA Foundation for Traffic Safety.

Traffic and Transport Psychology,
T. Rothengatter and R.D. Huguenin (Editors)

21

Why is Driver Impairment Difficult to Assess?

Karel A. Brookhuis and Dick de Waard

Introduction

The field of Traffic and Transportation represents a vulnerable niche in working society. This professional area is faced with an unacceptable number of accidents that concurs with an unacceptable level of economic and human cost. The consequences of the performance of "the driver" are central in this field. Every error, failure or lapse of attention may represent an antecedent to a traffic accident. It has been estimated that 90% of accident causation can be traced back to the driver (Smiley & Brookhuis, 1987).

The operationalisation of accident proneness centres on behavioural variables. The likelihood of spontaneous error may be related to the driver's energetical state, i.e. the psycho-physiological status of the individual with respect to background level of alertness, awareness, sobriety, physical health (Hockey et al., 1986). If the energetical state of the driver is inappropriate or insufficient to sustain a safe and accurate level of vehicular control, the driver is judged to be impaired.

The energetical status of the driver may be influenced by psychological factors such as boredom and physiological variables, e.g. muscular aches and pains. The majority of driver impairment represents both psychological and physiological effects. For example, drowsiness may be characterised by physiological symptoms (e.g. heavy eyelids, yawning) in conjunction with psychological changes such as attentional lapses, irritability and slow reactions to traffic stimuli. Similarly, an intoxicated driver is unable to sustain safe and accurate vehicular control due to psycho-physiological impact of alcohol on energetical status.

There is a broad agreement among transport professionals and the driving community about what constitutes unsafe or undesirable driving. It is just common-sense to pronounce that sleepy, intoxicated or sick drivers may constitute a safety hazard to themselves and other motorists. However, there are a number of theoretical problems surrounding the diagnosis of driver impairment below the anecdotal level. In the simplest case, the diagnosis of impairment due to alcoholic intoxication is straightforward. The amount of alcohol consumed may be measured by Blood Alcohol Content (BAC), which has an exponential relationship with accident likelihood (Borkenstein et al., 1974), such as shown in figure 1. Based on this relationship most countries have adopted a fixed level of BAC (mostly 0.5 promille) as a legal criterion. In other cases where the energetical state of the driver is inappropriate such as stress or fatigue, no equivalent index of impairment is available. However, a relationship similar as in figure 1 is likely (Brookhuis, 1998). This lack of an appropriate index may simply be a conceptual limitation. The individual often spontaneously perceives changes in energetical status in the absence of any explicit numeric scale or continuum. In the absence of an anchor scale (such as BAC in the case of alcohol or body temperature in the case of impairment due to a thermal stressor), the multi-dimensional character of driver impairment renders the concept susceptible to an undesirable level of indeterminacy. This ambiguity at the conceptual level inevitably creates related problems of measurement and interpretation. This limitation is particularly striking when we attempt to measure the impact of multivariate energetical states on complex skills such as driving.

These problems set the background to the present analysis and discussion. There are practical reasons to devise a logical and consistent framework for the evaluation of driver behaviour. For example, it is technically feasible to monitor and diagnose driver behaviour with respect to accident-prone behaviour (Brookhuis & Brown, 1992) using real-time sensor apparatus. However, the feasibility of this technical apparatus is dependent on a valid framework for the evaluation of driver impairment (Fairclough et al., 1993, Brookhuis, 1995a). In broader terms, a large number of research papers are published each year in the field of traffic psychology and a consensual framework to evaluate qualitative and quantitative aspects of driver impairment would aid comparisons between studies.

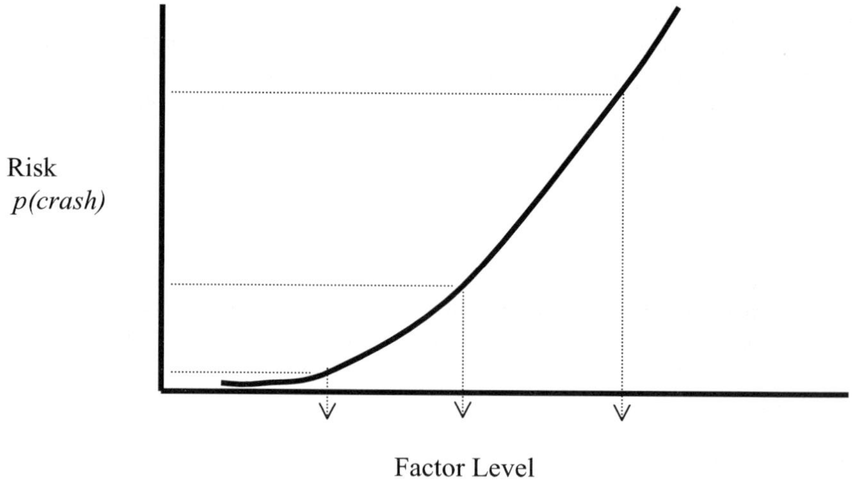

Figure 1. Relationship between the level of a factor (alcohol, fatigue, drug, etc.) and accident likelihood

What Constitutes Driver Impairment

The first step towards a definition of driver impairment is to establish accepted, valid distinction between 'normative' and 'impaired' categories of behaviour. One way to attain this goal is to induce impairment in a systematic and controlled fashion, therefore allowing us to study various levels on the continuum from normative driving to impairment. However, this process of categorisation is a contentious procedure as several alternative approaches are possible. A few techniques are feasible:

Inducing impairment

One technique is to manipulate the driving situation in such a way that it artificially induces impaired driving. The resulting data are then judged to be representative of impaired driving by definition and may be suitable as a benchmark measure for comparison. One straightforward method for inducing impairment is to have the driver consume a fair amount of alcohol, sufficient for a BAC above the legal level, and complete a journey in traffic. The detrimental effects of blood alcohol over the legal limit on traffic accidents are well documented while the effects on driving performance are demonstrated as well (Louwerens et al., 1987, Brookhuis, 1998). The data as collected during this test ride may be used to benchmark impairment relative to normative driving for a particular driver. Similarly it may be feasible to ask drivers to complete a driving task under conditions where they are impaired by depriving them of their perceptual senses. This technique involves an assessment of primary vehicle control under conditions where the driver's visual field is occluded (Godthelp, Milgram & Blaauw, 1984). When driver vision is totally occluded, the effects of "eyes off the road" time on lane keeping ability may be measured.

Accident precursors

An alternative technique would be to expose the driver to such a high level of a stressor that the driver is unable to sustain safe performance and drifts off-road or collides with another vehicle. Extreme forms of imposed visual impairments, as introduced De Waard et al. (1998) are feasible ways to induce stress in this sense. This approach has been used in a driving simulator by De Waard et al. (1998); they had subjects drive while they were distracted from the road by an extremely demanding, visual task.

High levels of fatigue could also serve as such according to Brown (1994, 1995), who proposed to define fatigue in terms of the consequences. There is some logic in reasoning that drivers are impaired if they are unable to avoid collisions or keep the vehicle on the road. Therefore, one may use the critical incident as a marker and analyse the period of activity prior to this incident via regression analysis (introduced in the SAVE project, see Bekiaris et al., 1997, Brookhuis et al., 1997). These techniques may ascertain which variable(s) are the strongest predictors of the critical incident.

Expert observation

In some countries in Europe, individuals that reach a certain age are required to subject themselves to examination by trained driving instructors, the case of the elderly drivers licensing. These professionals make an assessment of the individual's capability to drive safely based on this expert examination. Formalisation of expert observation may be used in order to develop a categorisation for "safe" versus "impaired" driving. A related example is the use of observation of drivers' facial activity in order to index fatigue (e.g. Ellsworth & Wierwille, 1994). In this example, a system of scoring facial symptoms of fatigue is designed and observers are "trained" to score directly from videotape.

Psycho-physiological criteria to define impaired driving

Impaired driving by definition implies that the driver is not fit to drive, as we have seen. This may be represented by psycho-physiological changes that may be used as a classification index to define levels of driver alertness. For example, EEG data may be used to index impending sleepiness while carrying out tasks like driving, independently from behavioural measures (Brookhuis et al., 1986, Åkerstedt et al., 1991). It is possible to collect concurrent data from driving behaviour and some well-defined psycho-physiological measures, and use the latter in order to categorise the former (Brookhuis, 1995b). Among those are heart rate and heart rate variability for effort and (mental) workload (Mulder, 1986, Mulder, 1992), facial muscles' activity for effort and emotional load (Van Boxtel & Jessurun, 1993), and eyelid position and activity for sleepiness (see also Brookhuis et al., 1998).

All these techniques are plausible and feasible to set up a valid categorisation, but none are without limitations. In the case of *inducing impairment*, there is an implicit assumption that all categories of driver impairment are equivalent. Hence, impairment due to alcohol is treated as interchangeable with other variables such as sleepiness. Whilst some researchers have emphasised the convergence of impairment variables on simple, laboratory tasks (Dawson et al., 1998), comparisons between different types of driver impairment have indicated key differences as well as similarities (Fairclough & Graham, 1999). The advantage of using alcohol in these conditions lies in its propaganda strength as a categorisation system based on legal and well-accepted criteria. The use of visual occlusion is a rarely used but valid attempt to measure decrements in lane-keeping performance by effectively "blinding" the driver to normal visual feedback. This method is suitable for the measurement of drivers' lane-keeping abilities but is very specific to this aspect of driving impairment and the ecological validity of this approach is suspect.

The technique described in *accident precursors* provides a direct link between either behavioural or vehicle input measures and examples of impaired driving. Whilst ethical considerations dictate that the techniques described in the first technique are usually the domain of closed circuit or simulator investigations, those in the second technique must always be performed in the simulator. This may raise the in principle valid questions regarding the perception of risk and drivers motivation to avoid accidents (see Farber, 1999, but also De Waard et al., 1999a, b). A second problem is the absence of any rational when one chooses what size of time window is appropriate to define the period prior to a critical incident, e.g. a small window of 1 minute or a larger window of 10 minutes. The use of a regression-type analysis may also be questionable as time-on-task may affect two concurrent measures of driver impairment (e.g. EEG and lane keeping) and therefore create the impression that the two are directly related to one another.

Both *psychophysiology* and *expert observations* take the emphasis from primary task measures to covert indicators of energetical state that do not directly reflect the quality of driver performance. The advantage of these measures is an assumption of increased sensitivity. In addition, psycho-physiological measures are traditionally used to classify human sleepiness and therefore, the same approach may be applied to those stages of reduced alertness that occur prior to full-blown sleepiness. The weakness is that both these techniques represent an indirect index of driver impairment.

It is possible to formulate 'composite' variables that represent a combination of different indicators of impairment. For example, psycho-physiological indicators may be more sensitive to the development of impairment than direct measures of primary task performance. These approaches to impairment measurement may be combined to produce an index of performance efficiency, i.e. the ratio between task input and performance output (Eysenck & Calvo, 1992). A composite measure was conceptualised by Meijman (1997) to represent the relationship between psycho-physiological mental effort (task input) and performance output. This index was applied to driving impairment to contrast the influence of two sleep deprivation regimes relative to a control condition (Fairclough & Graham, 1999). These data are illustrated below in Figure 2. The contrast between those subjects who had not slept (FullSD) and the other two groups is obvious from primary performance data. However, the composite variable reveals that the PartSD group (partial sleep deprivation) could only achieve equivalent performance to the Control group by investing a higher level of mental effort. These composite variables may represent a means of counteracting the weaknesses of individual measures.

The representation of driver behaviour is fundamental for the development of criteria and categorisation of impairment. These criteria are formulated to define the division, or "red line" between the normative and impaired examples of the primary task. These criteria may be formulated in either absolute or relative terms. The former relates to absolute values of behavioural measures, valid under all circumstances, the latter relates to individual differences. For an extensive explanation of the difference between absolute and relative criteria, see Brookhuis et al. (in press).

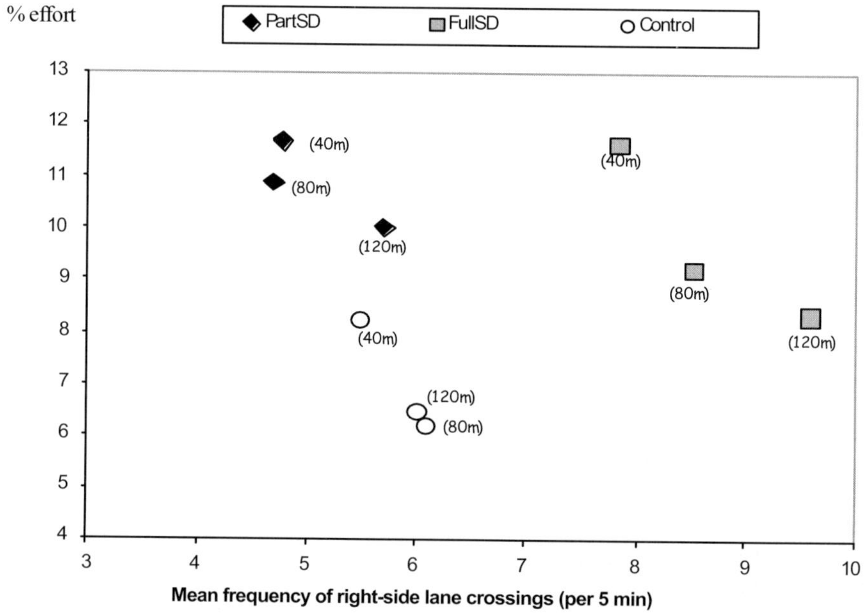

Figure 2. Performance efficiency index for three experimental groups across time-on-task; increase of x-values = poor lateral control of vehicle, increase of y-values = increased mental effort.

Many researchers have defined impaired driving as a statistically significant increase or decrease of a particular measure of driving. For example, in studies of in-vehicle displays a significant increase of vehicle lateral deviation would be assessed as an impairment effect resulting from attention distraction. In fatigue research, a significant decrease of steering reversal rate may be interpreted as impairment as the driver reduces the fidelity of steering control. This is a natural method for the categorisation of impaired driving in an experimental setting since most experiments contain control conditions or control subjects.

However, there are some problems defining impaired driving by statistical significance of a metric alone. The first one is the relation with accident likelihood (Risk, or *p(crash)*, as in figure 1). While this relation is exponential, which is at least for alcohol firmly established, the curve relating levels of a deficiency and a metric may seem to be linear (within a certain range probably then), or have an S-form, i.e. predominantly sensitive in a certain range as well. Moreover, the inter-individual variance is considerable, probably quite differently for the baseline or zero condition as compared to the impaired condition (e.g. Louwerens et al., 1987). This is illustrated in Figure 3. The metric measured might vary according to any of the curves as mentioned and depicted, depending on the paradigm used, while at the same time the variance is progressive with increases of the factor level for whatever construct under study.

The second problem concerns the consequences of signal-detection theory. In particular d-prime, i.e. in the present chapter the sensitivity of the impairment detection system, is relevant to the argument. Suppose the aim is to let the system discriminate drink driving from normal, sober driving by a simple, easily derived driving parameter, the amount of weaving, measured as the standard deviation of lateral position (SDLP). Taking the case of alcohol consumption has the inherent advantage of representing a benchmark, i.e. the relationship between BAC and accident likelihood (Borkenstein et al., 1964). Based on this relationship, in some countries the legal limit of BAC is 0.5 promille, in others it is still 0.8 promille. From the data of Louwerens et al. (1987), average SDLP's with these BAC's are known values. In the two examples in Figure 4, (a) describes (hypothetical) distributions of measured weaving of one particular driver in sober and drunk condition (0.8 promille), giving good separation with a small overlap. The driver in the example is called Mr. Average because his SDLP's at 0.8 and 0.5 promille match the average, "population" values as reported by Louwerens et al. (1987). Figure 4(b) describes the same driver who is now only marginally drunk (0.5 promille), showing a considerably smaller separation and larger overlap between distributions. In the first case, when Mr. Average is quite drunk (0.8 promille), the sensitivity of the impairment detection system is high, leaving a large area under both curves free of overlap. When Mr. Average is only marginally drunk (0.5 promille), the overlap is considerable and system sensitivity is much lower. Thus, the problem is clear; if Mr. Average with 0.8 promille is to be detected as drunk at all cost, occasionally the in-vehicle detection device, with (relative) criterion set at about 22 cm SDLP, will give false alarms in about (only) 10% of all cases. If false alarms have to be avoided completely, the detection criterion must be set at 24 cm SDLP, while drunk Mr. Average will then slip through in about 30% of the cases. At 0.5 promille things are much worse, avoiding false alarms means that Mr. Average, now marginally drunk, will slip through in at least 80% of all cases. Whereas from a safety perspective optimisation of detection would seemingly be preferable, drivers would quickly adapt to and neglect system warnings, but also be reluctant to accept a device that regularly gives false alarms, and it will be difficult if not impossible to turn this type of in-vehicle detection device compulsive. Mr. Average, however, could be forced to drive with a detection device, through court judgement after conviction for drunk driving.

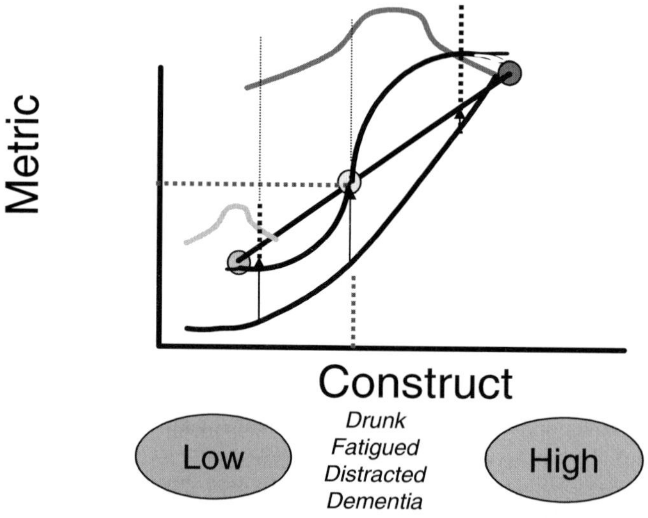

Figure 3. Relationship between the level of a construct representing a factor (alcohol, fatigue, attention, drug, etc.) and the metric that is selected to measure performance.

Categories of driving impairment

Back to the problem of definition concerning impaired driving. Often impairment is synonymous with the occurrence of an accident. While there can be little argument that certain categories of accidents (e.g. where the driver loses control of the vehicle and leaves the road) constitute impairment of driving skills, impaired driving per se does not inevitably lead to an accident. For example, an intoxicated driver weaving between two lanes benefits from either the absence of vehicles in the adjacent lane or the avoidance reactions of other road users. At the level of vehicle control, accidents where the driver bears the sole responsibility may result from either: (i) a loss of lateral vehicle control (e.g. lane weaving); (ii) an inappropriate use of lateral vehicle control (e.g. swerving into adjacent lane); (iii) an inappropriate use of longitudinal vehicle control (e.g. speeding, close following); (iv) concurrent occurrence of (ii) and (iii) (e.g. at overtaking); (v) concurrent occurrence of (i) and (iii) (e.g. skidding).

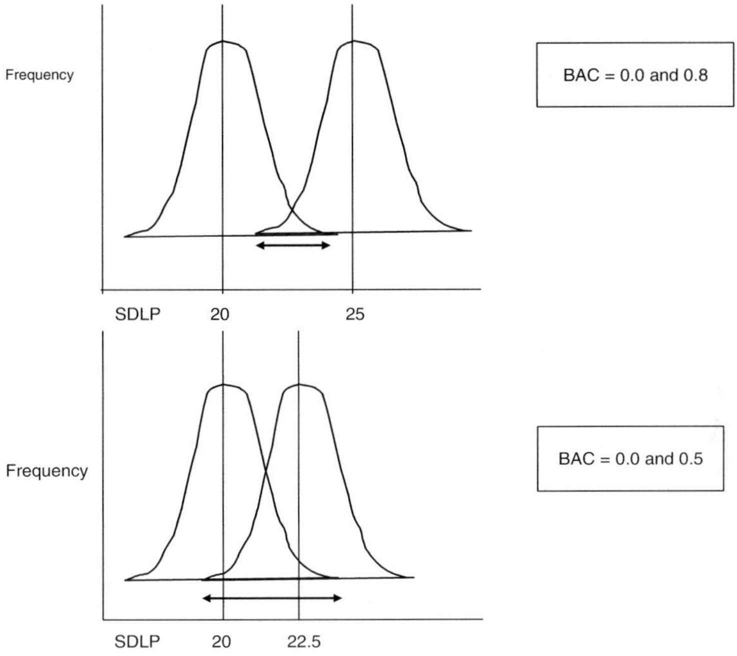

Figure 4. Hypothetical (approximately normal) distributions of measured weaving of one particular driver in sober and drunk condition (respectively 0.5 and 0.8 promille).

Taking a conceptual step back from traffic accidents, one could define impaired driving as those driver errors that may function as antecedents to actual accidents, as accident precursors. Harvey et al (1975) defined a driver error as "any action or lack of action by drivers that would require them or other road users to implement a correction in order to make the situation safe again". Harvey et al (1975) performed a roadside observation study of driver errors. Their eight most frequent errors and the categories of vehicle control associated with each are listed below. The five categories of vehicle control described above cannot exist in a vacuum. Therefore an attempt has been made to provide a series of referents in the driving environment to provide a context to the category of vehicle control.

This sub-set of driver errors may be used at a behavioural level to describe impaired driver performance. However, in order to be able to measure these errors, driving behaviour must be decomposed and operationalised into quantitative data. This translation shifts the definition of impaired driving from a behavioural level to a sensor level. In Table 2, vehicle measures have been substituted for the appropriate category of vehicle control.

These measures are the building blocks used to define and to characterise "impaired driving" at the sensor level. However, these measures merely describe the pattern of vehicle control in operation at any given time. They do not tell us if driving behaviour may be categorised as impaired or not. For this, we need the criteria, as was demonstrated before.

Table 1. Driver errors and vehicle control (from Harvey et al., 1975).

ERROR	*VEHICLE CONTROL*
Following too closely	Inappropriate longitudinal control relative to lead vehicle
Overtaking in face of oncoming traffic	Inappropriate lateral/longitudinal control relative to manoeuvre and vehicle in adjacent lane
Overtaking at junction	Inappropriate lateral/longitudinal control relative to location
Following too closely to overtaking vehicle	Inappropriate lateral/longitudinal control relative to lead vehicle and manoeuvre performed by lead vehicle
Changing lanes abruptly	Inappropriate lateral control relative to lane width
Straddling lanes	Loss of lateral control relative to lane width
Driving too fast for circumstances	Inappropriate longitudinal control relative to legal limit/traffic density

Table 2. Driver errors and vehicle measures.

ERROR	*VEHICLE MEASURES*
Following too closely	time headway to lead vehicle time-to-collision (TTC) to lead vehicle
Overtaking in face of oncoming traffic	Speed lateral position of vehicle time headway to vehicle in adjacent lane TTC to vehicle in adjacent lane
Overtaking at junction	Speed lateral position of vehicle TTC to "give way" line
Following too closely to overtaking vehicle	Speed lateral position of vehicle time headway to lead vehicle time-to-collision (TTC) to lead vehicle
Changing lanes abruptly	steering wheel activity speed lateral position of vehicle time-to-line crossing
Straddling lanes	steering wheel activity lateral position of vehicle time-to-line crossing
Driving too fast for circumstances	Speed

Integration

Individual measures have been discussed until now, such as SDLP, TTC, TLC, speed measures and steering wheel measures. Each of these measures has its value in determining driver impairment. However, an integrated diagnosis, or in other words a classification based on an integration of the flow of information from the whole lot of vehicle sensors, would potentially be much more powerful (De Waard & Brookhuis, 1991, Fairclough et al., 1993, Brookhuis, 1995a). Moreover, in the SAVE project several new, promising driver state related measures have been developed, i.e. an eye-lid closure sensor, a steering wheel grip sensor and a head position sensor, that certainly contributed. In this project (Bekiaris et al., 1997, Brookhuis et al., 1997), the processing of the impairment-sensitive sensor data has been realised through an Integrated Monitoring Unit, divided into three functional units, the vehicle sensors from which instantaneous driving data are collected, an advanced diagnosis or classification subsystem that analyses and interprets these data, and the storage / retrieval device which is used as a template of normal (normative) driving. The diagnosis or classification subsystem consists of a series of processing algorithms in sequence, centred around a Neural Network. The sequence consists of pre-processing by a suitable form of Principal Component Analysis, processing by an Artificial Neural Net (using a Barycentric Correction Procedure Sequential Learning Algorithm), after which a final diagnosis is performed with the aid of Fuzzy Logic (Hernandez, 1999). A series of validation experiments have been carried out to test and tune the system. Alcohol intoxication, serious fatigue and inattention have been subjected to classification procedures. It turned out that a correct diagnosis of at least 90% could be attained in case of impairment, however, only for individual drivers, based on their idiosyncratic, normative template. The reference to relative criteria appeared to be feasible for the conceptualisation of a driver impairment-monitoring device.

Conclusion

Several alternative schemes to approach monitoring impaired driving have been discussed, notably comparing performance with the decrement produced by illegal levels of alcohol intoxication and visual occlusion. It is clear, in principle, that driving after too much alcohol or blindfolded can only impair vehicle handling. However, these impairment manipulations are not equivalent and may produce specific effects which are not exactly generalisable to fatigue or illness etc. Nevertheless, the advantage of the alcohol manipulation is that most countries have prescribed a legal limit for alcoholic intake whilst driving. Therefore, the drunk driving case could have an exemplary function as both an impairment category in its own right and the nearest standard available for a legal definition of driver impairment.

The utilisation of a multidimensional approach (i.e. using psychophysiology, observation and direct measurement of driver performance for the assessment of impaired driving behaviour) has a number of advantages in terms of improved sensitivity and validity. The problems of sensitivity have been discussed with reference to absolute criteria and relative criteria. It has been argued that both criteria are necessary in order to fulfil the paradoxical goal of providing a definition of impaired driving which is consistent yet adaptable to inter-individual differences. However, within the current context, it is essential that driving performance itself functions as an anchor point for all other measures. The development of criteria to define driver impairment is necessary in order to: (i) define the validity of other indicators from different domains of measurement; and (ii) identify the magnitude of performance decrement to provide contextual information to a warning device.

Finally, a method has been proposed to index driver impairment (Brookhuis et al., in press). The approach described presents a decomposition of driver errors into operationalised measures of driver behaviour with the aim to monitor its safety. This analysis represents the first step towards the development of realistic criteria for determining impaired driving. The crucial aspect of criteria development concerns how to define the magnitude of change and those boundaries of driver impairment, which separate safety-critical changes from non-safety-critical changes. This is only the beginning, a potentially important step which, with the help of experts in the field, will hopefully lead to valid, integrated driver monitoring systems.

References

Åkerstedt, T., Kecklund, G., Sigurdsson, K., Anderzén, I., & Gillberg, M. (1991). Methodological aspects on ambulatory monitoring of sleepiness. In *Proceedings of the workshop Psychophysiological Measures in Transport Operations*. Köln: DLR, pp.1-21.

Bekiaris, E., Brookhuis, K.A., & De Waard, D. (1997). A system for Detection of Driver Impairment and Emergency Handling. In D. Roller (Ed.), *30th International Symposium on Automotive Technology & Automation* (pp. 223-231). London: Automotive Automation Limited.

Borkenstein, R.F., Crowther, R.F., Shumate, R.P., Ziel, W.B., & Zylman, R. (1964). The role of the drinking driver in traffic accidents. *Blutalkohol, 11*, suppl. 1.

Brookhuis, K.A., Louwerens, J.W., & O'Hanlon, J.F. (1986). EEG energy-density spectra and driving performance under the influence of some antidepressant drugs. In J.F. O'Hanlon & J.J. de Gier (Eds.), *Drugs and Driving*, (pp.213-221). London: Taylor & Francis.

Brookhuis, K.A., & Brown, I.D. (1992). Ergonomics and road safety. *Impact of science on society, 165*, 35-40.

Brookhuis, K.A. (1995a) Driver Impairment Monitoring System. In M. Vallet and S. Khardi (Eds.), *Vigilance et Transports. Aspects fondamentaux, dégradation et préventation.* (pp. 287-297). Lyon, France: Presses Universitaires de Lyon.

Brookhuis, K.A. (1995b). Driver impairment monitoring by physiological measures. In L. Hartley (Ed.), *Fatigue & Driving*, (pp. 181-189). London, Philadelphia: Taylor & Francis,.

Brookhuis, K.A., De Waard, D., & Bekiaris, E. (1997). Development of a system for detection of driver impairment. In C. Mercier-Guyon (Ed.), *Alcohol, Drugs and Traffic Safety, T'97*, (pp. 581-586). Annecy: CERMT,.

Brookhuis, K.A. (1998). How to measure driving ability under the influence of alcohol and drugs, and why. *Human Psychopharmacology, 13,* 64-69.

Brookhuis, K.A., De Waard, D., Peters, B., & Bekiaris, E. (1998). SAVE - System for detection of driver impairment and emergency handling. *IATSS Research, 22:* 37-42.

Brookhuis, K.A., De Waard, D., & Fairclough, S.H. (in press). Criteria for driver impairment. *Ergonomics.*

Dawson, D., Lamond, N., Donkin, K., & Reid, K. (1998). Quantitative similiarity between the cognitive psychomotor performance decrement associated with sustained wakefulness and alcoholic intoxication. In L. Hartley (Ed.), *Fatigue and Transport* (pp. 231-256). Amsterdam: Elsevier.

De Waard, D., & Brookhuis, K.A. (1991). Assessing driver status: a demonstration experiment on the road. *Accident Analysis & Prevention, 23,* 297-307.

De Waard, D., & Brookhuis, K.A. (1997). On the measurement of driver mental workload. In J.A. Rothengatter & E. Carbonell (Eds.), *Traffic and Transport Psychology*. (pp. 161-173). Oxford: Pergamon.

De Waard, D., Van der Hulst, M., & Brookhuis, K.A. (1998). The detection of driver inattention and breakdown. In P. Albuquerque, J.A. Santos, C. Rodrigues, A.H. Pires da Costa (Eds.), *Human Factors in Road Traffic II*. (pp. 102-108). Braga: University of Minho.

De Waard, D., Van der Hulst, M., Hoedemaeker, M., & Brookhuis, K.A. (1999a). Driver behavior in an emergency situation in the Automated Highway System. *Transportation Human Factors, 1*, 67-82.

De Waard, D., Van der Hulst, M., Hoedemaeker, M., & Brookhuis, K.A. (1999b). Reply to comments on "Driver behavior in an emergency situation in the Automated Highway System". *Transportation Human Factors, 1*, 87-89.

Eysenck, M. W., & Calvo, M. G. (1992). Anxiety and performance: The processing efficiency theory. *Cognition and Emotion*, 6, 409-434.

Fairclough, S. H., & Graham, R. (1999). Impairment of driving performance caused by sleep deprivation or alcohol: A comparative study. *Human Factors, 41,* 118-128.

Fairclough, S.H., Brookhuis, K.A., & Vallet, M. (1993). Driver state monitoring system DETER (V2009) (pp. 330-335). In *Advanced Transport Telematics, Proceedings of the Technical Days.* Brussels: Commission of the European Communities.

Farber, E. (1999). comments on "Driver behavior in an emergency situation in the Automated Highway System". *Transportation Human Factors, 1*, 83-86.

Godthelp, J., Milgram, P., & Blaauw, G.J. (1984). The development of a time-related measure to describe driving strategy. *Human Factors, 26*, 257-268.

Godthelp, J. (1988). Thesis. Soesterberg: TNO TM.

Harvey, C. F., Jenkins, D., & Sumner, R. (1975). *Driver Error* (Supplementary Report 149 UC). Crowthorne: Transport Research Laboratory.

Hernandez, N. (1999). Thesis. Toulouse: LAAS.

Hockey, G. R. J., Coles, M. G. H., & Gaillard, A. W. K. (1986). Energetical issues in research on human information processing. In G. R. J. Hockey, A. W. K. Gaillard and M. G. H. Coles (Eds.), *Energetics and Human Information Processing* (pp. 3-21). Dordrecht: Martinus Nijhoff.

Louwerens, J.W., Gloerich, A.B.M., De Vries, G., Brookhuis, K.A., & O'Hanlon, J.F. (1987). The relationship between drivers' blood alcohol concentration (BAC) and actual driving performance during high speed travel. In P.C. Noordzij and R. Roszbach (Eds.), *Alcohol, Drugs and Driving - T'86*, (pp.183-187). Amsterdam: Excerpta Medica.

Meijman, T. F. (1997). Mental fatigue. *International Journal of Industrial Ergonomics, 20*, 31-38.

Ministry of Transport and Communications Finland. (1998). *Guidelines for the evaluation of ITS projects*. Research report.

Mulder, G. (1986). The concept and measurement of mental effort. In G.R.J. Hockey, A.W.K. Gaillard and M.G.H. Coles (Eds.), *Energetics and human information processing* (pp. 175-198). Dordrecht, The Netherlands: Martinus Nijhoff Publishers.

Mulder, L.J.M. (1992). Measurement and analysis methods of heart rate and respiration for use in applied environments. *Biological Psychology, 34*, 205-236.

Smiley, A. & Brookhuis, K.A. (1987). Alcohol, drugs and traffic safety. In J.A. Rothengatter and R.A. de Bruin (Eds.), *Road users and traffic safety*, (pp. 83-105). Assen: Van Gorcum.

Van Boxtel, A., & Jessurun, M. (1993). Amplitude and bilateral coherency of facial and jaw-elevator EMG activity as an index of effort during a two-choice serial reaction task. *Psychophysiology, 30*, 589-604.

Wierwille, W.W. & Ellsworth, L.A. 1994, Evaluation of driver drowsiness by trained raters, *Accident Analysis and Prevention, 26,* 571-581.

Traffic and Transport Psychology,
T. Rothengatter and R.D. Huguenin (Editors)

22

Individual Differences in Driver Risk Acceptance During Sleep Deprivation

Joshua B. Hurwitz

Introduction

One of the major issues in driving research has been the effect of fatigue on driver performance (Wylie, Shultz, Miller, Mitler & Mackie, 1996). The impact of fatigue has been particularly acute in commercial driving. The pressures on commercial drivers often lead them to risk driving on less sleep than is recommended for safe and effective performance (Hanowski, Wierwille, Gellatly, Dingus, Knipling & Carroll, 1999). Given this situation, the challenge is to develop technologies that detect deterioration in performance due to fatigue to permit the implementation of interventions that mitigate this effect.

It is well known that fatigue impairs signal detection (Colligan & Tepas, 1986; Craig & Condon, 1985; Babkoff, Genser, Sing, Throne & Hegge, 1985; Colligan, 1983; Horne, Anderson & Wilkinson, 1983), sustained attention (Dinges, 1995; Dinges & Kribbs, 1991; Babkoff, Genser, Sing, Thorne & Hegge, 1985), and memory (Colligan & Tepas, 1986; Colligan, 1983; Colquhoun, 1982). Fatigue also increases the frequency of eye blinks, as drivers struggle to stay awake (Hargutt, 2000; Krüger, 2000), and microsleeps, as the body attempts to compensate for the sleep deficit (Dinges, 1995; Dinges & Kribbs, 1991). These effects are likely to influence how well drivers can process traffic and roadway information, leading to errors such as inattention to road signs, deterioration in lane following and running off roads (Najm, Mironer, Koziol, Jing-Shiarn & Knipling, 1995).

However, while fatigue is responsible for such impairments in information processing, it could also affect processes associated with decision-making. This effect is relevant because many accidents are associated with high-risk driving behaviours such as speeding and close following (Najm et al., 1995; West, French, Kemp & Elander, 1993). These so-called "intentional" errors (Parker, Reason, Manstead & Stradling, 1995; Reason, Manstead, Stradling, Baxter &

Campbell, 1990) relate more to the acceptance of risk-and to the general propensity to engage in novel, exciting and dangerous activities (Jonah, 1997; Zuckerman, 1979)-than to the ability to successfully maintain control of the vehicle and process information about the traffic environment.

Risk acceptance

Drivers accept risk by initiating dangerous manœuvres before having sufficient information to determine the consequences of those manœuvres. Consider, for example, a driver crossing an intersection. The driver accepts risk by crossing before determining the distances and speeds of other vehicles approaching along the cross streets. The driver may have the cognitive abilities to adequately make these estimates, but still lacks this information because of self-imposed time pressure.

Sleep loss may promote this strategy of favouring easier, automated, speeded responses over more difficult, controlled and more accurate responses (e.g., Soetens, Hueting & Wauters, 1992). Angus and Condon (1985) found on an inspection task that when the circadian rhythm is typically at its lowest, subjects tended to favour speed over accuracy. Evidence also suggests that fatigued subjects choose the easier response even when it is riskier than the more difficult one. Shingledecker and Holding (1974) found that fatigued subjects on a route-finding task chose easier routes over more difficult ones, even though there was a greater risk of failure associated with the easier routes.

While there are some obvious negative consequences when drivers choose fast, automated responses over slower, more controlled and less risky responses, these negative outcomes-accidents and violations-occur somewhat rarely (Najm et al., 1995). Furthermore, drivers are more likely to experience positive than negative outcomes as a consequence of risky behaviours. Drivers under time pressure are likely to accept risks such as speeding and not stopping at stop signs in order to achieve some goal, such as reaching their destination more quickly.

For sleep-deprived drivers, another incentive to accept risk might be to counteract the effects of sleep loss and remain engaged in the driving task. This is a reasonable assumption given results showing that performance under fatigue deteriorates greatest on tasks considered boring or uninteresting (Gaillard & Steyvers, 1989), and that incentives to perform well counteract fatigue effects (Horne, J.A. & Pettitt, A.N., 1985). Another incentive to accept risk might be for the sleepy driver to communicate negative feelings towards other drivers. Prior research indicates that fatigue has a negative effect on mood (Dinges, Pack, Williams, Gillen, Powell, Ott, Atpowicz & Pack, 1997). This effect could, in turn, influence tendencies toward the risky behaviours that are associated with road rage.

Measuring risk acceptance

While sleep deprivation may increase tendencies to accept risk, one obstacle to studying the relationship between fatigue and risk has been the lack of quantitative methods for measuring driver risk acceptance. Any risky driving activity could be attributable either to deterioration in processes that promote the perception of risk, or to increased acceptance of risk. Consider, for example, a fatigued driver who accepts dangerously small gaps with other vehicles when crossing an intersection. The driver's lack of sufficient sleep could have produced deficits in information processing that impaired his ability to judge the speeds and distances of those vehicles. On the other hand, fatigue could have made the driver more irritable and impatient, causing him to enter the intersection without leaving sufficient time to check for oncoming vehicles.

One approach taken by Hurwitz (1998, 1999) uses a mathematical driver performance model to assess risk acceptance in crossing intersections independently of input processes that affect risk perception. This model, called the DRIVE model ("Decision-making under Risk In a Vehicular Environment"), incorporates mechanisms for estimating crossing risk and for deciding whether to accept this risk. Prior studies with the model have shown that among all the parameters in the model, the one associated with the risk acceptance mechanism best accounts for individual differences in performance on a simulated intersection-crossing task. Furthermore, estimates of the value of this parameter relate to violation rates on drivers' official Motor Vehicle Records (Hurwitz, 1998, 1999).

The goal in the current study was to assess whether fatigue exacerbates driver risk acceptance, leading to increases in risk taking with increasing sleep deprivation. To achieve this goal, drivers performed the driving task at 3-hour intervals over a 36-hour period of sleep deprivation. The DRIVE model was fitted to their performance data, and risk-acceptance parameter estimates from the model were used to assess changes in risk with fatigue.

METHOD

Subjects

There were 24 subjects, 12 males and 12 females, with a mean age of 24.3 years, a standard deviation of 4.44 years, and a range from 18 to 34 years. Each subject received $590 at the end of the study for having completed the entire study.

Procedure

For the crossing task, subjects were presented with a PC-based simulation of a 3-dimensional scene depicting a "car" on a road approaching an intersection from the left side (see Figure 1). This scene was presented from the point of view of a driver waiting to cross the intersection. The subjects were instructed that they were playing the role of this driver, and that they could cross at any time by pressing a button on the joystick.

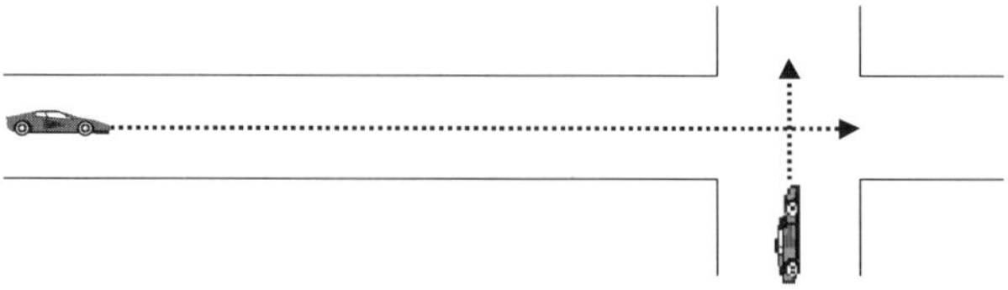

Figure 1. Diagram showing a bird's-eye view of the intersection crossing task.

Time pressure was implemented in this task by displaying a digital timer at the bottom of the screen. On each trial, the timer started at some value between about 3125 and 11500, and decreased at a rate such that it would reach 0 by the end of the trial if the subject made no response during the trial. The starting value depended on the conditions, and incorporated a random component to prevent the timer from acting as a cue on when to respond.

Overall, there were three possible outcomes on each trial. The subject's car 1) crossed safely in front of the oncoming vehicle, 2) crossed behind that car or 3) crashed into it. For outcomes 1 and 2, the subject received the number of points that were indicated on the timer when the response was made. For outcome 3, the subject lost four times the initial value on the timer.

Experimental design

There were four within-subject factors in the study: the starting distance of the oncoming car, the time available for the subject to successfully cross in front of that car, the time it took for the subject's car to cross the intersection, and the testing session. Regarding the first factor, the oncoming car approached the intersection from either 250 or 500 feet (76 or 152 metres) away. For the second factor, called the "Window of Opportunity", there were 0, 400, 900 or 2100 ms available for the subject to make a successful crossing in front of the oncoming car. For the crossing time factor, the speed of the subject's car was set so that, after the subject pressed the joystick button, it would take either 4 or 8 seconds for that car to cross the intersection.

Regarding the fourth factor, the subjects attended a number of testing sessions during the course of a week, and were given the same battery of tests during each session. They started with one practice session per day on Monday, Tuesday, Wednesday and Thursday, and then went through 13 fatigue sessions at 3-hour intervals starting Friday at 8:00 PM and going through Sunday at 8:00 AM. They were instructed to wake up anywhere from 6:00 AM to 8:00 AM on Friday, so, if this instruction was followed, they would have had 48 hours without sleep by the time the last fatigue session was completed on Sunday. Finally, the subjects participated in a follow-up session at 6:00 PM the following Tuesday, after having had two days to rest up from the fatigue sessions.

When this test session factor was combined with all the others (2 starting distances, 4 windows of opportunity, and 2 crossing times), there were a total of 288 conditions in the study (see Table 1 for the parameters of the crossing task). However, the analysis of driver risk acceptance presented below was limited to the first 6 testing sessions during sleep deprivation, for 96 conditions.

RESULTS

The analyses focused on measuring the joint effects of individual differences and fatigue on driver risk acceptance during the first night and morning of sleep deprivation. Risk acceptance in the crossing task was measured using the DRIVE model. This model is described in other papers (Hurwitz, 1997, 1998). Briefly, it predicts the probability of crossing at each moment in time, t, as the oncoming car approaches the intersection. This prediction is based on the model's "perception" of the risk inherent in crossing at t, and of its "propensity" to accept that risk.

Table 1. Experimental parameters for the crossing task, and resulting speeds for the oncoming vehicle.

Starting distance of the oncoming car from the intersection	*Time for the subject's car to cross the intersection (s)*	*Window of Opportunity (ms)*			
		0	*400*	*900*	*2100*
250 ft (76 m)	8	54 ft/s (16 m/s)	49 ft/s (15 m/s)	45 ft/s (14 m/s)	37 ft/s (11 m/s)
	4	107 ft/s (33 m/s)	91 ft/s (28 m/s)	77 ft/s (24 m/s)	56 ft/s (17 m/s)
500 ft (152 m)	8	107 ft/s (33 m/s)	99 ft/s (30 m/s)	90 ft/s (27 m/s)	74 ft/s (23 m/s)
	4	214 ft/s (65 m/s)	183 ft/s (56 m/s)	155 ft/s (47 m/s)	113 ft/s (34 m/s)

The model's risk perception at t derives from its estimate of how far the oncoming vehicle would be from the intersection if the crossing vehicle had reached the middle of the intersection after a response was initiated at t. To compute this "projected distance" requires an estimate of the oncoming car's speed and distance, and of the time it would take for the crossing vehicle to reach the other side of the intersection. Once the risk estimate is made, the model "decides" whether to accept this risk using the following decision function:

$$P_t = 1 - e^{-cD_t}$$

where P_t is the probability of crossing at time t, D_t is the projected distance of the oncoming vehicle at that time, and c is a free parameter ($c > 0$).

Note that when c is 0, the probability of crossing is always 0, so that the model is most conservative. As c increases, the crossing probability increases for a given value of D_t, and the required value of D_t to achieve a given probability of crossing goes down. For example, when c is 0.5 and the projected distance is 2 (arbitrary units), the probability of crossing is 0.63. If the value of c were 1, the projected distance would only have to be 1 to achieve the same crossing probability.

Implications for performance

The value of the risk acceptance parameter relates to the tendency to attempt to cross in front of or after the oncoming vehicle regardless of the traffic situation. Given the incentive system set up in the crossing task, an adaptive approach would be for drivers to wait a small amount of time at the beginning of a trial to estimate the speed of the oncoming vehicle. Then, to ensure obtaining a high point count, the optimal strategy when faced with a slow oncoming car would be for the driver to cross in front of that vehicle. When presented with a fast oncoming car, the driver should wait for that vehicle to cross the intersection first before pressing the mouse button. In this latter case, there would be sufficient time remaining after the oncoming vehicle crosses to obtain a relatively high point count.

Of course, the driver should also consider the speed of his or her vehicle and the distance of the oncoming vehicle when making the judgement to cross. If the driver's car is slower, then the speed of the oncoming vehicle should be correspondingly lower in order for the driver to cross in front of that vehicle. Similarly, if the oncoming car is approaching from a smaller distance away, then that vehicle's speed should also be lower for the driver to consider crossing in front of it.

For very small and very large values of the risk acceptance parameter, c, the model is less sensitive to the speed and distance of the oncoming vehicle and to the time required for crossing the intersection. The model simply either avoids crossing altogether (for small values of c), or always crosses almost immediately (for large values). In particular, a high value of c represents the tendency for some drivers to gamble that there will be a sufficiently large gap to allow for a safe crossing, despite the fact that they have not taken the time to estimate the size of that gap.

Model fits

The model was fit to the cumulative response probability functions for all 16 conditions of the driving task, and for data from each of the test sessions, using the method of least squares. Examples of such response functions are shown in Figure 2. The chart shows responses during the first six test sessions while the subjects were undergoing sleep deprivation. The chart shows the typical features of the intersection-crossing response function. Typically, between 50% and 80% of the responses occur in the first 1000 milliseconds of a trial, when many drivers are trying to cross in front of the oncoming vehicle. After this initial rise in the cumulative function, the function becomes flatter as the oncoming vehicle approaches to a distance at which most subjects avoid responding. After this plateau, the slope of the response function increases again as subjects cross behind the oncoming vehicle shortly after it has reached the intersection.

Another feature of responding is that the cumulative probability function is steeper when the window of opportunity is longer, and when the oncoming vehicle starts farther away from the intersection. The probability of initiating a crossing response 500 ms after a trial has started is 0.54 when the window of opportunity is less than 1000 ms, but goes up to 0.68 when it is 2100 ms ($F(1, 19) = 17.80$, $p < .001$, MSError = 0.001). Also, the probability is 0.47 when the oncoming vehicle starts 250 ft (76 m) from the intersection, whereas it goes up to 0.66 when that vehicle starts from 500 ft (152 m) away ($F(1, 19) = 18.57$, $p < .001$, MSError = 0.002). Both response patterns have been noted in previous studies (Hurwitz, 1997, 1998). While it makes sense that subjects would take more opportunities to cross in front of a slower oncoming vehicle, it is less clear why the starting distance would be a factor, since the opportunities to cross first are the same regardless of the starting distance.

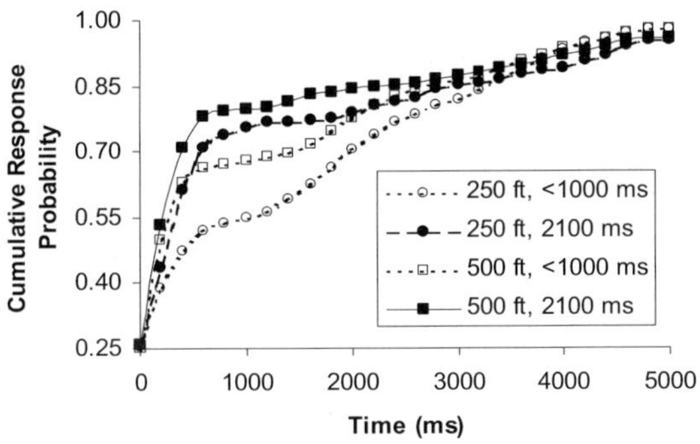

Figure 2. Cumulative response probability function for each starting distance (250 ft or 76 m, and 500 ft or 152 m) and window of opportunity.

Modelling individual differences

The first step in fitting the model was to estimate the best-fitting parameter values for all subjects. The next step was to hold all except for one of the parameters constant at these values, and then to fit the model again, allowing the value of the remaining parameter to vary across individuals. For a given parameter, the degree to which the fit improved when it was allowed to vary in this way represented how well that parameter accounted for individual differences in performance on the task.

Figure 3 displays the sum of squared errors for the individual-differences fits across all of the testing sessions. As in prior studies (Hurwitz, 1997, 1998), the results show that allowing the value of the c parameter to vary across individuals consistently produced the largest improvements in the fits, when compared to the other parameters in the model. This supports the hypothesis that individual differences in performance on this task are better accounted for by differences in risk acceptance than by differences in risk perception.

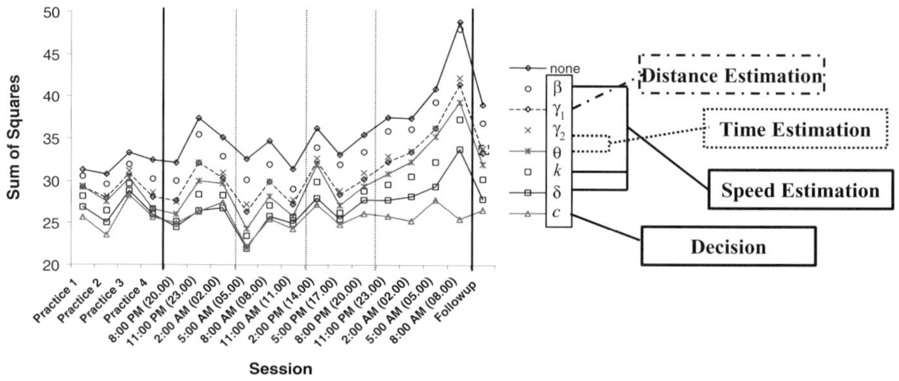

Figure 3. Individual differences model fits for the different model parameters across testing sessions of the study.

Effects of sleep deprivation

To evaluate how risk acceptance is affected by sleep deprivation, the subjects were divided into two groups based on their average risk-acceptance parameter estimates during the practice sessions. For this analysis, four subjects were not included because they had too much missing data, because they were outliers, or because they had not co-operated during the course of the study. Of the remaining 20 subjects, those placed in the high risk-acceptance group had an average parameter estimate during the practice sessions that was above the median. The remaining subjects were placed in the low risk acceptance group.

An analysis of variance was performed on the risk-acceptance parameter estimates of these two groups during the first night and morning of sleep deprivation. The factors for this ANOVA were Group (high vs. low risk acceptance during practice) and Session (8PM, 11PM, 2AM, 5AM, 8AM and 11AM). The results showed a significant main effect of Group ($F(1, 113) = 38.34$, $p < .001$, MSError = 0.02), but no effect of Session ($p > .05$). However, there was a significant interaction between Group and Session ($F(5, 108) = 23.48$, $p < .001$, MSError = 0.01; see Figure 4).

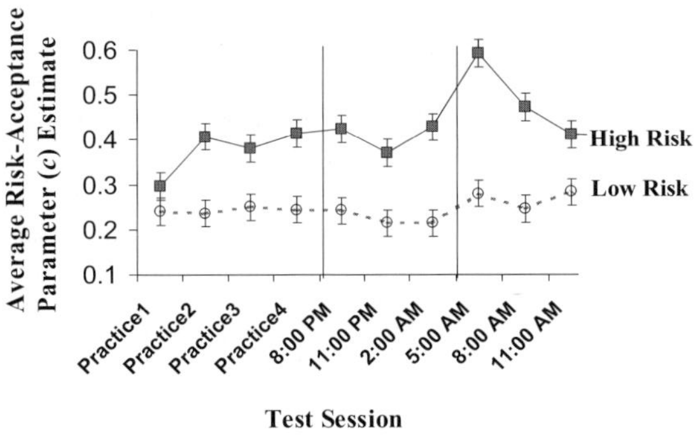

Figure 4. Average risk parameter estimates for the two risk groups across the practice test sessions, and the sessions on the first night and morning of sleep deprivation.

A comparison of the 11PM and 5AM results showed that there was a significant increase in the mean risk acceptance score of the high risk-acceptance group ($F(1, 112) = 7.29$, $p < .01$, MSError = 0.0011). A similar comparison for the low risk-acceptance group showed no significant effect ($p > .05$). A comparison of the 5AM and 11AM parameter estimates showed no significant effect for either group, but a trend toward a reduction in the estimate for the high risk acceptance group ($F(1, 112) = 3.18$, $p < .1$, MSError = 0.0011).

A third contrast analysis combined the previous hypotheses together. The foci of this comparison were that (1) the group showing lower risk acceptance during practice would continue to be lower during the 11PM, 5AM and 11AM test sessions, (2) this group would show no change in risk acceptance during these three sessions, and (3) the high risk-acceptance group would show increasing risk acceptance from 11PM to 5AM and decreasing risk acceptance from 5AM to 11AM. The results of this analysis were significant ($F(1, 112) = 28.8$, $p < .001$, MSError = 0.0011).

Part of the reason why the risk acceptance parameter increases in the high-risk group but not in the low-risk group can be seen in Figure 5. This figure shows the probability of crossing by 500 ms over the first six test sessions for the riskiest conditions of the crossing task. These were the conditions in which the starting distance of the oncoming vehicle was 250 ft (76 m) and the window of opportunity was less than 1000 ms. In these conditions, the high-risk group showed a higher crossing probability at 5AM, increasing from about 0.45 to 0.63, after which the probability decreased. The low-risk group stayed at a relatively low probability of crossing under these conditions.

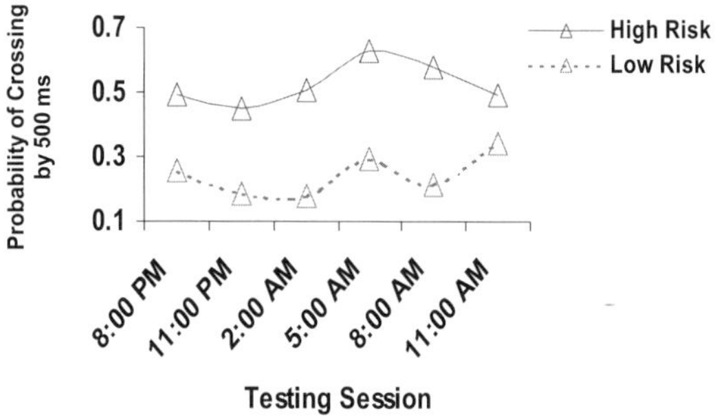

Figure 5. Changes in crossing probability over test sessions for each risk group and window of opportunity, for the short windows of opportunity (< 1000 ms) and the 250-ft (152-m) starting-distance condition.

Discussion

These results demonstrate how a model-based approach can be used to make inferences about the state of a driver based on his or her performance. They support the hypothesis that sleep deprivation exacerbates risk acceptance, and that the pattern of risk follows a circadian rhythm. Drivers who accepted more risk during practice trials showed increasing risk at 5AM during the first night of sleep deprivation. However, by late the following morning, their risk acceptance levels had decreased to the level observed during the previous evening.

The approach used here could be applied to the control of driver support functions in in-vehicle safety systems. One of the concepts underlying such systems is that hazard warnings to a driver-including advisories, alerts and alarms-would be adjusted based on the individual needs and state of that driver (Michon, 1993). The idea is that such systems would use driver performance measures to adjust parameters such as the timing, modality and intensity of such warnings.

Allowing in-vehicle systems to adapt in this way would require automated monitoring of the driver. Some current approaches require direct observation of drivers through video monitoring (Hargutt, 2000; Krüger, 2000). However, the approach suggested here-estimating model parameters using driver response functions-relates directly to performance of the driving task itself, rather than to evaluation of driver movements. Only some of those movements may be related to manœuvring the vehicle, and the challenge of such video monitoring will be to differentiate those that are relevant from those that are not.

Another advantage of the approach taken here is that driver performance is characterised in terms of higher-level processes underlying risk, rather than in terms of specific behaviours.

Accepting small gaps, close following, speeding and frequent overtaking are "symptoms" of a driving style that emphasises acceptance of risk. The DRIVE model incorporates the mechanisms underlying risk perception and acceptance, and performance is evaluated using estimates of model parameters. However, as a process model that simulates actual driver performance, this model reproduces some of the behaviours characteristic of drivers who are considered impulsive risk takers. In this way, the method used in this study is more parsimonious than traditional approaches that rely on a plethora of performance measures.

Future directions

While the study presented here provides evidence for the utility of the modelling approach in evaluating driver performance, the challenge will be to expand the modelling to include other hazardous driving situations. Estimates from a national sample of accidents suggest that intersection collisions account for almost 30% of all accidents. However, rear-end collisions accounted for just over 25% of collisions in this sample, and single vehicle roadway departure (SVRD) accounted for 20% (Najm et al., 1995).

Between these two latter collision types, there has been more work done to define algorithms for timing rear-end collision warnings (Burgett, Carter, Miller, Najm, and Smith, 1998) than for designing SVRD warnings. The algorithms for rear-end collision warnings take into account the delay in avoiding a collision due to driver reaction time to the warning. However, there are no assumptions about the processes underlying that reaction time. A driver performance simulation model that is analogous to the DRIVE model, incorporating perceptual and decisional components-but adding attentional elements as well-would help to determine how much of a response time to expect given the driver's previous performance and current state. In this way, such algorithms can be truly adaptive to the tendencies and conditions of the driver.

References

Angus, C. & Condon, R. (1985). Speed-accuracy trade-off and time of day. *Acta Psychologica, 58*, 115-122.

Babkoff, H., Genser, S.G., Sing, H.C., Thorne, D.R., & Hegge, F.W. (1985). The effects of progressive sleep loss on a lexical decision task: Response lapses and response accuracy. *Behaviour Research Methods, Instruments, & Computers, 17*, 614-622.

Burgett, A.L., Carter. A., Miller R.J., Najm, W.G., & Smith, D.L. (1998). *A Collision Warning Algorithm for Rear-End Collision* (Report number 98-S2-P-31). Washington, DC: National Highway Transportation Safety Administration.

Colligan, M.J. (1983). Shift work: Health and performance effects. In W.N. Rom (Ed.), *Environmental and occupational medicine* (Chapter 100). Boston, MA: Little, Brown.

Colligan, M.J., & Tepas, D. I. (1986). The stress of work hours. *American Industrial Hygiene Association Journal, 47,* 686-695.

Colquhoun, P. (1982). Biological rhythms and performance. In W.B. Webb (Ed.), *Biological Rhythms, Sleep, and Performance*. New York: Wiley.

Craig, A., & Condon, R. (1985). Speed-accuracy trade-off and time of day. *Acta Psychologica, 58*, 115-122.

Dinges, D. F. (1995). The performance effects of fatigue. *Proceedings of the Fatigue Symposium*. (p. 42). Washington, DC: National Transportation Safety Board.

Dinges, D. F., & Kribbs, N. B. (1991). Performing while sleepy: Effects of experimentally induced sleepiness. In T. H. Monk (Ed.) *Sleep, sleepiness, and performance* (pp. 98-128). New York: Wiley.

Dinges, D., Pack, F., Williams, K., Gillen, K., Powell, J., Ott, G., Aptowicz, C., & Pack, A. (1997). Cumulative sleepiness, mood disturbance, and psychomotor vigilance performance decrements during a week of sleep restricted to 4-5 hours per night. *Sleep, 20*, 267-277.

Hanowski, R.J., Wierwille, W.W., Gellatly, A.W. , Dingus, T.A., Knipling, R.R., & Carroll, R. (1999). Safety concerns of local/short haul truck drivers. *Transportation Human Factors, 1*, 377-386.

Hargutt, V. (2000). Eyelid movements and their predictive value for driver status. *Paper presented at the International Conference on Traffic and Transport Psychology*, Berne, Switzerland.

Horne, J.A., Anderson, N.R. & Wilkinson, R.T. (1983). Effects of sleep deprivation on signal detection measures of vigilance. *Sleep, 6*, 347-358.

Hurwitz, J.B. (1998). Modeling time-pressured risky decision-making. *Proceedings of the Association for Information Systems 1998 Americas Conference*. (pp. 249-251). Atlanta, GA: AIS.

Hurwitz, J.B. (1999). Process modeling of performance under simulated risk. *Proceedings of the International Training and Education Conference*, The Hague, The Netherlands.

Jonah, B. (1997). Sensation seeking and risky driving: A review and synthesis of the literature. *Accident Analysis and Prevention, 29*, 651-665.

Krüger, H-P (2000). Assessing the driver's state: A conceptual framework. *Paper presented at the International Conference on Traffic and Transport Psychology,* Berne, Switzerland.

Michon, J.A. (1993). Generic Intelligent Driver Support. Bristol, PA: Taylor & Francis.

Najm, W., Mironer, M., Koziol, Jr., J., Jing-Shiarn, W., & Knipling, R.R. (1995). *Synthesis Report: Examination of Target Vehicular Crashes and Potential ITS Countermeasure* (Rep. No. DOT HS 808 263), Washington, DC: U.S. Department of Transportation.

Parker, D., Reason, J.T., Manstead, A.S.R., & Stradling, S.G. (1995). Driving errors, driving violations and accident involvement. *Ergonomics, 38*, 1036-1048.

Reason, J., Manstead, A., Stradling, S., Baxter, J., & Campbell, K. (1990). Errors and violations on the roads: A real distinction? *Ergonomics, 33*, 1315-1332.

Shingledecker, C.A. & Holding, D.H. (1974). Risk and effort measures of fatigue. *Journal of Motor Behaviour, 6*, 17-25.

Soetens, E., Hueting, J., & Wauters, F. (1992). Traces of fatigue in an attention task. *Bulletin of the Psychonomic Society, 30*, 97-100.

West, R., French, D., Kemp, R., & Elander, J. (1993). Direct observation of driving, self reports of driver behaviour, and accident involvement. *Ergonomics, 36*, 557-567.

Wylie, C.D., Shultz, T. Miller, J.C., Mitler, M.M., & Mackie, R.R. (1996). *Commercial motor vehicle driver fatigue and alertness study: Technical summary* (Rep. No. FHWA-MC-97-001). Washington, DC: U.S. Department of Transportation, Federal Highway Administration.

Zuckerman, M. (1979). *Sensation Seeking: Beyond The Optimal Level Of Arousal*. Hillsdale, NJ: Erlbaum.

Traffic and Transport Psychology,
T. Rothengatter and R.D. Huguenin (Editors)

23

Compensation for Drowsiness and Fatigue

Volker Hargutt, Sonja Hoffmann, Mark Vollrath and Hans-Peter Krüger

Introduction

The actual discussion about driving models is dominated by the analysis of the different sub-tasks of driving (for example Donges ,1978 or Rasmussen 1986). These models are valuable tools for explaining variations in the driving performance according to different traffic situations and to differences between drivers. By focusing on driving performance they do not take into account another important precondition for successful driving: the maintenance of an activation level which is appropriate to the driving task. In fact, driving is a double task. The driver has to solve the "transportation task" (to get from A to B) and he or she has to regulate his or her activation level appropriately (Krüger, Neukum & Schuller, 2000)

Hockey (1993) designed a two-level model of control and stress regulation. He postulated a two main control loops. Loop A is seen as a "routine" control system maintaining behavioural stability. This system "compares feedback from current cognitive activity with the target state, and activates familiar (automatic) adjustments which modify behaviour until it matches the target". If the discrepancy between current state and target state is too high, loop B as supervisory level takes control over the adjusting processes. Either additional resources are recruited by introducing effort as compensatory mechanism or central motivational priorities are adjusted downwards in order to meet available resources. A shift from automatic to controlled processing is initiated.

An interesting question is how drivers regulate their activity level during long-distance driving. Studies examining long-distance driving have shown that two processes must be distinguished when looking at changes of driver state. At first a decrease in attention or vigilance can be detected which is usually caused by time on task, especially in monotonous situations. This loss of attention can normally be recovered by changing the situation. Subsequently, an increase in fatigue occurs which is related to the time of day, such as driving at night time. This essential loss of resources can usually only be recovered by regeneration processes such as sleep. Thus, the question can be formulated as follows: Do drivers employ different strategies to regulate their activity level depending on their state? A driving simulation experiment was conducted to investigate this issue. Time on task was manipulated to induce a change of attention without fatigue as well as a change of attention with fatigue. This manipulation was related to the duration of the driving task, which was the same for both experimental groups. To prevent the development of fatigue in the non-fatigue group, the experiment was not conducted late at night but in the evening. In order to create comparable conditions, the fatigue group did the experiment at the same time of day, in the evening. As fatigue could not be induced by using time of day as the manipulating factor, alcohol, well-known as a substance that sedates when low doses are taken, was administered.

Participants

Twelve participants took part in the experiment (two had to be excluded due to inadequate raw data). The mean age of the drivers was 22.5 years, ranging from 20 to 26 years old. Only drivers who had a minimum mileage of 5000 km per year, who had no hearing or sight handicaps, and who were not at risk of any kind of substance dependency, were selected.

Method

In order to examine the effects of driver state on the regulation of activity level, a two factor design was applied with time on task as the within subject factor and alcohol as the between subject factor (sober vs. alcohol). Five participants in each group were examined. The experiment was carried out in a fixed based driving simulator that provided a full car model, an environment model and a steering model (see Figure 1). The basic section of the route was a block with a length of 7.2 km. Three of these sections were administered. For this part of the route the participants were instructed to drive at a speed of 90 to 110 km per hour in order to make the difficulty comparable for all participants. The drivers were also instructed to stay in the middle of the right lane to avoid changing lanes.

Figure 1. Illustration of the setting and the environment of the simulation.

These three blocks - called "normal effort periods" (blue bars in Figure 2) - lasted approximately 15 minutes each and were followed by another block in which the participants were instructed to speed up until driving with maximum effort but without a decrease in accuracy - called "high effort periods" (red bars in Figure 2). The purpose of this section was to give the drivers the chance to compensate for possible loss of activation. Whilst driving, the participants had to complete an additional acoustic vigilance task. A clearly audible tone was presented at a regular interval of 1.7 seconds. The critical signal was a distraction tone of a different pitch (probability: 8 %). One of four buttons on the steering wheel was pressed to indicate detection of the critical signal. One trip consisting of three "normal effort periods" and one "high effort period" was further repeated 10 times (altogether 11 trips).

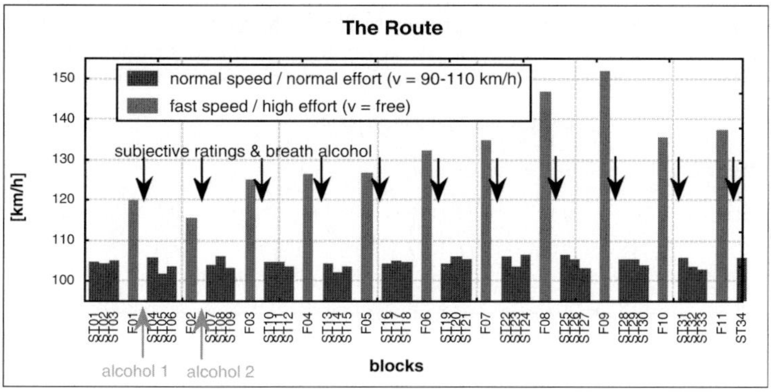

Figure 2. Description of the route exemplified by the speed profile of one subject. The blue bars indicate the "normal effort periods" with a speed limit of 100 km/h, and the red bars the "high effort period" without a speed limit.

There was a break after each "high effort period" in order to measure the BAC. Subjective feelings of attention and fatigue were also measured by asking the drivers "How was your level of attention?" and "How was your level of fatigue?". Answers were recorded on a Likert scale ranging from "very low" (1-3) to "low" (4-6) to "medium" (7-9) to "high" (10-12) and to "very high" (13-15). The participants were instructed to rate the "normal effort periods". In the first two breaks, alcohol, in the form of a drink consisting of orange juice and vodka, was given to half of the participants. By taking the total body water (TBW) into account, the target BAC of 0.5 ‰ was calculated as follows:

$$\text{amount of alcohol [g]} = \{[\text{desired BAC} + (0.15*1.5)]*1.3\} / 0.8.$$

Eye blink activity was measured to give a more accurate impression of the drivers' level of fatigue (see Hargutt & Krüger in this volume). The main parameters are the blinking pauses, the duration of single blinks, and the so-called eyelid opening level (see Figure 3)[i]

The main dependent measures were the BAC [‰], the subjective ratings of attention and fatigue [0-15], tracking performance measured by the standard deviation of lane position, attention performance measured by the reaction times in the vigilance task, and a fatigue-index calculated by an algorithm using eyelid-movements (see Hargutt & Krüger in this volume).

Procedure

Several days before the experiments, the participants filled out a questionnaire that controlled for any form of substance addiction as well as disqualification criteria such as hearing or visual handicaps. Before the actual examination could take place, each participant had to complete two training sessions on different days so as to prevent training effects during the experiment. Each training session lasted at least one hour. In the first training session participants were instructed to increase their driving speed to a speed at which they still felt safe. In the second training session the normal course, including the vigilance task, was driven.

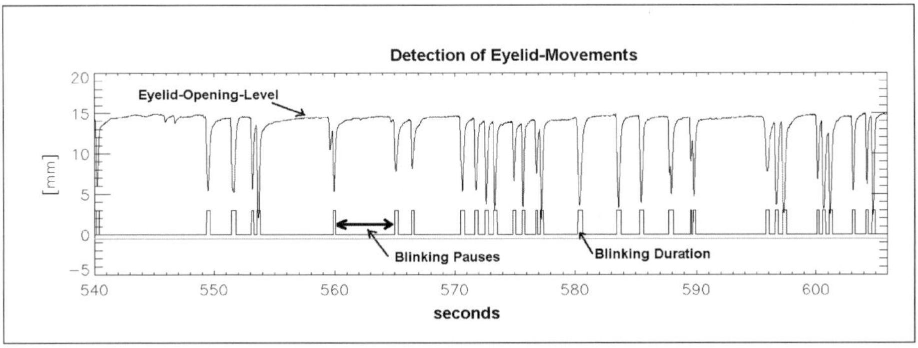

Figure 3. Illustration of the eyelid signal and the extraction of the main parameters.

On the day of the actual experiment the participants arrived at the institute at 5:00 p.m. First, the EEG electrodes and the sensors for eyelid movement detection were put in place. Second, the participants were seated in the car seat and given instructions regarding how to drive and how to do the vigilance task. The eyelid sensors were calibrated to the participants' closed eyes directly before starting the simulation. These preparations took approximately one hour and the experiment was started at 6:00 p.m. As mentioned above, after every "high effort period" (i.e. every 20 minutes) the simulation was stopped for a 2-3 minute break to measure BAC and to ask the participants about their subjective attention and fatigue. The alcoholic drinks were given to the participants of the alcohol group in the first two breaks. After completion of the eleven blocks the electrodes were removed and the experiment was over.

Method of Analysis

Firstly, mean and standard deviations were calculated for each of the 11 trips, for the normal and high effort periods separately. In a next step differences to the baseline (first trip) were calculated for each subject, again for normal and high effort periods separately. These values were compared with an ANOVA with one between factor (sober vs. alcohol) and one within subject factor (trip or time).

Results

There is a marked increase in BAC, with a decrease at the end, in the alcohol group (see Figure 4). Examination of the individual courses shows that the BAC peaks are always during trips 3 to 5 and that the BAC curves indicate a very comparable course over time.

In Figure 5, the subjective ratings of attention (left figure) show a significant decrease over time in both groups ($F(9,72)=3.13$, p = .003). The same pattern is indicated by an increase in reaction times on the vigilance task (main effect TRIP: $F(9,72)=3.78$, p = .001). Therefore, in both groups the subjective attention and the performance measure of attention decreases over time.

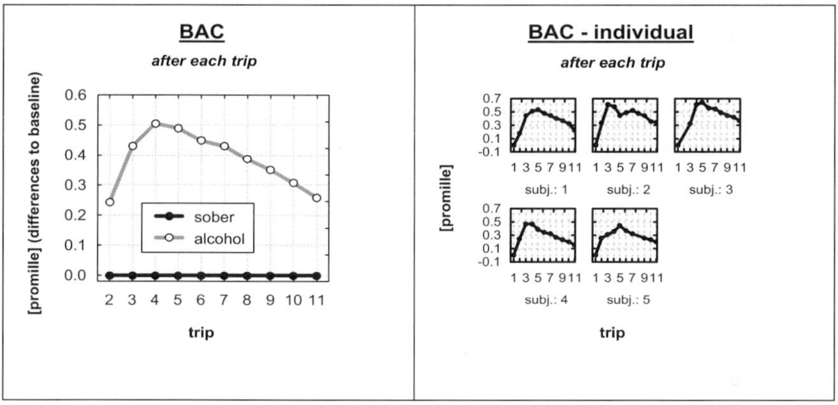

Figure 4. Left: Progression of the BAC compared to trip 1. Right: Individual BAC-Curve without baseline correction.

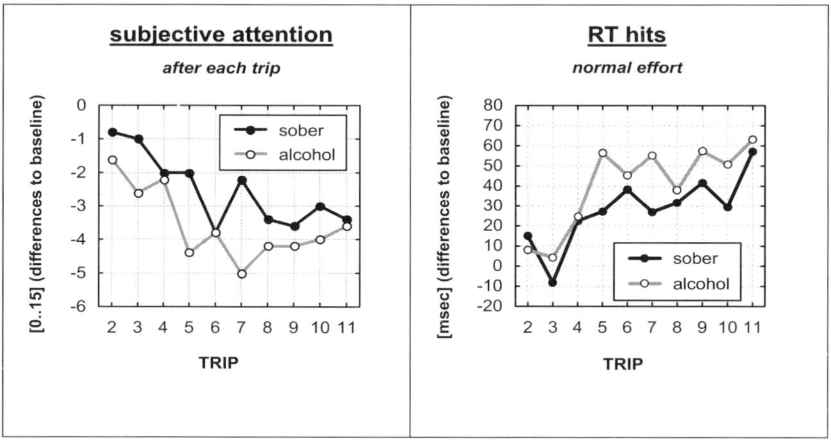

Figure 5. Left: Course of subjective attention (differences to baseline). Right: Course of the reaction times in the vigilance task as performance indicator of attention.

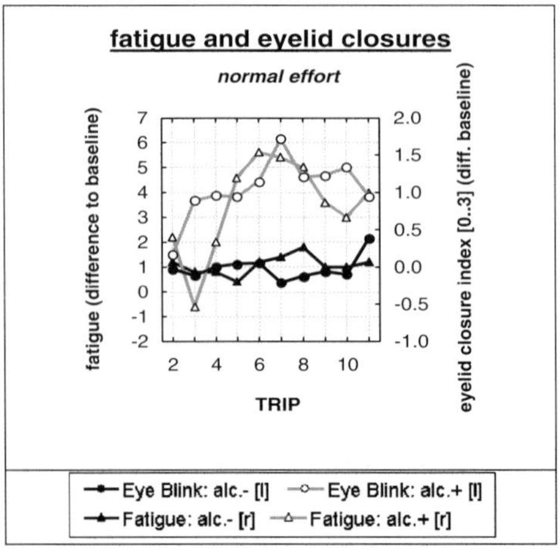

Figure 6. Fatigue and fatigue stages calculated with an algorithm based on eye blink activity.

The fatigue ratings (see Figure 6) are nearly exactly comparable to the change in fatigue indices based on the eye blink algorithm. There is a tendential increase in the subjective fatigue ratings over time ($F(9,72)=1.84$, p = .076). The fatigue index, which is calculated with the eyelid algorithm, shows a significant group effect ($F(1,7)=20.37$, p = .002)[ii] and a significant interaction effect ($F(9,63)=2.063$, p = .046). Both curves show a peak during the 6th to 7th trips, which indicates a delay of approximately 30 to 40 minutes compared to the peak of the BAC. It seems that both the feeling of fatigue and the physiological consequence of the blinking behaviour reflect processes which are not connected with the direct effect of alcohol but a delayed development of fatigue.

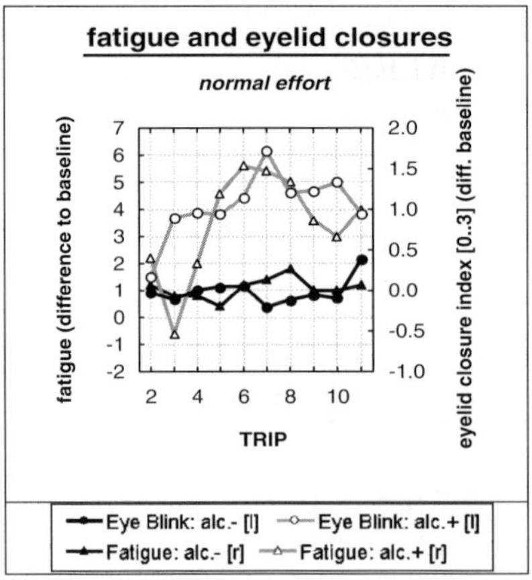

Figure 7. Fatigue and fatigue stages calculated with an algorithm based on eye blink activity.

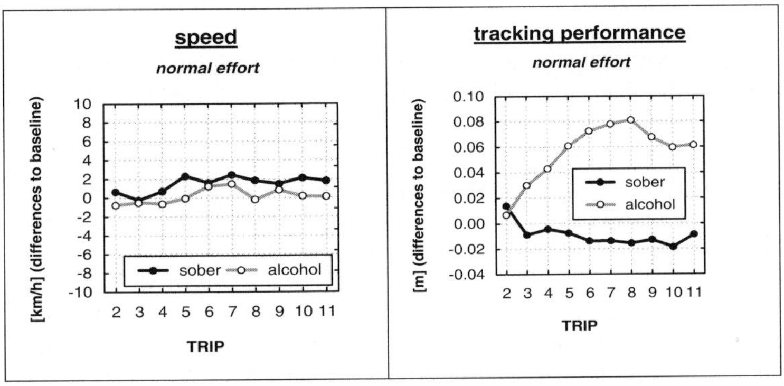

Figure 8. Course of mean speed (left) and tracking performance (right) during the normal effort periods.

The left graph of Figure 8 shows that the drivers followed the instruction to maintain their speed in the normal effort periods. However, the alcohol group has a worse tracking performance relative to the sober group ($F(1,8)=24.35$, $p = .001$). The strong interaction effect ($F(9,72)=7.25$, $p < .000$) means that the course of tracking performance over time differs between the two groups.

The same is plotted for the high effort periods in Figure 9. Both groups display an increase in speed ($F(9,72)=8.72$, $p < .000$), but there is variance between the two groups ($F(9,72)=2.36$, $p = .021$). It should be mentioned that speed is plotted as a difference to the first high effort period, so the absolute speed of the highest levels of approx. 160 km/h cannot not be seen. Furthermore the tracking performance of the alcohol group is again worse than the sober group (F(1,8)=6.44, p=0.035) and also deteriorates over time ($F(9,72)=2.37$, $p = .021$). The tracking performance of the two groups differs ($F(9,72)=2.30$, $p = .025$).

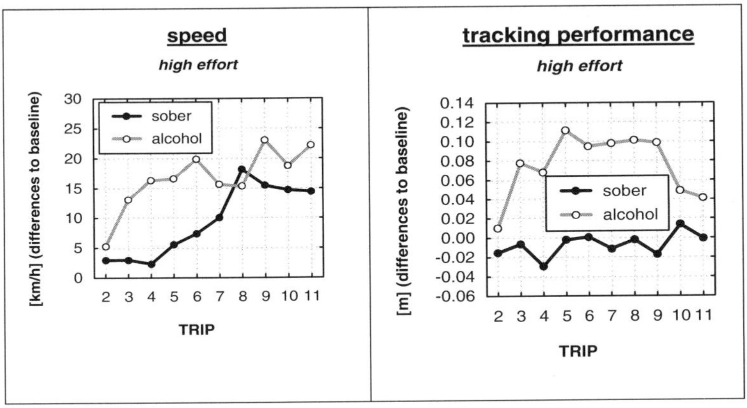

Figure 9. Course of mean speed (left) and tracking performance (right) during the high effort periods.

Discussion

The reported results suggest that continued driving leads to a loss of attention as indicated by subjective ratings and reaction times in a vigilance task, independent of alcohol. Subjective fatigue and fatigue measured by blinking activity only increases in the intoxicated group as a consequence of the sedating side effect of low doses of alcohol. Both groups steadily increase their speed during the high effort periods. This can be regarded as an attempt to compensate for loss of attention due to the monotonous situation. During periods of increased speed, the sober drivers manage to keep tracking performance stable, whereas the intoxicated drivers increase their speed at the cost of driving accuracy. This result firstly shows that drivers try to regulate their level of activation. A boring situation over a long period of time and a feeling that attention is decreasing because of the circumstances prompts drivers try to create a more interesting task by increasing task difficulty. Sober drivers are capable of this compensatory strategy because they are able to maintain driving accuracy. Intoxicated drivers also increase their speed to compensate for attention loss, but at the cost of tracking accuracy[iii]. Due to the fact that both groups show this compensatory behaviour, the loss of attention must be responsible for this and not the increase in fatigue. This particular experiment was conducted in the early evening so that no strong fatigue could be expected. Therefore, an interesting question is whether the same compensation strategies are applied when drivers reach extreme stages of fatigue.

Evidence for this second question is provided by a further experiment that was conducted between midnight and 4:00 am. The route was exactly the same and ten participants took part. Figure 10 shows that the driving speed of the high effort periods in low and medium stages of fatigue remains about 40 km/h higher than in the normal effort periods (speed limit of 100 km/h). However, in a very late stage of fatigue, indicated by very slow blinks and single sleep events, speed is reduced nearly to the level of the normal effort periods. This means that when a driver suffers from strong performance restraints due to extreme fatigue, the strategy changes from demand enhancement in order to work against a loss of attention to demand reduction! Perhaps the driver is aware that a further increase in task difficulty will more likely result in a dangerous situation than in prevention of attention loss. This behaviour is in accordance with the downward shift of goal in the model of Hockey (1993).

It can be concluded that in stages of vigilance decrements, compensation for loss of attention and moderate tiredness is characterised by attempts by the driver to increase speed and to achieve a kind of stimuli induced bottom-up activation. However, in late stages of fatigue - shortly before falling asleep - drivers adopt the strategy of demand reduction.

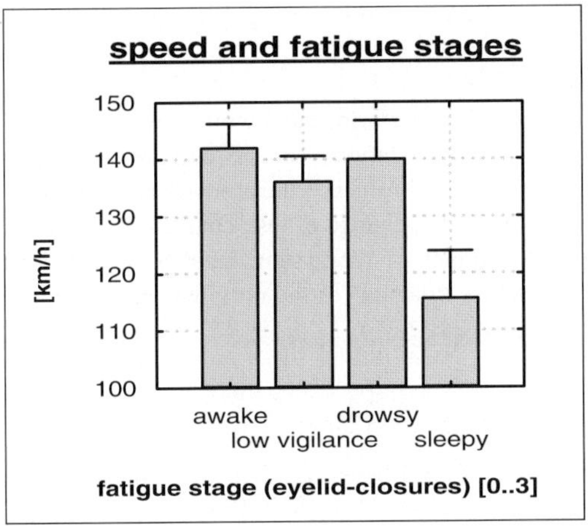

Figure 10. Mean driving speed depending on change of fatigue stages as measured by blinking activity.

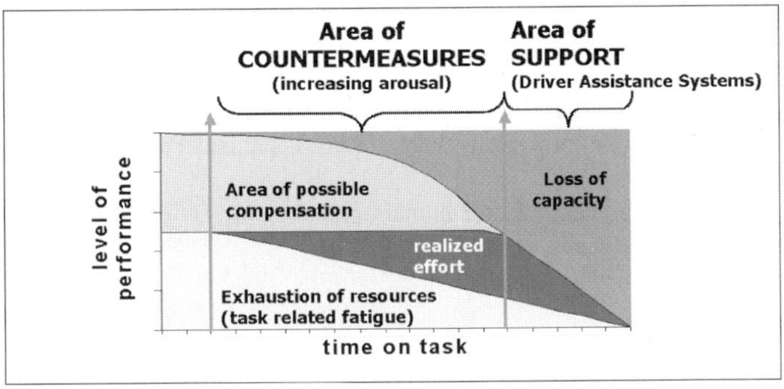

Figure 11. Illustration of effects of effort with respect to basic capacity of the human system.

The aforementioned results are illustrated in Figure 11. With time on task as the x-axis and performance as the y-axis, a normal (medium) level of performance at the beginning of a task can be assumed. This means that special effort would usually lead to a higher level of performance. After a certain amount of time, depending on the task characteristics, a kind of task related fatigue develops. Continued utilisation of resources leads to their exhaustion and should lead to a decrease in performance. With continued time on task (and due to circadian rhythms), the maximum capacity of the system also decreases. Introducing effort as a compensation strategy can cover the difference between the actual state of task-related fatigue and the capacity of the system. The detrimental effects of continued resource utilisation can be compensated for and performance remains stable. However, if the actual demands reach the capacity limit, effort is no longer efficient. The compensation strategy changes to demand reduction - the goals are changed.

In conclusion, if effort can maintain a constant level of performance, countermeasures against fatigue are possible. Detrimental effects of task related fatigue can be counterbalanced by changing the task or by introducing a new task in order to influence the activational state of the driver. Nevertheless, when the capacity limit is reached, a change of task characteristics cannot influence the activational system because the dynamics of the system have been lost. Thus support - perhaps through the use of driver assistance systems - is the only reasonable strategy to prevent situations leading to hazardous consequences.

REFERENCES

Donges, E. (1978). Ein regelungstechnisches Zwei-Ebenen-Modell des menschlichen Lenkverhaltens im Kraftfahrzeug. Verkehrsunfall und Fahrzeugtechnik, 24(3), 98-112.

Hargutt, V. & Krüger, H.-P. (2000). Eyelid Movements and their Predictive Value for Fatigue Stages. Proceedings of the International Conference of Transport and Traffic Psychology (ICTTP) 2000.

Hockey, G. R. J. (1993). Cognitive-energetical control mechanisms in the management of work demands and psychological health. In A. D. Baddeley & L. Weiskrantz (Eds.), Attention: Selection, awareness, and control: A tribute to Donald Broadbent (pp. 328-345). Oxford, England UK: Clarendon Press/Oxford University Press. xv.

Krüger, H.P., Neukum, A. & Schuller, J. (2000). A Workload Approach to the Evaluation of Vehicle Handling Characteristics. In: SAE. Human Factors in 2000: Driving, Lighting, Seating Comfort and Harmony in Vehicle Systems. SAE Technical Paper Series, No. 2000-01-0170.

Rasmussen, J. (1986). Information processing and human-machine interaction. Amsterdam: Elsevier Science Publishing Co., Inc.

---

[i] These three parameters combined provide a good description of different fatigue stages. The resulting values range from 0 (awake) to 3 (extreme fatigue). EEG and ECG were also recorded, but the results will not be mentioned here.

[ii] One subject in the sober group had to be excluded because the baseline trip could not be analyzed due to a bad raw signal.

[iii] The subjective ratings of performance indicate that drivers are aware of this loss of tracking accuracy (not reported here).

Traffic and Transport Psychology,
T. Rothengatter and R.D. Huguenin (Editors)

24

Cognitive/Neuropsychological Functioning and Compensation Related to Car Driving Performance in Older Adults

Rudi de Raedt and Ingrid Ponjaert-Kristoffersen

Introduction

Relevance of the study

As the mean age of the population in industrialised countries is rapidly increasing, a number of new problems are coming to the fore. These often relate to practical problems, but an understanding of the complex and multidimensional concept of ageing is a necessary precondition for proper analysis. One of the new scientific challenges concerns the older car driver, since senior drivers constitute a very rapidly increasing age cohort. From a neuropsychological standpoint, car driving is a very complex cognitive activity. Most of the time, its complexity is not experienced because many aspects of driving are highly automated. When a cognitive problem arises, however, a distortion of the complex information processing system can produce dangerous situations. It is a fact that during the ageing process considerable decreases can become evident in several domains of cognitive functioning. Car driving and ageing may be considered as an important issue, since elderly people are very vulnerable to accidents (McCoy, Johnstone & Duthie, 1989), while driving a private car may be crucial for independence and well-being (Huntley et al., 1986)

Given the rapid increase in the number of licensed older car drivers (Hakamies-Blomqvist, 1996), the fitness-to-drive assessment centre of the Belgian Road Safety Institute (CARA) has been increasingly confronted with questions concerning the driving ability of older persons. As it has become obvious that this segment of the population requires a specific approach, the Department of Developmental and Lifespan Psychology of the Free University of Brussels was asked to investigate this question in depth.

Ageing, cognition and car driving

An important research question was to investigate the possibilities of the cognitive approach with respect to fitness-to-drive screening procedures both at an in-depth assessment level and in primary healthcare settings. Although we hypothesise that more sophisticated in depth measures will provide much more detailed information, it might also be important to find easy-to-administer primary indicators for further referral when an older driver is suspected of cognitive problems that might interfere with safe driving.

From the outset of this project, a theory-driven top-down approach was adopted. Using models of driver behaviour and cognitive ageing, attempts were made to identify the cognitive skills relevant to safe car driving and to draw a picture of the influence of ageing on the cognitive information processing system with respect to car driving (De Raedt, 2000). Since these theoretical grounds must enable empirical research concerning the relationship between cognitive/neuropsychological functions and car driving performance, each function was operationalised by neuropsychological tests. For a few global functions, an easy-to-administer paper and pencil test was selected in addition to the more sophisticated computer-controlled tasks. The selected functions to be assessed were the visuo-perceptual and visuo-sensory function (movement perception and visual acuity), visuo-spatial function (with working memory component), the useful field of view (functional attention field), cognitive flexibility (alternating between different modalities), selective attention (with visual scanning and search), divided attention (tracking and scanning) and mental flexibility (suppression of automatic routines, focusing of attention).

Compensation

In the literature on ageing and car driving, compensation mechanisms are often mentioned as possible protective mechanisms (e.g. Hakamies-Blomqvist, 1993). It is at this level that elderly people should adjust their driving behaviour to external conditions and to their own capacities. This highlights important aspects of compensation strategies, such as tactical and strategic compensation (Michon, 1989). In the "successful ageing model" of Baltes and Graf (1996), selective optimisation with compensation is defined as a general strategy of mastery concerning the effective management of life in the face of age-related losses in mental and physical abilities. This model assumes that successful ageing is based on the interplay between "selection", "optimisation", and "compensation". Selection can be considered as a mechanism by which older people have to adapt the aspiration level of activities to their altered cognitive resources (strategic compensation). Avoiding complex traffic situations, not driving in the dark or through rain or fog are examples of this compensation behaviour. Optimisation involves maintaining high levels of functioning in selected areas by practice (mileage driven). Compensation involves situations that impose considerable mental or physical demands, in which alternative ways to reach goals can be substituted by adaptive behaviour (tactical compensation). Through an adaptive driving style, such as speed adaptation, keeping further from the car in front and anticipation, accidents might be avoided when cognitive/neuropsychological functions have declined.

Many authors suggest that compensation might be a very successful strategy to avoid car accidents (e.g. Christ, 1996), although this point has never been investigated empirically. Therefore, It may be important to measure both strategic and tactical compensation strategies and to investigate whether such strategies would be successful in avoiding accidents. A questionnaire was developed to measure strategic compensation (avoiding difficult driving conditions), and specific items were chosen on an evaluation grid for a real-world road test to evaluate tactical compensation (adaptation of driving style). Moreover, it was hypothesised that self-insight/metacognition and planning/problem-solving abilities would influence the use of compensation strategies. Accordingly, these aspects were operationalised using a questionnaire (to estimate self-insight concerning driving problems) and a planning test (random number generation).

General Methodology

Research sample

The research sample used to test our hypotheses concerning the correlation between cognitive functioning and driving consisted of older drivers referred to the CARA fitness-to-drive assessment centre. Since the objective of this project was to evaluate the influence of normal ageing on driving performance, healthy people without neurological disorders were selected. To evaluate the general medical condition, the standard questionnaire of CARA had to be completed by the family doctor. Colleagues from the University of Groningen focused their research on people who were suspected by their physician of major cognitive deterioration (Withaar, Brouwer, Bison & Ponjee, 1998). Our final sample consisted of 84 people aged between 65 and 96 years. Since many people were referred because of a change of insurance company or because of minor accidents, our research sample consisted of a well-balanced group of subjects with and without driving problems.

Dependent variables

A questionnaire was developed to identify the general characteristics of the research population as well as information on driving behaviour and car accidents that had occurred during the preceding 12 months. Only self-reported "at fault" accidents were considered as dependent variable. However, an additional in-depth interview was always conducted to ensure a maximum of correct data and to obtain detailed information on the precise conditions in which the reported car accidents had taken place.

Since another important dependent variable was the performance on a road test, a detailed evaluation grid was developed (the TRIP; Withaar et al., in cooperation with CBR and CARA). This detailed observation grid provides a means of comparing driving behaviour with specific cognitive functions. The psychometric qualities of this instrument were evaluated during our research, revealing an acceptable level of reliability. A very strict standardised protocol was followed for the entire procedure, the test order (neuropsychological tests) was randomised and the road test was carried out blind to the condition of the participants.

The Research Phases

First-tier screening battery

First of all, a short easy-to-administer screening battery was developed (De Raedt &.Ponjaert-Kristoffersen, 2000a). An important criterion was that this instrument had to be suitable for use in primary health care settings with minimum discomfort for elderly persons. A combination of the Trail test A, a clock-drawing task, the Mini Mental Status Examination of Folstein and a visual acuity test were selected for the battery. Age was entered as a fifth predictor variable. To evaluate the predictive power of our short screening battery, a cross-validated discriminant analysis was used with the judgement of the driving instructor after the road test (unconditionally fit to drive/not unconditionally fit to drive) as a dependent variable. Since our cross-validated analyses revealed that 85% of the subjects who were assessed as fit to drive and 80% of the subjects assessed as unfit to drive by the CARA driving instructors were correctly classified by the classification function based on the discriminant analyses, the potential usefulness of this instrument could be demonstrated. These results are in line with other research studies in which the usefulness of other short first-tier assessment tools were investigated (Janke & Eberhard, 1998). However, further research is needed to determine whether this instrument might also be suitable for a population exhibiting major cognitive decline. The prospective predictive power of the instrument could be evaluated on a future mixed population. However, it must be emphasised that, although specificity and sensitivity were high, this evaluation provides us with only a very rough indicator, since the separate functions, which might be crucial to the driving task, are not analysed in depth. This instrument can therefore be used only to evaluate the need for further referral to a specialised centre. When this rough screening reveals a problem, it is important to gain more insight into this problem. Detailed assessment procedures may be used to provide guidelines for rehabilitation or advice concerning traffic situations that should be avoided. This methodology enables a positive approach in which the possibilities for maximum mobility can be estimated.

The relation between cognitive/neuropsychological factors and driving

This initial study was followed by more detailed tests of top-down theory-driven hypotheses regarding the correlation between cognitive/neuropsychological functioning and car driving performance (De Raedt &.Ponjaert-Kristoffersen, 2000b). Correlations between specific neuropsychological tests and self-reported at-fault accidents during the preceding 12 months were investigated. Furthermore, the correlations between the same tests and a road test, independently assessed on the detailed evaluation grid, were analysed in depth. It could be seen that some tests showed a strong correlation with the results of the road test. The neuropsychological tests that showed the strongest correlation with the road test score were the movement perception test (r=.73) and the shrinkage in the useful field of view (UFOV) (r=.66). Moreover, 14 detailed hypotheses concerning the correlation between specific observations during the road test and specific cognitive functions were confirmed by significant correlations. Although some correlations were rather weak (r ranged between .37 and .70), these results are indicative for the correlation of certain aspects of driving behaviour with specific cognitive functions. These analyses highlight the potential usefulness of individual tests to obtain information on specific problems, since specific functions are related to specific observed driving problems. Moreover, a stepwise multiple regression model indicated that four tests (movement perception, useful field of view, cognitive flexibility and selective attention) could explain 64% of the variance in a road test score (r=.80). When we compare this to the correlation of our short first-tier screening battery with the road test score, which shows 47% shared variance, we can conclude that the more sophisticated tests offer substantial added value. However, the link between neuropsychological tests and accidents was less substantial. The regression model with accidents as a dependent variable yielded only 19% shared variability with two tests, selected by the stepwise model (cognitive flexibility and visuo-spatial function). It was therefore concluded that driving performance as observed during a road test where everyone is forced into difficult situations is easier to predict than a hazardous event such as a car accident.

Detailed accident analysis

Car accidents occur in various situations. However, almost every research project considers all accidents together as a dependent variable, without taking into account the kind of accident involved. We hypothesised that detailed accident analyses, taking into account the specific crash type, would yield better predictions (De Raedt &.Ponjaert-Kristoffersen, 2001). For these analyses, the neuropsychological tests and three factors of the evaluation grid of the road test (visuo-integrative, operational and tactical) were used as independent variables. The predictability of accidents, as calculated by classification functions based on discriminant models, increased from 62.9% (all accidents considered together) to 73.8 % (in the most detailed categories). Although this increase is not very high, it suggests that detailed analyses can provide greater insight into the relation between tests and accidents. Overall, the neuropsychological tests turned out to be better predictors of accidents than the different factors of the evaluation grid of the road test. This finding may be related to the fact that crucial factors such as visuo-spatial ability are covert processes that are difficult to assess in real-world driving situations.

The second-highest classification score (specific accident type versus no accidents) was observed for accidents occurring in situations where "traffic from the right has right of way when driving straight on", which was predicted by the UFOV test (73.5% correct classifications). Based on the visual TRIP scale, the same classification score was observed. This might be explained by the fact that the observation of oncoming traffic in the periphery of the visual field may be very crucial to this type of accident. A similar classification score (73.8%, highest score) was found for accidents occurring in situations where "traffic coming from the left has right of way, and when making left turns", which were predicted by the visuo-spatial test with working memory component. This can be explained by the fact that the decision to cross a road (mostly from a stationary position) is based on a dynamic situation. A correct spatial estimation has to be made in a continuously changing situation, which is highly dependent on working memory (Guerrier, Manivannan & Nair, 1999).

Strategic and tactical compensation

Since the predictability of accidents remains moderate, the effect of compensation strategies was evaluated in depth. Because driving is largely a self-paced activity with several opportunities to enhance safety, we were particularly interested in compensatory behaviour (De

Raedt &.Ponjaert-Kristoffersen, 2000c) To carry out this study, two measurements of compensation were selected based on the model of Michon (1989). Tactical compensation refers to adaptations in driving style to compensate for decreased cognitive capacities while driving. It was operationalised by specific observations during the road test: distance from the car in front, speed choice and anticipatory behaviour. Strategic compensation refers to the selection of driving conditions. To evaluate the former, a list of sixteen difficult driving conditions was presented to each of the participants, who were asked to indicate which situations they generally avoided (e.g. driving in the rush hour). The participants were divided into three groups based on their score in the road test: bad drivers, average drivers and good drivers. ANOVA'S revealed that in the group of bad drivers people without accidents during the preceding 12 months had significantly higher compensation scores (both tactical and strategic) than people with an accident history. This supports our hypothesis that the use of such strategies can be successful in avoiding accidents when cognitive functioning is impaired. Indeed, no difference in compensation was observed between crash-free subjects and subjects with prior crashes in the group of average and good drivers. Since in the poor-driving group strategic compensation was not related to mileage during the previous year, compensation seems to be unrelated to reduced mobility per se. However, our hypothesis that the implementation of compensation would be dependent on self-insight was not confirmed. A possible explanation may be that compensation is activated automatically as a reaction to cognitive overload and that enhanced safety is only a by-product and not the original purpose of such strategies (Hakamies-Blomqvist, 1993). Indeed, compensatory behaviour is also observed in tasks without safety risks (Welford, 1993). However, the tactical compensation score was correlated to the planning test (although it was only a weak correlation) in which the implementation of a new strategy while suppressing automatic actions was crucial. When the driving style has to be adapted while driving, it may be indeed important to suppress automatic routines (under time pressure). On the other hand, strategic compensation (selecting time of day, route, etc.) can be organised in advance without time pressure.

Since similar empirical research concerning the effects of compensatory behaviour is lacking, these results are of course in need of replication. However, they are indicative for the fact that compensation may be an important factor in the driving ability of older people. Moreover, since we have demonstrated that compensation can be measured, it may be important to give people with cognitive driving-related problems the opportunity (possibly during a third-tier assessment procedure) to undergo a road test in order to evaluate their potential for compensation. The important question as to why many older drivers do not resort to compensation strategies remains unresolved. Indeed, the group of bad drivers with an accident history revealed to be three times greater than the group without accidents. However, this observation is indicative for the need of rehabilitation programmes to enhance compensation behaviour.

General Conclusion

We believe that our research, which started on theoretical grounds, might be used as a starting-point for the application of procedures to evaluate older drivers. We started with a top-down driven theoretical analysis, which provides a means of identifying distinct cognitive subfunctions relevant to car driving. This methodology enabled to test hypotheses on the origins of driving problems often experienced by elderly people. This research can therefore be used as a platform for discussion concerning revalidation and re-adaptation programmes for elderly people with driving problems. In this way, this methodology is an interesting approach to an issue that is becoming increasingly topical.

The overall results of our research project highlight the relationship between cognitive functioning and driving performance in older people but also suggest that screening procedures must not focus solely on shortcomings but also on possibilities for maximum mobility. Since car driving is very important for the well-being and independence of older people, the decision concerning driving ability should be taken very carefully. On the other hand, when driving is no longer possible, attention should also be focused on coping with driving cessation (O'Neill, 1997).

REFERENCES

Baltes, P. B., & Graf, P. (1996). Psychological aspects of aging: Facts and frontiers. In D. Magnusson (Ed.), *The Lifespan development of individuals: Behavioral, neurobiological, and psychosocial perspectives* . Cambridge: University Press.

Christ, R. (1996). Ageing and driving - decreasing mental and physical abilities and increasing compensatory abilities. *IATSS Research* , *20*, 43-52.

De Raedt, R. (2000). *Cognitive/neuropsychological functioning and compensation related to car driving performance in older adults* (doctoral dissertation). Brussels: Vrije Universiteit Brussel.

De Raedt, R., & Ponjaert-Kristoffersen, I. (2000a). A short cognitive test battery for first tier fitness-to-drive assessment of older adults. Submitted.

De Raedt, R., & Ponjaert-Kristoffersen, I. (2000b) The relationship between cognitive/ neuropsychological factors and car driving performance in older adults. *Journal of the American Geriatrics Soceity, 48*, 1664-1668.

De Raedt, R., & Ponjaert-Kristoffersen, I. (2000 c). Can strategic and tactical compensation reduce crash risk in older drivers? *Age and Ageing, 29*, 517-521.

De Raedt, R., & Ponjaert-Kristoffersen, I. (2001) Predicting at fault car accidents of older drivers. *Accident Analysis and Prevention, 33*, 809-819.

Guerrier, J. H., Manivannan, P., & Nair, S. N. (1999). The role of working memory, field dependence, visual search, and reaction time in the left turn performance of older female drivers. *Applied Ergonomics, 30*, 109-119.

Hakamies-Blomqvist, L. (1993). Compensation in older drivers as reflected in their fatal accidents. *Accident Analysis and Prevention* , *26*, 107-112.

Hakamies-Blomqvist, L. (1996). Research on older drivers: A review. *IATSS Research, 20*, 91-101.

Huntley, J., Brock, D., Ostfeld, A., Taylor, J., Wallance, R., & Lafferty, M. (1986). *Established population for epidemiologic study of the elderly: Resource data book.* (NIH Publication nr. 86-2443). Bethesda: National Institute on Aging.

Janke, M. K., & Eberhard, J. W. (1998). Assessing medically impaired older drivers in a licensing agency setting. *Accident Analysis and Prevention, 30*, 347-361.

McCoy, G. F., Johnstone, R. A., & Duthie, R. B. (1989). Injury to the elderly in road traffic accidents. *The Journal of Trauma, 29*, 494-497.

Michon, J. A. (1989). Modellen van bestuurdersgedrag (Models of driving behaviour). In: C. W. F. R. van Knippenberg, J. A. Rothengatter and J. A. Michon (Eds.), *Handboek Sociale Verkeerskunde* . Assen/Maastricht: Van Gorcum.

O'Neill, D. (1997). Predicting and coping with the consequences of stopping driving. *Alzheimer Disease and Associated Disorders, 11*, 70-72.

Welford, A. T. (1993). The gerontological balance sheet. In. J. Cerella, J. Rybash, W. Hoyer and M. L. Commons (Eds.), *Adult information processing: Limits on loss* . San Diego: Academic press.

Withaar, F. K., Brouwer, W. H., Bison, S., & Ponjee, M. (1998). Autorijden bij ouderen met cognitieve functiestoornissen. In: P. W. Huijbers and M. M. Van Santvoort (Eds.), *Ouder worden '98; Nationaal Gerontologie* Congres. Utrecht: Nederlandse Vereniging voor Gerontologie.

SAFETY

DRIVER INFORMATION AND SUPPORT SYSTEMS

Traffic and Transport Psychology,
T. Rothengatter and R.D. Huguenin (Editors)

25

Driver Support Systems: Current Trends

Gilles Malaterre

Introduction

It is generally thought that modern cars and hence the driving task are experiencing a technological revolution that will solve most of the already identified problems, possibly create some new ones, but globally open up a new era to a transportation mode otherwise condemned by its own success and growth.

Enthusiastic predictions could be found as early as in 1986, at the very beginning of Prometheus for example. Several authors think (Amalberti, 1997) that slow improvements will eventually reach an asymptote that can be broken through only by the means of a drastic rearrangement of the system. Lannoy (1999) describes three successive steps, with regard to the development of the transportation system : (a) the nomological regime of truth, where laws regulate conflicts between road-users; (b) the ethological regime of truth, where the emphasis is on understanding behaviours, which are embedded in a complex system where numerous factors interact; (c) the technological regime of truth, where technology and telematics forward the best conciliation possible between individual and societal goals.

In this view, trying to solve old problems thanks to technology is almost nonsensical, as the whole system is on the verge of being completely reorganised, in a way that will make all these problems irrelevant. Nevertheless, after now some 15 years of research and development, we have the right to look back at what has been done, and try to understand why all these enthusiastic predictions have not yielded more operational products.

Driving-Aids Before 1985

The question of driver support systems is not new, and should be examined from a historic point of view. These systems concern every type of transport, and more generally every man-machine interaction, including industrial and everyday life activities. They were called job-aids in occupational psychology. The classic approach consists in identifying deficiencies, and trying to tackle them using available means, among which technology. This was a bottom-up approach.

Driving-aids, job-aids, assistance

The first definitions of driving aids were extensions of the notion of job aids, used in occupational psychology. Progressively, the concept of assistance was preferred, maybe because it suggests more intelligent and active participation. Actually, we find at least 4 different contents classified under the concept : (a) a technological system does something better than man (night vision, ABS), or provides him with information he has not naturally access to (blind corners); (b) a technological system acts as a second-line defence to prevent drivers from distraction or poor performance (collision warning, vigilance); (c) a technological system acts as a co-pilot, with whom the driver can co-operate. This will free him from tedious sub-tasks (stop and go), or on the contrary from tasks which could over-charge him in certain conditions (ACC); (d) a technological system imposes on the driver something he is not inclined to do (speed adaptation). This last meaning is somewhat misleading, assistance being generally associated with positive values, among which deliberate acceptance and direct improvement of comfort or safety for the final user, not only for society.

Assistance may concern driving itself but also the journey as a whole, vehicle usage (monitoring of different functions), or compliance with the rules.

Some examples of what has been done

Most of the systems proposed before 1980 concerned the driver or the vehicle. They can be classified as follows :

Driver condition: (a) vigilance : hand pressure on the steering-wheel, tilt of the head. These were simple and cheap, but resulted in numerous false alarms and did not detect all the low vigilance phases. Steering-wheel movements were heavily investigated, but were complex and not sufficiently reliable. Research on eyelid closure followed; (b) alcohol detectors : many of them existed, but their acceptance was very low. In some countries, they are imposed on alcohol offenders, if they want to get their licence back.

Vision: (a) anti-blinding ultraviolet internal lamps : put inside the wind-screen, were supposed to reduce glare. Magic, and completely inefficient; (b) polarised light : in theory very efficient but severe drawbacks were not overcome (energy consumption, necessity to have a special wind-screen or glasses, problem for pedestrians or unprotected drivers).

Navigation: The system ERG was tested, but had no commercial developments.

Speed and headway monitoring: (a) various alarms have been proposed and sold. Their purpose was to prevent the driver from involuntary speeding. The driver had to choose or store a reference speed, and overshooting this limit triggered an alarm, visual or auditory; (b) cruise controls of various type have existed for a long time, particularly in the US; (c) speed limitors were tested in France in 1978, with haptic pedals. They required a voluntary selection of the speed limit by the driver. Some technical problems remained, but above all their acceptance was low and there was no market; (d) Daimler Benz and Bosch tested a radar in 1980. It measured headways, displayed LEDs on the dashboard according to speed and distance, and delivered alarms in case of excessive closure speed. It had no action on throttle or brakes.

Lane markings monitoring: Some systems were proposed, which optically detected the white paint when the car pulled out of its lane. But they were unable to distinguish intended from unintended manoeuvres. They triggered alarms, but took no action.

Communication systems: (a) CB is not essentially a support system, but its considerable use by drivers (in the 70s) and above all by HGV drivers on different continents makes it worth mentioning. Before the GSM, it was the only means of communication between professional drivers, who used it (and still do) to warn each other of local hazards or police controls; (b) traffic info at a national or regional level, but also specialised channels used by network operators. The problem was the delay between the incident and its validation by a traffic centre, and the difficulty to limit the broadcast of the message to the area concerned; (c) The Tuffet system was experimented in France. It consisted of ferrite bars buried 10 cm under the carriageway and magnetic receptors under the cars. It worked on the principle of code bars, and was reliable and relatively cheap (the bars did not require power supply). It made it possible to display warnings on the dashboard when the vehicle approached bends, stops or dangerous locations. It could even display the current speed limit. Twenty years later, we can see that the concept was terribly modern.

As we can see, many ideas which are being developed now are not new. But these systems had a low degree of interactivity or adaptability. Except for CB and cruise controls, they had no commercial developments.

Explosion

In the eighties, several ambitious projects were launched in Europe, associating research institutes and industrialists of different countries. The first of these were Demeter, Europolis, Eureka, and particularly Prometheus (Program for European Traffic with Highest Efficiency and Unprecedented Safety) and Drive (Dedicated Road Infrastructure for Vehicle Safety in Europe). But the actual objectives were far from clear, and several car manufacturers joined the projects with scepticism, mainly concerned by not being left out if something important happened to come up. Some people thought that none of these overt objectives would be reached, but that these programs would boost sensor and actuator development, and would initiate international co-operations that would be useful for the car industry anyhow.

Yet, something really important was happening in Europe and a few years later in the US with IVHS (Intelligent Vehicle Highway System): the increase in traffic, congestion, delays, pollution had a negative impact on the quality of life and were threatening car development. These programs were an antidote to these adverse effects, and at the same time an opportunity to develop various sectors of industry, especially telematics. Furthermore, the end of the cold war created a need for finding civil applications for military technologies. We are far from the idea that new technologies would help to solve old and well identified problems concerning driver support. Much more was at stake, and a top-down approach was substituted to the former one. In fact, driver support is only a very small part of ITS. The goals of different actors were mixed in the same programmes, with a result which was not always clear (Industry, car manufacturers, end-users, public authorities).

R & D, Organisations, Architecture

At first, R & D programmes were launched, but there soon appeared a need for co-ordination, normalisation, global architecture. This is particularly true where telematics are concerned, when systems are based on co-operation between vehicles, between vehicles and infrastructure, or between vehicles and traffic centres. Three main organisations were set up at the beginning of the 90s. ITSA (Intelligent Transportation Society of America), VERTIS (VEhicle Road Traffic Intelligence Society), and ERTICO (European Road Telematics Implementation Co-ordination). Their common objective was to be a forum, where potential commercial partners could gather and exchange information and organise lobbying. Their status is not exactly the same on the three continents. VERTIS is a mirror of ITSA, offering exchanges and co-operation. ERTICO has a particular status, as participants hold shares. Some companies (particularly the international ones) belong to 2 or even the 3 organisations at the same time. Figure 1 below indicates the weight of these organisations, by number of participants.

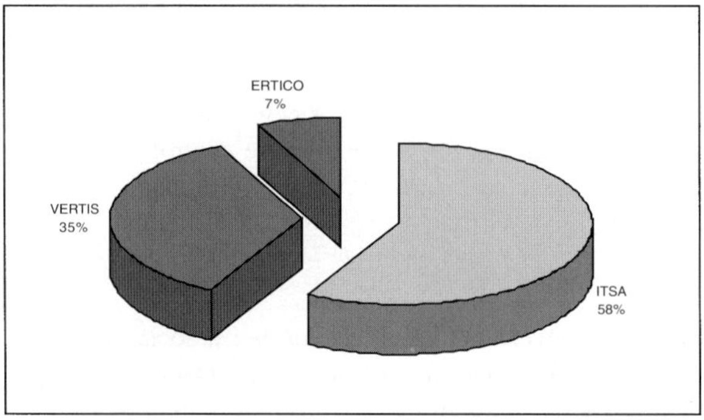

Figure 1. Participants in ITS, broken down by organisation (after Ygnace & Banville, 1998)

More than the number of participants, their types are interesting. Industry is dominant in VERTIS, but with the noticeable presence of 5 ministries. Public authorities are well represented in ERTICO. A quick examination of the particularities of each continent is necessary.

The US

The first programs started with IVHS, and a few years after ITSA was set up. IVI is part of ITSA but dedicated to driver assistance.

The aim of IVHS (Intelligent Vehicle highway System) was to reconcile car development with other societal goals (environment), to preserve individual liberty and foster industry (Ygnace & Banville, 1998). ITS America (Intelligent Transportation Society of America) was created in 1991, and was instrumental in co-ordinating several federal or regional programs, and in setting requirements for normalisation and standardisation. DSRC is a good example (DSRC standard agreement in the 5.8-5.9 giga band-width). Its scope is very large, driver support being only a small part of it. It concerns technology, systems and institutions. Some examples are as follows: automated red light enforcement, freeway and incident management, arterial management, traveller information system, transit management, cross-cutting technical issues, commercial vehicle operations (Salwin, 1996). A preference is now given to autonomous solutions, after the Automated Highway programs have been called off, mainly due to negative advice from TRB and from some car manufacturers, who preferred projects with shorter term applications, like IVI (Chanaron, 1999); IVI (Intelligent Vehicle Initiative) concerns support systems, generally called ADAS (Advanced Driver Assistance Systems). It is specifically focused on driver assistance, with a clear safety objective (Nuttall, 1998, Ferlis, 1999). NHTSA (National Highway Traffic Safety Administration) is strongly involved in it, jointly with FHWA. Seven topics have a high priority level (see Table 1):

Table 1. Priorities of IVI.

Priorities
Rear-end collision avoidance
Lane change and merge collision avoidance
Road departure collision avoidance
Intersection collision avoidance
Vision enhancement
Vehicle stability
Driver condition warning

Asia-Pacific

The main organisation is VERTIS (VEhicle Road Traffic Intelligence Society), but there are some specific organisations in Japan and in Australia. It was launched in 1994, as a mirror of ITSA. Its particularity is the strong investment of companies, particularly those in electronics and telematics, and also the participation of five ministries : Construction, Transportation, Post and Telecommunications, International Trade and Industry, Police (Anon. 1999).

A lot of importance has been given to architecture and normalisation. It is the most structured approach, the functions being classified in 9 areas, 21 user services and 172 user sub-services (Table 2). In Japan, navigation systems are much more developed than in other countries (5 millions already sold), and normalisation has been pushed much more than elsewhere. This has resulted in the implementation of road equipment, allowing communication, interactive functions, regulations, services to end-users etc. VERTIS provides a general framework that car manufacturers are required to comply with.

Europe

Several R & D programmes have been funded by the European Commission, among which, DEMETER, EUROPOLIS, PROMETHEUS (1986) and DRIVE (1991). ERTICO (European Road Telematics Implementation Coordination) was set up in 1991, with the encouragement of the European Commission (DG XIII). It is a non-profit company, with public/private partnerships. Participants hold shares, and have to pay an annual fee of 30,000 Euro. Its goal is "making ITS part of everyone's daily life". There are now 78 partners, broken down as illustrated in Figure 2.

Table 2. VERTIS classification.

Advances in Navigation Systems
1.1. route guidance 1.2. destination-related information
Electronic Toll Collection
2.1. Electronic toll collection
Assistance for Safe Driving
3.1. Provision of driving and road conditions information 3.2. Danger warning 3.3. Assistance for driving 3.4. Automated highway systems 3.5. Advanced cruise-assist highway system
Optimisation of Traffic Management
4.1. Optimalisation of traffic flow 4.2. Provision of traffic restriction information on incident management
Increasing Efficiency in Road Management
5.1. Improvement of maintenance operations 5.2. Management of special permitted commercial vehicles 5.3. Provision of roadway hazard information
Support for Public Transport
6.1 Provision of public transport information 6.2. Assistance for public transport operations and operations management
Increasing Efficiency in Commercial Vehicles Operations
7.1. Assistance for commercial vehicle operation management 7.2. Automated platooning of commercial vehicles
Support for Pedestrians
8.1. Pedestrian road guidance 8.2. vehicle-pedestrian accident avoidance
Support for Emergency Vehicle Operations
9.1. Automatic emergency notification 9.2. Route guidance for emergency vehicles and support for relief activities

ERTICO clearly states its goals : "Intelligent Transport Systems, or "ITS", are the marriage of information and communication technologies with the vehicles and networks that move people and goods. "Intelligent", because they bring extra knowledge to travellers and operators. In cars, ITS systems help drivers navigate, avoid traffic hold-ups and avoid collisions. On trains and buses, they let managers optimise fleet operation and offer passengers automatic ticketing and real-time running information. On the road network, ITS systems co-ordinate traffic signals, detect and manage incidents and display information, guidance and instructions to drivers." (web 2000).

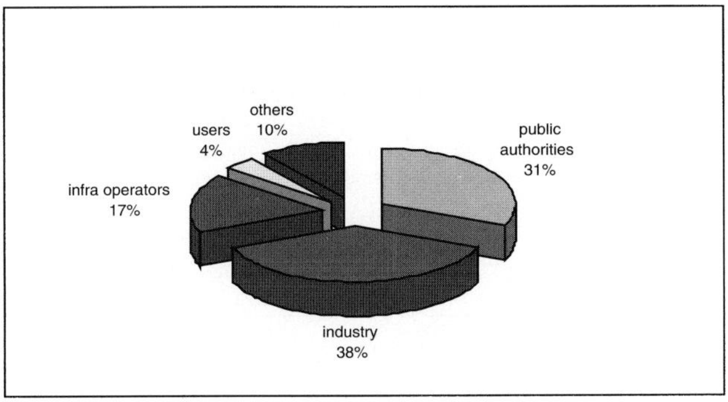

Figure 2. Partners in ERTICO (source : web, 2000).

All the activities are conducted on the initiative and responsibility of the partners. They cover navigation (GNSS : Global Navigation Satellite System), Multimedia applications, Digital Map Databases, Advanced Driver Assistance Systems and System Architecture. This last topic is a very important one, and has been dealt with by KAREN (Keystone Architecture Required for European Network) which followed SATIN (1994-1996) and CONVERGE (1996-1997).

A special emphasis is given to the evaluation of the systems (several actions engaged) and to the reactions of the end-users. Weissenberger (1999) pinpoints that society (needs) and technology must evolve at the same pace. Otherwise, the systems won't meet the market. A great importance is given to Human Factor considerations, in the sense that partners want "acceptable" systems (maybe more than "useful" systems...). As VERTIS, ERTICO is organised in services (Table 3). This type of classification has its own logic, which is not driver-centred. The support functions are scattered in different sub-sections, for example 1.9, 2.1, 2.2, 5.1, 5.2.

In 1997, the Council of Ministers agreed on a general strategy concerning the development of RTT in Europe. The first point was the following : "Road Transport Telematics (RTT) can benefit individuals, transport service providers, fleet Managers, road operators, policy makers and the environment. It can also create market opportunities for European industry and service providers."

Table 3. Services of ERTICO (web, 2000).

Traffic management
1.1. Access control
1.2. Dynamic speed adaptation
1.3. Environmental traffic & demand management
1.4. Incident management
1.5. Lane control (including speed management)
1.6. Parking management
1.7. Ramp metering
1.8. Re-routing
1.9. Road status monitoring
1.10. Traffic monitoring
1.11. Urban traffic control
1.12. Vulnerable road user facilities
Traffic and travel information
2.1. Pre-trip and on-trip information
2.2. Route guidance and navigation
Payment systems
3.1. Integrated payment
3.2. Parking payment
3.3. Payment for road use
3.4. Public transport payment
Public transport
4.1. Car pooling/sharing management
4.2. Congestion management
4.3. Demand-responsive public transport
4.4. Public transport priority
Security and emergency management
5.1. Breakdown and emergency alerts
5.2. Collision avoidance
5.3. Public transport security
5.4. Rescue services incident management
5.5. Winter maintenance
Freight and fleet management
6.1. Co-ordinated city logistics
6.2. Fleet and resource management
6.3. Freight management
6.4. Hazardous goods management
6.5. Operational planning management

We are close to the general goals of IVHS 6 years ago. Five priorities areas were set out for the period 1997-1999 : (a) RDS-TMC-based Traffic Information Services; (b) Traffic Data Exchange/Information Management the main action in these two areas is to create a framework for the use of technical standards and operating protocols. This should be done by means of voluntary Memoranda of Understanding between the actors involved. If this is not achieved by October 1997 the Commission will consider putting forward legislative proposals; (c) Electronic Fee Collection: the key action is to devise and implement a strategy to achieve convergence between existing and new systems to ensure an appropriate level of interoperability across Europe; (d) Human/Machine Interface: a code of practice will be developed to ensure on-board telematic devices do not impair driver performance or cause discomfort; (e) System Architecture: the aim is to define a European open system architecture.

In fact, 6 topics are being particularly investigated : RDS-TMC Traffic Information Services, In-Vehicle Route Guidance, Smart Cards for Automatic Payment, Collision Avoidance, Public Transport Priority, Public Transport Passenger Information. Several programmes are underway, with a special emphasis on standardisation, evaluation and human factor considerations (Glathe, 1998). Clearly, the partners want products which can be sold. The last big project to be mentioned is ROSETTA (Real OpportunitieS for Exploitation of Transport Telematics Applications). Its goal is precisely to bring together results and findings of 4th and 5th PCRD projects in order to support their effective application in Europe, to identify trends and to provide the feedback of user requirements for future developments. Here again, the emphasis is put more on acceptability than technology.

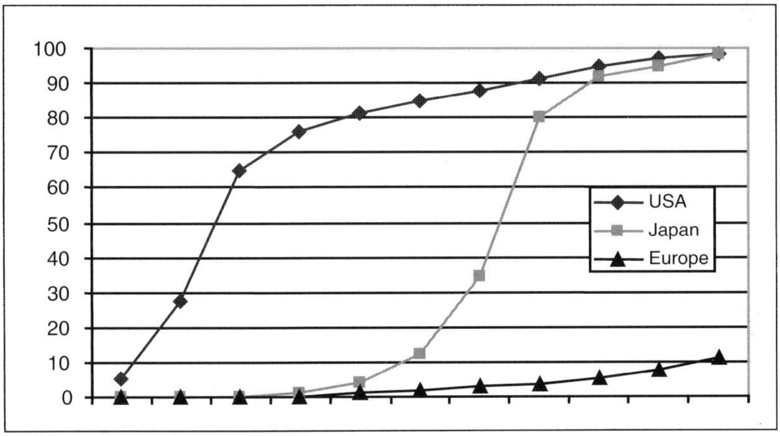

Figure 3. Percentage of equipment with automatic gear boxes in US, Japan and Europe, after Chanaron and Orselli (2000).

The development of AHS in a near future is questionable, at least in Europe where standardisation and legal problems are uneasy to solve (Chanaron & Orselli, 2000), and where the market does not seem ready. As an example, automatic gear boxes, which are absolutely necessary to automation, have difficulties to entering the European market :

The following examples are drawn out from Bishop (2000), Bursa (2000), Chanaron (1999), Little (1997), Spaak (1999), and different advertising and web publications. They are not exhaustive, and it is sometimes difficult to understand what is actually on the market and what is "almost" on the market. We know that "almost" may mean several years away (or never...). We can also notice that there is a gap between research and actual offer, even in advertising, based generally on traditional arguments : performance, low emissions, passive safety etc.

Ford

Ford is developing multimedia interfaces, and is working in a consortium on the definition of an Intelligent Data Bus. They want to put telematics in cars, and to promote assistance systems. Jaguar is the first to put an ACC on the market (coupé XKR), using a microwave radar sensor. The S type features an electronic messaging system, via radio FM. Ford plans to put internet in some models in a very near future. They are also working on Interactive Vehicle Dynamics, designed to correct trajectories in case of skidding.

GM

Buick used a fleet of 10 LeSabre for the demonstration in San Diego. The same vehicles are now being used for a 5-year research programme which started in 1999. Collision avoidance, crash warning systems and ACC will be grouped in a same package. An evaluation will be conducted with 120 drivers, each test drive lasting 2 or 3 weeks. Cadillac sells infrared night vision on its Seville and DeVille models (6000 already sold). These systems extend vision to 3 to 4 times the normal range of the headlights. They intend to propose a multimedia vehicle by 2001, with an access to internet (OnStar), a PC, Navigation, CD-rom, radio etc, all this driven by vocal command.

Toyota

Toyota has put two vehicles on the market : (a) an intelligent vehicle, with stability control, ACC, blind corners monitoring (Crown hardtop, Crown, Majesta, Progress markII, Chaser and Cresta), automatic gear downshifting when approaching bends (Celsior, Progres, Crown, Majesta), lane tracking, driver condition monitoring, pedestrian airbags; (b) a multimedia vehicle with navigation, Vehicle Information and Communication System (VICS), services (Monet) and Mayday system. An Autonomous Automated Driving System is under evaluation (lane following, forward obstacle detection, automatic lane changing).

Nissan

Same thing at Nissan, with two vehicles : (a) an intelligent vehicle, CW packages (Nissan and Mitsubishi), ACC; (b) a multimedia vehicle, navigation (Birdview), information and communication (Compasslink). They are still working on the 2D-ACC concept (stop-and go, ACC + lane-keeping + automated steering control)

Fiat

Fiat is known to be working on such topics as collision warning, emergency braking, emergency call, ACC, blind corner monitoring, lane keeping, driver monitoring, traffic info, navigation, vocal command, stop and go and tele-diagnosis. What is close to being marketed is not clear.

DaimlerChrysler

DaimlerChrysler is developing an Active Night Vision (different from the GM system which does not emit infrared beams). Its particularity is to detect animated targets and unanimated ones as well (stones...), and to be insensitive to the blinding effect of oncoming vehicle headlights. Chauffeur is still ongoing (electronic tow-bar between HGV), and about 10000 radars have been sold on HGV.

Renault

Renault will soon market an ACC. They have carried out a lot of research on vigilance, but up to now they don't offer any system in this field. But they sell products like Carminat (navigation, 1098 Euro), and services like Odysline (mayday and assistance through a call centre, 595 Euro + 30/month).

PSA

Citroën is marketing a multimedia vehicle (Xsara Windows), equipped with navigation, information and communication (VICS), and mayday systems. In addition, they work on vigilance, infrared night vision and ACC (C6 Lignage). Peugeot is working on ACC, lane-following, obstacle detection and night vision.

Trends

Japan is much more advanced in navigation systems (5 million already sold, 1.5 only in Europe). It has adopted a more structured and normalised approach, including road equipment. Its logic is to move step by step towards AHS. Nevertheless, the Japanese don't seem ready to accept any technological product whatever its price. Navigation corresponds to a need, it's less obvious for systems like ACC.

USA and particularly Europe prefer autonomous systems, with minor public investments. The logic is more to produce what can be accepted by customers and sold in the short term.

Car manufacturers develop packages of functions, using compatible technologies that can be implemented on a same car. Most of them adopt the same policy, with a multimedia vehicle and an intelligent vehicle. We can predict that multimedia vehicles will soon have a great commercial success, because they are pushed by the users' craze for telematics. It is predicted that 50% of cars will be telematics-capable by 2006.

We can have more doubts about assistance functions, few of them being ready and the need not being so clear. Car manufacturers are particularly careful about this because such systems can engage their responsibility.

Developments show up where profits are expected, or where public authorities are ready to impose systems upon the end-consumer. Services, traffic regulation, VICS, payment systems will continue to expand.

GPS (GNSS) seems a promising technology. The market is growing very fast, and the prices are decreasing by 7% a year. President Clinton suppressed Selective Availability in May 2000, authorising a greater precision for civil applications. Galileo is a major project in Europe. It is predictable that GNSS will continue to be developed for navigation systems but also for many other applications (alert, mayday etc).

Public authorities are required to organise and fund research on safety needs and driver behaviour, and carry out evaluations. The projects should now be "problem solving driven" and not "technology driven". At least is it said so.

Human Factors, Driver Behaviour

Everybody agrees now on the necessity to study driver behaviour and to analyse driver needs. A need is recognised concerning driver workload, especially when screens are used, and there is a clear tendency to develop vocal interfaces, (despite the fact that there have been several bad experiences in this field), or HUD. Recent examples (about 20 papers + expert opinions) can be found on a web forum which has been devoted to this question (see address below).

Often, it is thought that research on behaviours will help to solve the acceptance problems. Very seldom, researchers are questioned concerning the basic driving task itself and safety needs, which can be approached for example by the means of activity and accident analyses. Or when it occurs, immediate answers are required, in order to improve identified products, and make them adapted to drivers' needs and desires, and hence marketable. It seems that this difficulty to fund basic research exists on all continents.

Conclusion

It is likely that ADAS will spread rather slowly and will never concern a large segment of the market, mainly because there is not a strong demand among end-users. The scope is different with telematics, that is navigation, services, emails, internet, VICS etc, for which the demand is strong and the technologies ready. We were taken by surprise at first when cellular-phones invaded the planet and were used everywhere, including in cars. We have to be careful with this new technological wave. WAP is already present in Japan. Europe is adopting UMTS. GPS is developing very fast. We have very little time left to try to marshal and presumably limit the use of all these communication systems in cars.

References

Amalberti, R. (1997). Paradoxes aux confins de la sécurité absolue. Les interfaces hommes-technologie, février 1997.

Anon. (1997). Report to Congress on the National Highway Traffic Safety Administration ITS Program. US DOT.

Anon.. (1999). System architecture for ITS in Japan. National Police Agency, Ministry of International Trade and Industry, Ministry of Transport, Ministry of Posts and Telecommunications, Ministry of Construction.

Bishop, R. (2000). Intelligent Vehicle Applications Worldwide. IEEE Intelligent systems, Jan/Feb, 78-81

Bursa, M. (2000). Big names invest heavily in advanced ITS technology. ISATA magazine, December/January 2000, 24-30.

Chanaron, J-J. (1999). L'acceptabilité socio-économique des SIT (ITS) au Japon. Communication orale, METL, DRAST, 11 Juin 1999.

Chanaron, J-J., Orselli, J. (2000). Les marchés des automatismes de conduite. In Actes de la journée spécialisée "Quels futurs pour la conduite et la route automatiséees ? Ministère de la Recherche, Paris, 20 juin 2000.

Ferlis, R.A. (1999). Intelligent vehicle initiative : update for ITSA safety and human factors committee.

Glathe, H-P. (1998). Bringing advanced vehicle control to the market - a European perspective. Traffic Technology international, June/July 98, 71-73.

Nuttall, I. (1998). Moving ahead with safety. Discussing the Intelligent Vehicle Initiative. Traffic Technology international, June/July 98, 58-62.

Lannoy, P. (1999). Un siècle de préoccupations routières. Regard sociohistorique sur le traitement des problèmes engendrés par la circulation automobile. RTS, 65, 35-59

Little, C. (1997). The intelligent Vehicle Initiative: Advancing "Human-centered" smart vehicles. Public Roads, 61(2), 18-25

Salwin, A.E. (1996). Key findings from the Intelligent Transportation Systems (ITS) program. What have we learned ? Department of transportation, FHWA.

Spaak, M-L. (1999). Comment l'Italie freine l'hécatombe routière. Technologies internationales, 56, 19-22.

Weissenberger, S. (1999). Why ITS projects should be small. Intellimotion, 8, (1), 4-15.

Ygnace, J-L., de Banville, E. (1998). ITS : le champ des possibles. Contrat n° 96 MT 30-1 et 30-2.

APPENDIX

10 Useful internet sites

http://www.itsa.org/
http://www.iijnet.or.jp/vertis/
http://www.ertico.com/index.htm
http://www.driverdistraction.org

Glossary

ABS	Antilock Braking System
ACC	Autonomous Cruise Control
ADAS	Advanced Driver Assistance Systems
AHS	Automated Highway System
CARTS	Concertation and Achievements Report on the Transport Sector
CW	Collision Warning
DAB	Digital Audio Broadcast
DRIVE	Dedicated Road Infrastructure for Vehicle Safety in Europe
DSRC	Dedicated Short Range Communication
ERTICO	European Road Telematics Implementation Coordination
FHWA	Federal HighWay Administration
GNSS	Global Navigation Satellite System
GPS	Global Positioning System
GSM	Global System for Mobiles
HUD	Head Up Display
IDB	Intelligent Data Bus
ISA	Intelligent Speed Adaptation
ITS	Intelligent Transport System
ITSA	Intelligent Transportation Society of America
IVHS	Intelligent Vehicle Highway System
IVI	Intelligent Vehicle Initiative
KAREN	Keystone Architecture Required for European Network
NHTSA	National Highway Traffic Safety Administration
PCRD	Programme Commun de Recherche et Développement
PROMETHEUS	Program for European Traffic with Highest Efficiency and Unprecedented Safety
PROSPER	Project for Research On Speed adaptation Policies on European Roads
RDS-TMC	Radio Data System - Traffic Message Channel
ROSETTA	Real OpportunitieS for Exploitation of Transport Telematics Applications
RTT	Road Transport Telematics
SATIN	System Architecture and Traffic control INtegration
UMTS	Universal Mobile Telecommunications System
VERTIS	VEhicle Road Traffic Intelligence Society
VICS	Vehicle Information and Communication System

Traffic and Transport Psychology,
T. Rothengatter and R.D. Huguenin (Editors)

26

Behavioural Adaptation to an Advanced Driver Support System

Peter C. Burns

Introduction

The goal of the IN-ARTE system is to enhance vehicle safety and driver comfort by integrating the information available from several driver support systems. IN-ARTE acronym stands for the Integration of Navigation and Anti-collision for Rural Traffic Environments. This was a European Transport Telematics project (TR4014).

The IN-ARTE system integrates information from a digital road map, navigation system, anti-collision radar, lane recognition camera and other vehicle sensors. There were several expected benefits from the integration of this information. It was expected that it would help to improve performance of the individual support systems. For example, knowledge of the road layout around the vehicle could help to reduce the risk of false alarms from the forward collision warning radar. Integration was also expected to help extend the functionality of the existing systems. For example, integration of the vehicle speed sensors and speed limit information from the enhanced digital map database could provide intelligent speed adaptation (ISA) function that warns drivers when they exceed the speed limit. Another benefit of integration in IN-ARTE is that it can provide the driver with a unified human-machine interface (HMI). This would provide a standard display format and location rather than a set of independent systems with multiple displays situated in different locations. It would also enable the prioritisation and control of competing system messages.

Although the IN-ARTE system is designed to support drivers in maintaining safe control of their vehicle and being aware of the road traffic environment, there is a possible risk that this advanced driver support system may change the driving task and cause drivers to modify their driving behaviour. There is a potential risk for behavioural adaptation.

According to the Organisation for Economic Cooperation and Development (OECD, 1990), behavioural adaptation refers to those "...behaviours which may occur following the introduction of changes to the road-vehicle-user system and which were not intended by the initiators of the change". Mostly the term is used for unpredicted negative effects of long-term use. Estimates of the safety impact of new in-vehicle systems should not ignore behavioural adaptation. System designers must assume that behavioural adaptation will occur (Smiley, 1999) and the nature of these changes should be identified in case they are unsafe.

Typical behavioural adaptation is when safety improvements are compromised for improved mobility or when reductions in workload are exploited for greater productivity. Antilock brakes (ABS) provide a good case of behavioural adaptation. Fosser, Sagberg and Saetermo (1997) found, in an investigation of 213 taxi drivers, that drivers with ABS equipped cars drove with shorter following distances than drivers without ABS. This would constitute a negative behavioural adaptation because it is an unsafe side effect of the device's intended function (i.e., controlled braking). The better braking performance was used to drive faster and stop later.

The present study aimed to identify the occurrence of behavioural adaptation to the IN-ARTE system. Most research on driving support systems only take a 'snapshot' of behaviour with the system. This may not be long enough to capture instances of behavioural adaptation. Consequently, the present study had people drive with system for a week so that they would become very familiar with the system and have plenty of opportunity to use it appropriately or in unforeseen ways.

Method

Participants

Twenty experienced drivers aged 23 to 56 years with a median age of 30 years participated in this study. They had normal or corrected to normal vision and had been driving regularly for at least 5 years. There were 12 male and eight female participants split evenly between the two test groups. Ten drove with the IN-ARTE system and ten drove without the support system. Participants were recruited from within Volvo but were naïve to the exact nature of the study. They were given a pair of cinema tickets as an incentive to participate in this study.

Driving simulator

The driving simulator consisted of a static red Volvo 850. The simulated driving environment was projected on a cylindrical screen providing the drivers with a 135-degree field of view. The display had a height of 3 m and radius of 3.5 m. The vehicle was equipped with automatic transmission; hence no particular interaction with the gear shifting was needed, apart from going into Drive-mode when starting the test drive. The steering wheel in the simulator was equipped with an electrical torque engine to re-create some of the force feedback from turning the wheel.

IN-ARTE Human Machine Interface (HMI)

Table 1 describes IN-ARTE system HMI and functions. Driver support functions were split between safety critical and non-safety critical. The two levels of system function are listed in the first column: warning and intervention. The system presented both visual and auditory warnings. The visual icons and text were presented on a 5-inch colour display screen mounted on the centre of the dashboard (see Figure 1). The auditory speech warnings and rumble strip sound were presented through the car speakers.

The warning strategies used in this experiment were provided in IN-ARTE deliverable 4.1 (Bekiaris & Portouli, 1999). There are two levels of warnings followed by an intervention (see Figure 1). The low priority warnings are presented as traffic sign icons on the visual display screen. The higher priority messages are presented as speech messages (or tactile if implemented). For interventions, the vehicle slows itself down to avoid the hazard (with speech or tones).

Table 1. IN-ARTE system HMI and functionality.

Function	*Display*	
Warning	*Icon and text*	*Sound*
Speed reduction	Speed limit – "slow down"	
Stop sign	Stop sign – "slow down"	
Curve	Curve – "slow down"	
Lane exit	Lane exit – "stay in lane"	Rumble strip
Obstacle	Danger – "look out, obstacle"	Tone, spoken text
Intervention		
Speed reduction	Speed limit –"braking speed limit"	Spoken text
Stop sign	Stop sign – "braking, stop sign"	Spoken text
Curve	Curve – "braking, curve"	Spoken text
Obstacle	Danger – "braking, obstacle"	Spoken text

Scenarios

A static road network was designed for the IN-ARTE tests. It had a 37 km section of motorway and 26 km section of country road. A number of difficult traffic scenarios were planned in order to exercise the IN-ARTE driver support functions. There were 10 different routes designed with each route having a set of scenarios. Some of these scenarios were completely different, some were similar (e.g., front obstacle) and some were the same (e.g., stop signs). Some of these scenarios were specific to the road type (e.g., traffic lights only on the country road).

Different critical and non-critical scenarios occurred on the routes (e.g., front obstacle, speed changes & stop signs). Some of the scenarios were adaptive (e.g., the lead car would maintain a fixed distance ahead of the test vehicle) and others were fixed (e.g., lead car keeps a steady speed). The severity (i.e. opportunity for safe response) also varied within some types of scenarios.

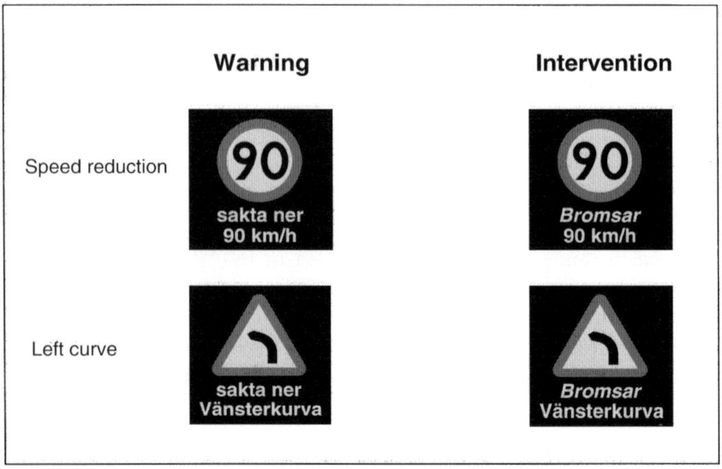

Figure 1. Warning and intervention displays.

Procedure

Participants were instructed to drive as they would normally, but that they were in a slight hurry. They were also told that they should try to respect the speed limits and obey traffic rules. Participants started with a practice drive and then drove 14 routes during five days (see Table 2). The experimental group had support from the IN-ARTE system for three days. They drove without IN-ARTE during the first and final two sessions. The IN-ARTE group was given a brief description of the support functions and HMI before their practice drive. Any questions they had about the system were answered. The Control group drove without IN-ARTE for the five days. Both groups drove on motorway and rural roads and encountered the same set of traffic scenarios.

All participants drove 324.5 km in total in the driving simulator. The IN-ARTE group drove 233.5 km with and 91 km without the support system. Thus a total of 6490 km of driving was logged on the simulator.

Participants completed a questionnaire at the beginning of the study to collect background information (e.g., age and driving experience). Participants were also asked to report their impressions of the IN-ARTE system on a questionnaire and during an interview at the end of the experiment. Participants signed a paper to give their informed consent to participating in the study. After their 5 days were completed, they were debriefed about the purpose of the research.

Analyses

Driver performance data from the vehicle was logged on computer. The data for all of the sessions was recorded. Information on the drivers' characteristics, subjective reports and attitudes were written down. A summary of the data was compiled and processed for analysis. Statistica, a statistical analysis software program, was used for the data analyses. The independent variables were exposure (before, during, after), road type (motorway, country road), support (with, without) and scenario (e.g., front obstacles, curves, traffic lights, stop signs). The dependent variables were warnings and interventions, critical incidents, speed, lane keeping and warnings.

Table 2. Test schedule.

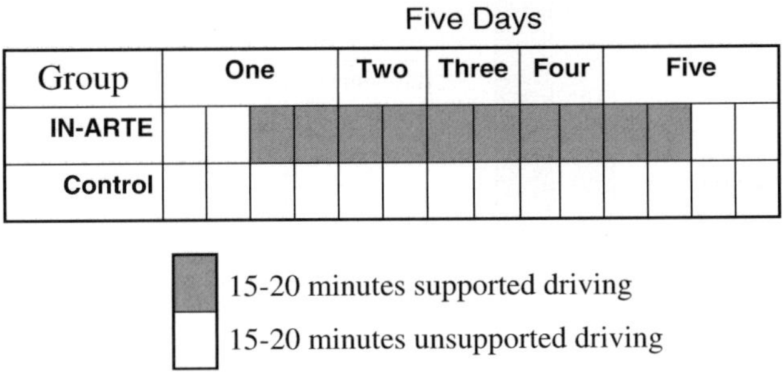

Driving performance was summarised across 1 km sections for both the baseline references and scenarios. No scenarios occurred on the baseline road sections; it was just a straight section of road without traffic. The data from the scenarios was identified in the simulator log files according to the distance where they occurred. For example, a baseline of motorway driving on the second day was taken from the 13.4 to 14.4 km section of motorway where no scenarios were planned. Performance at a stop sign was taken from the 22.5 to 23.5 km section of road that included the stop sign.

Results

Warnings and system interventions

The average number of warnings per route was calculated (see Figure 2). These warnings represent the situations when criteria for a warning were met (speeding, front obstacle or lane departure). Only the IN-ARTE drivers actually experienced the warning stimulus and only when the support system was activated. Otherwise no warnings were actually given. On average, the IN-ARTE driver had slightly more warnings per route than the control group BEFORE. The control group had more warnings than the IN-ARTE group during and AFTER. The same trend was observed for the interventions (see Figure 3). The majority of these warnings and interventions were for speeding.

Critical incidents

Overall, there were four crashes that occurred in this study. All occurred DURING and only in the control group. This was a statistically significant effect ($Z = 2.18$, $p < 0.05$). All of the drivers were males. The crashes took place on days 3 and 4 of the study. One of these collisions occurred on the motorway and three on the country road. All involved hitting a stopped or slow lead vehicle. Two of the collisions occurred in the same scenario; when the lead car was braking on a foggy country road.

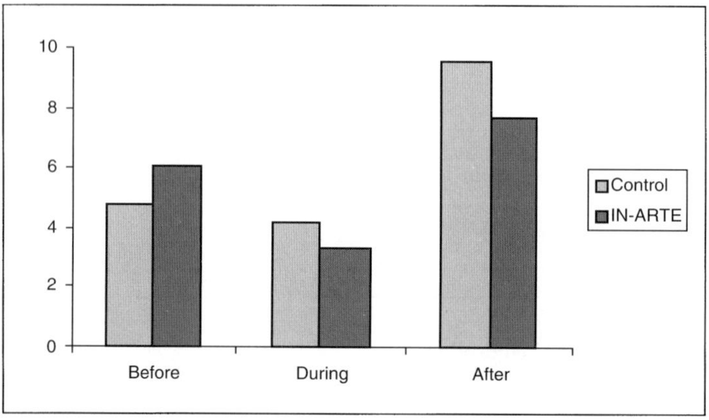

Figure 2. Average warnings per route by group and condition.

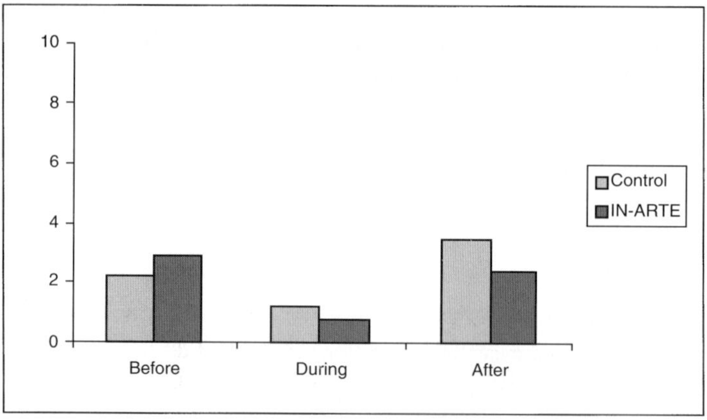

Figure 3. Average interventions per route by group and condition.

Lane keeping

A comparison was made in the mean standard deviation of lateral position for those routes where IN-ARTE system was on (DURING, depending on the test group). There was a marginally significant difference between the IN-ARTE and Control group for lane keeping on the motorway such that IN-ARTE drivers had less deviations ($F(1, 18) = 3.03, p < .10$), that is they stayed closer to the lane centre on average. This difference was significant on the country road baseline sections ($F(1, 18) = 6.43, p < .05$; see Figure 4). The same effect was observed in other scenarios (e.g., lead car braking and curve).

There was significantly more deviation in lateral position in the AFTER route than on the BEFORE route for both the IN-ARTE and Control groups ($F(1, 18) = 7.11, p < .01$). Overall, there was significantly more deviation in lane keeping performance on the country road than on the motorway ($F(1, 18) = 14.3, p < .001$). No significant differences in the number of lane departures were observed in this study.

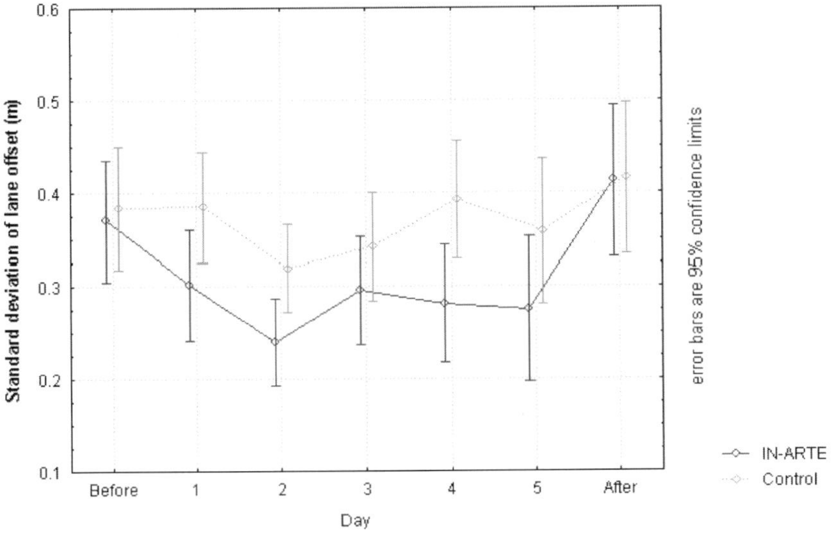

Figure 4. Lane keeping performance by day and group.

In Figure 4 and 5, the solid IN-ARTE line indicates the mean values for the 10 participants who drove with the system. In Figure 4 the mean values are for the standard deviation of lateral position. The dotted line represents the mean values for the 10 drivers in the Control group who never had support. The error bars are the 95% confidence limits around the means. The longer these bars, the more variation there is in the group's performance. The tests were run over 5 days. The 'Before' condition took place on Day 1 and the 'After' condition on Day 5. The 'Before' and 'After' conditions can be directly compared since the routes and scenarios were identical. The same applies for Day 1 and 5. Performance for days 2-4 should not be compared because they took place on different route segments.

Speed

Overall, there were no significant speed differences in the speed between the IN-ARTE and Control group. There was a significant interaction between group and condition such that the Control group drove significantly faster on the country road than the IN-ARTE group AFTER but not BEFORE ($F(1, 18) = 6.88$, $p < .05$; see Figure 5). This difference did not appear on the motorway. Instead, both groups drove significantly faster during the AFTER drive ($F(1, 18) = 13.72$, $p < .01$}.

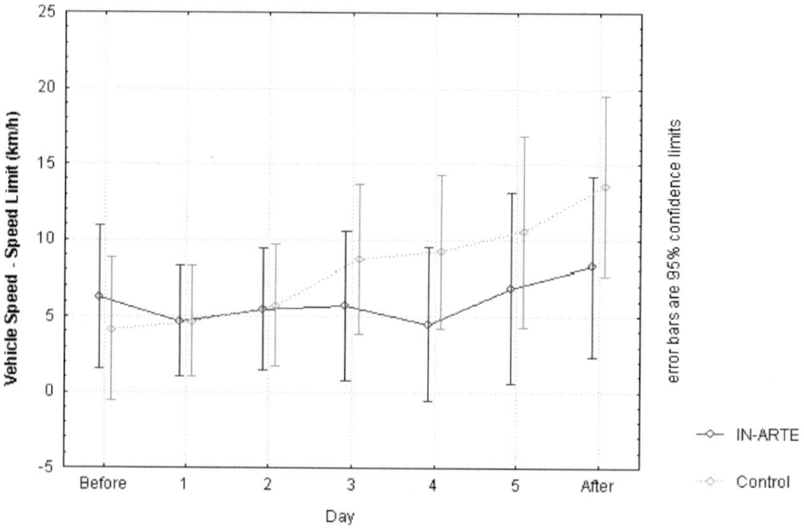

Figure 5. Speeding by day and group.

Discussion

In terms of the basic driving performance, a clear safety benefit was obtained from having support from the IN-ARTE system. None of the IN-ARTE drivers had a crash whereas four drivers in the Control group had crashes. There also seemed to be a safety benefit for 'normal driving'. On the baseline motorway and country road sections, where there were no critical events, lane keeping was significantly better when support from the IN-ARTE system was available. This difference also appeared during some of the critical events (lead vehicle brakes and sharp curve).

Lane keeping performance is a common indicator of unsafe driving (e.g., Hicks & Wierwille, 1979). Improved lane keeping performance is a positive result for the IN-ARTE system. While it would seem reasonable to predict that warning drivers to stay within the lane boundaries improves lane keeping, others have suggested that a lane departure warning system may cause poorer lane maintenance. It is possible that drivers will become complacent with a lane departure warning system and concentrate less on lane keeping because they know the system will warn them if they cross the lane boundary (Brown, 2000). This was not found to be the case.

Another important result was that drivers drove closer to the posted speed limit with the IN-ARTE system in many situations. Speeding is one of the most significant road safety problems. Intelligent Speed Adaptation (ISA), a speed limiting system with road side beacons, is considered by many to be the most promising ITS technology for improving road safety (e.g., ETSC, 1999). The IN-ARTE system offers another functional approach to ISA without the supporting road infrastructure.

For some scenarios on the country road (stop signs, curves, and traffic lights) the Control group exceeded significantly more of the activation criteria for warnings and intervention than the IN-ARTE group. Of course they had no feedback about this because they did not have the system to warn them. Nevertheless, their driving would be considered more dangerous in terms of the IN-ARTE warning algorithms.

There were changes in driving behaviour when using IN-ARTE. As described above, lane-keeping performance was significantly better and speeds were closer to the posted limit for some situations. Drivers also tended to adapt their behaviour so as to avoid warnings and interventions from IN-ARTE. There were also any carry-over effects of using the IN-ARTE system. Driving behaviour after using the system was different from driving before. Drivers tended to drive faster on the last day in some situations than on the first day. This may relate more to a familiarity with the driving simulator and some of the tests scenarios than the IN-ARTE system.

An interesting result was that the behavioural changes observed in this study seemed to occur at two levels of the driving task. Janssen (1979) and others (e.g., Michon, 1985) have made distinctions between the strategic, manoeuvring and control levels of driving. The strategic level involves activities like route planning. The manoeuvring level consists of conscious actions like passing or lane changing. The lowest level is control, which includes automatic, or reflexive driving actions like gear shifting and turn indicating. Lane keeping behaviour occurs at the control level of driving. This automatic behaviour only changed when the IN-ARTE system actively reminded drivers when they made an error. However, speed setting is a higher order conscious behaviour. Drivers make a choice about the speed they want to travel at and try to maintain that level. The IN-ARTE system appeared to affect this speed choice and this continued even after the support was removed.

Some of the test participants drove without IN-ARTE in their own cars during the test week. This driving outside of the laboratory may have had a disturbing effect on the results of this study. No estimate can be made of the amount of driving participants did outside of the laboratory or of the influence this had on their driving in the simulator. It is hoped that the specific configuration and context of the driving simulator, tasks and tests scenario would have been distinct enough such that there were minimal carry-over effects between the environments.

In conclusion, the IN-ARTE advanced driver support system appeared to only have a positive impact on driving behaviour. However, substantial field-testing is required to confirm these findings.

References

Bekiaris, E. & Portouli, E. (1999). Driver warning strategies, Internal deliverable ID4.1. IN-ARTE Project TR4014.

Brown, C. (2004). The concept of behavioural adaptation: Does it occur in response to lane departure warnings? *Chapter 3 of this Volume*

ETSC, (1999). *Intelligent Transport Systems and Safety*. Brussels: European Transport Safety Council.

Fosser, S., Saetermo, I.F., & Sagberg, F. (1997). An investigation of behavioural adaptation to airbags and antilock brakes among taxi drivers. *Accident Analysis and Prevention. 29* (3).

Janssen, W. H. (1979). Routeplanning en geleiding: een literatuurstudie [Route planning and guidance: a literature study], Soesterberg, The Netherlands: TNO Institute for Perception.

Hicks, T. G. & Wierwille, W. W. (1979). Comparison of five mental workload assessment procedures in a moving-base driving simulator, *Human Factors. 34*, 129-143.

Michon, J. A. (1985). A critical review of driver behaviour models. In L. Evans and R. S. Schwing (Eds.), *Human Behaviour and Traffic Safety* (pp. 487-525). New York: Plenum Press.

OECD (1990). *Behavioural adaptations to changes in the road transport system*. Paris: OECD Road Research Group.

Smiley, A. (1999). Behavioural Adaptation. Paper presented at the ITS Safety Test and Evaluation Workshop, IHRA-ITS. Washington, D.C.

Traffic and Transport Psychology,
T. Rothengatter and R.D. Huguenin (Editors)

27

The Effects of Different Display Types with Respect to Reading Numerical Information and Detecting Speed Change

Candida Castro and Tim Horberry

Introduction

Exceeding the speed limit contributes to nearly one-third of all fatal traffic crashes; it costs USA society more than $23 billion a year (US Department of Transportation, 1998). In even the most basic of cars there are, of course, more displays in a vehicle's dashboard than just a speedometer. However, from the point of minute-to-minute control of the vehicle's speed the Display is fundamental. They are often used to know the exact driving speed (reading numerical information) in order to check whether a vehicle is travelling under or over a certain velocity and to carry out any necessary adjustments (acceleration or deceleration). This information is crucial when driving, for instance, in rural neighbourhoods, when overtaking or in any driving situation where the speed limit prohibition plays a predominant role (e.g. due to traffic signs indications).

Any review of the classic human factors literature will find a plethora of recommendations and discussion for the effective visual display of dynamic information, much of which is applicable to the design of vehicle speedometers. Examples of this include Oborne (1995), Grandjean (1988) and Sanders and McCormick (1993). Although there are an almost unlimited number of possible designs for the display of speed information in vehicles, much of this literature usually, at the minimum, includes consideration of types of digital and analogue displays. For the analogue displays these are often considered as both circular and linear designs (either horizontally or vertically orientated).

For vehicle speedometers there have been a variety of studies comparing the effectiveness of digital and analogue versions, but these have produced varied results. For example, Walter (1991) found that drivers using analogue displays used their brakes more and glanced at the speedometer less than they do when using digital displays. Similarly, Kiefer and Angell (1993) who compared analogue and digital displays on driver performance speedometer, in terms of better speed control, reduced glance frequency and greater ability to detect events in the road environment. Haller (1991), however, found that reading time in two different experimental tasks, measured by eye movement recording, was less for digital versions when compared with the analogue versions. As a general conclusion, it is reported that digital types of displays are very quickly responded to (Nishi & Kadoo, 1994; Haller, 1991), but less effective in terms of detecting change (Galer, 1985; Bridger, 1995). So it must be concluded that the jury is still out regarding the 'best' type of display for speedometer information, and that the varying results of the different studies are probably mainly only due to differences in the experimental tasks and response measures.

Other recent studies have purely focused on analogue speedometers (Jindo & Hirasago, 1997). These authors justified not exploring digital Displays by arguing both that they had many degrees of freedom in styling, and the small use of actual digital displays. Their investigation tackled some interesting aspects with respect to analogue displays- such as the scale type, lettering, types of indicators and the starting point of the indicator. Their study obtained subjective evaluation scores about two criteria, the feeling of being easy to understand and the subjects' opinions about the speedometer design. They called the first factor 'clean-looking' and the second one 'luxurious'. From their results it can be concluded that both factors appear to influence the display's static impression, and correlations between the display design elements must be taken into account when developing analogue speedometers. However, their work did not measure any crucial driver behavioural variables nor did it contrast analogue displays with digital ones.

The need to design displays that will be totally understood by their users has been emphasised by Sanders and McCormick (1993). Moreover, when choosing the type of display to be used it is important that it is evaluated for effectiveness with the intended user group. This evaluation is usually a trade-off between the time taken to read the information, the accuracy of the receiver in interpreting the information correctly and the sensitivity of the display, that is the ability to detect small changes in the variable being measured (Oborne, 1995). This author reviewed literature and recommended the use of different displays for specific circumstances. For instance, when static presentations are shown, digital numerical displays produce fewer reading errors and faster reading times than the analogues ones. However, when dynamic situations (constantly changing) are shown, the performance digital displays deteriorated. It would be impossible to read numerical information that quickly changed because it can be blurred. Therefore, in real situations that involve constantly changing information analogue displays are widely employed. The pointer or needle provides help to the driver to obtain the information displayed. This performance is partially due to the movement of the pointer together with the rate of movement. A dynamic pointer usually provides enough spatial information to the driver to recognise whether the display moved to a higher or lower value from previously. In other words, this movement information allows the drivers to notice whether their cars are accelerating or decelerating sometimes without them having to read the exact numerical value that the Displays.

In addition to evaluating the overall type of display to be employed, it is also necessary to consider the specific design and complexity of the display. Again, many suggestions can be found in the human factors literature for effective designs with regard to complexity (c.f. Oborne, 1995). For example, Fowkes (1984) recommended that different displays in a car instrument panel should be more closely standardised in terms of their different types of pointer and scale markings. Similarly, in terms of the scale graduations with a display, Grandjean (1988) recommended that the height, thickness and distance apart of the graduations must be such that they can be read off with the least amount of error, and that the information presented to the operator is only what is needed - as unnecessary information might induce slower responses and more errors. Sanders and McCormick (1993) analysed several analogue displays designs, their recommendation included aspects such as: the numeric progressions of the scale, the length of scale unit, the design of scale makers and the pointers, how to combine scale features, scale size and viewing distance. Based on their advice, the measures for designing analogue displays are as follows: to employ a scale marker for every single scale unit to be read; the interval between marks should be constant, use a progression numerical system; the scale length should allow the reader's perceptual abilities to reliably discriminate the values; coloured pointers that partially contact the scale markers but not overlap them. Conversely, poorly designed speed displays can include those with a low number of scale markers and displays presenting excessive information.

As said above, car speedometers provide critical information to the driver, for instance, to control their speed within desired safety margins and to follow speed limit signs. From the foregoing it is thus critical that the time taken to check the speed, the Accuracy of the information received by the driver and the sensitivity of the display are essential requirements for good speedometer design. Most of the current car speedometers are circular, while only some speedometers (especially in sport cars) adopt a digital shape (although digital speedometers are increasingly used as part of in-vehicle route guidance systems, Srinivasan & Jovanis, 1997). Very few current car speedometers are linear or horizontal (an infamous example from the UK of this type from the past was the Hillman Imp´s speedometer). Additionally, in continental Europe the speed is displayed solely as kilometres per hour, whereas in the UK and many other countries vehicle speedometers the speed is not only showed as kilometres per hour but also as miles per hour. So, at the outset the UK vehicle speedometers adopt a higher complexity to include both types of velocity information. Therefore, variable criteria are applied when designing speedometers for different car models and countries.

Taking all these findings and recommendations into account, three experiments were carried out in order to test different types of Display and different levels of Complexity to establish their influence upon drivers' responses, using different tasks. Ultimately, the goal was to help understand the most effective display for showing speed information when driving. In other words, which display will promote the best performance in terms of reading numerical information and appreciating movement change. Table 1 shows the variable manipulated in the three experiments.

Table 1. The experiment sequence and main variables manipulated.

	TASK PERFORMED	*SPEEDOMETER DISPLAY*			*SPEEDOMETER COMPLEXITY*		
Experiment I	Under_Over 40	Circular	Horizontal	Digital	Low	Medium	High
Experiment II	Deceleration _Acceleration	Circular	Horizontal	Digital	Low	Medium	High
Experiment III	Under_Over 40 Deceleration _Acceleration	Circular	Horizontal	Digital	Low	Medium	High

EXPERIMENT I

The main aim of this experiment was to test which type of Display and which complexity would produce the best responses when the subjects' task was to read the information offered by the display when making a decision as to whether the speed shown on the display is over 40 mph or less than 40 mph. According to the previous research mentioned above, it was hypothesised that the digital types of displays would perform well on the response measures compared to the analogue ones, and that those speedometers with higher amounts of complexity would perform badly compared to simpler designs. It was also hypothesised that subjects would produce quicker RT when the speed displayed was nearer the decision point of 40 mph, according to Luce's Law (Luce, Bush & Galanter, 1965).

Method

Subjects. Eighteen subjects were employed. Their ages were between 25 and 50 years. All reported normal or corrected-to normal vision. All of the subjects held valid car licences.

Stimuli. The material used in this experiment consisted of speedometer images displayed on a computer screen. A complete list of all the stimuli used is presented in the Appendix I. The stimuli were displayed on the computer using the Micro Experimental Laboratory (MEL) software. The speedometer drawings varied according to the three main variables manipulated in this experiment (See these Drawings on the Appendix). Firstly, Display, three types were employed: analogue circular, analogue horizontal, or digital. Secondly, Complexity, three levels were used: low, medium or high. These varied according to the richness of the information and the scaling details. The information richness referred to the different measurement units to display the vehicle speed: miles or kilometres per hour. The scaling details referred to the gradation between the speed figures. In particular, the low complexity level consisted of simple display images where the speed was only shown as miles per hour information, and the marking scale format was minimal, i.e. only the main speed marks can be observed. In the medium complexity speedometers the speed was again only shown as miles per hour information, but the marking scale detail was more complex, i.e. five marks were displayed between the main speed marks. In the high complexity speedometers the speed was displayed both as miles as kilometres per hour and the scale detail was as rich as the medium complexity speedometers. Thirdly, Displayed Speed, four different speeds were employed: these were 29.5, 36.6, 43.5 and 50.5 mph.

Procedure. Each subject was tested individually. They sat in front of the monitor at a distance of 50 cm to the screen and were explained the instructions. For each trial a fixation point appeared. This point consisted of a small cross in the centre of the screen. Subjects were requested to keep their eyes fixed on this point. Shortly after a Display was shown. The subjects were to respond if the speed shown in the display was over 40 mph or less than 40 mph in each trial. Specifically, if the speed shown on the display was over 40 mph, then they had to press the key on the keyboard marked 'Over', as quickly as possible; if the speed shown on the display was less than 40 then they had to press the key on the keyboard marked 'Under', as soon as possible.

The fixation point was displayed for 400 ms. Afterwards, the speedometer was displayed until the subject made a response. This experiment had one practice block (5 trials) and two experimental ones (72 trials each) separated by breaks. The order of the stimuli presentation was randomly arranged for each block and subject.

Results

For the response measure of RT an ANOVA for Repeated Measures, 3x3x4 was performed. The within-subject factors manipulated were: Display (Circular, Horizontal and Digital); Complexity (Low, Medium, and High); Evaluated Speeds (29.5, 36.6, 43.5 and 50.5 mph). The results were as follows:

The main effect of Display was highly significant, $F(2,34)=10.05$; $p<.0004$. The fastest RT was found to the digital condition, 662.03 ms and the lowest RT was showed to the horizontal condition, 717.78 ms. For the circular one an intermediate RT was found, 692.06 ms. (See Figure 1).

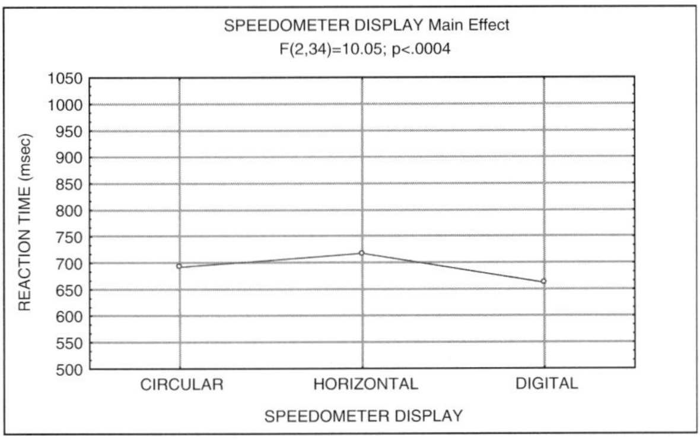

Figure 1. Mean RT for the three Displays from Experiment_I.

The main effect of Complexity was also significant, $F(2,34)=1.89$; $p<.002$. The faster RT were found either to the low (679.57 ms) and medium (675.12 ms) complexity levels, while the slowest RT was found for the high complexity condition (717.18 ms) (See Figure 2)

The main effect of the Evaluated Speeds was also significant, $F(3,51)=22.84$; $p<.0001$. The faster RT's were found at 29.5 mph (670.88 ms) and 50.5 mph (654.74 ms), while the slower RT's were found at 36.5 mph (715.58 ms) and at 43.5 mph (721.31 ms) (See Figure 3).

These were the only significant outcomes.

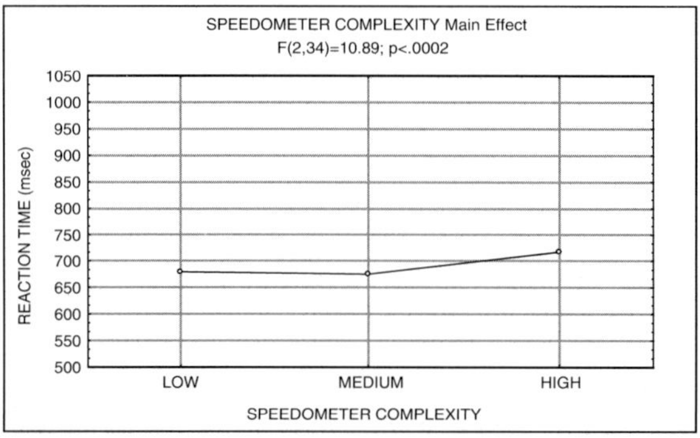

Figure 2. Mean RT for the three Speedometer Complexities from Experiment_I.

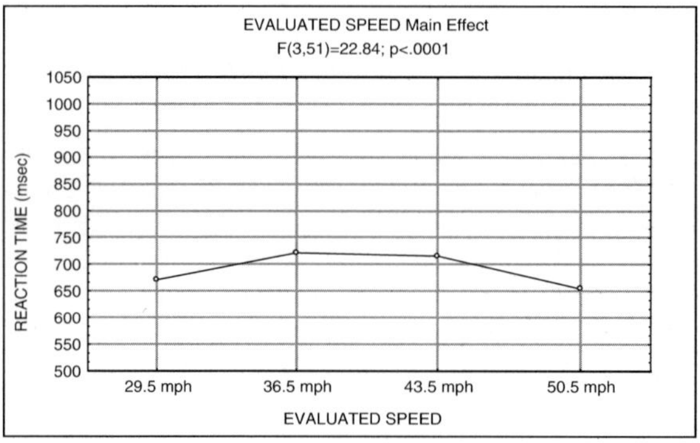

Figure 3. Mean RT for the four Evaluated Speeds from Experiment_I.

Experiment II

The main aim of this experiment was to test which type of Display and which complexity would produce the best responses when the subjects' task was to perceive small speed changes by paying attention to two speedometers and making a decision according to if the second Displayed a faster or slower speed than did the first one. As mentioned above, the sensitivity of the display was defined as the ability to detect small changes in the variable being measured. Following previous research, it was hypothesised that the digital types would be less effective in terms of discriminating change when compared with the analogue versions. In addition, speedometers with lower levels of complexity would perform better than those with higher levels of complexity.

Method

Subjects. Eighteen new subjects were employed. Their ages were between 25 and 50 years. All reported normal or corrected-to normal vision. All held valid car licences.

Stimuli. The same materials were used as in Experiment_I. Three Displays and three levels of complexity. The speeds displayed in miles per hour were the following pairs: 36-43, 36-50, 43-50 (acceleration); and 36-29, 43-36, 43-29 (deceleration).

Procedure. For each trial a fixation point appeared. Shortly after, they were shown two consecutive speedometer stimuli. The subjects' task consisted of paying attention to both speedometers and making a decision. For this decision, if the second Displayed a faster speed than the first one (acceleration), then subjects were instructed to press a key marked 'faster', as soon as soon as possible; similarly, if the second Displayed a slower speed than the first one (deceleration), then subjects were instructed to press a key marked 'slower'. The fixation point was displayed for 400 ms. The first speedometer was shown for 500 ms. Then, a black screen is displayed for 500 ms (SOA), afterwards the second speedometer was displayed until the subject made a response. This experiment had one practice block (5 trials) and four experimental ones (54 trials each) separated by breaks.

Results

For the response measure of RT an ANOVA for Repeated Measures 3x3 was performed. The within-subject factors manipulated were: Display (Circular, Horizontal, and Digital); Complexity (Low, Medium, and High). The results were as follows:

The main effect of Display was significant, $F(2,34)=9.58$; $p<.0005$. The fastest RT were found to the circular and horizontal conditions, 513.71 ms and 518.06 ms, respectively, and the lowest RT was showed to the digital condition, 574.41 ms. These results are displayed in Figure 4.

For RT, the main effect of Complexity and the interaction were not, however, significant.

EXPERIMENT III

The main aim of the final Experiment_In this series was to test which type of Display and which complexity would produce the best responses when subjects sequentially performed either a reading numerical information task or a detecting speed changes task. None of the previous work reported above has tried to combine both tasks. This is argued to be important, as during driving the driver must frequently perform both tasks at the same time. For instance, when driving along a highway and the driver detects a speed limitation sign due to an approaching junction then their task is to try to adapt their speed to that limitation. Not only must they know what is our current speed, but also they must glance at their speedometer constantly to know that the vehicle is slowing down. As with the first two experiments, it was considered interesting to establish the effects of the different speedometer complexities. Specifically, whether those speedometers with lower levels of complexity would perform better than those with higher levels of complexity.

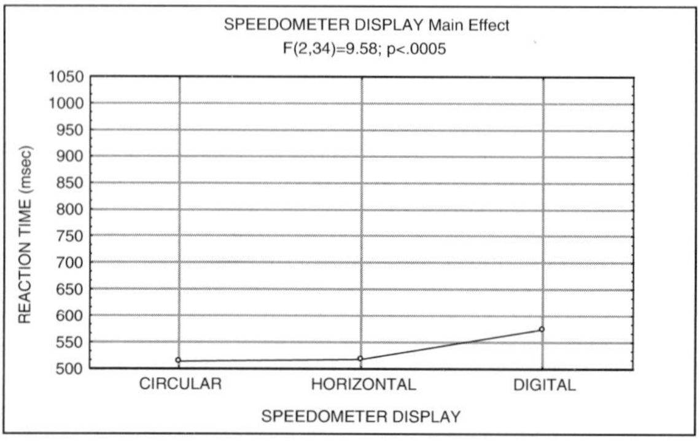

Figure 4. Mean RT for the three Displays from Experiment_II.

Method

Subjects. Eighteen new subjects were employed. Their ages were between 25 and 50 years. All reported normal or corrected-to normal vision. All held valid car licences.

Stimuli. The same materials were used as in Experiment_I. The same materials were used as in Experiment_I. Three Displays and three levels of complexity. The speed displayed were the following pairs: 57-64, 50-57, 50-64, 29-43 (all pairs were acceleration and the second value was over 40 mph); 29-36, 22-36, 22-36, 22-29 (acceleration and under 40 mph); 57-43, 50-43, 50-43, 57-50 (deceleration and over 40 mph); 29-22, 22-15, 50-36, 29-15 (deceleration and under 40 mph). These values were chosen to balance the speed intervals for each experimental condition.

Procedure. For each trial a fixation point appeared. Shortly after, the subject was shown two consecutive speedometers. Then the subject saw one of these two messages, "Deceleration-acceleration" or "Under-over 40 mph". This indicated the task the subject must carry out in each trial. Notice that the subject must retain all the information about the speed displayed in both speedometers because they did not know which task was being performed in the trial until after both speedometers had vanished. The fixation point was displayed for 400 ms. The first speedometer was shown for 700 ms. Then, a black screen is displayed for 500 ms (SOA) and the second speedometer was displayed for 700 ms. Afterwards one of these messages was shown ('Dec_Acceleration' or 'Under/Over_40'). It remained on the screen until the subject made a response. The experimental trial sequence is showed in Figure 5.

This experiment had one practice block (20 trials) and four experimental ones (72 trials each) separated by breaks.

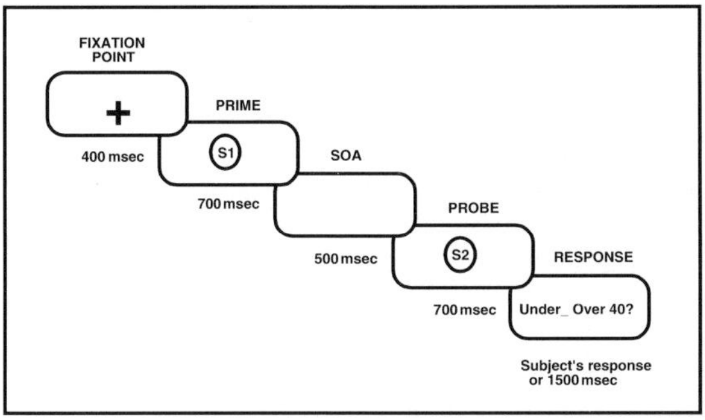

Figure 5. The experimental trial sequence in Experiment_III.

Results

The ANOVA for the RT of the three-factor experiment was a 3x2x3 repeated measures design: Display (Circular, Horizontal, and Digital) X Complexity (Low, Medium, and High) X Task Performed (Dec_Acceleration and Under/Over_40).

The main effect of Complexity was significant, $F(2,34)=8.38$; $p < .0011$. The fastest RT was found for the Medium complexity condition, 880.11 ms; while the slowest RT was found for the Low complexity condition, 927.34 ms and the High complexity condition, 924.4 ms (See Figure 6). The main effect of the type of Task Performed was significant, $F(1,17)=10.26$; $p < .0052$. The fastest RT was found for the Deceleration_Acceleration condition, 856.96 ms; while the slowest RT was found for the Under_Over condition, 964.27 ms (See Figure 7). The Display was marginally significant, $F(2,34)=3.22$; $p < .0524$. The fastest RT was found for the Circular condition, 893.92 ms; then, the Horizontal condition, 904.25; while the slowest RT were found for the Digital condition, 927.34 ms (See Figure 8). The two way interaction Display X Task Performed was also significant: $F(2,23)=4.72$; $p < .0155$ (See Figure 9).

The two way interaction Display X Complexity was significant $F(4,68)=10.23$; $p<.0001$ (See Figure 10).

These were the only significant outcomes.

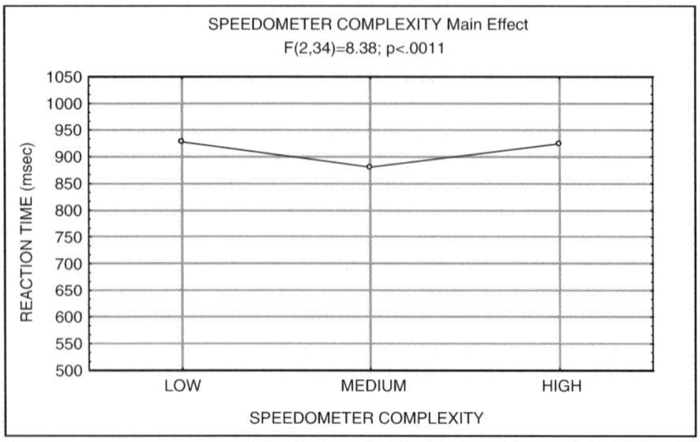

Figure 6. Mean RT for the three Speedometer Complexities from Experiment_III.

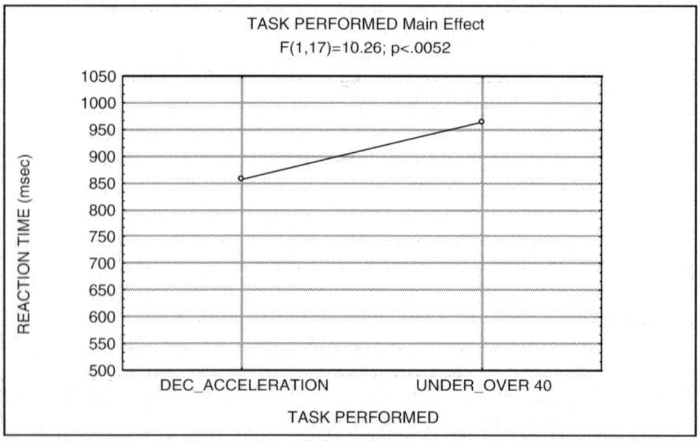

Figure 7. Mean RT for the two Tasks Performed from Experiment_III.

Overall Discussion

For Experiment_I the main results found that the digital speedometers produced quickest RT, followed by the analogue circular ones, and slowest were the analogue horizontal displays. In terms of display complexity, those displays with either a low or a medium complexity were responded to quicker than were those with a high complexity. Finally, when the speed displayed was closer to the task decision point (of 40 mph) it was responded to slower than when the speed was further away from this figure. The mean RT for this experiment was 680-700 ms.

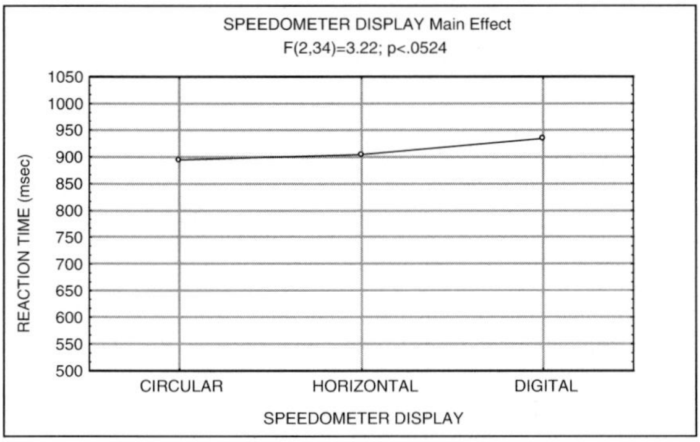

Figure 8. Mean RT for the three Displays from Experiment_III.

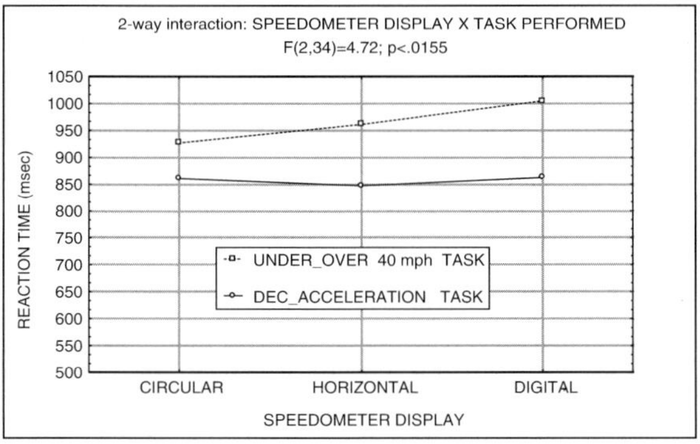

Figure 9. Mean RT for the three Displays X the two Tasks Performed from Experiment_III.

For Experiment_II the results found that the digital speedometers produced the slowest RT when compared with the analogue types. For display complexity, however, there were no significant differences obtained between the different conditions. The mean RT for this experiment was 500-550 ms. Therefore the Dec_Acceleration Task (Experiment_II) was performed quicker than was the Under/Over_40 Task (Experiment_I).

These results are therefore broadly in line with the previous literature (e.g. Nishi & Kadoo, 1994; Haller, 1991; Galer, 1985; Bridger, 1995) where it is reported that digital types of displays are responded to very quickly (as found in Experiment_I) but are less effective in terms of detecting change (as found in Experiment_II). Moreover, RT data in Experiment_I showed that high complexity displays were reacted to slower than were the low and medium complexity ones. These data support Grandjean's (1988) and Sanders and McCormick's (1993) findings. The other main result found in Experiment_I was that subjects produced quicker RT when the speed displayed was nearer the decision point of 40 mph. This corresponds with much previous work in cognitive psychology according to Luce's Law (Luce, Bush and Galanter, 1965).

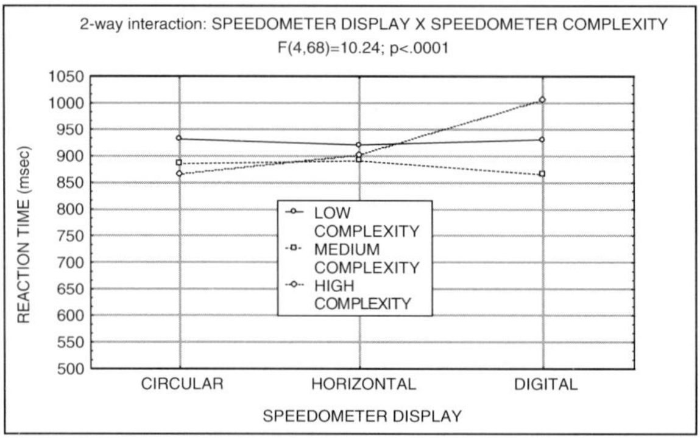

Figure 10. Mean R.T to the three Displays X the three Complexities from Experiment_III.

When comparing the two types of analogue speedometers, the circular type always produced 'better' results when compared with the horizontal type (i.e. it was responded to faster in both experiments). This in part may be due to subject being more familiar with circular speedometers. From the results obtained here, there seems little reason to recommend the use of analogue horizontal speedometers in terms of improving human performance.

For Experiment_III, when subjects retain the information needed to perform the Dec_Acceleration task the results found no significant main effects the RT measure for the different types of Display. However, when participants performed the Under or Over task, 'better' performance was found both for the Circular or the Horizontal displays compared with the Digital ones (as the interaction between Display and Task Performed showed). The results obtained in Experiment_I (that showed faster RT for digital displays) have not only disappeared but also a tendency in the opposite direction was found. When performing the same reading numerical information task in Experiment_I the digital display produced the fastest RT, whereas in Experiment_III it produced the slowest RT.

In addition, when subjects performed a detecting change task, the data found in Experiment_II were not replicated in Experiment_III. In the second experiment the digital display produced the slowest results, whereas in the third Experiment, the type of display does not affect performance. Taking into account all these data, it thus can not be reported that digital displays produced a good performance when drivers were required to sequentially carry out both tasks.

On the other hand, the Display X Task Performed interaction firstly highlights that the mean RT of these experiment were slower than those values obtained in the previous experiments. The uncertainly about which task have the subject to perform until both consecutive speedometer appeared could be partially responsible of that. Specifically, the subjects found it easier to perform the Dec_Acceleration Task than the Under/Over_40 Task; the RT were quickest for the sensitivity task than for checking the displayed speed, around 840-860 ms and 930-1010 ms respectively. This finding agrees with the previous results found in Experiment_I and II. The most relevant data that the Display X Complexity interaction showed was that the slowest RT to the Digital Display was when the Complexity was high. The digital speedometer was responded to slower when it had a high complexity level both compared to when it had a lower complexity and compared to high complexity analogue speedometers.

Of course, the experiments described here were undertaken in a laboratory using computer displayed images, thus they were low on ecological validity. In particular, the speedometers were not shown in a vehicle environment, or even a vehicle dashboard. Previous work (e.g. Labiale and Galliano, 1994) has shown that the context in which automobile symbols and displays are shown influences their visual recognition, thus some caution must be applied to the results obtained here. They do, however, provide a like-for-like comparison of different speedometer design variables while the subjects performed tasks that were similar to be encountered in driving situations (for example deciding whether the speed of the vehicle is above a certain level). So it is argued that a comparison between the different variables employed in these two experiments is meaningful.

Overall Conclusions

Overall, the results obtained in the three experiments reported here supported the previous literature. Digital displays were usually responded to quickly when the task is to read a value and make a decision based on it, but they are less effective when the task is to examine their sensitivity by how well speed changes can be detected. However, when performing both driving tasks sequentially, based on the obtain data it is not advisable to use digital displays. Analogue displays better fulfil the demands of both tasks.

Similarly, much of the previous literature has recommended keeping displays as simple as possible (e.g. Oborne, 1995). The experiments report here supported this, where those speedometers with either a low or a medium complexity were responded to quicker when compared with those versions with a high complexity. Speedometers in many countries (e.g. the UK) need to display speeds both as miles and kilometres per hour in the same dial, thus keeping this information as simple as possible in this situation is perhaps of even greater importance than it is for those countries that use only one speed measurement system.

When comparing the two different versions of the analogue displays used it was found that the circular speedometers performed better than the horizontal ones. They were responded to quicker for both tasks employed. Although familiarity may play a part in the results, it still appears that there are few grounds to recommend the widespread use of analogue horizontal displays.

Future research in this area could focus on the following topics. Firstly, using a dual task to examine speedometer performance combining either the reading of displayed velocity or detecting speed changes, with a tracking task. Secondly, testing the speedometers in more ecologically valid environments, for example testing the display as part of a vehicle dashboard.

Thirdly, using dynamic stimuli, that is, testing moving speedometers using video footage, virtual reality or real scenes.

References

Bridger, R. S. (1995). *Introduction to Ergonomics*. New York: McGraw-Hill.

Fowkes, M. (1984). Presenting Information to the Driver. *Displays, 5*(4), 215-223.

Galer, M. (1985). The Presentation of Information in Cars. Unpublished doctoral dissertation, University of Loughborough: UK.

Grandjean, E. (1988). *Fitting the Task to the Man*. London: Taylor & Francis.

Haller, R. (1991). Experimental investigation of display reading tasks in vehicles and consequences for instrument panel design. In A.G. Gale, C.M. Haslegrave, I. Moorhead and S.P. Taylor (Eds.), *Vision in Vehicles III*. Amsterdam: North-Holland.

Jindo, T., & Hirasago, K. (1997). Application studies to car interior of Kansei engineering. International Journal of Industrial *Ergonomics, 19*, 105-114.

Kiefer, R. J., & Angell, L. S. (1993). A comparison of the effects of an analogue versus digital speedometer on driver performance in a task environment similar to driving. In A.G. Gale, I.D. Brown, C. M. Haslegrave, H. W. Kruysse and S. P. Taylor (Eds.) *Vision in Vehicles IV*. Amsterdam: North-Holland.

Labiale, G., & Galliano, M. (1994). La reconnaissance visuelle des pictogrammes: Les effets de contextes. *Le Travail Humain, 57* (2), 163-177.

Luce, R. D., Bush, R., R. & Galanter, E. (1965). *Handbook of mathematical psychology*. (Vol. I). New York: Wiley.

Nishi, S., & Kadoo, A. (1994). Reading times of EFIS (electrical flight instrument system) by using eye mark recorder. *Reports of Aeromedical Laboratory, 35* (3), 63-75.

Oborne, D. J. (1995). *Ergonomics at Work* (3th edition). New York: Wiley.

Sanders, M. S., & McCormick, E. J. (1993). *Human Factors in Engineering and Design* (7th edition). USA: McGraw-Hill.

Srinivasan, R., & Jovanis, P. P. (1997). Effect of In-vehicle route guidance systems on driver workload and choice of vehicle speed: findings from a driving simulator experiment. In Y.I. Noy (Ed.) *Ergonomics and safety of intelligent driver interfaces*. Mahwah NJ: Lawrence Erlbaum.

US Department of Transportation (1998). Think. Available: http://www.nhtsa.dot.gov:80/people/outreach/safesobr/pub/think.pdf

Walter, W. (1991). Ergonomic information evaluation of analogue and digital coding of instruments in vehicles. In A.G.Gale, C.M. Haslegrave, I. Moorhead and S.P.Taylor (Eds.) *Vision in Vehicles III*. Amsterdam: North-Holland.

Appendix

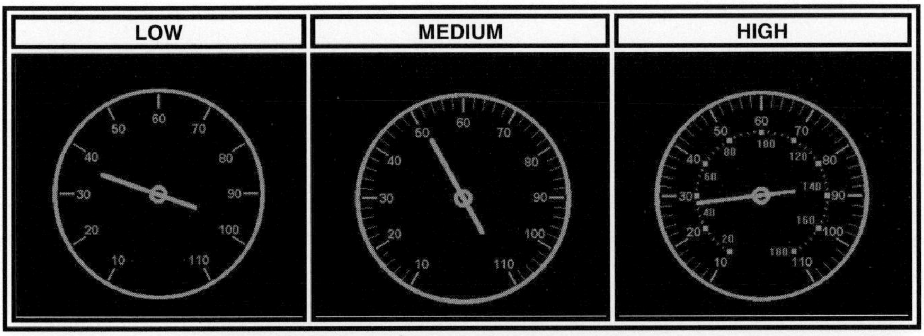
LOW
MEDIUM
HIGH

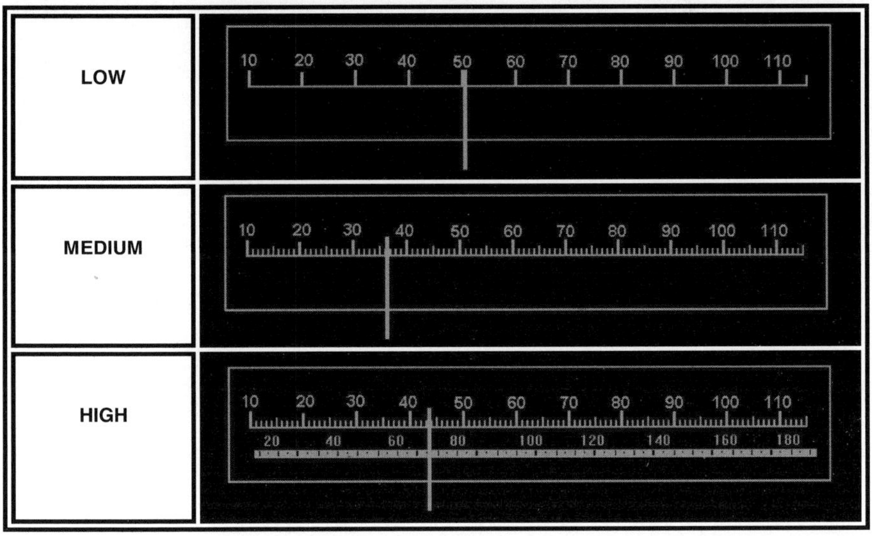
LOW
MEDIUM
HIGH

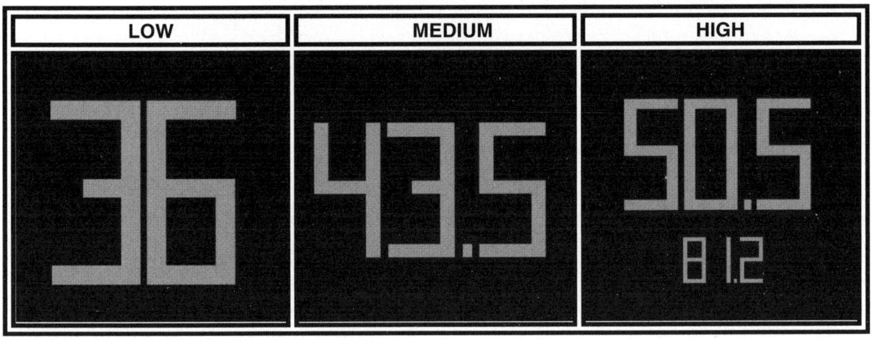
LOW
MEDIUM
HIGH
36
43.5
50.5
81.2

Traffic and Transport Psychology,
T. Rothengatter and R.D. Huguenin (Editors)

28

The Brake Activity of Car Drivers and that of an Automatic Brake System in Simulated Critical and Non-Critical Driving Scenarios

Lisbeth Harms and Jan Törnros

Introduction

Background

In the past decade driver support systems have been developed for a number of driving subtasks. Within the 4th European Telematic Application Programme the IN-ARTE project (TR4014) focused on integration of different driver support functions such as navigation, adaptive cruise control and anti-collision. Different support modes were also considered and both warnings and automatic interventions were subjected to simulator evaluations (see Martens & Van Winsum, 1999 for a full report). One evaluation study included anti-collision and adaptive cruise control as support functions and automatic brake interventions as the only support mode. Driver behaviour and workload were compared between supported and unsupported driving trials and driver acceptance of the system was investigated (see Törnros & Harms, 1999 for a full report). The present paper presents a post-hoc analysis of brake events recorded in this study.

Safety margins during catch-up and car following

Like many driver support systems for anticollision and adaptive cruise control the IN-ARTE system used a combination of headway and time-to-collision (TTC) for providing drivers, neglecting or ignoring safety margins, with timely brake interventions. Behavioural adaptation is a recognised problem with all driver support systems (Grayson, 1996) but it is often difficult to predict how behavioural adaptation to a particular system will develop. Using automatic brake interventions for driver support might result in reliance on the system, which would imply fewer brake actions and less care about safety margins - since the driver may leave this subtask to the system. On the other hand, finding brake interventions disturbing or just unpleasant, drivers might strive to avoid them and this would affect driving behaviour quite differently: Drivers being unfamiliar with the system would probably increase both brake frequency and safety margins in order to prevent brake interventions from occurring. Both in case of reliant and avoidant behaviour we would reasonably expect a trade-off between the activity of driver and that of the system.

Although drivers are able to perceive headway and TTC directly (Lee, 1976 see also Cavallo & Laurent, 1988) drivers may also take other factors into account in their judgement of acceptable safety margins. In a field study of truck drivers' following distances Fuller (1981) found that the truck drivers accepted shorter following distances (headway) during planned car following than in spontaneously occurring car following situations. Saad (1996) reported a similar finding. She asked drivers to comment on their own - video-recorded - behaviour on a motorway with dense traffic. Driver comments in combination with their behaviour strongly suggested that uncertainty was important to the drivers' general behaviour including also their accepted headway to lead cars.

Provided that a drivers' safety margin depend on the actual traffic scenario whereas the system uses a constant criterion in all traffic scenarios it is less likely that a simple trade-off between the driver's brake actions and the system's brake interventions will emerge. As the interaction between a driver and a driver support system is important both to driver acceptance of the system and to the necessary behavioural adjustments to it, we decided to perform a post-hoc analysis of the brake activity of the drivers and the system respectively in the above mentioned evaluation study.

METHOD

Subjects

Results from 16 subjects participating in the origibal study were selected for the present analysis. All drivers had normal driving experience. Their reported driving distance during the past year varied between 2,000 and 35,000 km.

Apparatus

The VTI driving simulator was used for the experiment. For a detailed technical description of the device see Nilsson, (1989) and Nordmark, (1990). A number of validations of the device (Harms, 1996 see also Harms et al. 1996) have reported acceptable behavioural validity of this device at the operational level (Allen, Lunefeld & Alexander, 1971).

The present study used a front-wheel driven Volvo with an automatic gearbox and a standard Swedish rural road i.e. a 9-metre wide road with one driving lane in each direction. The two lanes were separated by an intermittent centreline and the signed speed limit was 90 km/h except at a short section, which had a signed speed limit of 70 km/h.

The total driving distance for each subject was 100 kilometres including two practically identical road sections of 50 kilometres. Both road sections included 5 different traffic scenarios and 4 different road scenarios. Some traffic scenarios were presented repeatedly and subjects were presented with a total of 10 traffic scenarios in each trial.

Procedure

The subjects were instructed to drive the way they would normally do on a similar road and under similar conditions, but with the additional instruction that they should drive as if they were in a real hurry for an important appointment. In order to make the subjects familiar with the driving simulator and with the support system (brake interventions) they had a test drive prior to the experimental trials. All subjects performed two experimental driving trials, one with automatic brake interventions (supported driving) and one without automatic brake interventions (unsupported driving). The order of the two trials was balanced between subjects.

Results

The total number of brake interventions in supported driving trials were 424, corresponding to one intervention per 2 kilometres of driving. A high number of interventions (278) were due to speed violations (see table 1). The majority of the remaining ones (98) were related to scenarios demanding interaction with another vehicle (traffic scenarios) while road features accounted for the minority (48).

A brake intervention indicates that a certain pre-set safety criterion has been exceeded. Comparing the number of such criteria exceedings in unsupported driving trials with the number of actual brake interventions in supported ones a higher number of criteria exceedings was found in supported than in unsupported trials (Wilcoxon signed rank, $z = 3.35$, $p < .001$). The subjects' brake actions showed the reversed pattern: The subjects braked less frequently in supported driving trials (180) than in unsupported ones (235) (Wilcoxon signed rank, $z = 2.59$, $p < .01$). This observed trade-off is consistent with the reliance assumption.

Table 1. The number of brake events by agent (driver versus system) with and without system support. The shaded area represents brake interventions that would have been activated had the system been present.

	Supported driving		*Unsupported driving*	
Cause for Brake:	*Driver*	*System*	*Driver*	*System*
Too high speed	25	278	34	180
Road feature	40	48	43	47
Other vehicles	115	98	158	133
Brakes per agent	180	424	235	360
Total	604		235	

However, the total number of actual brake events increased dramatically in supported driving trials. Not surprisingly, too high speed accounted for the highest number of additional brakes in supported driving trials, but the same tendency was observed for traffic scenarios. Moreover, although traffic scenarios caused a higher number of brake actions in unsupported trials the subjects also exceeded the brake criterion more frequently in these trails. In unsupported trials the number of criterion exceeding was 133 whereas only 98 brake interventions were registered in supported trials (Wilcoxon signed rank, $z = 3.35$, $p < .001$). This finding is not consistent with a trade-off due to reliance on the system.

For a clarification of the interaction between the driver and the support system, we selected two traffic scenarios, an emergency scenario and a catch-up scenario, for further analysis.

Brake activity in an emergency scenario

Scenario description: During approach to a stationary car in the same lane, two closely following cars overtook the subjects. One of these cut into the driver's lane and braked hard whereas the other continued in the opposite lane at reduced speed.

The subjects were presented with the above-described scenario once in each trial. In unsupported trials it resulted in 3 collisions while 13 subjects managed to avoid a collision. The total number of brake actions was identical in the two trials. In supported trials a system intervention was activated only in 9 cases. Relating the brake events to the brake-onset of the lead car, we found that the subjects braked both prior to and after this brake-onset, whereas brake interventions occurred only after (see Figure 1).

All the subjects overtook the lead car a few seconds after it had seized to brake. Defining the "touch of the centreline with the left front tyre" as the onset of an overtaking manoeuvre quite a number of brake interventions, 11, were observed during overtake.

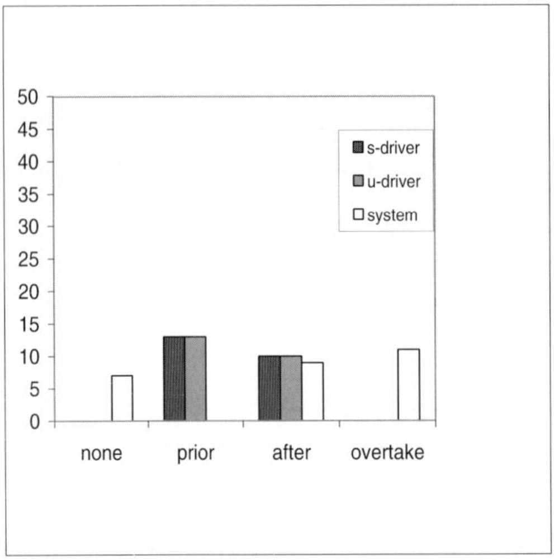

Figure 1. The number of brake events at subsequent stages of the emergency scenario distributed among the system and the driver in supported (s-driver) and unsupported (u-driver) trials respectively.

Brake activity in a catch-up scenario

Scenario description: The driver approached a slowly moving vehicle, which then reduced speed slightly but continuously. As no oncoming traffic was present the driver could adjust speed to the reduced speed of the lead car or overtake it. Subjects were presented with this driving scenario 3 times in each driving trial and no collisions with the lead car were registered.

In this driving scenario a significant increase in driver brake actions were observed in supported driving trials (Wilcoxon signed rank, $z = 2.39$ $p < .05$) (see Figure 2). Despite this in supported driving trials the system added 27 brake interventions to the total number of brake events. Again the majority of the subjects brake actions occurred prior to the onset of the brake of the lead car, while the system braked mainly after the onset of that and again quite a number of the brake interventions were observed during overtaking.

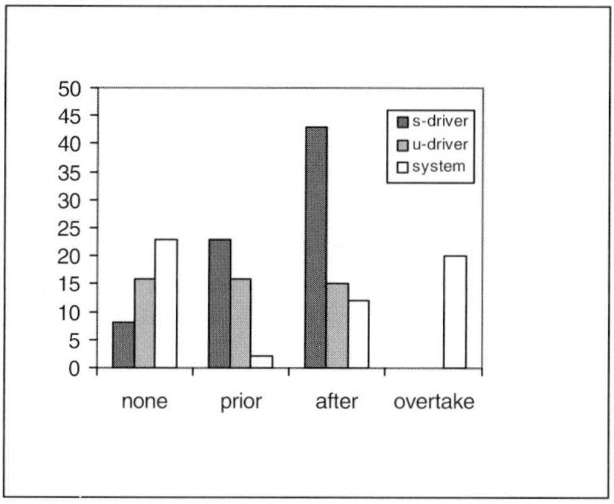

Figure 2. The number of brake events at subsequent stages of the catch-up scenario distributed among the system and the driver in supported (s-driver) and unsupported (u-driver) trials respectively.

Discussion

The analysis of brake events in the two selected driving scenarios reveals that the driver and the system used different criteria for braking. While the system used a constant safety criterion the drivers' criterion for braking apparently depended on the actual traffic scenario. This behaviour is consistent with driver behaviour in previous field studies (Fuller, 1981; Saad, 1996) finding that driver acceptance of safety margins, reflected in their brake behaviour, depended more on experienced uncertainty than on immediate perception. In the present study the drivers were generally cautious and they initiated a brake action as soon as the behaviour of another vehicle caused uncertainty. However, during overtaking the drivers frequently exceeded the safety criterion of the system. As a consequence in supported driving trials a driver initiating an overtaking manoeuvre frequently elicited a brake intervention. Thus in addition to the supportive brake interventions, primarily in emergency scenarios, a number of brake interventions, primarily during overtaking, conflicted both with the driver's intentions and with their behaviour.

The implication of this analysis to the design of brake algorithms for driver support systems is somewhat ambiguous: Of safety reasons it may not be worthwhile to use time margins that could jeopardise safe driving. It is, however important to avoid false alarms, that might lead drivers to counteract or compensate shortcomings of the system with unsafe driving behaviour. A partial solution to this problem, that used for the IN-ARTE protoytype, is to combine early warnings with subsequent emergency interventions. Another solution to the problem might be to continuously monitor driver behaviour and include also driver actions in the system algorithm, thereby following the principle of keeping the human agent in the control-loop.

References

Allen, T.M., Lunefeld. H., & Alexander, G.J. (1971). Driver Information needs. *Highway Research Record, 336*. Washington.

Cavallo, V., & Laurent, M. (1988). Visual information and skill level in time to collision estimation. *Perception, 17* (5), 623-632.

Fuller, R.G. (1981). Determinants of time headway adopted by truck drivers. *Ergonomics, 24* (6), 463-474.

Grayson, G.B. (1996). *Behavioural adaptation: a review of the literature*. (TRL Report 254). London.

Harms, L. (1996). Driving performance on a Real Road and in a Driving Simulator: Results of a Validation study. In A.G. Gale et al. (Eds.), *Vision in Vehicles V* (pp.19-26). Amsterdam: North-Holland.

Harms, L., Törnros, J. & Alm, H. (1996). Three studies of Behavioural Validity of a Driving Simulator - The impact of Face validity on vehicle control. *Paper presented on the Symposium on Design and Validation of Driving Simulators,* Valencia.

Lee, D.N. (1976). A theory of visual control of braking based on information about time-to-collision. *Perception 5*, 437-459.

Martens M. & W. Van Winsum (1999). Activation Criteria and warning strategies: Driving Simulator Results. IN-ARTE Project (TR4014), ID 7.1. Unpublished technical report. TNO Soesterberg.

Nilsson, L. (1989). The VTI Driving Simulator, description of a research tool. VTI-Reprint no. 150. Linköping.

Nordmark, S. (1994). Driving Simulators, trends and experiences. *Paper presented at the RTS Conference 1994*. VTI Reprint 204. Linköping.

Saad, F. (1996). Driver Strategies in Car Following Situations. In A. G. Gale et al. (Eds.), *Vision in Vehicles V*, (pp. 61-71).Amsterdam: North-Holland.

Törnros, J. & L. Harms (1999). Validation of the IN-ARTE system: A simulator Study of Driving with Brake Interventions on a Motorway and on a Rural Road. Unpublished technical report. VTI. Linköping.

Traffic and Transport Psychology,
T. Rothengatter and R.D. Huguenin (Editors)

29

Changes to Driving Behaviour in Conditions of Reduced Visibility Using an Infrared Vision Support System: Driving Simulator Evaluation Results

Philip Barham, Luisa Andreone, Antonella Toffetti, Daniela Bertolino and Johannes Eschler

Background

The need for driver vision support in conditions of reduced visibility

Problems associated with driving in conditions of reduced visibility, such as night, heavy rain and fog, are well documented. European car accident figures show that approximately 37% of accidents in Europe - which contribute to the 50,000 deaths that occur on Europe's roads each year - occur in conditions of reduced visibility. It is also well known that accidents at night are over-represented in relation to the number of miles that are driven in such conditions. Massie, Campbell and Williams (1995), using accident data from the USA, demonstrated that 10.4 fatal accidents occurred per 100 million miles driven at night, compared with only 2.2 per 100 million miles during the day. Furthermore, there are many people who feel uncomfortable with night-time driving, with more elderly drivers being particularly susceptible to such problems; this is because the ability of the eyes to adapt to low levels of illumination declines sharply with age, and this problem is compounded by slower reaction times. Research by Simms (1991) has shown that almost one in six drivers aged 70 and older never drove after the hours of darkness, and a lack of confidence in their ability to drive safely at night was often given as a reason for giving up driving altogether.

Thick fog, whilst being a comparatively rare occurrence, in both time and geographical location, is a particular problem, since it is not unknown for 100 or more vehicles to be involved in a single incident in such conditions. For example, on February the 13th 1996, between Brecia and Padova, Italy, an incident occurred in fog (visibility was reduced to less than 50 metres) which involved 300 vehicles. Eleven people were killed in this incident, with 300 other people seriously injured. Also that winter there were two other similar incidents in

Europe: between Turin and Milan an incident involving some 150 vehicles killed four people and seriously injured about 100 others, whilst in Belgium (near Deinz) 14 died and 60 were seriously injured in a pile-up involving 120 vehicles (La Stampa, 1996).

Whilst it might be hypothesised that a reduction in visibility will normally lead to a compensatory adjustment in speed in order to reduce the accident risk so presented, there is evidence to the contrary in the research literature. Sumner, Baguley and Burton (1977), for example, studied the effect of reduced visibility, caused by fog, on drivers' behaviour in a motorway situation; they found that speed adjustments made in such conditions were, in the case of more than half of the drivers studied, insufficient to enable them to stop within their visibility distance. The authors suggest that this explains why the percentage of fatalities and seriously injured persons in the UK, as well as the number of vehicles involved in each fog-related incident, are proportionately higher in fog than in other conditions. Similarly, Snowden et al (5) argue that, because reduced visibility lessens contrast within the road scene ahead, so removing many visual cues as to the car's velocity, the apparent speed of the vehicle slows, which, in turn, causes the driver to actually drive faster than usual. The phenomenon of a visual scene appearing to slow down has been demonstrated by these researchers in a laboratory using a virtual environment designed to simulate the view from a moving vehicle. Test subjects were asked to "drive" at a certain speed, without the aid of a speedometer, in visibility conditions that were described as "clear", "misty" and "foggy" (where the term "foggy" described the conditions of lowest contrast). The absence of a speedometer was a fairly realistic test condition, since, in foggy conditions, drivers are often reluctant to divert their gaze from the road scene ahead to the dashboard, which further exacerbates the problem of reduced visual speed cues. Snowden et al's results demonstrated a clear increase in driving speed as visibility was reduced.

Technological solutions currently offered

The DARWIN Project is one of a number of current initiatives within the automotive industry to seek to use night-time imaging technology for improving the safety of driving in conditions of low visual stimuli. The rationale behind the development of such a system is that drivers' ability to more readily detect objects in the road ahead in such conditions will enable them to react more quickly than they otherwise would to an emergency situation, thus reducing the risk of death and serious injury. The system will seek to achieve this end by using a Head-Down Virtual Image Display unit to project, onto the car's windscreen, a virtual image of the road scene captured by a far infrared camera. In the USA, Raytheon has developed an automotive far infrared camera for the Night Vision System of General Motors (USA), based on a very similar concept; the system is now on the market with limited availability as an option for the new Cadillac DeVille. GM's infrared sensor is pyroelectric, the presentation of images to the driver is done via a head-up display developed by Delco Delphi, and the image projector is installed behind the instrumentation panel.

Similarly, Jaguar Cars and DaimlerChrysler have led the development of night vision systems based on near infrared technology. Jaguar's system provides an interesting comparison, in human factors terms, with that developed by DARWIN, since the former utilises a contact analogue head-up display, whilst the DARWIN system aims to project images in front of the driver as a virtual image located in a head-down position. It is understood that Nissan, in Japan, is working towards a similar objective.

THE "DARWIN" PROJECT

DARWIN (Driving in AdveRse Weather and vIsibility coNditions) is a three-year project supported by the European Commission's BRITE-EURAM III Programme. The consortium's aim is to design, develop and evaluate a prototype driver vision support system, installed in a Lancia K demonstrator vehicle, by the end of the project, which is due to finish at the end of 2000. At the time of writing, this prototype has been duly installed in such a vehicle, and is soon to undergo human factors evaluations.

The DARWIN driver vision support system

With this system, images are captured by an infrared camera mounted in the grille of the car, projected from a unit located just behind the car's instrument panel, and displayed as a virtual image, using a head-up display unit, at the base of the car's windscreen. The objective is to provide a kind of "frontal mirror" in the periphery of the driver's view, in which information can be gathered without contact being lost with the road scene ahead (see Figure 1). Camera images are projected at a "virtual" distance in front of the driver in order to achieve a low eye adaptation time when the driver's attention switches between the virtual image and the scene ahead.

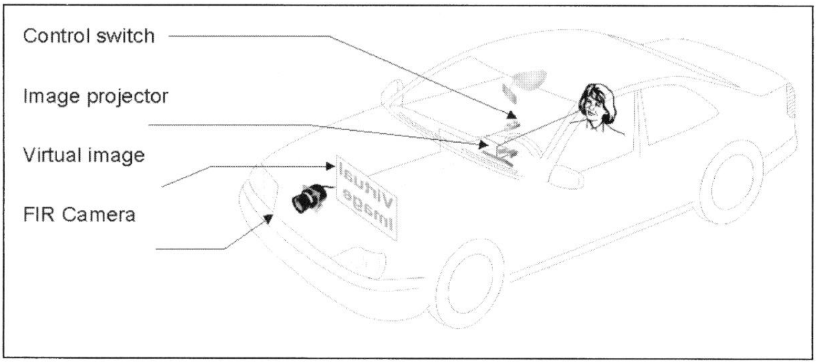

Figure 1. Conceptual diagram of the DARWIN system's head-down virtual image display.

Objectives of the human factors evaluations

The primary role of the simulator experiments, carried out during the first year of the project, was to initiate a learning process that would enable the project team to understand the issues involved with using such an imaging system in a car. In other words, it was intended that the findings from the simulator-based evaluations would both direct the drawing up of research protocols for the evaluations using a full-scale demonstrator vehicle, scheduled to take place in the third year of the project, and contribute to fine-tuning the design of the system itself. The trials, whilst evaluating the specific advantages of early detection of objects and incidents in the road ahead, also provided the opportunity to explore, generally, the extent to which using such technology might change users' driving behaviour when visibility is reduced. Of equal importance, of course, was the facility to investigate any potential disbenefits there might be in using such equipment, in terms, for instance, of the image having a distracting effect on the driver, and other human factors issues relating to the use of imaging technology in the driving environment.

The Human Factors Evaluations

Method

The evaluations were carried out using the Centro Ricerche Fiat driving simulator in Orbassano, near Torino. This driving simulator consists of a static vehicle placed inside a laboratory; it can be driven like a normal car. A computer-generated road scene is projected in front of the driver on a parabolic screen, with a viewing angle of 120°. Different driving scenarios may be simulated, in terms of type of road, number of obstacles, time of day and night, and whether visibility conditions are poor.

To simulate the infrared images of the DARWIN system, a black & white CCD camera with a viewing angle of 15° (an angle analogous to the field of view of the camera used for the first prototype of the system) was set up to capture images from the central monitor of the simulator's control room. For a thermal imaging effect, these images were transformed to negative, in real time. These were then sent to a frame grabber installed on a PC, dedicated real time image processing software made necessary adjustments and, finally, the images were sent to an image projector that was installed in the simulator's vehicle; images were then projected onto a transparent panel situated just above the fascia of the vehicle's dashboard. This set-up provided a very realistic mock-up of the DARWIN system's Human-Machine Interface (HMI).

A sample of 24 volunteer test subjects was set a task of following a car in front of them, with visibility reduced to approximately 30 metres. Subjects were asked to do this twice whilst recordings were being made; the only difference between the two runs was that a simulation of the system interface was available during one run, but not during the other. The rationale behind setting a car-following task was that it is common for a driver to follow close behind another vehicle when visibility is reduced. Since it is not possible to see ahead of this preceding vehicle, there is no prior warning of any emergency situation that might arise, and so no advanced warning that the car in front might suddenly stop. For these reasons, by far the most common type of collision in such conditions is the rear-end collision.

The path taken by the car in front was identical in all test runs, and was set by a researcher first driving the simulator car for one complete run. This ensured that all subjects followed exactly the same route throughout the simulation, thus recording the same mean speed for each run, and effectively eliminating speed as a dependent variable. The driving situation was that of a three-lane highway - with a hard shoulder - with no on-coming traffic or traffic coming from behind. The test route was punctuated by a number of obstacles and situations along the route, which occurred at exactly the same point in each test run. Of these, the current discussion is most interested in subjects' reaction to the vehicle in front having to brake sharply when encountering the wreckage of a two-car accident, as this caused the car that the subject was following to slow down suddenly, thus simulating an emergency situation.

The test protocol proceeded as follows: (i) The purpose and functionality of the DARWIN system, and the objectives of the evaluation, were briefly explained to the subject; (ii) The subject was asked to drive along the route in conditions of good visibility, and without a car in front to follow, in order to familiarise himself / herself with the functioning of the simulator's vehicle; (iii) The subject was asked to fill in a pre-trial questionnaire, asking for background information about driving experience, type of car driven etc; (iv) The subject was asked to perform the first car following exercise in poor visibility conditions, alternately with, and without, the support of the DARWIN system; (v) An eye test was administered, using a vision screener, to measure both near- and far-sighted binocular visual acuity; (vi) Each subject was asked to repeat "Step (iv)", either with, or without, the support of the DARWIN system; (vii) Each subject was asked to fill in an after-trial questionnaire, to elicit their views on the system that they had just used.

Key objective and subjective parameters

The simulator's software recorded data for nineteen parameters fifty times per second - those of most interest to the evaluation were : speed, braking force, "collision" flag, "off road" flag, and the precise position of both the test car and the car in front. From the latter data, it was possible to calculate the speed of the car in front, the headway between the two cars (this measurement being of key importance for safe driving), lateral deviation and lane encroachments.

Subjective feedback from volunteers was also important. With questions using a seven-point semantic scale, volunteers were asked to give their opinion on the usefulness of the system in poor visibility, the extent to which the system made them feel safer, the extent to which the presence of the system might have been distracting and how easy the system was to use. A number of questions on the technical features of the system were also asked, concerning, for example, the width of the "eye box", the width of the system's field of view etc..

RESULTS

A detailed analysis began with the separation of data recorded whilst the vehicle in front slowed to negotiate a hazard, from the remainder of the data set - this made it possible to examine the driving behaviour of volunteers when both following the car in front under "normal driving" conditions, and having to react to an emergency situation.

The effect of using the system during a simulated emergency situation was positive in terms of the number of collisions that volunteers had with the vehicle in front - which might be regarded as a useful "bottom line" indicator of potential safety benefits that might accrue through using such a system. Of the five instances of collisions being recorded when the car in front braked sharply, on encountering the wreckage of the two cars, only one occurred when the DARWIN system was available. Table 1 summarises the collisions and "near misses" that occurred during such episodes; these figures are cumulative, in that actual collisions are also counted as instances of headways of five metres or less, and so on.

Table 1. Number of collisions and "near misses" during a response to an emergency situation.

	With vision support system	*Without vision support system*
Collisions	1	4
Near misses		
Headway of 5m or less	5	11
Headway of 10m or less	11	33

This table shows headways of ten metres or less being reduced by a third, with near misses of five metres or less being more than halved when the DARWIN HMI was available. Whilst one individual was responsible for one collision both with and without this device, it is very interesting to examine the performances of the other three people who collided with the car in front, since, with the DARWIN system's support, they came no closer than 13 metres. This indicates a clear safety benefit among volunteers who demonstrated a propensity to be involved in a collision when driving, unaided, in conditions of poor visibility.

Frequency and harshness of braking were also used as indicators of whether the DARWIN system had a beneficial effect on subjects' driving during a simulated emergency. Using a percentage scale from 0% when the brake was not engaged, to 100% when the brake was applied fully, the mean braking force used by subjects when the car in front braked sharply was 77% with the DARWIN system and 86% without it.

There were no collisions during "normal driving", but a major research question here was whether the presence of the DARWIN system would have a behavioural effect on volunteers, expressed in headways (distance kept from the vehicle in front); the results of the simulations (See Figure 2) clearly show this to be the case, with mean headway during "normal driving" conditions being increased by 30% with the DARWIN system available. On an individual level, 22 (92%) of the 24 subjects recorded a longer mean headway when the DARWIN system was available.

In terms of frequency of braking, under "normal driving" conditions, 16 (67%) of the subjects used the brake more often when the system was not available, compared with six (25%) who braked more often when using the device; the corresponding mean braking forces were 59% and 51%, respectively.

It was also important to assess whether there were any negative safety implications for using the DARWIN system. There were three measures of interest in this part of the analysis: (i) The total number of lane encroachments; (ii) The mean position of the subject's car in relation to the centre of the lane; (iii) The mean absolute deviation from the centre of the lane. The key issue, of course, was the comparison between the value of these parameters when subjects did, and did not, have the DARWIN system available.

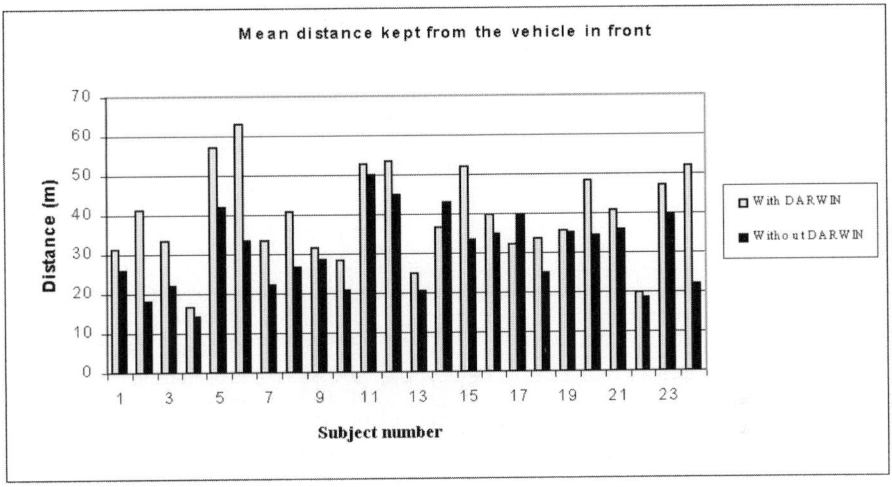

Figure 2. Variations in mean headway during "normal driving".

Whilst there was no significant difference in subjects' mean lane position with and without the DARWIN system, in terms of the total number of lane encroachments observed, all of the subjects recorded at least one lane encroachment during one, or most often both, of the test runs; the highest number of encroachments was 23. There were 14 subjects (58%) who encroached into the adjacent lane most often when the DARWIN system was not available, compared with only seven (29%) who encroached most often with the system. Using a Wilcoxon signed ranks test, this is a statistically significant difference (at a 94% level of significance). Altogether, there were 106 lane encroachments when the system was in use, and 143 encroachments when the system was not available.

As for the mean absolute deviation from the centre of a lane, there were 14 subjects (58%) who performed worse on this aspect of driving (i.e. showed greater lateral deviation) when the system was not available, compared with ten (42%) who showed the opposite tendency. If one ignores subjects whose mean absolute deviation figure was approximately the same both with and without the system (i.e. those for whom the two figures differed by 0.05 metres or less), then one is left with a sub-sample of 16 subjects; of these, no fewer than 12 (75%) deviated more when the DARWIN system was not available.

These results indicate that, not only was there no evidence here to suggest that using the DARWIN system hinders subjects' lane keeping ability, there were actually statistically significant indications that the system did in fact improve this aspect of their driving performance.

In terms of the subjective feedback received from the sample of volunteers, views on system usefulness, and whether or not they felt safer, were invariably positive, and the majority of the sample both found the system easy to use, and said that the image was not distracting. The results of the questionnaire that was administered immediately after volunteers had taken part in the evaluation are summarised in Figure 3.

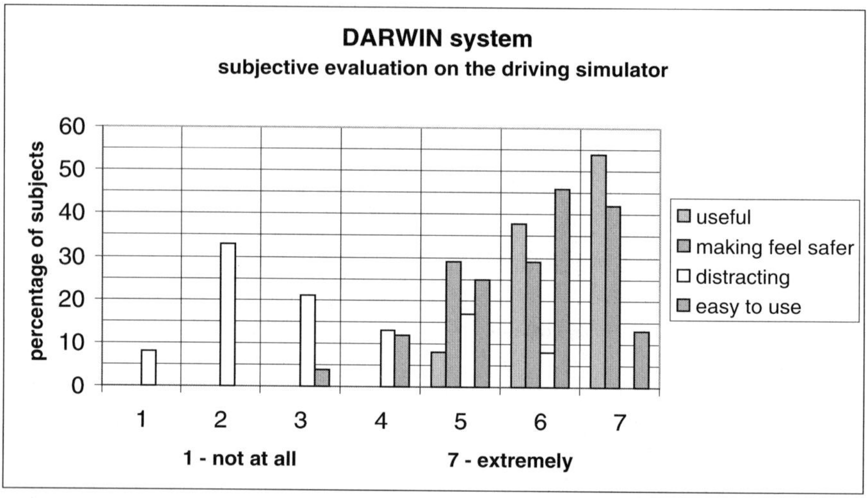

Figure 3. Volunteers' subjective views on the DARWIN system, when used in simulated conditions of poor visibility.

Discussion

When considering the limitations of the simulator evaluations, two obvious caveats refer to the fact that all simulations are an abstraction of reality and that the trials were carried out under artificial, laboratory conditions - volunteers were constantly aware that they were taking part in an experiment. A particular aspect of the trials reported here, however, is that the system under evaluation was itself a mock-up of how the first prototype will appear to the user. Whilst the device used for producing a virtual image in front of the driver was close to that which will be used in the DARWIN demonstrator vehicle, and the use of images in negative provided a good approximation of thermal images, there were important differences between the conditions experienced by participants in the simulations and those that will be experienced when using the DARWIN system in a real driving situation. Chief among these differences is the brightness and contrast of the simulated HMI and the environmental lighting conditions of the driving simulator - both of these conditions, and the way in which they interact, will be different when using the first prototype of the system in the demonstrator vehicle. Furthermore, although the dimensions of the simulated image, and the size of the system's field of view, were fairly representative of the forthcoming prototype, the properties of the eye-box were not accurate.

It is also possible to criticise the nature of the computer-generated simulation, in as much as it featured a driving scenario in which there was no on-coming traffic and no traffic travelling in the same direction as the subject, other than the car that the subject was required to follow. It could be pointed out, however, that the experiment was designed in order to focus on one particular aspect of driving - that of driving in traffic in conditions of much reduced visibility. In such driving conditions, much of the driver's attention will be absorbed in the dual tasks of lane-keeping and maintaining a safe headway to the vehicle in front - the simulation of driving with reduced visual stimuli was therefore very realistic. A more important limitation of the simulation of the road scene, however, was the fact that it was not possible to simulate brake lights on the car in front - the absence of this cue when this car slowed down made the task of following the vehicle, whilst at the same time avoiding a rear-end collision, even more difficult.

A general limitation of the evaluations was the fact that volunteers' exposure to the DARWIN system technology was very short-term. Each volunteer used the system for approximately five minutes, having never been exposed to it, or a similar system, before. Whilst this is unavoidable when dealing with evaluations of new (pre-prototype, in this case) equipment, it should be pointed out that nothing can be learnt about how people might use and interact with such a system once they have it in their own vehicle and have become thoroughly accustomed to it as part of their driving experience. Such questions can only be answered by the carrying out of long-term, longitudinal research. Such research would have to address issues such as risk compensation and "risk homeostasis" - i.e. will the net effect of using technology that enables the driver to see further ahead when visibility is reduced merely engender a false sense of security, thus encouraging higher speeds and actually compromise road safety ?

Conclusions

Whilst the main aim of the driving simulator evaluations was to provide key human factors information for the design of the DARWIN system, there is evidence, from the results of a car following task in conditions of considerably reduced visibility, that the system might have a positive impact on driving behaviour in such conditions. This is indicated by volunteer drivers' propensity to leave a larger gap to the vehicle in front of them, and is underlined in the significant reduction in collisions and near misses on the simulator when the DARWIN system was available to subjects. Subjective observations made during the evaluations showed that volunteers were unanimous in finding the DARWIN system both useful and easy to use, whilst, on balance, most people said that the system's image was not distracting for them, and that it made them feel comfortable and more safe when driving in conditions of poor visibility.

Acknowledgement

Partners in the DARWIN Project are the Centro Ricerche Fiat (Italy - co-ordinators), Robert Bosch GmbH (Germany), Vertex S.A. (France), CEDIP S.A. (France) and Cranfield University (United Kingdom). The authors of this paper would like to acknowledge the contribution made by Jenny Alexander, who assisted in the detailed analysis of the data, and by those who volunteered to take part in the experiments, since, without their input, the research would be meaningless.

References

Massie, D., Campbell, K., & Williams, A. (1995). Traffic accident involvement rates by driver age and gender. *Accident Analysis and Prevention, 27*, 73-87.

Simms, B. (1991). *Characteristics and driving patterns of drivers over seventy.* Carshalton, UK: Banstead Mobility Centre.

Snowden, R., Stimpson, N., & Ruddle, R. (1998). Speed perception fogs up as visibility drops. *Nature, 392*, (Apr.).

La Stampa. (Feb. 13th, 1996).

Sumner, R., Baguley, C., & Burton, J. (1977). *Driving in fog on the M4.* (TRL Supplementary Report 281). Crowthorne, UK: Transport Research Laboratory.

Traffic and Transport Psychology,
T. Rothengatter and R.D. Huguenin (Editors)

30

ATTITUDES TO TELEMATIC DRIVING CONSTRAINTS

Stephen Stradling, Michelle Meadows and Susan Beatty

INTRODUCTION

Intelligent Speed Adaptation (ISA) devices are part of a range of telematic driver support mechanisms currently vying for space at the roadside, and in the driving cabin and the engine control systems of next generation cars. An ISA system performs three functions: (i) measurement of vehicle speed; (ii) decision of a suitable vehicle speed; (iii) execution of speed adaptation (Sundberg, 2000).

Several different kinds of ISA have been trialled in Sweden, the Netherlands and the UK, the largest trial being the Swedish National Roads Administration programme which is currently monitoring 6000 adapted vehicles in Umea, Borlange, Lidkoping and Lund. There has been speculation that satellite controlled speed limiters may be required to be fitted in UK vehicles by 2010.

In-car technology is also available to measure the headway to the vehicle in front and to reduce vehicle speed until a larger headway is established. Thus the technology now exists to warn drivers when they exceed the local, posted speed limit; to automatically prevent them exceeding the posted speed limit; or even, in inclement conditions in specific locations, to restrict drivers to speeds below the speed limit; and to set a lower limit to their achievable headway to discourage close following. There has, however, been little research on drivers views of such abridgements of their autonomy when piloting their automobiles, though Comte (2000) has shown on both driving simulator and road test that automatic speed constraint may have maladaptive effects on driving style.

SAMPLE

In a recent study (Stradling, Meadows & Beatty, 1999) 791 English car drivers responded to a postal questionnaire (response rate: 21%). Table 1 shows that the sample covered a wide range of values on all the demographic variables: driver age, gender, socio-economic status, annual household income, and place of domicile; and on all the driving variables: years of driving experience, size of engine, age of car, estimated annual driving mileage, whether the car was employer-owned, and the extent of driving 'as part of your work'.

Table 1. Range of values on demographic and driving variables for 791 English car drivers.

Demographics	
Age	17 -> 83 years
Sex	M 61%; F 39%
SES	A/B, C1/C2, D/E, (economically) retired
Household Income	< £5K pa -> > £50K pa
Domicile	City, Town, Suburb, Village, Semi-rural & Rural
Driving Variables	
Driving Experience	1 year -> 60+ years
Engine Size	< 1 Litre -> > 2 Litres
Age of Car	1 year -> 10+ years
Annual Mileage	< 1K -> > 20K miles pa
Company Car	Yes / No
Drive As Work	Never -> Every working day

Usefulness and Acceptability of Telematic Devices

Respondents were asked '... to think about various systems that have been developed to automatically control certain aspects of your driving'. Judgements were requested of two types of systems - warning systems and override systems - each of which addressed three safety-critical situations - selecting appropriate speeds for prevailing conditions, close following, and speed limit breaches. This generates six types of telematic systems to be rated. Respondents rated the usefulness of each of the six systems on a 4-point scale from 'Very useful' to 'Not at all useful' and the acceptability of each of the systems on 4-point scales from 'Very acceptable' to 'Not at all acceptable'. Table 2 gives the distribution of ratings for each judgement.

A system that 'Warns you to adjust your speed to the conditions' was rated by a clear margin the most useful and by a narrow margin the most acceptable. A system that 'Automatically adjusts your speed so you keep to the limit' was considered the least useful and the least acceptable. Differences in judgements of both usefulness and acceptability were clearly related to the degree of intrusion of the system on the driver's control, autonomy and independence - and their freedom to violate the rules of the road. The more constraining the system the less favourable the ratings.

Characteristics of Car Drivers Finding Telematic Devices Useful and Acceptable

Composite usefulness and acceptability scores were computed for each respondent, averaging scores across the six control system scenarios. SPSS Answer Tree analyses were performed to determine the influence of each of the demographic and vehicle variables on the usefulness and acceptability scores for these warning and override systems. Table 3 summarises the influences on the usefulness ratings.

Table 2. Summary of usefulness and acceptability judgements of telematic control systems.

USEFULNESS [row %]	*V*	*F*	*NR*	*NAA*
Speed for conditions:				
Warns you to adjust your speed to the conditions	54	33	10	3
Automatically adjusts you to a safe speed for the conditions	43	33	16	9
Following distance:				
Warns if you are too close to the car in front	44	36	14	6
Automatically keeps you a safe distance from the car in front	45	30	17	9
Speed limit:				
Warns you if you're over the speed limit	49	35	12	4
Automatically adjusts your speed so you keep to the limit	38	28	22	13
ACCEPTABILITY [row %]	*V*	*F*	*NR*	*NAA*
Speed for conditions:				
Warns you to adjust your speed to the conditions	53	39	6	2
Automatically adjusts you to a safe speed for the conditions	38	34	18	9
Following distance:				
Warns if you are too close to the car in front	51	38	8	3
Automatically keeps you a safe distance from the car in front	39	35	18	9
Speed limit:				
Warns you if you're over the speed limit	52	37	8	3
Automatically adjusts your speed so you keep to the limit	34	29	23	15

V = Very *F = Fairly* *NR = Not Really* *NAA = Not at all*

Table 4 summarises the influences on the acceptability scores. The pattern for total acceptability ratings was substantially similar to that for usefulness ratings. Combining the two we may be reasonably confident that intrusion of telematic devices onto the driver's control, autonomy, independence, and freedom to violate the rules of the road will be more resisted by drivers under about 45, by male drivers more than by female drivers, by drivers from the higher social classes, from households with annual income greater than £30,000 pa, from the least experienced drivers, from high mileage drivers, and from those who drive as part of their work.

Evaluation of Telematic Devices and Speed Choice

Respondents had also been asked to indicate 'the speed at which you normally drive' and 'the speed at which you prefer to drive' on each of four different road types - motorways, other main roads, rural roads and suburban roads. The profile of those drivers finding telematic constraint unacceptable bears a number of similarities to that of drivers who nominated higher normal and preferred speeds (Stradling, Meadows & Beatty, 2001). The association between drivers' nominated speeds and their evaluation of devices designed to curb excess speed was examined.

Table 3. Influence of demographic and vehicle variables on car drivers total telematics usefulness scores.

Factor	*Influence*
Age Band	45+ > 23-45 > 17-23
Sex	F > M
SES	D/E, Retired > C1, C2 > A/B
Income	below £20K > £20-30K > £30K+
Domicile	no effect
Experience	1-3 years, less useful
Engine Size	2.0L+, less useful
Age of Car	4-7 years, less useful
Annual Mileage	below 8K > 8-20K > 20K+
Company Car	no effect
Drive As Work	Any, less useful

Table 4. Influence of demographic and vehicle variables on car drivers total telematics acceptability scores.

Factor	*Influence*
Age Band	45+ > 30-45 > 17-29
Sex	F > M
SES	D/E, Retired > C1, C2 > A/B
Income	below £20K > £20-30K > £30K+
Domicile	no effect
Experience	1-16 years, less acceptable
Engine Size	no effect
Age of Car	7+ years, less acceptable
Annual Mileage	below 8K > 8-20K > 20K+
Company Car	Yes, less acceptable
Drive As Work	Any, less acceptable

The most stringent control system evaluated was one which 'automatically adjusts your speed so you keep to the limit'. What were the speed choices of those drivers who were favourable and unfavourable towards such a system? The mean normal and preferred speeds on the four types of roads were tabulated for each response category of usefulness and acceptability rating in respect of this system. Results are shown in Tables 5 - 8.

Table 5. Mean nominated normal speeds on four road types by ratings of usefulness of automatic speed adjustment.

Speed would normally drive on: [m/hr]	*motorways*	*other main roads*	*suburban roads*	*rural roads*
Very useful	69	51	36	37
Fairly useful	71	51	35	40
Not really useful	73	54	36	42
Not at all useful	75	55	37	43
Mean	71.36	52.49	35.87	39.83
% increment: VU -> NAAU	9.03%	8.32%	4.23%	15.72%

Table 6. Mean nominated normal speeds on four road types by ratings of acceptability of automatic speed adjustment.

Speed would normally drive on: [m/hr]	*motorways*	*other main roads*	*suburban roads*	*rural roads*
Very acceptable	69	50	36	38
Fairly acceptable	71	52	36	39
Not really acceptable	73	54	37	41
Not at all acceptable	76	55	36	43
Mean	71.39	52.45	35.96	39.86
% increment: VU -> NAAU	10.35%	10.56%	1.38%	12.94%

Table 7. Mean nominated preferred speeds on four road types by ratings of usefulness of automatic speed adjustment.

Speed would prefer to drive on: [m/hr]	*motorways*	*other main roads*	*suburban roads*	*rural roads*
Very useful	70	52	37	37
Fairly useful	74	54	38	41
Not really useful	76	57	38	43
Not at all useful	78	59	38	45
Mean	73.69	54.76	37.40	40.61
% increment: VU -> NAAU	11.05%	12.94%	3.43%	20.22%

Each tabulation shows the per cent increment in nominated speed for those car drivers who find a system that 'Automatically adjusts your speed so you keep to the limit' 'Not at all' useful or acceptable over those who rate it 'Very' useful or acceptable (% increment: VU -> NAAU). These increments range from 10% to 20% across all road types except for suburban roads, and they were higher for preferred speeds than for normal speeds.

Table 8. Mean nominated preferred speeds on four road types by ratings of acceptability of automatic speed adjustment.

Speed would prefer to drive on: [m/hr]	*motorways*	*other main roads*	*suburban roads*	*rural roads*
Very acceptable	70	52	37	38
Fairly acceptable	73	54	37	40
Not really acceptable	75	57	39	43
Not at all acceptable	80	60	37	45
Mean	73.74	54.80	37.49	40.67
% increment: VU -> NAAU	13.75%	15.57%	1.20%	20.01%

Summary

A large sample of English car drivers rated the usefulness and acceptability of a range of telematic warning and control systems that could influence driver speed and headway. The more constraining the system the less favourable were the ratings.

Greater resistance to reduction in driver control and autonomy was shown: by drivers under about 45, by male drivers, by drivers from the higher social classes and from households with annual income greater than £30,000 pa, by the least experienced drivers, by high mileage drivers, and by those who drive a car as part of their work.

Those car drivers who found speed control by a system that 'Automatically adjusts your speed so you keep to the limit' not at all acceptable nominated higher normal and preferred speeds on motorways, other main roads, and rural roads. That is, those least likely to favour automatic speed regulation were those whose driving is most in need of it, and those who rated external regulation of speed as very acceptable were those whose driving was least in need of it.

References

Comte, S. (2000) New systems, new behaviour? *Transportation Research Part F, 3*, 95-111.

Stradling, S. G., Meadows, M. L., & Beatty, S. (1999) Factors affecting car use choices. Transport Research Institute, Napier University: Edinburgh, UK.

Stradling, S. G., Meadows, M. L., & Beatty, S. (this volume) Characteristics and crash-involvement of speeding, violating and thrill-seeking drivers.

Sundberg, J. (2000) Speed management. The need for an intelligent solution. *Traffic Technology International*, February/March 2000.

Traffic and Transport Psychology,
T. Rothengatter and R.D. Huguenin (Editors)

31

Driver Assistance Systems: Safe or Unsafe

Oliver Carsten

Introduction

We have just undergone a revolution in driving. Adaptive Cruise Control (ACC) is now on the market in Europe - it is available as an option on at least one Jaguar model and is predicted to be available shortly from a number of manufacturers. In Japan, ACC is already fairly commonplace. Traditional Cruise Control, which rather crudely maintains a driver-set speed, is not really viable on the crowded road of Europe or East Asia, since it is only operable in relatively free-flow traffic conditions. ACC extends traditional cruise control by adding a headway function, so that the vehicle accelerates to and keeps its set speed unless time headway will go below a preset minimum in which case the minimum headway is maintained by automatically reducing speed. Acceleration of the lead car is mimicked up to the maximum set speed. The function of ACC is to replace the driver in the task of car following particularly on motorways and other high speed roads.

ACC is revolutionary because this is the first time a major part of the driving task has been replaced by an automated system. With ACC in operation, the driver's task becomes lateral control of the vehicle, monitoring the functioning of the ACC system and resuming manual control in emergencies. And for the car manufacturers ACC is just the first step in a planned path towards fully automated driving, at least on some roads and in some situations (Zwaneveld et al., 1999). ACC will be supplemented by collision avoidance in longitudinal control and then by various warning and assistance systems for lateral control, including lane changes. Once a vehicle is capable of making autonomous decisions for both longitudinal and lateral control, then fully automated driving can become practicable.

If ACC is on the market, it is reasonable to assume that we know that the system is safe in general use, or rather we know that driving with ACC is not more unsafe than comparable driving without ACC. After all, the system has been in manufacturing development since the 1980s, test vehicles have been available since at least the early 1980s and there have been numerous studies of the implications of ACC and of driver behaviour with the system. Whether the assumption that safe operation has been verified is warranted is examined below.

Hypotheses Concerning ACC

Before reviewing the results of a number of studies of ACC, it is advantageous to construct a set of working hypotheses about how ACC might influence traffic safety. Such hypotheses can be categorised into two types: engineering hypotheses and behavioural and human factors hypotheses. Engineering hypotheses are those that depend on the engineering design of the system, e.g. on the values set for maximum acceleration, maximum speed and minimum headway. The major engineering hypotheses for ACC concern both speed and headway. In terms of speed, the hypothesis is that speeds will become more homogeneous both for an equipped vehicle (the system will control speed with less variation than a driver is able to do so) and in a given flow of traffic where the proportion of ACC-equipped vehicles is high. In terms of headway, the hypothesis is that headways will become more homogeneous (because they are controlled with greater precision by the system than by a manual driver) and that very short headways will perhaps be reduced (provide they are prevented by system design). Both the speed and headway effects imply smoother and therefore safer traffic flows.

The behavioural and human factors hypotheses on ACC are as follows:

- Automation of the driving task will reduce drivers' situation awareness, i.e. perception of the current situation, interpretation of the current situation and projection of the future situation (Endsley, 1995). Drivers will tend to rely on the system to monitor the traffic stream ahead.
- Drivers may misunderstand the performance envelope of the system. Drivers will not understand the limitations of the technologies underlying ACC or the constraints imposed by the designers on system operation. For example, after experiencing the fact that the system is capable of considerable deceleration (some ACCs have braking capability that encompasses 80 or 90 percent of the distribution of driver braking severity), drivers may interpret an ACC as a collision avoidance system. As a result, drivers may tend to be slow in resuming manual control when a critical situation does develop, anticipating that the ACC will be able to cope. This is what Fancher & Ervin (1998) have termed the "authority" issue - how much authority does the ACC have over the operation of the vehicle.
- Mode errors by the driver may arise: the driver may not be aware of whether the ACC is enabled or disabled, is in "pure" cruise control mode or in headway mode. After leaving a motorway the driver may forget that the ACC is still on.
- As stated above, with ACC one part of the driving task is now monitoring the operation of the ACC, both directly through whatever interface is provided by the car manufacturer, and indirectly through sensing system operation. One crucial aspect of such monitoring is the detection of faults and failures in the system. Bainbridge (1987) has pointed out the poor performance of humans in monitoring tasks.
- Behavioural adaptation may arise with ACC use. Behavioural adaptations were defined by an international expert group as "those behaviours which may occur following the introduction of changes to the road-vehicle-user system and which are not intended by the

initiators of the change" (OECD, 1990). One behavioural adaptation to ACC might be a change in lane choice, because some drivers disliked the operation of the system in headway mode.

- ACC may be used differently by different types of drivers, depending for example on age, experience, habitual driving style and attitudes. This would tend to negate the engineering effect of ACC in harmonising speeds and headways.
- With long-term use of ACC, drivers may loose skills particularly in car following. This might not matter if ACC were 100 percent reliable, but that is not currently the case - the technologies underlying ACC in the form of the headway radars, have some reliability problems particularly in bad weather.

All of these behavioural and human factors hypotheses indicate ways in which ACC might be detrimental to safety. The empirical evidence on these effects and on the engineering effects of ACC is reviewed below.

Verification of the Engineering Hypotheses

It could be argued that the engineering hypotheses can be verified by means of using simulation modelling to compare speed and headway distributions between ACC-equipped traffic and non-ACC traffic. But, since there are no human drivers in the loop is such modelling, the results will be open to question and may be treated as an artefact of the rules in the model. Far superior in terms of credibility are the results of field trials with ACC.

To date, there has been only one significant field trial of ACC, the Michigan "Field Operational Test" (Fancher et al., 1998; Fancher & Ervin, 1998). In this trial 10 cars were equipped with ACC and handed to drivers to use for their normal driving. Eighty-four drivers drove for two weeks with the ACC available to them in the second week. Twenty-four drivers drove for five weeks with the ACC available in the last four weeks. Thus there were 3.6 person years of driving with ACC available for use. ACC was in use for a total of 56,380 km (31% of the distance travelled) and 534 hours (18% of driving time).

The final report of the study states: "The data gathered in the FOT could be used to argue both for and against safety benefits. More headway time and a deceleration type of warning, if the driver is inattentive, certainly appear to be safety benefits. The possibility of inattention due to over reliance and over confidence as well as the possibility of slower or delayed reactions certainly appear to pose disbenefits. Given the limitations of presently available data, the net impacts on safety are unknown" (Fancher et al., 1989). Further on the authors specifically address the engineering hypotheses and state: "To the extent that safety is associated with longer headways and more uniform traffic, driving with this ACC system provides safety benefits." The qualification "this ACC system" should be noted: the drivers had the choice of three headways - 1.1 seconds, 1.5 seconds and 2.1 seconds - so that the shortest headway was longer than that chosen by many drivers in manual driving. Production systems are likely to have shorter minimum headways.

VALIDATION OF THE BEHAVIOURAL AND HUMAN FACTORS HYPOTHESES

In the discussion that follows, the hypotheses outlined above are grouped into pairs. For each grouping, the findings from appropriate research studies are provided. It should be noted that most of the studies cited have been carried out on driving simulators, in large part because of the ethical problems of creating safety-critical situations in real life.

Situation awareness and "authority"

In an experiment on the VTI driving simulator, drivers approached a stationary queue on a motorway (Nilsson, 1995). The ACC was set not to detect the cue so that the drivers had to detect the queue and slow down the vehicle appropriately. The design was a between-subjects design with ten drivers assigned to the ACC group and ten to the non-ACC group. In the ACC condition five drivers crashed into the queue; in the non-ACC condition one driver crashed.

A similar experiment was conducted on the HUSAT simulator at Loughborough University. drivers were exposed to a stationary queue at the end of a one hour driving session on a two-lane highway. Fifty-six drivers participated with half assigned to the ACC condition and half driving in the non-ACC condition. The result of the experiment was that minimum time-to-collision into the stationary queue was significantly shorter with ACC (Richardson, Ward, Fairclough & Graham., 1996).

Mode errors and monitoring

An experiment was carried out on the Southampton University driving simulator to investigate the effects of ACC failure on driver performance (Young & Stanton, 1997). When ACC failure was induced, one-third of the drivers collided with the lead vehicle, indicating that monitoring the functioning of the system is difficult and recovery from failure problematic.

Behavioural adaptation and driver type

An experiment was conducted on the University of Groningen driving simulator with 38 subjects (Hoedemaeker, 1999). The subjects first drove a motorway route without ACC and subsequently drove the same route three more times, each time with a different version of ACC out of a total of six alternative versions (the ACCs varied in terms of the set time headway and in terms of whether the system could be overruled in headway mode by use of the accelerator or brake). All the ACCs had sufficient "authority" to bring the vehicle to a safe stop. With ACC, speeds increased in both light and heavy traffic situations. Standard deviation of lateral position increased with ACC, particularly in heavy traffic, which is not likely to be beneficial to safety. Use of the left (fast) lane also increased with ACC, presumably because of the higher speed choice.

In the same experiment, differences were found by driving style. Fast drivers identified by the Driving Style Questionnaire of West, Elander & French (1992) increased their standard deviation of lateral position with ACC while driving in light traffic, whereas slow drivers decreased their standard deviation of lateral position in the same situation.

Driving style was also investigated in the Michigan Field Operational Test (Fancher et al. 1998). Here driving style was classified on the basis of actual speed and headway choice. From most aggressive to least aggressive, the categories were hunter/tailgaters, extremists, planners, flow conformists and ultraconservatives. It was found that the first group used the ACC relatively less often, in all probability because the system's minimum time headway of 1.1 seconds was larger than the drivers' preferred time headway of 0.6 to 0.8 seconds.

Loss of skill in the long term

There has been no long-term study of driver performance in ACC-equipped cars, so that the four weeks of driving with ACC in the Michigan trial remains the longest period of exposure. At the moment, therefore this issue remains unexplored.

Discussion: a Contrast Between two Vehicle Control Systems

There are two pioneer vehicle-control systems in operation on European roads. On the one hand, we have Adaptive Cruise Control which is promoted by the car manufacturers, has been under development for at least twelve years, for which there have no large-scale field trials to date (and since it already on the market, none are likely). Based on the review above, the safety effects of ACC are quite likely to be negative: virtually all the potentially negative behavioural hypotheses have been confirmed, so that there should be significant concerns about this system even if, with high penetration, speed and headway variance are reduced. ACC is available as an optional item now on at least one make of luxury car, with other manufacturers planning to introduce it shortly.

On the other hand we have Intelligent Speed Adaptation (ISA). This system, which can prevent exceeding a set speed, either the speed limit or a variable top speed adapted to local conditions, has been developed and promoted by part of the traffic safety community. ISA has been under intermittent development for more than 18 years and is undergoing very large field trials now in Sweden, though admittedly most of the trial vehicles are equipped only with advisory ISA. The safety impact of ISA is highly positive with a 36% reduction in injury accidents predicted for Great Britain with the introduction of a dynamic version that intervenes in vehicle control (Carsten & Tate, 2000). Predictions of when ISA will be on the market, let alone mandated by a national government, are anyone's guess.

It is also instructive to review the draft standard for ACC from the International Organization for Standardization (ISO). The proposed standard defines the set speed range for ACC as 18 km/h to 160 km/h, i.e. with a full range from slow urban driving at one end of the spectrum to a capability to massively exceed the highest speed limits on most countries' roads at the other end of the spectrum. The specified minimum time headway is 1.0 second, although at leas one car manufacturer is lobbying for a lower figure of 0.8 seconds. Such a number is well below recommended safe time headways of two seconds. Maximum longitudinal deceleration is 0.35 g, which to most drivers will give the appearance that the system can carry out emergency braking and is therefore capable of acting as a collision avoidance system. It is hard to defend these numbers on any rational grounds.

Conclusions

Before allowing new vehicle control systems to come on the market, it would be sensible to adopt the precautionary principle that there should be no fundamental change to the traffic system without assurance that safety is not harmed. In the case of these systems it is not feasible to devise a generic assessment which would immediately provide to researchers, the authorities and the public a clear indication of whether a new system meets reasonable standards of safety. The onus should therefore be on the manufacturers to provide adequate verification of the safety of their systems in everyday use, almost certainly through large-scale field trials. This is no more than is currently being required of ISA in order to demonstrate its capability to bring about benefits.

References

Bainbridge, L. (1987). Ironies of automation. In: J. Rasmussen, K. Duncan and J. Leplat (Eds.), *New Technology and Human Error*. Chichester and New York: John Wiley & Sons.

Carsten, O., & Tate, F. (2000). Final Report - Integration. Deliverable 17 of External Vehicle Speed Control. Leeds, UK: Institute for Transport Studies, University of Leeds.

Endsley, M.R. (1995). Toward a theory of situation awareness in dynamic systems. *Human Factors, 37* (1), 65(84.

Fancher, P., & Ervin, R. (1998). Adaptive cruise control field operational test. *UMTRI Research Review, 29* (4), 1-17.

Fancher, P., Ervin, R., Sayer, J., Hagan, M., Bogard, S., Bareket, Z., Mefford, M., & Haugen, J. (1998). Intelligent cruise control field operational test. Final report. Volume I: Technical Report. Ann Arbor: University of Michigan Transportation Research Institute..

Hoedemaeker, M. (1999). Driving with intelligent vehicles: driving behaviour with adaptive cruise control and the acceptance by individual drivers. PhD thesis, Delft Technical University. TRAIL Thesis Series 99/6, Delft University Press.

Nilsson, L. (1995). Safety effects of adaptive cruise controls in critical traffic situations. *Proceedings of the Second World Congress on Intelligent Transport Systems*, Yokohama. Volume 3, 1254-1259.

OECD (1990). *Behavioural adaptations to changes in the road transport system.* Paris: Organisation for Economic Co-Operation and Development.

Richardson, J.H., Ward, N.J., Fairclough, S.H., & Graham, R. (1996). PROMETHEUS/DRIVE AICC safety assessment: basic simulator. Confidential report. Loughborough, UK: HUSAT Research Institute, Loughborough University. [Cited in: N.J. Ward, Driver response to automated vehicle control. Proceedings of the 13th triennial congress of the International Ergonomics Association, June 29 (July 4 1997, Tampere, Finland (Vol. 1, pp. 280-282). Helsinki: Finnish Institute of Occupational Health.]

West, R., Elander, J., & French, D. (1992). *Decision making, personality and driving style as correlates of individual risk.* Crowthorne: Transport Research Laboratory.

Young, M.S., & Stanton, N.A. (1997). Automotive automation: effects, problems and implications for driver mental workload. In: D. Harris (Ed.), *Engineering psychology and cognitive ergonomics*. (Vol. 1 Transportation systems). Aldershot, UK: Ashgate.

Zwaneveld, P.J., Van Arem, B., Bastiaensen, E.G.H.J., Soeteman, J.J., Frémont, G., Bélarbi, F., Ulmer, B., Bonnet, C., & Gölliger, H. (1999). *Deployment scenarios for advanced driver assistance systems* (Report Inro/VK 1999-07). Delft, The Netherlands: TNO Inro.

SAFETY

ENFORCEMENT AND TRAINING

Traffic and Transport Psychology,
T. Rothengatter and R.D. Huguenin (Editors)

32

Questions for Psychologists Related to Enforcement Strategies

Stefan Siegrist

Introduction

There is no doubt that there is a strong association between the breaking of certain traffic laws and the loss of health. Non-compliance with speed and alcohol limits is a major cause of road accidents at individual as well as at group level (e.g. Evans, 1991).

On the other hand, enforcement of traffic laws has a positive effect on road user behaviour and consequently on safety level (overview e.g. in Zaal, 1994). Although there is evidence for best practice, there still remains considerable room for further improvement. Political and technological developments necessitate new recommendations for improved strategies and it is not yet clear how exactly enforcement should be combined with feedback, publicity campaigns and other supporting measures in order to achieve optimal results. The development of more efficient enforcement methods is also necessitated by the fact that in most countries nowadays, resources for traffic policing are shrinking.

While enforcement is neither the only nor the most efficient measure in the promotion of road safety - engineering usually offers more sophisticated solutions - enforcement will continue to play an important role in reducing traffic accidents as long as there is a minimal degree of freedom for road users. Specifically, as long as travel speed is not regulated by technical means, as long as there is no technical means to prevent a drunken driver starting a car engine, enforcement will play an important role.

Underlying Reasons for Non-Compliance with Traffic Rules

In order to know how to effectively change driver behaviour we must first study the psychological reasons for non-compliance. Various psychologists have attempted to classify different forms of errors in behaviour. According to Reason (1994), there are three major levels: ability-based, rule-based and knowledge-based. In contrast to the workplace situation (which is the main field of application for Reason's approach), behaviour in traffic is not only determined by the structure of the task. Further, road user behaviour is not only determined by safety considerations. Consequently, there are different causes behind the same kind of unsafe behaviour, and clearly different causes demand different solutions.

Several authors of traffic psychology papers have pointed out the central role of normative orientation, behavioural motives, the general social situation and the dynamics of the current social situation (e.g. Näätänen & Summala, 1976; Rothengatter, 1988) in determining behaviour in traffic. The most frequent cause of injuries in road traffic can thus be referred to as quasi-errors rather than errors in the execution of the task. Offences may indeed be a result of errors but they are mostly the result of certain attitudes, norms and motivations. Furthermore, we have to distinguish between conscious decisions not to comply with a regulation (which can be referred to as a violation) and not paying attention to the regulation (which is a quasi-error). Non-compliance with traffic regulations often reflects the influence of attitudes and motives that are contradictory to safe behaviour rather than a conscious decision to break the rules. Contravening the regulations does not necessarily mean that a driver has no respect for safety norms, nor that there is a lack of motivation to comply with the regulation in question. In some cases it may only mean that the desire to have pleasure is at the moment more dominant than other motivational factors. As a consequence, behaviour in traffic is affected by laws and enforcement work, to some extent, because they remind the driver of existing norms and values. If all road users were violators who did not accept the regulations and had negative attitudes towards compliance, enforcement would most likely have very little effect.

This evidence supports the theoretical notion of the Action Theory (e.g. von Cranach, Kalbermatten, Indermühle & Gugler, 1982), which maintains that higher-level processes have a more dominant effect on people's actions. Table 1 summarizes the causes of non-compliance and related objectives of prevention programs. It points to the need for enforcement strategies in road traffic addressing more than just the problem of deterring drivers from committing violations.

There is evidence for differences between drivers with respect to the amount of non-compliance as well to the causes of this behaviour (Gregersen & Berg, 1994; Parker, Reason, Manstead & Stradling, 1995): Differences between subgroups should be considered through target group specific enforcement strategies and safety programs.

So, our first question is: In psychological terms, what are the reasons for non-compliance and does it make sense to identify subgroups of drivers?

Table 1. Causes, types and prevention of unsafe behaviour.

Main cause of unsafe behaviour	*Type of non-compliant behaviour*	*Objective of prevention strategy (non-engineering measures)*
- ability - application of regulations - knowledge	error: task is wrongly executed	learning of basic skills (manoeuvring), regulations, specific knowledge and action strategies; aptitude-oriented selection
- attitudes	violation conscious decision to contravene the regulations	changing attitudes deter
- norms - attitudes - social influence	quasi-error: normative, motivational or social tendencies are more dominant than safety	show relevance of a regulation in a specific situation; increase road users' awareness of risk, increase social pressure to behave safely
- aptitude	quasi-error: lack of aptitude to decide whether to comply or not	identifying violators, analysing reasons for non-compliance, offering psychological support

How Enforcement Works and what Explanations Psychologists Offer

In order to monitor and improve the process of enforcement, it is essential to know why and how it works. One crucial factor seems to be the drivers' perceived risk of detection. There is general agreement and empirical support that visible surveillance decreases the rate of traffic offences. Increased enforcement leads to an increase in perceived probability of detection and is related to changes in driver behaviour (Figure 1).

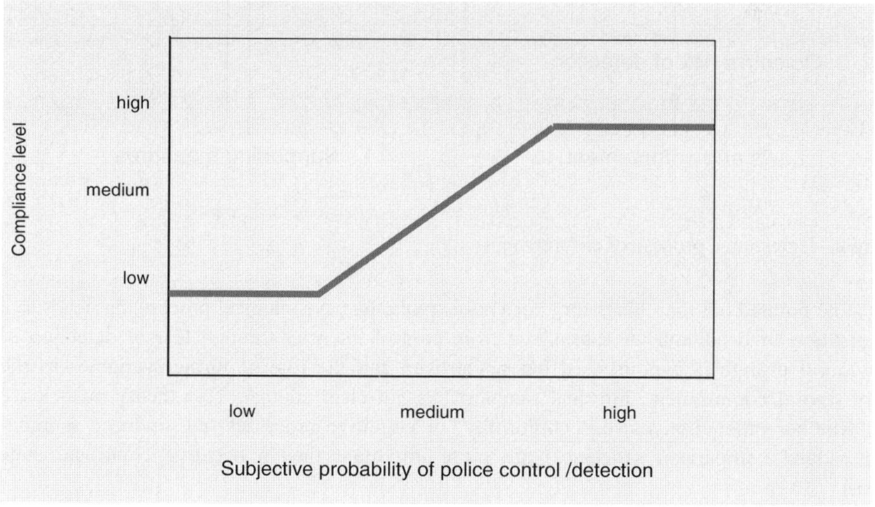

Figure 1. Relationship between subjective probability of detection and compliance level

In behaviourist terms, compliance is mainly a result of the fear of detection and the negative feedback that follows. In this sense the Deterrence Theory (Homel, 1988) attempts to describe or even explain road user behaviour as a function of traffic regulation enforcement, which is a type of social control. It is assumed that individuals will be deterred from taking a particular action by the threat of punishment. The threat of being detected in the act of contravening a regulation may be either real or perceived. General deterrence is the mechanism that influences all road users through the threat of police control and the probability of being checked and punished. Specific deterrence is the impact of a concrete experience of detection and punishment. This experience may be personal or that of a friend or family member. It is important to note that, according to the Deterrence Theory, individuals will only be deterred from contravening the regulations if they believe that the risk of detection is high. Many results that show the need for a minimal level of enforcement seem to support this theory. However, according to deterrence theory there are further measures different from police checks which have an influence on the perceived risk of detection or directly on behaviour (compliance level) (Figure 2).

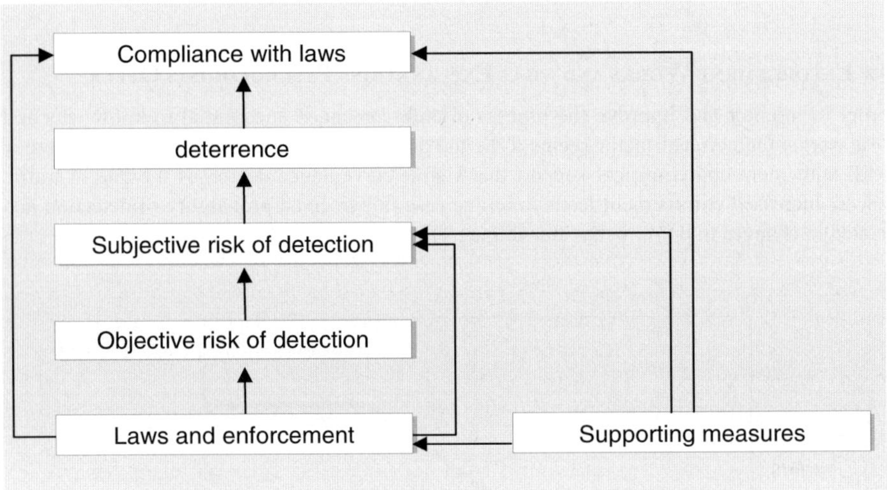

Figure 2. Deterrence process of enforcement

It must be pointed out that this theory does not explain the psychological process that leads to a modification of behaviour. A causal line from control intensity through fear of detection to behavioural change is hypothesised but not proven and the role of further variables in the theory (moral commitment, informal sanctions) is not clear enough. This theory must leave open whether other motives (e.g. conformity) or cognitive processes (e.g. induced memory effect, social comparison processes) are more important than a negative emotional state (threat).

The Theory of Reasoned Action (TRA) (Fishbein & Ajzen, 1975) and the Theory of Planned Behaviour (TPB) (Ajzen, 1985, 1988) offer a way of explaining the independent influences of subjective norms and attitudes on specific behaviour. The TRA and the TPB state that behaviour and analysis of behaviour should be based on intentional measures that are determined by attitudes and subjective norms. Attitudes are determined by beliefs and the evaluation of the outcomes of behaviour; they reflect the personal tendency of an individual to perform this behaviour. Subjective norms are determined by the individual's perception of social expectations to perform the behaviour (normative beliefs), weighted by his or her motivation to comply with these perceived expectations (motivation to comply). So subjective norms reflect the subjectively perceived influence of the social environment on the subject's behaviour. TPB (Ajzen, 1985, 1988) includes a third determinant of behavioural intention: perceived behavioural control (the ease of performing the activity or of avoiding it - volitional control). In terms of TPB, norms influence behaviour in so far as each individual is motivated to comply with this information and to the extent that he or she is able to do so.

Parker, Manstead, Stradling and Reason (1992) have demonstrated the ability of the Theory of Planned Behaviour (TPB) to account for a driver's intentions to commit four specific driving violations: drinking and driving, speeding, tailgating and overtaking in risky circumstances. Empirical evidence showed that the addition of perceived behavioural control led to a significant increment in the amount of explained variance in intentions, thus supporting this theory. The relationship between subjective norms and behavioural intention was stronger than that between attitudes toward behaviour and behavioural intention. Rothengatter (1988) shows that enforcement which increases the objective risk of detection can influence the level of compliance, although motivation and attitudes towards the prohibited behaviour (in this case speeding) remain unchanged. Contrary to other theories, TPB offers a possible explanation for this finding: obviously police control represents a social influence on the subjective norms. This interpretation is supported by the fact that posting the percentage of drivers complying with the law has a considerable effect on the compliance level (Rothengatter, 1988; Van Houten & Nau, 1983). A questionnaire survey of observed drivers showed that "these results cannot be solely attributed to an implied threat of apprehension as Shinar and McKnight (1985) suggest" (Rothengatter, 1988). At least the choice of speed seems not to be exclusively a result of detection probability, it also depends on the motivation of at least a part of the driver population to behave similarly to the majority. This means that regulations are a factor influencing road user behaviour, possibly independent of a road user's attitudes towards specific prohibited behaviour (speeding, drink-driving); the norm seems to have a positive effect on behaviour if the driver notices that compliant driving is common behaviour. This fact also supports the need to use additional measures, such as information campaigns.

Although psychologists have tried to explain this process they have not as yet succeeded. Deterrence theory does offer a way of describing the process of police intervention but - as it does not say much about the main psychological reasons for non-compliance - it is not able to explain the process and the necessary conditions for a lasting behavioural change. Social psychological theories, such as the theory of planned behaviour, cannot explain entirely why enforcement has an effect on driver behaviour. The probability of detection does not seem to be related to measures of attitudes. This also leads to the question of whether attitudes do at all play a role in human behaviour modification, or whether it is a epi-phenomena.

Because we don't know what kind of mechanism this perceived control level activates (fear of punishment; calculation of costs, remembrance of the rule in question; change/activation of a social norm) there is no agreement on what the structure and content of supporting measures should be: e.g. in parallel with an enforcement campaign should we communicate the objective enforcement level, the rate of punished drivers, the rate of drivers not breaking the law, the thinking of opinion leaders, show portraits of 'the offenders', the rule itself, the number of accidents and injuries, common goals related to safety and so on.

Further questions that traffic psychologists must consider are the following: What is the underlying psychological process relating drivers' perceived risk of apprehen-sion with success of enforcement? How significant are attitudes? Are they less important than most psychologists believe? Do we need psychological theories at all in order to improve enforcement effectiveness?

Psychologists' Contribution to Enforcement: Today and in the Future

Legislation is a political process and is therefore quite different in nature from traffic psychology, which is a social science. In order to influence the traffic system, traffic psychologists have to attempt to bridge these differences. The first step is to produce clear recommendations that can be integrated in prevention strategies at a local level. The following points summarizing the extent of existing knowledge, give some indications as to how enforcement procedures should be designed and which supporting measures enhance their effects (Figure 3).

The different regulations require that road user groups be categorised with respect to their willingness to comply, their actual behaviour and the reasons for persistent non-compliance. If compliance is not close to 100% a regulation must be enforced. Two strategies must be combined: a minimal level of highly visible enforcement and the detection of non-compliance. It is imperative that enforcement is conducted at a sufficiently high level in order to produce a desired level of subjective probability of detection. In order to enhance the effects of enforcement four supporting measures are necessary: (1) on a local level, drivers must be informed about the police activity (frequency and detection rate) and the level of compliance, (2) attitude-oriented campaigns must be conducted showing that safety is the main reason for the regulation in question, (3) communication of the level of traffic safety and the usefulness of enforcement for improving this level, (4) driver improvement or remedial training for groups with a high likelihood of recidivism. Preference should be given to punishment that is immediate and certain, which influences the psychological reasons for non-compliance and also prevents dangerous drivers from being allowed to drive.

Psychologists should also be engaged in designing future enforcement devices, which as a result of new technical developments will be quite different from those available today. Some suggestions are that: a) Driver behaviour could be monitored more intensively and perhaps continuously and in this way interludes between violation and sanction could become shorter. - b) Registered driver behaviour could be assessed according to the traffic situation and feedback could be given to the driver via in-vehicle devices. The feedback could be varied according to driver characteristics such as age and former driving violations. Non-compliant behaviour, such as not decreasing speed following feedback, could incur immediate punishment for example by automatically debiting the driver's bank account or by registering demerit points on his electronic driver license. Such systems have been under discussion and evaluated within large research projects as AUTOPOLIS (Harper, 1991).

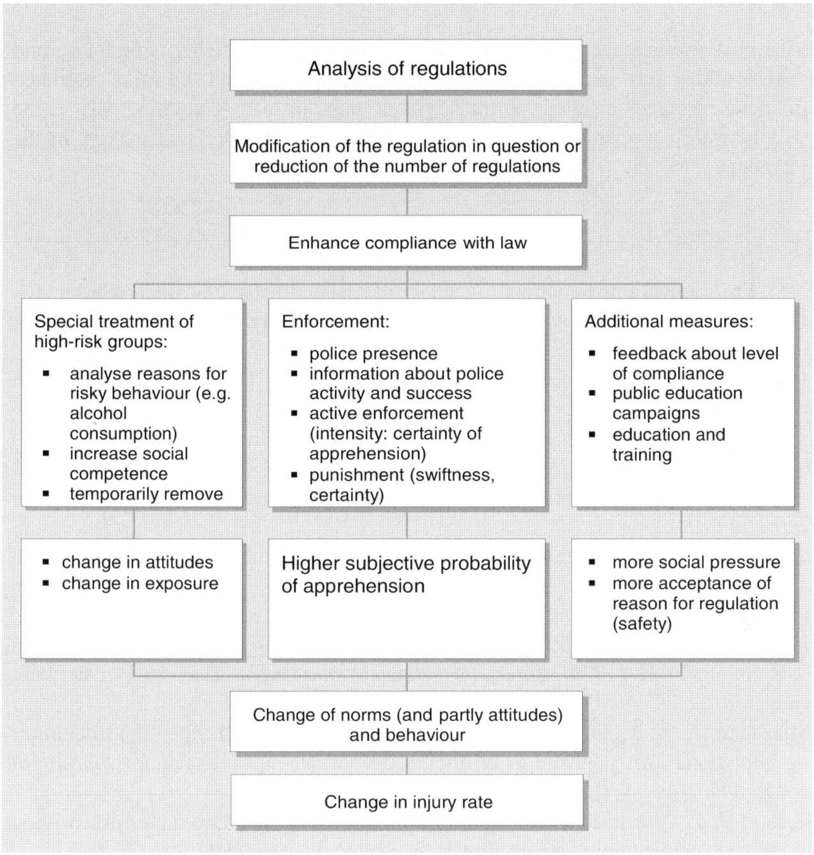

Figure 3. The logical structure of this integrated approach to non-compliance with traffic regulations

Although positive effects on traffic safety level may be expected, some questions with respect to driver reactions are still open: (a) Contrary to traditional or semi-automated enforcement, fully automated enforcement allows a systematic monitoring of driver behaviour so that feedback and sanctions will be based on more reliable measure. The question remains however whether acceptance of enforcement in general will consequently increase or whether drivers will react negatively against the idea of continuous monitoring? (b) According to the deterrence theory drivers must be exposed to enforcement and they must perceive that enforcement takes place. If they are permanently exposed to enforcement, will they still perceive that they are exposed and will a deterrence process be possible at all? (c) A permanent monitoring of driver behaviour might provoke a shift in responsibility. If drivers perceive the external influence on their driver behaviour as important and reliable, the perceived behavioural control (as described in TPB) might diminish. Hence, if they surrender themselves entirely to the judgements of the system, will more risky behaviour occur?

In summary, we pose the general question: In order to work towards higher compliance and lower injury rates, taking into account new technical developments and the more restricted human and financial resources available to traffic police units in many countries, what is the most useful advice traffic psychologists could give practitioners and decision makers in the field of enforcement ?

References

Ajzen, I. (1985). From intentions to actions: A theory of planned behaviour. In J. Khul and J. Beckman (Eds.), *Action control: From cognition to behaviour* (pp.11-38). Berlin: Springer-Verlag.

Ajzen, I. (1988). *Attitudes, personality and behaviour.* Milton Keynes, England: Open University Press.

Fishbein, M., & Ajzen, I. (1975). *Belief, attitude, intention and behaviour: An introduction to theory and research.* Reading, MA: Addison-Wesley.

Gregersen, N. P., & Berg, H. Y. (1994). Lifestyle and accidents among young drivers. *Accident Analysis and Prevention 26*, 297-303.

Harper, J. G. (1991). Traffic violation detection and deterrence: Implication for automatic policing. *Applied Ergonomics, 22*(3), 189-197.

Homel, R. (1988). *Policing and Punishing the Drinking Driver: A Study of General and Specific Deterrence.* New York: Springer Verlag.

Näätänen, R., & Summala, H. (1976). *Road user behaviour and traffic accidents.* Amsterdam: Elsevier.

Parker, D., Manstead, A. S. R., Stradling, S. G., & Reason, J. T. (1992). Intention to commit driving violations: An application of the theory of planned behaviour. *Journal of Applied Psychology, 77* (1), 94-101.

Parker, D., Reason, J. T., Manstead, A. S. R., & Stradling, S.G. (1995). Driving errors, driving violations and accident involvement. *Ergonomics, 38*(5), 1036-1048.

Reason, J. (1994). *Menschliches Versagen.* Heidelberg: Spektrum Verlag.

Rothengatter, T. (1988). Risk and the absence of pleasure: a motivational approach to modelling road user behaviour. *Ergonomics, 31*(4), 599-607.

Shinar, D., & McKnight, A. J. (1985). The effects of enforcement and public information on compliance. In L. Evans and R. Schwing (Eds.), *Human behavior and traffic safety.* New York: Plenum Press.

Van Houten, R., & Nau, P. A. (1983). Feedback intervention and driving speed: Parametric and comparative analysis. *Journal of Applied Behaviour Analysis, 16*, 253-281.

Von Cranach, M., Kalbermatten, U., Indermühle, K., & Gugler, B. (1982). *Goal-directed actions.* London: Academic Press.

Zaal, D. (1994). Traffic law enforcement: A review of the literature. Monash University, Accident Research Center, Australia.

Traffic and Transport Psychology,
T. Rothengatter and R.D. Huguenin (Editors)

33

Evidence for the Effectiveness of a High Enforcement Strategy: A Case Study from the Republic of Ireland

Ray Fuller and Emer Farrell

Introduction

The aim of an enforcement strategy is to discourage unsafe behaviour by changing its consequences - by imposing a penalty. To be effective, the strategy needs to create a sustained belief that violations will be detected and punished fairly (Mäkinen et al., 1999). That belief should in principle lead to an increase in compliance with targeted regulations and, in its turn, increased compliance should eventually become translated into a decrease in accident frequency and severity. Thus the model of the process of change mediated by increased enforcement has the elements indicated in Figure 1. For it to work, it requires ongoing co-operation and co-ordination amongst all of the agencies involved.

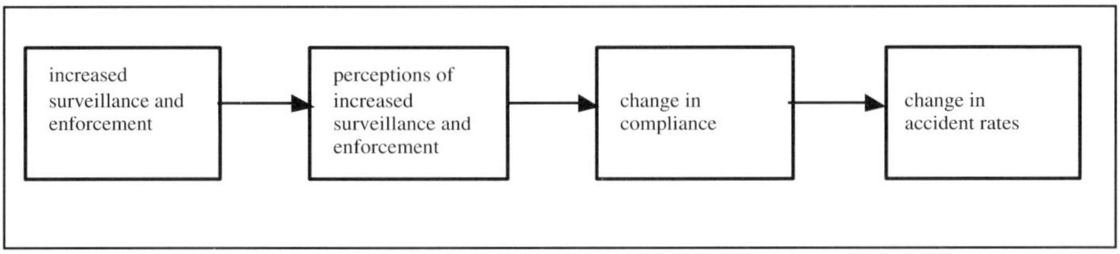

Figure 1. Conceptual model of how enforcement relates to behavioural change and accidents

Although the agents of enforcement are primarily police forces, there are others. There is the possibility offered by automated systems, providing for violation detection, recording and even the administration of a relevant penalty. Second there is the possibility of engineering measures, such as traffic calming, which can modify dangerous behaviour (such as high speed) by making it too difficult or physically punishing. It is not at all inappropriate that a colloquial name for the road hump should be the "sleeping policeman". Finally there are the possibilities provided by the process of social control - the social censure of others.

Ultimately, of course, there is hope in the development of a more pervasive safety culture amongst road users. High enforcement strategies can help this process by changing attitudes indirectly. First, as a result of enforcement, the road user's behaviour changes. Then, in order to be consistent with the changed behaviour, attitude change follows.

Operation Lifesaver (OL) is the name given to a high enforcement strategy targeting speeding, drink-driving and seat-belt wearing, initiated in one specific Police Divisional Area in the Republic of Ireland on July 14th 1997. The goals of this operation were to increase compliance with the law and thereby decrease the rate of traffic accidents and reduce accident severity.

Method

The basic design of the project involved a retrospective comparison of pre- and post-intervention levels of targeted behaviours and accident data in the Treatment area with pre- and post-levels in a matched Control area. The Control area was selected on the grounds of similarity to the Treatment area in mix of rural and urban areas, profile of road types, accident profile and proximity to the capital, Dublin.

Results

Levels of surveillance and enforcement

One indicator of levels of surveillance and enforcement comes from the number of traffic offences in respect to which proceedings were taken. Figure 2 shows the total number of traffic offence proceedings for the Control and Treatment areas for the years 1996 to 1998 (An Garda Síochána Annual Report, 1997; 1998). These numbers are of course in part a function of the rate of violation as well as intensity of surveillance and enforcement. It can be seen from Figure 2 that there was a large increase in proceedings in the Treatment area from 1996 to 1997 of approximately 22%. This contrasts with a reduction in the Control area of 9% and a national average reduction of 2% over the year. Furthermore, whereas in the Control area the level of proceedings remained essentially stable in 1998, a continuing increase was recorded in the Treatment area of about 13% over the 1997 value. This contrasts with a national average reduction of 10%. However, it should be noted that this analysis includes proceedings pertaining to all traffic offences and not just those pertaining to Operation Lifesaver.

Perceptions of increased surveillance and enforcement

The National Safety Council of Ireland (NSC) undertook a specific media campaign in the Treatment area to coincide with the onset of OL. This was designed to further the development of the perception of an increased probability of detection and penalty if committing a violation and to change attitudes towards the targeted offences of speeding, drink-driving and non-wearing of seat belts.

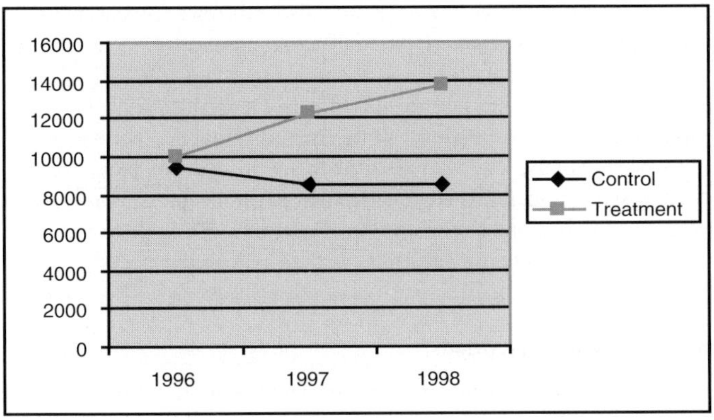

Figure 2. Number of traffic offences in which proceedings were taken, 1996-1998

Before describing that campaign, it should be recognised that as a focused intervention, it was situated in an historical and ongoing stream of national media campaigns directed towards increased road safety. In the year prior to OL, national campaigns by the NSC targeted anti-speeding, anti-drink-driving, wearing of seat-belts and the vulnerability of elderly pedestrians. Furthermore, in the one year period from the onset of OL, national campaigns continued to target anti-speeding, drink-driving and non-wearing of seat belts, as well as addressing pedestrian and motorcycle safety.

The primary medium used in the OL campaign was that of sheet poster, employed as a "point-of-danger" medium. Forty-eight sheet posters were located at various points along main roads in the Treatment area, depicting a Garda (police) officer using a speed camera with the caption "IT'S THE END OF THE ROAD FOR SPEEDERS" (see Figure 3). Twenty-five such posters were used during August and twenty-three during September and October 1997.

Figure 3. Roadside sheet poster used in the OL media campaign in the Treatment area

A supplementary radio campaign using a 30 sec message was also run over 2-week periods during the months of July and August 1997 with an estimated 30 spots per week.

Print media reinforced these campaigns. In the period 5th July to Dec 24th 1997, OL was mentioned on 23 separate occasions in a major national newspaper, a frequency equivalent to once about every 7 days. Not surprisingly, OL was also taken up by a local paper in the Treatment area, and it has been possible to contrast coverage in that paper with a similar type of local paper in the Control area. In the 6 months from July to December 1997, there were 13 reports of OL in the Treatment area paper and only one report in the Control area paper.

Comparative survey of knowledge and perceptions

Given the print, broadcast and other media coverage of OL in the Treatment area, and given the increased presence of police in traffic law enforcement, were there measurable differences in knowledge and perceptions between drivers in the Treatment and Control areas?

To answer this question, we obtained two convenience samples of drivers who agreed to participate and answer a series of questions posed to them on entry to a supermarket car park. One sample came from two towns in the Treatment area, and the other from two towns in the Control area. Overall 240 drivers were interviewed, 123 in the Treatment area and 117 in the Control area, with approximately equivalent age and gender distributions.

In the Treatment area, 46% of drivers said that they had heard of OL, and once prompted 73% could explain what OL was about. In the Control area, only 26% said they had heard of OL and this number rose to 32% who could explain what OL was about once prompted. Significantly more respondents had heard of OL in the Treatment area ((χ^2 = 10.44, df = 1, p<.01) and more could explain what OL was about, once prompted ((χ^2 = 41.45, df = 1, p<.001). Furthermore, in the Control area, only 15% of respondents could remember when OL started, contrasting with 55% in the Treatment area ((χ^2 = 7.89, df = 1, p<.01).

Drivers were asked if they felt that when OL was introduced they were more likely to be caught if committing any of the three targeted offences. Responses (in percentages) are presented in Table 1, below.

Table 1. Perceptions of likelihood of being caught for particular offences after introduction of OL (percentages)

	Treatment *more likely to be caught*	*Control* *more likely to be caught*
Speeding	70	51
Drink-driving	33	57
Seat-belts	42	29

Proportionally more drivers in the Treatment area felt they were more likely to be caught speeding and not wearing seat belts (Speeding (χ^2= 8.84, df = 1, p<.01; Seat-belts (χ^2 = 4.53, df = 1, p<.05). For drink-driving, proportionally more Control area drivers felt they were more likely to be caught once OL was introduced ((χ^2 = 13.82, df = 1, p<.001). This unexpected last result may be due to the fact that only a minority of drivers in the Control area were able to say what OL was about and few knew when it started, so most were presumably guessing about enforcement levels. This last finding perhaps represents a strong influence of the ongoing national campaign regarding drink-driving, reinforced by high enforcement blitz campaigns, particularly around the Christmas period, in the Control area, as well as in the Treatment area.

To explore the continuing effects of OL, drivers were asked if, in the last 6 months of 1998, they felt more or less likely to be caught if committing any of the three targeted offences, compared with before OL started. In the Treatment area, proportionally more drivers perceived themselves as more likely to be caught speeding ((χ^2= 3.60, df = 1, p<.05, 1-tailed) compared with before OL was introduced. For drink-driving, proportionally more Treatment area drivers perceived there to be no change from the time before OL ((χ^2 = 16.92, df = 1, p<.001). And for non-wearing of seat-belts, there was no reliable difference between Treatment and Control groups ((χ^2 = 1.10, df = 1, n.s.). Thus the continuing impact of OL seems to have been salient for speeding, less so for seat-belt wearing and least of all for drink-driving. However the proportions in each category for both areas are remarkably similar from 1997 to 1998, implying that the initial impact of OL, which clearly was different for the different targeted behaviours, was sustained through to the second year.

Changes in compliance

An Garda Síochána (the Police Authority) report the results of a study of compliance with speed limits in the Treatment area prior to the onset of OL and with a follow-up in October 1997, three months after the initiation of the high enforcement intervention (An Garda Síochána Management Journal, December 1997). In the initial sample 16,235 vehicles were monitored and 5,203 offences were recorded, indicating a non-compliance rate of 32.0%. The follow-up sample, which examined exactly the same routes, monitored 16,249 vehicles and found 4,463 offences, a non-compliance rate of 27.5%. A Chi Square analysis reveals that there is a statistically reliable difference between the pre- and post-samples in the proportion of drivers who are non-compliant ((χ^2 = 81.52, df = 1, p<.001). Thus the 4.5% increase in compliance detected after the implementation of OL is a significant one.

However, because of lack of availability of accessible data, we were able to compare compliance rates between the Treatment and Control areas only for seat-belt wearing over the years 1996 to 1998. It was possible to gain an estimate of compliance through accident records which indicate whether or not belts were worn at the time of the accident. Injury accident data for the Treatment and Control areas were examined for the months August to December and for the years 1996 through to 1998. It was found that there was a Treatment area advantage in 1996 which slipped in 1997 but then recovered in 1998, with a compliance rate of 87% (see Figure 4). However there were no significant differences between Treatment and Control areas for any year sampled. It should be noted that something like 65% of injury accident records were not complete in recording status of seat-belt wearing, and there may also be an interaction between seat-belt wearing and accident involvement (for example, culpable accident-involved persons may be less likely to wear seat-belts).

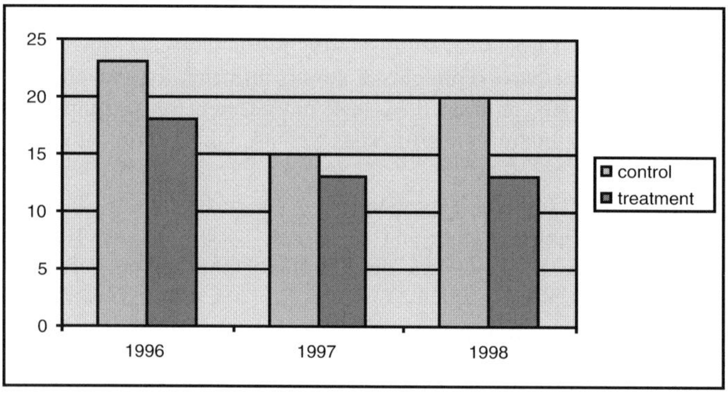

Figure 4. Percentage of drivers involved in all injury accidents not wearing a seat-belt

Changes in accident rates: analysis of hospital data

Because only a certain proportion of injury road traffic accidents (RTAs) are represented in the national statistics compiled from police reports, an attempt was made to estimate the effects of OL on the numbers of RTA victims presenting to the Accident and Emergency departments in a representative major hospital in each of the Treatment and Control areas. An analysis was carried out for the numbers of RTA victims retained or transferred over the years 1996 to 1999 and this revealed a significant difference between areas ((χ^2 = 10.21, df = 3, $p < .02$), with the numbers reducing over time in the Treatment area, but initially increasing and then decreasing in the Control area (see Figure 5).

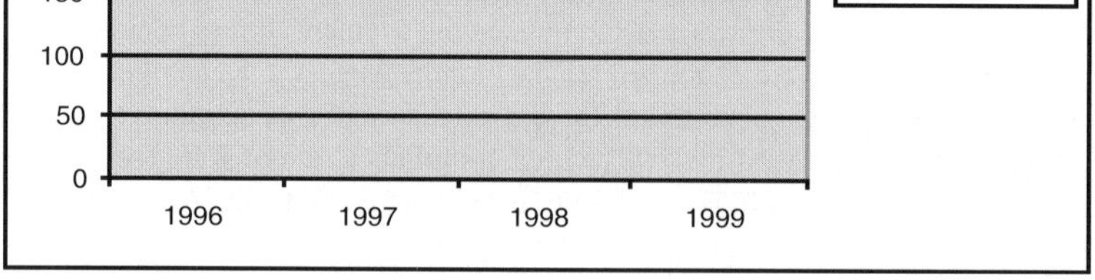

Figure 5. RTA victims retained in hospital or transferred.

Changes in accident rates: national road accident database

The national accident database is compiled from police records and, despite not capturing all injury accidents (as in other jurisdictions), provides a useful set of data for making comparisons over time. Since OL was introduced in mid July 1997, we can get a look at its possible immediate effects on accident casualties by comparing the 5 month period August-December 1997 with the previous equivalent period in 1996 and the subsequent equivalent period in 1998, in both the Treatment and Control areas. The year 1996 is a suitable starting point for this comparison as reporting requirements changed from this year, enabling a higher proportion of road accidents to be documented by the Gardai (estimated as an increase of about 17% (Bacon, 1999)).

The 5-monthly totals are given in Table 2. For fatalities, it may be seen that in the Treatment area there was a progressive decrease from 18 to 11 between 1996 and 1998, whereas in the Control area, there was a dramatic drop in 1997 (from 16 to 9), followed by a rise to 15 in 1998. However, there was no statistically significant difference in the relative frequencies for fatalities in each year (($\chi^2 = 2.01$, df = 1, n.s.). For serious injuries, there was a reduction in the Treatment area from 76 to 48 from 1996 to 1997, although a rise was noted in 1998, but not to the previous level. For the Control area, there was an increase in serious injuries from 1996 to 1997 which remained just about the same in 1998. Changes in relative frequencies over time for the two areas are statistically significant here (($\chi^2 = 6.80$, df = 2, $p<.01$, 1-tailed), offering good evidence for a safety impact of OL in the Treatment area. For minor injuries, the picture is not as heartening, however. From 1996 to 1998 there was a sizeable increase in the Treatment area of about 26% and in the Control area of about 18%. Proportional differences over years are again statistically significant (($\chi^2 = 15.65$, df = 2, $p<.001$), suggesting that there has been a greater deterioration in the Treatment area relative to the Control.

Table 2. Totals of fatalities and serious and minor injuries for Treatment and Control areas, 1996-98 (Aug-Dec)

	Aug-Dec	*Treatment*	*Control*
	96	18	16
Fatalities	97	15	9
	98	11	15
	96	76	37
Serious injuries	97	48	48
	98	58	47
	96	371	172
Minor injuries	97	367	246
	98	469	204

To examine further the effects of OL on injuries and fatalities, a second kind of comparison which can be made is between the years 1996 (last full year prior to introduction of OL and within the new reporting system) and 1998 (the first full year subsequent to the introduction of OL). The relevant annual totals are given in Table 3. Considering numbers of fatalities and injuries in this way assumes, of course, that differences in totals over the 3-year period are not simply due to proportionally different changes in the two areas sampled in population, vehicle registrations or kilometres driven. The data for new car registrations for 1997 and 1998 are consistent with this assumption, with an increase of 10% and 9.5% in the Control and Treatment areas respectively (Revenue Commissioners, Press and Public Relations Unit, September, 2000). There was no reason to suspect proportionally different changes in either population or mobility.

For fatalities, it may be seen that there was a drop from 1996 to 1998 in both Treatment and Control areas. The k test value for these data is 1.0, indicating that the decrease in fatalities in the Treatment area was the same as that in the Control area. Not surprisingly the associated (2 value was less then unity ((χ^2 <1.0, df = 1, n.s.), confirming no difference between the two areas. For serious injuries, there was a reduction in the Treatment area from 229 to 189, compared with a very slight increase in the Control area. For these data, k = 0.82, indicating a reduction of 18% in the Treatment area compared to the Control area. However the associated (χ^2 value was (χ^2 = 1.44 (df = 1, n.s), which was not statistically significant. For minor injuries, there was an increase in both the Treatment and the Control areas, although the increase was 9% more in the Control area (k = 0.91). The (χ^2 value here was also not significant ((χ^2 = 1.36, df = 1, n.s.), however.

Table 3. Totals of fatalities and serious and minor injuries for Treatment and Control areas, for the years 1996 and 1998

		Treatment	*Control*
Fatalities	96	44	40
	98	35	32
Serious injuries	96	229	109
	98	189	110
Minor injuries	96	878	435
	98	986	536

Taking the 5-month and whole-year analyses together, what may be concluded is that: (a) for fatalities there is an equivalent decrease in both the Treatment and the Control areas; (b) for serious injuries the Treatment area shows decreases, whereas the Control area shows at best no change and, if anything, increases; (c) for minor injuries there is an overall increase in both areas, but within this pattern there is some variability. There was an initial decrease in the Treatment area, followed by a rise, with the opposite pattern seen in the Control area. However taking the whole-year data, we see that the increase in the Treatment area is slightly less than in the Control area.

If we translate the proportional differences in casualty numbers between the Treatment and Control areas into an estimate of the saving in casualties between 1996 and 1998, we find that for fatalities there is no relative gain in the Treatment area; for serious injuries, there is a saving in the Treatment area of 41 serious injuries (i.e. 18% of the 1996 baseline) and for minor injuries, there is a saving in the Treatment area of 79 minor injuries (i.e. 9% of the 1996 baseline). Using current recommended average cost estimates for different categories of road accident (Bacon, 1999), these data translate into a saving of almost ten million euros. On the basis of estimates of the cost of implementing OL in the Treatment area, this represents a benefit to cost ratio of at least three to one.

Conclusions

Conclusions about the effects of OL must be tempered by recognition of the selective nature of the available data, the qualified nature of each data-set, the discrepancies between the different time-samples analysed and the general absence of statistically reliable changes in critical accident data. Clearly OL has had some noted effects, in particular in modifying driver expectations of the likelihood of being caught if speeding. Nevertheless this does not appear to translate into an equivalent shift in crash frequency.

This is partly, of course, because only a proportion of crashes have as a contributory factor some violation of traffic regulations. Although a major factor in road accidents is travelling at a speed in excess of what is appropriate for particular conditions of roadway, traffic and visibility, that speed need not be in excess of the posted maximum limit. Furthermore, the intervention of OL was situated in the context of ongoing national media campaigns relating to the very issues targeted by OL. To the extent that these campaigns were effective, they would have reduced any differences between the Treatment and Control areas.

So perhaps we should conclude on a positive note. There is some qualified evidence here that increased enforcement can work to reduce casualties. And its effects may be more subtle than those revealed in accident records alone, contributing to a slow, gradual shift in attitudes and values and behaviour, towards more responsible, and safer, roadway use.

Acknowledgements

The work for this report was assisted by a large number of agencies including An Garda Síochána, the National Safety Council, Our Lady of Lourdes Hospital (Drogheda), Naas General Hospital, the National Safety Council and in particular the National Roads Authority. The authors are, however, solely responsible for the contents of the report.

References

An Garda Síochána, Annual Report, 1997.

An Garda Síochána, Annual Report, 1998.

An Garda Síochána, Management Journal, December 1997.

Bacon, P. Study of the benefits and costs of the Government Road Safety Strategy 1998-2002, Dublin, 1999.

Mäkinen, T., Biecheler-Fretel, M.M., Cardoso, J., Goldenbeld, C., Fuller, R., Hakkert, S., Sanchez Martin, M.C., Skladana, P., Vaa T. & Zaidel D. Legal measures and enforcement, Espoo: VTI, 1999.

Revenue Commissioners, Press and Public Relations Unit, September, 2000.

Traffic and Transport Psychology,
T. Rothengatter and R.D. Huguenin (Editors)

34

The Development of Training Courses for Switzerland's Two-Phase Driver Training Model

Jacqueline Bächli-Biétry

Introduction

In all industrialised countries road accidents are the most common cause of death of young people aged between 18 and 24 years. In view of this in Switzerland additional measures to reduce the number of accidents are undisputed. In 1996 the Federal Department of Justice and Police passed the draft revision of the Road Traffic Act into the public debate phase. This draft bill includes the introduction of a two-phase driver training combined with a three year probation phase. This driving training model is now discussed and will be introduced probably in 2002, if accepted by government.

During this probation phase young drivers have to attend additional training courses, which have a length of 16 hours at most. Themes of this further training courses are the initial personal experiences during first driving practice; driving technique and knowledge about typically dangers in traffic (Schweizerischer Verkehrssicherheitsrat, 1995).

Whoever contravenes the road traffic regulations during this period of probation, such that it endangers other road users is required to undergo further training. Whoever offends a second time will be required to attend all courses again. Those who complete the probationary phase without contravening the regulations and have attended the requisite additional training courses will receive the full driving license for an indefinite period.

At this moment in Switzerland practical driver training is not obligatory. All beginners have to follow eight theory lessons that promote road sense (not only about the law but also about dangerous situations in traffic). These theory lessons are called „Verkehrskundeunterricht" (VKU). After passing the driving test, the driving license is issued for an indefinite period.

The aim of the project introduces here is to draw up concrete specifications for the additional training modules. These specifications were based on the current state of knowledge concerning the causes of accidents and the behaviour of young drivers as well as on experiences with various training models in other countries. Furthermore, young novice Swiss drivers were surveyed orally and in writing about their opinions concerning their driving training, their driving experience to date and what they would like to see included in the second training phase.

Current State of Knowledge about Causes of Accidents of Young Drivers

In papers published on the subject of young driver's characteristics and causes of accidents univariate as well as multivariate approaches are found explaining the increased accident-proneness of young road users. All agree that youthfulness is a much more important factor than inexperience (Schulze, 1996; Keskinen, 1996).

The increased threat to young people becomes more understandable if their development-specific motivational background is considered. This is an especially difficult phase in life, when young people need to release tensions and discover their own limits. Driving cars presents an opportunity to react to such a state of tension and to find out how far one can go. As the capability of young drivers to asses dangerous situations is not as well developed as that of older people, the risk-taking behaviour of young people is notorious. Young drivers also do not believe that they are vulnerable; they believe that they would survive all dangerous situations.

However, in multivariate approaches various authors came to the conclusion that not all young people are vulnerable to the same extent, but that there are certain groups that are especially at risk. A special type of lifestyle characterises these groups. Often these are masculine young people with a low education level, and a predilection for alcohol (Gregersen & Berg, 1994; Schulze, 1996).

For the second training phase it seems appropriate to combine training with imposing conditions, that is to say to ensure that the process of gaining experience after passing the driving test is accompanied by restrictions and conditions and, on the other hand, to deliberately initiate learning processes and to enable active experience formation. Practical training modules that only deal with purely technical behaviour - overcoming danger - have been shown to have negative effects on risk-taking behaviour because they are followed by an increased sense of safety, resulting in risky behaviour to become more frequent (Gregersen, 1996).

Results of the Inquiry

The experiences and opinions of young novice drivers were obtained by means of semi-standard interviews and a written survey. The interview findings provided the basis for the design of the questionnaire. The questionnaire was sent to 1,150 young novice drivers in Switzerland. The recipients had been in possession of a driving licence for a car or a motorcycle for between 6 and 12 months. The response rate was 53.3%. As a reward we used cinema vouchers.

The questionnaire was aimed to answer the following questions:

- What experience had the young drivers in the first 6 to 12 month when they drove on their own and what reasons they see for their experiences?
- What are the opinions of the young drivers to the obligatory theoretical lessons and what do they think about the two-phase driver training model.
- Is it possible to find differences between groups of young drivers concerning their opinions and their wishes concerning the two-phase driver training model.

Below the main results of the inquiry are described. Table 1 shows that the young drivers mentioned many critical events:

Table 1. Critical events during first-time unsupervised driving (N= 610)

Event	*Yes (%)*	*No (%)*
Loosing control of the car	36.0%	64.0%
Near accident	58.6%	41.4%
Accident (500 Fr. and more)	13.0%	87.0%
Fine for speeding	18.8%	81.2%

No differences between male and female young drivers were found in the frequency of occurrence of these critical events. This result clearly indicates that further training after passing the driving test is urgently necessary.

The responses to the question about the causes to which these events are attributed show that young drivers are not very self-critical (Table 2).

Table 2. Attribution of critical events (N=610)

Attribution	*often (%)*	*sometimes (%)*	*never (%)*
Seen the danger too late	2.1%	60.0%	37.8%
Not comply to the rules	1.6%	32.8%	65.6%
Loosing control of the car	0.2%	21.2%	78.6%
Risk-taking behaviour	4.1%	22.0%	73.9%
Chance (coincidence)	3.6%	59.6%	36.9%
Other people's fault	21.0%	59.8%	19.2%

The young drivers said that mostly other people's behaviour were the reason for the critical events. Coincidence and a lack in the perception of danger were less often mentioned. Over 80% mentioned that training that promotes road sense during the first practice phase would be useful for first-time driving experience (Table 3). The fact that over 50% mentioned that they would visit the theory lessons even if they were not obligatory can be interpreted as a clear sign of acquiescence. Concerning these two questions male students were much more critical than young drivers with a lower educational level. All in all, the comments on the two-phase model were rather sobering. The three-year probation phase was approved by 40% of the sample. Female and less educated young drivers were more positive than male young drivers and students. The acceptance of the obligatory theoretical lessons in the second phase is dependent on the cost. If it would be free, much more of the young drivers would agree (70% and 17%). The evaluation of the advanced training showed that practical driving courses - for example anti skid-courses - would be favoured against discussion and working groups. Car drivers wish an action-oriented form of further training. Theoretical instruction tends to be considered as boring and useless.

Table 3. Opinions about theoretical lessons and the two-phase training model (N=610)

Theory and two-phase model	*Yes (N, %)*	*No (N, %)*
Positive effect of theory lessons	80.8%	19.2%
Voluntary visit to theory lessons	50.5%	49.5%
Approve probation phase	40.5%	59.5%
16 hours theory free	71.6%	28.4%
16 hours theory not free	17.1%	82.9%

Concretization of the Further Modules

Basic thoughts

In creating an obligatory advanced training course there is the problem that the form of training favoured by young novice drivers - who have a distinct preference for track training -- leads to an increase in the sense of safety and thus may increase danger. This presents the difficult pedagogic task of designing a course that on the one hand accommodates the needs of young people by including practical driving elements, whereas on the other hand it should contain - from a psychological viewpoint more significant - emotional and motivational components that comparatively are given more significance.

That age is much more important for the accident risk of young people indicates that all young people should be educated after the driving test. The results of the lifestyle-analysis should be interpreted that only certain special target groups should be educated. In our concept we will not promote a programme for only the most endangered young people as it is not possible to identify the endangered individuals and the reasons of this increased risk are unknown. The fact that the most endangered groups often are lead by their emotions has to be considered in the second phase of education. Rational arguments are not effective.

Objectives of the advanced courses

The objectives of advance training courses are to improve the social responsibility of young people and to promote awareness of their own behaviour. It should therefore result in greater road safety

- By improving danger cognition (perception, recognition and evaluation of danger);
- By self reflection of the own motives;
- By encouraging empathy and the ability to communicate;
- By reducing the exposure of danger.

Formal elements of the 16 hours of advanced training

It is proposed to introduce three modules, each lasting for a total of 5 hours. The course modules are independent of each other so that they can be attended in any order. A two-person team will present each of the three modules: A specialist with psychological and pedagogic training and a specially trained traffic instructor (usually a highly qualified driving instructor) will work together. Only in this way it will be possible to set the required complex psychological processes in motion. Class size should be limited to 10 or 12 persons.

Ideally, the premises where the courses are held should allow to work and discussion to take place in small groups. The practical driving exercises require a large car park or a route that must be driven for exercise and observation purposes. Participants must provide their own vehicle for the training course.

Each of the three modules is dedicated to a subject that is related to the high risk faced by the young novice driver. The following main subject areas are proposed: Speed (risk), concomitant circumstances and night-time driving (alcohol). The structure of the modules is always the same. A motivational opening and a definition of the conditions of the collaboration are followed by a personal-experience of self-awareness section where the emphasis is on action. Experiences are then discussed in the group and on an individual basis, and the participants are urged to practise self-reflection. Each course module contains a practical driving section, a cognitive section and socio-motivational section. In principle, more emphasis is put on emotional and motivational subject matter than on cognitive elements. When dealing with the emotional an motivational subject matter the procedure must always moving from the general - affecting everybody - to the specific - affecting the individual course participant -- in order to avoid resistance. To increase acceptance, at least part public funding of these courses must be considered.

Methods

Discussion, teamwork and self-awareness questionnaires are the communications methods that were chosen for exerting emotional and motivational influence. As far as possible, class instruction is replaced by instructional discussions. Cognitive subject matter is backed up wherever possible by personal experience. In case of the practical driving elements, it is necessary to ensure that the feeling of safety is not enhanced by practising to the point of perfection. Rather, the practical driving section serves as the main attraction of the course and makes it easier to get into the social and motivational subject matter.

The pilot experiment proved to be successful for both presenters and course participants. Evaluation showed that the important objectives had been met using the proposed course type that the participants felt they had been taken seriously and were considering a behavioural change.

The proposed course type was tested using the course module „speed/risk" -summarised in Table 4 - in a test run with 12 participants.

Table 4. Test of the speed/risk module

Part	*Subject matter*	*Presenter*	*Duration*
Motivation	a) Conditions of collaboration b) Course timing c) Getting to know one another by means of interaction games	Educational sociologist Driving instructor	25 min.
Emotional-motivational part (personal)	Self-observation sheet (speed and risk)	Educational sociologist	20 min.
Driving experience	a) Introduction to practical training and movement b) Breaking exercises	Driving instructor	60 min.
Cognitive part	a) Audio visual knowledge test b) Test solution with explanations	Driving instructor	45 min.
Break (lunch or evening meal)			75 min.
Emotional-motivational part (general)	a) Interaction game b) Brainstorming (reasons for driving too fast) c) Summary of the reasons (entire class)	Educational sociologist	40 min.
Driving experience	a) Introduction to practical training and movement b) Practical driving exercises (experiencing practical strategies)	Driving instructor	60 min.
Emotional-motivational part (personal)	a) Working in small groups (avoidance strategies) b) Summary of strategies (rentire class) c) Individual evaluation of sociopedagogic test, drawing profile d) Implementing the knowledge gained, developping own strategies	Educational sociologist	70 min.
Evaluation of the course	a) Evaluation b) Questionnaire c) Discussion	Educational sociologist Driving instructor	15 min.

References

Gregersen, N. P., & Berg, H. Y. (1994). Lifestile and accidents amog young drivers. *Accident Analysis and Prevention, 26*, 297-303.

Gregersen, N. P. (1996). Young drivers' overestimation of their own skill-an experiment on their relation between training strategy an skill. *Accident Analysis and Prevention, 28*, 243-250.

Keskinen, E. (1996). Warum ist die Unfallrate junger Fahrerinnen und Fahrer höher? In *Junge Fahrer und Fahrerinnen*. (Berichte der Bundesanstalt für Strassenwesen. Mensch und Sicherheit, Heft M 52). Bergisch Gladbach: Bundesanstalt für Strassenwesen.

Schweizerischer Verkehrssicherheitsrat (1995). *Ausbildung der Neulenker*. (Schlussbericht der Projektgruppe). Bern: Schweizerischer Verkehrssicherheitsrat.

Schulze, H. (1996). *Lebensstil und Verkehrsverhalten junger Fahrerinnen und Fahrer*. (Heft M 56). Bergisch Gladbach: Bundesanstalt für Strassenwesen..

SAFETY

SELECTION AND REHABILITATION

Traffic and Transport Psychology,
T. Rothengatter and R.D. Huguenin (Editors)

35

Driver Selection and Improvement in Austria

Rainer Christ, Elisabeth Panosch, Birgit Bukasa

Introduction

Road safety is less a technical but rather a human factors problem. The majority of accidents are not caused by problems of the vehicle, bad road conditions, etc. but rather by the behavior of drivers. There are two principle approaches in order to influence the driver: Adjusting the traffic system to the driver or adjusting the driver to the traffic system. While the system centered approach aims at creating those road conditions that reduce the chance of accidents in advance resp. reduce the severity of accidents, the individual centered approach directly focuses on the traffic relevant performance and personality aspects as well as on the attitudes and behavior of single drivers. Driver selection and driver improvement are measures that belong to the latter approach.

Nowadays, in Austria driver selection and driver improvement are well established and approved measures for certain groups of drivers. Due to its special indication about 0,5 percent of the Austrian driving population has to undergo driver selection each year. About the same percentage of drivers has to take part in a driver improvement program annually.

History of the Measures

Development of driver selection

One of the main goals which initiated and supported the foundation of the Kuratorium für Verkehrssicherheit (Austrian Road Safety Board) by the insurance companies in 1959 was the implementation of driver selection in Austria. Klebelsberg was one of the pioneers of driver selection in Austria and head of the Institute of Traffic Psychology of the Kuratorium für Verkehrssicherheit for years. Research and development in the field of driver selection (e.g. Klebelsberg & Kallina, 1963; Klebelsberg, Biehl, Fuhrmann & Seydel, 1970) as well as growing road safety problems resulted in increased awareness and appreciation of this measure in Austria.

In order to cope with the growing number of subjects to be assessed group testing procedures had been introduced first, followed by computerized testing. The first generation of computerized test devices for driver assessment - the ART 90 (Act & React Test System) - had been introduced in daily testing in 1981 (Kisser & Wenninger, 1983) leading to highly standardized and objective testing procedures as well as to the realization of new test dimensions like peripheral perception (Bukasa & Risser, 1985) as well as new traffic related questionnaires (Felnemeti, Gheri, Krainz, Schmidt & Wenninger, 1987).

Although driver selection had been implemented as decision aid in driver licensing issues in the road traffic act for decades, in most of the cases it was up to the licensing authorities and the medical doctors to decide whether they require a psychological expertise or not.

In 1997 an important change took place when the Driving Licence Health Act (Führerscheingesetz-Gesundheitsverordnung), a supplement of the Austrian Driving Licence Law (Füherscheingesetz), came into force: For the first time, psychological assessment became compulsory for drivers with a BAC of 1,6 ‰ and more as well as for professional drivers who apply for a licence for passenger transport (buses).

In 1998 a new generation of psychological test devices for driver assessment developed at the Kuratorium für Verkehrssicherheit, - the ART 2020 (Bukasa, Wenninger & Brandstätter, 1997) - had been introduced in daily testing. This development includes several innovations on the psychological, technological and administrational level above all the introduction of multimedia assisted test instructions and reality based testing. Multimedia assisted test instructions refer to the concept of observational learning explaining the individual task of the tests visually and acoustically while at the same time it is demonstrated on the monitor. Thus, higher test fairness for people who learn in different ways, e.g. visual, acoustical, as well as higher test fairness from a cross-cultural point of view had been achieved (Wenninger & Bukasa, 1999). Reality based testing refers to the concept of low fidelity simulation covering several aspects: More complex and/or dynamic tests including driving scenarios scenes and more realistic response modes using a steering wheel and pedals with enhanced user interaction.

Development of driver improvement

Rehabilitation programs for imprisoned traffic offenders stood at the beginning of driver improvement in Austria in 1975 (e.g. Höfner 1976; Klebel, Michalke & Schmidt, 1977). Already two years later - in 1977 - driver improvement courses for traffic offenders had been implemented in the road traffic act. Yet, in analogy to driver selection, the licensing authorities were free to decide whether to impose driver improvement measures or not. Good results with these courses (e.g. Schützenhöfer & Schmidt, 1977; Michalke, 1979; Gheri, Schmidt & Zuzan, 1980; Zuzan & Ruby, 1986) as well as an evaluation study which showed a reduction of recidivism rate of 50 percent (Michalke, Barglik-Chory & Brandstätter, 1987) brought this measure into discussion as an instrument to reduce the novice drivers' accident risk.

When licence on probation came into force in 1992 driver improvement for offending novice drivers was one of the key elements. For the first time driver improvement was introduced as an obligatory measure for negatively suspicious novice drivers during the probation period. In this regulation certain quality standards of the courses, the setting and the qualification of the psychologist had been implemented. In 1997 driver improvement became a compulsory measure for all drivers in case of licence suspension due to a BAC of 1,2 ‰ and more. Thus driver improvement gained increased importance as a mean to reduce the recidivism rate of traffic offenders, especially with regards to DWI (e.g. Kaba, Panosch, Lager & Bartl, 1995; Panosch, 1996).

Organizational and structural change

Due the increased relevance of driver selection and driver improvement and the growing number of subjects to be assessed and rehabilitated a couple of organizational issues had to be changed, too.

At the beginning both measures - driver selection and driver improvement - had been financed by the insurance companies or public sources. Later on the drivers themselves had to pay for assessment and driver improvement. Until 1997 the Kuratorium für Verkehrssicherheit was the only or at least by far the biggest provider of these services. During that time the development of the necessary instruments (tests and test devices for driver assessment as well as new rehabilitation programs for driver improvement) and the support for evaluation and validation studies was raised from the budget of this organization.

Since 1998 the number of organizations authorized to carry out driver assessment and driver improvement increased up to five. The increased number of providers and the tendencies towards market orientation raised the need for quality regulations regarding the organizations which carry out driver assessment and driver improvement.

The following issues was determined by law: (a) Providers have to have a uniform organizational structure for providing services all over Austria; (b) Providers have to assure the quality of driver assessment and driver improvement; (c) Only specially qualified psychologists who completed defined curricula are allowed to work in driver selection and driver improvement; (d) Applicants for new assessment and driver improvement centers have to follow authorization procedures.

Concept of Driver Selection

In Austria, driver selection is part of the licensing system that demands physical and psychological fitness in order to get a licence. The Driving Licence Health Act (Führerscheingesetz-Gesundheitsverordnung, 1997) specifies that driver selection aims at verifying the subjects' capabilities with respect to driving a motor vehicle and to his or her willingness to adapt to traffic regulations (minimum requirements).

There are two main groups who have to undergo driver assessment[1]:

(a) "Problem" drivers, e.g. due to drunken driving, drug abuse, psychiatric, neurological or other medical indications, age related problems, failing the driving licence examination several times.

(b) "Higher responsibility" drivers, i.e. drivers who apply for passenger transport (buses).

There are four variants of examinations depending on the reasons for driver assessment:

(a) Complete driver assessment (traffic specific performance and personality)
(b) Short psychological assessment (screening regarding performance and personality)
(c) Restricted driver assessment (either to performance or personality only)
(d) Driver assessment focussing on maturity (personality and psycho-social development).

According to the Austrian Driving Licence Health Act a complete driver assessment demands the examination of the following aspects:

Performance dimensions: Observation capacity and ability to gain an overview of a situation, reactive behavior, in particular reaction speed and certainty of decision and reaction, as well as stress-resistance of the reactive behavior, concentration capacity, sensory-motor coordination, intelligence and memory capacities.

Personality dimensions: Social responsibility, self-control, emotional stability, willingness to take risks, tendency towards aggressive interaction in road traffic, emotional relation to cars.

The relevance of these dimensions for safe driving are based on numerous research findings on driver behavior during the last decades (see also Brenner-Hartmann and Bukasa, 2001). The dimensions are assessed by means of performance tests, personality tests and a personal interview.

The results of the entire psychological assessment and the corresponding conclusions regarding the fitness to drive a car have to be documented in an expertise. This expertise is a decision aid for the licensing authorities regarding the question whether a person's licence is regranted or not.

Concept of Driver Improvement

Driver improvement is conceptualized as an attitude and behavior modification training in order to prevent further traffic offences. The focus of the approach is more therapeutic and less pedagogic/didactic. Therefore, driver improvement courses can be carried out by specially trained psychologists only as already mentioned above. Driver improvement trainer not only have to be psychologists according to the professional law of psychologists (Psychologengesetz) which exists since 1991. Moreover, further qualifications are required

[1] 95% of the clientele in driver assessment is assigned by the licensing authorities; only 5% are sent by private companies (e.g. public transport, emergency transport, VIP transport). Therefore, only the obligatory assessments will be considered.

which are defined in the traffic law, like 1600 hours practice in traffic psychology, 160 hours theory in traffic psychology and 160 hours in intervention methods.

Generally, courses are carried out in group settings because group processes, feed-back from peers are important elements for initiating self mirroring, self reflection and behavior modification. The Austrian Road Safety Boards program, for example, is an integrative training program structured as a modular system (Schmitt, Teske et. al.,1992). Thus, specific units for different group compositions and individual indications are available. There are modules for initiating and intensifying group dynamic processes, for non directive therapeutic interventions, for self-reflexion and self-assessment, for verbalization of ones emotions, etc. Moreover, psychodramatic and cognitive-behavioral elements are applied.

Actually, there are different programs for alcohol and non-alcohol offenders as well as for novice and experienced drivers (e.g. Spoerer, Ruby, Hess 1994; Bartl, 1995; Spoerer, Christ, Siegrist, 1998). Driver improvement courses last for 12 to 15 units (à 50 min.) in 4 to 5 sessions which are distributed over a period of 4 - 6 weeks. Group size ranges from six to ten participants. In case of novice drivers with severe offences apart from DWI a specially trained driving-school instructor is present during a test ride, observing the participant´s driving behavior and giving feedback afterwards in the group setting. In specific cases, like participants who do not speek German at all resp. sufficiently well, deaf and dumb clients, stutterers, or clients who are not able to participate in group sessions due to other reasons. In this case 5 individual sessions per 50 min. are carried out.

In the near future, a special Driving Licence Driver Improvement Act (Führerscheingesetz-Nachschulungsverordnung) in analogy to the Driving Licence Health Act for driver selection will be established. This driver improvement act will specify, amongst others the conditions of the setting, efficiency proof, quality control and fees.

Evaluation Studies of Driver Selection

The Austrian Driving Licence Health Act not only demands that the psychological tests are adequate for driver selection, show sufficient reliability and objectivity, have adequate norms but also that the tests have to be valid with regard to traffic safety criteria.

Validation studies in driver selection have a long tradition at the Kuratorium für Verkehrssicherheit starting with Klebelsberg, Biehl, Fuhrmann und Seydel (1970), followed by validation I with volunteer drivers along with the introduction of the ART 90 test system (Risser, Schmidt, Brandstätter, Bukasa and Wenninger, 1983) and validation II with drivers from daily routine testing (Bukasa, Wenninger & Brandstätter, 1990). In these validation studies numerous significant correlations between the test battery of the Kuratorium für Verkehrssicherheit and driving behaviour elements with correlations up to .60 had been found. Moreover, validity checks for subgroups of drivers had been carried out, e.g. senior drivers (Christ, 1996; Christ & Brandstätter, 1997). Regarding traffic related personality tests several validation studies had been carried out as well using mainly data from the personal interview (e.g. reported accidents, fines, attitudes regarding own offences, offences apart from traffic) as external criteria. Several significant results between the traffic related personality scales and the external criteria had been found. The results are documented in Bukasa, Wenninger & Brandstätter (1990); Hutter, Bukasa, Wenninger & Brandstätter (1997); Hutter & Brandstätter (1996) and Hutter, Braun, Bukasa, Ponocny-Seliger, Schermann, & Wenninger (2000).

For the new multimedia test system ART 2020 two validation studies regarding the traffic related performance tests have been carried out at the Kuratorium für Verkehrssicherheit as yet (Bukasa, 1999).

Criterion Validation with Driving Behaviour

In this study, the test results of the ART 2020 performance test battery were taken on the predictor side. On the criterion side, the actual driving behaviour was the main criterion. Driving behaviour was measured by an observer who systematically observed and recorded certain predefined driving behaviour elements based on the Vienna Driving Test (Risser & Brandstätter, 1985; Brandstätter, 1989). The study was carried out on driver assessment clients (non-voluntary group). At first, the test subjects went through the test routines on the ART 2020 test system. After this, they had to carry out the driving test on the road. The data were gathered between November 1997 and March 1998.

Due to the sample size of 120 subjects, the interdependence of the predictor and the criterion variables has been exclusively analysed on a correlative basis. Because of the significant influence of the subjects' age that plays a moderating role for the relations between test and driving behaviour variables, the correlations were once more determined with the subject's age being removed by means of partialization.

The validity verification by comparing to actual driving behaviour supplied numerous significant correlations between performance test variables as predictors and differential driving behaviour categories in their negative form as criteria. All these correlations show the correct tendency, i.e. poorer performance test results were associated to increased inadequacies in a subject's driving behaviour. Despite the role of a subject's age in the relationship between predictor and criterion variables, a considerable number of the statistically meaningful correlations between test and driving behaviour variables could be confirmed even after adjusting for the age factor. A summary of these validation results is presented in Table 1.

Table 1. Correlations between tests and driving behaviour variables

driving behaviour	intelligence	memory	perception	concentration/ attention	reaction	amount of significant correlations	number of significant correlations
inappropriate speed	X (x)	X (x)	X	X (x)	X (x)	**.18-.38** (.22-.28)	**12** (7)
driving speed exceeding the legal limit		X	X			**.22-.25** -	**2** -
insufficient distance to the car in front				X (x)	(x)	**.18** (.20-.25)	**1** (2)
insufficient slowing down at intersections and turns	X		X (x)	X (x)	X (x)	**.19-.36** (.21-.31)	**10** (8)
incorrect operation of turn signals	X	X (x)	X (x)	X (x)	X (x)	**.19-.36** (.19-.39)	**17** (12)
inadequate behaviour when driving curves	X	X	X (x)	X (x)	X (x)	**.19-.39** (.19-.25)	**17** (5)
inadequate behaviour at traffic lights			X (x)			**.25** (.28)	**1** (1)
insufficient safety measures for crossing road-users				X (x)	X (x)	**.18-.25** (.19-.25)	**5** (4)
hesitant when changing lanes	X	X (x)	X	X (x)	X (x)	**.23-.53** (.24-.49)	**17** (14)
inadequate lane-changing before making a turn	X	X	X (x)	X (x)	X (x)	**.20-.44** (.19-.43)	**17** (15)
inadequate behaviour when not having the right of way		X (x)	X	X	X (x)	**.21-.61** (.18-.57)	**15** (10)
inadequate behaviour toward pedestrians				X (x)	(x)	**.26-.34** (.18-.34)	**2** (4)
errors in keeping to the lane	X	X (x)	X	X (x)	X (x)	**.24-.57** (.19-.46)	**17** (10)
insufficient lateral distance to other cars	X (x)	X	X	X (x)	X (x)	**.18-.34** (.18-.23)	**12** (5)
number of sign. correlations (age corrected sign. correlations)	**8** (2)	**9** (6)	**18** (7)	**19** (16)	**91** (67)		**145** (98)
amount of sign.correlations (amount of age corr.sign.correl.)	**.19-.30** (.18-.22)	**.19-.36** (.21-.24)	**.19-.48** (.19-.28)	**.20-.48** (.19-.36)	**.18-.61** (.18-.57)		

Extreme group validation

Test validation based on the reason for being assigned to driver assessment (i.e. differentiating between the subjects who are repeated driving test failures and those applying for special licences with increased driver responsibility, such as bus drivers, ambulance drivers etc.) was a further approach in criterion validation. During the observation time between July 1998 and February 2000, the data of a random sample of these two groups had been analysed.

The extreme group comparisons yielded highly significant differences in the ART 2020 traffic specific performance tests almost throughout (see table 2). This result can be seen as particularly positive, since despite an otherwise contrary trend with regard to age (i.e. younger subjects achieving better test results), the older group of the persons with increased driver responsibility showed better results in all performance tests than the younger driving test failures.

Table 2. Summary of extreme group comparisons

			extreme group criterion				
performance	*tests*	*test variables*	*MV; driving test failures*	*n*	*MV; increased responsib.*	*n*	*p*
intelligence	MAT	correct answers	6.80	151	10.35	117	0.000
memory	GEMAT	correct answers	19.00	15	21.29	24	0.012
concentration/ attention	Q1	total number of reactions	620.55	146	702.85	108	0.000
		percentage incorrect	2.15	146	1.35	108	0.016
	FAT	total number of reactions	471.87	41	483.26	30	0.672
		percentage incorrect	3.82	41	2.56	30	0.049
perception	LL5	total number of answers	30.42	159	33.62	117	0.000
		percentage incorrect	5.35	159	2.84	117	0.002
	TT15	correct answers	33.20	133	36.75	116	0.000
reaction	DR2	decision time	565.49	159	533.74	118	0.000
		reaction time	800.43	159	715.27	118	0.000
	RST3	run1: correct reactions	105.28	149	107.23	108	0.000
		run1: percentage incorrect	3.16	149	1.49	108	0.000
		run1: omissions	1.31	149	0.32	108	0.000
		run2: correct reactions	89.81	149	102.78	108	0.000
		run2: percentage incorrect	9.19	149	3.92	108	0.000
		run2: omissions	14.77	149	3.78	108	0.000
		run3: correct reactions	97.46	149	105.63	108	0.000
		run3: percentage incorrect	7.11	149	2.53	108	0.000
		run3: omissions	7.56	149	1.30	108	0.000
co-ordination	SENSO	run1: duration large deviations	3.52	21	1.61	53	0.036
		run1: duration small deviat.	6.78	21	5.11	53	0.015
		run2: duration large deviations	7.14	21	3.56	53	0.001
		run2: duration small deviatiat.	7.51	21	6.51	53	0.017
		run3: no. of counter-steerings	0.43	21	0.15	53	0.021

On the whole, the results of the different validation studies carried out until now yielded empirical evidence for the significance of the ART 2020 psychological tests that are used in driver assessment.

EVALUATION STUDIES OF DRIVER IMPROVEMENT PROGRAMS

Besides the above mentioned study of Michalke et al. (1987) recent Austrian evaluation studies confirmed the reduction of recidivism rates of about 50% (Bartl, Esberger & Brandstätter, 1997; Schützenhöfer, Krainz, 1999). These results go in line with related findings in German studies (Utzelmann & Jacobshagen, 1997; Winkler, Jacobshagen & Nickel, 1988).

In addition to these general evaluation approaches a study on the effectiveness of different course elements has been conducted as well (Christ, 1996). From October 1995 to April 1996 an almost complete sample of all driver improvement courses of the Kuratorium für Verkehrssicherheit has been subject to detailed data collection. A large number of potential factors which are considered to be relevant for personal changes had been considered (see figure 1).

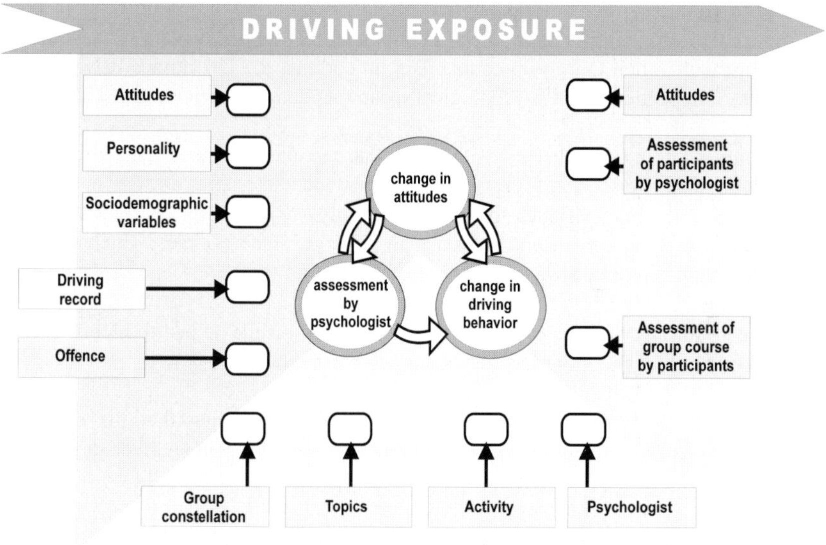

Figure 1. The design of the evaluation study

The figure above gives an overview of all collected data. One set of data (left column) describes the participant before the course, the column on the right stands for data which were collected at the end of the group courses. Another data set (bottom) describes the course characteristics. The study allows the comparison of three different effect measures (center of the figure). Attitude changes have been measured on four different scales, a recidivism prognosis concerning each participant on various risk dimensions has been made by the trainers and finally real recidivism data have been collected for a two years follow up period.

For each of the three most frequently used course models ("DI" Driver Improvement for repeated alcohol offenders, "A"-course for novice drivers with alcohol offences and "V"-course for novice drivers with other traffic offences but alcohol) the determinants were searched for which support course success or impede success (Christ, Eibel, Brandstätter & Smuc, 2000).

The results show that there is little variation between the participant characteristics and course characteristics measured and the recidivism of participants for the classical Driver Improvement courses for repeated alcohol offenders. This fact indicates that all participants benefit about the same way independent from the very course they attended. In fact these course model has been improved over years and is a well designed concept, and, at the time of the study period a fairly homogeneous clientele has been selected by psychological procedures for participation (Christ 2001).

A bit more variation of the course success is explained by participant characteristics if the "A"-course for young alcohol offenders is considered. Especially participants with some more extreme personality traits (reduced self reflection, self control) higher scores concerning additional traffic violations and participants who felt stressed during the group sessions benefit less from the course. This gives some indication how to detect novice drivers who would need more specific measures then the group course. But, in contrast to "DI" novice drivers have to attend the course independent from psychological recommendation or selection (Christ, 2001).

Concerning courses for novice drivers with other than alcohol offences the course success varies more with characteristics of the participant and characteristics of the course itself. Concerning the course characteristics the results strongly support a psychological approach with a focus on life-style, habits and attitudes in general, since courses which paid more attention on these issues proved to be more successful (Christ, 2000).

In general, success for any of these courses can be found, and results helped to identify the very improvement potential for the more recent developed course models.

From the methodological point of view it is also worth mentioning that the correlations between recidivism-rate and the other parameter chosen to measure course effects are low. This indicates the need for a careful selection of effect measure in this kind of studies.

References

Bartl, G., Esberger, R., Brandstätter, Ch. (1997). Unfallbilanz nach fünf Jahren Führerschein auf Probe [Accident records - five years after the introduction of driving license on probation]. *Zeitschrift für Verkehrsrecht, 42*, 9.

Brenner-Hartmann, J. & Bukasa, B. (2001). Psychologische Leistungsüberprüfung bei der Fahreignungsbegutachtung [Psychological performance testing in driver-aptitude-judgement]. *Zeitschrift für Verkehrssicherheit, 47*, 1-8.

Bukasa, B. (1999) ART 2020 - Das neue Multimedia-Testgerät für die Fahreignungsbegutachtung [ART 2020 - The new multimedia test-device for driver-aptitude-testing]. In F. Meyer-Gramcko (Hrsg.), *Verkehrspsychologie auf neuen Wegen: Herausforderungen von Straße, Wasser, Luft und Schiene* (I). 37. BDP-Kongreß für Verkehrspsychologie (381-401). Bonn: Deutscher Psychologen Verlag.

Brandstätter, Ch. (1989). Die Wiener Fahrprobe. Anwendungsmöglichkeiten multiplikativer Poisson-Modelle in der Fahrverhaltensbeobachtung [The Vienna driving test. applicability of multiplicative Poisson-models in driver-behaviour-observation]. Unveröffentlichte Dissertation, Universität Wien.

Brandstätter, C., Christ, R. (1992). Die Validität verkehrspsychologischer Testverfahren in der Fahreignungsdiagnostik bei Senioren [The validity of traffic-psychological test-procedures for driver aptitude testing of elderly drivers]. Psychologie in Österreich. *Mitteilungen der österreichischen Sanitätsverwaltung, 93*, 5, 125-128.

Bukasa, B., Risser, R. (1985). Die verkehrspsychologischen Verfahren im Rahmen der Fahreignungsdiagnostik [Traffic-psychological procedures for driver-aptitude-testing]. Kleine Fachbuchreihe des KfV. Wien: Literas.

Bukasa, B., Wenninger, U., Brandstätter, C. (1990). Validierung verkehrspsychologischer Testverfahren [Validation of traffic-psychological test-procedures]. Kleine Fachbuchreihe des Kuratoriums für Verkehrssicherheit, 25. Wien: Literas.

Bukasa, B., Wenninger, U., Brandstätter, C. (1997). Entwicklung eines neuen Testinstrumentariums zur Durchführung verkehrspsychologischer Fahreignungs-untersuchungen [The development of new test-instruments for traffic psychological driver-aptitude-testing]. In Baumgärtel, F., Wilker, F.-W. & Winterfeld, U. (Hrsg.), *Innovation und Erfahrung. Analysen, Planungen und Erfahrungsberichte zu psychologischen Arbeitsfeldern*, (137-144). Bonn: Deutscher Psychologen Verlag.

Christ, R. (1996). Evaluation of measures in Austria to reduce the risk of young drivers. Paper presented at the ICTTP Conference, Valencia.

Christ, R. (1996b). Ageing and driving - decreasing mental and physical abilities and increasing compensatory abilities? *IATSS Research, 20*, 43-52.

Christ, R., Brandstätter, C. (1997). Die Diskussion um die Fahreignung älterer Kraftfahrer zwischen Glaubenskrieg und empirischem Fundament [The discussion on the driving aptitude of elderly drivers between religious war and empirical basis]. *Zeitschrift für Verkehrssicherheit, 43*, 1, 10-19.

Christ, R., Eibel, M., Brandstätter, C., Smuc, M. (2000). Driver-Improvement, Evaluation der Nachschulungskurse. *Basisbericht zur Datenerhebung und Operationalisierung der Messgrößen* [Driver Improvement, Evaluation of Driver-Improvement courses. Main report on data collection and operationalisation of the coefficients]. Wien: Kuratorium für Verkehrssicherheit.

Christ, R. (2000b). Driver improvement courses for novice drivers in Austria. What determines the effect? *Recherche, Transports, Securité, 67*, Avril. Juin , 21-38.

Christ, R. (2001). Driver-Improvement, Evaluation der Nachschulungskurse. Kurse für alkoholauffällige Fahranfänger - Faktoren und Bedingungen, die den Kurserfolg begünstigen. Vergleiche zu den verschiedenen evaluierten Kursmodellen (A,V,DI) [Driver-Improvement, Evaluation of Driver-Improvement courses for novice drivers with alcohol offences - factors and determinants favouring course success. A comparison of the various evaluated course models (A,V,DI)]. Wien: Kuratorium für Verkehrssicherheit.

Felnemeti, A., Gheri, M., Krainz, E., Schmidt, L. & Wenninger, U. (1987). Verkehrspsychologische Beurteilung von Persönlichkeitsmerkmalen im Hinblick auf die Fahreignung. Einsatz von Fragebogenverfahren in der Fahreignungsdiagnostik [The judgement of personality traits from traffic psychological view concerning driving aptitude. The use of questionnaires in driver selection]. Kleine Fachbuchreihe des KfV, 22. Wien: Literas.

Gheri, M.F., Schmidt, L., Zuzan, W.D. (1980). Driver Improvement. Durchführung eines Problemorientierten Trainingsprogrammes und seine Bewertung durch Teilnehmer und Trainer [Driver Improvement. Implementation of a problem-focused training-program and it's assessment by participants and trainers]. Wien: Kuratorium für Verkehrssicherheit.

Höfner, K.J. (1976). Driver Improvement - Entwicklung psychologischer Maßnahmen zur Rehabilitation von Verkehrsstraftätern [Driver Improvement - Development of psychological measures aiming at rehabilitation of traffic law offenders]. Zeitschrift für Verkehrssicherheit 22, 4, 194-195.

Hutter, M., Bukasa, B., Wenninger, U. & Brandstätter, Ch. (1997): VPT.2 - Verkehrsbezogener Persönlichkeitstest Version 2. Testhandbuch - Kurzfassung. 2. überarbeitete und ergänzte Auflage [VPT2 - A traffic related personality test, 2nd version. Test manual - short version. 2nd improved and completed edition]. Wien: Kuratorium für Verkehrssicherheit.

Hutter, M. & Brandstätter, Ch. (1996): Neue Testanalysen zu FRF und VIP [New test-analysis on FRF and VIP (test for risk factors and item-pool on traffic related attitudes)]. Wien: Kuratorium für Verkehrssicherheit.

Hutter, M., Braun, E., Bukasa, B., Ponocny-Seliger, E., Schermann, W. & Wenninger, U. (2000): TAAK - Testverfahren für alkoholauffällige Kraftfahrer. Testhandbuch - Kurzfassung. [TAAK - A psychological test for alcohol offenders in traffic. Test manual - short version]. Wien: Kuratorium für Verkehrssicherheit.

Kaba, A., Panosch, E., Lager, F., Bartl, G. (1995). Bericht über Erfahrungen mit Nachschulungen (Paragraph 64a KFG) und begleitenden Maßnahmen (Paragraph 73 Abs. 2a KFG) [Report on experience with Driver Improvement (Paragraph 64a Driving law) and accompanying measures (Paragraph 73 Abs. 2a Driving law)]. Wien: Kuratorium für Verkehrssicherheit.

Kisser, R., Wenninger, U. (1983). Computerunterstütztes Testen im Rahmen der Fahreignungsdiagnostik (Act & React Testsystem ART-90) [Computerised testing in driver selection]. Kleine Fachbuchreihe des Kuratoriums für Verkehrssicherheit, 20. Wien: Kuratorium für Verkehrssicherheit.

Klebel, E., Michalke, H., Schmidt, L. (1977). Driver Improvement. Erste Erfahrungen mit einem Gruppentraining für alkoholauffällige Verkehrsstraftäter [First experience with a group training for alcohol offenders in traffic]. *Zeitschrift für Verkehrsrecht, 24*, 6, 180-188.

Klebelsberg, D. & Kallina, H. (1963). Verhaltensanalyse des Kraftfahrers [Analysis of driver behaviour]. Kleine Fachbuchreihe des Kuratoriums für Verkehrssicherheit, 8. Wien: Kuratorium für Verkehrssicherheit.

Klebelsberg, D., Biehl, B., Fuhrmann, J. & Seydel, U. (1970). Fahrverhalten: Beschreibung, Beurteilung und diagnostische Erfassung [Driving-behaviour: description, judgement and diagnostic recording]. Kleine Fachbuchreihe des Kuratoriums für Verkehrssicherheit, 5. Wien: Kuratorium für Verkehrssicherheit.

Michalke, H. (1979). Problemorientiertes Training für alkoholauffällige Kraftfahrer [Problem-focused training for alcohol offenders in traffic]. In W.D. Zuzan (Hrsg.), *Erster*

Internationaler Workshop Driver Improvement. Psychologische Behandlungsmodelle für verkehrsauffällige Kraftfahrer (144-161). Wien: Kuratorium für Verkehrssicherheit.

Michalke, H., Barklik-Chory, Ch. & Brandstätter, Ch. (1987). Driver Improvement. Effizienzkontrolle von Gruppentrainingsmaßnahmen für alkoholauffällige Kraftfahrer [Driver Improvement. An evaluation of group-training for alcohol offenders in traffic]. Wien: Kuratorium für Verkehrssicherheit.

Panosch, E. (1996). Sonderformen der Nachschulung von Fahranfängern in Österreich [Special settings for driver improvement of novice drivers in Austria]. In B. Schlag (Hrsg.), *Fortschritte der Verkehrspsychologie 1996*. 36. BDP-Kongreß für Verkehrspsychologie. Bonn: Deutscher Psychologen Verlag, 301-305.

Risser, R. & Brandstätter, Ch. (1985). Die Wiener Fahrprobe. Freie Beobachtung [The Vienna driving test. Free observation]. Kleine Fachbuchreihe des Kuratoriums für Verkehrssicherheit, 21. Wien: Literas.

Risser, R., Schmidt, L., Brandstätter, Ch., Bukasa, B. & Wenninger, U. (1983). Verkehrspsychologische Testverfahren und Kriterien des Fahrverhaltens [Psychological test procedures and criteria of driving behaviour]. Unveröffentlichter Forschungsbericht. Wien: Kuratorium für Verkehrssicherheit.

Schmitt, A., Teske, W., Anderle, F.G., Bartl, G., Gheri, M., Kaba, A., Krainz, E., Michalke, H., Panosch, E., Schützenhöfer, A., Strigl, K., Walser, B. & Zuzan, W.D. (1992). Integratives Trainingsprogramm für allgemein verkehrsauffällige und alkoholauffällige Fahranfänger [An integrated training program for traffic law offenders and alcohol offenders in traffic]. Wien: Kuraorium für Verkehrssicherheit.

Schützenhöfer, A., Krainz, D. (1999). Der Einfluss des Alkoholisierungsgrades beim ersten Alkoholdelikt auf die Rückfallwahrscheinlichkeit [The impact of the BAC-level at the first alcohol offence upon the probability of recidivism]. *Zeitschrift für Verkehrssicherheit, 45*, 2, 68-73.

Schützenhöfer, A., Schmidt, L. (1977). Driver Improvement - Verbesserung des Verkehrsverhaltens auffälliger Kraftfahrer - Grundlagen und Erfahrungen [Driver Improvement - Improvement of driving behaviour of conspicuous drivers - basic assumptions and experience]. *Zeitschrift für Verkehrssicherheit, 23*, 2, 73-74.

Spoerer, E., Ruby, M., Hess, E. (1994). *Nachschulung und Rehabilitation verkehrsauffälliger Kraftfahrer* [Improvement and rehabilitation of traffic law offenders]. Faktor Mensch im Verkehr, 35. Braunschweig: Rot-Gelb-Grün.

Spoerer, E., Christ, R., Siegrist, S. (1998): Driver Improvement in Europa [Driver Improvement in Europe]. In: Bundesanstalt für Straßenwesen (Hrsg.) *Driver Improvement. 6. Internationaler Workshop*. Referate des Workshops 1997. Mensch und Sicherheit, Heft M93. Bergisch Gladbach.

Utzelmann, H.D., Jacobshagen, W. (1997): Validation of the German system of diagnosis and rehabilitation for traffic offenders. In: Rothengatter, T., Carbonell Vaya, E. (Eds.): *Traffic and Transport Psychology. Theory and Application*, (p. 435-444). Pergamon.

Wenninger, U., Bukasa, B. (1999). Einführung multimedial unterstützter Testinstruktionen unter Anwendung softwareergonomischer Prinzipien [Introduction of multimedia supported test-instruction applying software-ergonomic principles]. In F. Meyer-Gramcko (Hrsg.), *Verkehrspsychologie auf neuen Wegen: Herausforderungen von Straße, Wasser, Luft und Schiene* (I) (p. 402-405). 37. BDP-Kongreß für Verkehrspsychologie. Bonn: Deutscher Psychologen Verlag.

Winkler, W., Jacobshagen, W., Nickel, W.-R. (1988): Wirksamkeit von Kursen für wiederholt alkoholauffällige Kraftfahrer [The effectiveness of courses for repeated alcohol offenders]. Unfall- und Sicherheitsforschung Straßenverkehr, Nr. 64. Im Auftrag des Bundesministers für Verkehr von der Bundesanstalt für Straßenwesen, Bergisch Gladbach.

Zuzan, W.D., Ruby, M. (1986). Psychologische Maßnahmen zur Rehabilitation verkehrsauffälliger Lenker [Psychological measures for the rehabilitation of traffic law offenders]. *Blutalkohol, 86, 23,* 4, 280-288.

Traffic and Transport Psychology,
T. Rothengatter and R.D. Huguenin (Editors)

36

Driver Selection and Improvement in Germany

Hans D. Utzelmann

Driver Selection by Medico-Psychological Assessments

In the German system of driver selection and improvement an interdisciplinary team of psychologists and physicians try to cope with the risks inherent in drivers with alcohol offences and in those with a high level of demerit points in the central register of offences in Germany. The medico-psychological assessments are integrated in the administrative laws considering the withdrawal and regranting of driver licences. Figure 1 shows the system for the case of DWI offenders.

Besides performance and reaction tests, a kind of clinical interview especially developed for this purpose are the psychological instruments used in the psychological part of the assessments. These instruments and the criteria to decide whether the driver is fit or unfit for driving are described in a handbook valid in principle for all companies working in this field. There are criteria for recommending different kinds of driver improvement measures too. The distribution on the different kinds of cases shows Figure 2.

In the meantime, there are a lot of different kinds of driver improvement measures for the above mentioned target groups. There are courses which are approved by the administration; for these courses a quality system and an accreditation are necessary because the certificate of participation leads to the regranting of the licence. For non-approved courses, accreditation is neither necessary nor possible. Their effect must be proved by a medico-psychological assessment in each single case before a new licence can be regranted by the administration. For further information to these points see Nickel (2004).

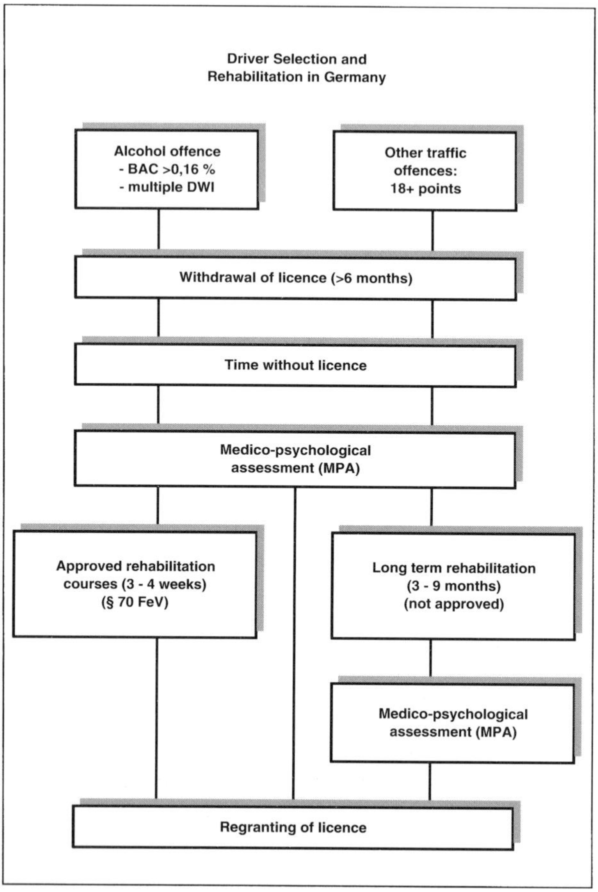

Figure 1. The system for the case of DWI offenders.

Quality Assurance and Evaluation

Quality of assessment and driver improvement measures are documented by internal quality assurance systems and additionally by an accreditation procedure according to EN 45013 under the responsibility of a special branch of the Federal Highway Research Institute (BASt) and their psychologists.

Evaluation studies have clearly shown that this system of driver selection and improvement leads to a reduction in relapses and accidents and thus to an important increase in traffic safety (Utzelmann and Jacobshagen, 1997).

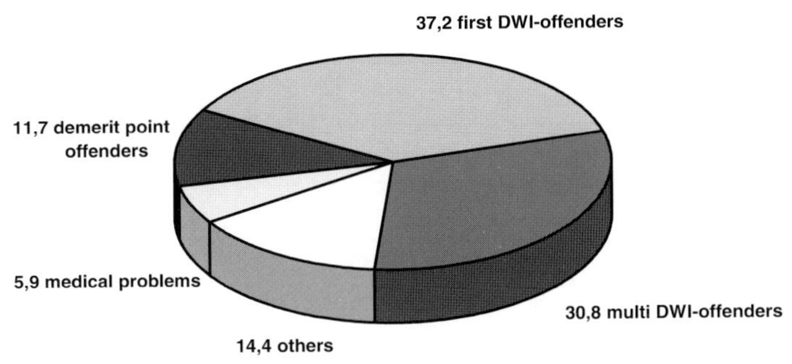

Figure 2. Distribution of medico-psychological examinations in Germany 1995

Principles of the Psychological Interview

The principles of the psychological assessment will be outlined by using the example of DWI drivers. By describing the methods, questions and decision criteria it will be possible to understand what are the topics of a driver improvement course, too. There are no "tests" in the sense of standardized inventories or personality questionnaires. And only in special cases with doubts well founded by the analysis of the records or by the medical assessment there will be proved the psycho-physical state of a testee (reaction time, concentration, orientation, attention, stress tolerance). This may be in cases of high age or of unusual frequency or course of an accident.

The centre of the psychological assessment is an interview. The character of this interview is that of a behaviour analysis as well known from the behaviour therapy. In so far the steps are to analyse (see for example the classical publication of Kanfer, 1980): Stimulus, Organism, Response, Contingencies, Consequences.

The main question then is the description of the history of the problem behaviour, e. g. the development of the drinking behaviour to alcohol abuse or even alcohol addiction (Figure 3). Next question then is whether and when the testee has understood that he has got a problem and what he has decided to do. The last question is if the attitude and behaviour changes are the right ones (i. e. alcohol abstinence or controlled drinking), and if they are so strong and stable and well founded by motivations, so that the psychologist can predict for the future time no major risk for a new drink-driving offence.

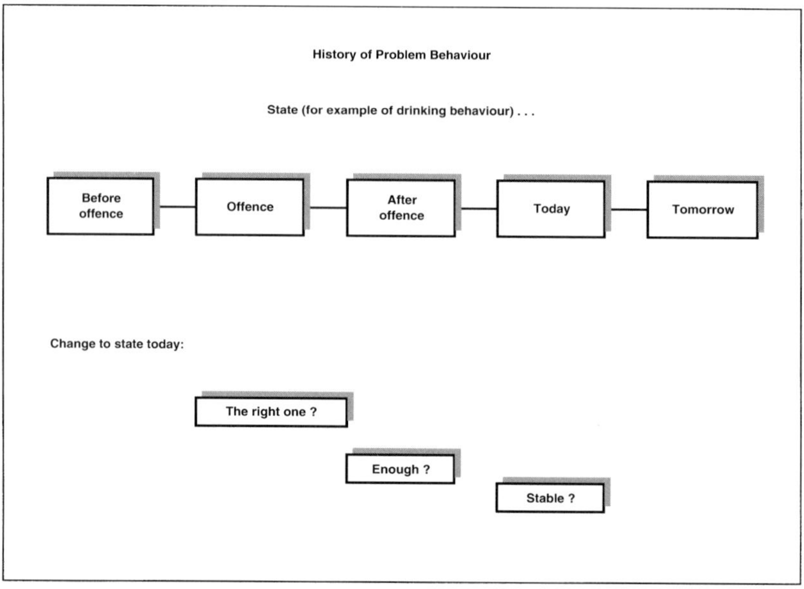

Figure 3. History of problem behaviour

In this interview for example with an alcohol offender the following themes and questions are discussed: Is the testee still drinking alcohol excessively? Has he got back the ability to control drinking alcohol? Is he an acute or a sober alcohol addict? Has he changed his habits regarding drinking and driving? Has he got back control of problem situations and is he now able to avoid excessive drinking? Is there sufficient acceptance of social norms? Are the psycho-motor abilities sufficient for driving? Are approved courses or other measures able to correct the problems in a sufficient way?.

There is an interview according to a handbook for the interviewer (VdTÜV, 1993) to each of these topics. The handbook does not determine a uniform course of questions; there are only determinations of themes which are to treat at any point of the interview. Furthermore there are principles of interview techniques and hints for avoiding faults in the assessment procedure. Techniques for testing and evaluating the truth (Ekman, 1985; Undeutsch, 1990) are an important part of the handbook on the one hand as well as techniques for founding the basis for a trustful atmosphere in the conversation on the other hand.

Besides the handbook for the conduction of the interview there is a list of decision criteria. According to Utzelmann and Jacobshagen (1997) as best predictors have proven in a study with more than 2000 testees with alcohol offences: (a) control of alcohol consumption, (b) control of "drinking and driving" conflicts, (c) a (positive) development of drinking habits.

Besides these decision criteria the following biographical datas proved as good predictors: (a) age (younger driver have more relapses), (b) time between DWI offences (short distances in the past mean high future relapse rates), (c) other traffic offences than DWI come together with high relapse rates, (d) alcohol related criminal offences outside traffic are related to DWI relapses as well as driving without licence or hit and run offences.

Conclusions

We have statistics showing that our german system of driver selection and improvement prevent alcohol offences and accidents in a remarkable size (Utzelmann and Jacobshagen, 1997). We are sure that the decline of the number of alcohol accidents and alcohol related withdrawals of licenses in Germany is - beside other causes - an effect of the system of driver selection and improvement, too. And the acceptance of the system for the testees themselves becomes better with the development of helpful measures as driver improvement courses and with the enrichment of the selection procedure by counselling methods.

References

Ekman, P. (1985) .*Telling Lies*. New York and London.

Kanfer F.H.(1980). Self Management Methods. In Kanfer, F. H. & Goldfried, A. P. (Eds.), *Helping People Change*. New York.

Nickel, W.-R. (2000). Licensing, Assessment and Rehabilitation. Lecture at ICTTP2000 in Bern. CD, Swiss Council for Accident Prevention bfu, Bern.

Undeutsch, U.(1990). Zur Verwertbarkeit und Glaubhaftigkeit von Probandenäußerungen. In: Nickel, W.-R., Utzelmann, H. D. & Weigelt, K.-G.: (Eds.) *Bewährtes sichern - Neues entwickeln.* Köln.

Utzelmann, H.D. & Jacobshagen, W. (1997). Validation of the German System of Diagnosis and Rehabilitation for Traffic Offenders. In Rothengatter, J.A. & Carbonell Vaya, E. (Eds.), *Traffic and Transport Psychology - Theory and Application*. Oxford: Pergamon.

VdTÜV (Ed.) (1993). Die Exploration als diagnostische Methode im Rahmen der Fahreignungsuntersuchungen in den Medizinisch-Psychologischen Untersuchungs-stellen. In: *TÜVIS-Prüfgrundlagen*, Band 2, (unpublished).

Traffic and Transport Psychology,
T. Rothengatter and R.D. Huguenin (Editors)

37

Regrant the Licence Earlier? Effects of Accelerated Assessment and Rehabilitation within the Legal Ban Period of DWI Drivers in Northern Germany

Wolfgang Jacobshagen

Introduction

Germany runs a nation-wide assessment and rehabilitation system for traffic offenders, founded in the fifties. In 1999, it got a new legal background while adapting the German licence system to EU-rules.

In case of DWI, drivers who have reached a BAC of .16 % or have been registered twice with DWI within 5 years have to be assessed and licence authorities base their decisions on the results of the Medical-Psychological Assessments (MPA). In 1999, around 95,000 clients with alcohol involved had to be assessed (for details see Jacobshagen 1997, Jacobshagen & Utzelmann 1998; Utzelmann & Jacobshagen 1997, Nickel 1993, 1997).

Normally, authorities may start administrative work for the regranting of the licence earliest three months before the end of the court-set ban period. Assessment may earliest take place one month before the end of the ban period is reached. As there are different obstacles, not only bureaucratic ones, this schedule is often quite theoretical.

Table 1. Prolongation of the court-set formal ban period

Prolongation of the court-set formal ban period (mean 405 days) for standard MPA-clients	
	additional days
Positive MPA-classification:	269
Course recommendation:	212
Negative MPA-classification[1]	428

[1] Only persons with registered reinstatement of licence within the 36 month follow up.

The mean formal ban period (starting at date of DWI), covering 431 standard cases in the project was 405 days[2], but was severely prolonged until effective reinstatement of the licence. According to the results of the assessments, prolongations are recorded as follows:

Bearing this in mind and taking into account that earlier psychological intervention may be more effective when administered while things are still fresh in client's mind, traffic ministries of north German countries and the Medical Psychological Assessment Institute of TÜV Nord Group decided to test the effects of starting the reinstatement process earlier, modifying the assessment process, too. (That was abbreviated BUSS, which means in German "Beratung, Untersuchung und Schulung innerhalb der Sperrfrist", i.e. "assessment, counseling and schooling within the ban period". The research project to accompany this was named INTEVA.) Practically, this meant to cancel the above mentioned time limits, to define a second short date with the client for a final interview before handing out the expertise (in case of positive tendency) and to give more precise practical hints for rehabilitation in case of a negative result of the assessment. In the latter case clients were able to start relevant measures, such as attending addiction-counsellors and joining self-help-groups, earlier and could manage to be successful in a second assessment within the formal ban period. Even when transgressing this limit, there would be a large portion of time saved, anyway. Even for clients recommended to take a standard rehabilitation course (such as model LEER, see p.e. Winkler, Jacobshagen & Nickel 1988, Nickel 1990, Nickel, Jacobshagen & Winkler 1987, Kroj 1993, Spoerer & Ruby 1996, Spoerer, Ruby & Jensch 1997, Jacobshagen 1998) there should be a more comfortable schedule within the ban period.

Thus, we hoped to reduce the recidivism quota significantly and to help the clients to get back their licences earlier.

---

2 To explain the German sanction system for the foreign reader shortly: courts put out fines in day's wages (very seldom jail) and add a minimum ban period. Licence authorities have to check later on if to reinstate the licence with another legal background, focusing the future risk of the driver, with assistance of MPA under defined conditions. Main parameters for the sanctions of courts are first or multiple DWI and having caused an accident or not. In the project, we found the following mean sanctions in Niedersachsen (Lower Saxony):

subgroup		*number of days wages (mean = 60 DM / 30,70 Euro)*	*ban period following DWI-day (in days)*
first DWI	routine control	33.7	348
	with accident	43.3	382
multiple DWI	routine control	50.5	455
	with accident	57.3	464

(Accidents seem to provoke a bipolar effect: they may rise the sanction, when others are victims, but can also lower it, when the driver himself is badly injured. The latter can be interpreted as a kind of „natural" sanction which is added to the legal one.)

The Acquisition of the Clients

In spite of wellspread information among court offices, licence authorities, advocates and the assessment-centers themselves the resonance among potiental clients for the experimental group was smaller than anticipated. Only 9.6 % of 30,010 clients, who had to be assessed because of DWI during the experimental period in the federal land of Niedersachsen (Lower Saxony) joined the experimental group. This caused difficulties in the time schedule, but can be seen positively, too, as the remaining control group was thus nearly not affected. It was quite clear that altering a routine process as reinstallation of the licence was not as simple as we had hoped.

A lot of clients of the control group, later confronted with the modified version to get the licence back, expressed that they would have taken the opportunity when having been informed in time.

Effect of the BUSS-System on the Standards of the Counsellors

Anticipating the effects of protruded assessment, we were looking forward to get lower rate of positive results of the assessments. We estimated fewer persons would have already stabilized reduced drinking habits. This should reduce the rate of course recommendations, too, and more clients were awaited to get recommendations of harder measures such as individual therapy or joining self-help-groups against alcohol misuse.

The counsellors did not get any instructions to alter their standards when assessing experimental clients. But indeed, they did, as can be seen in Figure 1. Interviewing the counsellors, this was explained as effect of new "intermediate" instruments to stabilise clients with positive tendency, such as studying literature or doing some "homework" until the scheduled final contact with the counsellor, in which the positive expertise should be handed over, if no new negative facts would contradict. This final contact itself was reason to formulate more positive results of assessment, as in case of "emergency" the result could be altered in a "last minute way". More votes claiming "course recommendation" were explained by assuming stronger effects of courses when administered earlier. Finally, it has to be accentuated that there wasn't any increase of negative votes in spite of the fact that the counsellor did not have to formulate a written negative expertise but only had to give a founded oral advice, which in the end saved a lot of time.

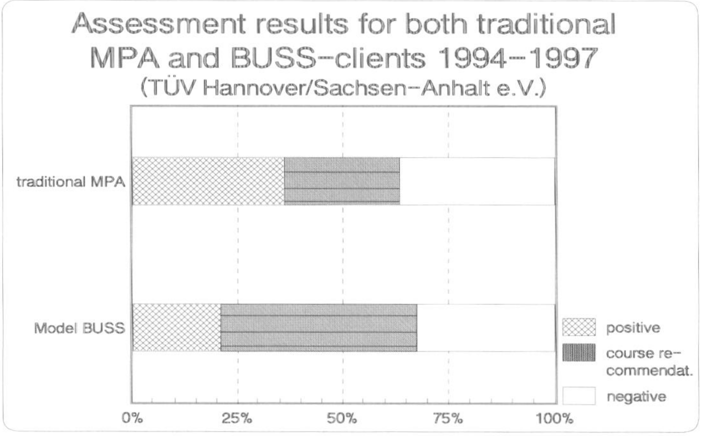

Figure 1. Assessment results for MPA and BUSS-clients

Method and Results

Main aim of the project was to find out, how traffic safety is affected when the effective ban period is significantly shorter. As random recruitement of experimentals could not be administered in this field, we firstly had to secure that main population parameters of experimentals and controls were comparable. To evaluate the assessment process itself, around 200 variables concerning biography and assessment results were collected. Within our time schedule, we thus collected 871 experimentals and 863 controls in the region of Niedersachsen, while 965 experimentals, covering a strongly reduced variable set, were added mainly from the federal land of Schleswig-Holstein.

Comparability of experimentals and controls

To compare both subgroups legitimately, a majority of risk-relevant variables should not differ significantly. This was reached on the following variables

(a) gender (8 % females)
(b) around 30,000 km driven yearly before losing the licence (this is significantly higher than mean kilometers driven in Germany)
(c) around 9 kms driven until alcohol control or accident
(d) comparable distributions of the incident times during the day
(e) the frequency of driving without licence, "hit-and-run" and criminal offences in the record does not differ
(f) reported duration of the drinking event is equal
(g) the same relation of fresh and remaining alcohol was reported

(h) changing of alcoholic beverages during the drinking event was 58.4 %
(i) rating of drinking habits by the adviser culminated at 4.3 on a scale ranking from 1 (abstinent) to 6 (alcohol addict)
(j) estimation of maximum BAC to be reached after assessment is 0.12 %
(k) Gamma-GT was registered around 21 u/l
(l) in the drinking history, ages of first permanent drinking and first severe intoxication are equal
(m) intellectual capacity is rated as equal
(n) vocational training was successfully finished by around 80 %
(o) unemployment rate was 6.8 % (experimentals) and 8.4 % (controls)
(p) duration of formal ban period was around 400 days for both groups

There are significant differences in following variables:

(a) 5.9 % German-rooted immigrants from eastern countries and Russians among experimentals vs. 1.0 % among controls
(b) BUSS-clients have a higher education level
(c) BUSS-clients did not tend to abandon the learned profession
(d) BUSS-clients did not change jobs as much as controls in the last 10 years
(e) BUSS-clients have more seldom professions known as close to alcohol drinking
(f) number of day's fines are slightly different with 41 vs. 39 ($p < 0.05$)

Some more significant differences are shown in the following figures.

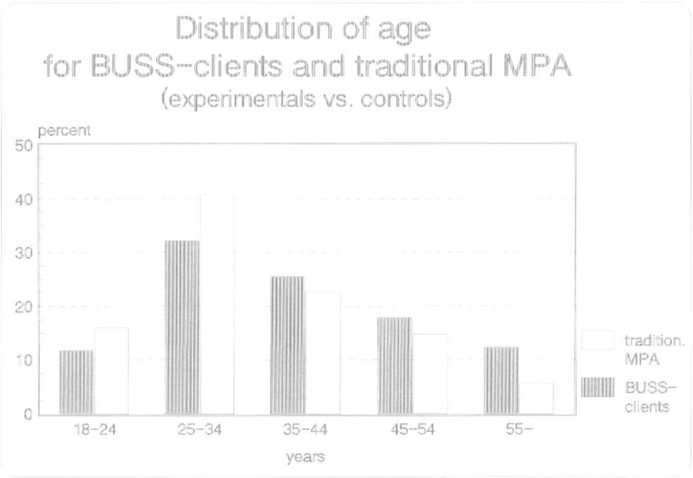

Figure 2. Distribution of age for BUSS-clients and traditional MPA

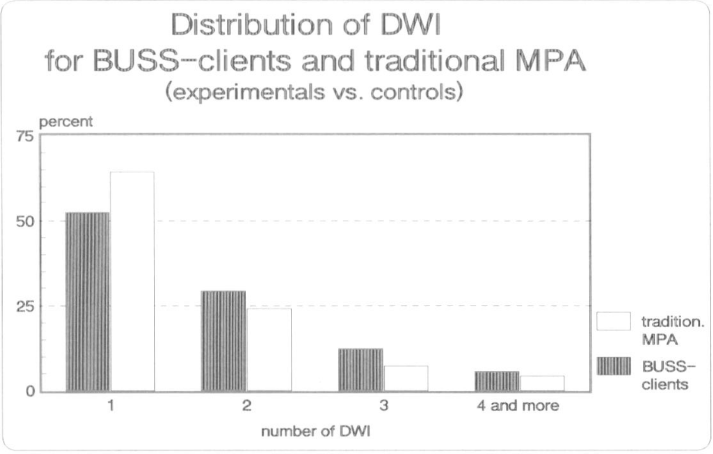

Figure 3. Distribution of DWI for BUSS-clients and traditional MPA

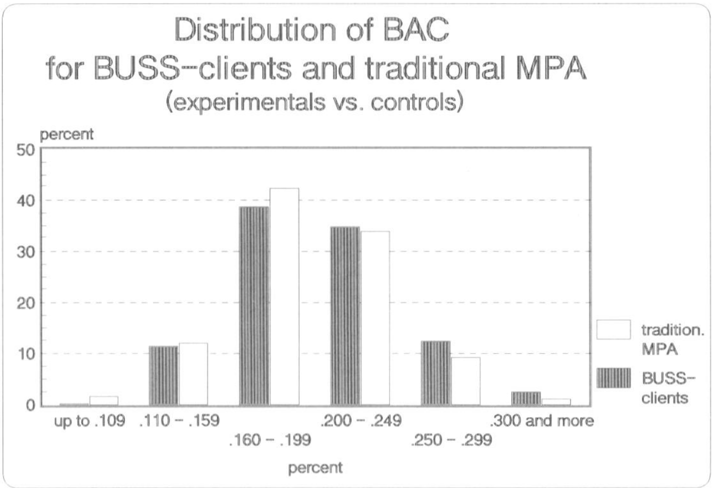

Figure 4. Distribution of BAC for BUSS-clients and traditional MPA

All in all, this means that insignificant differences dominate. Concerning the special variables with higher risk indication shown in the pictures, we can estimate that the effects compensate: BUSS-clients are less often young drivers with their elevated risk of relapse, but otherwise they reach meanly higher BACs and among them there are more persons condemned twice ore even more with DWI, indicating a traditional higher risk of reconviction. This means that BUSS-clients can in no way be defined as having a higher a priori risk of relapse.

Time schedules after DWI (experimentals vs. controls)

The second aim of the project was to increase the system effectiveness by reinstating the licence earlier in case there will be no negative effects on traffic safety. The main durations after the DWI can be seen in Table 2.

Table 2. Durations after DWI (experimentals vs. controls [i]) in Niedersachsen.

days from ... to ...	*experimentals M (s)*	*controls M (s)*	*significance t-test*	*difference*
DWI - day of validity of court sentence	107 (64)	126 (98)	***	19
DWI - end of ban period	390 (126)	405 (232)	n.s.	15
DWI - reinstatement of licence				
positively assessed	392 (105)	674 (566)	***	282
course recommendation	388 (118)	617 (496)	***	229
negatively assessed (only those with later reinstatement within the follow up period of 36 months)	597 (233)	833 (516)	***	236
day of validity of court sentence - medical-psychological assessment (MPA)	172 (91)	444 (492)	***	272
MPA - end of ban period	119 (82)	-174 [ii] (455)	***	293

[i] without repeated assessment after last DWI among controls, as those were not allowed in the BUSS group; N (experimental) ≥ 598 / N (control) ≥ 431; [ii] negative value means prolongation of the ban period; significance levels (two tailed): $p \leq .05$ *; $p \leq .01$ **; $p \leq .001$ *** ;not significant: n.s.

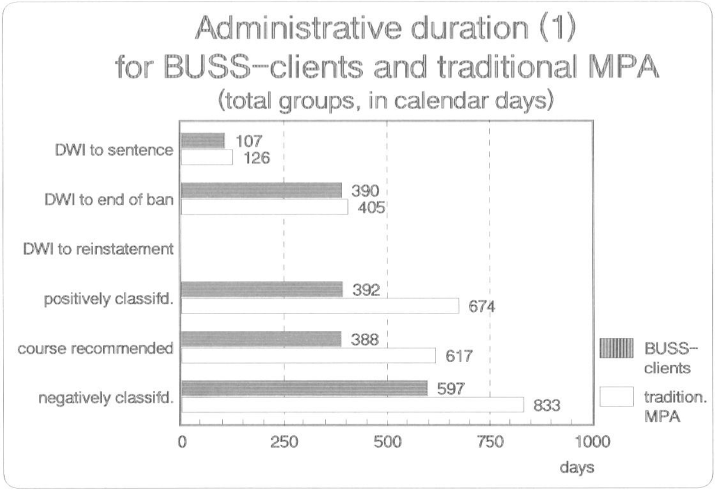

Figure 5. Administrative duration (1) for BUSS-clients and traditional MPA

The following has to be emphasised:

(a) BUSS-clients get their valid sentence faster (see also Figure 5)
(b) the time from DWI to end of ban period is not different in both groups
(c) for the clients, the time from DWI to the effective reinstatement is most relevant. Fact is that positively assessed BUSS-clients as well as those with course recommendation get their licences back exactly at the end of the formal ban period, while controls have to wait more than 200 days in addition. Negatively assessed BUSS-clients usually don't get their licence back at the end of the ban-period, but have an effective time without licence of 697 days, which is significantly shorter than the controls with 833 days. This means 428 additional days of delay.
(d) if we add all kinds of assessment results, it can be shown that 90 % of BUSS-clients have their licences reinstated 24 months after the end of the formal ban period, while the percentage for the controls is only 70. At the end of the formal ban period 65 % of the BUSS-clients were successful, while only 8 % of controls had managed to get their licences back.

Figure 6 shows further relations concerning the time consumption of experimentals vs. controls.

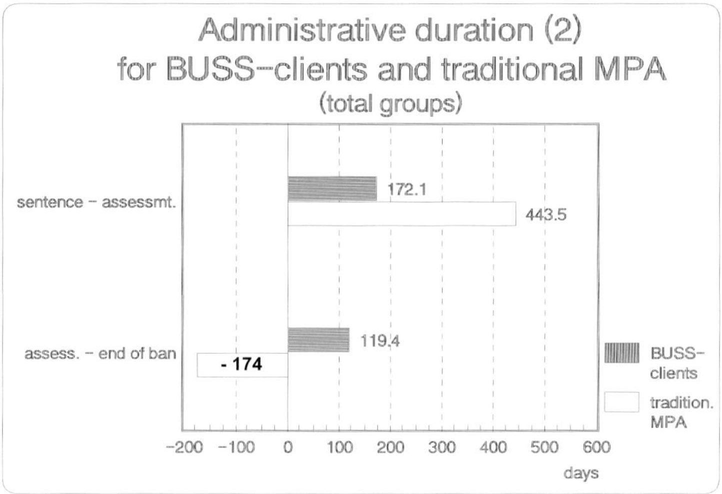

Figure 6. Administrative duration (2) for BUSS-clients and traditional MPA

All in all, it can be stated that on the background of comparable reaction of the justice on both experimentals and controls5, BUSS created a large time benefit for the clients.

Relapse rates collected by the CTR (Central Traffic Register)

Discussing effectiveness in the field of assessing and rehabilitation, a time span of 36 months follow up plus 6 months additional time for administrative purposes has been approved. This secures compatibility with former studies in Germany, too, and rises the reliability of the criterion. It has to be emphasised at this point, that according to the high rate of undetected DWIs in general, the criterion of legal relapse is poor. But: there is no better one available.

Concerning 36 months follow up after reinstatement of the licence, we had to extrapolate for the negatively assessed ith later reinstatement after a new MPA, as the project did not run indefinitely. We assume that this way is legitimate, as the relapse curve of DWI seems linear during the first 3 years. It also has to be added that this excluded negatively assessed persons with a longer delay of reinstatement to be followed up, as they had their licence not reinstated at the end of data collection. Thus, relapse rates of negatively assessed persons have to be interpreted carefully.

Table 3 shows relapse rates and number of persons followed up in the subgroups as well as results of former studies ALKOEVA (Winkler, Jacobshagen & Nickel 1988) and EVAGUT (Jacobshagen & Utzelmann 1996, 1998)

Table 3. Relapse rates (%) at 36 months follow up after reinstatement of the licence.

		result of MPA		
sample	*year of assessm.*	*positive*	*course recommendation*	*negative with delayed reinstatement*
BUSS-clients TÜV Nord*)	94 - 95	4.6 (241)	4.8 (351)	2.4 (247)
BUSS-clients TÜV HaSA**)	94 - 96	6.0 (134)	6.8 (458)	6.2 (179)
controls TÜV HaSA**)	94 - 96	6.5 (200)	8.3 (327)	4.4 (57)
EVAGUT northern region ***)	87 - 89	12.3 (485)	12.7 (408)	24.8 (151)
ALKOEVA northern region ***)	79 - 83	18.1 (364)	13.2 (212)	--

( ) number of persons in the sub-samples;
*) lands of Schleswig-Holstein, Mecklenburg-Vorpommern, northern Niedersachsen;
**) land of Niedersachsen;
***) lands of Niedersachsen, Schleswig-Holstein, Bremen

Statistically the differences of the relapse rates in the project are not significant at all. This doesn't meet results of intermediate calculations which seemed to support the initial hypothesis that earlier psychological intervention provides a plus in traffic safety. If we don't accept that the direction in the data still conforms with the initial hypothesis and that significance may be lowered by influence of altering the BAC-limit in Germany in the meantime, we really can stress the fact that clients have a substantial shorter ban period without influencing traffic safety negatively. This may indicate that the system should be altered according to the setting proved in the project.

The "good" relapse rates of the negatively classified clients have to be especially explained, as this could devaluate the results at first glimpse. As "EVAGUT" shows, this kind of relation to positively classified persons and those with course recommendation is a newer trend. This may be caused by the actual strategy of the advisers, not only forcing some more months without licence into the clients (meanly around one year), but also giving them practical hints what to do to reinforce their qualification to drive without alcohol individually. In the project, this aspect was emphasised, as negatively judged experimental clients did not get a written negative expertise, but a founded oral advice about what to do, fixed in a service booklet. This practice may cause this very homogeneous relapse pattern in the project. It makes clear that a highly differentiated system of measures has a better effect than a standard one to cover all DWI offenders.

Recommendations were used as follows in Table 4.

Table 4. Recommendations for negatively classified clients

recommendation	*proportion of*	
	BUSS-clients %	*traditional MPA-clients* %
recording a written drinking pattern	2.2	1.3
reading about „drinking and driving“	6.0	1.3
traffic-psychological therapy	10.4	6.0
consult ambulant addiction-adviser	62.3	51.3
join a self-help-group (p. e. AA)	55.2	33.3
consult common life-aiding institution	14.9	13.8
psychotherapy	11.2	6.0
additional psychotherapeutic measures	3.4	1.3
medical controls (p. e. liver parameters)	61.6	39.7
stationary addiction therapy	4.9	5.2
absolute & permanent alcohol abstinence	64.2	42.7

Since the existence of the ALKOEVA-project (data collected around 1980), relapse rates of DWI have gone down in Germany. This could eventually be traced back to harder standards of the counsellors from ALKOEVA-period to EVAGUT-period (data collected 1987 to 1989) , but since then there has been a stabilisation. Interpretation like "communicating pipes" now fails. The decrease can be seen as effect of an advanced system in the meantime, as p. e. common standards for the counsellors have better spread and administered. These standards have been evaluated in the project EVAGUT (Jacobshagen & Utzelmann 1996,1998). In addition, a general decreasing trend has been detected since the eighties, as figures of the CTR and local police statistics point out. (Bildungsinstitut der Polizei 1999, see picture 7). Decreasing police activity could also be taken into account, as proportion of accidents among DWIs slightly rose to INTEVA project (see Figure 8). This parameter correlated highly negatively with the number of chemical test devices used for roadside controls in the ALKOEVA-period. But: this alone cannot be responsible for the overall effect.

We prefer to interpret the trend as a multiple cause effect, in which modifications of the legal background, such as already forcing first DWI-clients with BACs from .16 % to the MPA, may have additional effect.

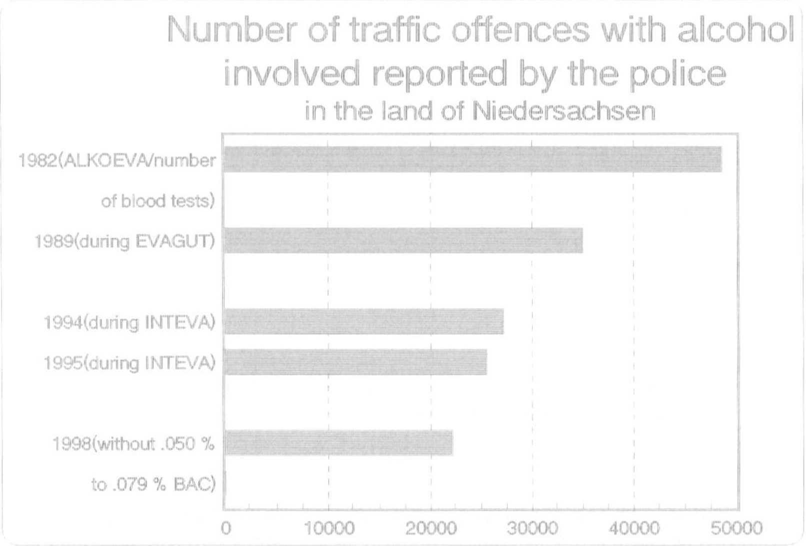

Figure 7. Traffic offences with alcohol

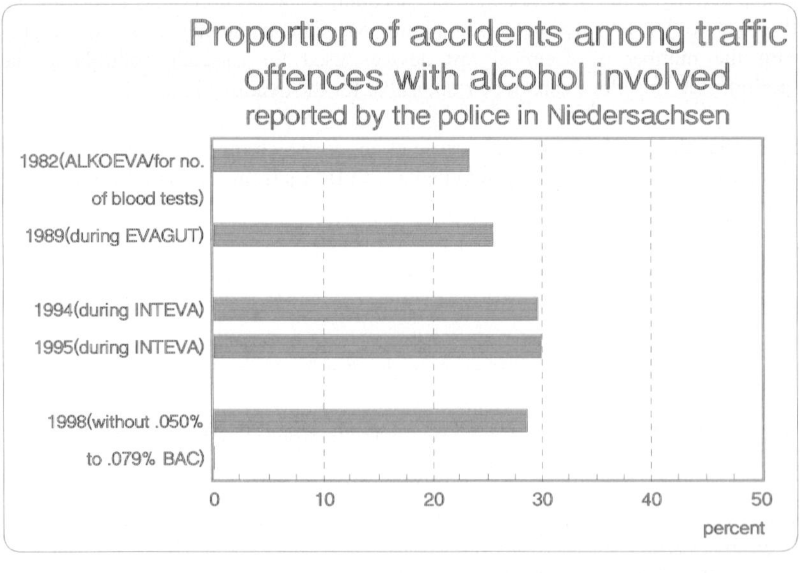

Figure 8. Accidents among traffic offences with alcohol

Summary And Conclusions

The BUSS model was mainly intended to rise traffic safety by focusing the clients to reflect their alcohol problems at an early stage and in an individual manner. This ranged from studying written material over standardised rehabilitation courses to joining professional alcohol therapy and/or attending self help groups regularly. Secondly, the model was designed to shorten the from time to time heavily prolonged ban periods. In the experimental /-control group design BUSS participants were compared with controls, having participated in standard MPA procedure. Main parameters of the groups show that this could be done in a methodically correct way.

Statistical comparisons show that there is no decrease of traffic safety with model BUSS, but a rise, hoped for following intermediate calculations, could not be secured statistically. This may be due to the introduction of a .05 % BAC limit in Germany in the last period of the observation time, possibly disturbing the original setting. But mainly, there is no negative effect on traffic safety.

On the other side, the strange shortening of the ban period does not produce any harm, and makes clear that the court-set timing must not be artificially prolonged. (The effect of cutting this period, too, could not be studied, as only a few clients managed to shorten this setting, convincing the judge that their individual risk was minimised).

All in all, results encourage to transfer constituting elements of BUSS into the standard system.

Compared with former results, it has to be pointed out that negative assessed clients with licences reinstated later, following a second, positive assessment, do not constitute a higher risk than those with a positive judgement or those with a course recommendation. This indicates that the recommended heavier psychological and medical measures for this subgroup of clients worked effectively. In earlier periods, when reinstatement was barely delayed, the risk of relapse of this subgroup was raised, in spite of a (second) positive assessment. This points out that an individual fine-scaled palette of measures, worked out in the assessing process, can homogenise the residual risk of this group of clients to a level acceptable to society.

Beside this, a general decreasing trend of DWI relapses in Germany has to be emphasised. This may be due to different causes, such as better public knowledge of the problems on drinking and driving, economic problems among the clients mainly involved, but also to a more developed re-licensing system. This should be further improved, systematically integrating specialised traffic psychological freelancers and clinical addiction specialists for the clients of the more negative part of the distribution.

References

Bildungsinstitut der Polizei Niedersachsen / FF Verkehr [Police Academy of Lower Saxony, Traffic Dept.] (1999). Personal message.

Jacobshagen, W. (1997). Medical-Psychological Assessment in Germany: System, Classification Results, Recidivism Rates and Validity of Predictors. In: Risser, R. (Ed.) *Assessing the Driver Contributions to a workshop on Driver Diagnostic and Selection* Brunswick: Rot-Gelb-Grün-Verlag.

Jacobshagen, W. (1998). Nachschulungskurse für alkoholauffällige Fahranfänger nach dem Modell NAFA in Deutschland: Klientel, Kursdurchführung, Wirksamkeit und Akzeptanz. [Training courses for beginner drivers with alcohol offences. An evaluation of the NAFA model in Germany with regard to its clientele, course procedures, effectiveness and degree of acceptance.] In Driver Improvement 6. Internationaler Workshop Mensch und Sicherheit Heft M 93 Bundesanstalt für Straßenwesen: Bergisch-Gladbach. (English text available from the author)

Jacobshagen, W. & Utzelmann, H. D. (1998). The medical-psychological assessment procedures for drivers with alcohol offences and drivers with a high penalty-point status. Empirical results concerning their effectiveness and diagnostic reliability. Cologne: Verlag TÜV Rheinland. [German version: Jacobshagen, W. & Utzelmann, H. D. (1996). Medizinisch-Psychologische Fahreignungsbegutachtungen bei alkohol auffälligen Fahrern und Fahrern mit hohem Punktestand. Empirische Ergebnisse zur Wirksamkeit und zu deren diagnostischen Elementen. Cologne: Verlag TÜV Rheinland.]

Kroj, G. (1993). Rehabilitation of drunken drivers in the Federal Republic of Germany. In: Utzelmann, H. D., Berghaus, G. & Kroj, G. (Eds.): *Alcohol, Drugs and Traffic Safety - T92* (Vol 1., pp.378-384). Cologne: Verlag TÜV Rheinland.

Nickel, W.-R. (1990). Programs for the rehabilitation of drinking driving multiple offenders in the Federal Republic of Germany. In: Wilson, R. J. & Mann, R. E.(Eds.): *Drinking and Driving: Advances in Research and Prevention.* New York: Guilford.

Nickel, W.-R. (1993). Licensing and medical psychological assessment in Germany. In: Utzelmann, H. D., Berghaus, G. & Kroj, G. (Eds.): *Alcohol, Drugs and Traffic Safety - T92* (Vol 1., pp. 246-250). Cologne: Verlag TÜV Rheinland.

Nickel, W.-R. (1997). Rehabilitation Of Drunk Drivers - Program Effectiveness And Quality Control. In: Risser, R. (Ed.) *Assessing the Driver Contributions to a workshop on Driver Diagnostic and Selection*, (pp. 102-112). Brunswick: Rot-Gelb-Grün-Verlag.

Nickel, W.-R., Jacobshagen, W. & Winkler, W. (1987). Evaluation of the effectiveness of treatment programs for DUI recidivists in the FRG. In: Noordzij, P. C. & Roszbach, R. (Eds.): *Alcohol, Drugs and Traffic Safety - T 86* (pp. 561-565). Amsterdam: Elsevier Science.

Spoerer, E., Ruby, M. & Jensch, M. (1997). Back to the Wheel. Theory and practical experience in the rehabilitation of traffic offenders. Series 'Faktor Mensch im Verkehr' Vol. 40. Brunswick: Rot-Gelb-Grün-Verlag. [German version: Spoerer, E. & Ruby, M. (1996). Zurück ans Steuer. Theorie und Praxis der Rehabilitation auffälliger Kraftfahrer. Brunswick: Rot-Gelb-Grün-Verlag.]

Utzelmann, H. D. & Jacobshagen, W. (1997). Validation of the German System of Diagnosis and Rehabilitation for Traffic Offenders. In: Rothengatter, T. & Carbonell Vaya, E. (Eds.): *Traffic & Transport Psychology / Theory and Application* (pp. 435-444). Amsterdam, New York, Oxford, Tokyo: Pergamon.

Winkler, W., Jacobshagen, W. & Nickel, W.-R. (1988). Wirksamkeit von Kursen für wiederholt alkoholauffällige Kraftfahrer. [Effectiveness of training courses for repeated DWI drivers.] Unfall- und Sicherheitsforschung Straßenverkehr, 64. Bergisch-Gladbach: Bundesanstalt für Straßenwesen.

Traffic and Transport Psychology,
T. Rothengatter and R.D. Huguenin (Editors)

38

Driving Tests - Test Reliability, Consistency of Candidates Performance and other Issues

Chris J. Baughan and Helen Simpson

Introduction

In the British practical driving test, the examiner chooses one of several set routes. Driving is continuously monitored for 48 categories of predefined errors, and examiners are trained to assess each as a dangerous, serious or more minor fault. Serious or dangerous faults are those judged to involve potential or actual danger, and candidates making one or more of them fail the test. The candidate has to demonstrate a hill start and two out of a possible three reversing manoeuvres. At the time of the study, the test lasted about 37 minutes, there was no upper limit placed on the number of minor faults that candidates were allowed to make, and all candidates had to demonstrate a simulated emergency stop. Tests are carried out by the Driving Standards Agency (DSA) - an Executive Agency of the Department of the Environment, Transport and the Regions (DETR). As part of a wider project commissioned by Road Safety Division, DETR to review the driving test, TRL conducted a study of test-retest reliability.

At first sight, the mechanism by which the test seeks to achieve a safe and competent driver population is that of driver selection or screening: drivers who do not meet the test standard are not allowed to drive unsupervised. In practice, only a small proportion of the population is permanently excluded from solo driving. Most people who fail the test simply take more training and practice, and take the test again; repeating the process until they pass. Thus it can be seen that the test's main function is to influence the amount and quality of training and practice accumulated by learner drivers before they are allowed to drive solo. The importance of this function is underlined by the fact that, in Britain, the licensing system does not require learner drivers to take any specified amounts of training or practice.

The Reliability of Driving Tests

Components of unreliability

DSA examiners are trained to help them to make reliable assessments of candidates' performance. In addition, examiners are regularly monitored: a more senior examiner sits in the back of the car, marks the test independently, and compares notes with the test examiner afterwards. Results from about 350 such check tests were collected as part of this study, and indicate an extremely high level of between-examiner agreement on test outcome. However, even if examiners' assessments are perfectly reliable (such that an examiner observing a given test drive would always assess it in the same way, and would agree with the assessments made by all other examiners) there are several reasons to expect that the driving test may have rather limited reliability. For example: (i) The test is subject to several quasi-random components such as weather, traffic conditions, specific traffic incidents and choice of test route, each of which may influence the outcome; (ii) The probability that a fault will be made during a test is likely to depend on the number of opportunities there are for that fault to occur; (iii) At the time of the test, task performance is likely to be unstable since candidates have accumulated only limited amounts of experience (Groeger & Clegg, 1994). In other words, a candidate's underlying error rate is still likely to be fairly high, and possibly fluctuating with time, (iv) As pointed out previously (e.g. Baughan, 1998), a test may tend to induce candidates to take just enough training and practice to bring them to a moderate probability of passing. This would inevitably lead to low reliability (as measured by test-retest agreements) irrespective of test content and examiner consistency.

Is Test Reliability Important?

A test with zero reliability for actual candidates (i.e. people who book a driving test in the course of learning to drive) could tell us nothing about their competence or accident liability, and would provide no basis for withholding or granting a licence. However, the test could still have good 'consequential' validity (in the sense of having the desired beneficial effect on road safety and driver competence) if it induced candidates to have sufficient training and practice. To do this, the test it would have to be reasonably reliable in failing potential candidates who are at an earlier stage of learning and who would be unsafe or incompetent as unsupervised drivers. If we accept underlying error rate as an index of a candidate's driving performance, the test would have to be reliable in failing potential candidates with error rates substantially higher than those typical for actual candidates.

Although a test with low reliability for actual candidates could be fulfilling its main function of maintaining standards of training, safety, and competence, high reliability is still desirable for reasons of efficiency and perceived fairness.

A test - retest study

A test-retest study was undertaken as part of the project (Baughan & Simpson, 1999). Candidates who had already booked a driving test at one of 20 test centres were asked if they would be willing to take a second driving test within a few days of the first. The 366 participants were not told the result of the first test, or given any feedback on how they had done, until after they had completed the second. At the end of the second test they were given a pass certificate if they had passed either or both the tests. The second examiner was not told the result of the first test until after the second test had finished. Test routes and times were allowed to vary as would happen normally with test bookings, to ensure that these sources of variability were included. For most test pairs it was stipulated that a different examiner would take each test. In five test centres, the examiner allocated was allowed to vary without restriction, yielding 38 test pairs using the same examiner for both tests. Participants did not have to pay for the second test and, if they used a driving school car, the school's fee for accompanying the candidate to and from the second test was also paid by the study. Following the second test, both the candidate and the instructor were handed a short questionnaire. 279 candidate questionnaires and 319 instructor questionnaires were completed and returned.

Table 1 shows the main results. Sixty four per cent of candidates received the same result in each test, 20% failed the first test and passed the second, and 16% passed the first but failed the second

Table 1. Results of test-retest study (Frequencies [% in brackets])

Results of 1st test	*Results of 2nd test*				*Total*	
	Pass		*Fail*			
Pass	80	(22)	57	(16)	137	(37)
Fail	75	(20)	154	(42)	229	(63)
Total	155	(42)	211	(58)	366	(100)

The pass rate for the first test was 37.4% and for the second test was 42.3%. This difference is not statistically significant, but may indicate a learning effect. If so, it could be argued that without this learning effect the proportion of people passing test 1 who then go on to fail test 2 would be even nearer to 50%.

Examiners were asked to rate the level of pass or fail into one of 6 categories: 'a very good/exceptional pass', 'a clear, solid pass', 'a borderline pass', 'a borderline fail', 'a definite/clear fail' and 'hopeless, nowhere near the required standard'. Tables 2 and 3 indicate that the rated level of performance in the first test does not predict the likelihood of a candidate passing or failing the second test.

Table 2. Level of pass in first test compared with result in second test

Level of pass in 1st test (rated by examiner)	*Result of 2nd test*		*Total (freq.)*
	*Pass**	*Fail**	
Borderline pass	56	44	48
Clear pass or better	60	40	89

**Cell entry = % of row*

After the second test candidates were asked to indicate how they thought they had done immediately after the first test. Of those who expressed a view, 52% reported thinking they had probably or certainly passed, and 48% that they had probably or certainly failed. Table 4 shows their actual test results.

Table 3. Level of fail in first test compared with result in second test

Level of fail in 1st test (rated by examiner)	*Result of 2nd test*		*Total (freq.)*
	*Pass**	*Fail**	
Borderline fail	32	68	184
Clear fail or worse	38	62	45

**Cell entry = % of row*

Table 4. Candidates' assessment of performance in first test

Candidates' assessment of performance in the first test	*Actual result*		*Total (freq.)*
	*Fail**	*Pass**	
Certain pass	36	64	28
Probable pass	38	62	102
Probable fail	84	16	58
Certain fail	89	11	63

**Cell entry = % of row*

Candidates who reported having thought they had probably or certainly passed were more likely to have done so than other candidates ($p<0.001$), although over a third of those who thought they had passed were wrong. Candidates who thought that they had probably or certainly failed the first test were generally right. This might have caused the study to overestimate the degree of disagreement between test-retest outcomes, with people who (generally correctly) thought they had failed the first test being strongly motivated to obtain a different result in the second one.

Explaining test-retest inconsistency

In principle, all the sources of inconsistency listed earlier could have contributed to the results shown in Table 1. Between-examiner effects are unlikely to explain much of the inconsistency - results of the check tests mentioned above show very high levels of agreement on test outcome. In fact, much of the inconsistency is almost certainly to do with some candidates coming forward for test when they are only just good enough to pass if they drive at their best. In other words, their rates of making serious and dangerous faults are such that, though they may get away without making one during a given test, there is a reasonably high probability that they will make one in another test.

A simplified model of a driving test

Some insight into the effect of individual candidates' underlying competence on the reliability of a driving test, and on its ability to identify and fail people with unacceptably poor underlying competence, can be gained by examining a simplified model of a driving test.

In this simplified model, the level of driving competence reached by a test candidate is characterised by that individual's underlying expected error rate. The test aims to fail candidates whose expected error rate exceeds some threshold. To do this it observes the candidate driving for a given period, counts the number of errors actually made, and fails candidates who reach or exceed a stated number of errors. For the purposes of the model, a candidate's errors are assumed to be generated by a Poisson process - i.e. a candidate's expected error rate is the mean of a Poisson distribution. Such a model can be used to explore test-retest reliability (measured as proportion of test-rest agreements) and probability of misclassification (i.e. failing candidates who have expected error rates below the desired threshold, or passing those with error rates above the threshold). It can show how these are influenced by test duration, error frequency, pass mark, and threshold error rate.

Table 5. Cumulative Poisson probabilities.

	Poisson intensity (expected events per time interval)							
r	*0.1*	*0.2*	*0.5*	*1*	*2*	*3*	*4*	*8*
1	.095	.181	.394	.632	.865	.950	.982	1
2	.005	.018	.090	.264	.594	.801	.908	.997
3		.001	.014	.080	.323	.577	.762	.986
4			.002	.019	.143	.353	.567	.958

Cell entry = probability that r or more events will occur in the specified time interval

Table 5 shows cumulative Poisson probabilities i.e. the probability that r or more events will occur in a stated interval of time. Suppose that a test is intended to fail candidates with expected error rates per test of 1 or more, and that the failure criterion is one or more actual errors committed during the test. The first row of Table 5 shows the test will correctly fail at least 98% of candidates with expected error rates of 4 or more, and will correctly pass over 90% of candidates with expected error rates of 0.1 or less (the table entry shows that 9.5% of candidates with an a expected error rate of 0.1 will fail). However, a rather high proportion (39%) of candidates with an expected error rate of 0.5 will be incorrectly failed, and (100-86.5) = 13.5% of candidates with an expected error rate of 2 will be incorrectly passed.

Maximum test-retest agreements (i.e. assuming no other sources of unreliability) for candidates with given expected error rates can also be calculated from Table 5. For example, it shows that candidates with an expected error rate of 0.5 per test have a probability of 0.394 of failing each test. Their probability of obtaining agreeing results in a test-retest study (if the only source of unreliability is their non-zero error rate) would therefore be the probability of getting two passes + the probability of getting two fails, i.e. (1-0.394)2 + 0.3942 = 0.522. In other words, even with no other sources of unreliability acting, the test would yield only 52% test-retest agreements for such candidates. The first row of Table 6 shows the results of similar calculations for other expected error rates, and indicates that test-retest agreements remain rather low over a wide range of expected error rates.

Given a distribution of expected error rates for the population of candidates, the model can be used to predict the proportion of agreements in a test-retest study, and the proportions of candidates who will be correctly failed and incorrectly failed by the test.

Table 6. Percentage of test - retest agreements for different expected error rates

Failure criterion	*Expected errors per test (Poisson intensities)* 0.1	0.2	0.5	1	2	3	4	8
1 error	83%	73%	52%	53%	77%	90%	96%	100
2 errors	99%	96%	84%	61%	52%	68%	83%	99%

Tables 7 and 8 show the results of doing this for a distribution similar to the one actually found in a large study of test errors carried out as part of the project. The failure criterion is 1 or more errors and, for Table 8, the test is aiming to fail candidates with an expected error rate per test period of one or more.

Table 7. Simple model: test-retest reliability

First test	*Second test* *Pass*	*Fail*	*Total %*
Pass	18	16	34
Fail	16	50	66
Total %	34	66	100

Cell entry = % of all candidates

The pattern of test-retest agreements is not dissimilar to that shown in Table 1 for the real driving test. Given the assumptions being made, this degree of similarity is probably spurious. However, the model result does show that high levels of unreliability may be inherent in an 'error counting' test based on observing infrequent errors.

Table 8 shows that the model test makes an 'incorrect' decision for 26 per cent of candidates. Like the test-retest agreements, this result depends on the choice of the population distribution of expected error rates - i.e. the distribution of test candidates' driving ability. There are, of course, degrees of incorrectness in pass-fail decisions. It does not really matter if people with expected error rates close to the test threshold are misclassified by the test, but it is important for the test to fail people with much higher error rates and to pass people with much lower ones. As already discussed, Table 5 gives some insights into the ability of a test to do this.

Improving the reliability of the driving test

As stated earlier, the driving test could still be performing its main function of inducing training and practice despite the pattern of test-retest disagreement shown in Table 1. Nevertheless, good reliability is desirable for the reasons outlined. Also, a test with good reliability and good discriminatory power is likely to be more effective in inducing training and practice.

'Wrong decisions' in the simplified model occur because of the difficulty inherent in using observed errors to estimate underlying error rates. Test-retest disagreements stem from a similar problem - the fact that a candidate with a constant underlying error rate will produce different numbers of errors in different tests.

In principle, these problems could be addressed by increasing the numbers of errors observed during the test, i.e. by increasing the duration of the test or by basing the test on errors that are less severe and therefore more frequent.

The likely effects of increasing the duration of the test can be explored using the model, on the simplifying assumption that a candidate's expected error rate per unit time will remain unchanged. Under this assumption, if the test duration is doubled then a candidate's expected number of errors per test will also double. Table 5 shows the effect that this would have on candidates at each expected error rate. For example, a candidate with an expected error rate per test of 2 in the table has a probability of being failed (i.e. of making one or more errors) of 0.865. In a doubled test, the same candidate would have an expected error rate per test of 4. Assuming that the failure criterion for the double length test is also doubled (to two or more errors), row 2 of the table shows that the candidate would now have a probability of failure of 0.908. Similarly, for a candidate with an expected error rate of 0.1 (i.e. 0.2 for a double length test), the probability of an (incorrect) failure would reduce from 0.095 to 0.018. The test would become somewhat better at failing people with high error rates, and passing people with low ones.

The second row of Table 6 shows the effect on test-retest reliability. Candidates with expected error rates of 2 and 0.1 per standard length test would have rates of 4 and 0.2 in a doubled test. Their test-retest agreements would improve from 77% to 83%, and from 83% to 96% respectively.

One disadvantage of the above approach is the cost of a longer test - especially since the failure criterion for this type of test can only be an integer number of errors. If it were to change to two errors, duration would have to be approximately doubled to maintain the current overall pass rate. A second problem is that the lengthened test would have to pass candidates who made one error. DETR and DSA have made it clear that it would be unacceptable to pass candidates who make such error classified as serious or dangerous during the test, though it would allow a lengthened test to be more effective than the current one at failing candidates with a high rate of serious or dangerous errors and passing those with low error rates.

An alternative would be to base the test on less severe, more frequent errors. Potentially, failing candidates who make more than a given number of minor errors could improve the ability of the test to detect and fail people with unacceptably high underlying error rates. Such a change was made to the test in May 1999, based on evidence that minor errors show an ability to detect candidates who have a raised accident liability (Maycock & Forsyth, 1997). On the above argument, it could also improve reliability and discrimination.

The above approaches to improving consistency are to do with improving the ability of a test to estimate a candidate's true expected error rate. Another approach to improving consistency would be to persuade people to delay taking the test until their driving skills have improved - i.e. until their error rate is lower (driving more consistent). It is therefore important to understand how people decide when to come for test. It seems possible that people might see it as worth attempting the test early, knowing that they will probably fail, but knowing also that if they do pass they will not have to pay for any more driving lessons. If this is going on, the question arises of what would happen if the consequences of failing the test were made more severe. If the cost of a re-test were increased, or if there were a long, compulsory, delay between test and re-test, would people then delay coming for test until they were more sure of passing it? If so, test pass rate would increase, test-retest consistency would improve, the standard of novice drivers would improve, and numbers of retests would decrease.

To gain some insight into this, we conducted exploratory interviews with eight instructors, and with 16 candidates who had applied for a driving test. The findings indicated that the candidates generally had not come forward for test before they thought they were ready. 'Ready' was thought of in terms of feeling competent and reasonably confident, with driving 'coming naturally' and the instructor feeling able to relax somewhat. However, it did not necessarily mean that candidates thought they had a high probability of passing the test, since they thought that 'test nerves' and chance occurrences during the test, would intervene. In other words, candidates felt ready for the test, but did not feel in control of the test outcome. If these results are typical of test candidates, they indicate that there is not much scope for using retest fees and delays to persuade people to postpone coming for test, because candidates do not think that taking more training and practice will greatly improve their probability of passing. It will therefore be desirable to examine how perceived control over test outcome can be improved. This may not be straightforward, and other ways of increasing pre-test experience may be much more effective.

A third way of attempting to improve test reliability is to change the test so as to reduce the opportunity for chance events and route/traffic differences to influence the outcome. The probability that a candidate will make a serious or dangerous fault, and therefore fail the current driving test, will depend on the number of opportunities for a fault to occur during the test. This will vary to some extent from test to test (for example, because of varying weather and traffic conditions), introducing an element of inconsistency. Possible ways of reducing this include (a) standardising test routes, (b) assessing performance only on those parts of routes that are standardised and ignoring what happens on other parts of the route, and (c) allowing good performance to cancel-out faults, so that the test score becomes the proportion of times that the candidate gets things right. Tests involving such elements have been introduced in the USA and Australia (e.g. McKnight, 1992). Arguments sometimes raised against introducing such tests in Britain include the fact that test routes are already fairly well standardised, and a concern that a highly prescriptive and standardised test may reduce the opportunity for examiners to use their skill and judgement in assessing the test drive.

Tests involving examiners' overall judgements of skills or competencies have been introduced in, for example, Sweden (Mattsson, 1999) and Western Australia (Drummond, 2000). In principle, this approach may avoid some of the potential disadvantages of tests based on observing errors, but it may also introduce its own difficulties associated with the reliability with which examiners are able to make the necessary judgements. More evidence is needed on this. Examiner's ratings are themselves presumably based to an extent on the errors observed during the test, so that these approaches may not in the end be so different from the British errors-based approach.

Other Approaches to Improving Novice Driver Safety

In Britain, the driving test is the main way of inducing learner drivers to build up training and experience before driving solo. This is asking a great deal of a driving test and, to achieve some of the desired improvements in training and experience, the test may need to be supplemented by other measures. Measures to encourage a more structured approach to learning and the gaining of more pre-test experience may, for example, be much more effective than changes to the test alone. Logbooks for learner drivers may prove useful here; a voluntary logbook scheme was introduced by the Driving Standards Agency in 1999.

It is also difficult for a test to include in its pass/fail criterion those variables that influence the discrepancy between supervised driving performance during the test and subsequent driving behaviour. We therefore need to consider measures to reduce or change exposure during early solo driving, and to exercise a continuing supervisory influence over the way drivers choose to behave once they have passed their test. Any such changes would still need to allow drivers to gain the experience needed to reduce their accident liability. Britain's scheme under which drivers revert to learner status if they accumulate six penalty points within two years of passing the test is an example of such a measure.

Measures to influence pre-solo training and experience, control exposure during early solo driving or influence the behaviour of novice drivers, have been introduced in other countries; often as part of graduated licensing systems. They include curfews, passenger restrictions, zero alcohol for novice drivers, extended periods of learning to drive, requirements for various types of logged experience, specified pre and post-test training, and requirements for violation-free periods, or passing of a second driving test, before leaving a probationary phase of solo driving. Evidence for the effectiveness of these measures has been reviewed by Baughan and Simpson (in press) as part of this project.

Conclusions

In the British licensing system for car drivers, the driving test is the main mechanism for inducing learner drivers to accumulate training and experience.

Test-retest reliability of the practical driving test is rather low, with inconsistent performance on the part of the candidate being an important source of test-retest disagreements. This does not mean that the test is failing to induce good training and practice, or that there is anything wrong with the way the test is carried out. Nevertheless, an improvement in reliability is desirable.

Potential sources of unreliability include: (a) Candidates having moderate ability (i.e. error rates around the test threshold) and (b) Other factors associated with variations in test events and conditions.

A simplified model of the test can give some useful insights into how the test's reliability, and its ability to identify and fail candidates with unacceptable underlying error rates, may be influenced by test duration, the population distribution of error rates, the severity/frequency of errors included, and the pass-mark and target error rate.

To achieve some of the desired improvements in training and experience, the test may need to be supplemented by other measures designed to encourage a more structured approach to learning and the gaining of more pre-test experience.

It is difficult for a test to include in its pass/fail criterion those variables that influence the discrepancy between supervised driving performance during the test and subsequent driving behaviour. We therefore need to consider measures to influence exposure during early solo driving, and to exercise a continuing supervisory influence over the way drivers behave once they have passed their test. Many graduated licensing systems have elements intended to achieve such objectives.

Acknowledgements

The work described in this paper was undertaken by the Transport Research Laboratory under a contract placed by Road Safety Division, Department of the Environment, Transport and the Regions. Any views expressed are not necessarily those of the Department. The authors would like to thank Mr Robin Cummins (DSA Chief Driving Examiner), Mr Trevor Wedge and many other Driving Standards Agency staff for their invaluable help with this project.

References

Baughan, C.J. (1998). Review of the practical driving test. In G.B. Grayson (Ed.), *Behavioural Research in Road Safety VIII.* Crowthorne: Transport Research Laboratory.

Baughan, C. J., & Simpson, H. (1999). Consistency of driving performance at the time of the L-test, and implications for driver testing. In G.B. Grayson (Ed.), *Behavioural Research in Road Safety IX.* Crowthorne: Transport Research Laboratory.

Baughan, C. J., & Simpson, H. (in press). *Graduated licensing - a review of some current systems.* (TRL Report). Crowthorne: Transport Research Laboratory.

Drummond, A. E. (2000). Paradigm lost! Paradise gained? An Australian's perspective on novice driver safety. In *Proceedings of the DETR Novice Driver Conference.* Bristol, UK, June 2000.

Groeger, J.A., & Clegg, B.A. (1994). Why isn't driver training contributing more to road safety? In G.B. Grayson (Ed.), *Behavioural Research in Road Safety IV.* Crowthorne: Transport Research Laboratory.

Maycock, G., & Forsyth, E. (1997). *Cohort study of learner and novice drivers. Part 4: Novice driver accidents in relation to methods of learning to drive, performance in the driving test and self assessed driving ability and behaviour.* (TRL Report 275). Crowthorne: Transport Research Laboratory.

Mattsson, H. (1999). Competency-based training and testing of advanced skills in Sweden. In *Proceedings of the ICBC Driver Testing Forum.* March, 1999. Insurance Corporation of British Columbia. Victoria, B.C. Canada.

McKnight, A.J. (1992). *Driver licensing in Victoria.* (Report 27). Clayton: Monash University Accident Research Centre.

Traffic and Transport Psychology,
T. Rothengatter and R.D. Huguenin (Editors)

39

Accident Proneness: The History of an Idea

Frank A. Haight

Introduction

During the First World War, the British government established the Industrial Fatigue Research Board (IFRB later known as the Industrial Health Research Board IHRB). There had been concern with the number of accidental deaths and injuries in the war production industries. In the course of its dozen or so years, the Board investigated myriad aspects of the subject, an early example what is now called ergonomics. One of these studies forms the basis for the present discussion.

In one of the volumes published by the Board, mathematicians discovered a curious anomaly in the data. To understand the importance – to them – of the discovery, we should remember that mathematical description of random events was at that time less than twenty years old. It started with the work of Von Bortkiewicz on death by horse-kick in the Prussian Army. In essence, Von Bortkiewicz showed that the number of such deaths, per year, or per division could be almost exactly described (or, in modern terminology modeled) by the *Poisson Distribution*, a formula discovered nearly hundred years earlier for a different purpose by an eminent French mathematician.

After the work of Von Bortkiewicz (but before the establishment of the IFRB) the Poisson Distribution was applied to a considerable number of different random phenomena: demographic data, gas molecules, particle counting in the plane, telephone traffic (then in its infancy), particles in solution, deaths from malaria, enteric fever among many others. With only trivial exceptions, the Poisson Distribution was a success: It fit the data to perfection. Furthermore this was accomplished with only a single parameter, the mean number of occurrences, to be estimated.

By the time World War One came along, a Poisson Distribution was universally regarded as a unique characterization -- virtually a definition -- of complete randomness in time or in space.

Because of its theoretical foundations it still is. With this background, both theoretical and empirical, we can imagine the consternation among the mathematicians working with IFRB when they found a distribution of Accidents that was seriously non-Poisson. Either the accidents were not occurring at random, or the Poisson frequencies were somehow not behaving as theory – and earlier data – suggested that they should.

We may suppose that this anomaly was of interest to only a small group of people, and that the work of the IFRB – and of the war – continued on its usual course. With such a tantalizing puzzle, a solution was soon found. A paper by Greenwood and Woods (1919) showed that a better fit was obtained with a different distribution – the "negative binomial". For those who cared about such matters, this was a source of considerable satisfaction.[1] The puzzle remained: Why wasn't the Poisson distribution performing in the way it should? About a year later (papers were published quickly in those days) Greenwood jointly with a prominent mathematician Yule (1920) discovered the answer: a new theoretical model.

A brief description of the model goes as follows: The accident experience of each woman working with six inch shells is indeed Poisson – as everyone agreed it should be – but with the value λ (the average number of accidents) differing from person to person. It was then a fairly simple calculation (and one which we now give as an exercise to students) to show that the negative binomial probabilities for the entire collection of workers must result.[2]

The whole episode might have been confined to the world of mathematics, but for the fact that a really exciting name was invented few years later. The individual values of each woman's λ was denoted *accident proneness.* Now the story becomes more complicated.[3]

The Search for a Measure

"Accident proneness" had a nice ring to it. The difficulty was that no one knew how to determine its value for a given individual. It provided a challenge to the psychology profession to devise a way to measure it, just as one can measure height, weight and perhaps even intelligence. If each individual has a unique λ-value, his or her accident proneness, it should be a reasonably simple matter to find out what that value is, by devising clever tests, perhaps physiological, more probably psychological.

The search began as early as the work of the IFRB, initially by Farmer and Chambers (1926, 1929). In their first paper, the connection between accident experience and sickness was correlated with nine clinical tests.[4] Their conclusions were that "there is something called accident proneness, related to poor aestheto-kinetic co-ordination and nervous instability", but only slightly connected with sickness, and further that there is a clear correlation between major

---

[1] The negative binomial distribution has two parameters, and so would be expected to provide a better fit. Here I am trying to describe the reasoning of 80 years ago, not to justify it.

[2] One additional assumption is involved: that the distribution of lambda is what we now call the *gamma.*

[3] I'm not sure who should get credit for the name. My best guess is Ethel Newbold, or perhaps G. Udny Yule

[4] Called simple reaction, simple co-ordination, choice reaction, complications, cover up, distraction, changed position, selective, dilemma.

and minor accidents.[5] The second paper continued with thirteen "psycho physical" tests.[6] The conclusions deserve to be quoted: "Even when the tests are weighted, they fail to give correlations of sufficient magnitude to warrant the assumption that they measure more than a portion of the factors involved in objective criteria. It is clear that the accident rate for any period less than the whole working life must be an imperfect measure of an individual's accident proneness. The longer the period of exposure, the nearer does the accident rate tend to be a true measure of accident proneness".

The search for a reliable measure of accident proneness continued for some thirty years. Hundreds of papers were subsequently published, appearing in such prestigious journals as the Journal of the Royal Statistical Society, Biometrics, the Psychological Bulletin, Psychometrics, Journal of Applied Psychology, and the Journal of the Institute of Actuaries. These authors covered the spectrum of fame up to and including such distinguished figures as Jerzy Neyman (see Bates & Neyman, 1952) and Franz Alexander (1949). The latter, by the way, decided that all accidents were deliberate, so that the elusive λ was a measure of a death wish rather than of mere clumsiness.

None of the experiments produced a positive, replicable result that correlated substantially with accident experience of individuals. Perhaps the most convincing evidence may be found in the many volumes published by the IHRB, reporting on tests that had been proposed, each with its tabulation of results. One that is quite comprehensive (Report No. 34, Newbold 1926) has thirty tables, at least half of which bear captions starting with the words "Correlation between..."

Public Acceptance

Now the story takes a different turn; the expression accident proneness leaked into the popular press, and thus into public opinion, and then into politics. The latter, in the United States, often means Congressional hearings. By 1938, a mere twenty years after its discovery, in hearings before the United States House of Representatives produced a considerable document, Motor Vehicle Conditions in the United States (US Congress, 1938). This fat book contains a section "The Accident Prone Driver" The findings were rather far reaching. For example, "There exists among the general population of drivers, a small group who are definitely accident prone and a much larger group who are just as definitely accident free. Given a drivers' histories one can predict their histories in the other half of the experience, either prospectively or retrospectively."

For public agencies accident proneness was an appealing concept. If accidents could be shown to be confined to this small proportion of "bad drivers", measures to combat accidents could be enormously simplified – and cheaper, too. Essentially all that would be needed would be detection and license cancellation. The report goes on to justify accident proneness on the basis

[5] In the 1960's I was rather struck by this conclusion, and thought that the best clue to future serious accidents might be the scratches and dings on a vehicle.

[6] Called dotting, pursuit meter, choice reaction, interrupted pursuit meter, coordination, steadiness, rectangles, strip, cube, linguistic intelligence, number setting, stereoscopic, dynamometer.

of contagion, specifically that the distribution of intervals between accidents "was not normal, as it would be if the first accident had no effect on the driver's propensity toward another." [7]

This view which might be called the U. S. official view at the time, dominated political thinking and public opinion, not only in the federal government but also in state and local agencies, and I believe in other countries as well. It hardly needs to be emphasized that it was almost entirely unsupported by any research available at the time. Since there was little to support the proposition scientifically, the ever-imaginative popular press invented something, which we will call The Great Percentage Fallacy.

It was claimed, no doubt with good reason, that a small percentage of drivers were involved in a large percentage of accidents. This small number of villains was proclaimed to be the hitherto missing group: the accident prone drivers. Of course, even in the beginning no knowledgeable person believed this beguiling argument.

The Percentage Fallacy can be shown to be wrong in any one of a number of ways. We mention briefly three of them. First, *any* model will involve unequal distribution of accidents, except a supernatural accident bookkeeper who allots one to a customer. One might as well call the losers at Monte Carlo "poverty prone".

The second argument against the fallacy is given by Moore (1956) "Attempts have sometimes been made to justify the concept of accident proneness by statements such as 'one-third of drivers have two-thirds of the accidents'. . . Statements of this type are no proof of the hypothesis, as the following example will show. In 1952 there were roughly 6 million licensed drivers in Great Britain and in the same year some 200,000 mechanically propelled vehicles were involved in personal injury accidents. That is, not more than 200,000 drivers had accidents, from which we deduce that 4% of drivers had 100% of accidents. In one hour in 1952, on the other hand, an average of 25 drivers had accidents, that is, 0.004% of drivers had 100% of accidents."

With this simple example Moore shows that the Fallacy depends on the length of the survey period. The supporting argument is time sensitive; shorter periods give sharper contrasts. The relatively late publication of Moore's paper gives a clue that the official view was still widely accepted as late as the 1950's.

The third difficulty with the official version is even more important, because it has implications for the entire accident proneness concept, and leads to a quite different model. Let's consider the Monte Carlo situation once again. For a person to be truly poverty prone, it would be necessary for that person to lose money not only today, but also tomorrow and the day after. In fact, in the original negative binomial formulation, this point has been entirely omitted. Suppose the 4% of drivers were involved in 100% of accidents in 1952; how about 1953, where presumably another 4% of drivers were involved 100% accidents. Was it the same 4% or an entirely new cohort?

---

[7] Actually, the distribution of intervals in a Poisson process is exponential, a concept that is often difficult to grasp. Even Rutherford, in an early paper, tried to force the normal distribution on exponential data.

In other words, if we plot the number of accidents experienced by an individual during one time period on the x-axis, and during another on the y-axis, will the points form exactly a straight line? If not, then what is the correlation coefficient? Is there in fact a meaningful correlation between the experience in consecutive time periods? In sports, there certainly seems to be, for the individual outcomes do not seem to be independent and random. The sense of accident proneness also implies a condition or personal quality that is relatively stable over time.

This "correlational model" was discussed in one of the last IHRB publications. Farmer and Chambers (1939) proposed the idea, but confessed that it is hard to interpret a correlation for non-normal data. Actually the data is not only non-normal, but based on samples too small to be meaningful, since an individual's accident experience does not usually reach statistically significant quantities.[8]

The argument between correlation and negative binomial models continued for a bit (see, for example Maritz, 1950) but veered away into mathematical abstraction. The reason may be the conclusion of Blum and Mintz (1951): "The major effort is to reduce accidents, not to wait for successive periods."

There were many mathematical results arising from the accident proneness hypothesis. For example Irwin (1941) proved that the negative binomial distribution could equally well be obtained from a hypothesis of "contagion", meaning that each accident increased the probability of another. Arbous and Kerrich (1951) call this the "burnt fingers model" and continue to provide an elaborate mathematical analysis, including its implication for bivariate analysis.

Interlude: Why so Popular?

The slogan, if not the concept of accident proneness was an instant hit with the public in the 1920's and 1930's, and still resonates in the popular press to some extent. Having been taken up by public and the media and confirmed by government, the lack of evidence was irrelevant. Principal investigators could be depended on to provide that.[9]

In support of the hypothesis, there were many people, both in and out of government willing and able to produce reports of success. Academic scholars have been known take a sample of their students to administer a test to find out which were accident prone, and then, as well as they and their funding permitted, follow up the crash experience of those sampled. The results

[8] At one time I tried to overcome the sample size sample size difficulty by correlating entire towns accident totals in consecutive years. As I remember it, some 500 towns, with populations varying from 10,000 to 25,000 yielded a correlation coefficient approximately 0.017.

[9] This might be a good place to point out that the safety profession does seem to be somewhat slogan-prone: in addition to "accident proneness" we have suffered various other pithy mottos: "defensive driving", "road rage", "killer drunk", "risk homeostasis", "Holiday Death Toll", "zero vision", "road hog" &c. Any one of these might be a good topic for a dissertation on popular culture in some department of anthropology.

were typically not positive, and frequently so inconclusive as to indicate that more research was needed to locate this elusive quantity.[10]

In the domain of popular opinion, accident proneness became a household word. It seemed to have the backing of government and was frequently found in press coverage of accidents. It had the advantage of being "proved" by bar charts, endorsed by impressive mathematical expressions. It seemed to the traffic safety panacea, the "cheap effective measure". It still lingers as a generic expression for personal injury. If A drops a brick on B, then A is guilty, but B is accident prone.

Destruction of accident proneness

During and after World War II, authors of scientific papers began to destroy all the ideas on which accident proneness had been based. After all, the entire concept, was balanced on the point of a pin – a minor statistical anomaly. Subsequent papers supporting the idea were now shown to be vulnerable, logically, statistically and experimentally.

One of the first dissenters was Johnson (1946). In this important paper he critiques and criticises over two hundred earlier studies. He shows that the statistical analyses were almost all invalid, inappropriate, inadequate or irrelevant. He asserts that the conclusions were logically unwarranted. He discusses the weakness and absurdity of psychological tests of driving ability. Very little of the buoyantly confident literature of the pre-war period escapes Johnson

The 1950's were especially rich in careful analysis of the accident proneness concept. Arbous and Kerrich (1951), although perhaps not as impetuous as Johnson, nevertheless carry on in much the same vein, destroying the literature of the 1920-1938 period. He (Arbous wrote the first part) was aware of the IFRB literature, and praises Newbold, Greenwood and Yule; the first of these "must still be regarded as almost complete summaries of our existing knowledge of this phenomenon." The uncritical acceptance of proneness as a proven fact is attributed to Farmer and Chambers; if this is true, one must add that they had myriad helpers. The relationships between causes (contagion, proneness, chance) and effects (Poisson, negative binomial, correlation) are also analyzed as to the logical structure.

Some of Arbous' conclusions are "The above findings lead one to conclude that the 'accident-prone Percy' is a figment of the imagination resulting from wishful thinking" . . . ."It is to be lamented that statements of this type should be allowed to acquire a mantle of respectability by being accepted for publication in journals of repute." . . . . "Self deceit of this type has never produced any results worth having." Strong words, indeed, but in my view quite justified.

[10] "The tendency has always been strong to believe that whatever received a name must be an entity or being, having an independent existence of its own. And if no real entity answering to the name could be found, men did not for that reason suppose that none existed, but imagined that it was something particularly abstruse and mysterious."

Needless to emphasize, he believes that the idea of removing the high accident people from the population will have little or no effect on subsequent accident totals.[11]

Adelstein (1952) covers much the same ground, with much the same conclusions, but in his case based on analysis of primary data. He chose the most hazardous occupation that would provide adequate sample size (1,452 accidents) – the men working as shunters on the South African railways over an eleven year period in relatively homogeneous circumstances. He found that age and experience had an effect on accidents among those recently employed, but that the effects "rapidly diminish". Adelstein also studies home accidents of the shunters as well as the correlation between time periods. In a dense paper of 56 pages, he covers many aspects of the problem.

"With respect to injury, during the first five years, chance factors are sufficient to explain the data. Those men who have been observed for five years show more evidence that proneness plays a part, and in those 122 men observed for eleven years, there is stronger evidence for differing degrees of proneness. But the correlations between different periods is small, and the factor of proneness . . . is probably of small practical importance, in comparison with chance factors which play a predominant part. . . . There is no evidence of correlation between industrial and home injuries, or between industrial accidents which cause injury and those which cause damage to property. There is no evidence of correlation between minor and major injuries. . . . No good evidence is available that the same men tend to repeat the same kind of accident. When men who have most accidents in their first year of exposure are compared during the next three years with the remaining men, it is found that the mean rates do not differ significantly."

The Counter-Revolution

By the late 1950's, accident proneness, although soaring in popular imagination, had fallen into disrepute in serious discourse. It is difficult today to use the expression in the title of a paper and expect that paper to be published in a good journal. Reflecting on the problems encountered in using accident proneness as explanatory variable: (a) First, beginning with IHRB material, the "differences" for example were so small as to be inconsequential; (b) There has never been a clear-cut successful way to measure proneness; (c) The craze during its early years was so extreme and then so violently refuted that it became difficult to take seriously in academic circles.

The expression continues in popular usage, and may continue to do so for some time. This may be due to the reluctance of the vernacular press to feature negative results. In this respect newspapers are worse even than scientific journals.

---

[11] In my opinion the negative results do not mean that accident proneness does not exist; actually I would guess that it does. As one of the earliest writers remarked, "After all, some people do have clumsier fingers than others." I think that perhaps the clumsy ones find a way to compensate so that we can't easily identify them. We would then have a quantity λ that exists but that can't be measured. I don't see any logical difficulty with that. I am sure that there are plenty of things that exist, but can't be measured: love, for example, and duty.

As accident proneness faded, it was struck a fatal blow by the emergence of two charismatic figures, Ralph Nader and William Haddon. Haddon, from an important government position[12] asked why, if we can ship eggs without damage, we can't do the same with people, and introduced the ideas of occupant protection. One can see these ideas developing in an early paper (Haddon 1961): "As accidents under present conditions are inevitable and will be to some extent for a long time to come, the vehicle should be designed to be fail safe, that is to be safe to have accidents in." Somewhat later in a 1970 paper, after leaving the Federal government he wrote "It is basic to the reduction of highway losses that there is no present evidence that vehicle crashes can be eliminated or even adequately reduced in numbers in the foreseeable future." This guess has been partly borne out thirty years later.

Nader (1965), piggybacking on these ideas wrote a best selling polemic showing that vehicle design was important, and by implication, that driver characteristics much less so – and in any case less amenable to manipulation.

There was also political support. The popular senator, Daniel Patrick Moynihan (1964), in a glowing tribute to Haddon's theories, wrote "Accidents are the only remaining major cause of human death and disablement still substantially viewed[13] by educated and uneducated alike in terms of ignorant superstition." Quite a good summary of accident proneness, if that is what he had in mind.

This emphasis on injury avoidance tended to discount human factors in general, and the role of the driver in particular. "Accidents will happen"[14] was the philosophy. Diagnosis and removal of drivers has been shown to be unproductive, so the argument went. Instead let's concentrate efforts on vehicle crashworthiness and occupant protection.

The 1960's, 1970's and 1980's were the heyday of vehicle, roadway and environmental modification. These, I should add, are well known to readers and were, it is fair to say, overwhelmingly successful. That story is told in many other places – one might especially mention news releases -- and I don't propose to recapitulate the details.[15]

The Driver Again Emerges

Within the past fifteen or twenty years, the driver as a factor in accidents has gradually started to re-emerge, among other things providing us with some interesting comparisons with the accident proneness period. I believe that there are at least two important trends that reinforced each other in producing the renaissance of the driver.

---

[12] Director of the National Highway Safety Board, forerunner of the present National Highway Traffic Safety Administration.

[13] Douglas C. Toms, Director, National Highway Safety Bureau (quoted in Automotive Industries 143(3)22, August 1, 1970)

[14] Curiously enough, also the slogan of the earliest days, before IHRB.

[15] I will, however, insert a published remark of one NHTSA administrator of the period. "I think we can almost eliminate deaths on the highways, except for pedestrians and those caused by dune buggies and motorcycles." Douglas C. Toms, Director, National Highway Safety Bureau (quoted in Automotive Industries 143(3)22, August 1, 1970)

First, as occupant protection became increasingly successful, and at the same time increasingly costly, the opportunities for improvement became smaller and smaller.[16] By the 1990's roads and vehicles in industrialized countries were generally in quite good condition. Seat belts, air bags, frangible construction, combined I hasten to add with driving style maturity, an aging population and increasing urbanization have combined to propel injury and fatality rates ever lower. This is particularly true for rates based on distance traveled.

The second factor was the re-discovery of a suitable villain that everyone could blame. This time it was the drunken driver, or occasionally even the drinking driver.[17] This tendency was strongest in places where alcohol was already under suspicion as morally unwelcome. Reading the published literature on drunk drivers is strangely reminiscent of the similar literature on accident prone drivers, and makes one wonder what are the similarities and what are the differences between these two grievous attributes.

What is the difference between the drunk driver and the accident prone driver? First we can measure the former (except for the tricky problem of catching him/her), but our experience as outlined above shows how difficult, if not impossible, it is to measure the latter. This means that compensation after drinking is not quite so easy as compensation for clumsy fingers. If I am not gravely mistaken, compensation possibilities after drinking have never been seriously investigated.[18] The accident prone driver could presumably escape, since no reliable test had been invented.

Second, the accident prone individual, if he/she exists does not bring the moral outrage attached to the drunken individual.[19] If anything, people who stumble or who have clumsy fingers are sometimes even looked upon sympathetically It is "not their fault", whereas drunkenness is.

Third, the treatment that society sends to the drunk driver is overwhelmingly punative, whereas the accident prone driver might be told simply "be more careful next time." It is obvious that the law treats them differently. Punishments for drink driving are among the most severe, even where no damage or injury are involved. Like prostitution, both drunk driving and accident prone driving are prima facie "victimless"; in one case a crime, and in the other not. (Until the moment in both cases when damage to the perpetrator or to other road users occurs.)

---

[16] Of course, the automobile industries and the safety establishments very likely have new and sophisticated devices on their drawing boards. It seems to me unlikely that these devices, even at their best, will be able change the safety in cars as much as they have improved in the preceding half-century.

[17] Not entirely, however. The speeding driver, the aged driver, the youthful driver and the discourteous driver have also had their share of attention, and very recently the angry driver. Note however that drunk, angry, youthful and discourteous are viewed as bad people; whereas the aged merely accident prone.

[18] There have been many studies using alcohol and steering around traffic cones, but none I believe offering $1,000 for a successful completion of the trial.

[19] The public image of drunk drivers involves injuring others rather than, as Ross (1992) points out, primarily themselves. This image has been ruthlessly exploited in public relations campaigns.

Another factor to consider when guilt is assigned after a crash: The police are trained to observe the driver[20], and more specifically the "alcohol involved" driver. Typically, they do not look for faults in road design, ergonomics of vehicle control systems or other less visible factors. The reporting form often has a box called 'driver' and cause 'drunk' and these are easy to check off. Further along the path of justice, drunken driver is usually easy to convict. The incompetent traffic or mechanical engineer, who by the way might also have been drunk, is not.

CONCLUSION

In my view, if we want to construct a model for "causes" of road accidents (as distinct from the cause of any individual accident), we could consider a triage: (a) Those factors which are internal to the driver, (b) Those specifically external to road, vehicle and other environmental factors. (c) those which are neither, but purely random. In this context, random means "cause impossible to know".

My experience, both with the concept of accident proneness and with the statistics of the Poisson distribution, convinces me that (c) has been greatly under-estimated both in public understanding and in research. Unfortunately many people think that, if no blame can be attached, no countermeasure can be prescribed. This is shown to be false by experience with lightening rods; we don't know where and when lightening will strike, or what is "at fault". The lightening rod is analogous to the seat belt in ameliorating the effect of a class (c) event.

I think that statistical tabulations over the past century provide data near enough to Poisson to suggest an underlying random distribution as to time, and place. If this is true, the search for the accident prone person was essentially looking for not only for a needle in the haystack, but also for a particular needle among thousands of others.

The further we go back in motorization, whether in the history of a specific country or in the collection of countries world wide, the greater the importance of (a) and (b). As we work toward ameliorating these two, the intent would be that eventually 100% of accidents would be in category (c), modelled exactly by the Poisson distribution. Even if this is turns out to be true it contains no implication for intervention: "accident prevention" or "saving lives" or "unintended loss erosion". These efforts are properly designed to change the average value of lambda. Tinkering with individual values is not particularly fruitful, as shown not only by the experience with accident proneness but by many other types of evidence.

Caveat

In this paper, to avoid plunging into mathematical digression I use lambda (λ) to denote both the average value and an individual value. The consequences of the accident proneness episode have been more significant for mathematical probability than for traffic safety. An entirely new paper could be devoted to that subject.

---

[20] A policeman once told me "I don't care if there is a ten foot hole in the middle of the road, it is the driver's job to stay out of it."

References

Adelstein, A. M. (1952). Accident Proneness: A criticism of the concept the concept based on an analysis of shunter's accidents. *Journal of the Royal Statistical Society, Series A, 115,* 354-410.

Alexander, F. (1949). The accident prone individual. *Public Health Reports, 64,* 357-362.

Arbous, A. G., & Kerrich, J. E. (1952). Accident statistics and the concept of accident proneness. *Biometrics, 7*, 340-342

Bates, G. E., & Neyman, J. (1952). Contributions to the theory of accident proneness. I An optimistic model of the correlation between light and severe accidents II. True or false contagion. *University of California Publications in Statistics, 1,* 215-253.

Blum, M. L., & Mintz, A. (1951). Correlation versus curve fitting in research on accident proneness: Reply to Maritz. . *Psychological Bulletin, 47,* 444-445.

Farmer, E., & Chambers, E. G. (1926). *A psychological study of individual differences in accident rates.* (Industrial Fatigue Research Board Report No. 38). London: Medical Research Council.

Farmer, E., & Chambers, E. G. (1929). *A study of personal qualities in accident proneness and deficiency.* (Industrial Fatigue Research Board Report No. 55). London: Medical Research Council.

Farmer, E., & Chambers, E. G. (1939). *A study of accident proneness among motor drivers.* (Industrial Fatigue Research Board Report No. 84). London: Medical Research Council.

Greenwood, M., & Yule, C. V. (1920). An inquiry into the nature of frequency distributions representative of multiple happenings, with particular reference to the occurrence of multiple attacks of disease or repeated accidents. *Journal of the Royal Statistical Society, 89,* 255-279.

Greenwood, M., & Woods, H. M. (1919). *The incidence of industrial accidents upon individuals with specific reference to multiple accidents.* (Industrial Fatigue Research Board Report No. 4). London: Medical Research Council.

Haddon, W. (1961). Research with respect to fatal accident causes; Implications for vehicle design. *Society of Automotive Engineers, 336A.*

Haight, F. A. (1965). On the effect of removing persons with N or more accidents from an accident prone population. *Biometrika, 52,* 298-300.

Haight, F. A. (1967). *Handbook of the Poisson Distribution.* New York: John Wiley.

Irwin, J. O. (1941). Comments on the paper "Chambers, E. C. and Yule, G. U. Theory and observation in the investigation of accident causation." *Journal of the Royal Statistical Society (Supplement), 7,* 89-109

Johnson, H. M. (1946). The detection and treatment of accident prone drivers. *Psychological Bulletin 43,* 489-532

Maritz, J. S. (1950). On the validity of inferences from fitting of Poisson and negative binomial distributions to observed accident data. *Psychological Bulletin, 47,* 434-443.

Moore, R. L. (1956). Accident proneness and road accidents. *Journal of the Institute of Automobile Assessors, 8,* 32-37

Moynihan, D. P. (1964). A plague of our own. *The Reporter.*

Nader, R. (1965*). Unsafe at any speed; the designed-in dangers of the American automobile.* New York: Grossman.

Newbold, E. M. (1926). (Industrial Fatigue Research Board Report No. 34). London: Medical Research Council.

Ross, H. L. (1992) *Confronting drunk driving.* New Haven and London: Yale University Press.
US Congress (1938) *Motor Vehicle Conditions in the United States; Part 6, The Accident-Prone Driver*. (House Document No. 462), 75th Congress, 3rd Session., Washington, DC: US Government Printing Office.

MOBILITY AND ENVIRONMENT

Traffic and Transport Psychology,
T. Rothengatter and R.D. Huguenin (Editors)

40

Psychological Motivation of Pro-Environmental Travel Behaviour in an Urban Area

Maria Johansson

Introduction

The environmental and health consequences of motorised traffic contradict several objectives of the Agenda 21 as well as Swedish objectives of environmental quality (Swedish Environmental Protection Agency, 1999; United Nations Conference on Environment and Development, 1993). The problems related to urban travelling could, amongst others, be reduced if people chose less polluting means of transportation, such as public transport, cycling or walking instead of driving a car.

Environmentally hazardous behaviours have been approached by antecedent strategies aimed at preventing the behaviour as well as consequence strategies, where actual behaviours are either rewarded or penalised (Dwyer, Leeming, Cobern, Porter & Jackson, 1993). However, often the best results have been achieved by combining these strategies (Gardner & Stern, 1996). Assuming that the transition from car driving to less polluting means of transportation may be facilitated by internal motives, in the present project the potential of an antecedent approach to pro-environmental travel behaviour was investigated. The focus was on emotional aspects related to car driving and the influence of the physical environment was of special interest. The general aim was to increase the understanding of the underlying attitudes of daily travel behaviour in an urban area and how attitudes related to pro-environmental travel behaviour can be promoted. The aims were addressed in two empirical studies. In the first study it was hypothesised that a) attitudes towards traffic and environment would be more strongly related to acceptance of traffic restrictions and travel behaviour than factual knowledge and b) that the environmental load in the physical living environment would influence acceptance and behaviour. The second study built on the results of Study I and accordingly it was hypothesised that attitudes towards and knowledge about traffic and environment may be promoted among children and adolescents by simulating environmental and health consequences of various choices of transportation.

The theoretical framework

As an overall frame for interpretation of the empirical results Küller's (1991) model for human - environment interaction was applied, since this model in addition to the social and individual aspects also includes the perception of the physical environment.

According to the model it was assumed that choice of transportation is the outcome of a basic emotional process that is initiated by the need to make a journey, activation. The orientation process involves the availability of different means of transportation and the location of the destination. The various alternatives of transportation are then evaluated by the state of the physical and social environment and mediated by the individual factors. If the choice of transportation is experienced as rewarding this will result in a feeling of control, otherwise, the next time the individual is likely to choose another means of transportation until control is finally established. It is likely that this process is conscious the first time a certain journey is made. However, once control has been established, the choice may become habitual, until any of the environmental or individual circumstances are changed. There may also be considerable variation in importance of the various factors over the life cycle. Such differences will include the individual mediators.

Study I

Participants

According to the theoretical model the first study may be regarded as a description mainly of the interacting individual and physical aspects in urban travelling. It was carried out as a questionnaire survey in a sample of 422 adult residents between 18 and 80 years (response rate 51%) in Lund, Sweden. The sample consisted of 42 per cent men and 58 per cent women (M = 40 years). In addition to the Lund residents a sample of 122 local politicians and civil servants (response rate of 51%) was sent an abbreviated version of the questionnaire.

The physical environment

Lund is a city of approximately 70,000 inhabitants in south of Sweden. Traffic is the main contributor to air pollutants and noise in the city and about 600 persons are injured in traffic each year (Trivector, 1998). Approximately 40 per cent of the households in Lund own a car (children older than 18 years, who lived with their parents, have been counted as separate households) (Lunds Kommun, 1999). Several bus routes cover the area and 98 per cent of the inhabitants have less than 500 metres from their home to the closest bus stop (Lunds Kommun, 1995). There is a long tradition of bicycling and it has been estimated that approximately 20 per cent of the transport mileage in Lund is made by bicycle (Linderholm, Ljungberg & Carlson, 1993). Two districts, differing in traffic density, were selected for the study, the City Centre and the North Common.

Measurements and statistical analyses

The residents' questionnaire covered travelling in terms of the annual driving distance and travel behaviour defined as the number of journeys and choice of transportation for various destinations during one week. Travel behaviour was translated into an index of environmental load, which could vary between one (all journeys made by foot or cycling) and five (all journeys made by car). Journeys made by public transport and combinations of means of transport were coded in between. Further a 10-item version of Küller and Laike's (1993) scale of acceptance of traffic restrictions was included in the questionnaire. The individual mediators included were factual knowledge about traffic and environment, which was investigated by questions about the local as well as the global situation, and attitudes toward traffic and environment issues, assessed by 14 modified Likert scales. The residents were also asked about their resources in terms of driver's licence and access to a car. Finally some questions about background information such as age, gender, socio-economics and health status were included. The version sent to civil servants and politicians included the scale of acceptance, knowledge and attitude items and a few items for background information. Data were treated with analysis of variance, factor analyses and regression analyses in SPSS (SPSSx, 1986). Due to the large sample the level of significance was set to $p = .01$.

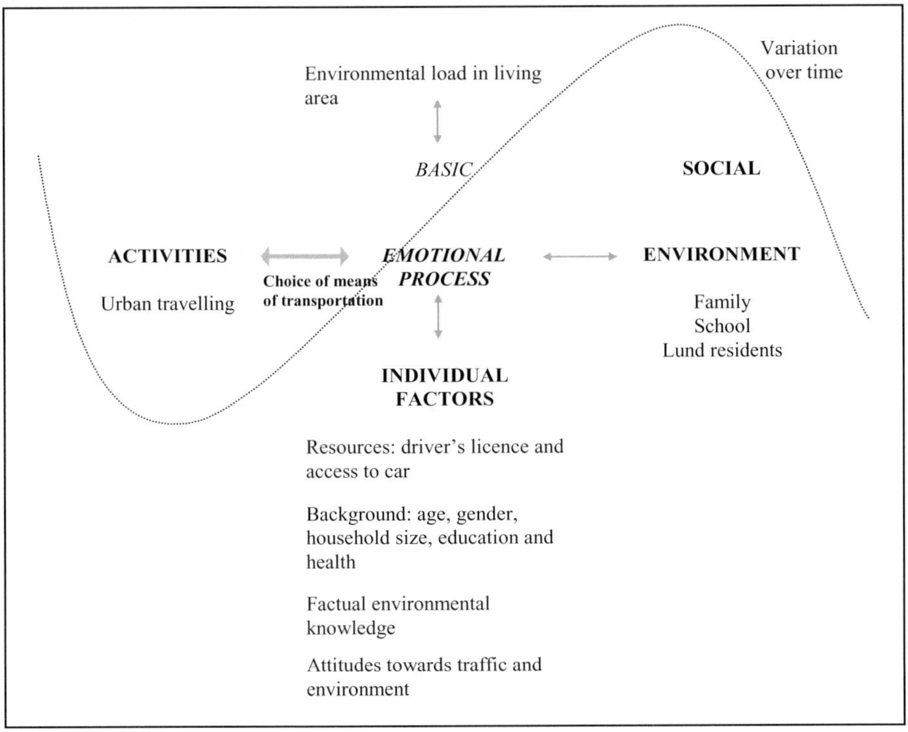

Figure 1. A model of factors influencing the basic emotional process behind choice of transportation (adapted after Küller, 1991).

Results of study I

In order to reduce the number of item and form psychologically meaningful constructs the attitude scales were entered into a factor analysis. An orthogonal solution with four dimensions was arrived at, accounting for 48 per cent of the variance. Factor I was interpreted in terms of environmental concern on a societal level, whereas factor II described the attitude towards public transport. Factor III expressed the perceived hazard level of traffic and the personal efficacy in dealing with its environmental impact. Factor IV described a personal concern about health and environment. A second factor analysis included an additional four scales that required holding a driver's licence and access to a car. In this analysis a fifth factor appeared, car affection, indicating an affective aspect of car driving.

In analyses of variance it was found that acceptance of traffic restrictions as well as driving distance and travel behaviour did differ between people with different attitudes. Those who felt concern for the environment, but little affection for the car caused less environmental impact (both $p < .001$). The acceptance of traffic restrictions was higher in those who scored high in environmental concern ($p < .001$), reported high hazard perception/low efficacy ($p < .001$) and scored low in car affection ($p < .001$). A tendency for greater knowledge to induce more acceptance of traffic restrictions was also noticed ($p = .02$). No significant relation was found between knowledge or physical living environment, and driving distance and travel behaviour.

In order to study the importance of the physical environment, knowledge and attitudes compared to resources and background a series of hierarchical regression analyses were carried out. Between 37 and 46 per cent of the variance in driving distance, travel behaviour and acceptance could be explained. The variables of particular interest for the study: living area, environmental knowledge and attitudes, intentionally were given the least favoured positions. Table 1 shows that resources and background variables accounted for most of the variance in driving distance and travel behaviour, but in the latter case, attitudes also contributed. Acceptance was mainly explained by attitudes and again a tendency was found for knowledge to explain some of the variance. However the physical environment did not contribute at all.

Table 1. Hierarchical regression analysis for driving distance (N=149), personal travel behaviour (N=157), and acceptance of traffic restrictions (N=161) among Lund residents.

	R^2 change					*R^2*
	Resources	*Background*	*Area*	*Knowledge*	*Attitudes*	
Driving distance	.34***	.07**	.00	.01	.02	.46***
Individual behaviour	.21***	.18***	.00	.01	.09***	.49***
Acceptance of traffic restrictions	.07**	.06*	.02	.03*	.21***	.37***

Resources=driving licence and car; Background=gender, age, civil status, children, distance to work, health causes and oversensitiveness to air pollution; Attitudes=environmental concern, public transport, hazard/efficacy perception, personal concern and car affection. * *p<.05*, ** *p<.01*, *** *p<.001*

A similar result was achieved in an analysis including also the politicians and civil servants, with attitudes accounting for 19 per cent and knowledge for five per cent of the variance in acceptance.

Comments

The major conclusion from this study was that the attitudes seemed more important than factual knowledge to acceptance of traffic restrictions as well as to travel behaviour. Another interesting result was that differences in traffic load in the physical living environment seemed to have no impact. This is contrary to indications of other studies and it was therefore thought to be due to small difference in the perception of the environmental effects between the two areas (Arcury & Christianson, 1990; Gärling & Sandberg, 1990).

Study II

Participants

The second study was an intervention study. According to the theoretical model it constitutes an attempt to induce change in the individual mediators attitudes and knowledge by manipulating the physical environment as an outcome of the choice of transportation. The manipulation was carried out in a computerised gaming simulation. Considering that an antecedent educational strategy seems most efficient in preventing polluting travel behaviour in a long-term perspective, we turned to children and adolescents (Gardner & Stern, 1996).

A sample of 288 children at junior level and adolescents at senior level were reached through contacts with schools in Lund (response rate 92%). The schools were selected from the City Centre and suburban residential areas, corresponding to the North Common. At the end of the semester, seven pupils could not complete the post-test, because they had moved from the class, attended special education or were on vacation. As shown in Table 2 the pupils in each age group were divided into treatment group and control groups.

Table 2. Pupils in treatment and control groups taking part in the intervention study.

	Children		*Adolescents*	
	Treatment group	*Control group*	*Treatment group*	*Control group*
N	58	71	102	57
Mean age (years)	7:10	7:11	13:10	13:10

Materials

The computerised gaming simulation "Traffic Jam" introduced in the treatment group was designed to show the environmental consequences of various choices of transportation. It was considered more important to focus on emotional aspects than to present extensive factual information about ecology (Johansson & Küller, in press). In brief the player meets a town where the inhabitants have severely impaired the environment and their own health by devastating choices of transportation. The player is to guide the inhabitants towards pro-environmental travel behaviour through a hero figure, who serves as a model of modal choices. Throughout one week the player is given a number of daily journeys to be completed within a set time limit. The environmental consequences of the players' choices are calculated from contemporary data of Swedes' travel habits and local measures of environmental impact caused by various means of transport. At the end of each day the player as a feedback is informed of the current state of health and the environment.

Measurements, design and procedures

The dependent variables, attitudes of environmental concern, hazard perception and car affection, as well as factual environmental knowledge, were measured by questionnaires specifically developed for children and adolescents (Johansson, 2000). The experimenter visited each participating class on two occasions for pre-testing of attitudes and knowledge. After pre-testing, classes were matched and assigned to treatment respectively control groups. The gaming simulation was then installed at computers in the schools of the treatment group, whereas the control group began working with alternative computer assignments. During the intervention period, which lasted approximately four weeks, each pupil in the treatment group worked with Traffic Jam on four different occasions and pupils in the control group in a similar way worked with their computer assignments. Two post-tests of attitudes and knowledge were completed approximately four weeks after the intervention period had terminated. After the Christmas Holidays two copies of the adult attitude questionnaire and an attached return envelope were distributed to the pupils, to take home to their parents.

The collected data were treated by means of analysis of variance, repeated measures in SPSS (Norusis & SPSS, 1993). The level of significance was set to $p = .05$.

Effects of the intervention

In the post-tests administrated one month after the intervention period had finished, no significant improvements could be seen in the indices of factual environmental knowledge.

Among the children as a group, the computerised gaming simulation did not contribute to increased environmental concern or hazard perception, nor to decreased car affection. Instead hazard perception went in the opposite direction and in comparison to the control group decreased (interaction $p < .05$). Among the adolescents Traffic Jam turned the common tendency of decreasing pro-environmental attitudes into an increased concern for the environment and a stronger perception of traffic as hazardous to environment and health in the treatment group (both interactions: $p < .05$). The attitude towards the car was not affected by the intervention.

Comments

The study confirmed the importance of evaluating environmental education materials on various age groups. The gaming simulation was partly successful and showed persistence over time among the adolescents, but it cannot be recommended among children for educational purposes. It therefore seems necessary to develop strategies better adapted to this age group.

It has been claimed that to be effective, environmental education must take on a holistic view and last over many years (Utbildningsdepartementet, 1994). Palmer and Neal (1994) claim that environmental education should include education for the environment, about the environment and in or through the environment. Obviously, the gaming simulation educated for the environment only, and to be of value it should be combined with other methods.

General Conclusions

The results of the project shows that the physical and social environment should allow for more pro-environmental means of transportation and make the car a less attractive alternative. The relation between acceptance and travel behaviour, and the identified attitudes, but also to some extent knowledge, implies that parallel to planning for pro-environmental alternatives and restrictions for the private car, educational strategies should be applied. Preferably such strategies should not only present facts and figures but also include the emotional aspects of the problem (Iozzi, 1989; Zimmerman, 1996). It might be successful to strengthen environmental concern and underline the idea of the car as hazardous and at the same time play down the affection for the private car.

Since travel behaviours tend to become habitual, it might be rewarding to promote attitudes related to pro-environmental travel behaviour at an early age (Verplanken, Aarts, A. Van Knippenberg, & C. Van Knippenberg, 1994; Verplanken, Aarts, A. Van Knippenberg, & Moonen, 1998). In the early teens environmental concern and hazard perception could be promoted by using a computerised gaming simulation where the consequences for health and environment of choice of transportation is shown by visible and auditory feedback of an emotional kind. Among children, however, other methods of promoting pro-environmental attitudes need to be considered.

References

Arcury, T. A., & Christianson, E. H. (1990). Environmental worldview in response to environmental problems. Kentucky 1984 and 1988 compared. *Environment and Behavior, 22* (3), 387-407.

Dwyer, W. O., Leeming, F. C., Cobern, M. K., Porter, B. E., & Jackson, J. M. (1993). Critical review of behavioral interventions to preserve the environment: Research since 1980. *Environment and Behavior, 25* (3), 275-321.

Gardner, G. T., & Stern, P. C. (1996). *Environmental problems and human behavior.* Boston: Allyn & Bacon.

Gärling, T., & Sandberg, L. (1990). Faktorer som påverkar bilhushålls avsikter att resa miljövänligt [Factors influencing the intention of households with car to pro-environmental travelling]. Umeå: Umeå Universitet, Trafik och Transport forskningsenheten.

Iozzi, L. A. (1989). What research says to the educator part one: Environmental education and the affective domain. *Journal of Environmental Education, 20* (3), 3-9.

Johansson, M. (2000). Identification and promotion of attitudes related to pro-environmental travel behaviour. Unpublished doctoral dissertation, Lund University, Lund, Sweden.

Johansson, M., & Küller, R. (in press). Traffic Jam - psychological assessment of a gaming simulation. *Simulation & Gaming.*

Küller, R. (1991). Environmental assessment from a neuropsychological perspective. In T. Gärling and G. W. Evans (Eds.), *Environment, cognition and action: An integrated approach*, (pp. 111-147). Oxford: Oxford University Press.

Küller, R., & Laike, T. (1993). Metamorphosis in traffic behavior. In C. Mazis, C. Karaletsou and K. Tsoukala (Eds.), *Proceedings of the twelfth biennal conference of IAPS*, Vol. 5, (pp. 61-65). Thessaloniki: Aristotle University of Thessaloniki, Publications Office.

Linderholm, L., Ljungberg, C., & Carlson, P. (1993). Bättre cykeltrafik i Lund [Improved bike traffic in Lund]. Lund: Trivector.

Lunds Kommun (1995). Gatu- och trafiknämndens verksamhetsberättelse [Annual report from Lund Municipality street and traffic committee]. Lund: Author.

Lunds Kommun (1999). Statistisk årsbok [Statistical yearbook]. Lund: Author.

Norusis, M. J., & SPSS Inc. (1993). *SPSS for Windows*. Chicago: SPSS Inc.

Palmer, J., & Neal, P. (1994). *The handbook of environmental education.* London: Routledge.

SPSSx User's Guide (1986). New York: Mc Graw-Hill.

Swedish Environmental Protection Agency (1999). Fifteen. Sweden's objectives for environmental quality -the responsibility of our generation. Solna: Author.

Trivector (1998). LundaMats - ett helhetsgrepp för miljöanpassat transportsystem i Lund. Sammanfattning [LundaMats- a comprehensive approach to a environmentally adapted transport system in Lund]. Report 8:1998. Lund: Author.

United Nations Conference on Environment and Development (1993). The Earth Summit the United Nations Conference on Environment and Development 1992, Rio de Janeiro. London: Graham & Trotman.

Utbildningsdepartementet (1994). Kursplaner för grundskolan [Curriculum for basic education (in Sweden)]. Stockholm: Author.

Verplanken, B., Aarts, H., Van Knippenberg, A., & Moonen, A. (1998). Habit versus planned behaviour: A field experiment. *British Journal of Social Psychology, 37*, 111-128.

Verplanken, B., Aarts, H., Van Knippenberg, A., & Van Knippenberg, C. (1994). Attitude versus general habit: Antecedents of travel mode choice. *Journal of Applied Social Psychology, 24* (4), 285-300.

Zimmerman, L. K. (1996). Knowledge, affect, and the environment: 15 years of research (1979-1993). *Journal of Environmental Education, 27* (3), 41-44.

Traffic and Transport Psychology,
T. Rothengatter and R.D. Huguenin (Editors)

41

Car Use: Lust and Must

Linda Steg

Introduction

The car is much more than just a means of transport. The way people talk about their cars, and the way cars are advertised make perfectly clear that the car is also a status symbol and that people can express themselves by means of their car. Moreover, driving is adventurous, it gives pleasure, thrill, and excitement. However, car use is still predominately explained through cognitive behaviour models that focus on instrumental factors related to car use, such as its speed, flexibility, and convenience. It is acknowledged that some deeper motives having to do with affect and symbolic functions of cars are playing important roles as well (e.g., Marsh & Collett, 1986; Sachs, 1984), but the supposed significance of these deeper motives is mainly based on theoretical reasoning. Little systematic research has been done on different (categories of) motives for car use. Yet, some recent empirical studies suggest that car use might be better explained when these deeper motives are taken into account too. For example, Stradling, Meadows and Beatty (1999) reported two affective benefits of car driving: being independent and getting a sense of personal identity from driving a car. It appeared that people who value these affective benefits of car use more are less inclined to reduce their car use. Sandqvist and Kriström (2001) found that people who indicate that car driving enhances the quality of their life are more likely to posses and drive a car. They conclude that people buy and drive cars simply because they like to, and not (only) because they have a real utilitarian need for a car or a practical reason to drive. Steg, Vlek and Slotegraaf (2001) also suggest that car use is attractive because of its affective and symbolic functions, next to its instrumental values.

Dittmar (1992) contends that material possessions, such as motor cars, represent instrumental values as well as by symbolic values. The symbolic values refer to the identity of a person. They are twofold: the expression of the self, and a social-categorical expression indicating one's social position or group membership. Moreover, according to Dittmar, the use of material goods might fulfil three functions: instrumental, symbolic, and affective. Applied to car use, this implies that car use has an instrumental function (i.e., it enables activities), a symbolic function (i.e., the car is a means to express yourself or your social position), and an emotional function in connection with deeper, non-instrumental needs and desires. Note that these three functions might be intertwined, e.g., an instrumental motive may also serve as an emotional function.

Dittmar's (1992) propositions seem to be well in line whit everyday practice of automobile marketing. In advertisements, TV-commercials and specific automobile magazines, it is apparent that, either explicitly or implicitly, appeals are made to people's sensitivities to power, control, self-esteem and social status. Car advertisements focus strongly on emotions and feelings evoked by car use. Cars are advertised by using slogans as 'How adventurous are you?', 'The hidden power', 'Your favourite toy', 'Go to the beach with your Spanish lover'. In contrast to car advertisers, governments follow a rather different approach. They focus on the instrumental function of cars, like travel time and costs. Attempts to reduce the use of motor cars will be more effective if they are directed at the main motives for car use.

Based on Dittmar's propositions and an explorative study on motives for car use, a motivational model to explain car use was developed (see Steg, Brand, Rooijers & Vlek, 1998; Steg & Tertoolen, 1999; Steg et al., 2001). This model distinguishes three classes of motives for car use: instrumental, social and affective (see Figure 1). Instrumental motives refer to the convenience or inconvenience of car use, and to the more or less objective consequences of car use, such as its speed, flexibility, safety and environmental problems resulting from car use. Social motives refer to the fact that people can express themselves and their social position by driving a car, that people can compare their car and car use with others, and to social norms. Affect refers to various emotions that are evoked by using a car, that is, car use may potentially alter people's mood and people might anticipate these (positive) feelings when making travel choices.

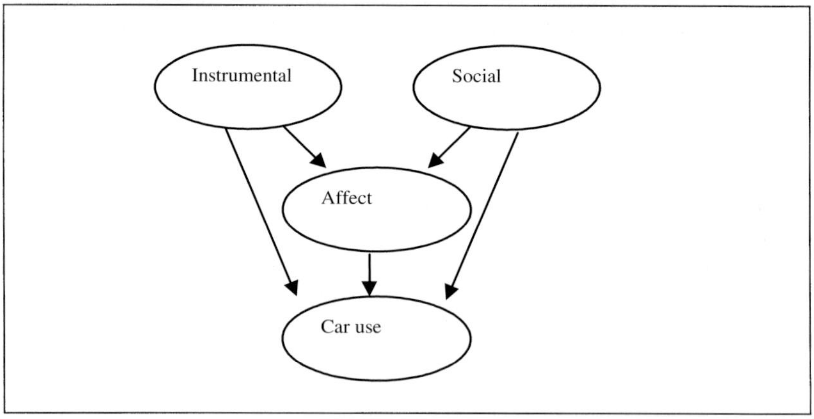

Figure 1. Motivational model to explain car use

Each of these three categories of motives are the subject of distinctive psychological theories and models, and measures of each of the motives categories have been developed based on these theories and models. Attitude models (e.g., Fishbein & Ajzen, 1975; Ajzen, 1985) usually focus on instrumental motives. It is assumed that attitudes are dependent on beliefs on outcomes of a specific behaviour and evaluations of the importance of those outcomes. In most study, especially beliefs on instrumental outcomes are measured (e.g., costs, time, flexibility; see Steg, 1996, for an overview).

Three theories on social motives might be relevant to explain car use. First, social comparison theory implies that people continuously compare their possessions, behaviour and opinions with those of others (Festinger, 1954). Generally, people aim to be superior to others, while not being too deviant. Individual differences exist in the extent to which people are inclined to social comparisons. Second, the self-presentation theory (e.g., Schlenker, 1980) proposes that people present themselves in a way that is congruent with their self-image. This theory is relevant because people might get a sense of personal identity from driving a car (see also Dittmar, 1992). Third, the theory of normative conduct (Cialdini, Kallgren & Reno, 1991) stresses the importance of social norms in influencing behaviour. Two types of social norms are distinguished: injunctive norms (i.e., perceptions of expectations of others) and descriptive norms (i.e., perceptions of what others actually do).

Affect might influence behaviour, for people might anticipate emotions that are evoked by behaviour (such as car use; Manstead & Parker, 1995). According to Russell and colleagues, affective reactions can be categorised on two dimensions: pleasure and arousal (e.g., Mehrabian & Russell, 1974; Russell & Lanius, 1984). Russell claims that all human emotions are based on a combination of pleasure and arousal.

The main goal of this study was to examine to what extent instrumental, social and affective motives contribute to the explanation of car use for commuting during rush hours. Furthermore, it was examined which group differences exist in the evaluation of the three kinds of motives for car use between groups differing in car habit and socio-demographics.

Method

Respondents and questionnaire

A survey study was conducted in September 1999. All respondents lived in or around Rotterdam, a region in the Netherlands often confronted with traffic jams. Only respondents who regularly travelled during rush hours were asked to participate; 52% of them were willing to do so. The mean age of respondents was 42 years; 73% of the respondents were male. The socio-demographic characteristics of the sample were comparable to those of a similar study among car users who often are confronted with traffic jams (Bureau Goudappel Coffeng, 1997).

Respondents were send a questionnaire on, among other things, their car use for commuting, their motives for car use, their possibilities to use alternative modes of transport, and their evaluation of policy scenarios. The results on the availability of alternatives and the evaluation of policy scenarios are not discussed here. A detailed overview of the study design, respondents, and results is given in Steg et al. (1999).

Measures

The measures of instrumental, social and affective motives were based on common measurements in Social Psychology (see Introduction).

Instrumental motives. The measure of instrumental motives was based on an 'expectancy-value' model (e.g., Fishbein & Ajzen, 1975; Ajzen, 1985). Respondents indicated whether using a car during rush hours is cheap, fast, independent, safe, environmentally friendly, easy, comfortable and private. Scores could range from 1 'very unlikely' to 5 'very likely'. Furthermore, they indicated whether these aspects are important for their travel behaviour; scores could range from 1 'not important at all' to 5 'very important'. Previous research revealed that these aspects contributed strongly to the (un)attractiveness of car use (see Steg et al., 2001). For each aspect, scores on both variables were multiplied. Next, the mean product score over the aspects was computed. Scores on 'instrumental motives' could vary from 1 'negative' to 25 'positive'. The reliability of this scale was high (Cronbach's α = .87). On average, respondents judged the instrumental motives not positively, but also not negatively (M = 12.1).

Social motives. Three indicators of social motives were used. Social comparison and self presentation was measured by a seven item scale (i.e. 'I will not easily travel by bike or bus when all my colleagues travel by car', 'I do not like travelling by public transport if all my colleagues travel by car', 'Travelling by car suits me better than travelling by bike or public transport', 'I pay attention to what kind of car others drive', 'I like to know which transport mode others use to commute', 'I pity people who do not commute by car' and 'I feel ashamed when I do not commute by car'). A principal components analysis revealed that all seven items loaded high on the first factor (r > .43). Therefore, the mean score on the seven items was computed. Scores on this variable could vary from 1 'car is not important for self presentation and no social comparison' to 5 'car is very important for self presentation and strong social comparison'; Cronbach's α of this scale was .64. On average, car use appeared not to be very important for the self presentation, and people did not strongly compare their car use with others car use (M = 1.8).

Two kinds of social norms were distinguished, i.e. perceptions of expectations of others (injunctive norms) and behaviour of others (descriptive norms; Cialdini, Kallgren & Reno, 1991). First, respondents indicated what they think other people expect them to do, i.e. 'My family thinks I should not commute by car', 'My colleagues would think it is peculiar not to commute by car' and 'My friends think the problems of car use during rush hours are exaggerated'. Scores could vary from 1 'strongly disagree' to 5 'strongly agree'. It was not possible to create a new, reliable scale on the basis of the scores on these items. Apparently, these reference groups do not have the same beliefs. Therefore, scores on the three 'injunctive social norms' were examined separately. Scores on the first item were recoded as to make a high score reflect a pro-car norm. Mean scores on the three items were 2.0, 1.7, and 2.5, respectively.

Second, respondents indicated how their friends, family and colleagues, respectively, travelled to work. Scores on the variable 'descriptive norm' were based on the mean score on these three items and could vary from 1'others never drive to work' to 5 'others always drive to work', Cronbach's α of this scale was .62. On average, most other people commuted by car ($M = 4.0$).

Affect. As said before, affective appraisals may be categorised on two dimensions: pleasure and arousal. Therefore, two indicators of affect were distinguished. Respondents indicated to what extent various emotions are evoked when they are commuting on five point scales. The following three items assessed the degree of pleasure: angry - happy; unsatisfied - satisfied, annoyance - pleasure. The mean score on these three items was computed; scores could vary from 1 'not pleasurable' to 5 'very pleasurable'. Cronbach's α of this scale was .81. Arousal was based on the items tense - relaxed; hurried - peaceful; aroused - calm. Again, mean scores were computed; scores could vary from 1 'not arousing' to 5 'very arousing'. Cronbach's α of this scale was .70. On average, respondents evaluated car use as not pleasurable nor annoying ($M = 2.8$) and as not very arousing ($M = 2.8$). Next, respondents indicated whether they felt in control when driving a car for commuting (no control - control and dependent - independent). Again, mean scores were computed; scores on this variable could vary from 1 'no control' to 5 'in control'. Cronbach's α of this scale was .69. On average, respondents felt in control while driving ($M = 3.9$).

Car use. Respondents indicated how often they commuted, and how often they used their car for commuting. The percentage of car trips for commuting was used as the dependent variable in the analyses.

Results

Correlations between car use and motives for car use

Apart from the variables 'pleasure' and 'the expectations of friends', all motives appeared to be significantly related to car use (see Table 1). In general, the more positive respondents evaluated the motives, the more often they commuted by car. Car use was especially related to the behaviour of others (descriptive norms). The more respondents thought others commute by car, the more respondents thought colleagues and family expect them to drive to work, the more they compare themselves with other and the more important car use is for their self presentation, the more often they drove to work. Moreover, the more often respondents commuted by car, the more favourably they evaluated the instrumental motives, and the more they feel in control when driving. Arousal was negatively related to car use, i.e., the more often the respondents drive to work, the less arousing car use is to them. Apparently, car use was evaluated as arousing because driving in heavy traffic and traffic jams is stressful.

Explaining car use

Table 2 shows that 28% of the variance in the percentage of car trips could be explained by the motives for car use. Especially social motives (behaviour of others, expectations of family, and social comparison and self presentation) and affect (arousal) contributed to the explanation of car use. Respondents commuted more often by car when others also drive to work, when their family expects them to do so, when they compare their car use with others and think using a car suits them, and when they think car use is less arousing (i.e. stressful). Instrumental motives, expectations of colleagues and friends, pleasure, and feelings of control did not contribute to the explanation of the percentage of car trips.

Table 1. Pearson's product-moment correlations between motives and car use

	% car trips
Instrumental	
Instrumental motives	.24***
Social	
Social comparison and self presentation	.17*
Descriptive norms (behaviour of others)	.40***
Expectations colleagues	.22*
Expectations family	.31**
Expectations friends	.06
Affect	
Pleasure	.10
Arousal	-.23**
Control	.25**

*** $p < .001$; ** $p < .01$; * $p < .05$

Table 2. Stepwise regression of car-use motives on percentage of car trips for commuting.

Motive	R^2	R^2*-change*	*F-change*	β
Descriptive norm (behaviour of others)	.16	.16	20.13	.30
Expectations family	.20	.04	5.83	.23
Arousal	.24	.04	5.25	-.21
Social comparison and self presentation	.28	.04	5.11	.19

Differences between respondents groups

First, it was examined whether group differences exist in motives for car use between groups differing in car habit. Two groups were distinguished: respondents who only commuted by car (59%), and respondents who also (or only) used other means of transport (41%). Table 3 shows that, in general, habitual drivers evaluated the motives for car use more positively than infrequent car users did. Respondents who always commuted by car evaluated the instrumental motives more positively, indicated that others more often use their car too, that their family expects them to drive to work, and thought that car use is less arousing (stressful) than respondents who also use other modes of transport did.

Furthermore, differences in the evaluation of the motives were found for groups differing in socio demographics. Table 4 shows that male respondents evaluated some of the social and affective motives more favourably than female respondents did. Male respondents compared their car use more often with others and think the car is more important for their self presentation than women did. Men also thought car use for commuting is less stressful and they felt more in control when driving a car than women did. Table 5 reveals that younger respondents (20 - 30 years) evaluated car use as more pleasurable than the other age groups did (i.e. respondents older than 31 year). Finally, the higher income groups more strongly thought that colleagues expect them to travel by car than the lower income groups did (see Table 6).

Table 3. Differences in motives for car use between habitual car users and infrequent drivers.

Motive	*Habitual drivers*	*Infrequent drivers*
Instrumental motives[1]	12.8	11.0
Descriptive norm (behaviour others)[2]	4.3	3.7
Expectations family[2]	4.3	3.8
Arousal[3]	2.7	2.9

Note: [1] *Scores could vary from 1 ='negative' to 25 'positive'.* [2] *Scores could vary from 1 'anti car' to 5 'pro car'.* [3] *Scores could vary from 1 'not arousing' to 5 'very arousing'.*

Table 4. Gender differences in motives for car use.

Motive	*Men*	*Women*
Social comparison and self presentation[1]	1.9	1.6
Arousal[2]	2.7	3.1
Control[3]	4.0	3.6

Note: [1] *Scores could vary from 1 'anti car' to 5 'pro car'.* [2] *Scores could vary from 1 'not arousing' to 5 'very arousing'.* [3] *Scores could vary from 1 'no control' to 5 'in control'.*

Table 5. Differences between age groups in motives for car use

Motive	*20-30 years*	*31-40 years*	*41-50 years*	*50 years and older*
Pleasure	3.2	2.7	2.6	2.8

Note. Scores could vary from 1 'not pleasurable' to 5 'very pleasurable'.

Table 6. Differences between income groups in motives for car use.

Motive	*< Dfl 3500*	*Dfl 3500-4500*	*Dfl 4500-5500*	*> Dfl 5500*
Expectation colleagues	1.4	1.6	1.8	2.2

Note. Scores could vary from 1 'anti car' to 5 'pro car'.

Conclusions

On average, respondents did not evaluate car use during rush hours very favourable. Even so, a majority of the respondents (i.e., 59%) always commuted by car, while only 15% never commuted by car. This may partly be due to the fact that no feasible alternatives are available. However, 49% of the respondents indicated that it would be possible for them to commute by other means of transport (see Steg et al., 1999). Apparently, commuting by car is still more attractive than travelling with alternative modes of transport. This might be an important point to address in future research.

Car use is significantly correlated with all three categories of car use motives. The more positively respondents evaluated the instrumental, social and affective motives for car use, the more often they commuted by car. Interestingly, respondents used their car less often when they think car use is stressful (arousing in a negative sense). Only social and affective motives contributed significantly to the explanation of car use. So, differences in car use especially result from differences in the evaluation of the social and affective motives, and not from differences in the importance of the instrumental function of car use. These results suggest that policy makers should take these social and affective factors into account when developing and implementing car travel reduction policies. In this study, we focussed on commuting traffic. These trips might be considered as highly functional. Social and affective motives might even play a more significant role when making trips for other purposes, e.g., trips for recreational or social purposes.

Several group differences were found in the evaluation of the car-use motives. Respondents who always commuted by car evaluated specific instrumental, social and affective motives more positively than respondents who also used other modes of transport did. Furthermore, men evaluated social and affective motives more positively than women did. Especially men perceived the car as a symbol to express their personality and they appeared to have a stronger affective relationship with their car, while women thought car use is more stressful than men did. Hardly any differences were found in the evaluation of the various car-use motives between different age groups and income groups. However, younger respondents evaluated car use as more pleasurable than older respondents did, while the higher income groups more strongly thought their colleagues expect them to commute by car than the lower income groups did.

The results of this study suggest that the three classes of car-use motives are multi dimensional constructs. Within each class of motives different specific motives for car use may be distinguished, and each of these specific motives might contribute to the explanation of car use. For example, all three kinds of social motives, i.e., the behaviour of others (descriptive norms), the perception of expectations of family (injunctive norm), and the extent to which respondents compared their car use with others and thought car use suits them (social comparison and self presentation) appeared to contribute to the explanation of car use. Future research should examine the different motive categories in more detail. Especially the role of social and affective motives should be examined more extensively, for these have not often been studied in traffic psychology. This study did not incorporate all relevant instrumental, social and affective motives for car use. Future research might focus on factors such as power, positive arousal (kick of car use), personality, and territoriality (e.g., Fraine, Smith & Zinkiewicz, 2000). Furthermore, future research could examine instrumental, social and affective motives for other means of transport and examine whether car use is more (or less) attractive than other travel modes because of its instrumental, social and/or affective values. Moreover, future research can be directed at examining the role of instrumental, social and affective motive in explaining car use (and/or the use of alternatives modes of transport) for other trip purposes.

Acknowledgements

This study was supported by a grant from the Ministry of Transport and Public Works, The Netherlands. A full description of the research is given in Steg, Uneken & Vlek (1999).

References

Ajzen, I. (1985). From intentions to actions: A theory of planned behavior. In J. Kuhl & J. Beckman (Eds.), *Action control: from cognitions to behavior*. Heidelberg: Springer.

Bureau Goudappel Coffeng (1997). Marktprofiel van de filerijder. Eindrapport [Profile of the driver confronted with traffic jams. Final Report]. Deventer, The Netherlands: Bureau Goudappel Coffeng.

Cialdini, R.B., Kallgren, C.A., & Reno, R.R. (1991) A focus theory of normative conduct: a theoretical refinement and reevaluation of the role of norms in human behavior. In L. Berkowitz (Ed.), *Advances in Experimental Social Psychology, 24*, 201-234.

Dittmar, H. (1992). *The social psychology of material possessions: To have is to be*. Hemel Hempstead, UK: Havester Wheatsheaf; New York: St. Martin's Press.

Festinger, L. (1954). A theory of social comparison processes. Human Relations, 7, 117-140.

Fishbein, M., & Ajzen I. (1975). *Belief, attitude, intention and behavior: an introduction to theory and research*. Reading: Addison-Wesley Publishing Company.

Fraine, G., Smith, S., & Zinkiewicz, L. (2000). The private car: A home on the road? In R. McLure (Ed.), *Readings in injury prevention and control: Proceedings of the third national conference on injury prevention and control* (pp. 63-66). Brisbane: Centre of National Research on Disability and Rehabilitation Medicine.

Manstead, A.S.R., & Parker, D. (1995). Evaluating and extending the theory of planned behaviour. In W. Stroebe & M. Hewstone (Eds.), *European Review of Social Psychology* (Vol. 6, pp. 69-95). Chichester, England: John Wiley & Sons.

Marsh, P., & Collett, P. (1986). *Driving passion: the psychology of the car*. London: Cape.

Mehrabian, A., & Russell, J.A. (1974*). An approach to environmental psychology*. Cambridge (Mass.): MIT Press.

Russell, J.A., & Lanius, U.F. (1984). Adaption level and the affective appraisal of environments. *Journal of Environmental Psychology, 4*, 119-135.

Sachs, W. (1984). *Die Liebe zum Automobil. Ein Rückblick in die Geschichte unserer Wünsche.* Reinbeck bei Hamburg: Rowohlt.

Sandqvist, K., & Kriström, S. (2001). Getting along without a family car. The role of automobile in adolescents' experience and attitudes. Part I. Inner city Stockholm. Stockholm, Sweden: Institutionen för individ, omvärld och lärande.

Schlenker, B.R. (1980). *Impression management: The self-concept, social identity, and interpersonal relations*. Monterey, CA: Brooks/Cole.

Steg, E.M. (1996). Gedragsverandering ter vermindering van het autogebruik. Theoretische analyse en empirische studie over probleembesef, verminderingsbereidheid en beoordeling van beleidsmaatregelen [Behaviour Change for Reducing the Use of Motor-Cars. Theoretical Analysis and Empirical Study on Problem Awareness, Willingness-to-Change and Evaluation of Policy Measures]. Doctoral Dissertation, Faculty of Psychological, Pedagogical, and Sociological Sciences, University of Groningen, The Netherlands. (in Dutch).

Steg, E.M., Brand, A.B., Rooijers, A.J. & Vlek, C.A.J. (1998). Affective motives for car use. An extensive summary (COV 98-05). Groningen, the Netherlands: Centre for Environmental and Traffic Psychology, University of Groningen.

Steg, L., & Tertoolen, G. (1999). Affective Motives for Car Use. In: PTRC, Transport Policy, Planning and Practice. *Proceedings of the European Transport Conference* (Proceedings of Seminar B, pp. 13-27). London: PTRC.

Steg, E.M., Uneken, E., & Vlek, C.A.J. (1999). Diepere drijfveren voor het autogebruik in de spits. Betekenis van psychologisch motieven voor het verkeers- en vervoerbeleid [Intrinsic motives for car use during rush hours. Significance of psychological motives for traffic policies] (COV 99-08).Groningen/Rotterdam, the Netherlands: Centre for Environmental and Traffic Psychology, University of Groningen/Adviesdienst Verkeer en Vervoer.

Steg, L., Vlek, C., & Slotegraaf, G. (2001). Instrumental-reasoned and symbolic-affective motives for using a motor car. *Transportation Research Part F, 4,* 151-169.

Stradling, S.G., Meadows, M.L., & Beatty, S. (1999). Factors affecting car use choices. Edinburgh, UK: Transport Research Institute, Napier University.

Traffic and Transport Psychology,
T. Rothengatter and R.D. Huguenin (Editors)

42

Is Employees' Achievement Motivation and Performance Affected by Commuting Stress?

Herbert Gstalter and Wolfgang Fastenmeier

Introduction

In recent years there have been two steady developments as far as commuting to work is concerned: The average distance between home and working place has been growing and correspondingly the modal split has been changing. Fewer trips can be accomplished by walking or cycling and the proportion of car use is still growing compared with the public transport sector. For safety and environmental reasons, this development should be stopped. The German Traffic Safety Council started an initiative to install mobility consultants in large organisations to encourage the use of public transport, manage commuting teams of employees and provide buses etc. The role of these consultants could be strengthened, if it were possible to show that employees arrive at their workplaces in a suboptimal condition because of strain as an after-effect of stress through commuting long distances in the car. Therefore, a study was developed to investigate the influence of commuter stress on mood, achievement motivation and mental fitness. The study design and some selected results are presented below.

Study Design

Twohundred-and-twenty subjects from 7 different companies and organisations took part in the study. All organisations were based in Munich or its surroundings. The dependent variable was the motivational and mental state of the subjects when they arrived at their working places, i.e. their mood, mental capacity and achievement motivation. This state may be influenced by the commuting experience immediately before, but also by various other variables like the situation at home on that particular morning before the trip, or the work situation and its anticipation by the subjects and of course by various personal characteristics. These components are shown in a simplified manner in Figure 1.

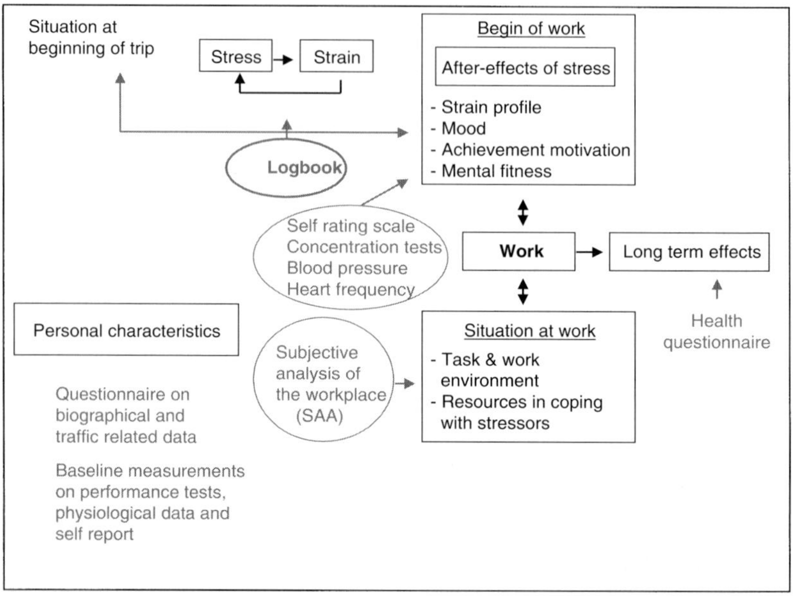

Figure 1. Study design.

To assess the condition of the subjects, we used a shortened version of an approved self rating scale (Nitsch & Udris, 1976). The subjects had to decide, how good their present condition was, by choosing from 20 descriptive adjectives. These could be merged to two dimensions in the computation giving estimates of the motivation and ability to work. Afterwards a concentration test ("d2", Brickenkamp, 1976) was administered to the subjects. Their blood pressure and heart frequency were also measured.

During the study all our subjects had to keep a travel logbook which played a central role in the collection of data about trips to work. They had to answer questions concerning the situation and their condition immediately before they started the trip (about sleep duration and quality, if they still felt tired or not, if they had had breakfast etc.). Directly after reaching their workplace, the subjects had to score on different items that described their trip to work and to scale how comfortable or stressful it had been. There were two versions of the logbook (one for car-driving and another for public transport). Both versions were a mixture of standardized items in a fixed format and open comments.

To assess the working situation of our subjects, we constructed a 12-item mini questionnaire about stressors and resources at work. This questionnaire is in the tradition of Udris & Alioth (1980). Another short questionnaire dealing with state of health and psychosomatic complaints had to be answered by the subjects at the beginning of the study. At the same time, information was collected about important biographical data, traffic related attitudes, characteristics of the route to work etc.

Biographical information, the description of the working environment and the health questionnaire were obtained at the beginning of the study. The same process was used to gain baseline measurements on the physiological data, the concentration task and the self-rating scale. Each subject kept the logbook for ten working days. The measurements at the workplace after the trip were taken three times for each subject.

Results

Subjects

The subjects travelled to work during the study in their normal fashion. In the computation we split the total sample into commuters and non-commuters. The commuters were defined as the subgroup of subjects taking 45 minutes or more for their trip to work. This distinction is of course arbitrary; we chose it because Costa, Pickup & Dimartino (1988) used this distinction and we wanted to be able to compare the results of both studies. This procedure resulted in 38% "Commuters" (30% car drivers, 70 % public transport users) and 62% "Non-Commuters" (58% car drivers, 42 % public transport users). 59.5% of the subjects were male.

Health and psychosomatic complaints

There was no significant relationship between trip duration and general state of health. But on specific health problems, commuters had worse self ratings than non-commuters: they more often suffered from problems with the back, the eyes, the respiratory and the gastrointestinal systems. In the commuter group, the health problems were significantly more severe within the car commuter subgroup.

Psychosomatic complaints displayed a fairly similar pattern (see Table 1). The comparison of all commuters to non-commuters did not show large differences (exception: nervousness), but between short and long car-trips the frequency of complaints differs significantly to the disadvantage of the car commuter subsample. Commuters with long car-trips clearly suffered more often from tiredness, sleep problems, lack of concentration, nervousness and anxiety. This is of course a condensed view of the actual condition of the subjects and cannot be regarded as a proof of a causal relationship between commuting as a cause and health problems as effect. Only longitudinal studies could clarify this relationship. The pattern of complaints is, however, quite similar to that found in other studies on commuter health (e.g. Costa et al., 1988).

Situation at the beginning of the trip

According to our hypothesis there was no difference in the fitness between car users and public transport users in the morning, but commuters felt worse compared to non-commuters. Commuters got up half an hour earlier and their sleep duration was 30 minutes shorter. Whereas the majority of non-commuters had breakfast at home in the morning, the commuters did not. The condition of the commuters is obviously worse before the trip. The non-commuters can sleep longer, feel more cheerful after waking up and have more time to have a snack at home.

Table 1. Psychosomatic complaints of commuters and non-commuters, related to use of car or public transport.

Do you often suffer from:	*Total*	*Commuters*			*Non-Commuters*			*Car Total*	*Public Transp. Total*
		Car	*PT*	*Total*	*Car*	*PT*	*Total*		
Tiredness	41,8	56,3	47,3	49,3	38,2	45,3	41,3	41,7	46,3
Sleep problems	22,3	43,8	25,5	29,6	17,6	26,4	21,5	22,6	25,9
Nervousness	20,5	43,8	27,3	31,0	14,7	15,1	14,9	20,2	21,3
Concentration problems	20,0	31,3	20,0	22,5	17,6	18,9	18,2	20,2	19,4
Anxiety	13,2	31,3	14,5	18,3	10,3	17,0	13,2	14,3	15,7

In contrast to the commuting car-drivers, commuters in the public transport systems can substitute the lack of sleep at least in part during the trip; the same holds true for eating. Indeed, 35 % of the public transport commuters reported in their logs that they had slept in subways, trams or buses.

Strain caused by the trip to work

The well-known fact that strain rises as a function of trip duration can be confirmed once more: Commuters felt significantly more strained than non-commuters (ANOVA, $p < .001$). Subjects with high strain ratings are most frequent in the subgroup of car commuters, revealing that the combination of long trips and car use is responsable for the maximum strain scores. In total, there is no significant difference between the travel modes. The effect of trip duration on the strain scores thus proves to be much stronger than that of travel mode.

Although the amount of strain reported is comparable, the stressors in the car are different from those in public transport. Figures 2 and 3 summarise the stressors that had been reported in the logbooks and that significantly (ANOVA, $p < .05$) influenced the result of the last item in the logbook: "How much do you feel strained by the trip?", that had to be answered on the 6-point rating scale.

Some of the strain influencing factors work in the same way, independently from travel mode: Feeling fit in the morning and starting the trip in nice weather conditions obviously operate as resources in coping with stressors during the way to work. The opposite is true for bad weather conditions and long trip duration: these factors are strain inducing in all travel modes. But, of course, mode specific stressors could be detected as well.

For car drivers, e.g. high traffic volumes represent a significant stress factor. High density traffic situations tend to be more complex, last longer and may create frustration and fear of arriving late at work. The proportion of high volumes and congestion was higher for the commuters. We assume that these situations occur mainly on the radial roads combining the city with its surrounding. So, commuters are not only exposed longer but also to more frustrating traffic conditions. Another source of stress for car drivers are daily annoyances such as construction sites, detours and quite often the behaviour of other traffic participants. Hazards have only been reported by 5% of the subjects, but their influence is significant. To our surprise the most important annoyances reported by the car drivers were foul and exhausted air inside the car and noise. Car commuters complained about bad air twice as often as noncommuters. It could be interesting to take a closer look at a possible link between these complaints and the increased health problems of long-trip commuters, that have been documented in the literature and are confirmed by our data (e.g. coughing, skin troubles, eye problems, respiratory system).

The typical troubles of public transport use are well-known to everybody and have often been documented: Draught, crowding, noise, microclimatic conditions, unpleasent smells are limiting the degree of comfort in trains and buses. The number of reported annoyances was doubled compared to car driver´s logbooks. The trip specific pattern of troubles was narrower in public transport; day to day variations of stressors were much stronger in car driving.

Subjective evaluation of the working situation

Subjects with good working conditions (low number of stressors and high resources) rated their state much more favourably in the self rating-scale than those with worse working conditions. Differences were significant for ratings of achievement motivation, readiness for social contact, social appreciation, self confidence and mood. Thus, the task and work environment has a very strong influence on people`s feelings even at the beginning of the working day. Subjects with positive evaluations concerning their work were slightly, but not significantly less strained by the commuting process.

State of the subjects at the end of their trip to work

No significant differences could be found compared to the baseline values. Neither blood pressure nor concentration task performance changed and neither did the self-rating scale show any significant changes. That holds true for all subgroups, meaning that the subjects´ condition at the beginning of the working day was not worse than during the course of it. More surprisingly, we did not find differences between commuters and non-commuters; their fitness, mood and achievement motivation was comparable.

Finally, we split the sample into those, who felt strained by the commuting process (and told us so in the logs) and those who didn`t. As this analysis indicated, these subgroups differed clearly in the rating scales in the expected direction. The correlation between the logbook rating of strain through the trip and the overall self-rating score was $r=0.3$, meaning that about 10 % of the variance in the self-rating scale can be traced back to commuting strain. This is a significant, but not a large influence. That fits in with the fact that only 25% of our subjects rated their trips as "very" or "somewhat" stressful. One explanation lies in a strong selection effect: Whereas the majority of the car-drivers called car-driving "relaxing", the public transport users mostly rated it as "stressful" (compare Table 2).

Besides, more than 35% of the public tranport users answered that they wanted "to avoid stress" when they were asked to give reasons for their choice of travel mode. That means that most subjects had found an adequate or "convenient" (Stradling et al., 2000) way to manage their travel to work.

Table 2. Distribution of answers to the question: "Is car-driving stressing or relaxing?"

	Stressful	*Relaxing*
Car drivers	34%	66%
Public Transport users	73%	27%

What is even more crucial to mention is: taking into account the considerable differences between the commuters and non-commuters in the morning, the trip to work was, for many subjects, more of a resource than a stressor. Indeed, the public transport commuters used the time to doze or even sleep (35% told us so), thus compensating at least in part their sleep deficiency. The missed breakfast was also available for most of them in the subway or tram. The car drivers became more alert on their way, being engaged in a relaxing routine activity and getting away from an unfavourable point in their circadian rhythm.

Discussion

Do these results mean, that commuting to work cannot be regarded as a stressor? Despite the results, we have to limit the validity of the general statement with respect to the following aspects: (i) At least 23% of the subjects felt greatly or somewhat strained and scored significantly worse on the self-rating scale. At least a strong minority did not manage to avoid commuting stress that affected their condition on the arrival at the workplace; (ii) There was considerable intra-individual variance in the logbook stress ratings, showing that situational factors on the road strongly influence the commuters condition; (iii) The selection effect with respect to travel-mode choice is a very important explanation variable. Nearly all our subjects really had that choice, meaning that they owned a car and could also use a public transport line from their homes to work. In rural areas in particular this possibility does not exist; (iv) It is likely that the more complicated way of life, that long-distance commuters have, due to more limited time-budgets will show effects in the home and familiy situation first and only later in the working situation; (v) Commuter stress will strongly increase in interaction with other stressors like shift-work, or for females with a stressful role in the family.

References

Brickenkamp, R. (1976). *Test d2 - Aufmerksamkeits-Belastungstest*. Göttingen: Hogrefe.

Costa, G., Pickup, L., & Dimartino, V. (1988). Commuting- a further stress factor for working people; evidence from the European Community. *International Archives of Occupational and Environmental Health, 60*, 371-385.

Nitsch, J. R. & Udris, I. (1976). *Beanspruchung im Sport*. Wiesbaden: Limpert.

Stradling, S., Hine, J., & Wardman, M. (2000). Physical, cognitive and affective effort in travel mode choices. In ICTTP 2000, Abstracts, 70.

Udris, I. & Alioth, A. (1980). SAA - Fragebogen zur Subjektiven Arbeitsanalyse. In E. Martin et al. (Ed.), *Monotonie in der Industrie*. Stuttgart: Huber, 61-68.

Traffic and Transport Psychology,
T. Rothengatter and R.D. Huguenin (Editors)

43

Who Will Reduce Their Car Use - and Who Will Not?

Stephen Stradling, Michelle Meadows and Susan Beatty

Introduction

The 'traffic problem' in the UK was recognised as early as 1930 in the final 'Report of the Royal Commission on Transport' which noted:

"Speaking generally, there is no direction in which such a lack of vision has been evident as in the failure to cope with the great increase in the volume and speed of modern traffic in most of the great cities." (Cited in Jones, 1999).

Thus the 'traffic problem' is not a new problem, though its range, reach and impact on both urban and rural quality of life is now so pervasive as to demand solution. Its nature and extent was summarised by Transport 2000 in their Blueprint For Quality Public Transport (Transport 2000 Trust, 1997).

"Transport is in crisis. Current transport patterns have big environmental, social, and economic costs. Road casualties, pollution, noise, congestion, social isolation, damage to wildlife and the countryside, and resource depletion are just some of those costs. The argument for a sustainable transport policy has gained in force and urgency as evidence of environmental damage and of people's concern has mounted."

As the UK road system grinds towards gridlock, changes in transport thinking have necessarily taken place.

"Since the publication of the 1989 National Road Traffic Forecasts, with their predictions of exponential growth in traffic, there has been a shift in UK transport thinking away from a 'predict and provide' mentality, as the forecasts made it obvious that it would be impossible to build enough roads to satisfy demand. Instead, transport professionals have increasingly searched for ways to manage and reduce demand for private road transport." (Rye, 1998)

But if demand for private road transport is to be reduced, some changes in private car use will be necessary. This will require either fewer trips to be made overall so the number of car journeys reduces, though their relative standing in the mix of transport modes for personal travel may remain the same; or both the number and proportion of traffic miles made by car trips must be reduced, either by substituting another mode of travel, or by meeting journey purposes by travelling to nearer destinations. But transport joins up the places where people lead their lives, so reduction in use will only be achieved by private car users changing the organisation and articulation of their current patterns of life.

Motorists are naturally reluctant to do this, seeing themselves as TINA'd - There Is No Alternative. As a respondent in one survey put it: *"[We have a] nice house on an estate, but the nearest shop is four miles away, the nearest school is three-quarters of a mile away, the nearest pub is certainly a car drive."* (AA, 1998). Having made investment in the arrangements arising from current land-use planning - the separation and specialisation of location function - people see no viable alternative to continued car use.

Travel decisions are driven by the interaction of opportunity, obligation and inclination (Stradling, Meadows & Beatty, 1999, 2000a; Wardman, Hine & Stradling, 2001). In order to persuade individuals to reduce their private car use it will be helpful to know what they currently use their cars for, whether they would like to change their current level of car and public transport (PT) use, whether they think that circumstances will facilitate or impede any change of levels of use of the car or of alternatives to the car such as public transport, and which policy measures they might find effective in encouraging or coercing them to change. This paper addresses those questions using findings from a study of English motorists (Stradling et al, 1999).

Sample

Sevenhundredninety-one English car drivers responded to a postal questionnaire (response rate: 21%). Table 1 shows that the sample covered a wide range of values on the demographic variables: driver age, gender, socio-economic status, annual household income, and place of domicile; and on the driving variables: years of driving experience, size of engine, age of car, estimated annual driving mileage, whether the car was employer-owned, and the extent of driving 'as part of your work'.

Car Use

Both the number of journeys made by car in the UK and the proportion of all journeys that are car journeys have been inexorably increasing. The 'amplifier effect' of the car on personal mobility was noted by Begg (1998).

"Most car journeys were never made by public transport. The car's flexibility has encouraged additional journeys to be made. Households with one car make more than two-and-a-half times as many journeys each week as those without a car. And households with two or more cars make three-and-a-half times as many journeys."

Figures from the 1994/96 National Travel Survey (DETR, 1997: Table 2) make plain the changes in the UK in the last quarter of the 20th Century.

Table 1. Range of values on demographic and driving variables for 791 English car drivers.

Demographics	
Age	17 -> 83 years
Sex	M 61%; F 39%
SES	A/B, C1/C2, D/E, (economically) retired
Household Income	< £5K pa -> > £50K pa
Domicile	City, Town, Suburb, Village, Semi-rural & Rural
Driving Variables	
Driving Experience	1 year -> 60+ years
Engine Size	< 1 Litre -> > 2 Litres
Age of Car	1 year -> 10+ years
Annual Mileage	< 1K -> > 20K miles pa
Company Car	Yes / No
Drive As Work	Never -> Every working day

Table 2. Journeys per person per year in Great Britain 1975/76 to 1994/96[1].

	75/76	*85/86*	*89/91*	*94/96*	*% Change 75/76 - 94/96*[3]
Walk	325	350	328	303	-7
Bicycle	30	25	21	17	-43
Bus	107	83	73	65	-39
Rail + LU[2]	15	18	18	16	+6
Car	428	517	618	631	+47
Totals[3]	905	993	1058	1032	+14

[1] *Source: UK National Travel Survey.* [2] *London Underground* [3] *Added to original*

Bus and bicycle travel have declined substantially, walking and the use of rail and London Underground combined have remained relatively constant, while car journeys have increased by almost half as many again (+47%). Calculating the total journeys for each year reveals that this too is on the increase, by 14% in two decades. We are entering, in John Adams' felicitous phrase, a state of hypermobility (Adams, 1999).

For what purposes is the private car used? Analysis distinguished six main kinds of journeys for which our sample used their cars (Stradling et al., 1999, 2000a): (i) Driving as part of their work. Almost two-thirds of those in work (64%: 75% of males, 49% of females) said they drove a car 'as part of their work' at least some of the time (which proved to have implications for their safety on the road: Stradling, Meadows & Beatty, 2000b); (ii) Driving to and from work. 69% of car drivers in employment - 78% of those in full-time employment - used their car to travel to and from work 'every working day'; (iii) Child escort duties - ferrying children around, both to school and to other places; (iv) Life and network maintenance tasks such as shopping, visiting friends and relations, and evenings out; (v) Driving for holidays and weekends away; (6) Life enhancement activities such as voluntary work, hobby support or just driving for pleasure.

These are ordered here in likely decreasing degree of time pressure - or obligation to others. One complicating factor is multi-purpose trips ('trip-chaining'), which are more common amongst (multi-tasking) female than (mono-tasking) male drivers e.g., combining the school run and travel to work, a trip to the tip with the supermarket run.

The Road Traffic Reduction (UK Targets) Bill, debated in the Westminster Parliament on 30th January 1998, sought to propose targets for a reduction in total road traffic miles of 5% by 2005 and 10% by 2010, but for a government seeking transport policies to reduce car use, different targets may need to be set, and different strategies will need to be employed, for the reduction of private car traffic miles for each of these six different kinds of car use.

Preferred and Anticipated Changes in Car and Public Transport Use

The UK Government's July 1998 integrated transport White Paper 'A New Deal For Transport: Better For Everyone' asserted that "The mood is for change" (1.3, p. 10). Are UK motorists ready to reduce their car use? Respondents in our study were asked to consider their intentions for future car and PT use over the coming year. They were invited to rate their likely use and their preferred use of both.

The question rubrics read: "Over the next 12 months, I am likely to use the car ... "; "Over the next 12 months, I would like to use the car ... "; "Over the next 12 months, I am likely to use public transport ... "; "Over the next 12 months, I would like to use public transport ... ".

Ratings were on 7-point scales, with end-points labelled 'A lot less' and 'A lot more' and the mid-point labelled 'About the same'. Responses are here recoded to three categories 'Less' (scale points 1, 2, 3), 'The same' (scale point 4) and 'More' (scale points 5, 6, 7).

Crosstabulation of responses to the two 'car' variables (Table 3) shows that while 33% of the sample would like to use the car less, only 7% see themselves as likely to (bolded figures). Thus 26% (23 + 3) of the sample - a quarter of these motorists - would like to reduce their car use 'over the next 12 months' but see themselves as unlikely to do so.

Table 3. Crosstabulation of likelihood of and preference for car use 'over the next 12 months' showing total percents.

I am likely to use the car	*I would like to use the car*			
	Less	Same	More	Totals
Less	7	1	1	8%
Same	23	47	5	75%
More	3	6	7	17%
Totals	33%	54%	13%	*N* = 789

Crosstabulation of responses to the two 'public transport' variables (Table 4) shows that while 34% would like to use PT more over the next twelve months, only 5% of the sample (bolded figures) believed they were likely to. Thus 29% (3 + 26) of the sample would like to use PT more 'over the next 12 months' but did not think it likely that they would. This 29% of motorists represents a substantial potential - and currently frustrated - market for PT providers.

Table 4. Crosstabulation of likelihood of and preference for public transport use 'over the next 12 months' showing total percents.

I am likely to use pt	*I would like to use pt*			
	Less	Same	More	Totals
Less	11	3	3	18%
Same	5	44	26	75%
More	1	1	5	7%
Totals	17%	49%	34%	*N* = 760

Crosstabulation of car and PT use preferences (Table 5) indicates that only one third of the sample (34%: bolded figure) are happy as they are - they wish to use both car and PT 'the same' as currently. Thus two-thirds of this sample would like some change in the balance of their transport mode selection - a high level of volatility. 1 in 5 (19%: bolded figure) of this sample of car users would like to use the car less and PT more, but only 3% (Table 6) anticipate they are likely to. 5 out of 6 of those who would like to comply with current UK transport policy and switch some part of their travel from car use to PT use feel they are unlikely to do so.

Table 5. Crosstabulation of preferences for car and public transport use.

I would like to use pt	*I would like to use the car*			
	Less	Same	More	Totals
Less	4	8	6	17%
Same	10	34	4	49%
More	19	12	3	34%
Totals	33%	54%	13%	*N* = 765

Crosstabulation of likelihoods of car and PT use (Table 6) shows that 62% (bolded figure) indicated that both their car use and their PT use is likely to remain unchanged over the next 12 months. Thus 38% - over one third of these motorists - anticipate some change in their transport mode usage. However only 8% of these persons (3*100/38 = 8) anticipate that the change envisaged will be the UK Government's desired combination of a decrease in car use and an increase in PT use.

Judged Effectiveness of Policy Measures to Reduce Own Car Use

Steg and Vlek (1997) identified a variety of possible policy-driven sticks and carrots that could be used to either 'push' or 'pull' motorists out of their cars. Table 7 draws on their work to enumerate some examples. In our study we were interested in which of these inducements to reduce car use would be favoured by motorists, and also in which motorists would be most and least affected by them.

Table 6. Crosstabulation of likelihoods for car and public transport use.

I am likely to use pt	*I am likely to use the car*			
	Less	Same	More	Totals
Less	1	10	7	18%
Same	5	62	9	75%
More	3	3	1	7%
Totals	8%	75%	17%	$N = 763$

Table 7. Push and pull measures for encouraging motorists to reduce car use (after Steg & Vlek, 1997).

'Push' measures	*'Pull' measures*
Increase costs: raise fuel prices raise parking charges tolls by place (e.g. motorways) or time (e.g. peak hours) Decrease availability: no city centre car access reduce or eliminate city centre parking no new road building lower speed limits	Persuasive communications: anti car use propaganda Spread or reduce demand: stimulate flexi-time & teleworking Reduce procedural uncertainty: improve availability of information well publicised role modelling Improve alternatives: more and better cycle tracks, car pool lanes 'better' public transport vehicles and interchanges - cheap, clean, comfortable, convenient, fast, frequent, reliable, safe, weatherproof

Respondents were asked to indicate how effective they thought each measure would be in reducing their own car use. Using a 3-point response scale, motorists rated the 13 measures as 'Very effective', 'Fairly effective' or 'Not at all effective'. Table 8 gives the distribution of responses to the 13 items, arranged in descending order of endorsement as very effective.

The set of ratings was factor analysed using Principal Component Analysis. Two factors were extracted (Table 9), accounting for 53% of the variance, and factor scores saved for further analysis. The two factors clearly mirrored Steg and Vlek's (1997) distinction between 'pull' and 'push', or carrot and stick measures. The first factor grouped together all the measures which improved the attractiveness of the alternatives to car use ('pull'); the second factor grouped those measures which penalised continuing car use ('push').

This combination of factor structure and response distribution leads to two conclusions. First that it is not just the theorists but also the travelling public who clearly distinguish measures intended to pull them out of their cars by providing attractive alternatives from measures intended to push them from their cars by increasing costs or decreasing access (Table 9).

Second, it is plain that they prefer the former to the latter, judging pull measures substantially more likely than push measures to be effective in reducing their own car usage (Table 8).

Table 8. Rated effectiveness of pull and push measures in reducing own car use.

Please indicate how effective you think each of the following measures would be in getting *you* *to reduce your use of the car*	*Very effective*	*Fairly effective*	*Not at all effective*
More reliable public transport services	59	23	18
Much cheaper transport	42	29	29
Shorter overall journey times on public transport	41	35	24
Shorter interchange times on public transport	37	36	27
A ticketing policy so that 1 ticket covers different forms of transport	37	33	30
The closure of city centres to cars	29	28	43
More readily available information about public transport	27	41	33
Vouchers from employers to subsidise the cost of season tickets	27	27	47
Better cycling facilities	19	24	58
Fewer places to park the car	14	33	53
More expensive petrol	13	25	62
Road tolls	10	31	59
Public information campaigns about negative effects of car use	5	21	74

Table 9. Pattern matrix factor loadings: rated effectiveness of measures in reducing own use of car.

	F1	*F2*
Shorter overall journey times on public transport	.86	
Shorter interchange times on public transport	.85	
More reliable public transport services	.82	
Much cheaper public transport	.79	
More readily available information about public transport	.75	
A ticketing policy so that 1 ticket covers different forms of transport	.64	
Vouchers from employers to subsidise the cost of season tickets	.54	
Better cycling facilities	.48	
More expensive petrol		.80
Fewer places to park the car		.78
Road tolls		.76
The closure of city centres to cars		.68
Public information campaigns about negative effects of car use		.41

Responses to the item 'Public information campaigns about negative effects of car use' proved illuminating. Not only was this technique rated ineffective, but the factor analysis - unlike Steg and Vlek (1997) - grouped this item with the 'push' measures. It would seem that motorists react negatively to being dubbed polluters, to being told that they are part of the problem.

Who Would Be Moved from Their Cars by Pull and by Push Measures?

The influence of a number of the demographic and vehicle variables on respondents' 'push' and 'pull' factor scores was examined, using SPSS Answer Tree analysis, and these are summarised in Table 10 (full details are given in Stradling et al, 1999). 'Pull' measures were deemed as more effective by the young (17-21) and by drivers of smaller engined cars (<1.4 litres), as less effective by the (economically) retired and by rural and semi-rural dwellers, as much less effective by drivers doing a high annual mileage (>20,000 miles pa) and as less effective for those who drive as part of their work 'once a week' or more often. 'Push' measures are more likely to achieve a reduction in car use for the old, the poor and urban dwellers; and for low mileage drivers, drivers of smaller cars, drivers of older cars, and those not obliged to drive as part of their work.

Table 10. Comparison of influence of demographic and vehicle variables on rated effectiveness of pull and push measures to reduce car use.

Factor	*Influence of Pull measures*	*Influence of Push Measures*
Age Band	17-21: more effective	42-55: less effective, 55+: more effective
Sex	no effect	no effect
SES	Retired: less effective	no effect
Household Income	no effect	<£10K: more effective
Domicile	Rural, semi-rural: less effective	City, town: more effective
Engine Size	<1.4L: more effective	<1.4L: more effective, >1.8L less effective
Age of Car	no effect	>3 yrs: more effective
Annual Mileage	>20Kpa: (much) less effective	>14K: less effective
Drive As Work	>once per week: less effective	>once per month: less effective

And those residing out-of-town, driving medium and large cars, doing high mileage and required to drive as part of their work are less likely to be persuaded to reduce their car use by either type of measure.

Conclusion

As congestion on UK roads inexorably increases, a solution to 'the traffic problem' is urgently needed. The findings reported here identify a number of discriminable types of functional use to which the private car is put, and reduction in each of these uses will need different (and imaginative) solutions.

One in five English motorists (19%) would like to reduce their car use and increase their public transport use, enough to make a substantial difference to congestion on the roads, but only 3% think they are likely to. This discrepancy means there are many frustrated motorists. The different profiles of those who will be most affected by push measures, most receptive to pull measures, and most resistant to either type of measure have clear implications for transport policy makers in determining and targeting policies to reduce car use and enhance patronage of public transport. Of course hypothecation of revenues from 'push' measures to finance "pull' measures would materially contribute to solution of 'the traffic problem' in the UK in the twenty-first century, a solution which is currently desired by a substantial number of English car drivers.

References

AA Report (1998). The Great British Motorist 1998 by Mitchell, C. G. B., Lawson, S. AA Group Public Policy: Basingstoke.

Adams, J. (1999). Hypermobility. *Prospect, March 2000*, 27-31.

Begg, D. (1998). 'Car Free Cities'. In Reducing Traffic In Cities: Avoiding The Transport Time Bomb. 3rd Car Free Cities Conference, Edinburgh, June 1998.

DETR (1997). *National Travel Survey 1994/96*. HMSO: London.

Jones, H. (1999). 'Designing The Motor Car's Habitat'. In On The Road. The Art of Engineering in the Car Age. The Architecture Foundation: London

Rye, T. (1998). 'Can we make a business case for Employer Transport Plans?' In Reducing Traffic In Cities: Avoiding The Transport Time Bomb. 3rd Car Free Cities Conference, Edinburgh, June 1998.

Steg, L., & Vlek, C. (1997). The role of problem awareness in willingness-to-change car use and in evaluating relevant policy measures. In J.A. Rothengatter and E. Carbonell Vaya (Eds.), Traffic and Transport Psychology, (pp. 465-475). Oxford: Pergamon.

Stradling, S. G., Meadows, M. L., & Beatty, S. (1999). Factors affecting car use choices. Transport Research Institute, Napier University: Edinburgh.

Stradling, S. G., Meadows, M. L., & Beatty, S. (2000a). Helping drivers out of their cars. Integrating transport policy and social psychology for sustainable change. *Transport Policy, 7*, 207-215.

Stradling, S. G., Meadows, M. L., & Beatty, S. (2000b). 'Driving as part of your work may damage your health'. In G.B. Grayson, (Ed.), *Behavioural Research in Road Safety X,* Crowthorne: Transport Research Laboratory.

Transport 2000 Trust (1997) Blueprint For Quality Public Transport. London: Transport 2000.

Wardman, M., Hine, J., & Stradling, S. G. (2001). *Interchange and travel choice*. (Vol. 1, 2). Edinburgh: Scottish Executive Central Research Unit.

Traffic and Transport Psychology,
T. Rothengatter and R.D. Huguenin (Editors)

44

Perceptions of Car Users and Policy Makers on the Effectiveness and Acceptability of Car Travel Reduction Measures: An Attribution Theory Approach

Birgitta Gatersleben and David Uzzell

Introduction

Car use has many direct and indirect positive and negative effects on the quality of human life. On the positive side cars give people more freedom and comfort. Too many cars, however, cause congestion and air pollution.Various studies have shown that people are generally aware of the costs of increasing car use and they agree that it needs to be reduced (Gatersleben & Uzzell, 2000a; Nilsson & Küller, 2000; Steg & Vlek, 1997). However, few people appear to change their own behaviour. They often indicate that in their situation it is simply not possible to travel less or use alternative modes of transport. They attribute the fact that they do not reduce their car use to external factors: i.e., I want to, but I can't. In contrast, people who are asked to judge other people's behaviour are more likely to attribute it to internal dispositions; i.e., most people can but they do not want to reduce their car use. This paper examines the relationship between the causal attributions of car users and policy makers and their beliefs about the effectiveness of car travel reduction measures. If observers attribute car use reduction in terms of internal dispositions (willingness) and actors attribute it to external causes (ability) how does this effect their perceptions of the malleability of car use? Is it more likely that people will reduce their car use in response to various car travel reduction measures when they are (perceived to be) more willing or when they are (perceived to be) more able to reduce their car use?

Attribution theory

According to attribution theory (Heider, 1958; Jones & Davis, 1965) people try to make sense of their social environment by making causal attributions about another person's behaviour. Basically, an observer tries to decide whether the behaviour of another person is caused by internal dispositions or by external factors. When making attributions about a person's behaviour people tend to underestimate the effect of situational factors and overestimate the effect of personal factors (the 'fundamental attribution error'). But this does not appear to hold for one's own behaviour. People are more likely to attribute their own behaviour to external factors. According to the actor-observer effect described by Jones and Nisbett (1971) actors are more likely to attribute their own behaviour to situational factors (i.e., I want to but I cannot drive less), whereas observers are more likely to attribute it to personal disposition (i.e., he/she can but does not want to drive less). Various explanations have been suggested for the actor-observer effect. For instance, it has been proposed that actors may want to justify their own behaviour. An alternative explanation lies in cognitive factors. Observers do not have as much information about the situation as the actors themselves do. Observers may be more likely to attribute behaviour to stable dispositions because they have less knowledge about the variability of the actors' behaviour in different situations. This idea is supported by findings that people are more likely to attribute other people's behaviour to situational factors when they know the person better (Nisbett, et al, 1973). Another explanation could be the different perspectives of actors and observers. The actor mainly sees the environment whereas the observer focuses most attention on the actor.

The actor-observer effect explains why people usually attribute their own car use to external factors whereas people who are asked to make judgements about other people's car use often explain this in terms of internal dispositions. Little is know, however, about how the actor-observer effect is related to people's perceptions towards the malleability of behaviour. This is especially relevant for the decision-making processes of policy makers. How effective do they perceive various car travel reduction measures to be? Is the perceived effectiveness related to external or internal attributions of the use of cars by individuals or organisations? It is possible that policy makers believe that car use cannot be reduced because individuals and organisations can change, but they will not be willing to be persuaded to do so. This, however, would contradict an important part of their brief: to develop, implement and support policy measures.

In this paper we will examine the transport problems as perceived by residents, local businesses and local policy makers in Guildford, England. Guildford is a medium sized town in the UK. It lies approximately 50 km to the south-west of London in Surrey, a county in the prosperous south-east of England, a fact which is reflected in high car ownership figures. In 1990 there were .54 cars per person in Surrey, 1.5 times as many as the national UK average. In 1991 51% of the journeys to school in Surrey were made by car compared to 30% nationally (Surrey County Council, 2000).

Respondents were asked to what extent they believed various car travel reduction measures should be implemented in the town. It was expected that respondents would believe that most measures should be implemented. Secondly, we explore to what extent residents and organisations say they are able and willing to reduce their car use, and what local policy makers (as observers) think of the willingness and ability of residents and organisations to reduce their car use. It was expected that policy makers would believe that residents and organisations would be able but unwilling to reduce car use and that residents and organisations themselves would indicate that they are willing but unable to reduce their car use. Finally, we examined the relationship between the extent to which actors (car users) and observers (policy makers) attribute car use to external or internal causes on the one hand and their perceptions of the effectiveness and acceptability of car travel reduction measures on the other.

RESPONDENTS

Residents

In May 1999 a questionnaire was sent to 1500 households in the Borough of Guildford. To ensure that the sample was representative the questionnaire was sent to both urban and rural areas.

The questionnaires were accompanied by a covering letter in which the goal of the study was explained. Potential respondents were car users in each household. These people were asked to return the completed questionnaire to the University in the freepost envelope that was provided.

A total of 439 (a response rate of 30%) people returned a completed questionnaire. The mean age of the respondents was 44 years old. When the respondents were compared to population statistics of the borough the older respondents appeared to be slightly over-represented (Guildford Borough Council, 1995). Fifty-three percent of the respondents were male. Most of the respondents had a monthly income above the national average. This corresponds with the fact that Surrey is one of the wealthiest counties in the UK. The average mean income in Surrey in 1999 was £23,100 compared to £16,300 for England as a whole (Surrey County Council, 2000).

The average level of education of the respondents was higher than the average level of education in Guildford as presented in the 1991 Census report (Office of population census and surveys, 1994). About 15% of the respondents had a higher degree. A further 28% of the respondents had a first degree.

Because the questionnaire was directed towards car users 99% of the respondents owned one or more cars. The use of other travel modes than a car was very low among these people. About 42% of the households possessed two cars. A further 16% possessed three to five cars.

Businesses

In June 1999 a questionnaire was sent to 200 organisations in Guildford. The questionnaires were directed towards directors or managers within each organisation. A total of 89 people returned the completed questionnaire (a 45% response rate), reflecting a wide range of companies: small (e.g., shops, pubs), middle sized (e.g., health organisations, accountancy agents) and large (e.g., supermarkets and a hospital). Non profit organisations such as churches also participated. About 75% of the organisations were based in Guildford town centre. The size of organisations ranged from 1 to 2500 employees. About 30% of the organisations 'employed' 5 people or less. Thirty percent 'employed' between 5 and 25 people. Twelve percent 'employed' more than 125 people.

Policy makers

In September 1999 a questionnaire was sent to all 45 borough councillors and to 25 county councillors (with an electoral division in or near Guildford borough). A total of 35 councillors returned a completed questionnaire: 66% were borough councillors and 31% were county councillors. The average age of the respondents was 53 (with a range of 21 to 70); 54% were male; 83% of the councillors lived in the Guildford borough.

A similar questionnaire was sent to 64 Guildford borough officers. A total of 33 (a 51% response rate) officers returned the completed questionnaire. About 10% of the respondents worked for the chief-executive office, 13% worked in leisure, 23% in housing and health and 39% in planning. Of these respondents 74% were male. About 30% of the respondents were principal officers or senior officers, 7% were officers, 26% were directors or managers. Eight respondents did not indicate their position within the organisation. The mean age of the respondents was 43 years old (min = 21, max = 61). Just over 60% of the respondents lived in Guildford.

Final data set

To examine whether differences between the groups are statistically significant a new data file was created that included all 35 councillors, 33 officers and 89 organisations and a 25% random sample of the residents. The 25% random sample was taken because statistically valid tests can not be conducted when there is a disproportionate variation in group sizes[1]. The new data file contained only those variables that were comparable among the groups. The councillors and officers were combined into one group called local policy makers. Previous analyses showed that there were few differences between councillors and officers in their responses to the relevant questions. For the results of separate analyses see Gatersleben and Uzzell (2000b). The final data file consisted of 247 respondents: 67 policy makers, 91 residents and 89 organisations.

Measurement of Variables: Willingness and Ability to Change

The questionnaires were not the same for the three groups of respondents. Only those questions are discussed that were included in at least two out of the three questionnaires (i.e., the policy makers and either the resident's or the organisation's survey). The resident's questionnaire was the longest and included questions on issues such as car use, transport problems, transport generated air pollution, and car travel reduction measures (see Gatersleben & Uzzell, 2000a). The other questionnaires were shorter versions of this questionnaire.

The acceptability of car travel reduction measures was examined by asking residents, the policy makers and organisations for their degree of support (on a five point scale; 1 = totally unnecessary, 5 = very necessary) for the implementation of fourteen different car use reduction

[1] All the analyses presented in this paper were conducted three times with different random sub-samples. This did not alter the results.

schemes: e.g., 'increasing park and ride schemes', 'building more cycle lanes', 'raising parking charges' and 'implementing a toll for driving through Guildford town centre during peak hours'.

The perceived effectiveness of car travel reduction measures was measured by asking organisations how likely it would be that a company transport plan would be introduced in their organisation under different circumstances: 'an opportunity to create a product or service', 'regulation and fear of prosecution', 'cost pressure of taxes or charges' and 'incentives for voluntary action' (1 = very unlikely, 5 = very likely). Policy makers were asked to what extent they believed organisations would introduce a company transport plan under those circumstances (1 = very unlikely, 5 = very likely).

Residents indicated how they would respond to a variety of car travel reduction measures (e.g., 'increased parking charges, expanded park and ride schemes, the introduction of a toll). For instance, 'if parking charges would increase by £1 an hour how likely would it be that you would ... pay the charges, ... shop elsewhere, ... change your travel mode' (1 = very unlikely, 5 = very likely). Policy makers indicated how likely they believed it would be that residents actually reduce their car use under these circumstances (1 = very unlikely, 5 = very likely). Although the questions for residents and policy makers were not completely identical there were three measures for which responses could be compared. Both groups were asked how likely it would be that residents would 'use expanded park and ride schemes', 'change their travel mode if parking charges were increased' and 'cycle if the cycle network was expanded'. For the latter, residents were asked three questions ('let their children cycle to school', 'cycle into the town centre' and 'cycle more for pleasure') on the basis of which one scale was computed (by calculating the mean score) indicating the extent to which respondents (and their children) were likely to use an expanded cycle network ($\alpha = .82$).

To examine the causal attributions people make of their own and others' car use residents and organisations were asked to indicate to what extent they thought it would be possible and to what extent they would be willing to try to reduce their car use (in their organisations) (5-point scales: 1 = absolutely not willing/possible, 5 = very willing/possible). Policy makers indicated to what extent they believed residents and organisations were willing (1 = not at all, 5 = very willing) and able (1 = not at all, 5 = very able) to reduce their car use.

Results

What car travel reduction measures would respondents like to see implemented?

The respondents' preferences for 14 car travel reduction measures are listed from the most preferable to the least preferable (according to the residents) in Table 1. As can be seen all three groups had the most positive attitude towards park and ride schemes, the introduction of school buses, school carpool schemes, work carpool schemes, and the provision of cycle lanes. They had the most negative attitudes towards restricted parking, the introduction of a toll and increased parking fees. A number of respondents commented separately that they did not believe such financial measure would make a difference. They believed that the local authority would only implement such measures for the sake of 'filling their own pockets'. On the whole, however, all respondents appeared to have a positive attitude towards most measures ($M > 2.5$).

Organisations appeared to have the most negative attitude, especially towards pedestrianisation, restricted parking, increasing parking charges and priority lights (see Table 1).

Table 1. Percentage of respondents thinking that certain car travel reduction measures should be implemented in Guildford? ($MF(28,416) = 2.04, p < .01$)

	Politicians *N = 62*	*Residents* *N = 72*	*Organisation* *N = 79*
Park and ride schemes	4.22	3.90	4.05
Introducing school buses	4.31	4.05	4.16
Car pooling schemes to bring children to school	4.08	4.15	4.24
Pedestrianising streets in Guildford town centre	3.84_a	3.83_a	3.35_b
Car pooling schemes for commuting to work	3.85	3.78	3.71
Providing cycle lanes in urban areas	3.79	3.80	3.59
Providing cycle lanes in Guildford town centre	3.72	3.52	3.52
Introducing an information campaign	3.87_b	3.54_a	3.85_b
Providing priority lanes for buses and taxis	3.61	3.55	3.43
Giving priority to buses and taxis at traffic lights	3.54_a	3.11_{ab}	3.22_b
Restricting parking in Guildford town centre	3.23_a	2.94_{ab}	2.54_b
Restricting parking in urban areas	2.90	2.73	2.46
Introducing a toll of around £2	2.52_a	2.39_a	1.86_b
Increasing parking fees by £1 an hour	2.49_a	2.13_{ab}	1.89_b

Note. 1 = totally disagree, 5 = totally agree. Means with different subscripts differ significantly (p < .05). Totals do not add up to 247 due to missing values.

The actor-observer effect and individual car use

More than 50 % of the residents said they would be willing to reduce their car use (33% would not be willing and 15% were neutral). Only 43% of the respondents believed it would actually be possible to reduce their car use. A further 47%, however, did not think it would be possible. When asked what types of trips respondents would change, most of them answered they would change their travel mode to work, or they would reduce weekend trips.

Few policy makers believed that residents would be willing to reduce their car use (13% agree, 64% disagree), but most of them (81%) believed that residents could do so if they wanted to. Figure 1 shows that, as expected, policy makers were less likely to believe that residents would be willing to reduce their car use than residents themselves said they were ($F(1,150) = 10.17, p < .001$). Residents were more likely to say that they were not able to reduce their car use ($F(1,150) = 19.04, p < .001$).

The actor-observer effect and car use in organisations

About 27% of the respondents from the organisations sample believed it would be possible to reduce car use in their organisation. When asked for what kind of trips this reduction could be achieved, 88% of the respondents mentioned commuting trips, 13% mentioned work trips and 12% mentioned trips made by clients/visitors/customers. Over half of the respondents from the organisation sample indicated that they would be willing to try to reduce car use in their organisation.

Eighty percent of the policy makers believed organisations could reduce their car use, but only 25% believed that organisations would be willing to do so. Figure 2 shows to what extent policy makers and organisations believed organisations would be willing and able to reduce car use. As can be seen, the groups did not differ in their perceptions of organisations' willingness to reduce car use. Both policy makers and organisations believed that organisations would not be very willing to reduce car use. There did appear to be a difference between the groups in the perceived ability of organisations to try to reduce car use. Councillors and officers believed organisations would be more able to reduce their car use than the organisations themselves said they were ($F\,(1{,}148) = 39.63, p < .001$).

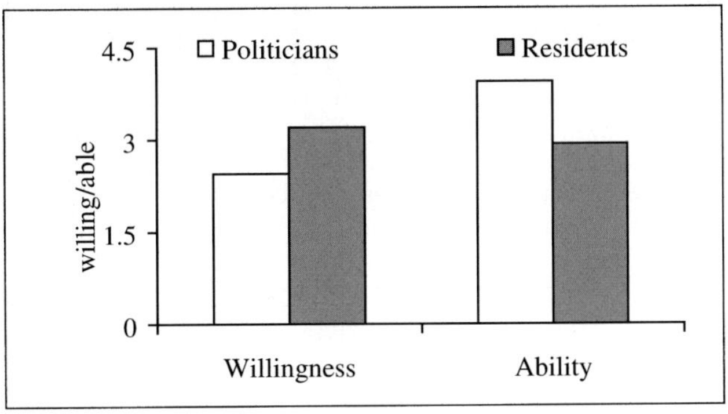

Figure 1. Perceptions of policy makers and residents on the willingness and ability of residents to reduce their car use (1 = absolutely not, 5 = absolutely).

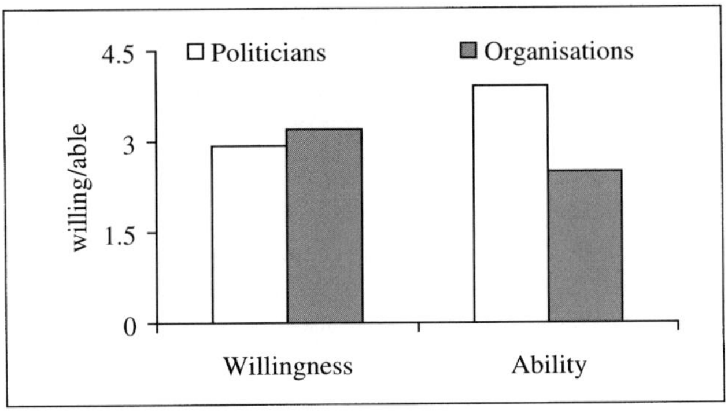

Figure 2. Perceptions of policy makers and organisations on the willingness and ability of organisations to reduce their car use (1 = absolutely not, 5 = absolutely).

How would residents respond to various car travel reduction measures?

As can be seen in Table 2 policy makers had a more positive view on the effectiveness of car travel reduction measures than did residents. Policy makers were significantly more likely then residents to believe that residents would use park and ride schemes (F (1,130) = 49.21, $p <$ .001). Moreover, policy makers were much more likely than residents to believe that increased parking charges would lead to the desirable behaviour changes (i.e., changing travel mode) of residents (F (1,130) = 7.10, $p < .05$). Beliefs about the extent to which residents would be willing to use expanded cycle facilities did not differ significantly between policy makers and residents.

Table 2. Expected responses to transport policy measures.

	Policy makers *N = 66*	*Residents* *N = 89*
Use expanded park and ride schemes*	3.74	2.41
Change mode due to increased parking charges*	3.12	2.66
Use expanded cycle network	3.22	2.89

Note. Variables are measured on a 5-point scale, 1 = very unlikely, 5 = very likely.
** means differ significantly*

Table 3. Correlations between the likely behavioural responses of residents to policy measures and their willingness and ability to reduce car use.

	Policy makers		*Residents*	
	Willing	Able	Willing	Able
Use expanded park and ride schemes	.21	.00	.17	.08
Change mode due to parking charges	.32**	.39**	.22	.16
Use expanded cycle network	.09	.39**	.36**	.27*

* $p<.05$, ** $p < .01$

Table 3 shows that the more policy makers attributed residents' reduction of car use to internal dispositions (willingness) the more they believed that expanded park and ride schemes and increased parking charges would change their behaviour (although only the correlation for parking charges is significant). The more car use was attributed to external factors (ability) the more policy makers believed parking charges and an expanded cycle network would change resident's behaviour.

The extent to which policy makers believed residents were able and willing to reduce their car use appeared to be positively related to their believe that residents would change their travel mode in response to parking charges. But perceived intentions to use cycle facilities were only related to external attributions (perceived abilities) and not to internal attributions (willingness). Moreover, perceived intentions to use park and ride were only related to willingness and not to abilities.

The question can be asked whether these results say anything about the views of policy makers on the types of people for whom different measures may be effective It could be argued that cycling facilities may be more relevant for those who do not have a car-dependent life-style: people who are able to reduce their car use; e.g., do not have children to bring to school, don't need to carry things, are fit enough to cycle and have the time to do so. Park and ride schemes may be more relevant for people who do rely on using their car. Whether or not people would use a park and ride scheme may depend on their willingness to reduce car use, but their ability to reduce car use may not be relevant. The results seem to support this suggestion.

How would organisations respond to various measures?

Table 4 shows to what extent policy makers and organisations believed that organisations would implement a company transport plan under certain circumstances. Organisations appeared to believe significantly more often than policy makers that they would implement a company transport plan if this would enable them to create a new product or service (F = 26.96(1,137), p<.001). Policy makers were also more likely to think that organisations would implement a transport plan if regulation would require them to do so (F (1,137) = 18.02, p < .001) or if they were faced with cost pressures of taxes and charges (F (1,137) = 23.20, p < .001). There was no difference between policy makers and organisations in their beliefs about the effectiveness of an awareness raising campaign or incentives for voluntary action.

Table 4. Expected responses to transport policy measures.

	Policy makers *N = 66*	*Organisations* *N = 89*
An opportunity to create a product or service*	3.26	2.31
Regulation and the fear of prosecution*	3.87	3.01
Cost pressure of taxes or charges*	3.85	2.81
Awareness of best practice	3.06	3.16
Incentives for voluntary action	3.21	3.12

Note. Variables are measured on a 5-point scale, 1 = very unlikely, 5 = very likely.
** means differ significantly*

Table 5. Correlations between the likely behavioural responses of organisations to various measures and their willingness and ability to reduce car use.

	Policy makers		*Organisations*	
	Willing	Able	Willing	Able
Opportunity to create product/service	.25*	.08	.39**	.32**
Regulation and the fear of prosecution	.20	.32**	.40**	.42**
Cost pressure of taxes or charges	.20	.12	.38**	.51**
Awareness of best practice	.28*	-.18	.58**	.49**
Incentives for voluntary action	-.12	-.19	.47**	.43**

* $p<.05$, ** $p<.01$

Table 5 shows that the more organisations said they would be able to reduce car use the more often they indicated that they would be likely to implement a company transport plan (under any circumstances). For the observers (the policy makers), however, internal and external causes of behaviour have different effects. The more policy makers attributed an organisations intention to implement a transport plan to internal dispositions (willingness) the more effective they believed persuasive measures would be such as 'creating a opportunity' and 'awareness of best practice'. On the other hand, the more policy makers attributed organisations' behaviour to external causes (ability) the more effective they believed a negative measure 'regulation and the fear of prosecution' would be.

It appears that policy makers believed that positive and persuasive measures would be more effective for those organisations that are willing to try to reduce car use, independent of weather they are able to do so or not. Negative measures may be more effective for organisations that are able to reduce car use, independent of whether they are willing to do so or not.

Conclusions and Discussion

As expected it was found that almost all respondents (residents, organisations as well as policy maker) believed that something needs to be done about the local transport problems. It was also shown that most car users (residents as well as organisations) indicated they would be willing to reduce their car use but that they are not able to do so. On the other hand, policy makers believed that car users were able to reduce their car use but not willing. This is in line with the actor-observer effect which would predict that observers (policy makers) attribute car reduction behaviour to internal dispositions whereas actors (residents and organisations) attribute their behaviour to external factors.

This paper showed that attribution theory can be helpful in describing the (perceived) willingness and ability of individuals and organisations to reduce their car use. However, the study also raised new questions. Firstly, more research is needed to examine the relationship between the attribution of actors and observers and the effectiveness of behaviour change measures. Obviously correlational studies such as the one presented in this paper cannot determine any causal relationship. Experimental studies where, for instance, people are placed into the position of actor or observer are needed to determine such relationships. Moreover, this paper revealed that the relationship between the actor-observer effect and perceptions of the effectiveness of behaviour change strategies varies with different types of strategies. For instance, it was found that policy makers believe that positive and persuasive measures may be more effective for organisations that are willing to change, independent of whether they are able to do so or not. Negative measures were perceived to be more effective for those who are able but not willing to reduce car use in their organisations. For car travel reduction measures directed towards individual car users we also found that the relationship between attributions and the perceived effectiveness of such measures varied. However, the relationship was less consistent. It should be noted, however, that this study examined only a few car travel reduction measures. Further studies are necessary to verify the results. Moreover, such research could help to develop new models and theories that link attribution theory to theories on behaviour change strategies (e.g., De Young, 1993).

On a more practical level, it seems worthwhile to examine to what extent the perceptions of policy makers are related to the policy decisions they make. To what extent do attribution processes play a role in the actual decision making process? Moreover, it is important to examine how close the perceptions of policy makers are to the truth. It seems likely that the perceptions of policy makers influence their decisions at least to some extent. Providing policy makers with more insight into the actual malleability of car use could, therefore, improve decision making processes on car travel reduction measures.

References

De Young, R. (1993). Changing behaviour and making it stick: the conceptualisation and management of conservation behavior. *Environment and Behavior, 25*, 485-505.

Gatersleben, B., & Uzzell, D. (2000a). Residents' perceptions of transport problems and sustainable solutions in Guildford (GBCRS report 1). Unpublished GBC report University of Surrey, Guildford, UK.

Gatersleben, B., & Uzzell, D. (2000b). Perceptions of transport problems and sustainable solutions in Guildford; the view of elected members and Guildford Borough Council officers (GBCRS report 3). Unpublished GBC report, University of Surrey, Guildford, UK.

Guildford Borough Council (1995). *Guildford Borough Population profile*. (Planning and monitoring report 7/95). Guildford, UK: Guildford Borough Council.

Heider, F (1958). *The psychology of interpersonal relations*. New York: Wiley.

Jones, E.E., & Davis, K.E. (1965). From acts to dispositions. *Advances in Experimental Social Psychology, 3*, 1-24.

Jones, E.E., & Nisbett, R. (1971). *The actor and the observer: divergent perceptions for the causes of behavior*. Morriwtown, NJ: General learning Press.

Nilsson, M., & Küller, R. (2000). Travel behaviour and environmental concern. *Transportation Research Part D, 5*, 211-234.

Nisbett, R.E., Caputo, C., Legrant, P., & Maracek, J. (1973). Behaviour as seen by the actor and as seen by the observer. *Journal of Personality and Social Psychology, 27*, 154-165.

OPCS (Office Of Population Census And Surveys, 1994). Ward and Civil Parish Monitor, Census 1991, Surrey. CEN 91, WPC 40, London, OPCS.

Steg,L., & Vlek, C. (1997). The Role of Problem Awareness in Willingness-to-Change Car Use and in Evaluating Relevant Policy Measures. In: J.A. Rothengatter and E. Carbonell Vaya (Eds.). *Traffic and Transport Psychology. Theory and Application*, (pp. 465-475). Oxford: Pergamon.

Surrey county Council, 2000). Surrey Trends: Average income Available on http://www.surreycc.gov.uk/council.html

Traffic and Transport Psychology,
T. Rothengatter and R.D. Huguenin (Editors)

45

The Prediction of Travel Behaviour Using the Theory of Planned Behaviour

Sonja Forward

Introduction

Recent years have witnessed a growing interest in non-motorised modes of transport, due in large part to concerns over the negative side effects of car usage. The increased levels of traffic have already resulted in many European cities suffering from serious problems in the areas of: safety, congestion and pollution.

Many of our travel routines are influenced by a number of factors such as socio-economic, demographic, together with needs and attitudes. An important step in the direction of developing general concepts for the implementation of supportive measures for walking and cycling would therefore be to collect enough background information about the traveller him/herself.

The prediction of travel behaviour from knowledge of peoples attitudes have been under investigation for some time but was perhaps most popular in the 70's and 80's (Stopher, 1996) when a number of different approaches were used (Everett and Watson, 1987). In general, the results were unsatisfactory and in 1979 Dumas postulated that there was no accepted theory of travel behaviour that includes attitudes, which can be used to predict behaviour. Subsequently, many researchers turned to other areas of research (Stopher, 1996). However, poor results would appear to be methodological and not as a result of the relationship between attitude and behaviour not existing.

One theoretical model of attitudes, which addressed this problem, is the Theory of Planned Behaviour (TPB) (Ajzen, 1985). It has been used to predict a range of behaviour. Initially the main area of interest was related to health (see, Forward, 1994) but in recent years it has also been used to also explain behaviour related to transportation including modal choice.

The theory includes three major factors: attitudes; subjective norm and perceived behavioural control. A behavioural intention is regarded as a sufficient immediate cause of behaviour and describes motivation.

The model predicts the personal decisions (intentions) of a behaviour based on attitudes toward the act, subjective norms and perceived behavioural control. Behaviour refers to an observable act. Attitudes include all salient beliefs about the consequences of the act weighted by an evaluation of those outcomes. Subjective norms are the summed product of an individuals belief about significant others expectations weighted by the motivation to conform to them. Perceived behavioural control refers to a person's perception about his/her own capability to perform an act and does not deal with the amount of control a person actually has. It is a function of control beliefs and perceived facilitation. The control belief may be based on past experience, own or others, and/or second hand information. Habits, like all other variables not included in the Theory of Planned Behaviour, are said to act indirectly on behaviour mediated by attitudes, subjective norm and perceived behavioural control.

Ajzen (1988) assumed that perceived behavioural control reflects past behaviour and would therefore mediate the effect. Nevertheless, subsequent research does not always support this hypothesis (Beck & Ajzen, 1991; Bagozzi & Kimmel, 1995; Norman & Smith, 1995; Quine & Rubin, 1997; Bunce & Birdi, 1998). A direct effect on behaviour was found by Bagozzi and Kimmel (1995) and in the study by Norman and Smith (1995) it was the only variable which made a significant contribution to the final regression equation. Furthermore, it has been found that perceived behavioural control and past behaviour do not interact in their influence on intentions (Bagozzi and Kimmel, 1995; Norman and Smith, 1995) and sometimes the effect of habit is greater than that of perceived behavioural control (Verplanken, Aarts, van Knippenberg & Moonen, 1998). Based on the above evidence it is difficult to rule out the importance of habit and an expanded version of the TPB was therefore explored in this study

Although the model has been used to predict modal choice, studies in the area have not, in the main, been conducted within a broad theoretical framework. If attitudes are being measured it is usually in isolation and/or without the rigorous methodology proposed by Ajzen in 1988. The aim of the studies presented in this paper was therefore to assess how well the theory could predict travel behaviour and if it could be regarded as an accepted theory of travel behaviour.

In this paper results from two different studies using the TPB will be presented. The first one ADONIS[1] was funded by the European Community within the 4th framework and the second one was a replication of the first[2]. The aim was to analyse cross-cultural differences with regards to attitudes and discuss how well the Theory of Planned Behaviour helped to predict modal choice.

---

[1] ADONIS is an acronym for "Analysis and Development of new Insight into Substitution of short car trips by cycling and walking

[2] A more detailed description of these studies can be found in Forward, 1998a and Forward, 1998b.

Method

Participants: In the first study 354 people of both sexes, 183 males and 171 females, took part in this study (135 from Amsterdam; 100 from Barcelona, 119 from Copenhagen and 188 from Gothenburg). The average age was 38 years, with an age range of 18 to 68 years. In the second study carried out in Gothenburg 188 people took part, 83 women and 105 men. The average age was 41 years, with a range of 21 to 69 years.

Procedure

The attitude study carried out within the framework of ADONIS was based on an extended version of the Theory of Planned Behaviour (TPB) covering attitudes, social norms, perceived control and habit. Salient background information was collected, including: gender, age, occupation, working hours per week, income, education, main user of private car and means of transport at their disposal. The questions it contained therein had been formulated with the aid of three pilot studies, carried out in Barcelona, Amsterdam and Copenhagen. In each city, ten persons were invited to discuss different modes of transportation. The most common and frequent assertions were subsequently included in the final questionnaire.

Each city drew approximately 1000 telephone number randomly from a telephone directory covering the survey area. Citizens in the different cities were then contacted by phone and asked if they travel up to 5 km on a regular basis and if they possessed a current driving licence. If the answer was affirmative the nature of the study was explained.

The interviewer went through a travel diary and a trip was recorded if it exceeded 300 m3. Three days later the same people received a mailed questionnaire. In the survey a scenario was presented, whereby the person concerned was asked to give an opinion on three different forms of travel: walking, cycling and driving a car, all of which started from the home to a destination 2.5 km away.

A measure of attitudes was obtained by including eleven items about: health and fitness, comfort, relaxation, freedom, time, environment, cost accidents, threat, parking and theft. Subjective norm was assessed by asking if people in general, who are important to them, would approve or disapprove of themselves engaging in the activity, referents included friends, partners and family. Perceived behavioural control was measured by asking how easy or difficult it would be, if they had the resources required and if a number of factors such as being in a hurry, heavy traffic, dry weather, night-time and luggage could prevent them from using the suggested mode of transport. The intention measure contained two questions: "I plan to" and "I will try". All the items listed above were scored from 1 to 7 using the so-called Osgood scale. Habits were measured by asking how frequently they had used the different modes of transport over the last two months. In addition, demographic and socio-economic factors were collected.

The second study carried out in Gothenburg was a replication of the first hence the same procedure was used with the exception of the pilot study.

RESULTS

The return rate of the questionnaire in Study 1 was 69% (Amsterdam 135; Barcelona 100; and Copenhagen 119) and in Study 2 it was 82%.

The socio-economic background varied somewhat between the different cities. In Amsterdam the incomes were higher than the other four cities. In Barcelona the level of education was lower and more of them worked part-time. In Copenhagen the average age was slightly lower than in Gothenburg and Barcelona and fewer of the participants had access to a car. Finally, in Gothenburg the participants were more likely to be professionals. No differences were found with regard to gender.

Prediction of intention

To examine the way in which intention depends on one or more of the variables as measured by the Theory of Planned Behaviour a regression analysis (stepwise) was performed. The first variable to enter the equation was attitudes followed by subjective norm and perceived behavioural control respectively. In accordance with the theory belief based measures were used in the analyses (Ajzen, 1988). Table 1 presents the relative weights of the model components in the prediction of intention to walk a distance of 2,5 kilometres.

Table 1. Multivariate regression analysis of intention to walk.

City	*Variables*	R^2	*Beta*
Amsterdam	PBC	.53	.73**
Barcelona	PBC	.15	.30**
	SN	.21	.26*
Copenhagen	PBC	.21	.38***
	A	.25	.23*
Gothenburg	PBC	.23	.33***
	SN	.30	.23***
	A	.32	.20*

Abbreviations: PBC=perceived behavioural control; SN=subjective norm; A=attitudes. ***$p < .001$; **$p < .01$; *$p < .05$

Table 1 shows the result of the regression analysis where the dependent variable was represented by intention, and the independent variables by attitude, subjective norm and perceived behavioural control. The variables within the model accounted for 21 - 53 percent of the variance in intention to walk a distance of 2.5 km. The variable that had the highest explanatory value was, in all cities, perceived behavioural control. In Barcelona and Gothenburg this was followed by subjective norm and in Copenhagen by attitudes. Attitudes also helped to increase the value in Gothenburg with another 2 percent. Table 2 presents the relative weights of the model components in the prediction of intention to bike a distance of 2,5 kilometres. Table 3 shows that the variables within the model accounted for 22 to 58 percent of the variance in intention to drive a distance of 2,5 km. In all cities the variable that had the highest explanatory value was perceived behavioural control. In Amsterdam the inclusion of attitudes contributed another 6 percent and in Copenhagen subjective norm added 4 percent and attitude yet another 2 percent.

A further assessment was made to determine the effect of socio-economic and demographic variables. The results showed that these variables failed to make any significant contribution to the model except for walking in Gothenburg. In this city, gender contributed to the prediction of walking. When this variable was added to the equation the explanatory value increased from 32 to 39 percent. The findings from this study showed that the women in Gothenburg were better educated, had lower incomes, were younger, worked fewer hours per week and that fewer of them had access to a car. Further analysis was therefore carried out to determine if any of these factors co-varied with the effect of gender and the intention to walk. However, the results showed that women were more likely to walk and that this was irrespective of their socio-economic background and if they had access to a car or not.

Table 2. Multivariate Regression Analysis of Intention to Bike.

City	*Variables*	R^2	*Beta*
Amsterdam	PBC	.47	.68***
Barcelona	PBC	.22	.47***
Copenhagen	PBC	.44	.66***
Gothenburg	PBC	.53	.73***

*Abbreviations: PBC=perceived behavioural control; SN=subjective norm; A=attitudes. ***p <.001; **p <.01; *p <.05.*

Table 3. Multivariate regression analysis of intention to drive.

City	*Variables*	R^2	*Beta*
Amsterdam	PBC	.43	.46***
	A	.49	.32***
Barcelona	PBC	.22	.46***
Copenhagen	PBC	.43	.50***
	SN	.47	.22**
	A	.49	.17*
Gothenburg	PBC	.58	.76***

*Abbreviations: PBC=perceived behavioural control; SN=subjective norm; A=attitudes. ***p < .001; **p < .01; *p < .05.*

Table 4. Multivariate regression analysis of intention to walk.

City	*Variables*	R^2	*Beta*
Amsterdam	PBC	.53	.50***
	Habit	.61	.36***
	SN	.62	.13*
Barcelona	Habit	.21	.42***
	SN	.31	.33***
Copenhagen	Habit	.27	.38***
	PBC	.32	.27**
Gothenburg	Habit	.33	.40***
	PBC	.39	.26***
	SN	.42	.18**

*Abbreviations: PBC=perceived behavioural control; SN=subjective norm; A=attitudes. ***p <.001; **p <.01; *p <.05.*

An additional aim of this study was to assess if the addition of habit improved the prediction of modal choice. In the regression analysis habit was therefore entered into the equation as the fourth variable. Table 4 presents the relative weights of the model components in the prediction of intention to walk a distance of 2,5 kilometres. Table 4 shows that habit made the greatest contribution in three of the four cities. The exception was Amsterdam where perceived behavioural control still made the greatest contribution. The total variance explained was 31 to 62 percent. Attitude made no significant contribution to the prediction. Table 5 presents the relative weights of the model components in the prediction of intention to bike a distance of 2,5 kilometres.

Table 5. Multivariate regression analysis of intention to bike.

City	*Variables*	R^2	*Beta*
Amsterdam	Habit	.76	.85***
	SN	.78	.14**
Barcelona	Habit	.38	.53***
	PBC	.47	.31***
Copenhagen	Habit	.47	.43***
	PBC	.54	.37***
Gothenburg	PBC	.53	.47***
	Habit	.60	.37***

Abbreviations: PBC=perceived behavioural control; SN=subjective norm; A=attitudes. ***$p < .001$; **$p < .01$; *$p < .05$.

Table 5 shows that habit was the most important variable in three of the four cities. The exception was Gothenburg where perceived behavioural control accounted for most of the variance. However, perceived behavioural control was also important in Barcelona and Copenhagen although to a lesser degree (9 and 7 percent respectively). In Amsterdam it was excluded and replaced by subjective norm which added 2 percent to the equation. The total amount explained by the model varied from 47 to 78 percent.

Table 6 presents the relative weights of the model components in the prediction of intention to drive a distance of 2,5 kilometres. Table 6 shows that habit and perceived behavioural control best helped to explain the intention to drive a distance of 2,5 km. In three of the four cities habit was the most important one followed by perceived behaviour control. In contrast perceived behavioural control was the most important one in Amsterdam and here habit only accounted for 5 percent of the total variance. Subjective norm made a small (3%) but significant contribution to the prediction in Copenhagen. In total the model explained 35 to 69 percent of the variance.

Further analysis, using Pearson's correlations coefficient, looked at the relationship between the variables within the model and habit. The results showed that the link was strongest to perceived behavioural control and intention. Table 7 shows the result from this analysis. Table 7 shows that habit and intention was closely related followed by perceived behavioural control. The variable most remote from habit was subjective norm.

A final assessment was made when also socio-economic and demographic variables were added to the equation. The results showed that these variables did not improve the prediction of modal choice over and above the variables already included.

Table 6. Multivariate regression analysis of intention to drive.

City	*Variables*	R^2	*Beta*
Amsterdam	PBC	.43	.31***
	A	.50	.32***
	Habit	.55	.27***
Barcelona	Habit	.26	.39***
	PBC	.35	.22**
Copenhagen	Habit	.50	.45***
	PBC	.53	.26*
	SN	.56	.16*
Gothenburg	Habit	.60	.47***
	PBC	.69	.43***

Abbreviations: PBC=perceived behavioural control; SN=subjective norm; A=attitudes. ***$p < .001$; **$p = <.01$; *$p < .05$.

Table 7. Correlations between habits and the variables within the TPB.

	Walking				*Biking*				*Driving*			
	A	SN	Pbc	I	A	SN	Pbc	I	A	SN	Pbc	I
Amsterdam												
Habit	.23	*ns*	.57	.64	.29	*ns*	.67	.82	.35*	*ns*	.57	.57
Barcelona												
Habit	.24*	*ns*	.45	.48	*ns*	*ns*	.30	.60	*ns*	*ns*	.36	.49
Copenhagen												
Habit	*ns*	*ns*	.49	.52	*ns*	.27	.67	.67	.44	.37	.70	.70
Gothenburg												
Habit	.39	.25	.46	.53	.43	.30	.69	.70	.32	.18*	.70	.77

Abbreviations: A=attitudes; SN=subjective norm; PBC=perceived behavioural control; I=intention; ns= non significant; *$p < .05$ *all others at a level of* $p < .01$.

Discussion

One of the objectives with this study was to test how well the Theory of Planned Behaviour explained modal choice. A number of different regression analyses were conducted, where intention represented the dependent variable. Three separate analyses were carried out: the first was to show how well variables in the model explained intention to walk, bike and drive, the second, what effect habit had, and finally the third, the effect of socio-economic and demographic factors.

The contribution of attitudes, subjective norm and perceived behavioural control towards the prediction of intention was assessed using a regression analysis (stepwise). The results showed that perceived behavioural control explained most of the variance regardless of mode of transport followed by attitudes and then subjective norm. For walking the model explained 21 - 53 percent of the variance, for biking 22 - 53 percent and for driving 22 to 58 percent.

In this project, an expanded version of TPB was used which also included habit. When this variable was added to the analysis the explained variance increased and habit became in all cities the most important predictor of biking. With regard to walking and driving the same applied to three of the four cities. With the inclusion of habit the explained variance for walking went up by approximately 9 percent (7 - 10%), for biking up by 18 percent (7 - 31%) and for driving up another 9 percent (6 - 13%).

The principle conclusion drawn from this result is that habit has an impact on future behaviour over and above the variables already included in the model. However, this is not, by itself, very useful when we want to explain behaviour since it only tells us that it has been carried out in the past. Although it does suggest that other factors plays an important role and therefore need to be identified..

In this study we also found that habit and perceived behavioural control were related to each other. This could suggest that regular practice makes the person more competent which in turn increases his or her own perceived behavioural control. This would then be in accordance with Ajzen (1988) who argued that the perceived behavioural control mediated the effect of habit. Nevertheless, in nine out of twelve equations habit contributed more to the prediction of modal choice than perceived behavioural control. In two of those it even disappeared from the equation, becoming less important than subjective norm. Hence, these results tend to lean towards supporting those who argued that the effect of habit is greater than perceived behavioural control (Verplanken et al., 1998) rather than being mediated by the same. Although it was not as Norman and Smith (1995) found the only variable making a significant contribution.

Further assessments were also done to determine the effects of socio-economic and demographic variables for the prediction of intention. The addition of this information to the equation did not improve the prediction of modal choice except for walking in Gothenburg. In this city gender explained an additional of seven percent of the variance. It could therefore be argued that these variables mainly have an effect via the variables already included in the Theory of Planned Behaviour, which would be in agreement with the theory itself (see Forward, 1994).

In general the model was most successful in explaining travel behaviour in Amsterdam and least successful in Barcelona. However, it is interesting to note that when habit was included the biggest increase happened in Barcelona especially with regard to biking and driving. There can be any number of reasons for this but one could be that people in Barcelona had lower education than the others and perhaps less experience with these kinds of surveys. In addition to this biking was almost non-existent in this city and therefore they do not consider biking as a mode of transport. Another plausible explanation could be that some of the content of the questionnaire got lost in the translation but this was later ruled out after a qualified translator looked at the English and the Spanish versions. However, discussions with psychologists in

Spain confirms that the model is less successful when used in Spain as compared to other countries something which certainly is worth finding the answer to.

Conclusion

The aim of these two projects was to suggest means by which short car journeys could be substituted by walking and cycling. Travel behaviour is influenced by sociological and psychological factors and without an accurate understanding of the aforementioned any attempt to reach this goal would fail. The study therefore assessed the attitudes and travel behaviour in four different cities with different levels of walking and cycling, in order to provide a more comprehensive description of travel behaviour.

Various measures have been taken to increase the use of non-motorised transport although without a proper tool for assessment very little can be said about the result.

The studies used an expanded version of the Theory of Planned Behaviour in which habit was included as an extra variable. The results showed that the extended model explained between 31 to 78 percent of the variance, which is more than satisfactory. Without the extra variable the predicted power decreased somewhat, 21 to 58 percent. It could therefore be argued that the Theory of Planned Behaviour (with or without habit) is a useful model to assess travel behaviour. The study also demonstrated that socio-economic and demographic variables did not contribute to the prediction of the intention to walk, bike and drive. It could therefore be concluded that it would be wrong for transport researchers to concentrate on socio-economic and demographic variables unless they also incorporate traveller attitudes, perceived behavioural control, subjective norm and habits.

References

Ajzen, I. (1985). From intentions to actions: A theory of planned behaviour. In Kuhl, J. and Beckmann, J. (Eds.). *Action-control: From cognition to behaviour*. Heidelberg: Springer.

Ajzen, I. (1988). *Attitudes, personality and behaviour*. Milton Keynes, UK: Open University Press.

Bagozzi, R. P., & Kimmel, S. K. (1995). A comparison of leading theories for the prediction of goal-directed behaviours. *British Journal of Social Psychology, 34*, 437-461.

Beck, L., & Ajzen, I. (1991). Predicting dishonest actions using the theory of planned behaviour. *Journal of Research in Personality, 25*, 285-301.

Bunce, D., & Birdi, K. S. (1998). The theory of reasoned action and theory of planned behaviour as a function of job control. *British Journal of Health Psychology, 3*, 265-275.

Dumas, J. (1979). Traveller attitude-behaviour implications for the operation and promotion of transport systems. *Transportation Research Record 723*, 64-71.

EMO. (1991). Enquiesta de mobilitat obligada, 1991. (Travel diary). Institut d'Estadistica de Catalunya, Barcelona, 1992.

Everett, P. B., & Watson, B. G. (1987). Psychological contributions to transportation. In D. Stokols and I. Altman. (Eds.). *Handbook of environmental psychology*. New York: Wiley.

Forward, S. E. (1994). Theoretical Models of Attitudes and the Prediction of Driver's Behaviour. Report 434, Uppsala University, Uppsala; Sweden.

Forward, S. E. (1998a). Behavioural factors affecting modal choice. Project ADONIS UR-96-SC.326. European Commission under the Transport RTD Programme of the 4th Framework Programme. Publ. Swedish Road and Transport Research Institute, Linköping, Sweden.

Forward, S. E. (1998b). Val av transportmedel för korta resor: Göteborgarnas resvanor och attityder. (Translated into English "Modes of transport on short journeys: attitudes and behaviour of the inhabitants of Gothenburg"). Report 437, Swedish Road and Transport Research Institute, Linköping; Sweden.

Gatunämnden. (1988). Cykelprogram för Göteborg - Slutrapport. (Program for cycling in Gothenburg - Final report).

Ministry of Transport. (1995). Cities make room for cyclists. Ministry of Transport, Public Works and Water Management, The Hague.

Norman, P., & Smith, L. (1995). The theory of planned behaviour and exercise: An investigation into the role of prior behaviour, behavioural intentions and attitude variability. *European Journal of Social Psychology, 25,* 403-415.

Quine, L., & Rubin, R. (1997). Attitude, subjective norm and perceived behavioural control as predictors of women's intentions to take hormone replacement therapy. *British Journal of Health Psychology, 2,* 199-216.

Stopher, P.R. (1996). Household travel surveys: New perspectives and old problems. Paper presented at the Conference on Theoretical Foundations of Travel Choice Modelling, Stockholm, Sweden.

Verplanken, B., Aarts, H., van Knippenberg, A., & Moonen, A. (1998). Habit versus planned behaviour: A field experiment. *British Journal of Social Psychology, 37,* 111-128.

APPENDIX 1: DESCRIPTIONS OF CITIES

Amsterdam

The proportion of trips on foot in Amsterdam is 23% (Ministry of Transport, 1995). In Amsterdam clearly marked footpaths and some pedestrian areas exist. Various 30 km/h zones are gradually being implemented. It does not have a pedestrian policy. A fairly large proportion of trips in the Netherlands are made by bike (between 23-43%) which reflects its long tradition in cycling. The proportion of trips by bike in Amsterdam is 28% (Ministry of Transport, 1995). Extensive works to improve and expand the network for cyclists started in the 1980s. The aim was/is to enable the cyclists to travel across the city quickly, safely and comfortable. The proportion of trips by car is 37% (Ministry of Transport, 1995). Paid parking is being introduced and 30 km/hr zones are gradually being installed.

Barcelona

The proportion of journeys on foot is 33% (EMO, 1991). The city of Barcelona has narrow streets, some of them with pavements others not. It has also some areas for pedestrians only. During the last two decades mobility policies in Spain have mainly concentrated on improving facilities for the driver. As a consequence of this policy fewer trips are now made by foot and more by car. Today the municipality of Barcelona has started to pay more attention to pedestrian needs, with improvements to pedestrians' conditions having been promised. The proportion of trips by bike is < 1% (EMO, 1991). In the 1990's 60 km of cycle lanes and paths have been created in Barcelona. Many of these lanes are not separated from motorised traffic which have resulted in cars also using this space. Plans exist to improve cyclists' conditions. The proportion of trips by car is 24% (EMO, 1991). Approximately 1 million vehicles cross the municipal borders every working day. From having given almost total attention to driving, a shift in policy has been seen in recent years, giving car users lower priority. Restricted areas have been introduced and in some places car lanes have become places for pedestrians.

Copenhagen

The proportion of trips on foot was 15% (Ministry of Transport, 1995). The city of Copenhagen has an extensive network of pedestrian pavements. Normally pavements are on both sides of the road although in some areas, with high concentration of pedestrians, a third pavement has been added in the middle. The city has also a fairly large area for pedestrians only. Several policies already exists which are aimed at encouraging more non-motorised traffic. Denmark has, like the Netherlands, a long tradition of cycling and the percentage of bicycle trips in the whole country is between 18-35%. The proportion of trips by bike in Copenhagen is 26% (Ministry of Transport, 1995). Most major roads have cycle paths, sometimes on both sides of the road. Cycle paths are less frequently alongside roads with low traffic intensity. In some places cycle lanes across junctions are clearly marked, in others the paths cease before the intersection. Several policies exist which show a strong commitment towards non-car traffic. The proportion of trips by car is 37% (Ministry of Transport, 1995). The city of Copenhagen has a relatively low car density which has resulted in that parking is generally on-street or on private property. Traffic calming is widely used and the speed is not normally more than 30 -

40 km/h. In one area, called a "shared area" it is normally below 15 km/h. A "Healthy City Plan" exists which aims to reduce the adverse effects of traffic such as: accidents, noise and air pollution.

Gothenburg

The first cycling network plan was decided in 1975. Since then, this network has been expanded in accordance with this initial plan. Since 1994, the local authority has allocated an average of 20M SEK per annum for maintenance and expansion of the cyclist lane network. This has resulted in relatively successful expansion of the cycle network today, both within the city centre and further afield within the suburbs. The overall extent of the network has about the same width or coverage as the main network for motor traffic, and embraces the entire city (Gatunämnden, 1988). Over a relatively short period of time, following practical implementation of the initial plan, the volume of cyclists more than doubled (1978-82). Since then, this volume remained unchanged until 1984, when the trend swung downwards to today's relatively low level. How many cyclists there are in the Gothenburg region, has not been determined so far. However, rough estimates indicate that 12% of all trips or short journeys are made by bicycle.

Traffic and Transport Psychology,
T. Rothengatter and R.D. Huguenin (Editors)

46

Public Acceptability of Travel Demand Management

Bernhard Schlag and Jens Schade

Aims of the TransPrice Project

This chapter reports a survey of the public acceptability of transport pricing carried out as part of the European Commission, DG VII (now DG TREN), project TransPrice (Trans-Modal Integrated Urban Transport Pricing for Optimum Modal Split; Keranen, Schade, Schlag & Vougioukas, 1999; TransPrice Consortium, 2000). Based, among others, on the EC green paper 'Towards fair and efficient pricing in transport' (1995) TransPrice aimed to demonstrate the potential benefits of several demand management and mode-choice pricing measures by modelling and real-life applications. The method used was to examine the potential user response as well as the road traffic operational, socio-economic, financial and behavioural effects of pricing measures by means of travel behaviour analysis and stated preference analysis and by a traffic simulation for several alternative trans-modal pricing scenarios. One of the main purposes was the analysis of the acceptability which the demonstrated or proposed new measures got or would get if introduced.

Opinions and intentions of transport user groups (essentially the general public) are often not canvassed when proposed traffic demand management (TDM) initiatives are being considered for implementation. However, public acceptability is an important precondition for successfully implementing new TDM systems. One aim of the TransPrice project was to measure the responses of mainly urban car drivers to various TDM scenarios, especially to different road pricing schemes at a general level. This part of the project was conducted by means of a common survey questionnaire which was based on the theoretical framework explained by Schlag and Teubel (1997) and Schlag (1998).

In the following descriptive total results of the acceptability surveys will be reported, as well as results on cross-site comparisons between the eight TransPrice sites: Athens, Madrid, Como,

Leeds, York, Helsinki, Goteborg and Graz. The first five sites were model as well as demonstration sites. The last three sites were considered only feasibility-study-sites. As a part of the Stated Preference Survey an attitudinal questionnaire was filled in at every site before the implementation of any measure. An acceptability questionnaire was completed at demonstration sites and in the city of Graz afterwards.

Public Acceptability Surveys

Survey methodology

Among the public there is a broad awareness of mobility related problems and of the necessity and urgency to act. The following issues determining the public acceptance of urban transport pricing options can be identified[1]: (i) People must know and understand projected measures. They also should be aware of the background (e.g. to pay the true costs of transport - including external costs), of the aims (e.g. to improve traffic conditions, to reduce congestion, environmental objectives, safety considerations) and of how specific measures are implemented in practice; (ii) At present the awareness for different demand management options is rather low; "Improve public transport" and "Restrict driving" are the most widely known measures, (iii) If pricing mechanisms to influence travel behaviour are applied, revenues will inevitably arise. An important issue with regard to the acceptance of pricing schemes is how this money will be used, (iv) It is necessary that people themselves perceive regulatory policies such as transport pricing as meeting equity considerations. If not, they perceive this policy as unjust and unfair, and acceptance will be hard to reach. Moreover perceived injustice creates a motivation to readjust personal costs (lower) and benefits (raise) so that the cost-benefit-relation compared with other users is again perceived as fair.

The following issues are addressed in the questionnaire which was applied in six different European cities (Athens, Madrid, Como, Leeds, York and Graz): (i) Problem perception: People's perception of traffic related problems like congestion, air pollution, parking problems, and safety; (ii) Information about TDM options; (iii) Acceptability of TDM options; (iv) Equity: respondents' expectations about costs and benefits; (v) Intentions: respondents' intentions if the use of urban roads is to be charged.

The following general TDM measures had to be evaluated by the respondents: (i) Reducing parking space, (ii) Increasing parking cost, (iii) Cordon pricing (Drivers pay (a fixed toll) to use the roads when they enter e.g. the inner city), (iv) Distance based pricing (Drivers pay dependent on the distance travelled by car), (v) Congestion pricing (Drivers pay only on congested roads - a variable amount depending on the level of congestion), (vi) Improving public transport, (vii) Park & ride, (viii) Access restriction (Restriction of driving in various Rareas of the city, except for residents and delivery vehicles), and (ix) A transport package (Package approach) which considers revenue allocation.

The questionnaire asked for a rating of a given set of measures into four levels (four-graded-scale). To obtain a single average value for each question, a weighted sum was calculated on

[1] For a more detailed theoretical structure of acceptability issues see Schlag & Teubel, 1997; Schlag, 1998 or Schade, 1999. Results of former studies are taken, among others, from MIRO, 1995; Bartley, 1995; Jones, 1995.

the basis of codings (e.g. 1 = absolutely not acceptable; 2 = not acceptable; 3 = acceptable; 4 = absolutely acceptable).

The total TransPrice sample consisted of 1459 respondents (Table 1). In the five demonstration cities only car drivers were asked, thus probably reflecting a part of the population with rather conservative attitudes for most of the questions posed. The Graz sample differed from the other five samples and included users of all modes, not only car drivers. The total sample of all six sites reflects the gender-distribution in the car driving population well - with the exception of Graz and of the small York sample.

Table 1. Sample sizes.

	Total	*Athens*	*Madrid*	*Como*	*Leeds*	*York*	*Graz*
Sample size	1459	116	239	177	300	91	536
Female	629	47	78	70	110	48	276
%	(43.1)	(40.5)	(32.6)	(39.3)	(36.7)	(52.9)	(51.3)
Male	830	69	161	107	190	43	260
%	(56.9)	(59.5)	(67.4)	(60.7)	(63.3)	(47.1)	(48.5)

Results

The descriptive results for all TransPrice sites are presented in two ways: (i) Total, all site results are added up to one total result and (ii) Site for site, allowing for comparisons between the different sites.

Problem perception. All the items mentioned were at least partly perceived as a problem. Traffic congestion and a lack of parking space were perceived as the most pressing problems in the six European cities (by car drivers in the five demonstration sites, except for the mixed Graz sample). On average roughly 80% of all respondents rated these two issues as problematic. The persons interviewed also considered environmental problems as relevant, in particular air pollution from motor vehicles.

Table 2 shows for each site the percentage of respondents who rated the items as "somewhat a problem" or "a very serious problem". There were considerable differences in problem perception between the six sites. In Athens all states were rated as a problem by nearly all respondents. On average problem perception was significantly higher in southern cities (Athens, Como and Madrid), whereas in Leeds and York problem ratings were relatively low and modest in a consistent manner. Only traffic congestion was rated as a problem by a majority at all six sites.

Figure 1 shows mean values of problem perception from all six sites together.

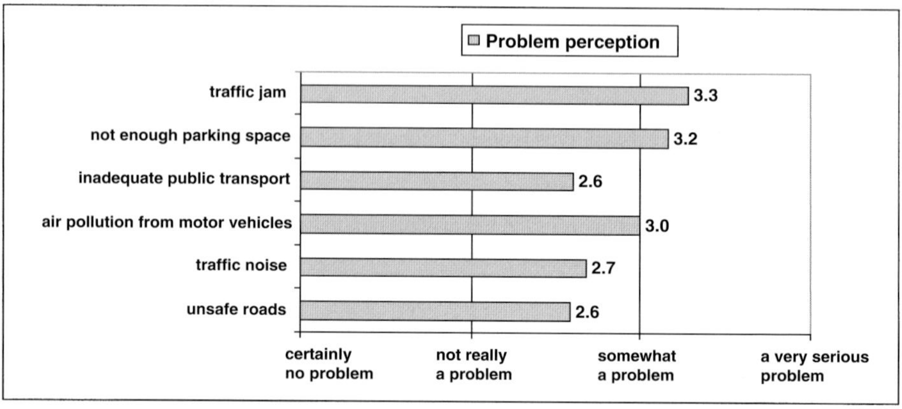

Figure 1. Total problem perception (mean).

Table 2. Problem perception at all sites (percentage of rated as a problem).

Traffic related problems	*Problem perception*						
	Total						
1. traffic congestion	85	Athens 100	Como 94	Graz 92	Madrid 89	Leeds 68	York 55
2. not enough parking space	78	Athens 100	Como 94	Madrid 88	Graz 86	Leeds 45	York 44
3. air pollution from motor vehicles	72	Athens 100	Graz 84	Como 76	Madrid 76	Leeds 49	York 40
4. traffic noise	60	Athens 97	Graz 79	Como 71	Madrid 69	Leeds 21	York 14
5. inadequate public transport	56	Athens 99	Graz 63	Madrid 51	Leeds 47	Como 46	York 24
6. unsafe roads	52	Athens 90	Madrid 83	Como 67	Graz 49	York 18	Leeds 16

Information about demand management options. Table 3 shows the frequency distribution on the information question for the five demonstration sites (without Graz). The overall information level was rather low. The best known measures were "improve public transport", "park & ride" and "access restriction". Pricing measures were the least known measures. With the exception of cordon pricing (known at least by around half of the respondents) pricing measures were unknown to three fourths of the car drivers asked.

Acceptability of demand management options. Table 4 shows the percentage of support[2] for the different TDM measures. The data should be considered with care, because people had experience with only some of the TDM measures. They could only respond on a hypothetical

[2] "support" means respondents' ranking as "acceptable" or "absolutely acceptable"

basis when it comes to pricing measures. This is also reflected by the very low values of information about pricing measures in Table 3.

Table 3. Information about demand management options (total without Graz; in %).

DM measure	*know a lot about this scheme*	*know somewhat*	*know nothing at all*
reducing parking space	15.6	34.7	49.7
increasing parking cost	17.6	41.4	41.0
cordon pricing	11.6	44.9	43.4
distance based pricing	6.5	21.7	71.7
congestion pricing	7.4	17.3	75.1
improve public transport	31.5	50.7	17.8
park & ride	31.2	43.7	25.0
access restriction	27.5	49.9	22.6

Table 4. Ranking of acceptability (Confirmative response in %).

TDM measure	*Support (in percent)*						
	Total						
1. improve public transport		Athens	Como	Leeds	Madrid	Graz	York
	94	100	98	97	95	90	86
2. park & ride		York	Leeds	Como	Madrid	Graz	Athens
	91	94	92	92	91	87	85
3. access restriction		York	Como	Leeds	Athens	Madrid	Graz
	68	92	76	70	65	64	37
4. reducing parking space		Madrid	Graz	Athens	Como	Leeds	York
	19	32	25	18	15	14	8
5. cordon pricing		Como	Madrid	York	Athens	Leeds	Graz
	19	24	20	20	16	16	16
6. increasing parking cost		Madrid	Athens	Graz	Leeds	York	Como
	16	27	19	17	17	7	7
7. congestion pricing		York	Madrid	Como	Graz	Leeds	Athens
	16	23	17	16	15	14	11
8. distance based pricing		Athens	Como	Madrid	Graz	York	Leeds
	12	20	12	11	11	10	8

"Pull"-measures, such as improvements in public transport and introduction of park & ride were accepted by almost all of the respondents with little variation between the sites. People seem to prefer innovations which give them additional chances or choices. The only restrictive (or "Push"-) measure which could be designated as accepted by the majority is some kind of access restriction. In York "access restriction" was accepted by more than 90% of the respondents. Only in Graz "access restriction" got no substantial support. Perhaps access restriction was more accepted than pricing measures because of equity concerns: access restriction seems to be perceived as more just. All other measures, which are all price-based except for "reducing parking space", were refused by a vast majority.

But considering the little information about price-based measures one may argue, that the respondents accepted only those measures they felt to be well informed about. And as is known now from Norwegian experiences, after the introduction of cordon pricing the (low) acceptability before implementation (rated on a hypothetical basis of expectations and not on the basis of real experiences) tends to shift to more positive acceptance values within the first 10 years (see e.g. Schade et al., 2000). Thus, the degree of support for or opposition to the measures when implemented is not yet visible.

The differences between the sites in the acceptability level seem to be rather small. In general, opposition to parking restrictions and most price-based measures was a little stronger in Northern cities (Leeds, York). In York park & ride and access control received particularly high and reducing parking space as well as restricting parking costs the lowest support. Despite this there was some support for congestion pricing by around a quarter of the respondents in York. Cordon pricing was supported by a quarter of the respondents in Como. In Athens all parking and pricing measures were accepted by a fifth of the respondents. In Madrid restrictive parking measures were accepted by around a third of the interviewees and, in addition, a High Occupancy Vehicle (HOV) lane now implemented gained high acceptability values. In future there could be a chance to combine HOV lanes with pricing in a way similar to „value pricing" on Californian interurban routes: drivers who are willing to pay substantial charges could be allowed to use HOV lanes, too.

The anticipation of advantages and disadvantages when a pricing scheme would be introduced differed strongly between the sites. But, despite of the predominantly negative acceptability ratings for any kind of pricing measures, respondents did not only expect disadvantages. In Leeds and York even a slight majority expected advantages. Above all, many respondents expected environmental improvements, better public transport and more attractive city centres to result from road pricing.

When it comes to behavioural intentions in the case that some kind of road pricing is introduced only a minority would pay and not change their own behaviour in one way or the other. Most respondents consider adapting their behaviour to the new situation and stated they would drive less and use car-pooling, public transport or bicycle more. Beneath mode shifts people would intend to drive at less tolled times or on less tolled roads. But a substantial and between the cities very different proportion of respondents also considered strongly opposing reactions, such as joining an anti-pricing movement.

Support for a transport package including cordon pricing. Respondents were asked whether, on balance, they would support the following package (cp. Jones, 1991):

"Charge motorists a fee for driving in the inner city and use this money to provide: much better quality of and lower fares for public transport, plus measures to improve the urban living conditions, plus better facilities for pedestrians and cyclists."

Results are shown in Table 5.

Table 5. Support for a transport package (in %).

Traffic demand management measure	*Support (in per cent)*						
Package approach (cordon pricing plus revenue allocation)	Total 45	Athens 64	York 53	Como 53	Leeds 44	Graz 41	Madrid 36
Cordon pricing	Total 19	Athens 16	York 20	Como 24	Leeds 16	Graz 16	Madrid 20

Compared to the level of acceptability for a single measure like cordon pricing, there was a considerable increase in support for a transport pricing package. The proposed transport package was completely supported by 45% of all respondents. In Athens, York and Como even a majority of respondents would support such a pricing package.

Only around a third of the respondents who supported the package had also supported cordon pricing on its own. In this survey it can be seen that support for cordon pricing trebled when it was presented as the pillar of a package of measures which improve alternative modes of transport and provide a safer and more pleasant environment. For gaining higher acceptability for pricing measures earmarking of revenues is one essential precondition.

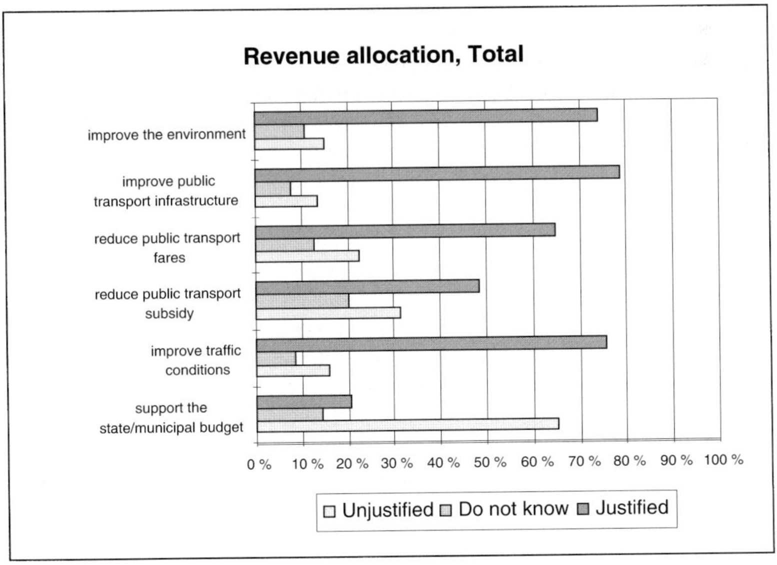

Figure 2. Preferred revenue allocation.

Hypothecation of revenues. If clear earmarking of revenues for well accepted aims substantially raises acceptability for proposed measures including a pricing component, which revenue allocation would be preferred by the public? Some attitudinal questions added to the Stated Preference Surveys before implementation of the site specific measures were to give an impression on preferred hypothecation of revenues and methods of payment.

The majority of respondents strictly disapproved of the revenues to be used to support state/municipal budgets in general. However, they agreed with the money to be used for improvements of the public transport infrastructure, of traffic conditions and of the environment (Figure 2). The most popular method of payment for road-use charges was a prepaid electronic card (and similar: electronic monthly Transport cards) which can be used for other purposes as well. The least popular was paying the toll in cash. Electronic credit card received also a low ranking.

References

Bartley, B. (1995). Mobility Impacts, Reactions and Opinions. Traffic demand management options in Europe: The MIRO Project. *Traffic Engineering and Control, 36*, 596-603.

Commission of the European Communities (1995), Towards fair and efficient pricing in transport: policy options for internalising the external costs of transport in the European Union. Green Paper, Brussels.

Jones, P.M. (1991). Gaining public support for road pricing through a package approach. *Traffic Engineering and Control, 4*, 194-196.

Jones, P.M. (1995). Road pricing: The public viewpoint. In B. Johansson, L.G. Mattson (Eds.), *Road Pricing: Theory, Empirical assessment and Policy*. Boston, Dordrecht, London: Kluwer.

Keranen, M., Schade, J., Schlag, B., & Vougioukas, M. (1999). Public Acceptability. TransPrice - Transmodal integrated transport pricing for optimum modal split. Deliverable 6: Report to Commission of the European Communities, DG VII, Helsinki, Dresden, London.

MIRO (1995). MIRO Final Report. Deliverable 8 to Commission of the European Communities, DG XIII DRIVE Programme, Brussels.

Schade, J. (1999). Individuelle Akzeptanz von Straßenbenutzungsentgelten (Individual acceptance of road tolls(. In: B. Schlag (Ed.): *Empirische Verkehrspsychologie*. (pp. 227-244). Lengerich, Berlin: Pabst Science Publ.

Schade, J., & Schlag, B.; Giannouli, I.; Beier, A. (2000). Acceptability of marginal cost road pricing. AFFORD Deliverable 2C: Report to EC DG VII. Dresden, Helsinki.

Schlag, B. (1998). Zur Akzeptanz von Straßenbenutzungsentgelten [Acceptance of road user fees]. *Internationales Verkehrswesen, 50* (7/8), 308-312.

Schlag, B., & Teubel, U. (1997). Public acceptability of transport pricing. IATSS Research. *Journal of the International Association of Traffic and Safety Sciences, 21* (2), 134-142.

TransPrice Consortium (2000). Final Report and Summary. Deliverable 9 to Commission of the European Communities, DG VII, London.

Traffic and Transport Psychology,
T. Rothengatter and R.D. Huguenin (Editors)

47

EVALUATIONS OF BIKE AND WALK SYSTEMS

Anita Gärling and Björn Berle

INTRODUCTION

To achieve a sustainable society several propositions and programs have been presented in which the necessity to reduce automobile use has been declared (SOU 1997:35; U.S. Department of Transportation, 1994). However, the world's automobile population is growing at a much faster rate than the human population. In the 1950´s, there were about 50 million vehicles on Earth, by 1994 the vehicle population had grown to almost 600 million, and if the present trend continue there will be over 3 billion vehicles on Earth by the year 2050 (Sperling, 1996). Besides from granting users freedom, privacy, and convenience, the usage of automobiles also threatens our environment. In dumping carbon dioxide and other climate-altering greenhouse gases into the atmosphere, automobiles cause severe ill effects on the environment.

To reduce the ill effects cleaner fuels have been developed and fuel catalysts have been implemented. However, these measures do not affect the emission of carbon dioxide, a major contributor to the greenhouse gases. Substituting current gasoline-powered automobile fleets with environmental sounder fleets seem more realistic but still too far away to have any major effect in the near future. However, earlier research has revealed that there is, at least theoretically, a substantial potential in changing shorter automobile trips into biking and walking (Pucher et al., 1999; Vejdirektoratet, 1995).

Yet, to get automobile users to substitute even shorter trips with biking and walking is a tremendous challenge. First, becoming bikers and walkers have to be offered bike and walk systems. Secondly, those systems have to be accepted. The former is not, at least in the western larger cities, a problem but the latter. The knowledge of how bike and walk systems are perceived are very scarce (Forester, 1994). Are present systems accepted? Do users perceive them as useable? If not, this might be an explanation of current relatively low usage. To enhance biking and walking as means of transportation knowledge of users' perceptions might be of substantial value.

To find out what users really think about current bike and walk systems a heuristic evaluation method might be used (Nielsen, 1992, 1994; Nielsen & Molich, 1990). In this a set of representative scenarios of a (computer) system is set up to be evaluated in terms of what is good and poor with respect to the (computer) system's usability. The goal of the evaluation is to "debug" the (computer) system as effectively as possible. In the present study this "debugging" procedure is applied to current bike and walk systems.

METHOD

Respondents

Respondents were volunteers from a random sample drawn from the Swedish National Registration Database of men and women aged 20 to 70 years living in the greater Göteborg area, Sweden and male and female traffic-engineers identified through their employers.

Mail-back questionnaires

Mail-back questionnaires were in October and November 1998 administered to 900 randomly sampled men and women (users) and to 78 male and female traffic-engineers (experts). Of the 146 (40.4 %) respondents who in the mail-back questionnaire stated an interest in further participation 49 users (45.7 %) and 30 experts (80.5 %) participated in an experimental study (VCR show). Experts were more educated than users and females more than males, $F(2, 76)=6.1, p<.01$, and $F(1, 76)=5.7, p<.05$. (Table 1).

Table 1. Sociodemographics.

	Experts (n=30)		*Users (n=49)*	
	Females (n=14)	*Males (n=19)*	*Females (n=24)*	*Males (n=22)*
Age (M years)	35.2	47.6	37.2	36.7
University degree	10	12	12	4
Access to at least one car	13	16	15	14
Driving license	14	19	23	18
Prefer biking over walking	7	12	10	11

Bike and walk VCR shows

The heuristic evaluation method chosen was VCR recordings. A representative set of bike and walk systems located in the greater Göteborg area, Sweden was selected for the study. The systems were varied on physical design (e.g. paths, lanes, routes (UCLA, 1972)) and location (e.g. in the city core or in the outskirts of the city). The recordings were made during daylight hours in October 1998. Information in the recordings of area type was deleted before combination into a bike and a walk VCR show. Seven different area types were included (Table 2) and the types were exposed in the same order in both shows.

Table 2. Area types.

Area no	*Definition*	*Explanation*
1	Roadway	Walk, bike, and car traffic mixed
2	Sidewalk	Separate walk area, bike and car traffic mixed
3	Bike/walk path	Walk and bike areas separated from each other and from car traffic
4	Bike/walk route	Walk and bike areas shared but separated from car traffic
5	Distanced bike/walk path	Walk and bike areas separated from each other and from car traffic
6	Distanced bike/walk route	Walk and bike areas shared but distanced from car traffic
7	Short cut	Not planned/built area

Procedure

Respondents interested in further participation were contacted by phone and informed about the VCR shows. In the laboratory, the respondent was instructed to picture her/him biking or walking to work, for shopping, or for exercise in the areas shown. In doing this she/he was asked to state his/her opinions of the bike or walk areas aloud. She/he was informed that the show was going to be paused whenever she/he stated an opinion and that she/he was going to be asked to identify the area in question among 7 different drawings of area types. Furthermore, the respondent was asked to assess the quality of the area in its present appearance as well as in darkness and in snowy and rainy climate. The assessments were given on 9-point graphical scales without verbal end-points. The stated opinions were taped and transcribed and categorized[1] afterwards. The experiment took 60-120 minutes to accomplish and was run November 1998 through March 1999. The respondents were acknowledged with theatre tickets.

Results

Correspondence between believed and actual area type

At each statement the VCR show was paused and the respondent was asked to identify the area in question. An analysis of variance showed that the correspondence between believed and actual area type differed significantly between area type, experts and users, and conditions, $F(6, 2030)=61.4$, $p <.001$, $F(1, 2030)=4.1$ and 5.5, $p <.05$. Area 7 was most often and area 4 least often correctly identified. The correct area type was more often identified by the experts and more often in bike conditions (Table 3). Furthermore, the area type was more often identified by experts in shopping errands, more often by females in walk conditions, and more often by females in work errands, $F(2, 2030)=7.2$, $p <.001$ and $F(1, 2030)=5.2$ and 3.8, $p <.05$.

[1] A random sample of 10 % of the statements was independently categorized by a second person. The correspondence between the two categorizations was 73 %.

Table 3. Correctly identified areas (%).

	Experts (n=810 statements)		*Users (n=1,247 statements)*	
Area no	*Walk (n=360)*	*Bike (n=450)*	*Walk (n=640)*	*Bike (n=607)*
1	82.8	70.0	55.9	53.3
2	62.5	75.4	64.8	76.2
3	68.1	75.6	62.3	73.8
4	10.8	2.9	4.6	4.5
5	73.8	86.7	82.7	87.1
6	91.2	85.7	68.7	76.8
7	87.5	100.0	90.6	86.1

Statements and bugs

A total of 2,130 statements were registered. On average the respondents made 26.7 (6-56) statements per show. No significant differences between experts and users, gender, conditions, or errands were found. An only opinion, or a bug, was uttered in 1,755 (82.4 %) of the statements, two in 248 (11.6 %), three in 84 (3.9 %), four in 33 (1.5 %), five in 8 (0.4 %), and six in 2 (0.1 %) of the statements. A total of 3,364 bugs were registered and categorized into 13 different domains; good and poor accident risk, good and poor aesthetic design, good and poor physical design, good and poor safety (e.g. assaults and other criminal acts) design, good and poor social design, temporary hindrance, descriptions and questions. More than half of the bugs (56.1 %) referred to some kind of poor design within the system. More, and more negative bugs, were stated by users than by experts, more by males than by females, and more by those who attended the walk VCR show than by those who attended the bike VCR show. Furthermore, more bugs were stated for roadways (1) and least for short cuts (7). Most of the bugs belonged to the domain of poor physical design (24.1 %), next most to good physical design (22.1 %), and third most to temporary hindrance (12.2 %). In the domain of poor physical design the most mentioned bug was poor direction for use, in good physical design good direction for use, and in temporary hindrance parked vehicles.

No significant effects were reached in the domains of descriptions and questions. In the domain of poor (e.g. increased) accident risk experts more often mentioned parked vehicles, $F(1, 20)=7.9$, $p<.05$, while no significant effects were reached in the domain of good (e.g. decreased) accident risk.

In the domain of poor aesthetic design the bug ugly/unpleasant yielded two significant interaction effects. This bug was more often mentioned by experts in work errands than in the other types of errands and more often by female experts than male experts, $F(2, 79)=4.0$ and 5.5, $p<.05$, respectively. The bug beauty/pleasantness in the domain of good aesthetic design differed reliably between area types, $F(6, 178)=2.3$, $p<.05$. Walk and bike areas separated from each other and from car traffic were perceived as more beautiful/pleasant and experts in bike conditions perceived the areas as more beautiful/pleasant, $F(1, 178)=5.9$, $p<.05$.

In the domain of poor physical design male users more often mentioned the bug visibility, $F(1, 50)=7.3$, $p<.05$. In the domain of good physical design experts more often mentioned the bug direction for use, $F(1, 70)=5.1$, $p<.05$. This bug was also more often mentioned for walk and bike areas separated from each other and from car traffic in bike conditions and by females in walk conditions, $F(2, 70)=7.27$, $p <.01$ and $F(1, 70)=5.20$, $p <.05$, respectively. The bug width/space in the same domain was more often mentioned for walk and bike areas separated from each other and from car traffic and more often in shopping errands, $F(5, 56)=5.2$, $p <.05$ and $F(2, 56)=11.7$, $p <.01$, respectively. Furthermore, the bug width/space was more often mentioned for the same area in bike conditions, in shopping errands, by experts in shopping errands, by expert males, by males in bike conditions, and more often by males in shopping errands, $F(3, 56)=6.6$, $p <.05$, $F(4, 56)=5.7$, $p <05$, $F(2, 56)=6.1$, $p <.05$, $F(1, 56)=21.6$, $p <.001$, $F(1, 56)=10.3$, $p <.05$, and $F(2, 56)=7.5$, $p <.05$, respectively. The bug verdure in the same domain was more often mentioned by female users and the bug paving more often by users in bike conditions and in exercise errands, $F(1, 52)=6.0$, $p <.05$, $F(1, 60)=6.1$ and $F(2, 60)=5.3$, respectively, $p <.05$.

No significant effects were found in the domains of poor and good safety design or in the domain of poor social design. However, in the domain of good social design the bug people/activities was more often mentioned in shopping errands in walk and bike areas separated from each other and from car traffic and in walk conditions in shopping errands, $F(5, 52)=5.3$ and $F(2, 52)=7.3$, $p <.01$.

Finally, in the domain of temporary hindrance the bug construction area was more often mentioned for roadways, the bug parked vehicles for walk and bike areas separated from car traffic, and the bug noise in work errand, $F(4, 43)=5.9$, $p <.01$, $F(2, 38)=5.1$, $p <.05$ and $F(6, 79)=2.6$, $p <.05$, respectively. Moreover, experts mentioned the bug construction area more often for roadways and the bug parked vehicles was mentioned more often in bike conditions in work errands, $F(1, 43)=9.2$, $p <.01$ and $F(2, 79)=4.0$, $p <.05$, respectively.

Quality assessments

At each pause in the VCR show the respondent assessed the quality of the area in question (e.g. in its present appearance), in darkness, and in rainy and snowy climate. The quality was assessed as higher in its present appearance, as higher for walk and bike areas separated from each other and from car traffic and as lowest for short cuts (Table 4).

The quality in the present appearance was assessed as higher in bike conditions, as higher in shopping errands, and as higher by females, $F(1, 2101)=5.1$, $p <.05$, $F(2, 2101)=10.2$, $p <10.15$, and $F(1, 2101)=13.2$, $p <.001$, and experts assessed the quality in the present appearance as higher in shopping errands, $F(2, 2101)=8.4$, $p <.001$. In rainy climate there were significant differences between errands and between gender, $F(1, 2100)=29.\ 6$, $p <.001$ and $F(2, 2100)=3.81$, respectively, $p <.05$. The quality in rainy climate was assessed as higher in exercise errands and higher by males and as higher by males in walk conditions, by experts in shopping errands, by males in shopping errands, and as higher in bike conditions in shopping errands, $F(1, 2100)=7.1$, $p <.01$, $F(2, 2100)=6.5$, $p <.01$, $F(2, 2100)=7.8$, $p <.001$, and $F(2, 2100)=10.6$, $p <.001$, respectively. The quality in darkness was assessed as higher by experts, in exercise errands, by males, $F(1, 2101)=5.4$, $p <.05$, $F(2, 2101)=8.1$, $p <.001$, and $F(1, 2101)=59.55$, $p <.001$, respectively. Moreover, by males in walk conditions, by experts in shopping errands, by males in shopping errands, and in bike condition in shopping errands,

$F(1, 2101)=19.6$, $p<.001$, $F(2, 2101)=10.0$, $p<001$, $F(2, 2101)=3.8$, $p<.05$, and $F(2, 2101)=7.2$, $p<.01$, respectively. Finally, in snowy climate users and males assessed the quality as higher than experts and females, $F(1, 2098)=9.0$, $p<.01$ and $F(1, 2098)=39.2$, $p<.001$, and as higher by male experts, by males in bike conditions, by users in exercise errands, and by males in exercise errands, $F(1, 2098)=9.1$, $p<.01$, $F(1, 2098)=7.5$, $p<.01$, $F(2, 2098)=4.0$, $p<.05$, and $F(2, 2098)=11.8$, $p<.001$, respectively.

Moreover, the quality assessments increased and decreased, respectively, with the number of positive and negative bugs included in the statement. Furthermore, within a statement the quality assessment of negative bugs is counteracted by number of added positive bugs (e.g. the impact of a negative bug are compensated by the impact of added positive bugs) (Table 5).

Table 4. Quality assessments (W=work errands, S=shopping, and E=exercise errands).

	Expert statements (n=819)						*User statements (n=1,282)*					
	Walk (n=375)			*Bike (n=444)*			*Walk (n=623)*			*Bike (n=659)*		
	W	*S*	*E*	*W*	*S*	*E*	*W*	*S*	*E*	*W*	*S*	*E*
Current	4.9	4.9	4.6	4.5	5.6	5.2	4.9	5.0	5.1	4.5	5.4	5.4
Rain	4.5	4.4	4.0	4.0	5.2	4.4	4.0	4.0	4.8	4.1	4.4	4.6
Darkness	4.0	4.6	3.9	3.8	5.0	4.6	3.8	3.7	4.6	3.9	4.2	4.4
Snow	4.5	4.1	3.9	3.7	3.9	3.9	3.7	4.0	4.7	3.7	3.8	4.2

Table 5. Impact of positive bugs on negative.

	A negative bug	*Two negative bugs*	*Three negative bugs*	*Four negative bugs*	*Five negative bugs*
Present	3.98	4.00	4.37	3.84	2.50
Plus 1 positive	5.33	5.09	4.64	4.57	3.67
Plus 2 positive	6.28	5.86	6.00		
Plus 3 positive	6.78	6.25	6.40		
Plus 4 positive	7.00				
Rainy	3.52	3.44	3.79	3.32	2.38
Plus 1 positive	4.28	4.53	4.14	2.86	3.33
Plus 2 positive	5.21	5.41	5.11		
Plus 3 positive	5.94	4.75	5.20		
Plus 4 positive	5.83				
Darkness	3.46	3.17	3.48	3.32	2.38
Plus 1 positive	4.10	4.20	3.73	2.86	3.33
Plus 2 positive	4.98	4.50	4.78		
Plus 3 positive	4.94	4.88	5.40		
Plus 4 positive	4.67				
Snowy	3.32	3.07	3.56	2.95	2.50
Plus 1 positive	3.86	4.26	3.86	2.86	2.33
Plus 2 positive	4.60	5.19	4.89		
Plus 3 positive	5.39	4.62	4.80		
Plus 4 positive	5.33				

Discussion

The "debugging" procedure elicited abundantly many bugs, about one per minute, when it was applied to the current bike and walk system of Göteborg, Sweden and a majority of the elicited bugs were stated in a negative mode. Users stated more, and more negative bugs, and more bugs were stated in the walk conditions as well as for roadways. Moreover, users assessed the quality of the systems as lower and they were also less good in identifying the different areas.

If the stated single bugs were lumped together according to their content (e.g. parked vehicles regardless of domain forms one group, direction for use another, a.s.f.) the largest group was beautiful/pleasant followed by direction for use, paving, and verdure. Clearly the aesthetic aspect is very important in the perception of bike and walk systems but also direction for use seem to be of great importance. Although most of the direction for use of a system is given in road signs and road markings some are given in the physical design of the system itself. If direction of use is misinterpreted this might result in confusion, which, in turn, might result in lower assessments and lower perceptions of usability of the systems (e.g. lower usage) because of feelings of incompatibility with the system in question.

The results obtained in this study should, of course, be evaluated with a clear understanding of its limitations. Even though Nielsen & Landauer (1993) state that the most important bugs in a (computer)system are identified within the first five evaluations generalization of these results should be done with care. The number of subjects that participated was relatively, at least regarding the subgroups, low, though exceeding five, and the method used clearly needs further development and refinements to be fully usable in other areas of research than in the computer sciences.

However, to increase perceived usability and perceived quality of current bike and walk systems, and maybe use of bike and walk as means of transportation, improvements of direction for use could turn out to be quite meaningful. Moreover, some improvements might easily be reached without much cost and within a quite short period of time. However, further research is needed to more precisely uncover users' negative and positive perceptions of current direction for use. Moreover, more attention paid to the desires and demands of the public, or the common users, in the planning process of new, and the redesign of older, bike and walk areas might also be worthwhile. In the end it is always the users' decision whether to use, or not use, bike and walk systems that make up its usage level.

Acknowledgements

This research was funded by a grant to the first author from the Swedish Transport and Communications Research Board (#1998-220). Thanks to Lena Fritzell and Maria Blomqvist for assistance in collecting and coding the data and the respondents for sharing their knowledge and experience with us.

REFERENCES

Forester, J. (1994). A review of the national bicycling and walking studies, Report from the Cycling Transportation Engineering, CA, USA.

Nielsen, J. (1992). Finding usability problems through heuristic evaluation. In P. Bauersfield, J. Bennet, and G Lynch (Eds.), *Proceedings of the CHI '92 Conference on Human Factors in Computing Systems* (pp. 373-380). NY: Association for Computing Machinery.

Nielsen, J. (1994). Heuristic evaluation. In J. Nielsen and R. L. Mack (Eds.), *Usability Inspection Methods* (pp. 25-62). NY: Wiley.

Nielsen, J., & Molich, R. (1990). Heuristic evaluation of user interfaces. In J. Carrasco Chew and J. Whiteside (Eds.), *Proceedings of the CHI '90 Conference on Human Factors in Computing Systems* (pp. 249-256). NY: Association for Computing Machinery.

Nielsen, J., & Landauer, T. K. (1993). A mathematical model of the finding of usability problems. In S. Ashlund, K. Mullet, A. Henderson, E. Hollnagel, and T. White (Eds.), *Proccedings of the INTERCHI '93 Conference on Human Factors in Computing Systems* (pp. 206-213). New York; NY: Association for Computing Machinery.

Pucher, J., Komanoff, C., & Schimek, P. (1999). Bicycling renaissance in North America? Recent trends and alternative policies to promote bicycling, *Transportation Research Part A, 33*, 625-654.

Sperling, D. (1996). *Future drive: Electric vehicles and sustainable transportation.* Washington, DC: Island Press.

SOU 1997:35. (1997). Ny kurs i trafikpolitiken: Slutbetänkande av Kommunikationskommittén [Heading for a new Transport Policy: Final Report by the Government Commission on Transport and Communications], Stockholm: Norstedts.

University of California (UCLA), Los Angeles. Institute of Transportation and Traffic Engineering, 1972. Bikeway planning criteria and guidelines. UCLA-ENG-7224. Los Angeles, CA.

U.S. Department of Transportation. (1994). *Long range transportation program.* Washington, DC: Bureau of Transportation Statistics.

Vejdirektoratet. (1995). Cyklens potentiale i bytrafik [The potential of the bicycle in city traffic]. Trafiksikkerhed og Miljo: Rapport 17, Denmark.